THE EUROPEAN POWERS AND
THE GERMAN QUESTION
1848–71

THE EUROPEAN POWERS AND THE GERMAN QUESTION
1848-71

WITH SPECIAL REFERENCE TO ENGLAND AND RUSSIA

BY

W. E. MOSSE

1969

OCTAGON BOOKS

New York

First published 1958

Reprinted 1969
by permission of the Cambridge University Press

OCTAGON BOOKS
A DIVISION OF FARRAR, STRAUS & GIROUX, INC.
19 Union Square West
New York, N. Y. 10003

LIBRARY OF CONGRESS CATALOG CARD NUMBER: 74-76002

Printed in U.S.A. by
NOBLE OFFSET PRINTERS, INC.
NEW YORK 3, N. Y.

CONTENTS

PREFACE

THE German question in the nineteenth century has been studied in the past almost exclusively from the point of view of Prussia. Bismarck's diplomacy, in particular, has been accepted as the primary—if not indeed the sole—motive force in European affairs from the moment of his appointment as Prussian Prime Minister. This Germano-centric approach has several disadvantages of which perhaps the most serious is that it is incapable of explaining why the older powers acquiesced in the establishment of the German empire instead of combining to prevent its emergence. It is difficult to accept the view that Bismarck's diplomacy, however skilful, should by itself have been sufficient to prevent the formation of hostile coalitions. In fact, there can be no doubt that, in order to answer the question, it is necessary to study, in their own right, the policies of the other powers. This is true in particular with regard to England and Russia, each of which was capable of exercising a powerful influence detrimental to Prussian aspirations. A study of the international background to the German question, moreover, must throw some light on two prevalent if conflicting views: that Germany had to win her place among the nations in the face of a hostile Europe, and that it was consistent Russian support which made possible the creation of the German empire. It is the purpose of this book to re-examine the reaction of the powers to the German national movement and to show the considerations—often wholly unconnected with the affairs of Germany—which helped to determine their conduct.

In preparing this book I have had the benefit of much generous assistance. I have to acknowledge the gracious permission of Her Majesty the Queen to make use of material from the Royal Archives in Windsor Castle. I wish, at the same time, to express my gratitude to the staff of those archives for their unfailing kindness. I am indebted to Countess Mountbatten of Burma for permission to use material from the Broadlands Papers and to her archivist, Mrs Blois, for making it available to me. I have to thank for their assistance the staffs of the Public Record Office in London and the Haus- Hof- und Staatsarchiv in Vienna. A period of research at the latter archives was financed with the help of a grant from the Central Research Fund of London University. The Carnegie Trust for

PREFACE

the Universities of Scotland and the Publications Committee of Glasgow University by a joint guarantee made possible the publication of this book. I am greatly indebted to Professor Lilian Penson and Dr George Bolsover for reading the manuscript and for many valuable suggestions. Last but not least, I wish to thank my colleague Dr James Tumelty for his unfailing help and encouragement at every stage of the enterprise.

W. E. M.

University of Glasgow
October 1957

ABBREVIATIONS
USED IN THE FOOTNOTES

AAE Archives du Ministère des Affaires Etrangères, Paris.

AHR The American Historical Review.

APP Die Auswärtige Politik Preussens 1858–1871, 10 vols. (Oldenburg, 1932 *et seq.*).

BFSP British and Foreign State Papers.

EHR The English Historical Review.

Foundations H. Temperley and L. M. Penson, *Foundations of British Foreign Policy* (London, 1938).

GE Bismarck, *Gedanken und Erinnerungen* (popular edn., Stuttgart, 1913).

GP Die Grosse Politik der europäischen Kabinette (Berlin, 1922–6).

GW Bismarck, *Gesammelte Werke*, 6 vols. in 8 (Berlin, 1924 *et seq.*).

HHSAPARRR Haus- Hof- und Staatsarchiv, Wien, Pol. Arch. Russland, Russie, Rapports.

HHSAPSDiRMPM Haus- Hof- und Staatsarchiv, Wien, xxxx 275 Präsid. Sektion Dep. 1 R.M. Protokoll Ministerratsprotokoll.

HT Henderson Transcripts (in the Cambridge University Library).

Jomini *Etude diplomatique sur la guerre de Crimée* (St Petersburg, 1878), Russian official publication attributed to Baron Jomini of the Russian Foreign Ministry.

Origines Les origines diplomatiques de la guerre de 1870–71, 29 vols. (Paris, 1910 *et seq.*).

PRO Public Record Office, London.

QVL The Letters of Queen Victoria.
First Series 1837–1861, ed. A. C. Benson and Viscount Esher (London, 1908).
Second Series 1861–1885, ed. G. Buckle (London, 1926).

RA Royal Archives, Windsor Castle.

SR The Slavonic Review.

WSA Württembergisches Staatsarchiv, Stuttgart.

INTRODUCTION

THE modern movement for the political consolidation of Germany, destined to produce the momentous results known to history, sprang from the failure of the Germanic Confederation of 1815 to meet the needs and aspirations of important sections of German society. Intellectuals inspired by the literary and political nationalism of the Romantic Age, enterprising industrialists seeking wider markets, advocates of Prussian leadership and critics of particularism alike were dissatisfied with the political order created by the Congress of Vienna. There arose in the years after 1815 a widespread desire for the closer union of Germans through a strengthening of Germany's political organization.

Any step towards political consolidation of Germany raised a number of distinct if interrelated issues. A closer integration of the German states would necessitate the reform or abrogation of the existing Federal Constitution. This was not an easy matter. The procedure for constitutional change laid down in the treaty of Vienna[1] put a heavy premium on the particularism of the lesser German states.[2] Moreover, reform of the Constitution, although in the first place a purely German matter, was linked with non-German interests. Austria was not a purely German state; the kings of Denmark and the Netherlands were members of the Confederation in respect of Holstein and Luxemburg. Furthermore, the treaty of Vienna declared the Confederation to be 'perpetual'.[3] Any attempt, therefore, to abrogate the Federal Constitution might afford the signatories a pretext for intervention.

The difficulties in the way of reform were aggravated by the secular rivalry of Austria and Prussia. The former claimed the leadership of Germany, the latter demanded parity with her rival. Neither government was likely to waive its pretensions; neither would, in normal circumstances, be able to impose its will upon the other. With the interests, policies and ambitions of Austria and Prussia in irreconcilable conflict, federal reform by agreement was a virtual impossibility. Moreover, both Austria and Prussia were not merely German but also European powers[4]

---

[1] In articles LVIII, LIX and LX.

[2] The treaty of Vienna, embodying the distribution of votes, is printed in *The Great Treaties of the Nineteenth Century*, ed. Sir A. Oakes and R. B. Mowat (2nd impression, Oxford, 1921), pp. 37 ff.

[3] In article LIII. *Ibid.* p. 64.

[4] It is significant that the emperor of Austria and the king of Prussia had become members of the Confederation 'for all their possessions which anciently belonged to the German Empire' (*ibid.*).

who conducted their foreign policies independently of each other and of the Confederation.

These difficulties of German consolidation were further aggravated by the problem of nationality. If—in accordance with accepted liberal and romantic theories—language was made the basis of political allegiance, far-reaching consequences must follow. The application of the principle of nationality must produce the break-up of the polyglot Habsburg monarchy with the German-speaking subjects of the Emperor joining their German brethren in the new German national state. That state would also absorb territories which had for centuries been associated with other non-German states. Such were the Duchies of Holstein and Schleswig, the first exclusively German in speech and sentiment, the second partially so, yet linked with the Danish monarchy. Such was Alsace, German-speaking province of France. Such might become the Baltic provinces of Russia, German by the character of their ruling and commercial classes. Conversely, the creation of a German state based on the principle of nationality would raise in an acute form the problem of the Poles living in the Prussian province of Posen (Poznan); it might revive in its entirety the thorny Polish question. The reorganization of Germany in accordance with national principles threatened to set fire to the four corners of Europe.

Finally, the emergence of a strong German state in the heart of the European continent would profoundly modify the European equilibrium. Austria and France would be the two powers most immediately affected by this event but England and Russia also would feel its repercussions, whilst Italian national aspirations might be vitally affected. German weakness under the aegis of dualism had become a permanent feature of the European States' System; German strength threatened to create a major political upheaval. The emergence of a new great power, in fact, could not but affect the interests and policies of all the others. It was bound to frustrate the objects and arouse the opposition of some at least of the older powers.

Such were the main problems arising from the movement for German consolidation. Some, like constitutional reform and Austro-Prussian rivalry, were largely, though not exclusively, internal; others, like the application of the principle of nationality and the modification of the European equilibrium, affected the concert of Europe at large and Germany's neighbours in particular. It is the latter rather than the former aspects with which this study is primarily concerned.

The movement for the national consolidation of Germany first assumed European importance during the year of revolutions; its inability— apparent by 1850—to find an acceptable substitute for the Germanic Confederation marked the end of the first acute phase of the German question. During the years which followed, attention was focused first on the eastern and later on the Italian question, both of which exercised an indirect—although by no means negligible—effect on German affairs. After 1863 the achievements of Roon, Moltke and Bismarck revived the German question in a new and dramatic form; by 1871 the new German empire had replaced France as the leading power of continental Europe.

Each of the active phases of the German question has given rise to a problem of great historical interest. With few exceptions, German historians have argued that the failure of the great national movement of 1848-9 was due, to a greater or lesser extent, to the hostile intervention of Europe. This view has indeed been disputed but continues to hold the field.[1] A review of the available evidence is overdue both to determine the attitude adopted by the cabinets of Europe and to assess its influence on events.

The second phase of the German question raises an issue of a different kind. The reorganization of Germany culminating in the proclamation of the German empire at Versailles involved perhaps the most far-reaching modification of the European equilibrium between the Congress of Vienna and the dissolution of the Habsburg monarchy. A development of this magnitude affected directly or indirectly the interests and policies of every European state. It is a remarkable fact that Prussia was able not only to defeat her principal rivals in isolation but to achieve her triumphs without provoking a coalition of the type which had all but destroyed her in the days of Frederick the Great. Bismarck's diplomacy, a major factor in achieving this result, has been abundantly studied; the European situation in which he was able to perform his miracle has received less attention.

Yet Bismarck's skill alone is insufficient to explain the absence of hostile coalitions. Not all the strings were pulled by the wizard in Berlin: each cabinet had its own interests and ambitions and pursued its own policies. If the powers refrained from combining against Prussia, the reason on more than one critical occasion lay in considerations completely unconnected with German affairs. In consequence, to understand their conduct in the German question, it is often necessary to analyse the general objects of their diplomacy.

I

Whilst it is not difficult to see in what manner the creation of a strong German state would touch the interests of France, the concern of England and Russia in the matter is less immediately apparent. Yet the two powers on the flanks of Europe were affected almost as vitally as Germany's immediate neighbours. Anglo-Russian rivalry and dissension had been, at least since the beginning of the Palmerstonian era, a permanent feature of the diplomatic scene. Distrust, caused by political rivalry and ideo-

[1] For a discussion of the views expressed by German historians about the attitude of Europe towards the movement for the closer integration of Germany see appendix A.

3

logical conflict, reigned supreme in London as it did at St Petersburg. It all but dominated the policies of the two governments, who as a result tended to view all major changes in Europe in the light of their antagonism. The German national movement, therefore, raised some important questions. How would a new German power align itself in the struggle between England and Russia, liberalism and autocracy? What influence would the new state have on the 'solution' of the perennial eastern question? The new power might tip the scales between England and Russia, decide issues with which it had little concern; the future of Turkey and Central Asia, even of India herself, might be decided on the 'battlefields' of Germany.

From the Russian point of view the emergence of a powerful state in Germany would create a further problem. Should its creation result in a weakening of Austrian influence in Germany, it was not improbable that the energies of the Habsburg monarchy would be increasingly directed towards expansion in the Balkan Peninsula; Austro-Russian rivalry in that area would be intensified. Here again, a new Germany, not perhaps directly interested herself, might hold the balance and decide the issue.

While the implications of German consolidation for England and Russia were so momentous, their attitudes in turn would be vitally important for the fate of the German national movement. The attitudes of France and Austria towards German affairs were largely if not wholly determined by long-standing traditions; England and Russia, less bound by traditional influences, had a larger freedom of action. Without direct and immediate interests at stake in the convulsions of Germany, they might, at any moment, turn the scales in the embattled diplomacy and warfare of Austria, Prussia, France and Italy. As Bismarck knew only too well, vital decisions affecting the future of Germany might be made at St Petersburg or London.

II

Russia, during the first half of the nineteenth century, had come to exercise a powerful influence in German affairs. That influence rested on the twofold basis of strategic strength and dynastic ties. The union between the Russian empire and the 'Congress Kingdom' of Poland set up in 1815 had permanently established Russian armies within two hundred miles of both Berlin and Vienna. Occupied by Russian armies, Poland outflanked the capital of the Habsburgs and was a pistol pointed at the heart of the Prussian state. Dynastic ties and the known conservative and legitimist views of Alexander I in his last years, of Nicholas I and of his son after him, made the tsar the chosen protector of many of the lesser German princes and even of the Hohenzollern rulers of Prussia. Austro-Prussian rivalry within the Confederation lent weight to the views of a ruler who might sway more than one vote in the Federal Diet; the lesser German states, impartially distrustful of Austria and Prussia alike, were often ready to listen to advice from St Petersburg. The strength of the Russian position in Germany (based on German particularism and the strategic control of Poland) was secured by the treaty of Vienna. It is not surprising, therefore, that under Nicholas I and Nesselrode Russian diplomacy took its stand on the provisions of that treaty; from the Russian point of view, in the 1840's, any change in the existing state of affairs could only be for the worse.

A policy of maintaining the settlement of 1815 in the interest of Russian strength blended harmoniously with the conservative and legitimist ideologies professed at St Petersburg after 1820. It was, in fact, the same enemy which menaced both the authority of legitimate governments and the bases of Russian power. A unitary national movement in Germany threatened to destroy alike the princely dynasties and the internal divisions which secured Russia's influence. Revolutionary designs on Schleswig and Holstein menaced not only the legitimate authority of the king of Denmark but also Russian interests in the Baltic. Moreover, western liberals and democrats supported the aspirations of the Polish gentry which endangered the integrity of the Russian empire itself; the triumph of revolutionary German nationalism would act as a spur to Polish national sentiment. The triumph of any liberal, national or democratic movement in Germany would not only subvert legitimate authority but weaken Russian influence in Europe. Apart from any legitimist principles which successive tsars might profess and any sympathies they might feel for close relatives on German thrones, the Russian national interest appeared to demand the maintenance of the *status quo* in Germany.

England, unlike Russia, had little interest in preserving existing arrangements. Not only was the Germanic Confederation a weak and clumsy body of doubtful value in the event of French aggression; Metternich's conservative system served all too successfully the purpose—for which indeed it might have been almost specifically created—of protecting the flank of Russia. The Polish insurrection of 1830–1 had revealed all too clearly the value to Russia of the German defensive barrier. However, whilst the old Confederation had acted mainly as a shield for Russia a Germany reorganized under liberal (and probably Prussian) auspices, might play a very different role. Such a Germany, 'western', parliamentary and predominantly Protestant, would be England's 'natural ally' against Cossack despotism, French encroachments and the spread of Catholic influence. Hatred of Russian tyranny might turn her into a defender of Turkey. She might even make it possible for England to 'do something for the Poles'. In this way, the European equilibrium, disturbed by the alliance of the eastern monarchies might be restored. Russia would be deprived of strategic advantages, hampered in her development and all but expelled from Europe. The consolidation of a *liberal* Germany, therefore, would serve the purpose of British diplomatic strategy.

5

For England as for Russia, the decisive aspect of German consolidation was thus ideological. Whilst a strong liberal Germany would be invaluable to British diplomacy, a Germany reorganized under conservative auspices would promote the security of Russia. In either event, both England and Russia had a vital stake in the organization of the great strategic area in the heart of the European continent. On the future orientation of Germany might depend—in no small measure—the outcome of their rivalries in Asia as well as in Europe.

III

The German problem might be solved in several ways, differing in the fundamental principles involved and in their ideological and political significance. Germany might be reorganized on the basis of nationality and language and endowed with liberal parliamentary institutions; that was the dream of professors and journalists, poets and liberal deputies. A different form of consolidation might be achieved under the auspices of Prussia. This seemed likely to involve a Prussian conquest of Germany (there was little chance of voluntary political union under Prussian leadership). Such a conquest would be the work of a regular monarchical government and a Prussian reorganization was likely to take dynastic and conservative forms. Prussian leadership, moreover, might well involve the exclusion of Austria from the new state. This would give the new Germany a predominantly Protestant character. Consolidation under Austrian leadership was another possibility. This would in all probability be founded on conservative principles and be the result of the agreement between the emperor of Austria and the major German princes other than the king of Prussia. Such a revived and modernized 'Holy Roman Empire' would be predominantly Catholic, largely defensive and, almost certainly, incompatible with the continued existence of Prussia as a European power. It was doubtful whether such a result could be achieved by peaceful means. Finally, there was the possibility of a dualistic solution with Prussia leading Germany north of the Main and Austria leading the south. In this diarchy each of the component parts was likely to be monarchical and conservative. Whatever links might be established between them, rivalry based on political and religious differences was likely to continue.

Each of these possible solutions had its peculiar difficulties or disadvantages. The liberal-national form of reorganization with the object of uniting all German-speaking populations was likely to have the most revolutionary consequences. Austrian hegemony, the 'Empire of Seventy Millions', would involve the most serious disturbance of the balance of power in Europe. The integral Austrian and Prussian solutions were likely to be achieved only as the result of civil war; even a genuine dualism might be difficult to establish by peaceful means as the Habsburgs were unlikely to give up without a struggle their traditional claim to leadership. Almost any attempt to create a more compact German state was likely to raise the European question of Schleswig-Holstein and the future of the Danish monarchy. Any solution except one of pure dualism would reduce the power and influence of France and deprive her of the possibility of playing a part in German affairs.

In their policy towards any such attempts, therefore, European statesmen had to consider not only the general impact of a new power on the existing States' System but also the particular implications of the specific solution proposed. The policies of the non-German powers must be shaped to a large extent by their attitudes towards the different facets of the German national movement.

The Russian government, both on ideological and on practical grounds, would prefer a dynastic to a parliamentary approach. A dynastic solution was, on the whole, likely to be conservative, and if Prussian or dualist, need not affect the vital question of Poland. A Germany led by Prussia was certain to maintain the solidarity of the partitioning powers; in a dualist Germany, the Prussian part at least would oppose Polish aspirations. Germany led by Austria was likely to become a dangerous rival in the Balkans; Prussia, on the other hand, had no direct interest in the affairs of south-eastern Europe and was more likely to tolerate Russian expansion. On the other hand, Prussia as the leader of Germany was likely to weaken the Danish monarchy by absorbing Schleswig and Holstein and thus bring closer the spectre of a Scandinavian union. If, therefore, the German national movement must needs issue in the abrogation of the federal constitution, genuine 'dualism' appeared from the Russian point of view to be the least objectionable substitute. Should this prove unattainable, a Prussian Germany was to be preferred to an Austrian one. It was less likely to prove 'unsound' on the Polish question, and the weakening of the Danish monarchy was a lesser evil than an active 'German' policy in the Balkans. With all its disadvantages, however, even an Austrian empire was still to be preferred to a liberal, national and democratic state, which was bound to be anti-Russian, would raise in an acute form the questions both of Poland and the Duchies, and might become the spearhead of an anti-Russian crusade.

The general considerations influencing British statesmen were of an opposite nature. A moderately liberal and parliamentary solution was preferred to one that was military or purely dynastic. Parliaments would be almost certain to have pro-British and anti-Russian majorities. They might prove amenable to doctrinaire arguments in favour of free trade. They were likely to oppose military adventures and appeared, on general grounds, to be the most satisfactory form of government. A liberal-national form of organization, therefore, appeared desirable, as long as democratic extremism could be kept in check. In addition to a preference for a cautious liberalism, which accorded so well with British interests there was another guiding principle which influenced British policy. There survived in England a distrust, inherited from the days of the Armada and the *Roi Soleil*, of the Papacy, France and Austria. The maintenance of Prussia as a strong European power representing the Protestant interest was therefore held to be an important object of British policy. Any Austrian solution of the German question might leave England as the only bulwark of protestantism and freedom. British policy, therefore, inclined to the side of Prussia rather than Austria; any solution, to be fully acceptable to England, must be both Prussian and liberal. The Prince Consort and Queen Victoria dreamt of a liberal Prussia transforming Germany into a great liberal, parliamentary and Protestant empire. This solution, moreover, must if possible be achieved by peaceful means. The prospect of civil war in Germany raised at once the spectre of French intervention in an attempt to satisfy ambitions of long standing. Even Russia, closely interested in German affairs, might be tempted to intervene. Finally, British policy was influenced also by commercial considerations. Prussia was the leading spirit of the German *Zollverein* which was pursuing a policy of protection denounced by the doctrinaire free-trader as well as the hard-headed British industrialist. British policy, therefore, would aim at a reduction of German tariffs and would try in favourable circumstances to barter political support for economic concession.

Such were some of the general considerations underlying the day-to-day policies of Russian and British governments in their dealings with the movement for German consolidation. Russia, ideally, required a Germany that was dualist and conservative, England one that was unitary and liberal. Each had a double object and each was to see the realization of half its aspirations. The fate of the German national movement in its turn would depend to an important degree on whether it could devise forms of organization not totally unacceptable to other powers. The reorganization of the Confederation was unlikely to succeed without at least the neutrality of either Russia or England.

For England as well as for Russia, the stakes in the German question were high. An alliance between England and a rejuvenated Germany would end Russian dreams of Constantinople and the Straits and indeed Russia's days as a major European power. On the other hand, were Germany to ally herself with Russia, the latter would become all but invulnerable to western attack and a Russian solution of the eastern question would be simply a matter of time. Small wonder that German affairs were anxiously watched in St Petersburg as well as in London.

The ultimate alignment of a consolidated German state was uncertain and unpredictable. Within Germany, there was a deep division between those desiring a Russian alliance and advocates of a western orientation. Neither history nor German traditions of diplomacy provided a clear-cut answer. Germany, situated in the centre of Europe and facing both east and west,[1] had developed a dual foreign policy, particularly since Russia and Prussia had emerged as European powers. From the age of Louis XIV to that of Napoleon I, German energies had been absorbed by the struggle—both in the west and the east—against the preponderance of France. In the process, Germany had co-operated with England as well as with Russia. Allied to England, one or other of the German powers had, at different times, defended the Low Countries and Hanover as well as the European equilibrium. At the same time, Austria had more than once joined Russia in attempts to expel the Turk from Europe and eradicate French influence in Poland, whilst Prussia had collaborated with Russia in destroying the Polish Commonwealth. The struggle against Napoleon had, for a moment, united the two traditions, but with the Holy Alliance and the ascendancy of Metternich and Nicholas I the eastern orientation prevailed. The revolutions of 1848 once more reopened the question: the 'westerners' in Germany took heart: the east was on the defensive. With the new fluidity inside Germany, her future alignment had become once again a matter of European interest and concern.

[1] At an earlier age, the antithesis in German policy had been between a southern and an eastern orientation.

PART I
THE AUSTRO-RUSSIAN ALLIANCE

CHAPTER I

THE POWERS AND THE GERMAN REVOLUTION, 1848-51

O N 4 March 1848 Alphonse de Lamartine, Foreign Minister of the revolutionary French Republic, issued his famous manifesto calling for the resurrection (*reconstruction*) of the oppressed nationalities of Europe. One 17 March Heinrich von Arnim-Suckow, Foreign Minister in the revolutionary Prussian government, announced that the foundation of his policy would be the restoration of 'old Poland' (des 'alten Polen') as a bulwark (eine 'Vormauer') against Russia and to strengthen Prussian ties with England and France.[1] A week later, the king of Prussia reluctantly authorized the 'national reorganization' of the Grand-Duchy of Posen. A Polish National Committee was brought into existence, and local Polish committees were formed in the towns and villages of the province.[2]

Arnim's Polish policy formed part of a larger design. Prussia supported by revolutionary France and sustained by British sympathy would assume the leadership of Germany. German national aspirations would be satisfied by the acquisition of Schleswig and Holstein. Prussia would completely detach herself from Austria and would leave the Habsburgs to fight their own battles in Italy and Hungary. A breach with Russia must be risked: Germany, France and Poland backed by the sympathies of England need not fear a war even with the hosts of Nicholas. In the name of liberty and the happiness of peoples, Prussia would lead liberal Europe against despotic Russia.[3]

Arnim's policy was accepted enthusiastically by German liberal opinion. The *Kölnische Zeitung* wrote about 'emancipation' from St Petersburg and about the 'flaming hatred of Russia' filling the hearts of Germans. The *Augsburger Allgemeine Zeitung* went so far as to attribute the outbreak of the revolution primarily to the policy of subservience to Russia.[4] Meyendorff, the Russian minister in Berlin, complained to his chief of 'the blind hatred unleashed in Germany against Russia'.[5] The German national movement, led by the liberals of the south-west and the Rhineland and acting through the revolutionary Prussian government,

---

[1] A. Scharff, *Die Europäischen Grossmächte und die Deutsche Revolution 1848–1851* (Leipzig, 1942), p. 14.
[2] H. von Sybel, *Die Begründung des Deutschen Reiches durch Wilhelm I* (4th ed. München and Leipzig, 1892), vol. I, p. 147; and Scharff, *op. cit.* p. 17.
[3] *Ibid.* p. 14.
[4] L. B. Namier, *1848: The Revolution of the Intellectuals* (London, 1946), p. 49.
[5] *Ibid.* p. 60.

thus made its entry—significantly—on the stage of European history with a plan for an aggressive and revolutionary crusade on behalf of the Poles against imperial Russia.

In raising the Polish question, the German revolution had touched a vital Russian interest. When a British diplomat proposed to Meyendorff some expedient for satisfying Polish aspirations, he received a reply which revealed the vital importance of Poland for the Russian empire.

'Look, I said to him, what would you say if it was proposed to you to restore the independence of Ireland?' 'Oh, he replied, that is impossible for us.' 'Well, I said, if Poland was an island, the combination you suggest might perhaps be feasible. But Poland, as understood by the Poles, extends to the mouths of the Vistula and Duna, as well as to the Dnieper at Kiev and at Smolensk. Such a Poland enters Russia like a wedge, destroys her political and geographical unity, throws her back into Asia, puts her back two hundred years. To prevent the establishment of such a Poland, every Russian will take up arms as in 1812 and fight without counting the number of his foes.'[1]

For a moment it seemed as if the tsar would take up the German challenge. On 14 March, under the fresh impact of revolution in Berlin, he had issued his famous manifesto[2] which appeared to foreshadow intervention in the west. However, when the first anger had worn off and the tsar's emotion cooled down under the influence of the sober Nesselrode[3] the policy which emerged was expectant and defensive. It was summed up by the Chancellor: 'Rester l'arme au bras et se défendre soi-même, voilà à quoi est réduit notre tâche.'[4]

This cautious policy was soon justified by events. Early in April, the Poles of Poznania attacked the German inhabitants of the province and alienated German sympathies. The French government declined to enter an alliance with Prussia for the restoration of Poland. The British attitude was cool.[5] As early as 8 April Meyendorff could inform Nesselrode that he considered the Polish movement no longer a threat; it remained, how-

[1] Meyendorff to Nesselrode, 27 March/8 April, *Peter von Meyendorff. Ein russischer Diplomat an den Höfen von Berlin und Wien. Politischer und privater Briefwechsel 1826–1863,* ed. O. Hoetzsch (Leipzig, 1923), vol. 2, p. 67.
[2] Summarized in K. Stählin, *Geschichte Russlands von den Anfängen bis zur Gegenwart,* vol. 3 (Berlin, 1935), pp. 492 f.
[3] Chancellor and Minister of Foreign Affairs. Meyendorff also urged caution: 'Surely we do not want to provoke Prussia, nor hurt German feelings; we shall not undertake any hostile act or serious demonstration, but we shall preserve a strictly defensive attitude and leave to our enemies the guilt of aggression' (Meyendorff to Nesselrode, 25 March 1848, Namier, *op cit.* p. 60).
[4] Nesselrode to Meyendorff, 6 April 1848, Meyendorff, *op. cit.* p. 79.
[5] Palmerston informed the British minister at St Petersburg that British public opinion strongly favoured the Poles. '...but we, the Government, will never do anything underhand or ungentlemanlike in those matters. I wish we could hope that the Emperor might of his own accord settle the Polish question in some satisfactory manner' (Palmerston to Bloomfield, 14 April 1848, E. Ashley, *Life of Viscount Palmerston 1848–1865* (London, 1876), vol. 1, pp. 91 f.; cf. also Namier, *op. cit.* pp. 62 ff.).

ever, a nuisance which would prove intolerable in the long run.[1] Meyendorff received instructions to widen the breach between the two nationalities.[2] As the Germans' Polish enthusiasm waned and was replaced by interest in Schleswig-Holstein and an all-German Parliament, the first international crisis provoked by the German revolution died down.

II

Arnim's Polish plans formed part of a larger design by which Prussia with French and British backing would assume the lead of liberal Germany. On 21 March, Frederick-William IV issued the famous proclamation in which he placed himself at the head of a united Germany.[3] In the face of widespread opposition, however, he consented to leave the task of uniting the 'fatherland' to an all-German assembly about to come into existence. On 31 March, the pre-Parliament at Frankfurt began its deliberations, superseding the Federal Diet established by the Federal Acts of 1815. In consequence, the German question was about to become an issue of European politics.

The attitude of at least one European power towards this development had already been considered. In the preceding autumn, Palmerston had drawn up a memorandum discussing this very subject.[4]

There can be no doubt [he had written] that it is greatly for the Interest of England to cultivate a close political Connection and alliance with Germany, as it is also the manifest interest of Germany to ally itself politically with England. The great Interests of the two are the same.

England and Germany were threatened by the same danger, 'an attack from Russia or from France separately, or from Russia and from France united'.[5]

England and Germany therefore have mutually a direct interest in assisting each other to become rich, united and strong and there ought not to be in the mind of any enlightened Man of either Country any feeling of jealousy as to the Progress made by the other Country in Civilization and Prosperity.

The only friction between the two countries arose from the protectionist policy pursued by the German *Zollverein*, 'which without doing any good

---

[1] *Ibid.* p. 65.

[2] Nesselrode to Meyendorff, 21 April 1848, *Lettres et Papiers du Chancelier Comte de Nesselrode 1760–1856*, ed. A. de Nesselrode (Paris, n.d.), vol. IX, p. 85.

[3] Printed in Sybel, *op. cit.* p. 143.

[4] Memorandum by Palmerston for Prince Albert, 16 September 1847, printed in Th. Martin, *The Life of H.R.H. the Prince Consort* (London, 1875 *et seq.*), vol. I, pp. 447 ff.

[5] This was a view which went back at least to Castlereagh who in 1815 had declared it an object of British policy that 'Germany might again be confederated in the same system, to render it an impregnable bulwark between the great States in the East and West of Europe'. Extracts from Speech in House of Commons on 20 March 1815, in C. K. Webster, *British Diplomacy 1813–1815* (London, 1921), p. 397.

to Germany is intended to cripple, and to a certain degree does cripple the Trade and manufactures of England'.

The latter was certain, even though British trade had in fact increased in spite of the *Zollverein*. As long as the *Zollverein* continued its protective system, the public in England would look upon it as 'a League founded in hostility to England'; and the British government would have an interest in keeping out of it any North German states which had not already joined. In fact, 'any English Ministry would be thought to have much neglected its Duty and to have sacrificed the Commercial Interests of the Country...' if it did not make every proper effort to prevent the non-member states from joining the *Zollverein*.[1] Palmerston, therefore, considered that whilst the political interests of the two countries were virtually identical, there was a clash between them in the economic sphere. The events of March 1848 would force the Foreign Secretary to decide whether to give priority to political or economic considerations.

No one who knew Palmerston could doubt the outcome. On 23 March, the Foreign Secretary issued his instructions to the British representative in Frankfurt:

The plan to which you allude for the reconstruction of the German Diet and Confederation has as you have seen in the papers to-day been more fully developed by the King of Prussia in his proclamation, and we wish you to support as far as you properly can without any direct or unfitting interference any plan which has for its object to consolidate Germany and give it more unity and political vigour.[2]

Russian diplomacy, for reasons widely different from those of Palmerston, favoured the consolidation of Germany under the leadership of Prussia. The surrender of Frederick-William, far from invalidating this solution, only served to enhance its importance in Russian eyes. The defence of authority, Meyendorff reported, had become more important than ever.

In spite of the blind hatred unloosed against us [he wrote] I do not cease to promote with all my efforts and counsels anything which may prevent Germany from breaking up....If a chance remains of saving Germany, it is from here [Berlin] that the impulse must come. God grant that the effort may be successful! The feebler and more divided Germany becomes, the more open she will be to republican influences, the closer the danger approaches our frontiers. May the Germans, enlightened about their true interests, understand that Russia can wish only to see Germany powerful and united, and that, having no propagandist aims in Germany

---

[1] This passage, taken in isolation, has been held to show that British policy towards the consolidation of Germany was dictated by economic jealousy. Palmerston's memorandum stands almost alone among British documents of the period in discussing economic questions connected with the rise of Germany. Moreover, Palmerston's subsequent utterances and the whole course of British policy show that economic issues were not a dominant influence.

[2] Palmerston to Strangways, Private, 23 March 1848, the Broadlands MSS. (at Broadlands). Copy.

herself, she merely wishes that the France of 1848 may not exercise her propaganda in Germany to our disadvantage.[1]

Germany and Prussia must be strong as a bulwark against France. Prussia alone could prevent the French from establishing a German republic and then moving to help the Poles.[2] Far from desiring to see Germany divided, Russia wished to see her strong and united.[3]

Bismarck was later to assert that during the days which intervened between the south-German revolutions and that in Berlin, the Prussian monarchy was the only remaining legitimate force in Germany. The German princes at that time would have accepted the leadership of Prussia and agreed to sacrifices 'on the altar of the fatherland' similar to those made by the French nobility on 4 August 1789.[4] Had the king of Prussia finally crushed the revolution in Berlin, Nicholas I would have raised no objection to the reorganization of Germany under Prussian leadership. His sympathies were originally with Prussia rather than Austria, even if they did not extend to the personality of Frederick-William IV.[5]

Meyendorff's correspondence suggests that this was, if anything, an understatement. The fear of republicanism and of an alliance between France, revolutionary Germany and Poland was such that, at least down to the end of April, Russian diplomacy would gladly have supported any form of monarchical order in Germany. The opportunity offered to the German dynasties and to the king of Prussia in particular was perhaps even greater than Bismarck believed.

Both British and Russian diplomacy thus viewed without disfavour the beginnings of the movement for the reorganization of Germany. Palmerston wished to see a strong liberal Germany able to withstand French revolutionary republicanism and the reactionary pressure of Russia; Nicholas I, Nesselrode and Meyendorff wished to promote the consolidation of a strong conservative Germany which would act as a bulwark against the French Republic. British diplomacy was ready to encourage any moderate programme of unification whether at Frankfurt or Berlin; that of Russia would have preferred to operate through the Prussian monarchy and an anti-revolutionary ministry in Berlin. These aims were not irreconcilable. Both England and Russia, remembering the great French Revolution and the Napoleonic Wars, wished to see a Germany able to repel French revolutionary ideas and possible French aggression; compared with this the details of Germany's future organization were of

---

[1] Meyendorff to Nesselrode, 7/19 March 1848, Meyendorff, *op. cit.* p. 49.
[2] The same to the same, 7/19 April and 13/25 April 1848, *ibid.* pp. 77 ff.
[3] The same to the same, 19 April/1 May 1848, *ibid.* p. 81.
[4] Bismarck, G(*edanken und*) E(*rinnerungen*) (popular ed. Stuttgart, 1913), vol. I, p. 59.
[5] 'so würden wir von dem Kaiser Nicolaus nach dem Zusammenbruch Oestreichs keine Schwierigkeiten in der Neubildung einer haltbaren Organisation Deutschlands erfahren haben. Seine Sympathien waren ursprünglich mehr nach Berlin als nach Wien gerichtet...' (*ibid.* p. 60).

secondary importance. The German national movement, therefore, began under international auspices which were not entirely unfavourable; neither England nor Russia was opposed on principle to the consolidation of Germany as such. If the British government was more inclined to support the moderate party at Frankfurt whilst that of Russia looked to the Prussian monarchy, it seems certain that any moderate attempt to reorganize Germany would have enjoyed the sympathy of at least one of the great European powers. On the other hand, both the British and Russian governments were agreed in opposing radical, democratic and republican tendencies, Nicholas and Nesselrode, with grim determination, Palmerston and the British cabinet with 'diplomatic' disapproval.

III

The attitude of the powers towards the reorganization of Germany was modified by the appearance of the Schleswig-Holstein question. It is of some importance to understand correctly the connection between this question and that of German reorganization. The hostility shown to Germany in the question of the Duchies has been accepted almost universally as opposition to the German national movement as such. There was indeed a connection between the two but they were not identical and the relation between them is more complex than is commonly supposed.

On 24 March 1848, the Provisional Government of the Duchies proclaimed at Kiel issued a declaration that 'We will join in the movement for German unity and freedom with all our might'.[1] Since the Duchies formed part of the Danish monarchy, this was a revolutionary act and one moreover of international significance.

The rising in the Duchies was greeted with enthusiasm throughout Germany; conservatives, liberals and radicals joined in demonstrations of sympathy. Arnim, in his desire to vindicate Prussia's claim to leadership in Germany, decided to aid the rebels. On 24 March, therefore, Frederick-William IV formally announced his support for the claim of Schleswig and Holstein to an order of succession different from that in the rest of the Danish monarchy.[2] This meant that, on the death of the childless king of Denmark, the Danish monarchy would break up; Schleswig and Holstein would become independent of the government in Copenhagen.[3]

[1] 'Wir werden uns mit aller Kraft den Einheits- und Freiheitsbestrebungen Deutschlands anschliessen.' Scharff, *op. cit.* p. 29.
[2] The question of succession after the death of the childless king of Denmark was the formal issue between the Danish government and the estates of the Duchies which had been under discussion for a number of years. The Danish government had proposed to separate the two Duchies, incorporating Schleswig with its mixed population with the rest of the monarchy by abrogating its traditional order of succession. Holstein, already a member of the Germanic Confederation, was to be allowed to separate herself from the rest of the monarchy.
[3] Sybel, *op. cit.* p. 223. For the following, *ibid.* pp. 146 and 223.

On 9 April, Danish troops attacked rebel detachments and forced them back to the river Eider which formed the boundary between the two Duchies. The following day, Prussian troops crossed the Eider and began the invasion of Schleswig. On the 12th, the German Federal Diet recognized the Provisional Government of the Duchies and called on Prussia to obtain Danish consent to the inclusion of Schleswig in the Germanic Confederation. Shortly afterwards the National Assembly in Frankfurt admitted deputies from the Duchy. The king of Denmark appealed to the powers against this violation of his sovereign rights. On 23 April, Prussians and Holsteiners attacked and dispersed Danish troops in Schleswig. On 2 May the border fortress of Fredericia surrendered to the Germans and the invasion of Jutland began.

The support given by Germany to the rebel subjects of the king of Denmark had aroused indignation at St Petersburg. Meyendorff received orders to warn the Prussian government that a full-scale invasion of Jutland would 'gravely affect the interests of all the Baltic Powers and tend in its effects to destroy throughout the north the equilibrium established by the treaties. This was an eventuality which Russia could not admit.'[1] Russia had a right—indeed a duty—to ask Prussia to give up a policy not founded on any principle of justice. The tsar, therefore, must demand the immediate cessation of hostilities. Failure to comply with this request would suggest that Prussia meant to destroy the Danish monarchy. This would make a rupture with Russia inevitable.[2] For the time being, however, Russian diplomacy would be cautious.[3] The course finally adopted would depend on the attitude of the British government.[4]

In the meantime, British policy also was being formulated. In response to separate requests from Arnim, the Confederation and the Danes,[5] Palmerston had turned his attention to the subject. He outlined his views in a letter to the Queen. His aim, he explained, was to secure assistance for halting the Germans whilst there was still time to prevent the outbreak of general war. He wished, if possible, to preserve the *status quo*; as far

[1] '...que l'invasion, étendue au Jutland, porterait une grave atteinte aux intérêts de toutes les Puissances riveraines de la Baltique et tendrait par ses conséquences à rompre dans tout le Nord l'équilibre politique établi par les traités. La Russie ne saurait admettre une telle éventualité.' Nesselrode to Meyendorff, 26 April (O.S.) 1848, printed in F. de Martens, *Recueil des Traités* (St Petersburg, 1888), vol. VIII, p. 375.

[2] 'Dans ce cas, liés que nous sommes par nos actes de garantie, nous nous voyons dès aujourd'hui dans la nécessité de lui faire connaître que cette conduite de sa part devra infailliblement amener une rupture entre la Russie et la Prusse' (*ibid.*).

[3] Nesselrode feared that if Russia gave direct assistance to Denmark, she would rouse against herself the national sentiment of all Germany and perhaps revive the Polish question. Advice to be prudent was therefore given to Denmark as well as Germany. When Denmark asked for Russian mediation, the tsar replied that he would always support her against unjust and exaggerated German demands but would not act as mediator. When Denmark and Sweden asked for armed Russian intervention to support their demand for an armistice, they received a negative reply (Scharff, *op. cit.* p. 32).

[4] Nesselrode to Meyendorff, 27 April 1848, Nesselrode, *op. cit.* p. 88.

[5] Scharff, *op. cit.* pp. 36 f.

as Schleswig was concerned, England appeared bound by treaty to do so.[1] The British government, therefore, supported Russian efforts at Berlin and Frankfurt to try and restrain the Germans. France, watchfully neutral at first, ended by joining England and Russia.[2]

Threatened with complete isolation, the Prussian government decided to yield. Early in June, it announced the evacuation of Jutland; on 26 August, it signed an armistice with Denmark at Malmö. Arnim's plan to exploit Schleswig-Holstein in the interest of Prussia's German policy had been frustrated by European opposition.

In the question of the Duchies, the Russian attitude had from the start been hostile to Prussia and Germany. That of England had at first been neutral.[3] In the end, however, her diplomatic pressure had been added to that of Russia in an attempt to end hostilities and restrain Prussia and Germany from pressing to the full their military advantage. To what extent did these attitudes, which were to become more pronounced in the later phases of the dispute, betoken hostility to the reorganization of Germany? There can be no doubt that for the Germans the incorporation of the two Duchies in a reconstituted German state was an integral part of the movement for national consolidation. Schleswig and Holstein for German liberals and nationalists had become the symbol of their struggle for unity. For the deputies in Frankfurt a reorganization of the fatherland based on the abandonment of the Duchies was unthinkable. Therefore, from the German point of view, hostility to their policy in Schleswig automatically implied hostility to the movement for German unity.

From the point of view of Nicholas I and Palmerston, however, there was no apparent reason why a reorganization of Germany should necessarily involve the destruction of the Danish monarchy. Only by admitting the principle, anathema to Nicholas I and Palmerston alike, that a reorganization of Germany demanded the union under a single political authority of all German-speaking populations, could it be argued that the incorporation of Schleswig formed a necessary part of German consolidation. This was a principle no European government was prepared to admit.

---

[1] Palmerston to the Queen, 18 April 1848, in H. C. F. Bell, *Lord Palmerston* (London, 1936), vol. II, p. 8.   [2] Scharff, *op. cit.* pp. 43 ff.

[3] It is interesting to note that among the suggestions for a compromise solution during this period was one that Schleswig should be divided on ethnographical lines and that southern Schleswig and Holstein should then participate in the future organization of Germany. The proposal was welcomed by the Russian government. Nesselrode considered it the best way for 'getting decently out of this unfortunate complication' (*ibid.* pp. 40 f.). This suggestion put forward by England and Russia should dispose of the legend that the two countries adopted a one-sided anti-German policy in the Schleswig-Holstein dispute. The Austrian government also recommended this solution but it failed because the two parties to the dispute could not agree on points of detail (*ibid.*). Later Palmerston proposed that Schleswig should be given a separate constitution independent of Denmark and Germany alike. This solution was favoured also by Russia and received some support in Copenhagen but it was firmly resisted by the Provisional government of the Duchies and the German administration in Frankfurt (*ibid.* pp. 48 f.).

Nor, in practice, did it seem impossible to increase Germany's political effectiveness without adding to her territory. Even the old Confederation had never been unduly hampered by the fact that it did not include territories like the eastern portions of the Prussian monarchy. Therefore, whilst it might be desirable to strengthen Germany, there were less objectionable ways of doing this than through the incorporation of the Duchies. From the point of view of the European powers hostility to German proceedings north of the Eider need not involve opposition to German consolidation. Conversely, sympathy with the movement for the reorganization of Germany did not necessitate approval of German action in the Duchies. From a European point of view at least, the question of Schleswig was quite distinct from that of German unification.

In spite of this, however, the decisions taken at Berlin and Frankfurt with regard to the Duchies were to exercise a profound influence on the attitude of the powers towards both the Prussian government and the authorities in Frankfurt. The future of the Duchies was not to be settled till 1850, and the treaty of London, which put an end to this phase of the dispute, was not to be signed until 1852. There were to be two further bouts of fighting, accompanied by European pressure on the Prussian and German authorities. The German national movement would not, for another two years, renounce its support of the Duchies in their struggle for independence or union with Germany. This inevitably drew upon it the ill-will of Nicholas I, of the British government and of France. The question of Schleswig, by providing a source of constant friction between Germany and the non-Germanic powers, induced the latter to adopt a more critical attitude even towards purely internal attempts to reorganize the German nation. As long as any strengthening of Germany was certain to be accompanied by renewed support for the rebellious subjects of the king of Denmark, the cabinets of St Petersburg and London had some grounds for hesitation and an inducement to favour a return to the *status quo*. It is in this sense that the question of the Duchies was truly called 'a fateful question for the German revolution and for the German policy of Frederick-William IV'.[1] From the European point of view, the 'German question' and that of the Duchies were not inseparable. Nevertheless, the two were closely connected in practice, and opposition to Germany's Danish policy influenced the European attitude towards German reorganization.

IV

Whilst the cabinets of Europe were occupied with the first phase of the Schleswig-Holstein question, representatives of Germany were meeting in the Paulskirche to draw up a new constitution. On 28 June the National

[1] Scharff calls it a problem 'das zu einer wahren Schicksalsfrage der deutschen Revolution und der deutschen Politik Friedrich Wilhelms IV werden sollte' (*op. cit.* p. 29).

Assembly set up a Provisional Executive authority for the whole of Germany; on the following day, archduke John of Austria was elected to head it with the title of 'Reichsverweser'.[1] The creation of a new all-German government was an event of European importance. Legal continuity with the old Diet had indeed been carefully preserved, but even the most elaborate constitutional forms could not conceal the fact that the new authority was in its essence of revolutionary origin. Moreover, the National Assembly had associated itself with German policy in the Duchies. It had sanctioned the incorporation of Schleswig in Germany and shown marked intransigence during the negotiations for an armistice.

In the circumstances, the Russian reaction at least could hardly be in doubt. Nesselrode, exasperated by the attitude of the Provisional administration in the question of Schleswig, declared that Russia would withhold her recognition because it was impossible for any self-respecting government to have dealings with the men of Frankfurt.[2] If they were allowed to carry out their designs, the territorial arrangements in Germany (*la circonscription de l'Allemagne*) would be completely changed. Moreover, as these had been laid down by the treaties of 1815, other powers also would have a say in the matter.[3] As to Prussia, people in Berlin seemed more frightened of Frankfurt than of St Petersburg. The time for threats had passed and the moment come to prepare for action.[4] If the six great governments[5] were to mobilize their forces, and to reach an understanding, Frankfurt would have to yield. It would then be possible to establish on secure foundations the unity of the Danish monarchy so much desired by all. Otherwise the National Assembly would exercise despotic sway in Germany.[6]

The British attitude also was influenced by German policy in Schleswig. Early in July, Heinrich von Gagern, the influential President of the German National Assembly, appealed to the British government to recognize the archduke in the most formal manner customary among sovereigns 'and so obtain a mark of countenance and encouragement for Germany in her progress towards Constitutional Government which would be most highly prized by the German nation'.[7] Palmerston's reply

---

[1] Sybel, *op. cit.* pp. 169 ff.

[2] 'Il est impossible pour un cabinet qui se respecte d'avoir affaire aux hommes de Francfort.' Nesselrode to Meyendorff, 19 August 1848, Nesselrode, *op. cit.* p. 152.

[3] The same to the same, 12 August 1848, *ibid.* p. 144.

[4] The same to the same, 19 August 1848, *ibid.* p. 151.

[5] 'les grands six gouvernements', by which Nesselrode presumably meant those of Russia, England, France, Austria, Prussia and Sweden.

[6] Nesselrode to Meyendorff, 10 September 1848, *ibid.* p. 172.

[7] Gagern expressed a hope that British recognition would precede that of Russia: 'And as the Germans have no wish to come before the world in their new shape under the patronage of Russia but a great wish to make their first foreign stay the friendship of England, the President trusts the Queen will view the matter in the same light.' It was hoped to make the new Empire or Confederation of Germany 'the chief continental ally of England in place of Austria'. 'This policy is calculated to render Germany equally indepen-

was not encouraging. Cowley, then British minister at Bern, was indeed ordered to proceed to Frankfurt, but only as an unaccredited diplomatic representative. Recognition was withheld on formal grounds:

The Diet which was constituted in accordance with the provisions of the Treaty of Vienna, and to which a British Minister has hitherto been accredited, has dissolved itself, and although that Diet by its last act devolved upon the Arch Duke John as Reichsverweser the functions with which the Diet itself had been invested, yet the Arch Duke John has been invested by the German Parliament at Frankfurt with only a temporary and provisional character and that Parliament has not as yet determined what is to be the final and permanent arrangement for the Supreme Authority of United Germany.

At Frankfurt, in his conversations with German statesmen, Cowley was to express

the deep Interest which the British Government takes in the welfare of Germany, and the sincere and earnest wish which the British Government forms that the deliberations in which the representatives of Germany at Frankfurt are now engaged, may lead to results conducive to the Prosperity, the Happiness, the Strength and Independence of the German Nation.

Three matters might arise in discussions with German leaders. 'With the Political Arrangements which the Germans may think fit to adopt for their own organization the British Government has no Right and no wish to interfere.' However, when the time should arise for discussing the commercial arrangements which might be proposed for Germany, Cowley would receive instructions

with a view to recommend to the Germans that liberal and enlightened system of Commercial Policy which the Progressive Diffusion of Political Knowledge has convinced all reflecting men is sound in Theory and which the experience of late years has proved to be advantageous in Practice.[1]

The only matter of pressing European interest upon which it appeared necessary at present to express an opinion was the proposed armistice between the German and Danish forces in Schleswig-Holstein. Her Majesty's Government hoped that the armistice agreed on between the governments of Prussia, Denmark and Sweden would be concluded before Cowley reached Frankfurt,

but if that should not have been the case, and if any Sanction or Authority from Frankfurt should be requisite for the Conclusion of that Armistice, you will omit no Effort for the Purpose of persuading those with whom the giving of that Sanction rests to grant it without further Delay.

dent of France and Russia, and to combine naturally enough with the friendly relations she will desire to keep up with Belgium, Hungary and her other immediate neighbours' (Strangways to Palmerston, 12 July 1848, Broadlands MSS.).

[1] Whenever an opportunity offered of conversing on these matters, Cowley was to point to the recent example of England 'as affording a Proof that Moderate Import Duties are the most productive in Revenue, and tend to improve Native Industry by the spur of competition'.

A prolongation of hostilities in the Duchies could not fail to lead to 'serious and extensive Embarrassments'.[1]

Palmerston's hopes were doomed to disappointment. Strangways[2] had already found occasion to comment on the 'other-worldliness' and pedantry of the German constitution-makers.

...The extraordinary and undue weight laid upon words, and upon the order of words in phrases where the Sovereignty of the People and the Power acknowledged to be left to the Princes come in contact, is absurd and ridiculous and the most important questions are lost or modified for the sake of some word of small real import which happens not to please the Left.[3]

The reports of Cowley confirmed these observations.

I have really scruples in committing to a despatch all that is to be said upon the state of affairs here, and upon the character of the men, who have undertaken to conduct them. The affairs themselves seem to be getting into greater confusion every day—and as to the Ministers a more useless inefficient body of men were never brought together....

It was the Foreign Minister in particular who had aroused his scorn:

What answer can you make to a Minister of Foreign Affairs who says 'What do you think we are afraid of—war? I am not sure that war is not the *best thing* for us. It must at all events settle the question of Unity at once'! In short they are a parcel of children who want whipping and caressing alternately.[4]

It is small wonder that Palmerston began to doubt the prospects of German unity: 'As to German unity that vision seems fast dissolving but probably the efforts made to realize that phantom may lead to a reconstruction of the Confederation in some form better adapted to the present state of Germany.'[5] Doubts deepened as August passed into September; indeed the attempt of the Diet to disavow the Prusso-Danish armistice roused Palmerston to heights of scornful fury. Cowley was invited to ask some members of the Diet, known to him, 'in civil terms' 'whether they are mad and really intend to disavow the Sleswig-Holstein armistice. If they are deliberately determined to rush into Conflict with all Europe, including, as it seems, Prussia, well and good, let them take the consequences. Quos Deus vult perdere dementat prius.' Should Cowley meet any member 'who may still be in his sane senses', he was to represent to him the possible consequences for Germany.[6]

By the autumn of 1848 the old governments were daily gaining ground. The revolutionary spirit was ebbing. The Assembly and Government in Frankfurt were losing whatever importance they had possessed. It was

---

[1] Palmerston to Cowley No. 1, 29 July 1848, Draft, Broadlands MSS.
[2] The British Minister previously accredited to the old Federal Diet.
[3] Strangways to Palmerston, Private, 28 June 1848, Broadlands MSS.
[4] Cowley to Palmerston, Private, 21 and 27 August 1848, *ibid.*
[5] Palmerston to Bloomfield, 18 August 1848, quoted in Bell, *op. cit.* p. 3.
[6] Palmerston to Cowley, Private, 8 September 1848, Broadlands MSS. copy.

becoming clear that the real decisions about the future of Germany would be made in Vienna and Berlin. The role of Frankfurt was played out. Relations between the German provisional government and those of Russia and England had been dominated by the question of the Duchies. It was this above all which had earned for the National Assembly the violent animosity of the Russian government and the scorn and disapproval of Palmerston. It was this, moreover, which had cemented the 'unnatural' Anglo-Russian entente[1] and reduced British sympathy for the liberal and national cause in Germany. The German National Assembly, dependent as it was on the support of German public opinion, had no choice in the matter. It was forced to support the inhabitants of Schleswig and Holstein. It is equally certain, however, that it was above all German intransigence in the question of the Duchies which provoked the hostility of the powers towards the National Assembly and its government.

V

During the second half of 1848 the sands of the revolution were steadily running out. On 17 June Windischgrätz recaptured Prague for the Habsburgs; during the 'June Days'[2] Cavaignac defeated the Paris revolutionaries. On 25 July Radetzky routed the Piedmontese at Custozza, on 6 August he entered Milan. These events paved the way for counter-revolutionary advances in Germany: on 30 October, revolutionary Vienna surrendered to the forces of Windischgrätz; on 1 November the strong man of the counter-revolution, Prince Felix Schwarzenberg, became Prime Minister. On the same day, Frederick-William IV appointed a conservative ministry under Brandenburg and a week later General Wrangel's troops re-occupied Berlin. In December, Ferdinand I abdicated in favour of his nephew Francis-Joseph; the Prussian assembly was dissolved and a new constitution promulgated by decree. On 10 December, Louis-Napoleon was elected President of the French Republic.

The revolutionary forces, however, still held out in many parts of Europe. The Magyars remained in arms; Manin's Venetian Republic continued to fight for its existence; Piedmont was preparing to re-enter the lists.[3] The question of the Duchies remained unsettled, and democrats and republicans were active in many parts of Germany.

In fact, the victories of reaction during the summer of 1848 had ushered in a period of 'dual power' during which the revolutionary movement was

---

[1] It is interesting to note that Nesselrode showed extreme reluctance to take any action over Schleswig without the co-operation of the British government. 'Nous ne prendrons définitivement notre parti que lorsque nous saurons ce que l'Angleterre fera' (Nesselrode to Meyendorff, 27 April 1848, Nesselrode, *op. cit.* p. 88). Russia will not speak at Frankfurt except in conjunction with England (the same to the same, 12 August 1848, *ibid.* p. 144).

[2] 23–6 June.

[3] On 9 August she had been forced to accept the armistice of Vigevano.

steadily losing momentum, whilst the old authorities had not yet regained full control. This phase of the revolution was to last until the spring of 1849, when Frederick-William's refusal of the imperial crown,[1] the recall of the Austrian deputies from Frankfurt[2] and the Prussian rejection of the imperial constitution[3] opened the way for the final triumph of counter-revolution in Germany. The suppression of democratic and republican risings in June 1849 set the seal on the defeat of the German revolution.

During the period of 'dual power', three rival programmes for the reorganization of Germany competed for public favour. The first was that of Gagern and the moderate groups in the Assembly, who wished to reconstruct the Confederation under the joint auspices of Frankfurt and Prussia. By the end of January 1849, the draft of a new constitution had been virtually completed and on 27 March it was resolved to establish a hereditary monarchy. On the following day, Frederick-William IV was elected emperor of Germany. In the meantime Austria, excluded from Germany by the constitution-makers of Frankfurt, had devised a programme of her own. A new constitution promulgated on 7 March[4] proclaimed the empire an indivisible unitary state. Two days later, the Austrian government demanded the admission of the new state to the German Confederation. At the same time, it proposed a new federal constitution which excluded all elements of popular representation and reduced Prussia to the position of one of six German 'groups'. Finding it difficult to accept the programme of either the moderate democrats at Frankfurt or of Schwarzenberg in Vienna, Frederick-William IV proposed the creation of a federal state under Prussian leadership, based on an understanding between the German princes and the moderate majority of the National Assembly. The situation was simplified when Berlin and Frankfurt failed to reach agreement. This became evident in April and was followed by the eclipse of the Assembly, the 'Reichsverweser' and the Frankfurt authorities. As a result, Prussia and Austria were left face to face to settle Germany's future.

Developments in Germany were anxiously watched at St Petersburg. In the Russian capital, the renascence of Austria was greeted with satisfaction. Nesselrode waxed enthusiastic about the character and policies of Schwarzenberg.[5] He felt that the survival of the Habsburg monarchy was a vital Russian interest.[6] Were not the generals commanding against

[1] Announced on 3 April 1849.
[2] On 5 April 1849.
[3] On 21 April 1849.
[4] It was dated 4 March 1849.
[5] '...Schwarzenberg mène les affaires à merveille. Alles was aus dem österreichischen Kabinet kommt hat Hand und Fusz [sic]...' (Nesselrode to Michael Chreptovich, 15 January 1849, Nesselrode, *op. cit.* pp. 212 f.).
[6] 'Nous ne pouvons pas laisser crouler la monarchie autrichienne; c'est une question vitale pour nous. Maintenant qu'elle commence à se relever et que nous voyons à la tête de ses affaires des hommes de cœur et d'esprit, dont les principes doivent nous inspirer de

Austria in Italy, Hungary and Transylvania Poles? Since the restoration of Poland lay at the bottom of all the troubles, the interests of Russia were linked with those of Austria;[1] the Hungro-Polish conspiracy was as dangerous to the one as to the other.[2] Anything which strengthened the Austria of Schwarzenberg would be of advantage to Russia. It was therefore considered at St Petersburg that Austro-Prussian co-operation offered the only hope for the future of Germany.[3] The tsar desired the union (*Einigkeit*) of Germany but without unity (*Einheit*), firm Austro-Prussian co-operation, and a strong executive not based on popular sovereignty. He was opposed to the mediatization of the lesser states and to a federation based on the ideology of Frankfurt.[4] There was, however, no thought of active Russian intervention in German affairs.[5]

It was the policy of Prussia which caused anxiety at St Petersburg. Whilst Meyendorff was indefatigably urging the Prussian government to conciliate Austria and break with Frankfurt, a Prussian circular note of 23 January seemed to foreshadow Prussian co-operation with the National Assembly. 'Union not with Austria but with the revolution' was the Russian comment. Nesselrode, with deep regret, began to contemplate the possibility of Austria's exclusion from Germany and even of civil war.[6]

During April and May, revolutionary risings occurred in Thuringia, Saxony and western Germany; a wave of unrest also swept over Prussia. In the face of these developments, Prussian policy took a sharp turn to the right. On 21 and 28 April, the Prussian government rejected the imperial constitution drafted at Frankfurt.[7] On 26 May, the governments of

la confiance, il est de notre intérêt de l'aider dans la tâche si difficile qu'elle a encore à remplir' (the same to the same, *ibid.* p. 212).

[1] 'Preuve évidente que le rétablissement de la Pologne est au fond de tout cela, et que, par conséquent, notre cause et nos intérêts sont intimement liés à ceux de l'Autriche...' (Nesselrode to Meyendorff, 1 April 1849, *ibid.* pp. 227f.).

[2] Nesselrode to Chreptovich, 16 May 1849, *ibid.* p. 239.

[3] '...c'est la seule ancre de salut [*sic*] pour l'Allemagne' (Nesselrode to Meyendorff, 26 December 1848, *ibid.* p. 204).

[4] Report by Rochow, the Prussian personal military attaché to the tsar, quoted in Scharff, *op. cit.* pp. 101f.

[5] 'Dans cette situation si incertaine, ce qui nous convient de plus, à nous, Russie, c'est de nous maintenir dans notre attitude et de nous mêler le moins possible des questions qui ne nous touchent pas de très près' (Nesselrode to Meyendorff, 15 February 1849, Nesselrode, *op. cit.* p. 219).

[6] When discussing a rebuff administered by Prussia to Austria he wrote: 'Je crains que cette faute ne soit irréparable et qu'elle n'amène une scission, voire même une guerre civile en Allemagne' (the same to the same, 21 February 1849, *ibid.* p. 222). Meyendorff wrote despairingly: 'Well then, let her [Germany] organize herself as she thinks best, so long as the war with Denmark is ended. We shall see later in what relations to the new government to place ourselves' (Meyendorff to Nesselrode, 27 March/8 April 1849, Meyendorff, *op. cit.* p. 185).

[7] Sybel comments on this rejection: 'Es war die Vernichtung, und leider die von preussischer Hand vollzogene Vernichtung aller Hoffnungen, an welchen das Herz der Nation seit einem Jahre gehangen hatte' (Sybel, *op. cit.* p. 317).

Prussia, Saxony and Hanover jointly proposed to the other German states the adoption of this same constitution greatly modified in a conservative sense. The king of Prussia was to head the new Federation.[1] During June, Prussian troops crushed insurrectionary movements in south-western Germany. Nesselrode was sanguine. Already during May, he had written to Meyendorff: 'If events continue to move at the present rate, I foresee a return to the triple alliance of Toeplitz and Münchengrätz.'[2]

Nesselrode's optimism was premature. The new German constitution elaborated at Berlin was permeated by a spirit of moderate liberalism and provided for a unitary state with executive power vested in the king of Prussia. The Russian chancellor considered this constitution, 'fabricated' in Berlin, to be detestable.[3] More serious even than Prussian 'constitutionalism' was the resumption of German activity in the Duchies. On 23 February, the Danish government had unwisely denounced the armistice of Malmö. On 3 April, German forces under a Prussian general had resumed military operations. At a fateful meeting of the Prussian cabinet on 1 May, it was decided that Prussia's 'military honour' demanded a determined prosecution of the war. In these circumstances, Nicholas I addressed himself to the king of Prussia. In a firm personal letter, he demanded a complete rupture with Frankfurt and the end of the Danish war. If the war went on, Russia would have to seek an understanding with France. This eventuality, disagreeable to Germany, Prussia could still forestall.[4] In a covering letter, Nesselrode wrote that Russia would await the king's reply before adopting an attitude hostile to Prussia and Germany. A Russian fleet was getting ready to assist the Danes in the defence of their islands, but Russian intervention would, for the time being, be limited to naval action.[5] Frederick-William, moved to tears by the tsar's letter, replied that he could not order his troops to retreat before a beaten enemy.[6] The Russian government thereupon decided to suspend all dealings with Prussia until the end of the Hungarian campaign.[7] General Rauch, sent to Warsaw to appease the tsar, found that Nicholas appeared to regard war with Prussia as almost inevitable.[8] He was moving towards friendship with Austria and a mission to Warsaw undertaken by Schwarzenberg and the young Francis-Joseph had better success than Rauch's. Nesselrode recorded that relations with Austria were becoming

[1] Saxony and Hanover accepted the arrangement on condition that the two south-German kingdoms also agreed to join.
[2] Nesselrode to Meyendorff, 16 May 1849, Nesselrode, op. cit. p. 239.
[3] Nesselrode to Chreptovich, 12 June 1849, ibid. p. 254.
[4] Copy in Meyendorff, op. cit. pp. 197f.
[5] Nesselrode to Meyendorff, 10 May 1849, ibid. pp. 95f. Nesselrode explained that a campaign on land would be imprudent before the end of the Hungarian campaign (ibid.). In fact, no fewer than 120,000 Russian troops were at this time engaged in the campaign in Transylvania and Hungary (Stählin, op. cit. p. 514). [6] Scharff, op. cit. p. 122.
[7] Nesselrode to Meyendorff, 22 and 23 May 1849, Nesselrode, op. cit. pp. 240f.
[8] Cf. Scharff, op. cit. p. 124.

very cordial.[1] This, however, did not yet mean that the tsar had given his blessing to Schwarzenberg's German policy. On the contrary, he still favoured a dualist system under which Germany should be divided along the river Main. Prussia should take the lead in the anti-revolutionary campaign; she would receive Russian support if an end was put at once to the campaign in the Duchies. Otherwise, the troops intended to protect Prussia would cross her borders, the Russian fleet would land troops in Schleswig, and German ports would be blockaded.[2]

Although the tsar had no intention at this moment of declaring war on Prussia,[3] his threat, combined with Franco-British diplomatic pressure, made a deep impression on Frederick-William. The Prussian commander in Denmark was ordered to delay his advance. On 10 July, under heavy diplomatic pressure from Russia, England and France, Prussia and Denmark concluded a six months' armistice and signed preliminaries of peace.[4] The tsar expressed satisfaction at the Prussian concessions, the Russian squadron withdrew from Danish waters, and Russo-Prussian tension relaxed.[5]

VI

The Prusso-Danish agreement appeased not only the tsar; it also induced Palmerston to abandon his reserve respecting Prussia's German policy. Three days after the signature of the armistice, the Foreign Secretary told the British minister in Berlin that the Cabinet had, for the last twelve months, watched with intense interest the progress of events in Germany 'with reference to the great question of German Unity'. Although it had been felt that these events were of extreme importance as bearing upon the general interests of Europe,

yet the questions debated in regard to these matters have been in their immediate origin and application so purely German...that Her Majesty's Government have purposely abstained from departing, with respect to these affairs, from the position of anxious observers of what was passing.

[1] Schwarzenberg was following a policy of careful restraint in the question of the Duchies. He held the view that, as a European power, Austria should remain neutral in the German-Danish conflict and work for an early settlement.

[2] Scharff, op. cit. pp. 125f.

[3] Rochow soon understood from his conversations with the tsar that the Russian squadron had been sent to Danish waters merely as a demonstration. It would facilitate a Danish retreat from the mainland and might attempt to prevent a German landing on Zealand. Beyond this, Nicholas would not go (ibid. pp. 126f.).

[4] German forces would evacuate Jutland. Schleswig would be administered by three Commissioners, a Prussian, a Dane and an Englishman. The northern half of the Duchy would be occupied by Swedish, the southern by Prussian troops. In any final settlement, Schleswig would be given a status different from that of either Holstein or Denmark proper.

[5] At the same time, the tsar firmly refused a Prussian invitation to act as mediator in the Austro-Prussian dispute. This is the first—if by no means the last—Prussian attempt to invoke the tsar's arbitration in purely German affairs. For months to come, the king of Prussia and his advisers would continue to press the proposal. The tsar steadily declined to act as arbitrator.

Even now, although matters had been much simplified by the course of events, the British government 'would not wish to take any direct or active part, by advice or otherwise, in the discussions still going on'. With this qualification, however, they were prepared to give their blessing to the plan of German unification proposed by the Prussian government. That plan 'would no doubt be advantageous to the German People, with reference both to their internal Interests, and to their Foreign Relations, and it would consequently on that account be advantageous to Europe at large'. It seemed to assure 'that separate nationalities would, to a certain degree, be preserved' and it appeared to combine in its organization 'many of the advantages of Unity without destroying those moral springs of action which derive their strength and elasticity from feelings of local nationality'.

At the head of such a league there must of necessity be a state possessing separate and individual importance and consideration, 'and in the present posture of affairs in Europe, Prussia seems to be the only German State qualified to assume such a position'. Hanover, Saxony, Württemberg and Bavaria were not of sufficient magnitude and power, 'and the peculiar condition of Austria, past, present and future, seems to oppose obstacles of a grave character, to prevent that Power from being the Head of a United Germany'. The head of such a German league should not only be 'a substantively powerful state', but should also be 'heart and soul German'. It should be biased by no foreign interest and should be swayed by no foreign influences. The government of the Austrian empire, however, must frequently have been guided in its political course by influences 'altogether foreign to Germany'. Moreover, the present distressed and uncertain position in which Austria was placed with regard to her internal affairs obviously disqualified her for the moment from being accepted as the head of the German organization. As regards her future condition, whatever might be the issue of her war with Hungary, the result of that war must either revive the pre-existing objections to her headship or must create objections of a new and stronger kind.

It therefore appeared to the British government that if Germany was to be organized on a principle of intimate union, such an organization could be effected only under the leadership of Prussia

and it is most desirable for the working out of such a scheme, that Prussia should disarm the jealousies and allay the fears of the smaller sovereignties by respecting their Political Existence, and by not expecting from them any sacrifices which would be incompatible therewith.

A German league so formed under the leadership of Prussia might enter the closest possible alliance with Austria for all purposes of common defence. Their joint action would be none the less sincere because the two bodies politic mutually abstained from interfering with each other in regard to matters belonging to internal organization and administrative detail.[1]

The British government, therefore, favoured the consolidation of Germany under Prussian leadership. Considerations of commercial policy had dropped into the background. There was no sign of anxiety about possible Anglo-German naval rivalry in the future.[2] Palmerston's only doubt arose from the Germans' evident inability to unite: 'There can be no objection to the idea of German union except that no one seems able to achieve it.'[3]

After the truce with Denmark, therefore, the chances for the realization of Radowitz's[4] programme were not unfavourable. Austria continued to be occupied in Hungary. Russia, engaged in Hungary and the Danubian Principalities,[5] was, for the moment, immobilized. The British attitude was sympathetic. The tsar, moreover, was ready to concede to Prussia, at the very least, a preponderant influence in northern Germany. In the circumstances, possible French displeasure need cause little anxiety as long as the Germans agreed among themselves. If, at this juncture, Hanover and Saxony at least had given Prussia their unqualified support, she could now have secured what she would not in fact achieve until 1866 at the price of two campaigns. If Bavaria and Württemberg also had agreed to co-operate with the northern states, even the results of 1870 might perhaps have been anticipated without a policy of 'blood and iron'. In fact, it now depended almost entirely upon the German governments what advantages Germany would gain from British diplomatic support, Russian preoccupations in the Balkans and the general European *détente* following the Prusso-Danish armistice.

---

[1] Palmerston to Westmorland, 13 July 1849, printed in V. Valentin, *Bismarcks Reichsgründung im Urteil englischer Diplomaten* (Amsterdam, 1937), pp. 500ff.

[2] Early in November 1848 Cowley had a conversation with Prince Adalbert of Prussia who was to organize the imperial German navy. The Prince had expressed a desire to visit England. Cowley assured him that there was no foundation for rumours that England viewed with disfavour the creation of a German fleet. It would be many years before a German navy could become an object of jealousy. In any case, British and German interests would probably be the same. England need not fear the rise of a naval power which, in his opinion, would be called on always to defend the same cause as the ships of Her Majesty the Queen (Cowley to Palmerston, 5 November 1848, *ibid.* pp. 39f.).

[3] 'Es ist gegen die Idee eines Deutschen Reiches nichts einzuwenden, als dass niemand es scheint zustandebringen zu können' (Report by Bunsen of 29 July 1849, Scharff, *op. cit.* p. 134).

[4] General Joseph Maria von Radowitz, called to Berlin on 22 April 1849 to assist Frederick-William IV in his plans for the reorganization of Germany under Prussian leadership.

[5] Disturbances in the Principalities had provoked a joint Russo-Turkish occupation.

VII

The opportunity was missed never to return. It was missed through German disunion. By the end of 1849, Germany stood poised on the brink of civil war.[1] In the face of this growing tension, both sides appealed for Russian support. Late in May 1850, Frederick-William sent his personal adjutant Edwin von Manteuffel and his brother the Prince of Prussia to meet the tsar near Warsaw.[2] Schwarzenberg also made his way to Skierniwice. Nicholas tried to reconcile the differences of the two parties. He told Manteuffel that a civil war in Germany would be contrary to the treaties and that he would not permit it. He would lend his support to the party which stood closest to the treaties. An invitation from Manteuffel, that he should act as mediator, Nicholas firmly refused. In

[1] The causes of German disunion can be indicated here only in outline. They were essentially the revival of Austria and the refusal of the secondary German states to give support to Prussia.

The Austrian recovery took place during the late summer of 1849. On 18 July the Austrians re-entered Budapest; on the 31st, the Magyar forces suffered a decisive defeat; between 11 and 13 August their commanders negotiated the surrender of Vilagos. On 24 August negotiations were opened for the surrender of Venice. Three days later, Manin departed into exile. By the end of the month, the Habsburg empire had finally 'weathered the storm'. Schwarzenberg could turn his undivided attention to the affairs of Germany.

Prussia also had strengthened her position. By October the whole of northern and central Germany and Baden had accepted the programme of the Prussian 'Union'. Hanover and Saxony, however, had entered the 'Union' reluctantly at a time when the Prussian army was the only defence of the princes against republicanism and democracy. With the reduction of the revolutionary danger and the revival of Austria, their kings eagerly sought an opportunity to recall the mandate entrusted to Frederick-William IV at a moment of crisis. On 5 October the Council of the 'Union' discussed the date for elections to the all-Union parliament (Reichstag). The delegates of Hanover and Saxony opposed the holding of elections but were outvoted. 15 January 1850 was fixed as the date for elections. Hanover and Saxony protested. On 20 October the representatives of the two kingdoms announced that they would no longer take part in the affairs of the 'Union'. In consequence, Prussia was now left alone with Baden and the lesser central- and north-German states.

In a circular of 12 November Schwarzenberg solemnly announced that the Federal Constitution of 1815 remained the basis of relations between the German states. On the 28th, he informed the Prussian government that the 'Union' was incompatible with the Federal Acts and therefore unconstitutional.

Both sides then tried to organize their forces. The Prussian government tried to organize its 'Union', named the Erfurt Union after the centre of its activities, whilst Schwarzenberg attempted to reconstitute the old Federal Diet at Frankfurt. Complete deadlock resulted.

Germany was now divided into two rival camps. On the one side stood Prussia, supported by Baden and the lesser states of northern and central Germany, on the other the league of the four kings (Bavaria, Württemberg, Saxony and Hanover) backed by Austria. During the autumn, Austria was concentrating military forces in north-western Bohemia and Vorarlberg. Prussia, although unprepared from a military point of view, was determined to defend the Erfurt Union.

In the end, an open clash was averted, but this was another of the wars postponed but not avoided. The war was fought—with a very similar grouping—in the summer of 1866. However, the relative military strength of the two sides had greatly changed in the interval.

[2] Frederick-William told Meyendorff: 'Je vais envoyer le Prince de Prusse à Varsovie, parceque le moment est venu où je dois appeler à une décision de l'Empereur entre l'Autriche et moi' (Meyendorff to Nesselrode, 11/23 May 1850, Meyendorff, *op. cit.* p. 300). For the following cf. Scharff, *op. cit.* pp. 184ff. and Sybel, *op. cit.* pp. 383ff.

conversation with Schwarzenberg, the tsar urged the need for agreement with Prussia. The Austrian statesman was able to gain his sympathy by consenting to a division of Germany into a Prussian and an Austrian sphere.[1] When he asked, however, that Russian troops should occupy Galicia in the event of an Austro-Prussian war, he met with a firm refusal.

After the discussions in Warsaw, direct Austro-Prussian negotiations were resumed, but in his desire to preserve the Erfurt Union, Frederick-William declined Schwarzenberg's conciliatory overtures. On 17 July he finally rejected the Austrian offer of a dualist settlement in return for the abandonment of the Union.

Schwarzenberg, in the meantime, had gained a major diplomatic success. Impressed by his counter-revolutionary arguments,[2] the tsar in a note of 24 June had given his blessing to the inclusion of the entire Habsburg monarchy in the Germanic Confederation.[3] He admitted that, in exchange for abandoning northern Germany to Prussia, Austria might create a new political unit embracing the monarchy and the states of southern Germany. This Russian decision greatly strengthened the hand of Schwarzenberg.

A few days later Prussia, in her turn, tried to improve her European position. She signed a treaty with Denmark leaving the Duchies to their fate. It was not a moment too soon: the tsar had made his arbitration in Germany dependent on the conclusion of peace with Denmark[4] and the Franco-British attitude in the impending conflict might also turn on Prusso-Danish relations. With a heavy heart, therefore, Frederick-William belatedly sacrificed the Duchies to the international needs of his German policy.

The Prussian withdrawal, however, did not end the conflict in Holstein, where the inhabitants continued to resist the Danes. It was this which offered Schwarzenberg an opportunity to confirm himself in the tsar's good graces. He informed the Russian government of his willingness to use his 'Diet' in Frankfurt for the reduction of the recalcitrant Holsteiners under the terms of the Treaty of Berlin.[5] The king of Denmark, he declared, should appeal to Frankfurt for 'mediation'. Schwarzenberg, moreover, was able to gratify another Russian wish. On 2 August, a Protocol had

---

[1] Schwarzenberg felt that it was undignified to draw the tsar into a purely German dispute. He declared that it was ridiculous and disagreeable to submit purely German differences to foreigners after they had 'for two years talked foolishly (*gefaselt*) about the unity, independence, power and greatness of Germany'. He expressed surprise that the Prussian government did not appear to share this feeling.

[2] In a memorandum of 6 June he had skilfully explained that a strong central Europe under Austrian leadership would be a powerful bulwark against revolutionary currents from the West.

[3] This was against the advice of Meyendorff, who had consistently warned his government against Schwarzenberg's 'Empire of Seventy Millions' (Meyendorff, *op. cit. passim*).

[4] At Warsaw, he had again urged a speedy settlement and warned Manteuffel that he was bound by guarantees given to Denmark and might have to send his fleet to her assistance.

[5] Article IV of the treaty of Berlin signed between Prussia and Denmark on 2 July 1850 authorized the king of Denmark in his capacity as duke of Holstein to call upon the Germanic Confederation to restore his authority in the Duchy.

been signed by the representatives of England, France, Russia, Sweden and Denmark, guaranteeing the integrity of the Danish monarchy. Both Prussia and Austria had been invited to adhere, but whereas Bunsen, the Prussian minister in London, refused to do so, the Austrian representative added his signature on 23 August after the other signatories had admitted an Austrian reservation respecting the rights of the Germanic Confederation. This constituted a further success for Schwarzenberg, for not only had he succeeded in establishing a further claim on the tsar's goodwill but also in deepening Prussia's isolation. Holstein thus remained the Achilles heel of Prussia's German policy.

The tsar, in fact, blamed Prussia for her intransigence and considered her conduct proof that she intended to set herself against the whole of Europe. The moment was critical: a Russian squadron was cruising in the Baltic, ready to join Swedish naval forces in intervention on the coast of Holstein. Denmark had appealed to England and France for military assistance. Military talks had been initiated between Austria and Bavaria. Tension was increased when on 2 September Schwarzenberg's assembly in Frankfurt constituted itself as a regular *Bundestag*. In reply, Frederick-William on 14 September appointed Radowitz, the protagonist of the Erfurt Union, as his Minister of Foreign Affairs. Radowitz was detested at St Petersburg and his appointment had the effect almost of a declaration of war.

At the beginning of October, the situation was further aggravated by a severe conflict between the Prussian government and the authorities in Frankfurt.[1] As a result, Austrian, Prussian and Bavarian troops were

---

[1] At the beginning of September, the inhabitants of Electoral Hesse had risen against their ruler. The Elector in his difficulties had appealed for assistance to the 'Bundestag' in Frankfurt. Regardless of the fact that Electoral Hesse was formally a member of the Prussian Union, the 'Bundestag' on 21 September decided to support the Elector, if necessary by force of arms. On the 26th, a Prussian Crown Council unanimously decided that, rather than permit this, Prussia must occupy the Electorate herself. On 15 October the Elector formally asked the 'Bundestag' for military assistance and on the following day the assembly resolved to grant his request.

Electoral Hesse gained its importance from the fact that it was wedged between the eastern and western portions of the Prussian monarchy, and straddled the direct line of communications between Berlin and Cologne. Under the old Confederation, Prussia had exercised a dominant influence in the Electorate. She had secured the right to use two roads running across the country as military routes (*Etappenstrassen*), to assure military communications between Berlin and the western provinces.

The crisis in Electoral Hesse was not the only cause of dispute. Late in September, Nesselrode announced that Russia would officially recognize the 'Bundestag' as soon as it had ratified the treaty of Berlin and taken active steps to secure its execution with regard to Holstein. Early in October, the 'Bundestag' duly ratified the treaty. The Prussian government challenged the right of the assembly to act on behalf of the Confederation. When Schwarzenberg proposed a federal execution in Holstein under the authority of his 'Bundestag', Prussia declared such action to be 'illegal', and announced her intention to resist it by force of arms.

On 11 October Francis-Joseph signed a treaty of alliance with the kings of Bavaria and Württemberg. A military conflict seemed certain.

converging on Hesse, where a clash seemed imminent. In this situation, the parties in the dispute once again addressed themselves to the tsar. Prussia as before took the lead and for the third time in two years an envoy from Frederick-William took the road to Warsaw to state his case to the emperor Nicholas.[1] The choice fell on Brandenburg, the Prime Minister, who on the afternoon of 17 October had a long conversation with the tsar. Nicholas once again emphatically refused a suggestion that he should mediate in the conflict. He declared that he wished well to both Austria and Prussia and would not interfere in their quarrel in any way. At the same time, he praised the Elector of Hesse for appealing to the 'Bundestag' and called for the disarming of Holstein. The latter, it appeared to Brandenburg, was the key to his policy. In a subsequent conversation, the tsar proposed that Prussia herself should 'pacify' the Duchy and added that he would regard resistance to measures which the 'Bundestag' might take with this object in view as a personal insult to himself. He would reply to such action with military preparations. He would, in any case, recognize the 'Bundestag' as soon as it took the first step towards a pacification. In conversation with Rochow, Nicholas added that he would watch quietly whilst Prussia organized her Union and Austria her 'Bundestag' but neither must interfere in the other's province. Both Hesse and Holstein belonged to the sphere of the 'Bundestag'.

In the meantime, Francis-Joseph and Schwarzenberg also had arrived at Warsaw. The latter had come in a conciliatory frame of mind and agreement was reached between him and Brandenburg about a way of settling the dispute.[2] The settlement which the Prussian Prime Minister brought back from Warsaw caused the resignation of Radowitz and two of his colleagues. On 6 November, Brandenburg himself was dead.[3]

VIII

The agreement between Schwarzenberg and Brandenburg came too late to avert a crisis over the twin questions of 'Bundestag' execution in Hesse and Holstein. On the evening of 5 November, Frederick-William ordered a general mobilization which was announced the following day. Two days later, shots were exchanged between Prussian troops in Hesse and Bavarian forces approaching their positions on the military roads. On the 10th, the Austrian minister in Berlin declared that he would demand his passports unless the Prussians evacuated Hesse. On the same day, the tsar

[1] For the following cf. Sybel, *op. cit.* vol. 2, pp. 6ff.; and Scharff, *op. cit.* pp. 215f.
[2] It was agreed that Prussia would shelve her Union for an indefinite period. In return, Austria would waive her demand for Prussian recognition of the 'Bundestag'. The future constitution of Germany would be discussed in 'free conferences' by representatives of the German states. Agreement was reached on some parts of the constitution; others were reserved for the conference.
[3] His place was taken by Otto von Manteuffel, the conservative Minister of the Interior.

replied in severe terms to a further appeal from Frederick-William. On the 11th, Alexander Gorchakov presented his credentials as Russian minister to the 'Bundestag'.

On 15 November, the Prussian government formally proposed to its allies the abrogation of the Erfurt constitution. This action, however, could not resolve the crisis: the forces of the 'Bundestag' destined to carry out federal execution in Hesse and Holstein continued to be held up at the Prussian military roads. To make matters worse, the government of Brunswick, through which the federal contingent must pass on its way to Holstein, announced that it did not recognize the 'Bundestag' and would resist the passage of federal troops. In reply to an appeal from the duke of Brunswick, the Prussian government declared in Vienna that Brunswick was acting within her rights and would receive Prussian support. A warlike speech from the throne, read by Frederick-William on 21 November, reverberated through the length and breadth of Germany.

The tsar stigmatized the speech as warlike and revolutionary. Four Russian army corps in Poland were once again placed on an active footing.[1] The Russian minister in Berlin declared that the tsar would regard any attempt to obstruct the execution in Holstein as a personal affront. A conflict in Hesse he would regard as a *casus belli*. The Prussian minister was preparing to leave St Petersburg.

In face of the danger from Russia, Frederick-William appealed to England for support. Radowitz hastened to London to ask for an alliance of which the British government should itself dictate the terms. There was only one condition: there must be no collaboration with revolutionaries.[2]

The Prussian appeal led to an exchange of views between the Court and the Foreign Secretary. The Queen was in favour of giving support to Prussia and German liberalism against despotic Austria. Had not England promised protection to the Italian states against the Habsburgs in 1847? '...Consistency would require that we should now...throw *our weight* into the scales of *Constitutional* Prussia and Germany....' British representatives in Germany with the sole exception of Cowley at Frankfurt were, unhappily, 'warm partisans of the *despotic* league against Prussia and a German Constitution and *for* the maintenance of the old Diet under Austrian and Russian influence'. 'Ought not Lord Palmerston to make his agents understand that their sentiments are at variance with those of the

---

[1] Russia had begun military preparations on 28 October. After pacific assurances had been received from the Prussian government, all military preparations had been cancelled on 12 November.
[2] Frederick-William declared that he would never enter into alliance with 'Frankreich oder Sardinien, mit Roten und Gothaern, Königsmördern und Kaisermachern' (*ibid.* p. 233). This, however, did not prevent him from telling the *Flügeladjutant* of the king of Hanover that he could choose his alliances where he wanted, that England and France were at his disposal and that Hungary and Italy only waited for a sign (*ibid.* p. 253).

English Government?'[1] Palmerston replied that whilst he remained a partizan of 'rational and sound Constitutional Government' in Germany, he could not see that this was at present in danger. Austria would be quite unable to re-establish despotic government in a nation so enlightened and attached to free institutions as the Germans now were. The danger seemed to lie rather in the opposite direction, that of universal suffrage among people 'who had been, some wholly and others very much, unaccustomed to the working of representative Government'. Moreover the conflict between Austria and Prussia could 'scarcely be said to have turned upon principles of Government so much as upon a struggle for political ascendancy in Germany'. In Berlin, at Dresden and in Baden the Prussian government had, no doubt very properly, employed military force to re-establish order. With regard to the affairs of Hesse, the ground taken by Prussia was not so much a constitutional as a military one.[2]

Some days later, Palmerston elaborated his views in a letter addressed to Cowley. 'German affairs are indeed come to a state of chaos. The only thing that seems pretty clear is, that all parties are more or less in the wrong. But Prussia seems to bear away the palm in this respect....' Her course had been 'dishonest, inconsistent and irresolute and weak' and with regard to the Duchies she had, throughout, acted 'with the greatest duplicity and bad faith'. '...In regard to German affairs, her only object from beginning to end seems to have been her own aggrandisement which, at moments when much was within her grasp, she had not the courage or steadiness successfully to pursue.'[3] Her partizans tried to make out that the contest between her and Austria was one between constitutional and arbitrary government. In fact it was no such thing. It was ' only a conflict between the two leading Powers in Germany as to which should be politically preponderant'.

The British government had had no objection to seeing Prussia take first place. '...On the contrary, a German Union embracing all the smaller states, with Prussia at its head, and in alliance with Austria as a separate Power, would have been a very good European arrangement.' But when the empire was offered to Prussia, the king shrank from the hazardous position thus proposed to him and declined to accept it till he should be

---

[1] The Queen to Palmerston, 18 November 1850, R(oyal) A(rchives) in Windsor Castle, B 11/143a, printed in *The Letters of Queen Victoria* (hereafter quoted as *QVL*), 1st series, ed. A. C. Benson and Viscount Esher (London, 1908), vol. 11, pp. 274f. Where documents from the Royal Archives are published in this series, the reference will be given in brackets.

[2] Palmerston to the Queen, 18 November 1850, RA, B 11/143b (*QVL, loc. cit.* pp. 275f.).

[3] It is interesting to note that similar views were expressed at St Petersburg. In the spring of 1850 the tsar had told the Prussian minister that a determined Prussian attack in the summer of 1848 might have produced results. These would not have been just results, but at least results gained in honest battle. What was intolerable was Prussia's attempt to gain advantages from revolution and general confusion (Scharff, *op. cit.* p. 173).

asked to do so by the sovereigns. 'That decided the question, for it was pretty certain that the Sovereigns would never trouble him with such a request.' The empire having thus been negatived, Prussia ought to have taken at once the only alternative course. She should have agreed with Austria to reconstruct the German confederation on the principles of the treaty of 1815 'with such modifications as the establishment of parliaments in Prussia and Austria, and all the other states, might render necessary'.

Instead of this, Prussia went on pottering about an Erfurth [sic] Union, which never could end in anything but smoke, and then she chose deliberately to expose herself to the humiliation of being obliged, by military threats, to retreat step by step from all the positions she had taken up in regard to almost all pending affairs.

All this was lamentable and proved afresh that honesty was the best policy. What Austria meant, remained to be seen. In the meantime, enormous armies had been put into the field on both sides just as winter was setting in 'and without any intelligible question to fight about'. The one thing both sides should do forthwith was to send these useless soldiers home 'to their stoves and provisions stores'. 'In the meanwhile, Russia on one side and France on the other[1]...must be inwardly chuckling at seeing Germany come down in so short a time from *Einheit* to intense exasperation and to the brink of civil war.'[2]

In a letter to Russell, the Prime Minister, Palmerston outlined the attitude England should adopt in the event of an Austro-Prussian war:

The likelihood is that if such a war should break out the sympathies of this nation would be in favour of Prussia, Protestant and liberal; but there is a wide distance between sympathy and active assistance. The interest of England and I should say of Europe generally would be that out of such a war Prussia should come unscathed and if possible enlarged and strengthened.

Were war to be forced on Prussia, he should be glad to see it turn to her advantage but the odds would be fearfully against her. Supposing then that the nation sympathized with Prussia and that it was generally felt that British interests were identified with her success, would Parliament and the public support the government in taking part even on such grounds in a war between the states of Germany?

I think certainly not. To send a land force to co-operate with the Prussians against Austria would be out of the question, and our naval co-operation would be of small assistance. If our alliance is sought for with reference to such a conflict we should probably say that we could not promise it without the consent of Parliament; that Parliament would not be likely to give its consent and certainly would not by anticipation without knowing the grounds of the war in which it was asked to promise to take part.

[1] As so often, Palmerston here showed a very incomplete appreciation of Russian motives. The prospect of civil war in Germany was viewed at St Petersburg with genuine distress.
[2] Palmerston to Cowley, 22 November 1850, printed in E. Ashley, *op. cit.* vol. I, pp. 242 ff.

However, a war begun between the German states might draw France and Russia into its vortex. This would, indeed, alter the nature of the conflict '...but on this supposition also it would not be prudent for us to make prospective promises or engagements, and we should keep ourselves free to act according to the course of events'. To all these motives for avoiding commitments might be added the consideration 'that the course hitherto pursued by the Prussian Government has not been marked by so much prudence, steadiness and consistency as to justify us in promising to follow her future steps blindfold'.[1]

Palmerston's attitude condemned Radowitz's mission to failure in advance. Indeed, Radowitz had to report to the king of Prussia that he had found no support for the idea of an alliance. The Tories, although frightened of an extension of Russian influence in central Europe and a revival of French ambitions on the Rhine, inclined to the Austrian side. The Whigs, the Cabinet and even the Court itself had lost much of their earlier enthusiasm for German unity. Prussian policy in the Duchies was universally condemned. No sympathy was felt for Prussia in a conflict apparently over a convention about military roads in Hesse.[2] Palmerston had warned against hostilities in a matter of this kind: Prussia no longer represented a cause which would justify a war. If there was a conflict, England would remain neutral so long as Russia did the same. She would enter no preliminary engagements and her attitude would be influenced by that of France. In a Congress, England would stand by Prussia in the German question, provided the problem of the Duchies had received a satisfactory solution.[3]

Whilst Frederick-William IV was negotiating unsuccessfully in London, Schwarzenberg had decided to force the issue. By an ultimatum delivered at Berlin on the morning of 25 November, Prussia was summoned to notify within forty-eight hours her readiness to permit the passage of federal troops across the Prussian barrier in Hesse. The 'federal' commander received instructions to advance on Kassel[4] on the 27th and to break Prussian opposition.

It is well known how, at the last minute, Schwarzenberg reluctantly agreed to postpone the military advance and meet a Prussian representative at Olmütz.[5] Meyendorff, who had unrivalled opportunities for

---

[1] Palmerston to Russell, 26 November 1850, *The Later Correspondence of Lord John Russell*, ed. G. P. Gooch (London, 1925), pp. 35f.

[2] Russell wrote to Stockmar: 'Even now, when Electoral Hesse has as good and sacred a cause as ever roused the sympathies of free men, these sympathies are all deadened and destroyed by the interference of Prussia. Not for the sake of Justice and Freedom, but for a good military position and the Etappe roads. I am as sorry as an Englishman can be for these costly, perhaps fatal errors' (Russell to Stockmar, 22 November 1850, *ibid.* pp. 34f.).

[3] Scharff, *op. cit.* pp. 233f. and 237f.

[4] Kassel, which the federal forces were to occupy, lay north of the Prussian barrier, whilst federal forces were advancing from the south.

[5] For the following see Sybel, *op. cit.* pp. 56ff.

observation, ascribed his change of plan to the language of Palmerston[1] and the ambiguous attitude of Louis Napoleon.[2] Meyendorff was invited to accompany Schwarzenberg to Olmütz. It needs no retelling how, thanks largely to the skill of the Russian diplomat, agreement was reached on all disputed matters and embodied in the celebrated 'Punctuation'.[3] On 1 December Frederick-William reluctantly accepted the agreement: the danger of war was averted.

IX

In accordance with the terms of the 'Punctuation', Austria and Prussia issued a joint invitation to the German states to discuss constitutional reform. On 23 December, representatives of the German governments met at Dresden. Schwarzenberg again put forward his ambitious plan for a future Germany under Austrian leadership; Prussia, in self-defence, insisted on the principle of parity. The two views proved irreconcilable and in the end it was decided to return to the arrangements of 1815. The representatives of the German states once again took the road to Frankfurt to operate as best they could the clumsy constitution it had proved impossible to replace.[4] Within a year, Schwarzenberg was dead. On the surface at least, Germany reverted to the internal stagnation in political matters and international weakness which the various proposals for reform had been designed to remedy.

The final phase of the discussions had raised in an acute form the international problem of Schwarzenberg's 'Empire of Seventy Millions'. This had attracted the attention of the chanceries. On 3 December, Palmerston informed Westmorland that the entry of the entire Habsburg monarchy into the Confederation would raise issues which could not be settled without consulting the powers which had signed the treaty of Vienna.[5] The British government would require detailed explanations

[1] From Olmütz, Meyendorff explained to Nesselrode the reasons for Schwarzenberg's decision to accept a conference: 'Je place au premier rang le langage ambigu de Lord Palmerston qui, tout en déconseillant la guerre à la Prusse, dit assez haut qu'elle représente à ses yeux le principe de liberté politique, cher à la nation anglaise, tandis que la Russie et l'Autriche sont des puissances réactionnaires qui tendent à détruire les constitutions' (Meyendorff to Nesselrode, 15/27 November 1850, despatched from Olmütz on 17/29 November, Meyendorff, *op. cit.* p. 345). [2] *Ibid.*

[3] Meyendorff's comment on the 'Punctuation' throws an interesting light on Russian policy: 'Elle a été le complément de ce qui avait été fixé à Varsovie, et c'est à la légitime influence de notre Empereur que l'Allemagne et l'Europe ont dû la paix...notre intervention a été non seulement une bonne action, mais aussi un bon calcul' (Meyendorff to his brother Georg, 9/21 December 1850, *ibid.* p. 361.

[4] Meyendorff considered it a disgrace that the German governments had proved as incapable as the Parliament in Frankfurt of reorganizing Germany (Meyendorff to Nesselrode, 22 March/3 April 1851, *ibid.* p. 397). Schwarzenberg also considered the outcome a pitiful confession of bankruptcy and a triumph for the enemies of Germany (H. von Poschinger, *Preussens Auswärtige Politik 1850–1858* (Berlin, 1902), vol. 1, p. 131).

[5] Palmerston considered 'that the Germanic Confederation is not a Union formed solely by the voluntary association of the states that compose it, and which therefore can be

before it could form an opinion.[1] France declared more bluntly that she considered Schwarzenberg's programme at variance with the treaty of Vienna.[2]

Russia alone of the major powers was willing to accept the Austrian solution. The tsar, confirmed in his favourable dispositions by the oft-repeated argument that a powerful Germany led by conservative Austria would prove a bulwark against revolution, stood loyally by his declaration of 24 June. Nesselrode surprised the British minister at St Petersburg by the declaration that Russia did not oppose the Austrian plan.[3] Indeed, the Russian government now considered Germany's future constitutional arrangements a purely internal matter.[4] When invited by the French government to intervene on behalf of the lesser German states, Nesselrode replied that what Europe needed was agreement between Austria and Prussia. He felt certain that these powers would deal fairly with the lesser members of the Confederation. No outsider had a right to interfere. The best advice, therefore, which he could give to the French government would be to ignore completely all German developments during the period of reconstruction. That was the policy of the Russian government.[5]

However, faced with growing French opposition,[6] the Russian government began to modify its views. Nesselrode became convinced that internal and external opposition made the Austrian programme impracticable. He asked Meyendorff to tell Schwarzenberg that, in a conflict with

altered and modified at the absolute will of those States. . . . The German Confederation . . . is the result and creation of a European Treaty concluded at Vienna in 1815, and it forms part of the general Settlement of Europe which that Treaty established and regulated.' It therefore appeared to the British government 'that no important change can properly be made in the character and composition of the Confederation without the consent and concurrence of the Powers who were Parties to the Vienna Treaty of 1815' (Palmerston to Westmorland, 3 December 1850, FO 64/312, no. 210 draft).

[1] The British government considered 'that it would be premature for them . . . to pronounce a definite opinion either for, or against, the proposed change, because much in regard to the opinion they might form upon it, would depend upon the Regulations to be established for the Confederation and upon the reciprocal Rights, obligations and federal Functions of the Component States. But Her Majesty's Government deem that Great Britain is entitled to expect that, before anything final is done in regard to this matter, the British Government should receive from the Governments of Austria and Prussia full explanations as to the nature and object of the contemplated change, and as to the Reasons which make it desirable, and that a clear statement should be given as to the degree, if any, of interference which is in any case proposed to be exercised by one or more Members of the Confederation or by the aggregate Body in the internal Affairs of any States belonging thereto, and in any difference which may arise between Sovereigns and Subjects' (ibid.).

[2] Louis-Napoleon had expressed his misgivings about Schwarzenberg's proposals in August 1850 in conversation with an Austrian diplomat. Early in December, the Prussian minister in Paris reported that he was determined to prevent their realization (Scharff, op. cit. p. 275). [3] Ibid. p. 281.

[4] In Dresden 'as it were, the German family was assembled'. No foreigner had the right to meddle in their deliberations (Rochow to Manteuffel, 22 December 1850, ibid. pp. 281 f.).

[5] The same to the same, 31 December 1850 and 8 January 1851, ibid. pp. 282 f.

[6] In February and March 1851 Louis-Napoleon, in conversations with the Austrian minister, demanded 'compensations' if France was to abandon her opposition to Schwarzenberg's programme (Hatzfeldt to Frederick-William IV, 2 March 1851, ibid. p. 288).

France, Austria must not count on Russian support. Austrian policy was producing an Anglo-French *rapprochement* which it was necessary to fore-stall.[1] On 12 April, Nesselrode finally announced that the Russian government no longer favoured the plan.[2] In consequence, Schwarzenberg's programme had lost all chance of acceptance; a return to the old Confederation became the only solution.

The question of the Duchies, so closely linked with that of German reorganization, did not receive its 'definitive' solution until the following year. On 28 January 1852, after prolonged negotiations, Frederick VII of Denmark formally resumed the government of the Duchies. In a proclamation to his newly restored subjects, he promised separate representative bodies for the component parts of the monarchy. On 8 May, the powers signed the celebrated treaty of London proclaiming the integrity of the Danish monarchy to be a European necessity and regulating the succession on the death of the present king. Although the treaty was signed by all the major powers, there was one ominous absentee: the Germanic Confederation. As far as that body was concerned, the treaty had no legal existence. The Estates of Holstein also entered a protest. In face of rising national sentiment among Germans and Danes alike, the settlement reached was—to say the least—precarious.

IX

The German revolution of 1848 thus ended in the restoration of 1851: the Germanic Confederation of 1815 received a new lease of life; so did the historic Danish monarchy; so also did the 'neo-Holy Alliance' of Austria, Prussia and Russia.[3] Nicholas I and Nesselrode, therefore, had secured the principal objects of their policy; they had prevented an outbreak in the Congress Kingdom of Poland; by their intervention in Hungary they had assured the survival of the Habsburg monarchy; they had contributed in a large measure to the preservation of the Danish monarchy; they had prevented the outbreak of civil war in Germany and helped to preserve the dualist system of the old Confederation. The triumph of Russia seemed complete. The system of 1815, of which she was the champion, had been challenged by liberals, republicans, democrats and nationalists; it had survived their onslaught. In spite of some constitutional survivals in Germany and of such innovations as Schwarzenberg's unitary constitution, the 'restoration order' remained in essence that of 1815.

If the restoration settlement of 1851 constituted a Russian victory, it was by the same token a major British defeat. Germany, Italy and

[1] Nesselrode to Meyendorff, 16 and 25 March 1851 and 12 April 1851, Nesselrode, *op. cit.* vol. x, pp. 34ff.
[2] Meyendorff to Nesselrode, 2/21 April 1851, Meyendorff, *op. cit.* pp. 398f.
[3] On 16 May 1851, Austria and Prussia had concluded a secret defensive alliance. This had completed the 'restoration settlement' in Germany.

Hungary had returned to their former allegiance. Conservatism and absolute rule had triumphed in Vienna and Berlin.[1] The three eastern monarchies—whilst they remained united—occupied a dominant position in Europe. Not the least galling of British defeats was the failure of the German liberal movement caused above all by Frederick-William's 'gran rifiuto'. The high hopes raised by the early successes of German liberalism had been disappointed. The Protocol of London was small consolation for failure to see the consolidation of a strong, constitutional and pro-British German state.

The political basis of the restoration settlement had been the tsar's support of Schwarzenberg which had enabled the Habsburg monarchy to salvage its positions first in Hungary and later in Germany. Indeed, the risings of the Magyars and Italians had—for a time—destroyed Austria's position as a German power. This had left the field to her Prussian rival. For a time, only the particularism of the frightened princes had stood between Prussia and the undisputed leadership of Germany. At the decisive moment, however, the Prussian government faltered. Divided counsels brought about an inability to choose between a policy of collaboration with the moderate revolutionaries and one of anti-revolutionary reaction. Frederick-William, feeble and vacillating, refused to make a choice between the system of Palmerston and that of Nicholas. He rejected co-operation with the National Assembly, yet would not lead an anti-revolutionary crusade. The result was disastrous to Prussian aspirations. Whilst Palmerston turned away in disappointment from the king's feeble and possibly insincere Prusso-German constitutionalism, the tsar, unable to conceal his disgust at Prussia's ambiguous policy, in the end chose Schwarzenberg and Francis-Joseph to lead the German counter-revolution. The result of this was a settlement under Austro-Russian auspices, which represented the interests of Austria, Russia and the German princes. The return to the arrangements of 1815 put an end both to Prussian dreams of leadership and to British hopes of constitutional consolidation in Germany.

Prussia's defeat was caused in no small degree by the interaction of the German question with that of Schleswig-Holstein. In fact, Prussia was forced to pay a heavy price for her policy of humouring the nationalist aspirations of German liberalism. Her action in the Duchies alienated the sympathies of England and France. It brought about the diplomatic co-operation of the other powers and her own complete isolation. In particular, her conduct gave grave offence at St Petersburg. Next to the security of Poland, the preservation of the Danish monarchy formed perhaps the most important single objective of Russian diplomacy. The tsar, therefore, was unwilling to tolerate acts which threatened the integrity of Denmark. He did not conceal his indignation at Prussia's policy. It

[1] The Prussian constitution of 5 December 1848 had been promulgated by royal edict.

43

was this which had offered Schwarzenberg his opportunity. Strong in his 'correct' attitude towards the Danish question, he was able to gain the goodwill of Nicholas and with it Russian support for his policy in Germany. The Duchies thus became a stepping-stone to the restoration of Austrian influence in Germany.

If Austria owed the recovery of her German position in part to Schwarzenberg's skilful 'exploitation' of the Dano-German conflict, she owed it no less to the Russian intervention in Hungary. That intervention was caused by concern for the security of Poland and was not therefore directly connected with Germany. Yet, paradoxically, the subjection of Hungary in its consequences formed perhaps the most far-reaching foreign intervention in German affairs. The subjection of Hungary was the necessary prerequisite of Austria's return to Germany. It could be claimed, therefore, that Austria's survival as a German power and the consequent return to dualism in German affairs was simply a by-product of the Polish question. It was this which, to some extent, caused the failure of the German revolution.

That failure, whilst not unwelcome in Paris, caused keen disappointment in London[1] and gave no great pleasure even at St Petersburg. The British government had hoped for a defensive consolidation of Germany, the tsar for sincere Austro-Prussian co-operation in the face of France and revolution. The final restoration of a precarious balance within the old Confederation, therefore, marked the failure of Palmerston and Nicholas alike. The British failure, however, was the greater of the two: the new Germany was neither strong nor constitutional. The tsar could console himself with the reflection that the restored Confederation, if weak, was at least monarchical and conservative.

Neither England nor Russia resorted to active military intervention—except for the indirect effects of Russian action in Hungary. Both had been cautious in their diplomacy. The British government, whilst expressing its sympathies in general terms, had refrained from discussing details. Only in the question of Schwarzenberg's programme—a European as much as a German issue—had Palmerston departed from his policy of passive benevolence.

The Russian government had consistently indicated its 'natural' preference for conservative and anti-revolutionary solutions. Like that of

[1] Russell squarely placed the blame for this failure on the shoulders of the Germans themselves. He replied to Stockmar's complaint that the Germans had been abandoned by the British government:

'It is not for forty millions of people to complain that they could not obtain good government because England has looked coldly upon them. Their own mistaken wishes and blundering action must bear the blame. Had they set to work heart and mind to throw off the old Metternich *incubus* they would surely have succeeded. But they set their wits to work and their courage to fight for a bit ∪f conquest—to deprive the King of Denmark of Sleswig, which neither justice nor England could tolerate. But to the German ambition they added a Prussian ambition...' (Russell to Stockmar, 22 November 1850, Gooch, *op. cit.* pp. 34f.).

England, it had abstained from expressing opinions on matters of detail. During 1848 and 1849, it departed from its passivity only with regard to the 'European' question of Schleswig-Holstein. Russian naval demonstrations and diplomatic warnings, whilst they may have influenced Prussia's policy towards Denmark, had little direct bearing on the future organization of Germany.

Throughout the summer and autumn of 1850 Nicholas maintained his attitude of critical detachment—as far at least as the constant importunities of Frederick-William IV and the counter-insinuations of Schwarzenberg would permit. He refused repeated Prussian invitations to mediate in the conflict. Instead, a gentle pressure was applied impartially at Vienna and Berlin to bring about an Austro-Prussian *entente*. The inducement of Russia's moral support was held out to the party which should prove itself the more conservative and pacific. Only the immediate threat of civil war in Germany finally induced the tsar to concentrate his forces and announce that he would fight the aggressor. The threat of force was employed also to induce Prussia to leave the Duchies to their fate.

As soon as the integrity of Denmark was saved and civil war in Germany averted, Russian policy resumed its passive role. It is significant that Meyendorff refused Schwarzenberg's invitation to accompany him to the final conferences in Dresden.[1] Russian diplomacy was at pains to emphasize that German reorganization was a purely internal affair. The tsar was prepared to sanction even an arrangement prejudicial to Russian national interests.[2] If a settlement could be obtained only at the price of accepting Schwarzenberg's proposals, he was ready to pay that price. Had Austria and Prussia agreed to include the entire monarchy in the Confederation, he would have raised no objection. Again, had the two powers decided to divide Germany between them, Russian approval was assured. The result of 1866 could have been achieved at any time without opposition from Russia.

The importance of ideological elements in Nicholas's foreign policy has often been discussed. Following Schiemann,[3] older historians tended to

---

[1] Rochow to Manteuffel, 22 December 1850, Scharff, *op. cit.* p. 282.

[2] On hearing that the Russian government no longer favoured Schwarzenberg's proposal, Meyendorff wrote to Nesselrode: 'A mon point de vue je n'avais jamais jugé que l'entrée de l'Autriche en Allemagne fut avantageuse, ni à l'Autriche, ni à l'Europe, ni à l'Allemagne, ni surtout à la Russie. Cependant quoique l'Empereur dans sa bienveillance pour l'Autriche voulait bien ne pas s'y opposer, il ne m'appartenait pas de le faire. Mais j'ai pu dans mon fort intérieur ne pas m'affliger de voir cette combinaison abandonnée pour le moment' (Meyendorff to Nesselrode 9/21 April 1851, Meyendorff, *op. cit.* pp. 398f.). Nesselrode had earlier explained that in his attitude towards Schwarzenberg's proposals the tsar had been guided not by considerations of their political usefulness or dangers but by his friendship for Austria and the desire to help her out of her difficult position with regard to Prussia (Nesselrode, *op. cit.* pp. 39f.).

[3] Th. Schiemann, *Geschichte Russlands unter Nikolaus I* (Berlin, 1919), vol. 4, pp. 137ff. The view was strengthened by Alexander Gorchakov's strictures on the policy of his predecessor.

emphasize the anti-revolutionary nature of Russian policy at this time. More recently others, following Friese,[1] have argued that the tsar's ideological language served as a cloak for real political interests. The reaction against the older view, although a healthy one, can in fact be carried too far. It is certain that Nicholas I was a man of principle. His readiness to sanction the entry of the entire Habsburg monarchy into the German Confederation shows that his policy was not dictated by narrow Russian interests alone. Even the desire for a close Austro-Prussian understanding sprang from considerations which were not exclusively Russian.[2] In any case, the antithesis between ideology and national interest is, at least in its extreme form, a false one. The two interact and policy, as a rule, is a compound of both. Success in the ideological field means increased political power. Moreover, from the Russian point of view, a conservative policy in Germany combined in perfect harmony the claims of ideology and national self-interest. It is idle to speculate which was the more important in the minds of Nicholas and Nesselrode.

British policy also was influenced to no small extent by ideological promptings. It was German constitutionalism as much as national consolidation which had found favour in England. The Court and sections of public opinion thought of the German problem in terms which were almost exclusively ideological. What they saw was a struggle between ordered freedom and despotism, the British and the Russian 'ways of life'. Yet liberal British constitutionalism like anti-revolutionary Russian conservatism agreed with national self-interest. A constitutional reorganization of Germany would strengthen the European centre. A liberal Germany was expected to adopt a liberal commercial policy. Idealism and self-interest, as in the case of Russia, happily coincided.

Throughout the course of the German revolution it was only a common

[1] Ch. Friese, *Russland und Preussen vom Krimkrieg bis zum Polnischen Aufstand* (Berlin, 1931).

[2] Meyendorff drew Nesselrode's attention to the fact that a close understanding of Austria and Prussia might not be in Russia's interest. In a prophetic passage, he declared:

'L'affaire danoise pourra nous en donner un avant-goût. Dès que l'Autriche et la Prusse réunies prennent cette affaire en main, nous ne voudrons plus soutenir le Danemarc avec autant de vivacité qu'en 1848, d'abord parceque ces deux puissances ne font plus de la politique révolutionnaire, mais aussi nous ne voudrons pas leur tenir à toutes deux une langue comminatoire' (Meyendorff to Nesselrode, 14/26 January 1851, Meyendorff, *op. cit.* p. 372).

'...le scandinavisme et le germanisme s'entendront toujours assez tôt contre nous, précisément comme l'Autriche et la Prusse malgré tout ce que nous avons fait pour les réconcilier' (*ibid.*).

Meyendorff considered that from the point of view of *Realpolitik* Russia had no interest in seeing Prussia and Austria either strong or united:

'Une politique moins élevée aurait laissé les voisins de la Russie s'entregorger et aurait cru trouver des éléments de force dans leur affaiblissement mutuel. Mais notre cabinet a senti et envisagé dans cette guerre le triomphe assuré de la révolution, sachant que la Prusse aurait dû fatalement faire cause commune avec elle. Ceci posé, notre intervention a été non seulement une bonne action, mais aussi un bon calcul' (Meyendorff to his brother Georg, 2/21 December 1850, *ibid.* p. 361).

interest in the preservation of the Danish monarchy which disguised the basic antagonism existing between Russia and England. The 'conservatism' of British diplomats in Germany[1] and particularly of Westmorland in Berlin[2] contributed to this result. In fact, the autumn and winter of 1849 had seen the battle royal over the fate of the Hungarian refugees in Turkey, the spring of 1850 the incident associated for ever with the name of Don Pacifico. Palmerston, by this time, had become in Russian eyes a 'ferocious beast', disturber of the peace of Europe.[3] British diplomacy, at the same time, watched with growing distaste the triumph of Austro-Russian reaction in Germany. The return to the neo-Holy Alliance paved the way for the *rapprochement* of England and France.

During the revolutionary crisis, the tsar had come to realize as never before the community of interests which bound together Russia and the Habsburg monarchy. Nationality was the common enemy: there was an intimate link between the affairs of Hungary and those of Poland. Again, the years of upheaval appeared to have reinforced the need for conservative and monarchical solidarity: the cabinet of Vienna had shown a greater awareness of the fact than had the pseudo-liberals of Berlin. Schwarzenberg, above all, had stood forth as the champion of the reaction, a man far superior to Manteuffel, the uninspiring Minister of Frederick-William IV. For Nicholas, therefore, Austria had become the natural partner in defending the restoration settlement.

On the surface at least, that settlement appeared to be solidly based. Monarchical governments were everywhere in the ascendant. The Spielberg housed the malcontents of the Habsburg dominions; Hungary, Poland, Italy and the Duchies were alike subdued and quiescent. Revolutionary Paris had been 'tamed'. Yet Nicholas and Nesselrode might well have wondered whether their structure was as solid as it seemed. Was not Schwarzenberg himself alleged to have declared that Austria would one day astound the world by the greatness of her ingratitude? How long, in fact, would the Austro-Russian alliance resist the strain a revival of the eastern question must necessarily produce? How long would Schwarzenberg maintain his ascendancy in Vienna in the face of liberal currents which could not be wholly suppressed? How long could Russia successfully hold the balance between Austria and Prussia with their rival ambitions in Germany? Moreover, liberal sentiments and national aspira-

---

[1] The Queen had complained to Palmerston of what she considered the Austrian bias of British diplomats. The Queen to Palmerston, 18 November 1850, RA, B 11/143a (*QVL*, loc. cit. pp. 274f.).

[2] Meyendorff wrote to Nesselrode: 'Westmorland me seconde de son mieux non seulement dans l'affaire danoise, mais aussi pour celles de l'Allemagne' (Meyendorff to Nesselrode 25 November/7 December 1849, Meyendorff, *op. cit.* p. 242; cf. also the same to the same, 8/20 March and 15/27 March 1850, *ibid.* pp. 275 and 279).

[3] 'Mais tant que cette bête féroce, comme vous l'appelez fort justement, présidera à la politique extérieure de l'Angleterre, il n'y a pas de repos à espérer pour l'Europe' (Nesselrode to Meyendorff, 18 February 1850, Nesselrode, *op. cit.* p. 286).

tions had survived everywhere in Europe. A Bonaparte ruled France. British policy remained enigmatic, incalculable and subtly hostile to the Austro-Russian system. Last but not least, Nesselrode's 'ferocious beast' was rampant, smarting under the sting of temporary defeat. The restoration settlement was, in fact, precarious, and nowhere more so than in Germany. As long as the system of Nicholas and Schwarzenberg survived, German national and liberal currents might cease to be a political force; the destruction of that system would at once reopen issues which the triumph of reaction had seemed to close for many years to come.

CHAPTER 2

THE END OF THE AUSTRO-RUSSIAN *ENTENTE* AND THE DEFEAT OF RUSSIA, 1853-6

THE settlement which terminated the revolutions of 1848 had been shaped in important respects by international relations. The 'solution' of the Danish question rested on an understanding between England, Russia, France and Sweden; that of the German problem on the *entente* between Nicholas I and Schwarzenberg. In fact if not in name the revolutionary movements of 1848 had ended in arrangements hardly less international than those which closed the Napoleonic era. Like the order created at Vienna, that of the second restoration was propped up by a European structure in which Russia played a prominent part. It would be shaken to its foundations if any of the props were pulled away. This is what happened between 1853 and 1859. During this period there took place developments unconnected with Germany which were yet to exercise a decisive influence on the evolution of German affairs.[1] A study of international relations between 1853 and 1859 shows the origin of conditions which made possible the 'second revolution' of the later 1850's and 1860's.

The Crimean War and the Franco-Austrian War of 1859 destroyed in their cumulative effect the diplomatic and military foundations of the restoration settlement. They created diplomatic constellations at once less rigid and more favourable to the national aspirations repressed in 1849. The powers affected above all by the change were Russia and Austria, the twin pillars of the restoration edifice. Russia's weight in European affairs was greatly diminished by the outcome of the Crimean War and by her known exhaustion and need of repose. Moreover, the treaty of Paris reduced Russian interest in the affairs of central Europe. The gaze of the Russian cabinet was now obstinately fixed on the Black Sea and the Balkans. Immediate expansionist energies found an outlet on the Amur and in the Caucasus. Austria, during the Crimean War, sacrificed Russia's friendship to the desire to expel her from the Danubian Principalities. Buol's policy of cutting the links which united the two empires destroyed the basis alike of Austria's international position and of the restoration settlement.

These changes in the position of Russia and Austria were underlined by

[1] It has been claimed with some justification that 'The real stake in the Crimean War was not Turkey. It was central Europe; that is to say, Germany and Italy.' A. J. P. Taylor, *The Struggle for Mastery in Europe, 1848–1918* (Oxford, 1954), p. 61.

important changes of personnel. Schwarzenberg died in 1852. Three years later Nicholas I followed him to the grave. With Schwarzenberg the Habsburg monarchy lost not only the chief architect of its revival but also its last great statesman (with the possible exception of Andrássy). From now on, successive Ministers of lesser stature would wrestle with little success with the growing difficulties of the situation. The death of Nicholas I in its turn removed a figure of unrivalled prestige, the main defender of the old order in Russia and in Europe. Some months after his disappearance Nesselrode, who with Metternich had nursed the system of Vienna from its infancy, made way for a younger man. Alexander II lacked his father's personality and prestige; the impetuous Gorchakov replaced but inadequately his cautious and experienced predecessor. After 1855 there was no longer a recognized leader of the conservative forces in Europe. Only secondary figures were left as defenders of the existing order. They proved themselves incapable of rallying the scattered forces of genuine conservatism in the face of Napoleon, Cavour and Bismarck,[1] the standard-bearers of nationality and change. What is more, both in Russia and Austria the successors of the great conservative leaders, carried away alike by the *Zeitgeist* and the lure of *Realpolitik*, abandoned the system of 1815 which their predecessors had restored. Buol and Gorchakov in turn unwittingly assisted Napoleon in his efforts to upset the established order.

The principal agent in the destruction of the restoration settlement was Louis-Napoleon, emperor of the French since the end of 1852.[2] Napoleon was to wage two wars to overthrow the existing order. The first of these would lead to the exhaustion of Russia, the second to the enfeeblement of the Habsburg monarchy. Napoleon's mission, in the field of foreign policy, was to abolish the treaties of 1815 and restore France to a leading position in Europe. His chosen instrument for the attainment of these objects was the alliance of the western powers reinforced by an understanding with one of the eastern monarchies. By means of such a grouping Napoleon hoped to promote the cause of nationality in Europe, raise the prestige of his dynasty and extend the territory of France.

Palmerston, although he distrusted Napoleon and France, disliked and distrusted Russia even more and was a warm supporter of the Italian national movement. He was, therefore, not unwilling to co-operate with Napoleon first in humbling Russia and later in assisting Cavour. He hoped, at the same time, to utilize a close understanding with France to control and restrain the mercurial emperor of the French. British opinion, overwhelmingly anti-Russian and pro-Italian, was ready to support

[1] Bismarck, for all his conservative masquerading, had long outgrown his early conservatism. This was well understood by those true Prussian conservatives the brothers von Gerlach. Whilst no adjective can adequately describe the great man, his influence before 1866 was certainly revolutionary rather than conservative.

[2] It is a curious fact that the year 1852 saw both the death of Schwarzenberg and the final emergence of the man who was to usher in the new age.

Palmerston in the policy of alliance with France. Thus was renewed the understanding of the 'western powers' broken by Louis-Philippe and Guizot. It was to be the most important single factor in the destruction of the restoration system.

The Franco-British understanding came into existence during the early phases of the eastern crisis of 1853. The ensuing clash between Russia and the West, apart from the resulting realignment of forces, is significant because it gave the contestants a foretaste of the future German attitude in matters pertaining to the east. If the revolutionary period just past had given the Germans a glimpse of what they might expect from the powers in the event of a new movement for national consolidation, the eastern crisis would give the powers, in their turn, an inkling of Germany's attitude towards Anglo-Russian rivalry in the east.

In fact, neither Austria nor Prussia found it easy to take sides in the eastern quarrel. Both in Vienna and Berlin there were liberal elements favouring union with the west and conservative groups advocating support for Russia. The outcome of the struggles foreshadowed a significant realignment of the powers. In Vienna, the liberal trend represented by Buol and Bach eventually carried the day against the conservative military leaders. In Berlin, the cautious conservatism of Manteuffel triumphed over the Prince of Prussia and the *Wochenblatts-partei*. Austria chose the west and her representatives were to play a prominent part at the Congress of Paris by the side of the victorious allies; Prussia chose the east and barely gained admittance to the deliberations of the powers. The foundations both of Austro-Russian enmity and of Russo-Prussian friendship were well and truly laid. Events between 1853 and 1856 paved the way for the 'second revolution'.

I

On 5 May 1853 Menshikov, the tsar's special envoy who since 28 February had been negotiating with the Porte,[1] proposed to the Turkish government a treaty establishing a Russian protectorate over Turkey's Christian subjects.[2] He demanded acceptance within five days under threat of a Russian reoccupation of the Danubian Principalities. Advised by the British ambassador, the Turkish government rejected the Russian demand. Menshikov thereupon declared his readiness to accept the assurances demanded by his government in the form of a simple note. When this

---

[1] At the beginning of 1853, the tsar had sounded Sir Hamilton Seymour, the British minister, about the possibility of partitioning Turkey. The British government had returned a non-committal reply. Nicholas had then decided to apply direct pressure at Constantinople to secure the keys of the Holy Places for the Greek monks in Palestine and to gain for Russia the right to intervene in favour of the Greek Christians in the Near East.

[2] For the following cf. E. Heinrich Geffcken, *Zur Geschichte des Orientalischen Krieges 1853–1856* (Berlin, 1881), pp. 25ff.

proposal also was rejected, he declared that his mission was terminated and that diplomatic relations between Russia and Turkey were at an end. He left Constantinople with the declaration that Russia would regard any interference with the Orthodox religion and clergy as a hostile act.

On 28 May, the British government declared that in case of need it would give assistance to Turkey. Three days later, the Russian government announced its intention to occupy the Principalities as a pledge for Turkish acquiescence in the Russian demands. England and France, in reply, ordered their fleets to the mouth of the Dardanelles. On 3 July, Russian troops crossed the Pruth and proceeded to occupy Jassy and Bucharest. They did not cross the Danube, but a Russian administration was set up in the Principalities.

The Russian occupation of the Principalities aroused indignation in Constantinople and hostility in London and Paris. It created a situation in which the attitude of the 'Germanic' powers would be of the greatest importance. If Austria and Prussia gave diplomatic support to England and France, Russia was isolated; if they backed Russia, the cabinets of London and Paris would fail in their efforts to transform the Russo-Turkish dispute into a European question. Nicholas I, in the early phases of his diplomatic offensive, had felt confident of Austro-Prussian support. In one of his conversations with the British minister early in 1853, he had asserted: 'When I speak of Russia, I speak of Austria as well; what suits the one suits the other; our interests as regards Turkey are perfectly identical.'[1] During the summer, he had told the minister of France: 'A quatre vous me dicteriez la loi mais cela n'arrivera jamais, je puis compter sur Vienne et Berlin.'[2]

These hopes, at the time, had not been without foundation. During the early stages of Menshikov's negotiations, Buol had expressed full confidence in Russia's pacific intentions. His faith had been shaken by the manner and content of the Russian ultimatum, but he still nursed the hope that Menshikov might have exceeded his instructions and would be disavowed. That hope was dispelled when Meyendorff returned to Vienna at the beginning of June. Russia's occupation of the Principalities shattered the last illusions.

In Vienna the Russian occupation of the Principalities was held to touch a vital national interest. Had not Count Stadion in 1807 informed Sir Robert Adair that a Russian occupation of Moldavia and Wallachia would produce in Vienna an impression similar to that which might be created in London by a French occupation of the Isle of Wight?[3] Buol now told Meyendorff: 'My conduct with regard to the Eastern question is

---

[1] G. H. Bolsover, 'Nicholas I and the Partition of Turkey', [The] S[lavonic] R[eview], XXVII, no. 68 (December, 1948), p. 142.
[2] Geffcken, op. cit. p. 59.
[3] Ibid. pp. 55f.

inscribed on the map.'[1] The Austrian government therefore informed the cabinets of London and Paris that it regarded the integrity and independence of Turkey as an important Austrian interest. It would not promise Russia neutrality in a possible conflict. Moreover should an armed demonstration in defence of Turkish integrity become a necessity, Austria would carry out the necessary operations. In this manner, Austria had taken the first step towards the western camp. Schwarzenberg had proved his clear-sightedness when he had made his famous remark about her future 'ingratitude'. The tsar's ill-considered impetuosity had forced the Austrian government to move away from the Russian alliance. This was the beginning of an estrangement which was to last for nineteen fateful years. The Russian invasion of the Principalities thus became a remote source of Bismarck's later successes.

The attitude of Prussia also was unfavourable to the tsar. Although the king and his Ministers felt only the remotest of interests in the fate of the Danubian Principalities, and had little but humanitarian sympathy for the Christian subjects of the Porte, they yet admitted that the Russian occupation of Moldavia and Wallachia was an act of unwarranted aggression. They were, therefore, prepared to join in diplomatic action to secure a Russian withdrawal.

Threatened with diplomatic isolation, the tsar, who had hitherto insisted that Europe had no concern with the Russo-Turkish dispute, agreed that a settlement must be arrived at by the joint efforts of the European powers. The outcome of this *volte face* was the 'Vienna Note' of 1 August. In this note the representatives of England, France, Russia, Austria and Prussia agreed—or thought they agreed—on a solution designed to satisfy all parties. It was to be urged on the Turkish government for its acceptance. Before long, however, it became clear that the Russian government put on the loosely drafted document an interpretation differing from that of its partners. The British government in consequence decided that it had been the victim of Russian trickery and could no longer recommend at Constantinople the acceptance of the note.

The Russian interpretation of the 'Vienna Note' destroyed European confidence in the tsar's intentions and made a settlement through the concert of Europe impossible of attainment. Russia's concession in agreeing to a 'European' solution had been nullified by what was widely regarded as her duplicity.

In the meantime, an increasingly warlike spirit had developed at Constantinople. On 11 and 12 September demonstrations for war and riots took place in the Turkish capital. On the 23rd, the sultan made a warlike speech. Two days later, the Grand Council advised in favour of war, which was finally declared on 4 October. At dawn on the 23rd, Turkish troops crossed the Danube and attacked the Russian outposts;

[1] J. Klaczko, *The Two Chancellors* (London, 1876), p. 27.

on 4 November, the Russians counter-attacked; on the 30th, they destroyed a Turkish squadron in the Black Sea port of Sinope. The 'massacre of Sinope' caused an outburst of anti-Russian feeling in England; the attitude of the British and French governments became increasingly threatening.

In this situation, the tsar during a visit to Olmütz late in September, made a determined attempt to win over the emperor Francis-Joseph. He declared that he had not even contemplated the possibility of war. He had occupied the Principalities simply as a pledge and still hoped to avoid a conflict. His forces would not cross the Danube unless provoked. They would, however, conduct a vigorous campaign in Asia Minor.[1] The meeting at Olmütz formed the prelude to an effort to restore the alliance of Russia, Austria and Prussia. The two emperors and the king of Prussia met at Warsaw. During a further meeting at Olmütz, Nicholas and Francis-Joseph held discussions with the Prince of Prussia. The climax was reached when in a last desperate effort to secure Prussian support, the tsar paid a sudden visit to Berlin. It was to no avail. At one moment indeed Francis-Joseph, inspired by gratitude for past assistance and by the Russian sympathies of his military advisers, had agreed to an offensive and defensive alliance of the three powers. Frederick-William, however, rejected the proposal and Manteuffel informed Nicholas that it was in Prussia's interest to remain neutral. By maintaining an attitude of neutrality Prussia hoped to render a service to the cause of peace. Manteuffel, at the same time, informed the British minister that Prussia would sign no agreement with the tsar. The king, he explained, was haunted by fears of a French invasion of Prussia. In view of the Prussian attitude, Francis-Joseph also resolved to await events. By the end of October Nicholas knew the bitter truth that he would get no help from either Austria or Prussia. Indeed, after the 'massacre of Sinope', these powers took a further step: their representatives joined those of England and France in signing a Protocol which proclaimed the interest of the four powers in the preservation of Turkey.[2] This Protocol was transmitted to the Turkish government accompanied by an inquiry about the terms on which the Porte would be ready to discuss the conclusion of peace.

The declaration of 5 December, greeted at St Petersburg with pained surprise, forms a milestone in the collaboration between the Germans and the western allies. In fact, Austria and Prussia had now formally asso-

[1] Cf. Geffcken, *op. cit.* pp. 36f. For the following cf. Vicomte de Guichen, *La Guerre de Crimée (1854–6)*, (Paris, 1936), pp. 73 ff.

[2] The key sentence in the Protocol of 5 December 1853 declared: '...En effet, l'existence de la Turquie dans les limites que lui ont assignées les Traités, est devenue une des conditions nécessaires de l'équilibre européen et les P. P. soussignés constatent avec plaisir que la guerre actuelle ne saurait, en aucun cas, entraîner dans les circonscriptions territoriales des deux empires des modifications susceptibles d'altérer l'état de possession que le temps a consacré en Orient et qui est également nécessaire à la tranquillité de toutes les autres puissances' (*ibid.* pp. 84f.).

ciated themselves with Russia's enemies. It was the second rebuff which they had administered to the tsar.

England and France, in the meantime, had drifted into war with Russia. The Turkish government replied to the note of the four powers that it would not negotiate whilst Russian troops remained in the Principalities. The tsar, in spite of pacific advice from Meyendorff,[1] felt unable to withdraw his forces. The resources of diplomacy were virtually exhausted when on 22 December the British government accepted a French proposal that allied squadrons should enter the Black Sea. Between 3 and 5 January, allied vessels passed the Bosphorus. On the 12th, Seymour informed Nesselrode that they would 'require every Russian ship which they may meet with to re-enter a Russian port'.[2] This was more than the proud autocrat of all the Russias could stomach. On 4 February, after fruitless representations in London and Paris, the Russian ministers in those capitals were recalled. On the 21st, the British and French ministers left St Petersburg. On 14 March, the consuls of the two powers delivered notes summoning Russia to evacuate the Principalities before the end of April; four days later they received a negative reply; on 27 March, England and France declared war.

The outbreak of war drew attention to the strategic importance of Austria and Prussia. Prince Albert lucidly described the situation:

> The worst of the war is that we cannot bring it to an effective conclusion. Russia is a great and clumsy mass and the blows we can strike her in the few places which we can reach, will not make a great impression on her. If Prussia and Austria go with us, matters are different and the war becomes impossible for Russia.[3]

In these circumstances, it became the primary aim of Russian diplomacy to secure at least the neutrality of the two Germanic powers; by the same token, it became the basic object of allied diplomatic strategy to draw them into the war on the side of England and France.

On 30 January Orlov, the tsar's special envoy, presented to Francis-Joseph a personal letter in which Nicholas expressed his willingness to conclude an honourable peace and invited Austria, Prussia and Germany to adopt a neutral attitude.[4] Francis-Joseph asked for guarantees that Russian troops would not cross the Danube, that the Principalities would ultimately be evacuated, and that Turkish integrity would be respected. When Orlov refused these undertakings, the emperor declined to promise his neutrality and declared that his future policy would be based on the

---

[1] Meyendorff argued that the occupation of the Principalities forced Austria against her wishes to give a western orientation to her foreign policy and reminded his government that it had been a similar occupation which in 1806 had prevented her from coming to the assistance of Russia in the battle of Eylau. Geffcken, *op. cit.* p. 57.

[2] Quoted in H. Temperley, *England and the Near East: The Crimea* (London, 1936), p. 383.

[3] Geffcken, *op. cit.* p. 106. The crucial importance of the Germanic powers during the Crimean War is brought out by A. J. P. Taylor in *Rumours of Wars* (London, 1952), pp. 35 ff.

[4] For the following cf. Geffcken, *op. cit.* pp. 59 ff.

principles laid down in the declaration of 5 December. An appeal to Buol in the name of 'conservative interests' produced the rejoinder that these interests were best served by the defenders of Turkish integrity. On 8 February, Orlov left Vienna empty-handed.[1] Buol, moreover, wrote in a despatch to St Petersburg that the Russian occupation of the Principalities was unjust and that Russia must bear responsibility for the consequences. Austria began to concentrate her forces in the direction of the Principalities.[2]

The attitude of Prussia was hardly more favourable to Russia. In Berlin, there existed the usual division of opinion. Liberals of all shades were pro-British and anti-Russian;[3] Bonin, the Minister of War, was not averse to a campaign at the side of the western allies. On the other hand, the military camarilla surrounding the king was filled with admiration for Nicholas I and sympathized with the Christians under Turkish rule. The king, as was his wont, tried to steer a middle course.[4] Without actively supporting the western powers,[5] he yet firmly declined the Russian demand for a formal promise of armed neutrality.[6]

Late in February, England and France invited the two German powers to associate themselves with a summons to Russia to evacuate the Principalities. This invitation brought out the latent differences between the attitudes of Austria and Prussia. Whilst the Austrian cabinet gave effective diplomatic support to the western demand, that of Prussia adopted a policy of neutrality directed against France rather than Russia.[7] On 11 March, the king of Prussia informed Francis-Joseph of his intention

[1] Shortly afterwards, Francis-Joseph told Meyendorff that until Orlov's arrival he had believed in the tsar's peaceful intentions. Orlov's first words had changed his opinion: 'I was greatly shaken by this and must take my measures accordingly. Until then, it had been my intention to remain neutral. My present attitude, unlike that of Prussia, is not the result of secret negotiations with England. I have assumed no obligations but the vital interests of my empire impose upon me certain duties' (*Étude diplomatique sur la guerre de Crimée* (St Petersburg, 1878), Russian official publication attributed to Baron A. de Jomini of the Russian Foreign Ministry [quoted hereafter as Jomini], vol. I, p. 503).

[2] On 5 February, 25,000 men were despatched to the military frontier (the frontier zone bordering on Serbia and Bosnia). On 22 February, another 25,000 followed. The Austrian corps of observation in Transylvania was strengthened.

[3] Goltz, Pourtalès and their supporters had founded the *Wochenblatt* to advocate a liberal and anti-feudal policy both inside Prussia and abroad. Bunsen, the enthusiast of 1848, joined with British Ministers in drawing an 'ideal' map of Europe, in which the boundaries of Russia were moved significantly to the east. The prince of Prussia, one day to be William I, considered Russia the aggressor and advocated an anti-Russian policy.

[4] He told Bunsen: 'Prussia's position is too favourable and leaves the final decision too manifestly in our hands for me not to see this and to act accordingly' (Geffcken, *op. cit.* p. 71).

[5] In December 1853 he had sent Pourtalès to London to explain to the British Ministers that Prussia's neutrality was a gain to the common cause. This explanation had not been well received.

[6] A draft Protocol submitted by the Russian minister had moved him to indignation both by its contents and form. On 31 January, Otto von Manteuffel, the President of the Council of Ministers, declared the draft unacceptable.

[7] The difference between the Austrian and Prussian attitudes was largely the result of geography. Both countries had reason to fear Napoleon, the one in Italy, the other on the Rhine. For Austria, however, the threat in the Principalities was of more immediate urgency than that which might one day develop in Italy. Her immediate interests, therefore, lay on

to observe an absolute neutrality. He expressed pleasure at the report that Austria had decided to sign no convention with the western powers except in conjunction with Prussia. The two countries should conclude an offensive and defensive alliance for the duration of the war. Based on their common neutrality, this should provide for the joint defence of all their territories. In making these proposals, Frederick-William pursued a double object. He wished to prevent Austria from joining the western powers and dragging Germany into war with Russia. He also hoped to strengthen neutral Germany in the face of possible aggression from France. Prussia would, in case of need, help to defend Austrian possessions in Italy in return for Austrian assistance in the defence of Germany on the Rhine. An arrangement of this kind would enable both to withstand all possible pressure from France.

The Austrian government, conscious of the value of Prussian support in Italy, was not averse from the proposal. The alliance, moreover, might be used to strengthen Austria's eastern policy. As Francis-Joseph explained in his reply, a further Russian move in the Balkans might force Austria to occupy the Principalities. In that event, he would not declare war and his advance would stop at the river Pruth. If he were forced to act, a Prussian promise to defend Austria would deter Russia from attacking her.

Late in March, the Austrian government officially proposed the conclusion of an alliance. It also suggested a partial mobilization of German forces. Prussia in her reply stipulated that the alliance should be limited to the duration of the war. The question of armaments might be reserved for separate discussion. Agreement was reached on a defensive alliance. The *casus foederis* would arise in the event of an unprovoked attack on the territory of either power. It would occur also if one of the partners in defence of German interests and after consultation with its ally, should find itself forced to take offensive action. The Austrian government immediately invoked this clause, declaring that in conformity with the Protocol of 9 April[1] and in defence of German interests, it would demand at St Petersburg the evacuation of the Principalities.[2] It was prepared, if necessary, to enforce this demand, and relied on the support of Prussia. Frederick-William IV, angered by the rejection of a proposal for a settlement which he had submitted to the Russian cabinet, agreed to the

the side of the allies. Prussia, on the other hand, had no interest whatever in the Principalities. Her chief source of anxiety lay on the Rhine. In consequence, each of the two powers tried to influence the policy of the other. Austria spared no pains to draw Prussia and Germany into an anti-Russian coalition; Frederick-William and his entourage tried to turn to the West the attention of a neutral and united Confederation.

[1] On 9 April the representatives of England, France, Austria and Prussia had signed a Protocol at Vienna. It stated that although two of the signatories were now at war with Russia, they all agreed to adhere to the principles previously laid down. They desired the integrity of Turkey, the evacuation of the Principalities, safeguards for the Balkan Christians to be accorded by the sultan and the admission of Turkey into the concert of Europe.

[2] The situation bears a remarkable resemblance to that which arose in the summer of 1914.

Austrian request. An article to this effect was added to the terms of the proposed alliance. In addition, the two governments agreed to take offensive action to prevent Russia from incorporating the Principalities or crossing the Balkan range. On 20 April the treaty of alliance was signed by representatives of the two governments.

Having made these concessions to Austria and the western powers, Frederick-William, to show his strict neutrality, carried out a minor palace-revolution against the 'western' party in Berlin. Early in May, Bunsen was recalled from London, Bonin dismissed and the prince of Prussia relieved of his military duties. After 23 May the Prussian representative ceased to attend the conferences of the four powers in Vienna. The Prussian government thus dissociated itself from the efforts to mobilize the concert of Europe against Russia.

On 3 June, Buol summoned the Russian government to evacuate the Principalities. The tsar was asked to fix a date for the Russian withdrawal. This must not be made conditional on guarantees which Austria was unable to give. In a treaty with Turkey signed on 14 June, the Austrian government promised to take all necessary measures to secure the evacuation of the two provinces. It undertook not to conclude any agreement with Russia which was not based on the integrity of Turkey and the sovereign rights of the sultan. In return, until the conclusion of peace, the Porte transferred to Austria its sovereign rights in Moldavia and Wallachia. The news of this agreement caused indignation at Berlin. Buol was informed that it violated the treaty of 20 April. To a telegraphic message that Austrian troops had received orders to occupy the Principalities, the king of Prussia replied by declaring that he considered himself released from his obligations under the supplementary article of the treaty of alliance. The Austrian government thereupon cancelled the order to its forces.

Austria's conduct had aroused great bitterness at St Petersburg.[1] The tsar declared the old intimacy between the two empires to be at an end and taxed Austria with ingratitude.[2] The Austrian 'ultimatum' and the Austro-

[1] Esterházy, the Austrian minister, reported: 'Je m'abstiens...de répéter les propos qui circulent sur le compte de l'Autriche. Il est au dessous de notre dignité d'y faire attention. ...Néanmoins, c'est un fait constaté aujourd'hui que les sentiments qui animaient jusqu'ici la Russie pour l'Autriche étaient ceux d'un protecteur pour son protégé, sans égard pour la parité de leurs positions comme puissances européennes' (Esterházy to Buol, 9 June 1854, in Guichen, *op. cit.* pp. 158f.).

[2] Early in July, Esterházy was received by the tsar. He reported: 'L'Empereur... me reçut *fort froidement*. Après avoir posé sur la table la lettre de Notification que je lui avais remise, il me dit d'un ton sévère qu'il était vivement froissé de voir l'attitude hostile que Sa Majesté l'Empereur avait prise contre la Russie...; qu'il paraissait que l'Empereur, notre Auguste Maître, a ʌait entièrement oublié ce qu'il avait fait pour lui, et qu'enfin il était profondément peiné et blessé des préparatifs de guerre qu'on faisait contre ses armées en Autriche, que si la guerre devait éclater, Dieu serait juge entre les deux Souverains.... L'Empereur...continuant d'un ton irrité, me dit que la confiance qui avait existé jusqu'ici entre les deux souverains pour le bonheur de leurs Empires étant détruite, les mêmes rapports intimes ne pourront plus jamais exister' (the same to the same, 6 July 1854, *ibid.* pp. 159ff.).

Turkish treaty form another milestone in the collapse of the restoration settlement. From now on, it would prove all but impossible for Austria to regain the goodwill of the tsars. The Prussian government, on the other hand, need only persevere in its 'natural' policy of neutrality in order to stand out as the only European power that was not hostile to Russia.

Undeterred by Prussian and Russian indignation, Buol persisted in his policy of pressure to secure the evacuation of the Principalities. When Nesselrode declared that before Russia could withdraw she must have guarantees, he received the reply that Austria could make no promises on behalf of the western allies. She must insist on unconditional evacuation. In fact, the Austrian government was ready to expel the Russians by force. Austrian troops were assembling in Galicia and the Bukovina; military talks were opened with the western allies about co-ordinated action in the Balkans. The Russian military attaché in Vienna reported that Austria would be ready for action by the end of August.

At the same time, the Austrian government was working for closer association with England and France. Buol wished to conclude an offensive and defensive alliance. He desired, at the same time, to obtain a definition of allied war-aims lest Austria be drawn into an interminable war for objects which did not concern her.[1] He also asked for an undertaking that France would not disturb the *status quo* in Italy.

Drouyn de Lhuys, the Foreign Minister of Napoleon III, was eager to conclude an alliance which would shatter the system of Nicholas I. He was willing, therefore, to accede to Buol's request for a definition of war-aims. At the beginning of July, conversations took place in Paris from which emerged, in an embryonic form, the famous 'Four Points' which were to become the basis of negotiations. On 9 July Hübner, the Austrian minister in Paris, recommended to Buol the conclusion of a treaty between Austria and the allies.[2] On the 24th, he was authorized to enter into discussions with Drouyn. The negotiations for associating Austria with the allies were conducted between the representatives of France and Austria. They were only imperfectly revealed to the British government. On 26 July, the French chargé d'affaires communicated to the Foreign Secretary, the documents relating to the Franco-Austrian negotiations. Three days later, the British cabinet agreed to an exchange of notes turning the Four Points into a binding diplomatic instrument and to the proposed treaty of alliance between the three countries. The French drafts proved equally acceptable in Vienna and on 1 August the British minister recorded with delight: 'Buol agrees to proposed Notes and Treaty, in

---

[1] For this and the following cf. G. B. Henderson, *Crimean War Diplomacy* (Glasgow, 1947), pp. 158 ff.
[2] He had recommended 'un traité par lequel les puissances s'engageraient à consacrer tous leurs moyens d'action au but commun, dont le minimum se trouve défini par les quatre points' (*ibid.* p. 160).

short, buckles to everything.'[1] The association of Austria with the western allies appeared a matter of days.

It was at this moment that a decision taken at St Petersburg completely altered the aspect of affairs. The tsar had been convinced for some time that war with Austria was probable.[2] Such a war, however, boded ill for Russia: the Russian commander in the Balkans declared that an Austrian occupation of Wallachia would render his position untenable.[3] In the face of this opinion, the tsar began to waver. On 21 June and again on 6 July, Esterházy reported that the Russians would withdraw. Buol, before finally committing himself to alliance with England and France, resolved to wait and see whether the promised evacuation would in fact take place. He therefore spun out his negotiations on the pretext of some minor modifications proposed by England. On 5 August he finally informed the British and French ministers that he would sign the treaty only if Russia refused to evacuate the Principalities.

Buol, by this time, knew that the evacuation was already in progress. On 1 August, the son of the British minister in Vienna had written: 'Buol has a report (seemingly authentic) of the retreat of the Russians from Wallachia.'[4] In fact, the Russians had begun to withdraw on a large scale on 27 July. On 8 August, Gorchakov informed Buol that the tsar had ordered the complete evacuation of the Principalities. Without the use of force, Austria had obtained a major diplomatic triumph.

That day, Buol informed the allied ministers that he was prepared for an exchange of notes establishing the Four Points as the 'allied' basis of peace. At the same time, he excused himself from signing the proposed treaty of alliance on the plea that the evacuation of the Principalities had deprived it of its *raison d'être*. Austrian diplomacy secured a further triumph. The Four Points, formally proclaimed in notes exchanged on 8 August, limited allied war-aims. It seemed not impossible that Russia in her turn might yet be brought to accept them.[5] At the same time, Buol

---

[1] *Ibid.* p. 163.

[2] Cf. Esterházy to Buol, 6 July 1854, printed in Guichen, *op. cit.* p. 160. On taking leave of Gorchakov, who was to replace Meyendorff as Russian minister in Vienna, Nicholas I observed: 'I place in your hands my honour and that of Russia. I place full confidence in you but do not expect a favourable result from your efforts. I expect you to return within a month with the news of our break with Austria.' Geffcken, *op. cit.* p. 111.

[3] *Ibid.* p. 110.

[4] Henderson, *op. cit.* p. 164.

[5] The Four Points, as expressed in the notes of 8 August, declared: 'the three Powers are equally of the opinion that the relations of the Sublime Porte with the Imperial Court of Russia cannot be re-established on solid and durable bases' (i) if the Russian guarantee of the Principalities be not replaced by a European guarantee; (ii) if the Danube be not 'freed'; (iii) if 'the Treaty of 1841 be not revised in concert by all the High Contracting Powers in the interest of the Balance of Power in Europe'; and (iv) if the Christian subjects of the Porte be not placed under European rather than under Russian protection (*ibid.* p. 167). The final form of the note embodying the Four Points is attached to Westmorland to Clarendon, 8 August 1854, no. 293 in the P[ublic] R[ecord] O[ffice], FO 7/435.

had evaded any commitment which would oblige Austria to enter the war on the side of the western powers.

On 18 August the Austrian commander in Transylvania and the Banat issued a proclamation informing the inhabitants of Moldavia and Wallachia that, by virtue of an Austro-Turkish agreement, Austrian troops would occupy the Principalities. Two days later, Austrian forces entered the two provinces without meeting resistance. Generals Hess and Coronini took over the government in Bucharest.

The events leading up to the Russian evacuation of the Principalities had destroyed the understanding established by Nicholas I and Schwarzenberg. Resentment at St Petersburg at the methods employed by the cabinet of Vienna could not be allayed by the consideration that Austria's action had given Russia a major strategic victory.[1] In any event, Russia benefited from the Austrian occupation only so long as Austria maintained her neutrality. Were she to join the western allies, her forces in the Principalities would become at once a serious threat to the safety of Russia's southern provinces. The policy which had just culminated in the allied exchange of notes and the proclamation of the Four Points could inspire little confidence as to Austria's future intentions. It was far from certain whether she would be able to resist allied pressure to fight for war-aims to which she was a party. The action of Austria in first forcing Russia to relinquish her pledge and later seizing it herself could not but create a lasting resentment throughout the length and breadth of Russia.

The early months of the eastern crisis had thus profoundly changed the European situation. Austria and Russia were estranged. England and France were united. Austria appeared disposed to associate herself with the western powers. The inevitable consequence of these developments had been a *rapprochement* between Russia and Prussia. It seemed that in Berlin the cautious conservatism of the king and Manteuffel had triumphed over the 'Wochenblattspartei'. As a result, Prussia had, almost automatically, assumed the position previously occupied by her rival. Prussia alone now stood between Russia and complete isolation in Europe. The tsar knew that he owed to the cabinet of Berlin a debt of gratitude which it would be hard to exaggerate. The services rendered to Russia were none the less important for being unspectacular and fully justified the resentment against Prussia expressed in London and Paris.

The early months of the Crimean War had revealed important facts partly concealed by the collaboration of Schwarzenberg and Nicholas I. Whatever solidarity of conservative interests might exist between the cabinets of St Petersburg and Vienna, Russia and Austria were rivals in the Balkans. No such rivalry existed between Russia and Prussia. On the contrary, there was revealed a strong solidarity of interests between the

---

[1] The Austrians in the Principalities effectively protected southern Russia on the land-side as long as Austria chose to remain neutral.

Russian government and Prussian conservatives. Both were agreed in their fear of France and revolution, their dislike of German liberalism and their inflexible opposition to Polish national aspirations. Long before Bismarck had come to occupy a position of power, community of interests had established close sympathy between the cabinet of St Petersburg and the followers of the *Kreuzzeitung*. As far as the Russian government was concerned, Austria and Prussia had in fact changed places. Vienna, rather than Berlin, had become the centre of 'liberalizing' tendencies; the clash between Russia and 'Germany' had been transferred from the Duchies to the Principalities. A situation was beginning to emerge which differed in important respects from that established by the restoration of 1851.

II

The Russian evacuation of the Principalities and their occupation by Austrian troops was the first success of Buol's policy. Russian influence had been removed from the Danube, war in the Balkans had become unlikely and a broad neutral belt from the Baltic to the Black Sea had been interposed between the belligerents.[1] Following this achievement, the stage was set for the realization of Buol's second object, the conclusion of peace under the auspices of Austria. From now on, it was to be the principal aim of Austrian diplomacy to limit and define the allied war-aims and to impose them on the Russian government. In the course of this operation, Buol would try to crown his diplomatic structure by a permanent association between Austria and the western allies. In such a grouping he hoped to find security against the resentment of Russia,[2] the ambition of Prussia in Germany, the aspirations of Piedmont and the Italian sympathies of the emperor of the French.[3]

It was in pursuance of this policy that England, France and Austria had on 8 August exchanged notes setting out the Four Points as the basis of future negotiations with Russia.[4] The new Austrian action had heightened

[1] Circumstances, it was hoped in Vienna, might even enable the Austrian government to turn the temporary occupation of the Principalities into a permanent annexation. Cf. Friedjung, *op. cit.* p. 135; and F. Eckhart, *Die deutsche Frage und der Krimkrieg* (Berlin, 1931), p. 214.

[2] The emperor Francis-Joseph was soon to declare that 'he thought it necessary to provide for the future and that the present war should not end by a mere Treaty of Peace. He thought Russia would long bear ill-will to Austria for the part she had taken, and he wished to be united in a Treaty with the Maritime Powers, with a view to a permanent political system' (Russell to Clarendon, private, 23 April 1855, Clarendon MSS. in the Bodleian Library, Oxford).

[3] 'Man sieht', writes Friedjung, 'worauf das Absehen Buols gerichtet war und wodurch er die Richtigkeit seiner Politik erweisen wollte: er schuf für die durch die heilige Allianz gebotenen Bürgschaften einen entsprechenden Ersatz; man sollte ihm nicht nachsagen, dass er das Werk Metternichs zerschlug und nichts an dessen Stelle setzte.' H. Friedjung, *Der Krimkrieg und die österreichische Politik* (Stuttgart u. Berlin, 1907), p. 134.

[4] To make the proceedings acceptable to the British government, the notes of 8 August contained the proviso that if the events of the war favoured the allies, further supplementary demands might be put forward.

the indignation already felt at St Petersburg. When Esterházy invited Nesselrode to accept the Four Points as a basis of negotiation, the Chancellor expressed his disgust that the new demand should follow so closely Russia's conciliatory gesture in evacuating the Principalities.[1] The tsar, overcome by indignation drew up a 'projet de déclaration de guerre à l'Autriche'. Nesselrode dissuaded him by explaining that such a declaration would merely increase the number of Russia's enemies.[2] As a result, the Russian government contented itself with a blunt rejection of the Austrian proposal. Nesselrode declared that Russia would in no circumstances accept the Four Points as a basis of negotiation. Should adverse fortune oblige her to consent to them for a time, this would usher in not an era of peace but one of unending complications. What the allies understood by the 'interest of the European balance' was nothing less than the abrogation of all earlier Russo-Turkish treaties and the humiliation of Russia. Russia had just proved her love of peace by a sacrifice made to the special interests of Austria and Germany. The cabinet of Vienna had seen in this concession merely an opportunity for further far-reaching agreements with Russia's enemies.[3]

Russia's attitude was soon modified by events. Allied armies had landed in the Crimea without encountering resistance and on 20 September won the spectacular victory of the Alma. Rumour reported that Sevastopol had fallen. The news acted as a spur to Austrian diplomacy: Francis-Joseph expressed delight; Buol despatched congratulations to London and Paris whilst his language to the unfortunate Gorchakov became increasingly hostile.[4] Esterházy reported from St Petersburg that the tsar's dispositions were conciliatory.[5] The Austrian government decided to increase its pressure: Buol's despatches to St Petersburg became more pressing. Finally on 22 October orders were issued to place the Austrian army on a war footing. In face of these developments Nesselrode and the king of Prussia urged the tsar to consent to a further concession. Nicholas decided to yield. On 8 November a telegram from St Petersburg informed Buol that Russia would accept the Four Points. On the 17th Esterházy reported that he had received formal notification of the fact. Four days later the Austrian orders for mobilization were revoked except so far as they had already been carried out.

Buol, in the meantime, had resumed negotiations for an alliance with

---

[1] 'Est-ce ainsi', Nesselrode asked, 'que vous répondez aux sacrifices que nous vous portons en évacuant les Principautés? Comment, nous cédons aux instances de l'Autriche et dans ce même moment vous exigez de nouvelles concessions? Est-ce juste?' (Esterházy to Buol, 30 August 1854, Henderson, *op. cit.* p. 171). To the Prussian minister the Chancellor remarked that he objected less to the Four Points themselves than to the manner of their presentation at the moment when Russia was evacuating the Principalities (*ibid.* n. 3).
[2] If war was declared on Austria 'au lieu de trois ennemis nous aurons à lutter contre l'Europe entière' (*ibid.* p. 172).
[3] Geffcken, *op. cit.* p. 114. [4] Henderson, *op. cit.* p. 174 n. 3.
[5] For the following cf. *ibid.* pp. 177ff.

the western powers. He had met strong opposition from the russophile entourage of the emperor but, after threatening to resign, had finally carried the day. On 2 December the tripartite treaty between Austria, England and France was signed.[1] The treaty carried one step further Buol's policy of terminating the war in association with the western powers. It can hardly be claimed that it constituted 'a diplomatic revolution more far-reaching in its effects than that of Kaunitz',[2] for that revolution had already been accomplished.[3] None the less, the alliance was regarded throughout Europe as an important event. It was hailed in Paris as a decisive success in Napoleon's campaign to destroy the northern coalition, 'the main object of which since 1815 has been to keep France in check'.[4] It was held to herald the end of the Holy Alliance.[5] The tsar was deeply hurt and relieved his feelings by presenting to his valet a statuette of Francis-Joseph which had until then adorned his study. He asked Esterházy the famous question about the two most foolish kings of Poland.[6] Three months after the signing of the treaty Nicholas was dead. His sudden end was widely attributed to a 'broken heart' caused, next to military reverses, by the ingratitude of Austria.

III

Buol's policy was soon to receive a severe setback. Shortly after the death of Nicholas representatives of Austria, Russia and the western powers met in the famous Vienna Conferences to try and reach agreement on the interpretation of the Four Points already accepted by Russia. Buol, Drouyn and Russell,[7] the three principal allied representatives were, each for different reasons, eager to end the war. Under the auspices of Buol, they 'manufactured' an interpretation of the third point[8] at variance alike

---

[1] The most important provisions of the treaty were contained in articles I and V. By the first of these the signatories confirmed the Four Points and reserved the right to put forward supplementary demands. They agreed not to enter into agreements with Russia without previous consultation. By the second it was laid down that if peace had not been concluded before the end of the year, the signatories would consult together about the means most fitted to achieve the objects of the alliance (*ibid.* p. 184).   [2] *Ibid.* p. 154.

[3] In October, Buol had spoken of this diplomatic revolution as an accomplished fact (Westmorland to Clarendon, 18 October 1854, *ibid.* pp. 187f.).

[4] Cowley to Clarendon, 4 December 1854, *ibid.* p. 185.

[5] Benedetti then First Secretary of the French Embassy in Constantinople wrote: 'Politiquement, militairement, le traité du 2 décembre renverse tout et révèle un nouvel horizon. Vous avez blessé à mort la Sainte Alliance; vous venez la mettre en terre, avec enterrement de première classe' (Benedetti to Thouvenel, 10 December 1854, *ibid.* pp. 185f.).

[6] Who, the tsar was alleged to have asked, were the two most foolish kings of Poland? John Sobieski and himself, for they had both saved Austria (*ibid.* p. 188).

[7] Russell, at this time, was not a member of the government, having resigned from the office of Foreign Secretary in January 1855.

[8] The official Anglo-French interpretation of the third point declared: 'La révision du traité du 13 juillet 1841 doit avoir pour objet de rattacher plus complètement l'existence de l'Empire Ottoman à l'équilibre européen, et de faire cesser la prépotence de la Russie dans la Mer Noire' (*ibid.* p. 108).

with their instructions and with a secret Franco-British agreement.[1] This solution was criticized in London and Paris. On 4 May the British ambassador and the French Minister of War persuaded Napoleon to reject it. The British government followed suit. On 7 May Drouyn, the convinced advocate of a Franco-Austrian alliance, resigned his post as Foreign Minister.

Chastened by this experience, Buol decided to bide his time. He was now aware that only a decisive turn in the bitter struggle for Sevastopol could create conditions favourable to a resumption of negotiations.[2] When on the night of 8 September Russian forces evacuated Sevastopol, Buol summoned the French minister who was about to visit Paris. He outlined the terms of peace he was now prepared to recommend at St Petersburg. Towards the middle of October Bourqueney returned from the French capital with Napoleon's authorization to negotiate with the Austrian government. On 14 November Buol and Bourqueney initialled a memorandum laying down the terms on which Austria was to bring about peace in conjunction with the western powers. Russia must accept the neutralization of the Black Sea. The second point dealing with freedom of navigation on the river Danube was 'developed' to include a rectification of the frontier between Russia and Moldavia. A fifth point was officially added to the existing four stipulating the right of the belligerents at a future peace conference to make additional demands 'in a European interest'. Austria was to present these terms for acceptance at St Petersburg. In case of a refusal she would break off diplomatic relations. In addition it was laid down that Austria, France and England would conclude a tripartite treaty to guarantee the enforcement of a general treaty of peace.[3]

The Protocol of 14 November forms a landmark in the evolution of Austrian policy. The demand for a territorial cession which the Russian government would naturally attribute to Austrian malice, support for the policy of neutralization, the decision to submit these onerous terms in the form of an ultimatum and, last but not least, the resolve to enter a permanent association with England and France could not but make the breach between Vienna and St Petersburg final and irrevocable. It was the Protocol of 14 November which paved the way for the final 'renversement des alliances' by which Austria broke away from Russia and associated herself with the western powers.

[1] For the secret Franco-British agreement cf. *ibid.* pp. 108f.

[2] Towards the end of August, Buol had told a German diplomat: '...que les négociations de paix ne pouvaient être reprises qu'après une victoire décisive remportée par les uns ou par les autres et que, cet événement accompli, il fallait se presser de faire une nouvelle et sérieuse tentative de pacification' (Stockhausen to Lenthe, 13 September 1855, no. 70, Staatsarchiv Hannover 9, Türkei no. 27 H[enderson] T[ranscripts] in Cambridge University Library).

[3] Memorandum signed by Count Buol and M. de Bourqueney. Copy in Clarendon to the Queen, 19 November 1855, RA G 40/79.

By the middle of December the reluctant consent of the British government to the Austro-French agreement had been obtained. On the 16th, Esterházy left Vienna for St Petersburg bearing the terms of the Austrian ultimatum. He reached the Russian capital on the 26th and was received by Nesselrode two days later. Esterházy explained that the terms he was about to submit[1] were the result of a final effort (*d'un suprême effort*) to terminate the war. He had been sent not to negotiate but simply to transmit a document prepared by the Austrian government.[2] Any attempt to discuss modifications would make agreement impossible.[3]

Before replying to the Austrian summons the tsar called together his Council. With one dissentient voice members declared themselves in favour of accepting the ultimatum as a basis of negotiation.[4] At the same time, the territorial integrity of the empire must be maintained. Counter-proposals excluding the cession and the fifth point should be addressed to Vienna. This, Alexander later informed the Russian commander in the Crimea, constituted the extreme limit of concession. Simple acceptance of the ultimatum would have been an impossibility.[5] On 5 January Nesselrode transmitted this reply to Gorchakov in Vienna.[6] Two days later he told Esterházy that a conciliatory reply had been despatched. Since his words did not, however, imply an unconditional acceptance, Esterházy on instructions from Buol now read a further despatch explaining that any reserve or modification would be treated as a refusal. Rejection would infallibly be followed by a rupture of diplomatic relations.[7] On the 11th Buol received the Russian reply. The following day he told Gorchakov that it was unsatisfactory. Unless an unconditional acceptance was received before the 18th, the Austrian government, in pursuance of solemn engagements, would break off diplomatic relations with Russia.[8]

On 12 January it was known at St Petersburg that Austria had rejected the Russian counter-proposals. Three days later the tsar once again called

[1] Nesselrode had already learnt the terms of the Austrian ultimatum through a despatch from the Russian minister in Berlin received on 24 December. Cf. Geffcken, *op. cit.* p. 208.

[2] 'J'établis d'une manière catégorique que, quant à moi, je n'étais point arrivé à St Pétersbourg en *négociateur*, mais simplement comme *porteur* d'un travail du Cabinet de Vienne' (Esterházy to Buol, 29 December 1855, Guichen, *op. cit.* pp. 311f.).

[3] '...qu'aucune chance d'accomodement n'était possible du moment où elle [the Russian court] voudrait apporter des modifications au programme que je venais de lui remettre' (*ibid.*).

[4] For an account of the meeting of the Imperial Council on 1 January 1856, cf. A. P. Zablotski-Desjatovski, *Count P. D. Kisselev and his time* (in Russian), (St Petersburg, 1882), vol. III, pp. 3ff.

[5] Alexander II to M. D. Gorchakov, 6 January 1856, S. S. Tatishchev, *The Emperor Alexander II* (in Russian), (St Petersburg, 1903), vol. I, p. 184.

[6] Esterházy to Buol, telegram, 7 January 1856, H[aus] H[of und] S[taats] A[rchiv Vienna], P[ol.] A[rch.] R[ussland], x, fasc. 39, H.T.

[7] Buol to Esterházy, 16 December 1855, no. 2, confidential, *ibid.* fasc. 38 copy. The interview is described in Esterházy to Buol, 12 January 1856, no. 2 A–G, *ibid.* fasc. 39.

[8] Buol to Esterházy, telegram, 12 January 1856, *ibid.*

a meeting of his Council.[1] He found among his advisers general agreement that the Austrian terms must be accepted. Nesselrode read a detailed memorandum prepared by the Ministry of Foreign Affairs in which it was argued that although the empire was still in a condition to prolong the war, no favourable turn of events could be expected. The diplomatic situation was bound to deteriorate: Austria, Sweden and even Prussia[2] might join the ranks of Russia's enemies; an effective allied blockade supported by Austria, the Scandinavian countries and the German states would slowly strangle Russia and prejudice the future development of her economy. In the long run, her position would become untenable and she might be forced to conclude peace on terms more disadvantageous than those now proposed to her. By accepting the Austrian ultimatum, Russia would disconcert her enemies who reckoned on a refusal. The conclusion of peace would enable her to dissolve the hostile coalition composed of heterogeneous elements and held together only by the needs of a common struggle. France appeared sympathetic to Russia and Napoleon was clearly tiring of the policy into which he had been forced by the war. The Russian government must assist his efforts to emancipate himself from the British alliance. If Russia refused the present terms, she would drive the emperor of the French once more into the arms of England; if she accepted them, she would flatter his *amour propre* and make him the arbiter of the coming peace. This situation would enable both Russia and France, enlightened by their recent experiences, to give a new direction to their policies 'in which their interests and tendencies would find more favourable elements'.

The speakers who followed Nesselrode declared that continued resistance would lead to a harder and more humiliating peace which would weaken the country for many years to come. The Crimea, the Caucasus, even Finland and Poland might be placed in jeopardy. Compared to dangers such as these, the sacrifices now demanded were insignificant. Rather than face such risks, the ultimatum must be accepted.

The most interesting arguments for the conclusion of peace were those brought forward by Meyendorff. A continuation of the struggle, he argued, would bring Russia to the verge of bankruptcy. Already, the war had cost 3000 million roubles in extraordinary expenditure; receipts had fallen short

---

[1] The Council of 15 January 1856 is described in Jomini, *op. cit.* (Engl. ed. London, 1882), vol. II, pp. 366 ff. Cf. also Tatishchev, *op. cit.* pp. 186 f. and Meyendorff, *op. cit.* vol. III, pp. 214 ff.

[2] On 15 January the king of Prussia had telegraphed to the Prussian minister at St Petersburg: 'La Prusse doit s'approprier les propositions afin d'échapper à l'isolement; insistez pour qu'on les accepte, afin qu'elle ne soit pas mise dans la nécessité de rappeler son ministre. On fera, par contre, aux conférences tout pour amener une modification dans la délimitation territoriale' (Guichen, *op. cit.* p. 351). For a detailed study of the circumstances in which the tsar accepted the Austrian ultimatum cf. W. E. Mosse, 'How Russia Made Peace, September 1855 to April 1856', in *The Cambridge Historical Journal*, XI, no. 3 (1955), pp. 297 ff.

of anticipation; in more than one province there existed a serious shortage of agricultural labour; the productive capacity of the nation was impaired.

If the present costly struggle continued, Russia would eventually find herself in a position similar to that of Austria after the Napoleonic Wars. Exhausted by her struggle with the French revolution, she had then been forced to renounce all political initiative and to follow a policy of peace at any price. In a similar manner Sweden, after the wars of Charles XII, was exhausted and fell to the rank of a third-rate power. Such might hereafter be the fate of Russia if she decided to continue the present struggle. If, on the other hand, she now consented to a peace which did not impede the development of her resources and which did not prejudice her future, she would, with an economical system of government, be as strong 'in a few years' as she had been before the outbreak of war. She might then be able to accomplish what present circumstances would not permit her to do. Concluded now, a peace might only be a truce; postponed for a year or two, it might leave the empire in such a state of exhaustion that fifty years would be needed for its recovery. During that time, unable to face the prospect of war, Russia would be forced to observe scrupulously the terms of any treaty she might have been forced to sign. Many European questions, Meyendorff concluded, might be decided without or even against her. It was for this reason that he gave his vote for immediate unconditional acceptance.

The official advisers of the emperor Alexander II had with virtual unanimity declared in favour of peace. Other views, however, were expressed by those who did not share official responsibility.

The national feeling was wounded by the very idea of a humiliating peace. Russia was not conquered, she had still a numerous army gloriously tried; she had her recollections, her patriotism, her perseverance, the difficulties which her immense territory and her severe climate opposed to invasion; she might await the enemy at home, repeat the examples of 1812, leave him to exhaust himself in ineffective efforts, fatigue him by dint of patience, and await the favourable moment for crushing him.[1]

These and similar arguments in favour of Russia's traditional strategy were put forward 'with extreme vivacity' though 'without presenting either the maturity of opinions wisely weighed in the balance of cool reason, or the irresistible energy of uncontrollable passion which sometimes excites to the utmost the popular fibre'.[2] It was the Grand-Duke Constantine, the emperor's younger brother, who urged these views in a 'passionate discussion' (*discussion passionnée*), which took place after the meeting of the Council. The tsar, who in his heart of hearts agreed with his brother, spoke strongly in favour of peace. He pointed to the danger

[1] Jomini, *op. cit.* pp. 369f. [2] *Ibid.*

that Prussia might join the western powers, to the immense losses suffered by the Russian armies, to the difficulties of recruitment and to the exhaustion of Russia's finances.[1] In fact, he had resigned himself to the dishonour which he could no longer escape.

At 2 p.m. on 16 January Esterházy received from Nesselrode a written note announcing Russia's unconditional acceptance.[2] That evening in Vienna Buol learnt the news from a crestfallen Gorchakov.[3] Buol's diplomacy had gained a further success. The price of this achievement was the lasting estrangement of Russia. An audience Esterházy was to have had from the tsar was postponed an hour before it was due. It required several attempts on the part of Nesselrode before the tsar would appoint another date. When he finally received Esterházy his attitude was formal and reserved. He complained bitterly that it should have been Austria which had demanded the cession in Bessarabia. No explanations given by the Austrian envoy could dispel his indignation.[4] The tsar spoke not only for his Court, his advisers and his diplomats, but for at least the vocal part of his subjects when on a subsequent occasion he told Esterházy that Russia would never forget the services rendered to her by Austria in this crisis.[5] Russian diplomats were even more outspoken. Gorchakov, who had been treated badly by Buol, privately described the Austrians as 'infâmes gueux'[6] and declared Buol's conduct to be 'incroyable et inqualifiable'.[7] He dreamt of revenge for the humiliations inflicted on his country and himself[8] and did not hesitate to inform Buol of the fact. Orlov, soon to be Russia's first plenipotentiary at the Congress of Paris, spoke bitterly about the Austrians.[9] Lesser Russian diplomats, Budberg,

[1] Werther to Manteuffel, 27 January 1856, Guichen, *op. cit.* p. 351. In fact, Russia was approaching the end of her resources. A palace revolution was apprehended (*ibid.* pp. 299 and 303). The possibility of a popular rising was discussed (*ibid.* pp. 303 and 354). Meyendorff, in a letter shown to Cowley, gave 'a lamentable account of the disorganized state of the whole military department in Russia—it had completely broken down' (Cowley to Clarendon, private, 29 April 1856, Clarendon MSS.). Granville, during the coronation of Alexander II, was to write from Russia: 'They think themselves and acknowledge themselves to be much more beat than they are thought in the West to have been and there is a great deal of irritation on the subject' (Granville to Clarendon, private, 15 August 1856, *ibid.*).

[2] Esterházy to Buol, telegram, 16 January 1856, HHSAPAR, x, fasc. 39, HT.

[3] Geffcken, *op. cit.* p. 216.

[4] Esterházy to Buol, 6 February 1856, no. 10 A-B, HHSAPAR, x, fasc. 39, HT.

[5] 'La Russie n'oubliera jamais les services que l'Autriche lui a rendus dans cette crise' (quoted in Guichen, *op. cit.* p. 376).

[6] Geffcken, *op. cit.* p. 212.

[7] Seymour to Clarendon, 22 June 1856, no. 431, secret, FO 7/487.

[8] Whilst the fate of the Austrian ultimatum was still hanging in the balance, Gorchakov had exclaimed: 'Si j'étais près de l'Empereur, je serais capable de lui conseiller d'accepter: en trois ans la Russie aura repris ses forces et elle pourra alors tomber à bras raccourcis sur ce gouvernement perfide, qui a conseillé le morcellement de la Russie...' (Geffcken, *op. cit.* p. 212).

[9] After Orlov had passed through Berlin on his way to Paris, Budberg wrote to a colleague: 'Je puis certifier qu'à son passage ici, j'ai trouvé le comte Orlov irrité au point qu'il doutait s'il aurait assez de sang-froid pour se contenir aux conférences. Si le comte Buol, s'écriait-il, s'avise de me jeter le gant, je saurai le mettre à la raison' (Guichen, *op. cit.* p. 376).

Balabin, Stackelberg, spoke with one voice on the subject.[1] Hatred of Austria had become well-nigh universal.[2]

IV

During November 1855 the aged Nesselrode had drafted his letter of resignation.[3] In January Gorchakov had seen fit to inform Buol that he was about to become Minister of Foreign Affairs.[4] In February Nesselrode prepared a detailed memorandum on the policy which Russia should pursue after the conclusion of peace.[5] It was the political testament of the last important statesman to have participated in the reconstruction of Europe at Vienna.

If the coming negotiations, Nesselrode declared, led to the conclusion of peace, Russia must modify the political system she had followed until this time. The recent war had imposed upon the empire sacrifices the true effect of which could not yet be assessed. It was, however, clear that her recent exertions would oblige Russia to concentrate on her internal affairs and on the development of her material and moral resources. Since internal reconstruction must be the first concern of the Russian government, all diplomatic activity which might impede it must be carefully avoided.[6]

Until the recent war Russia's system of foreign policy had involved the obligation to maintain—if necessary by force of arms—the stipulations of the European treaties as well as those of agreements concluded with

[1] Budberg, a moderate and responsible diplomat told his Sardinian colleague: 'Pour le moment l'Autriche recueille quelques avantages de l'alliance du 2 décembre. Je ne saurais l'affirmer pour l'avenir. En s'éloignant de la Russie elle a fait un pas dans une voie semée d'écueils.... *Nous avons été mal recompensés de notre généreuse intervention en Hongrie*; je conviens qu'il nous est plus facile de pardonner à nos ennemis qu'à nos prétendus amis' (*ibid.* p. 356).
Balabin in his turn observed: 'L'Autriche sait à présent qu'elle a la paix, mais elle ne sait pas encore ce que celle-ci lui coûtera' (*ibid.*).
[2] Seymour reported to Clarendon: 'Between Austria and Russia a great Gulf has been fixed' (Seymour to Clarendon, 23 July 1856, FO 7/488, no. 526, secret and confidential). 'The greater number of English travellers with whom I have lately spoken are struck by the language not only of exasperation and hatred but even of menace which is employed by the Russians, so many of whom are to be met this summer at the German baths, in speaking of Austria. Many of them give it to be understood in an indirect but significant manner that not long will elapse before Austria will be made to pay severely for what in the apparently official language of Russia is termed "her unparalleled treachery"' (the same to the same, 8 September 1856, *ibid.* FO 7/490, no. 675).
[3] Nesselrode, *op. cit.* pp. 108f.
[4] Seymour to Clarendon, private, 15 January 1856, Clarendon MSS.
[5] The memorandum is printed in Nesselrode, *op. cit.* pp. 112ff., and with an additional paragraph (evidently interpolated in 1863), in Meyendorff, *op. cit.* pp. 217ff.
[6] 'La guerre a imposée au pays des sacrifices, dont on ne connaît pas au juste l'étendue et les conséquences. On peut toutefois se dire, dès aujourd'hui, qu'il en résulte pour la Russie une nécessité presqu'absolue de s'occuper de ses affaires intérieures et du dévelope-ment de ses forces morales et matérielles. Ce travail intérieur étant le premier besoin du pays, toute activité extérieure qui ferait obstacle, devra être soigneusement exclue.'

certain countries. In future for an unspecified period of time[1] such engagements must be entered only after first consulting the direct interests of Russia. Pacific in its general tendency, Russian policy would admit the possibility of war only after its evident advantage for the empire or its unavoidable necessity had been conclusively shown.[2] To carry out this system made necessary by internal needs, Russia must observe existing treaties[3] but avoid new obligations.

This policy must be applied also to Russia's relations with France. To enter at once into a formal alliance with that country would be to abandon prematurely the system prescribed by circumstances. Assured of Russian support, Napoleon would embark on enterprises in which it might not suit Russia to follow him as far as he would wish. A war in which he relied on revolutionary passions or oppressed nationalities must never receive Russian approval[4] much less her material assistance. In the true interest of the empire and the dynasty alike Russian policy must remain monarchical and anti-Polish.[5] Neither could Russia make common cause with Napoleon in an attempt to conquer the left bank of the Rhine. It should not be forgotten that Prussia alone of the powers had, during the present crisis, shown a firm determination not to be hostile to Russia.[6] By holding out to Napoleon the expectation that she would not join a hostile coalition, Russia would give him a token of her goodwill. This should be sufficient to secure his co-operation in the preservation of peace.[7] That must be the limit of Russia's engagements.

The extreme importance which Napoleon still attached to his relations with England justified the expectation that the Franco-British alliance would survive the present war. Its disintegration might be a slow process.[8] Russian offers of a *rapprochement* with France might, therefore, prove ineffective. They might present to Napoleon an opportunity for exciting well-founded suspicions at Berlin and renewed hostility in Vienna.[9] He might thus maintain and even extend his anti-Russian coalition. Amidst the uncertainties following the conclusion of peace some time must pass before it could be seen whether new political groupings were possible. Until then, it would be reckless to compromise, on the strength of Louis

---

[1] 'pendant un nombre d'années indéterminé'.

[2] 'Pacifique dans sa tendance générale, notre politique n'admettrait l'éventualité de la guerre que lorsque son inévitable nécessité ou son avantage évident pour la Russie aura été bien constaté.'

[3] 'il faut se maintenir ostensiblement sur le terrain des transactions existantes'.

[4] 'ne devraient jamais recevoir notre approbation'.

[5] 'notre politique doit, dans le véritable intérêt de la Russie et de la dynastie, rester monarchique et anti-polonaise'.

[6] 'la Prusse, seule de toutes les puissances, a fermement manifesté l'intention de ne pas nous être hostile'.

[7] 'pour obtenir en retour sa coopération efficace et décisive pour la paix'.

[8] 'ce ne sera que lentement et dans un avenir qu'on ne saurait déterminer'.

[9] 'une haine nouvelle'.

Napoleon's word, Russia's good and useful relations with Prussia[1] or to poison still further those with Austria which through necessity had been preserved at so heavy a cost.

The same necessity forced Russia, and would force her for a long time, to treat Austria with consideration.[2] Had they not seen the entire Confederation ready to rise in her defence? Moreover, there existed, since the Polish partitions a community of interests among the partitioning powers. The revolution in Poland had proved that it was Russia which most needed that solidarity. Before breaking entirely with a political system which had been followed for forty years not through a whim[3] but as a result of the irresistible force of principles and facts[4] it was necessary to recall that in politics all intimacy amounted to an engagement. Would it not be reckless and premature to base an entire political system on close alliance with a country which since 1815 had been the theatre of three revolutions? Two dynasties, more firmly established in appearance than that of Napoleon, had been swept away within twenty-four hours.

In summing up, Nesselrode repeated that the well-understood interests of Russia required that her policy should remain monarchical and anti-Polish. The *rapprochement* with France as a means of dissolving the anti-Russian coalition must be subordinate to these paramount needs. It must not take the form of an alliance unless this was dictated by favourable circumstances.[5]

Nesselrode's memorandum was a warning against the policy of a French alliance which he feared his successor would adopt. The aged chancellor knew that in spite of Austria's 'perfidy' a community of interests between the two empires required the maintenance of close relations between them. This was a fact which, although instinctively understood by the tsar, was hidden from Gorchakov. For years the new Foreign Minister would be the protagonist of a French alliance and the bitter enemy of Austria.

Gorchakov's appointment took effect on 17 April. It was ill-received in Russia and abroad.[6] Seymour, who had for some years been his colleague

---

[1] 'nos relations si bonnes et si utiles avec la Prusse'.

[2] 'de la ménager'.

[3] 'non par prédilection ou par caprice'.

[4] 'par la force irrésistible des principes et des choses'.

[5] 'si des conjonctures favorables le prescrivaient'. It is not difficult to guess the nature of the 'conjonctures favorables'. If Napoleon at the risk of breaking up his alliance with England, should be prepared to help Russia free herself from the shackles of the treaty, his assistance might justify even a Russo-French alliance.

[6] Budberg, the ablest of Russia's younger diplomats, declared: 'La nomination de Gortchakoff ne m'aurait pas surpris il y a deux ans. Elle m'étonne beaucoup aujourd'hui après ce qui s'est passé à Vienne. Il paraît donc que la phrase conserve son empire chez nous—c'est triste' (Budberg to Dmitri Nesselrode, 20 April 1856, Nesselrode, *op. cit.* pp. 132f.). Cowley, less suspect of partiality, wrote from Paris: 'Every Russian complains of Gortschakoff's appointment' (Cowley to Clarendon, private, 29 April 1856, Clarendon MSS.).

at Vienna, had formed a 'confirmed conviction of the unfitness of the new Minister for the post to which he has been raised'.[1] It is, indeed, well known that Gorchakov's approach to political problems was emotional, dramatic, 'feminine' and inspired by an almost pathological vanity. Unlike Nesselrode, his sober predecessor, he was to prove himself incapable of distinguishing between personal emotions and diplomatic facts. An emotional attachment to France and an almost equally 'personal' aversion to Austria concealed from the new minister much that his wiser predecessor had seen.

In spite of this, it is true to say that the practical effects of Gorchakov's appointment have perhaps been overrated. Gorchakov may have exaggerated when he described himself somewhat inelegantly as 'a sponge which yields at the pressure of the imperial hand the liquid with which it is filled'.[2] Yet Bismarck, who was later to enjoy unrivalled opportunities of watching the Foreign Minister in action, formed the impression that he was essentially an official carrying out his master's instructions.[3] Russian foreign policy in the days of Alexander II remained decisively the policy of the tsar. The transition from Nesselrode to Gorchakov, therefore, produced a change of emphasis and an accentuation of existing trends rather than a reversal of policy. The presence of Alexander II with his basically conservative instincts and his veneration for the memory of his father guaranteed a measure of continuity and acted as a brake on his impulsive minister. The tsar never overcame his distrust of Louis-Napoleon and it hardly needed the latter's tenacious refusal to abandon the British alliance to keep within modest bounds such *rapprochement* with France as Gorchakov might attempt.[4]

Apart from the continuity of policy resulting from the tsar's personal direction there was the fact that, after the Crimean War and the treaty of Paris, Russia's future course was clearly indicated by the needs of her situation. Three factors, above all, dictated the conduct of Gorchakov as they would have that of conservatives like Meyendorff or Budberg, or of

---

[1] Seymour to Clarendon, 11 June 1856, FO 7/486, secret and confidential. Seymour added: 'As a companion Prince Gortschakoff has all the necessary qualifications—as a Minister...he will involve himself in constant difficulties. He talks profusely and very well —but it is not in his power to keep silence—a talent possessed in so eminent a degree by his predecessor Count Nesselrode' (*ibid.*).

[2] Immediatbericht Bismarcks, 27 April 1859, in *Die politischen Berichte des Fürsten Bismarck aus Petersburg und Paris, 1859–1862*, ed. L. von Raschdau (Berlin, 1920), pp. 30f.

[3] 'Le prince Gortschakoff n'est pas l'homme à nourrir ou à suivre des convictions indépendantes et dépourvues de l'autorisation impériale. C'est un esprit actif et brillant, d'une conception prompte et facile, mais doué de cette souplesse nationale qui lui fait réfléter les moindres nuances des dispositions de son maître' (*ibid.*).

[4] Misled by the somewhat extravagant language of Walewski, Morny and Gorchakov, and by the equally exaggerated apprehensions expressed in London and Vienna, historians have persistently exaggerated the importance of the Franco-Russian *rapprochement* of 1856–9. It never alarmed Bismarck who not only believed that it would not damage Prussia but fully realized its necessary limitations.

opportunists like Orlov or Brunnow. Of the three 'inevitable' elements of Russian foreign policy the first was the need, so clearly expressed by Meyendorff and Nesselrode, to avoid entanglements or engagements through which Russia might be involved prematurely in another war. This conviction, a commonplace of Russian diplomacy,[1] was shared by the tsar himself. He told Orlov:

The treaty just signed in Paris which puts an end to the war and in consequence to the alliance directed against Russia, leaves us in an uncertain position with regard to our future policy. After her recent trials, Russia must concentrate on her own affairs and seek to heal by domestic measures the wounds inflicted by the war. For a period of time the length of which it is impossible to foresee, our entire policy must be based on this principle in order to achieve this beneficent result. We must eliminate all external obstacles which might stand in its way. Every effort of the emperor's servants must be directed to the realisation of this object.[2]

Gorchakov, therefore, merely expressed in a felicitous phrase a fact generally recognized by diplomats,[3] when he announced in his famous circular that Russia was not sulking but simply withdrawing within herself.[4] His mouthpiece Jomini would later declare that Russia's enforced withdrawal from Europe was perhaps the most momentous result of the Crimean War.[5]

[1] As early as November 1853, a Russian diplomat in conversation with a foreign colleague had delivered himself of the following opinion: 'Admettez que nous soyons forcés d'évacuer les principautés et de signer une paix comme nous n'en avons pas signé depuis un siècle. Nous aurions toujours à y gagner.... Car la question d'Orient une fois résolue d'une manière ou de l'autre, nous pourrions licencier les deux tiers de nos armées...et avec les économies que nous ferions de cette manière construire nos chemins de fer etc. En chosissant cette voie, nous regagnerions en dix ou vingt ans tout ce que nous aurions perdu et bien au delà' (quoted in Vitzthum von Eckstädt, *St Petersburg and London 1852-1864* (London, 1887), vol. I, p. 190).
The Grand-Duke Constantine had resigned himself to the necessity of concluding peace 'reconnaissant qu'avant de se livrer à de nouvelles entreprises, la Russie devait accomplir de graves réformes intérieures' (Werther to Manteuffel, 27 January 1856, quoted in Guichen, *op. cit.* p. 351).
[2] Memorandum approved by the emperor, 17/5 April 1856, quoted in Tatishchev, *op. cit.* pp. 199f.
[3] When Gorchakov in one of his wilder moments threatened Buol with a 'politique de vengeance', the Austrian Minister replied that he was not a believer in that kind of policy and that 'if Russia should be fortunate enough to obtain peace, she would find ample occupation for some years to come in healing her wounds, making railroads, opening banks, and the like domestic employments' (Seymour to Clarendon, private, 15 January 1856, Clarendon MSS.).
Palmerston also considered that the peace about to be concluded would leave Russia 'a most formidable Power' able in a few years' time, when she should by a wise internal policy have developed her immense natural resources, once again 'to place in danger the great interests of Europe' (Palmerston to Clarendon, private, 7 March 1856, *ibid.*).
[4] 'La Russie boude, dit-on. La Russie ne boude pas. La Russie se recueille' (Circular of 3 September 1856, quoted in Tatishchev, *op. cit.* pp. 229f.).
[5] '...it sufficed that Russia should withdraw from the affairs of Europe for her momentary absence to break the equilibrium and deliver up the general peace to the most dangerous disturbances' (Jomini, *op. cit.* p. 393).

The second basic feature of Russian policy after 1856 was dictated by history and national ambition. No true Russian could doubt for one moment that the recent setback was a purely temporary misfortune and that, after the necessary period of reconstruction, Russia would resume her traditional policy. On this issue, Gorchakov's language did not differ one whit from that of Meyendorff.[1] Brunnow's views in 1860 were the same as those expressed by Russian diplomats at the time of the Paris Congress.[2] Had not Alexander II resisted to the last a settlement which he considered dishonourable and had he not declared his signature of the treaty of peace to have been an act of cowardice which nothing would induce him to repeat?[3] There could be no doubt that the destruction of the treaty of Paris must be the immediate long-term object of Russian diplomacy. It must be followed by a full resumption of Russia's traditional policy.[4]

The third necessary element of Russian foreign policy on the morrow of the Congress of Paris was the obvious need to break up the hostile coalition and end the isolation of Russia. The means for this lay ready to hand in Napoleon's evident desire to improve his relations with Russia. A Russo-French *rapprochement* must loosen automatically the ties between France and England. It must weaken the precarious friendship of France and Austria. France was the member of the coalition least antagonistic to Russia in the eastern question, the only one whose interests it might prove possible to reconcile with those of Russia. Even Nesselrode

[1] In discussing the terms of peace, Gorchakov had declared: 'L'essentiel est d'avoir toujours deux objets en vue: que la défense des intérêts réligieux qui nous a mis les armes à la main, atteigne complètement son but,—voilà quant au présent; qu'aucune condition portant le germe d'un mal organique et pouvant arrêter le dévelopement providentiel des destinées de la Russie, ne soit admise dans le traité de paix,—voilà pour l'avenir' (Gorchakov to Olga Nicolaevna, 22 February/7 March 1855, W[ürttembergisches] S[taats] A[rchiv] [in Stuttgart], vol. cccIV, no. 42).

[2] Brunnow, Russia's most accomplished diplomatic technician, wrote: 'La Russie a besoin de réparer, de ménager, de concentrer ses forces avant d'être en mesure de soutenir avec succès une nouvelle lutte en Orient. Vous me l'avez dit, mon cher Prince, plus d'une fois: notre intérêt bien entendu nous recommande de laisser subsister le *statu quo* en Turquie, sans provoquer une catastrophe prématurément à nos risques et périls' (Brunnow to Gorchakov, private, most secret, 25 March/6 April 1860, printed in B. Nolde, *Die Petersburger Mission Bismarcks 1859–62* (Berlin, 1936), pp. 205ff.).

[3] Friese, *op. cit.* p. 20.

[4] One evening in Vienna, Gorchakov, come to present his letters of recall, was discussing political matters with some compatriots in the presence of Sir Hamilton Seymour. He had described Buol's policy as 'incroyable et inqualifiable' when Seymour interjected that it had been designed 'as well for finishing the war as for concluding a difficult question'. This remark had got the better of Gorchakov's discretion: '"To finish the question!", the Prince exclaimed with great eagerness, "to finish the question do you say? You will see whether the question is finished or not!"'

The Russians present looked astonished at this outburst and one appeared to press Gorchakov's arm. The new Foreign Minister, lowering his voice, explained: '"We of course have no intention of doing anything in the business, all I mean is that *la force des circonstances* is such that the question is further than ever from settlement...".' (Seymour to Clarendon, 22 June 1856, no. 431 secret, FO 7/487.)

whilst advising caution, had agreed that a *rapprochement* with France was a tactical necessity. His views were shared by the tsar. Gorchakov, in his impetuous way, wished to go further along this road, but the misgivings of his imperial master restricted his freedom of action. In fact, if the search for a closer understanding with France formed an 'inevitable' element of Russian diplomacy the limits of the new friendship were set by Alexander's distrust of Napoleon and by the French emperor's desire to preserve his alliance with England. The policy pursued by Gorchakov differed only in emphasis from the one a new Nesselrode would have followed in his place.

V

Perhaps the most important single effect of the Crimean War was the exhaustion of Russia and the need felt by her rulers for a period of recovery and reform. This meant that, in all matters not directly touching Russian interests, the Russian government would be less active than it had been in the days of Nicholas I. Gorchakov hardly exaggerated the importance of the Russian 'withdrawal' from Europe when he later ascribed to it a large part in the growth of Prussian preponderance.[1] The reduction of Russian influence and diplomatic activity altered the European balance and weakened the restoration settlement in the creation of which Russian arms and diplomacy had played so decisive a part.

The effect of this change was accentuated by the breach between Russia and Austria resulting from the diplomacy of Buol. Austria had indeed successfully defended her interests in the Balkans but had done so at the price of Russia's friendship. She now faced the risk of having to meet a new revolutionary crisis without the 'conservative' support which had saved her in 1849. She might still find German states willing to come to her assistance; the estrangement of the two eastern empires, none the less, held out new hope to the defeated revolutionary forces.

The transformation of diplomatic relations accompanying the Crimean War was further emphasized by the *rapprochement* of Russia and France. Louis-Napoleon had become emperor of the French in defiance of the treaties of 1815. It was the scarcely concealed object of his ambition to upset both the arrangements made at Vienna and the more recent restoration settlement. Yet the successor of Nicholas I and his new Foreign Minister were willing to facilitate Napoleon's task.[2] As a result,

[1] 'But who can say that Prussia would have dreamt of them [her 'exploits in four years and two campaigns'] and would have been able to accomplish them without the profound disturbances caused by the Crimean War in Europe? Probably no lesson so striking and so rapid was ever taught by the enchainment of facts and the logic of history' (Jomini, *op. cit.* pp. 389f.).

[2] It is a curious fact that both Austrian and Russian diplomacy in turn played a prominent part in upsetting the settlement of Nicholas I and Schwarzenberg. Buol broke with Russia and aligned Austria with England and France. Gorchakov would soon 'keep the ring' for Napoleon in a war which was to shake Austria to her foundations. In fact, both Buol and

the foundations of the restoration settlement had become as precarious as could possibly be imagined.

Gorchakov reacted with some violence against the 'system' of their predecessors. In each case the immediate reason for a change of 'system' was a direct political interest: the Russian occupation of the Principalities in the one case, that of destroying the anti-Russian coalition in the other. But there were, perhaps, also deeper reasons for the change. Both Buol and Gorchakov were representatives of that official 'liberalism' associated in Austria with the name of Bach, in Russia with that of the 'Tsar Liberator' himself. In Prussia, a similar 'trend' was soon to find expression in the 'New Era' and its Foreign Minister Schleinitz. Buol, Gorchakov, and Schleinitz, the three foreign ministers of the 'liberalized' eastern monarchies were alike sympathetic to reform at home and 'western' in their foreign policy. They represent a trend common to the three monarchies. It is therefore possible that the 'diplomatic' revolution of 1854–6, apart from its immediate political causes, was the manifestation of wider changes in central and eastern Europe. It may well be that it was the revulsion against the internal policies of Metternich and Nicholas at least as much as purely diplomatic causes which destroyed the 'Neo-Holy-Alliance'. It might be held that it was the desire of liberal groups temporarily in the ascendant in the three monarchies for 'liberal' western alliances which destroyed the restoration of Nicholas and Schwarzenberg. If this view is accepted it is no accident that Buol and Gorchakov, although bitter rivals, contributed in fact to the same result. Their policies, whether they realized it or not, were as tinged with 'ideology' as those of their predecessors. In each case, the 'new diplomacy' was opposed by conservatives who disliked both internal change and a 'liberal' foreign policy. These groups were pro-Russian in Vienna (and Berlin), pro-German at St Petersburg. There was a connection between domestic conservatism and support for the old diplomatic system as there was between 'liberalism' and the search for western alignments. The diplomacy of Buol and Gorchakov alike may have been merely a manifestation of the great battle waged in central and eastern Europe between 'liberal' and conservative forces.

PART II

THE SECOND REVOLUTION, 1857–67

CHAPTER 3

NAPOLEON III AND THE BEGINNINGS OF THE SECOND REVOLUTION: ITALY AND POLAND, 1857–63

THE six years following the Crimean War can be described without exaggeration as the second 'Napoleonic Age' in European affairs. The war itself, and the Congress by which it was concluded, placed the upstart emperor of the French on the pinnacle previously occupied by Nicholas I. Victorious in war, triumphant in diplomacy, Napoleon was courted by every government in Europe. No policy could be successful which failed to obtain his blessing. The cabinets of Vienna and Turin, of Berlin, St Petersburg, London and Constantinople, looked anxiously to the Tuileries where the 'sphinx' appeared to hold in its paws the future destinies of Europe. During the years which followed, the prestige of Napoleon did indeed lose some of its lustre but until the great diplomatic defeats of 1863 he continued to be the 'most powerful man' in Europe.

During the period of his 'preponderance' Napoleon in spite of occasional conservative 'deviations', consistently championed the cause of nationality in Europe. He gave military assistance to Cavour and diplomatic support to Romanian patriots, repeatedly tried to help the Poles and sympathized with the aspirations of the Magyars. His efforts during this period did not, indeed, directly affect the affairs of Germany, yet his support of nationalities created the conditions in which the German question could be reopened. The Napoleonic phase of the 'Second Revolution' made possible the Bismarckian phase which followed.

Three results in particular following directly from the activities of Napoleon were to affect the evolution of the German question. French policy made a decisive contribution to the isolation, defeat and second disintegration of the Habsburg monarchy. Distrust of Napoleon's designs accentuated the understanding between Russia and the Prussian conservatives in face of a renewed revolutionary threat. The same fear brought about the isolation of France and a *rapprochement* of Palmerstonian England, Austria, Prussia and Russia. The 'second Napoleonic Age' created the conditions for the Bismarckian solution of the German question.

I

The conversion of Russia from an ally into an enemy biding his time for revenge left Austria in a difficult position. At the end of June 1856 Seymour warned Clarendon of the precarious position of the Habsburg monarchy. Inside Austria, he observed, there were

heterogeneous elements which give no signs of coming together—men of various races who have no bond of union—general discontent in the Italian provinces—discontent in Hungary—distress among the manufacturing Classes—a financial state ...still very far from secure—and a new religious system[1] the effect of which remains to be shewn but which assuredly will not tend to improve the relations which for the last century have existed between Christians of various confessions.

Abroad, the picture was equally discouraging:

Russian interests alienated, indeed actually although not openly hostile—Prussia disliked and suspected—the rest of Germany perhaps less well affected to Austria than it ever has been since 1815—Piedmont desirous of nothing so much as for a fresh opportunity of re-entering the lists with her national enemy—and in the way of close and intimate Alliances, nothing but a very near intimacy with Rome and a close but necessarily most precarious alliance with France.

Taken at its best the French alliance rested upon the life of Napoleon 'and its warmest friend and promoter Baron Bourqueney has not hesitated to remark to me that observation has brought with it the unpleasant con-viction of its being already very little acceptable to his countrymen'.[2] In March Francis-Joseph in a letter to Buol had expressed misgivings about Napoleon's future intentions.[3] By the summer, his anxiety had deepened.[4] During the months which followed friction developed between the cabinets of Vienna and Paris. Napoleon showed a disconcerting tendency to take the Russian side in disputes about the interpretation of the treaty of Paris, whilst Austria adopted the opposite view.[5] A serious disagreement arose about the future of the Danubian Principalities. Napoleon strongly favoured their union,[6] whilst Buol considered that this development must

---

[1] The Concordat of 18 August 1855 by which the Roman Catholic Church 'was given a freedom from state interference and a control over education which it had not enjoyed since the worst days of the Counter-Reformation' (A. J. P. Taylor, The Habsburg Monarchy (new ed. London, 1948), p. 89).

[2] Seymour to Clarendon, 25 June 1856, FO 7/487, no. 443, confidential.

[3] 'Leider aber ahne ich eine Zukunft die ich mir kaum eingestehen möchte....Der Kaiser verdeckt nur unvollkommen Pläne, die eine sehr nachteilige Entwicklung herbeiführen könnten' (Quoted in Eckhart, op. cit. p. 215).

[4] Seymour to Clarendon, 23 July 1856, FO 7/488, no. 526 secret and confidential.

[5] For details of the disputes, cf. W. E. Mosse, 'Britain Russia and the Questions of Serpents Island and Bolgrad', in SR, xxix, no. 72 (December 1950), pp. 86ff.

[6] Napoleon considered that the union would be 'an act which would form an epoch in the history of those countries, and be a remarkable result of the war in which he was recently engaged, and of the Treaty by which this war was closed' (Bulwer to Clarendon, private, 17 August 1856, FO 195/507).

be opposed at any cost.[1] Relations between Austria and France rapidly deteriorated and Buol openly expressed his ill-humour.[2]

Tension between Austria and France coincided with a visible *rapprochement* between the cabinets of St Petersburg, Paris and Turin. The three governments were united by a common dislike of Austria.[3] A joint plan of action was agreed on at meetings between Napoleon and the tsar at Stuttgart and between Napoleon and Cavour at Plombières. The Austrians were to be expelled from northern Italy. France, in certain circumstances, would acquire Nice and Savoy. If the war ended in a Congress, the three states would jointly attempt to free Russia from the restrictions on her sovereignty in the Black Sea. Such were the terms finally agreed on between Napoleon and the tsar in the Franco-Russian treaty of 3 March 1859.[4]

Circumstances appeared to favour the accomplishment of Napoleon's designs. The benevolent neutrality of England seemed assured. Palmerston and Russell, supported by public opinion, were sincere friends of Italy. Derby's Tory followers who viewed with some distaste the weakening of Austria and the 'unholy alliance' between autocracy and revolutionary nationalism, were unlikely to find support for an anti-Italian policy. Prussia's attitude was doubtful but she seemed unlikely to intervene. Why should she defend Austria's Italian possessions? Could Austria pay the price of her support? Would not the tsar, who had undertaken to immobilize a part of Austria's forces, restrain German impetuosity? Would not British influence be exerted in the same direction?

Two untoward events caused Napoleon to hesitate. Early in 1858 Palmerston's ministry was replaced by one under Derby which might attempt, by diplomatic means, to prevent the outbreak of war. In the autumn, another change of ministry reduced Russia's influence in Berlin.

---

[1] Buol declared: 'Pour la France c'est une politique chevaleresque et de sentiment, c'est une question de vie ou de mort pour notre Empire' (de Heukern to Walewski, 1 July 1856, A[rchives du Ministère des] A[ffaires] E[trangères] in Paris, Autriche 464, unnumbered).

[2] The French chargè d'affaires reported from Vienna: 'Il existe ici une profonde inquiétude, une méfiance non dissimulée à l'endroit de la politique suivie par notre Cabinet...nos prétendus projets en Italie...notre alliance avec la Russie' (*ibid.*). Buol said to Bourqueney: 'We all know that upon Italian questions England is opposed to us, and on these we occasionally see you leaning towards England and against us, while upon the Russian questions you fail in giving us that support which England...does not cease to afford us' (Seymour to Clarendon, 23 July 1856, FO 7/488, no. 526, secret and confidential).

[3] Upon the resumption of diplomatic relations between Russia and Sardinia, Stackelberg, the Russian minister, significantly informed Cavour: 'Nos deux pays doivent être bons amis, car ils n'ont pas des intérêts qui les divisent, et ils ont des rancunes communes qui les rapprochent' *Cavour e l'Inghilterra* (Bologna, 1933), vol. II, pp. 21f. For a detailed account of the Franco-Russo-Sardinian *entente* cf. W. E. Mosse, 'The Russians at Villafranca', *SR*, xxx, no. 75 (June 1952), pp. 425ff.

[4] For a detailed analysis of the Franco-Russian negotiations leading to the conclusion of the treaty of 3 March, see B. H. Sumner 'The Secret Franco-Russian Treaty of 3 March 1859', *EHR*, XLVIII (London, 1933).

On the other hand Cavour, by skilful diplomatic manœuvring, had induced the Austrian government to place itself in the wrong in the eyes of Europe by a hasty ultimatum to Piedmont. Austria, at one stroke, lost the sympathies of the British government.[1] In these circumstances Napoleon finally decided to act.

French armies were successful in Italy but clouds soon gathered on the horizon. A wave of patriotic excitement reminiscent of 1840 swept over Germany. It now seemed possible that the Confederation might join Austria if French forces violated its territory in Italy.[2] German governments, at the same time, prepared to repel a French attack on the Rhine. Prussia mobilized six army corps and proposed in Frankfurt the mobilization of two federal corps as well. She also took steps to pave the way for an armed mediation of the neutrals. The tsar indeed tried to restrain German ardour but his efforts in this sense were accompanied by anxious inquiries in Paris about Napoleon's future intentions. In the face of these developments, Napoleon decided that the time had come to terminate his campaign.[3] On 8 July 1859 he signed the armistice of Villafranca. Three days later, agreement was reached on the preliminaries of peace. Austria undertook to cede Lombardy to Napoleon who, in his turn, would transfer the province to Piedmont. Napoleon's 'grand design' had ended in a transaction worthy of eighteenth-century cabinet diplomacy. The balance of forces in Europe appeared but little changed by an arrangement which, for a variety of reasons, earned almost universal disapproval.

II

Napoleon by his campaign in Italy had unwittingly unleashed forces far beyond his control. In the train of the Italian war, a movement reminiscent of 1848 swept over many parts of Europe and seemed to usher in a new age of national struggles. The peoples of Central Italy rose to expel their rulers. Magyar squires and burghers demanded with renewed insistence the withdrawal of Bach's German officials and the restoration of their ancient constitution. By the double election of Couza the inhabitants of the Principalities laid the foundations of the Romanian state. Liberal nationalists throughout the length and breadth of Germany

[1] Malmesbury, the Foreign Secretary, wrote: 'By this precipitate step the Cabinet of Vienna forfeits all claim upon the support or sympathy of England whatever may be the consequences that may ensue from it...' (Malmesbury to Loftus, 21 April 1859 in H. Temperley and L. M. Penson, *Foundations of British Foreign Policy* (London, 1938), p. 201).

[2] The frontier of the Germanic Confederation was held to coincide, rather remarkably, with that between the provinces of Venetia and Lombardy.

[3] Napoleon's position before Villafranca bears a curious resemblance to that of Bismarck before Nikolsburg seven years later. In each case a swift transaction between the belligerents forestalled an impending intervention from outside. In each case the settlement was 'moderate' and left open the possibility of a future reconciliation. An important difference in the two situations is that in 1866 Austria was defeated far more decisively than in 1859.

were organizing the celebrated 'Nationalverein'. Plans of federal reform were canvassed in every chancery. The demand was raised on all sides to enforce by a federal execution the just demands of the Germans in Schleswig and Holstein. Soon Garibaldi would raise southern Italy against the Bourbons, and the Poles would bid once again for national independence. A new 'age of revolutions' had dawned.[1]

It was evident to all Europe that this second movement of the nationalities had, like the first, originated on the banks of the Seine. However hesitant Napoleon's support of national movements, however ambiguous his dealings with the 'legitimate' powers, there could be no doubt that he was the inspirer of the movement. He had given encouragement and support to Cavour and Couza and had been ready to mobilize the Magyars and even a Polish legion against the Habsburgs. Even if, to preserve his friendship with Russia, he had adopted a 'correct' attitude during the early phases of the Polish movement, it was yet a matter of common knowledge that Paris was the capital of the Poles in exile. It was known that they were regarded with deep sympathy in France and that Prince Napoleon, *enfant terrible* of the Second Empire, warmly championed their cause.

It was not only Napoleon's encouragement of national movements which alarmed the principal chanceries. The French acquisition of Nice and Savoy raised the spectre of direct Napoleonic aggression to 're-draw the map of Europe'. The British government began to fear for the security of Belgium, that of Prussia for its territories on the left bank of the Rhine. The Austrian government prepared to meet a Franco-Sardinian attack on Venetia accompanied by a rising in Hungary. Uneasiness prevailed at St Petersburg about possible French plans for a future kingdom of Poland. The anxiety of the governments affected a wider public. In 1859 the Germans had steeled themselves to resist French aggression which they thought imminent; the following year, it was the turn of England to prepare in haste for a French attack believed to be impending. Early in 1860 Gorchakov had remarked to the French ambassador Montebello: 'Let me tell you as a friend that Europe needs peace. If you continue periodically to disturb that peace you will gradually end by inspiring everybody with a certain distrust. In the end, your best friends will break away from you.'[2] Some months later, Russell declared in the House of Commons:

...such an act as the annexation of Savoy is one that will lead a nation so warlike as the French to call upon its Government from time to time to commit other acts of aggression: and, therefore, I do feel that, however we may wish to live on the most

---

[1] By a curious coincidence, the ferment was not confined to the European nationalities. It was contemporaneous with the upheaval in Russia caused by the liberation of the serfs. It was closely followed by the civil war on the North American continent.

[2] Quoted in Nolde, *op. cit.* p. 103.

friendly terms with the French Government...we ought not to keep ourselves apart from the other nations of Europe, but that, when further questions may arise, we shall be ready to act with others and to declare...firmly, that the settlement of Europe, the peace of Europe, is a matter dear to this country, and that settlement and that peace cannot be assured if it is liable to perpetual interruption.[1]

Palmerston informed the French ambassador that he agreed with every word spoken by Russell. The conduct of Napoleon rendered all future confidence impossible. When Flahault rejoined that this meant war, Palmerston replied that if to tolerate Napoleon's misdeeds was the price of peace, then England was ready to fight.[2]

After 1859, therefore, suspicion of France and a desire to curb her ambition had become general. Europe felt threatened by the restless and unpredictable adventurer who controlled an army believed to be the strongest and best equipped on the continent.[3] There was in consequence a widespread desire to take precautions both military and diplomatic. The need was felt to avoid all complications which might enable Napoleon to 'fish in troubled waters'. In fact, in the face of resurgent national movements linked with French restlessness and ambition, 'conservatives' everywhere began to remember, as they had not done since the year of revolutions, the solidarity demanded by their common interest in the maintenance of peace and the defence of the *status quo*. Ideology, repudiated since the Crimean War, began once again to have some influence on the conduct of diplomatic affairs.

By 1860 Napoleon had become the 'bugbear' of European diplomacy. His Italian adventure had inaugurated that isolation of the Second Empire which would later prevent its co-operation with the other powers in restraining Bismarck and Prussia. The coolness which arose in 1859 and 1860 between France and her former 'allies' was scarcely less important in its consequences than had been Austria's fateful diplomacy during the Crimean War.

---

[1] Russell in the House of Commons on 26 March 1860. *Foundations*, pp. 211 f. The diplomatic tension was in some degree mitigated by the economic rapprochement following the Cobden Commercial Treaty signed in January 1860.

[2] *Ibid.* and Vitzthum, *op. cit.* vol. II, pp. 52 ff. In private Palmerston consoled himself with the reflection that the transfer of Nice and Savoy would unite Germany against Napoleon and would make the British people more willing to spend money on defence (Palmerston to Russell, 7 February 1860, Bell, *op. cit.* p. 248).

[3] When in the autumn of 1860 Palmerston realized for the first time how close, during the previous summer, Prussia had come to war with France, he wrote:

'...I had no idea that Prussia had such serious intentions of attacking France during the late Italian war as these papers disclose. Ma foi, elle l'a échappée belle. She would have been fairly trounced if she had carried her Intentions into execution, and her Rhenish Provinces would by this time have been Part of the French Empire' (Palmerston to Russell, 8 October 1860, *Foundations*, p. 250).

The mobilization of 1859 had revealed grave shortcomings in Prussia's military organization. These the Prince Regent was determined to remedy. In December 1859 he appointed Roon as Minister of War. The reform of the Prussian military system, the indispensable prerequisite of Prussia's later successes, was begun under the aegis of this remarkable man.

III

The defeats inflicted 'by proxy' at Magenta and Solferino quenched Russian thirst for the humiliation of Austria.[1] Napoleon's secretive and sudden proceedings at Villafranca increased the distrust which the tsar had for some time felt for his ally in Paris. The risings in Central Italy strengthened Alexander's misgivings about his own indirect encouragement of revolution. Moreover, the bankruptcy of his 'system' had sealed the fate of Buol who during May had been replaced by Rechberg, a pupil and admirer of Metternich.[2] The reception accorded to Archduke Albrecht of Austria during a visit to Warsaw in the autumn, revealed the change which had occurred in Russia's attitude. The way seemed clear for a resumption of normal relations between the cabinets of St Petersburg and Vienna.[3]

In December Count Thun, a conservative aristocrat, arrived at St Petersburg as Austrian minister with authority to meet almost any wish that might be expressed to him by the tsar.[4] An able and sincere protagonist of a revived Holy Alliance, he was well-received in the Russian capital. He was helped in his mission by the fact that the tsar's ideas were rapidly evolving in a conservative sense.[5] In the autumn Bismarck, who was detained in Germany, had learnt from St Petersburg that 'friendship with Austria was the horse on which Budberg hoped to ride into the Ministry'.[6]

[1] Bismarck, who shortly before the outbreak of war had become Prussian minister at St Petersburg, had written to his wife about Russian detestation of Austria: 'Wie die Oestreicher hier drunten durch sind, davon hat man gar keine Idee; kein räudiger Hund nimmt ein Stück Fleisch von ihnen...der Hass ist ohne Maasen und übersteigt alle meine Vermuthungen....die ganze russische Politik scheint keinem andern Gedanken Raum zu geben als dem, wie man Oestreich ans Leben kommt. Selbst der ruhige und sanfte Kaiser gerät in Zorn und Feuer, wenn er davon spricht' (Nolde, *op. cit.* p. 48).

[2] Rechberg had been chosen by Francis-Joseph in consultation with the aged Metternich. He had been Austrian representative at the federal Diet in Frankfurt and had proved himself a competent official of limited ability. A strict conservative and admirer of Metternich, he had opposed the policies of Buol and Bach. He believed in a gradual return to the alliance of the eastern monarchies and in Austro-Prussian dualism in German affairs. Cf. F. Engel-Jánosi, *Graf Rechberg* (Berlin, 1927), pp. 6ff.

[3] Gorchakov expressed his readiness for a reconciliation. The price for a restoration of friendly relations, however, must be Austrian support for a revision of the treaty of Paris. When asked what Russia would offer in return, he replied that a public reconciliation with Russia would be in itself of great benefit to Austria. If this exchange produced no immediate results, it did at least indicate Russian willingness to resume normal relations with Austria (*ibid.* p. 68). [4] Friese, *op. cit.* p. 213.

[5] The tsar wrote in the margin of a despatch reporting Napoleon's observation that French policy in Italy did not hurt Russian interests: 'Nos intérêts non, mais les principes que nous avons toujours soutenus, oui' (*ibid.* p. 212). He listened with approval to a remark by the Prussian chargé d'affaires that a government professing conservative principles could not make common cause with Napoleon and that the hope of attaching him to a system of peace and order was illusory (*ibid.*).

[6] Bismarck had heard 'dass "die Freundschaft mit Oestreich das Pferd sei, auf dem Budberg hoffe, in das Ministerium einzureiten"' (*ibid.* p. 214).

The efforts to restore friendly relations between Russia and Austria were not encouraged by Gorchakov. The Vice-Chancellor's attitude towards 'conservative principles' can be judged from the fact that he called on the Austrian government to abandon its 'Prinzipienpolitik'. The treaties of Vienna, he declared, had been broken (*durchlöchert*) so many times and for so long, that they could hardly be said any longer to exist.[1] A close understanding with Austria ran counter to his personal inclinations.[2] More seriously, Austria was now far too weak to lend Russia effective assistance in revising the treaty of Paris. Austria, in fact, was not considered 'bündnisfähig'.[3] Any understanding with her would antagonize Napoleon who could alone help Russia to achieve the objects of her policy.[4] Moreover, any attempt to restore the Holy Alliance would inevitably drive him back into the arms of England. The two western powers would then be able to lay down the law to Europe.[5]

Still Gorchakov considered it prudent to lend his hand to a superficial improvement of Austro-Russian relations. This would keep Austria from closer relations with England. It would please the tsar. Last, but not least, it might frighten Napoleon into paying the price of Russian friendship.

In spite of all Gorchakov's efforts, Russia and France were beginning to drift apart. Napoleon had dismissed the incompetent but russophile Walewski and replaced him by the abler Thouvenel who was no friend of Russia.[6] Gorchakov justly suspected the new Minister of wishing to settle the Italian question in conjunction with Palmerston and Russell. The tsar was offended both by the change of Ministers and by the Franco-British agreement on the transfer of Central Italy to Piedmont.[7] Yet Gorchakov still nursed hopes of achieving his aims in conjunction with the emperor

[1] Engel-Jánosi, *op. cit.* pp. 72f.

[2] Gorchakov would soon confide to Bismarck: 'Mais je vous avoue que pour les rapports intimes avec l'Autriche, je suis "chat échaudé"; je vous la laisse, arrangez-vous comme vous pourrez' (Bericht, 27 June 1860, Raschdau, *op. cit.* p. 130).

[3] In private, Gorchakov remarked picturesquely, if somewhat inelegantly, that he did not seek his alliances 'dans la pourriture' (Engel-Jánosi, *op. cit.* p. 73). To Olga Nicolaevna he wrote: 'Chercher des alliés parmi les agonisants, quand par là on se crée gratuitement des adversaires puissants, serait d'une politique par trop aveugle, et grâce au Ciel, nous n'avons pas encore la cataracte' (Friese, *op. cit.* p. 215). Kisselev, the ambassador in Paris, had called Austria a corpse (*cadavre*) (*ibid.* p. 214).

[4] Gorchakov wrote to Olga Nicolaevna in speaking of Austria: '...nous aurons pour elle quelques sourires, quelques paroles de consolation, mais nous réserverons les faits pour ceux qui peuvent servir efficacement les intérêts de la Russie' (*ibid.* p. 215).

[5] Kisselev argued that a new Holy Alliance would be weak since Austria in her present state was a corpse and Russia a paralytic (*paralytique*). Austria alone would benefit from a northern alliance. The superiority of the Maritime powers would hit most severely the commerce of Russia and Prussia (*ibid.* p. 214).

[6] Kisselev considered the change of Ministers as 'the destruction of the fruits of three years' labours to strengthen the alliance and mutual confidence' (*ibid.* p. 213).

[7] Gorchakov considered the fact that France had reached agreement with England without informing Russia as a breach of the understanding come to in Stuttgart between the tsar and Napoleon (*ibid.*).

of the French. After Napoleon had formally announced his intention of annexing Nice and Savoy[1] the British government proposed to Russia, Prussia and Austria a joint protest in Paris. The cabinet of St Petersburg ostentatiously held aloof declaring that the matter concerned France and Piedmont alone.[2] Gorchakov could claim with some justification that 'a word from St Petersburg had sufficed to frustrate British attempts to establish a coalition of the four powers against the government of France'.[3] The price for this service Gorchakov hoped to reap in the form of binding French promises to assist Russia in the east. An exchange of views about the possibility of co-operation took place between the two cabinets but Napoleon and Thouvenel were concerned above all with appeasing the wrath of England. Nothing was further from their minds than to commit themselves to an anti-British policy in the east. The negotiations proved abortive, Gorchakov was 'bilked' of his reward. In May, Garibaldi landed in Sicily. The tsar had appealed to Napoleon to prevent his expedition by the use of French naval forces but the appeal had been ignored.

The progress of the Italian revolution increased the tsar's distrust of Napoleon,[4] and strengthened his determination 'to remain faithful to the conservative principles which for thirty years have guided the policy of Russia'.[5] He still considered that Russia and Prussia could together tame Napoleon by putting upon him 'the chains of an alliance'[6] but in face of the Prussian refusal to accept this combination[7] his thoughts turned once again to the possibility of friendship with Austria. Gorchakov, disappointed at the trick which Thouvenel had played him, held admonitory and conservative language in Paris[8] and spoke not without bitterness of the proceedings of the French government.[9] Circumstances once again seemed to favour the policy of Rechberg.

Towards the end of June, Gorchakov told Bismarck that the Austrian government was making determined efforts to restore its alliance with Russia. The Austrian chargé d'affaires had informed him that his govern-

---

[1] In his speech from the throne on 1 March 1860.

[2] The cabinet of St Petersburg considered itself bound by the Stuttgart agreement of 1857.

[3] *Ibid.* p. 217.

[4] By the end of June, Bismarck could speak of 'cet éloignement primitif qu'a pour la France l'Empereur Alexandre qui par l'effet continu d'une défiance légitime prend de plus en plus la nature d'une forte antipathie' (quoted in Nolde, *op. cit.* p. 130).

[5] 'Je suis décidé', the emperor told Bismarck, 'à rester fidèle aux principes conservateurs qui depuis trente ans ont présidé à la politique de la Russie...' (Immediatbericht, 14 June 1860, Raschdau, *op. cit.* p. 114).

[6] 'C'est dans l'intention de rattacher l'Empereur Napoléon à un système plus régulier et plus légal qui je voudrais lui imposer les liens d'une alliance...' (*ibid.* p. 116).

[7] Friese, *op. cit.* p. 219.

[8] Cf. Bismarck's report of 27 June 1860, Raschdau, *op. cit.* p. 136.

[9] Bismarck reported: '...le Prince a manifesté beaucoup d'humeur à l'égard de la France qui selon lui pêche par trop d'habileté.' However, he added, 'la disposition du Prince Gortschakow tient plutôt du dépit amoureux' (Bismarck's report of 26 June 1860, *ibid.* pp. 130f.).

ment would do all Russia might require in the east if this would restore the old intimacy of the two governments.[1] In reply, Gorchakov had advised the Austrian government to reach an agreement with Prussia on German affairs.[2] At the same time he urged on Bismarck the need for a *rapprochement* between the cabinets of Berlin and Vienna.[3] Some improvement took place in Austro-Prussian relations. At the end of July, Francis-Joseph, the Prince-Regent of Prussia and their advisers met at Teplitz in Bohemia. They failed to agree on federal reform, but the tone of their discussions was friendly and there were expressions of Austro-Prussian solidarity in the face of possible dangers from France.[4]

News of the meeting caused lively satisfaction at St Petersburg. The tsar spoke of an Austro-Prussian understanding as 'a dam against the floods of revolution'.[5] Gorchakov made no secret of his approval. It was expected that concessions needed to cement the unity of Germany would be made by Austria, the weaker of the two powers. Her conduct in this question would be the touchstone of her sincerity and would show whether she had learnt from her recent experience.[6]

The increasingly friendly disposition of the Russian court towards Austria was reflected in a number of unexpected gestures. An Austrian military deputation which visited St Petersburg during the summer, was showered with official attentions; so were Revertera and Thun, the Austrian representatives in the Russian capital. On 18 August, the birthday of Francis-Joseph, Thun was received in audience by the tsar and delivered a cordial letter from his master. The audience was followed by an official dinner to which Thun was invited; Austrian decorations were worn; a cordial toast was drunk to the health of the Austrian emperor. It was the first official celebration of Francis-Joseph's birthday at St Petersburg since the Crimean War; moreover, Napoleon's birthday three days before had passed completely unnoticed.[7]

In these circumstances Francis-Joseph inquired at St Petersburg whether a visit from him during the tsar's stay at Warsaw in the autumn would be welcome. He received a cordial invitation. Shortly afterwards, the Prince-Regent of Prussia also was invited to visit Warsaw. The impression was widespread—especially in the lesser German capitals—that the Holy Alliance was about to be restored.[8]

Nothing, however, was further from Gorchakov's intentions. The Vice-Chancellor explained that his object was to effect a reconciliation

---

[1] 'qui, par ordre de son gouvernement, venait m'assurer que l'Autriche se mettrait entièrement à notre disposition pour tout ce qui concerne la politique d'Orient, si par là elle gagnait la chance de rétablir l'ancienne entente' (Bericht, 27 June 1860, *ibid.* p. 130).

[2] 'je réponds toujours par le conseil de s'addresser plutôt à la Prusse et de lui faire des concessions raisonnables dans les affaires fédérales' (*ibid.*).

[3] Nolde, *op. cit.* p. 132.

[4] *Ibid.* p. 133.

[5] Quoted in Friese, *op. cit.* p. 223.

[6] *Ibid.*

[7] *Ibid.* pp. 222f. and Nolde, *op. cit.* p. 133.

[8] Friese, *op. cit.* p. 223.

between Napoleon and the eastern powers. He spoke of 'the union of the Continental powers, the solidarity of Continental interests,[1] and expressed a wish that Thouvenel should join in the discussions. The cabinets of Berlin, Paris and Vienna had during the last three years accepted in principle a revision of the treaty of Paris;[2] England alone barred the way. Might it not prove possible to weld the continental powers into an anti-British league to promote the Russian object?[3] Gorchakov cared nothing for conservative principles and little for the affairs of Europe; his attention was concentrated almost exclusively on the affairs of the Ottoman empire.[4] The tsar, on the other hand, was concerned in almost equal degree with the interests of conservatism in Europe and the revision of the treaty of Paris. An association between the eastern monarchies and France, based on French promises of 'conservatism' in Italy and support for Russia in the East would reconcile the conflicting policies and combine the defence of conservative principles with the prosecution of Russia's national aims.

Thouvenel with his customary shrewdness had early realized the danger that the meeting of Warsaw might, in spite of Russian assurances to the contrary, give birth to a coalition directed against France. He had, however, taken the measure of Gorchakov and knew a certain way for preventing developments harmful to France. In September, Gorchakov received from the French government a memorandum with the promising title of '*Bases d'une entente confidentielle entre la France et la Russie*'.[5] This document, which spoke in pseudo-conservative language of French intentions in Italy and held out—albeit in the vaguest of terms—the prospect of Franco-Russian co-operation in the east, filled Gorchakov with a delight hardly justified by its carefully worded terms. It made him more than ever determined that the coming meeting in Warsaw must not become a demonstration directed against France. The tsar, still captivated by the idea of 'taming' Napoleon through an association with the eastern monarchies,[6] readily accepted his Minister's programme.

---

[1] *Ibid.* p. 226.

[2] The Prussian government had declared its support for any alteration in the treaty of Paris favourable to Russia but had refused to take any initiative in the matter (K. Rheindorf, *Die Schwarze-Meer (Pontus) Frage 1856–1871* (Berlin, 1925) pp. 27f., quoted in Friese, *op. cit.* p. 215).

[3] Friese, *op. cit.* p. 215.

[4] According to Bismarck's observation 'interessierte ihn [Gorchakov] jede unbedeutende Erscheinung im Orient oder in den südslavischen Ländern von Böhmen bis in den Balkan mehr als alle Nachrichten aus Italien' (*ibid.* p. 232).

[5] Printed in Nolde, *op. cit.* pp. 292f.

[6] It is curious to note with what remarkable tenacity it was believed that Napoleon could be 'tamed' by means of 'respectable' alliances. This had been the vision of Buol and Hübner; it was now adopted by Alexander II, Francis-Joseph and Rechberg. The most conservative statesmen used this argument to quieten their scruples about associating, in the interests of their own national policies, with a disreputable French adventurer. The argument contained large elements of wishful thinking and unconscious hypocrisy but also an element of truth. It was used by Palmerston when discussing the nature of the Anglo-French alliance and it is certain that friendly British influence did, on many occasions, restrain Napoleon. In 1863,

On 25 October the three monarchs and their ministers held their first political meeting.[1] Francis-Joseph complained of the policy of France with its encouragement of revolutionary movements in Hungary and Poland and its threat to Austria in Venetia. In private, he had already informed the Russians that in return for a promise of support against Napoleon he would agree to the abolition of the Black Sea Clauses. Alexander, who had listened sympathetically to Francis-Joseph's tirade, replied that he could not tie his hands by any engagement hostile to France or join a coalition against her. He wished to do everything in his power to reconcile the emperor of the French to the programme of European conservatism. He alone could defeat the European revolution. Gorchakov then read the Italian portion of Thouvenel's memorandum, explaining that it was a highly confidential document which revealed the intimate thoughts of the emperor Napoleon. It was accepted by the monarchs and their advisers as a basis for further discussion.

On the day of the meeting, the tsar received news of the serious illness of his mother. On the following day he left for St Petersburg. The conference was brought to a premature conclusion. A subsequent discussion of Thouvenel's memorandum was a purely academic exercise; so was the later correspondence between Paris and St Petersburg about an eastern *entente*. Napoleon and Thouvenel, after the successful annexation of Nice and Savoy, had no intention of antagonizing England for the sake of Gorchakov's ambitions in the east.

The conference in Warsaw thus marked a triumph for Thouvenel, a partial victory for Gorchakov and an almost complete defeat for Francis-Joseph and Rechberg. Thouvenel, seconded by the Russian Minister, had prevented a return to the policy of the Holy Alliance. Gorchakov had safeguarded his understanding with France and prevented a change in the direction of Russian policy. He had, however, been unable to establish a common front on the 'eastern question'. The Austrians had shown to the world that Russia was no longer their implacable enemy, but had failed to secure a guarantee for the joint defence of Venetia. Gorchakov would be glad enough to have Austrian support in the Congress which, he hoped, would one day reopen the 'eastern question'; in the meantime he had no intention of buying the support of a 'corpse' with concessions which would offend the powerful emperor of the French.

Thun had earlier complained to Bismarck that Gorchakov alone stood in the way of an Austro-Russian understanding.[2] During the winter of 1860, he spared no effort to undermine the position of the Vice-Chancellor. The support, however, which he obtained from Nesselrode

both the British and Austrian cabinets were to justify the later phases of their diplomatic action on behalf of the Polish insurgents by the need to prevent Napoleon from acting single-handed.

[1] For the following cf. *ibid.* pp. 143f.   [2] *Ibid.* p. 133.

and Meyendorff merely helped, if anything, to strengthen Gorchakov's position. The tsar was far from insensitive to the charge which might be brought against him that, in the interest of the Court and influenced by its German sympathies, he had abandoned the 'national' policy inaugurated by Gorchakov. Influential men had represented to him the great unpopularity with the public and the army of any attempt to restore the Holy Alliance. Public opinion, in effect, had not followed the conservative evolution of the tsar; active supporters of the German connection were forced to admit that military support for Austria in any circumstances was an impossibility.[1] Gorchakov had public opinion behind him when he informed a German minister that 'Russia would never take up arms for the preservation of this Austria'.[2] In fact, when in 1861 and 1862 movements among the Balkan peoples revived old rivalries, a marked coolness in Austro-Russian relations succeeded the *rapprochement* of the previous year. Once the spectre of universal revolution conjured up by the triumphs of Garibaldi had vanished, ancient antipathies resumed their sway. The Holy Alliance, which at one moment had seemed so near, had receded into the distance. Whatever the personal sympathies and antipathies of the tsar, Gorchakov, supported by public opinion, had secured the continuation of his 'national' policy. The interests of Russia would continue to take precedence over those of European conservatism. Rechberg's attempt to end the isolation of Austria and to secure against possible threats from Prussia, Italy and France at least the moral support of Russia had proved a disastrous failure. The restoration of 'normal' relations with St Petersburg was small compensation for sacrifices in the eastern question which Gorchakov had spurned with contempt. Rechberg and Francis-Joseph had to learn the bitter lesson that only the strong have friends. Napoleon, on the other hand, had the satisfaction of seeing that thanks to the skill of Thouvenel and the gullibility of Gorchakov, his 'system' had survived—at least in outward respects—the hazards of the Italian crisis; the relations of Russia, Austria, and France emerged but little changed from the test to which they had been subjected.

IV

In spite of the apparent return to the *status quo* of 1858 the Italian campaign and its aftermath had subtly altered the political atmosphere in the Russian capital. The policy of a close understanding with Napoleon was becoming steadily less acceptable to the tsar and had lost some of its glamour even in the eyes of Gorchakov. The emperor was at last beginning to doubt the possibility of restraining Napoleon's ardour in the cause of nationalities. French recognition on 15 June 1861 of the 'revolutionary' kingdom of Italy increased these Russian misgivings. What certainty was

---

[1] Friese, *op. cit.* p. 231.   [2] *Ibid.* p. 232.

there that Napoleon would not encourage an attack by Italians and Magyars on the enfeebled Habsburg monarchy? Might he not, on the other hand, repeat his attempt to reach an agreement with Austria, allowing her to occupy the Principalities in exchange for the cession of Venetia?[1] Moreover the Polish question, the Achilles heel of Russo-French friendship, was by 1861 coming uncomfortably to the fore. How long would the seemingly 'correct' attitude of the French government continue in view of Napoleon's longstanding Polish sympathies?[2] Gorchakov, in his turn, was becoming increasingly embittered as the hoped for fruits of 'his' understanding with France were withheld from his grasp through French co-operation with England not only in Italy but also in the east.[3] France, in fact, was gradually losing the position which, since Morny's mission in 1856, she had occupied at St Petersburg.

France's loss was the gain of Prussia, for as Napoleon abandoned his positions at St Petersburg, they were occupied by Russia's second ally. It is not without significance that the tsar's first reaction on hearing of the preliminaries of Villafranca had been a wish 'to make his relations with Prussia closer than ever'.[4] Some months later, he had openly documented this desire by a meeting with the Prince-Regent and his advisers at Breslau.[5] Alexander and Gorchakov had indeed used their visit principally in order to urge an improvement in Prusso-French relations, but the gesture involved in the tsar's visit to the Silesian capital was not to be mistaken. By the following summer the tsar, who was nothing if not sincere, could speak to Bismarck not only of 'the intimate alliance existing between the two courts'[6] but also of 'Prussia, my most intimate ally'.[7] It is true that these words were spoken in an attempt to reassure Bismarck about the nature of Russo-French relations; that the tsar was urging the need of improved Prusso-French relations; and that he advocated a triple *entente* of Russia, Prussia and France.[8] There was nothing anti-French in

[1] The proposal that Austria should give up Venetia in exchange for the Principalities was for many years favoured by England and France. It was repeatedly recommended at Vienna. The plan invariably caused alarm at St Petersburg. Its steadfast rejection by the Austrian government prevented any lasting *rapprochement* between Austria and the western powers, especially France. It established, by the same token, some bond between the cabinets of St Petersburg and Vienna.

[2] Early in 1861, Alexander was reported to have said of Napoleon in conversation with a Prussian General: 'Ja, er wird revolutionieren, wie in Italien, so in Ungarn und den Donauländern, zuletzt in Polen' (quoted *ibid.* p. 235).

[3] For Gorchakov's growing disappointment cf. *ibid.* pp. 241 f.

[4] 'die Beziehungen zu Preussen enger als je zu gestalten' (telegram by Bismarck of 16 July 1859, Raschdau, *op. cit.* p. 112).

[5] For the meeting at Breslau cf. Nolde, *op. cit.* p. 98.

[6] 'l'alliance intime, qui existe entre les deux cours' (Immediatbericht by Bismarck of 14 June 1860 (reporting an interview with the emperor of the preceding day), Raschdau, *op. cit.* p. 114).   [7] 'la Prusse, mon alliée la plus intime' (*ibid.*).

[8] 'Je vous dis franchement, que je désire établir une alliance entre la Prusse, la Russie et la France, parceque j'y vois en ce moment le moyen le plus simple et le plus efficace pour assurer le repos de l'Europe' (*ibid.* p. 115).

his attitude.[1] Indeed, in the realm of diplomacy, Russia still depended on France and the French alliance remained the basis of Gorchakov's calculations. Yet in the realm of sentiment at least the balance was inclining to the side of Prussia.[2] Russia, in fact, was like a man standing on his two legs and determined to continue to do so, yet gradually and almost imperceptibly shifting his weight from one leg to the other. If from its very nature the change was too slow and delicate for measurement, it yet produced over a period of time a significant transfer of weight.

There were good reasons why, after the cooling of Russian sympathy for Napoleon and France, the inheritance should readily pass to Prussia. These were historical, sentimental and political. A close understanding between Russia and Prussia was 'natural' in the sense that in spite of some ups and downs it had in fact existed since the two peoples had been comrades in arms in the struggle against the first Napoleon. There was nothing novel, forced or artificial in the attempt to develop this tradition. Moreover, a close understanding with Prussia offered a convenient outlet for the tsar's sincere monarchical, dynastic and conservative emotions,[3] his filial piety,[4] and his need for an unreserved exchange of views with a like-minded fellow monarch. In 1860 and 1861, the family ties which bound together the two 'branches' of the house of Hohenzollern were strengthened by three successive events: the death of the Dowager Empress of Russia, that of her brother, the king of Prussia, and the coronation of William I in Königsberg. No ties of this nature could ever be established between the tsar and Francis-Joseph,[5] let alone Napoleon.

[1] 'Une coalition contre la France serait un moyen désespéré, une anticipation du mal, que nous voulons empêcher...' (*ibid.* p. 116).

[2] It would be interesting to examine whether it is not a general phenomenon in the decline of an alliance that the spiritual *élan* disappears some time before the abandonment of the working arrangement; that there exists an intermediary stage at which mutual 'goodwill' has disappeared whilst the forms of the alliance remain. This can easily be observed in the history of the Anglo-French alliance after the Crimean War and is probably true of other partnerships as well. If this observation is correct, Tatishchev may well be right in noting that somewhere about the time of the meeting at Breslau, the Franco-Russian understanding passed from the phase of 'hopefulness' into that of interest and calculation.

[3] During Bismarck's first audience, the emperor had spoken of 'les sentiments qui m'attachent personnellement au Prince-Régent, à la famille Royale et, je puis dire, à la Prusse. Ces sentiments sont pour moi un héritage inaliénable, que je tiens de mon père et de ma mère; ils n'ont jamais varié, ils sont les mêmes aujourd'hui, et mon cœur souffrirait péniblement, si je voyais se refroidir ces relations, auxquelles de mon côté, j'apporte l'amitié la plus cordiale' (Immediatbericht by Bismarck, 17 June 1859, Raschdau, *op. cit.* p. 95).

[4] It is interesting to compare the 'hereditary' element in the German policy of Alexander II with Queen Victoria's rigid fidelity to the German policy of the Prince-Consort. There are many curious and perhaps not entirely accidental similarities in the German policies of the two sovereigns. The similarity even extends to such details as two Danish and therefore bitterly anti-Prussian daughters-in-law.

[5] Alexander, at the time of the meeting of the three monarchs at Warsaw, was beginning to develop a similarly emotional attitude towards Francis-Joseph also. He had told the French ambassador before the meeting: 'In meinen Augen ist der Besuch, den mir Kaiser Franz-Joseph in Warschau machen will, eine Schuld mir gegenüber. Er wird dort dieselben Zimmer bewohnen, dir er einst bei meinem Vater bewohnt hat' (quoted in Nolde, *op. cit.*

Moreover, as the tsar was never tired of explaining, his sentiments were based on sound political judgment. He assured Bismarck that, in desiring to see Prussia take the lead in Germany, he was guided by political convictions as much as by personal predilections.[1] An alliance with Prussia, he repeated three years later, was not only dear to his heart, but in his view alone represented the true interests of Russia.[2] Neither country had anything to claim or obtain at the expense of the other; they depended upon each other for the defence of similar interests against the manifold dangers resulting from the state of Europe.[3] Prussia alone stood between Paris, the hotbed of revolution, and the restive Poles. The Prussian government was fearlessly asserting its monarchical prerogatives in the face of parliamentary attack. Last but not least, it was the reorganized Prussian army which would, in case of need, fight to prevent a repetition of the year of revolutions. If for the tsar alliance with Prussia meant first and foremost a defensive understanding in the face of a common danger, Gorchakov in his turn hoped to reap advantages of a more substantial kind. Prussia had promised to support Russia's campaign against the Black Sea Clauses. A close understanding with her strengthened Gorchakov's hand in his dealings with the French government by making 'paralytic' Russia a more desirable partner in the eyes of Napoleon and his ministers.[4] Finally, it was the hope of combining a 'conservative' understanding with Prussia and friendship with 'doubtful' France which alone induced the tsar to sanction Gorchakov's policy. He would never—after his recent experiences—consent to a foreign policy based on an exclusive understanding with Napoleon. He could, however, still reconcile himself to a grouping in which Russia and Prussia would combine to restrain a dangerous ally.[5] Gorchakov, like his master, had

p. 138). However, Russian public opinion would not allow the tsar to indulge in such sentiments for the emperor of hated Austria.

[1] 'En réclamant en faveur de la Prusse l'initiative de la politique allemande, j'ai été guidé par mes convictions politiques, mais en même temps par les sentiments qui m'attachent...à la Prusse' (Immediatbericht by Bismarck, 17 June 1859, Raschdau, *op. cit.* p. 95).

[2] '...Am Schluss gab mir der Kaiser...in sehr bewegten Worten den Auftrag, Eurer Majestät bei meiner Ankunft in Berlin mündlich nochmals zu versichern, dass er unter allen Umständen entschlossen sei, an der innigen Freundschaft mit Eurer Majestät festzuhalten, und hierzu nicht nur durch die Bande des Blutes und die ererbten Neigungen seines Herzens getrieben werde, sondern auch das engste Bündniss mit Preussen als das allein den Interessen Russlands entsprechende erkenne' (Immediatbericht by Bismarck, 8 April 1862, Raschdau, *op. cit.* vol. II, p. 187).

[3] 'Von beiden Ländern, sagte Seine Majestät, habe keines auf Kosten des andern etwas zu gewinnen oder zu erstreben, sondern beide seien zu gemeinsamer Vertheidigung gleichartiger Interessen gegen mannigfache durch den gegenwärtigen Zustand Europas bedingte Gefahren auf einander angewiesen' (*ibid.*).

[4] 'We bring you Prussia' ('Wir führen euch Preussen zu') Gorchakov had somewhat exuberantly informed the French ambassador shortly after the tsar's meeting with the Prince-Regent in Breslau (quoted in Friese, *op. cit.* p. 211).

[5] Alexander II explained to Bismarck during the summer of 1860: 'C'est dans l'intention de rattacher l'Empereur Napoléon à un système plus régulier et plus légal que je voudrais lui imposer les liens d'une alliance; il vaut la peine au moins d'essayer si, en lui montrant

good reason to desire a state of affairs which, without forcing him to abandon his day-dreams, prevented an exclusive *tête à tête* with a restless and dangerous partner.

The causes making for a *rapprochement* between Russia and Prussia—or rather for a strengthening of their traditional ties—were, to a large extent, independent of personal sentiment. The effects of Bismarck's very intermittent stay at St Petersburg have been seriously overrated.[1] In fact, at the very beginning of his mission, the tsar affirmed his profound belief in the political advantages of Russo-Prussian friendship. Nor is the increased Russian consciousness of the 'revolutionary menace' to be attributed to any great extent to the activities of Bismarck. The growing 'conservatism' and 'Prussianism' of Russian diplomacy was the result of the Italian crisis and of anxiety about the future of Poland; Bismarck's personal contribution, however important, was far from being decisive. Finally, and perhaps most significantly, the period of Bismarck's mission was one of constant friction between the two governments. Their views diverged when Prussia threatened to intervene in Italy; they differed later when the Prussian government tried to form an anti-French alliance; they clashed again when, in 1861, the Russian government inaugurated a 'liberal' course in Poland. It is a travesty of the facts to suggest that it was during Bismarck's mission that the idea of common political interests again gained ground at St Petersburg. Bismarck's personal relations with Alexander II and Gorchakov were cordial but there is little reason to believe that similar relations would not have been established with any other representative of a friendly and allied monarch. There is no evidence whatever that Bismarck converted to the idea of a closer understanding any influential Russian who had previously doubted the wisdom of such a course. He was, in any case, preaching to the converted. Not a single

plus de confiance...on ne puisse le guérir de l'idée qu'il doit sans cesse remuer l'Europe pour se faire respecter et fasciner l'esprit des Français....

'A moi seul, je ne saurais suffire à la tâche que je me suis proposée; mais si j'étais assisté par la Prusse, il est très probable qu'en agissant d'accord, nous exercerions une influence très sensible sur les résolutions de l'Empereur des Français. C'est au régime de la paix et du principe conservateur qu'à l'aide du Prince-Régent je voudrais le rallier' (Immediatbericht by Bismarck, 14 June 1860, Raschdau, *op. cit.* vol. I, pp. 116ff.).

Even though the Prussian government consistently turned a deaf ear to these proposals, they reveal clearly enough one of the basic ideas of the policy pursued at this time by Alexander II.

[1] Nolde, in summing up the results of Bismarck's mission, does not hesitate to declare: 'Er hatte in Petersburg seine erste grosse Eroberung gemacht: hatte Preussen die russische Freundschaft gewonnen' (Nolde, *op. cit.* p. 198). Friese is more cautious in his judgment: 'Unermüdlich hat Bismarck daran gearbeitet, wieder das Gefühl dafür zu beleben, dass eine enge Verbindung Russlands und Preussens...im wohlverstandenen Interesse der beiden Staaten selbst liege. Und es ist ein ganz wesentlicher Verdienst seines Petersburger Aufenthaltes, dass er diesem Gedanken wieder stärker Eingang verschafft hat: dass er die politischen Kreise Petersburgs an die Vorstellung gewöhnt hat, dass ein mächtiges Preussen für Russland nicht ein unangenehmer Nachbar, sondern ein wertvoller Bundesgenosse und eine kräftige Stütze seiner Politik sein werde' (Friese, *op. cit.* p. 239).

Russian statesman or diplomat of importance opposed the Prussian connection. This was, indeed, perhaps the only point on which the partisans of Gorchakov and Kisselev agreed with the followers of Nesselrode and Budberg. If, therefore, the strengthening of Russo-Prussian ties must be attributed to individuals rather than the force of circumstances, it is to Napoleon that history must look for the cause. Bismarck, not without skill, took advantage of a following breeze.

Russia's attitude towards the question of federal reform—revived by the general quickening of national movements everywhere—was dominated by the desire to create a bulwark against France. In St Petersburg—as elsewhere—Austria, after her defeat in 1859 and the renewal of constitutional conflict in Hungary, was regarded as little better than a corpse. Prussia, on the other hand, even though her mobilization had revealed weaknesses in her military organization, remained an effective barrier between Napoleon and Poland. Her army, moreover, was in process of reorganization. It was clear, therefore, that whoever desired a strong Germany must welcome a strengthening of Prussia. Bismarck, indeed, used this argument to some effect[1] but it hardly needed his advocacy to convince the tsar and Gorchakov of so self-evident a fact. Already during Bismarck's first interview, the tsar had observed that he claimed for Prussia the right of initiative in German affairs.[2] When Austria attempted to re-establish friendly relations with Russia, she was told more than once that she must first make concessions to Prussia in Germany.[3] This view was expressed clearly by Gorchakov in a conversation with Bismarck late in 1861. The Vice-Chancellor then declared that the union and strength of Germany constituted an important Russian interest. Prussia was Russia's best friend in Germany. The Russian government, therefore, could only welcome German consolidation under Prussian leadership. Russia and Prussia had a common interest in the defensive strength and general welfare of Germany, both of which could advance only under Prussian direction. Guided by these considerations, he had repeatedly urged Austria to give up her anti-Prussian policy and help to create for Prussia a position which it would be worth her while to defend by force of arms. In this event, it would be Prussia's own interest—and not merely the letter of the federal acts—which would lead her to work together with Austria. The Austrian government would then be able to face its internal problems. If co-operation between the two powers was in this manner assured, England would be less anxious to cling to the French alliance; at present, conditions in Germany did not offer her any inducement to separate herself from France.[4]

[1] Friese, pp. 250f.
[2] Immediatbericht by Bismarck, 17 June 1859, Raschdau, *op. cit.* p. 95.
[3] Bismarck's reports of 27 June and 13 July 1860, *ibid.* pp. 127ff.
[4] Report by Bismarck, 23 November 1861, *ibid.* pp. 141f.

General support for German consolidation under Prussian leadership did not, however, involve automatic approval of any methods which Prussia might choose to adopt. When late in 1861 and during the early months of 1862 her government reopened the question of federal reform in an aggressive spirit, Gorchakov expressed alarm. He told Bismarck that however much he would rejoice to see Prussia 'at the head of a Federation strengthened by the union of its members',[1] he saw a danger that 'a too decisive attempt to achieve a goal in itself desirable and reasonable',[2] would drive the lesser German states into the arms of France.[3] The tsar in his turn warned Bismarck that an attempt might be made to give the German question a revolutionary solution which would be exploited by France.[4] He urged that serious conflict should be avoided and warned Austria to be conciliatory as Prussia enjoyed a material superiority.[5] This advice was offered with great prudence and without the appearance of an unwarranted interference on the part of the Russian government. Gorchakov announced rather sententiously that he would avoid his predecessors' mistake of meddling in purely German affairs.[6] Bismarck noted his lack of interest in matters concerning the Confederation. He seemed to regard these as 'a kind of Sanskrit' which no one could be troubled to elucidate.[7]

In fact, throughout 1861 and 1862 the energies of the Russian government were absorbed by the social upheaval occasioned by the liberation of the serfs. Bismarck observed that diplomacy had been put in 'cold storage'. Gorchakov lamented that circumstances made an active foreign policy a virtual impossibility. The task of Russian diplomacy, he declared, must be limited to preventing the formation of groupings which might prejudice Russian interests in the future.[8] Foreign policy now consisted merely of arabesques; the decisive events were domestic.

The policy of Russia during the diplomatic 'pause' which followed the creation of the kingdom of Italy, was, on the whole, restrained. The maintenance of friendly relations with Prussia and France prevented the formation of a hostile coalition, helped to restrain Napoleon and preserved

---

[1] 'an der Spitze eines durch Einigkeit gekräftigten Bundes.'
[2] 'ein zu entschiedenes Vorgehen nach einem an sich wünschenswerten und vernünftigen Ziele'.
[3] Report by Bismarck of 1 March 1862, Friese, *op. cit.* p. 252.
[4] Report by Bismarck of 8 April 1862, *ibid.*
[5] Report by Bismarck of 22 February 1862, *ibid.*
[6] Report by Bismarck of 27 February 1862, *ibid.*
[7] Report by Bismarck of 15 January 1862, *ibid.*
[8] Gorchakov wrote to Olga Nicolaevna: 'À mes yeux, la question intérieure domine toutes les autres. C'est là que nous devons concentrer tous nos efforts et toute notre énergie....Je considère la politique comme pouvant être réléguée sans aucun inconvénient au dernier plan. Ce sont des arabesques qui n'influent pas directement sur nos destinées. J'entends par là la politique *active*; celle *défensive*—c'est différent. Là il faut avant tout chercher à éviter des fautes et appliquer notre vigilance à prévenir des combinaisons qui pourraient nous nuire' (Gorchakov to Olga Nicolaevna, 6 July 1861 (O.S.), *ibid.* pp. 347f.).

the peace of Europe. Beyond this, Russian diplomacy could not go: the eastern question could not be reopened in earnest as long as close ties persisted between Paris and London: no new diplomatic grouping could be created whilst Austria was weak and despised, France unreliable and England unfriendly.[1] Prussian repugnance to any understanding with France had proved insuperable; in the circumstances, Russia could hope for nothing beyond the preservation of peace and the prevention of hostile groupings.

As far as the German question was concerned, Russia's first need was the maintenance of peace and the avoidance of revolutionary upheavals. As in the days of Nicholas the most urgent need was Austro-Prussian co-operation in a joint defensive policy. Austria, as the weaker of the two, must make such concessions as were needed to restore German harmony. She should recognize Prussian leadership in military affairs—without, if possible, destroying the sovereignty of the secondary states. Constitutional details were outside the scope of Russian interest and should be settled by the German governments. Hidden revolutionary dangers might lurk in the German situation; a strong monarchical Prussia seemed the best protection against another 1848. Whatever happened, Russia would interfere in the affairs of Germany only in defence of her most immediate interests.

The question of the Duchies alone seemed, for the moment, capable of directly involving Russia. In this question, her basic attitude had not changed since the days of Nicholas and Nesselrode. The integrity of the Danish monarchy was still regarded in St Petersburg as a major national interest.[2] However, the means available for defending this interest were no longer what they had been in earlier days: the strength and prestige of Russia had declined, her attention was absorbed by internal developments. Moreover, the idea of nationality, which had been anathema under Nesselrode, was quite acceptable to Gorchakov; Bismarck left St Petersburg with the conviction that the Russian government would not oppose an eventual partition of Schleswig along an ethnographic boundary.[3] In the circumstances it was certain that, should the question once

---

[1] Gorchakov, in 1861, had written to Olga Nicolaevna: 'C'est une triste époque que celle où nous sommes appelés à vivre et à agir! À l'heure qu'il est (sic) n'existe pas une seule Puissance de premier ordre qui, par sa valeur intrinsèque ou le caractère invariable de ses convictions, puisse servir de point d'appui à un Gouvernement probe et honnête comme le nôtre. On n'a que le choix entre la perfidie ou la défaillance' (Gorchakov to Olga Nicolaevna, 6 July (O.S.) 1861, *ibid.* p. 348).

It is interesting to speculate about the place assigned to Prussia in Gorchakov's analysis. Did he deny her claim to be a power of the first rank? It seems the only explanation, for he could hardly class her with perfidious England and Austria or untrustworthy France. It must be remembered, however, that Gorchakov was writing to an austrophile princess, whose antipathy to Prussia was to become notorious. Moreover, it was probably true at this time that Prussia was a useful partner rather than a first-class power in her own right.

[2] Cf. Friese, *op. cit.* pp. 248 ff.

[3] Report by Bismarck, 15 April 1862, *ibid.* p. 250.

again become an issue of European diplomacy, Russia's attitude would be less rigid than it had been between 1848 and 1851. It was equally certain that Alexander II would spare no pains to avoid a conflict with Prussia.[1] The activities of Napoleon and the renewed revolutionary ferment had created between the tsar and his uncle a 'spiritual' and moral solidarity which had become one of Russia's major diplomatic assets. It would not be sacrificed without the direst need.

V

Napoleon's Italian campaign not only produced a 'conservative' *rapprochement* and a closer Russo-Prussian understanding. It also helped to weaken the western alliance and to pave the way for the eventual isolation of France. The first loosening of the Crimean ties had, indeed, preceded the French annexation of Nice and Savoy, but it was that event which had struck the first serious blow at Franco-British friendship. The distrust aroused in England would prevent for years wholehearted co-operation between the western 'allies'. In face of this instance of French desire for aggrandizement, British opinion concluded that Napoleon's ultimate object must be further expansion in Belgium or on the Rhine. It was therefore necessary to take precautions. In 1861, in a private letter to Russell, Palmerston revealed his innermost thoughts on what was left of the once glorious alliance.

...The real Truth of the Relations of England to France is that the whole Drift of our Policy is to prevent France from realizing her vast Schemes of Extension and aggression in a great Number of Questions, and of Course our Success in doing so must necessarily be the Cause of perpetual displeasure to her Government and People. But we fulfill our Duty as long as we can succeed by Negotiation and Management so as to avoid Rupture and open Collision by restraining France by the Shackles of Diplomatic Trammels.[2]

In the summer of 1862 an Austrian agent reported to his government that the British Prime Minister continued to watch Napoleon's progress with undiminished distrust.[3] In the spring of 1863, Palmerston once again gave Russell the benefit of his reflections on Napoleon and France:

...Antwerp is quite as much in his Thoughts as Brussels and his real Object and that which lies at the Bottom of his Heart, as well as of that of Every Frenchman, is the humbling of England, the traditional Rival of France, and the main obstacle to French Supremacy in Europe and all over the world. The Emperor would wish to bring us upon our Marrow bones in the most friendly manner if we would let him do so, and it is our Business by making ourselves strong, to render it hopeless for him to attempt doing so in any other way.[4]

[1] *Ibid.*
[2] Palmerston to Russell, 8 February 1861, PRO 30/22, 21.
[3] Report by Apponyi, 13 July 1862, *Foundations*, p. 250.
[4] Palmerston to Russell, 7 April 1863, PRO 30/22, 14.

Palmerston's distrust, shared by the Queen, Russell and British public opinion, made wholehearted co-operation with Napoleon impossible.[1] On the contrary, British diplomacy now set to work to deprive Napoleon of any pretext for a policy of aggression. The defence of Germany against possible French encroachments became a major preoccupation of British ministers. It was this which made Palmerston anxious about Prussian policy in the Elbe Duchies: 'It may be doubtful whether Prussia is not falling into a Trap about her Quarrel with Denmark and whether France may not be lying in wait for a Rupture between those Parties to side with Denmark and threaten Rhenish Prussia.'[2] To obviate these dangers, the British government began to work for a defensive understanding of England, Austria and Prussia.

VI

The state of the Habsburg empire on the morrow of the Italian war held out little hope of active opposition to French encroachments in Europe. Hungary remained unappeased, the new kingdom of Italy coveted Venetia and would try to seize that province at the earliest opportunity. With the revival of the German national movement, Austro-Prussian rivalry was again becoming acute. Rechberg's attempt to find support at St Petersburg had produced but meagre results. Early in 1861, Bloomfield reported from Vienna: '...at this moment she [Austria] seems to me to be abandoned by every power except Turkey, and she feels that in Germany the ground is slipping from underneath her feet'.[3] It was not in a prosperous state that Austria approached her coming ordeals.

Rechberg in his predicament now sought in London the support denied him at St Petersburg. He complained to Bloomfield of England's coolness towards Austria, particularly in the affairs of Germany.[4] Apponyi, the Austrian ambassador[5] in London, asked Russell for British support on German questions. He explained that the cabinet in Vienna had long lost hope of ever agreeing with England on Italian matters. The settlement in the Principalities had shown how little British co-operation could be relied on in eastern affairs. Rechberg, therefore, was all the more anxious to know what attitude England intended to adopt in the affairs of Germany.[6]

---

[1] 'The great fault of Palmerston and Russell in their last ministry was the breach with France over the annexation of Savoy. During the next five years France and England were never really friends, and the results were seen in their failures over Poland and Schleswig-Holstein. It is quite plain that a strong Franco-British combination might have held Prussia and Russia in check' (*Foundations*, p. 286). 'The breach between Palmerston and Napoleon was complete, and became a serious hindrance to their future joint action in Europe' (*ibid.* p. 205).   [2] Palmerston to Russell, 21 January 1861, *ibid.* p. 250.
[3] Bloomfield to Russell, private, 18 April 1861, PRO 30/22, 40.
[4] Bloomfield remarked on 'these foolish dreams of the unfriendly disposition of Her Majesty's Government towards Austria and of the more favourable feelings entertained by you for Prussia' (the same to the same, private, 2 May 1861, *ibid.*).
[5] Late in 1860 the British Legations in St Petersburg and Vienna and the Austrian and Russian Legations in London had been raised to the status of Embassies. Two years later, England and Prussia took a similar step.   [6] Vitzthum, *op. cit.* p. 144.

The Austrian appeal for support did not fall on fertile soil. Palmerston had expressed the opinion that the Austrian government in not following British advice to sell Venetia to Italy was 'sliding deliberately towards its Ruin'.[1] The Austrians were 'pigheadedly blind to their own interests'.[2] Vitzthum, the Saxon minister in London, observed: 'The difficulty lies partly in the Italian sympathies of the English Ministers, partly in their doubts as to the present fitness of Austria for an alliance.'[3] Palmerston, in fact, was reported to have told Stratford that all he wished was that Austria should once again become strong. But he was said to have added: 'How can you wish that we should conclude an offensive and defensive alliance with a Power so threatened, from within and from without, as Austria is today?'[4]

In the circumstances, Rechberg's overture could receive but one reply. Russell declared that the Austrian government had taken 'needless alarm' with regard to British policy in the Principalities. They were equally mistaken in their view of British conduct in Germany.

> Her Majesty's Government also trust that Count Rechberg will explain what he means by English influence being used against Austria in Germany, for they have not interfered at all, or even expressed an opinion there. It must be for the States and Peoples of Germany to decide what changes, if any, are required in their Federal Constitution.[5]

This reply made Rechberg 'comparatively happy' but he could not conceal his disappointment at the attitude adopted by the British press towards Austria's constitutional experiments.[6] It was clear that Austria would receive no effective British support and would have to face alone the hazards of a dangerous situation. The British government, on the other hand, knew only too well that serious resistance to French encroachments could be hoped for only from Prussia.

VII

Anxiety about Napoleon's plans together with the evident weakness of Austria made a *rapprochement* with Prussia desirable in British eyes. On 6 November 1858 the Prince of Prussia had dismissed Manteuffel's conservative ministry and replaced it with the 'liberal-conservative' ministry

[1] Palmerston to Russell, 21 September 1860, Bell, *op. cit.* p. 267.

[2] The same to the same, 25 December 1860, *ibid.* p. 308. Palmerston expressed extreme irritation at the Austrian refusal to sell Venetia to Italy: 'To say that her honour and her interest forbid the transfer of Venetia for 20 million sterling is all *bosh*: and to say that the fortresses of the Mincio are the outposts and defences of Germany is about as rational as it was to say that Gatton and Old Sarum were the bulwarks of the British constitution' (the same to the same, 6 October 1860, Bell, *op. cit.* p. 266).

[3] Vitzthum, *op. cit.* vol. II, p. 60.

[4] *Ibid.* pp. 60f.

[5] Russell to Bloomfield, 29 April 1861, FO 120/389, no. 105.

[6] Bloomfield to Russell, private, 2 May 1861, PRO 30/22, 40.

of the 'New Era'. Schleinitz, a confirmed anglophile, had become Minister of Foreign Affairs. In his speech from the throne, the Regent had proclaimed that Prussia would henceforth seek 'moral conquests' in Germany, and would eventually merge herself in a constitutional German state. This declaration had revived British hopes. Germany might yet become England's principal ally in the defence of ordered liberty against revolutionary France and autocratic Russia.

In fact, the 'liberal' phase of Prussian policy was to prove of short duration. The Italian war and its conclusion revealed that Francis-Joseph would lose a province rather than pay the price of Prussian support. At the same time Palmerston and, less dogmatically, even Russell, refused to sanction the principal claim of liberal Germany—an alteration in the status of the Duchies.[1] Schleinitz and his colleagues, therefore, could satisfy neither Prussian patriotism nor the nationalist aspirations of German liberals.

Disillusionment with the foreign policy of the 'New Era' coincided with a turn towards conservatism inside Prussia. On 5 December 1859, Roon, father of the Prusso-German army and a fanatical conservative, had become Minister of War. On 9 February 1860 a law reforming the army was presented to the Prussian Diet. It was withdrawn in the face of opposition from the Deputies. In return, the Diet voted funds needed to keep Prussian forces on a footing of special preparedness until the following summer. The compromise proved short-lived. During 1861, the Prussian liberals organized themselves in the great German Progressive Party. In December they won the elections for a new Diet.[2] Late that year Schleinitz had to give up his post. Bernstorff, his successor, addressed to the German courts a note proposing in uncompromising terms a revision of the federal constitution in a sense favourable to Prussia. In March 1862 the majority of the Diet demanded that the budget should contain a more detailed account of expenditure. The Ministry resigned and King William dissolved the Diet. A new Diet, overwhelmingly progressive, refused to grant supplies for Roon's military reform. The king thought of abdication. In September 1862, as a last desperate measure, he called on Bismarck to form a government prepared to ignore the hostile majority in the Diet. For several months thereafter, Prussia appeared to stand on the verge of civil war.[3]

[1] It is curious that whilst Palmerston charged the Austrian government with 'pig-headedness' for its refusal to sell Venetia, he himself was showing an almost equal blindness in his rigid defence of the London treaty of 1852.

[2] Frederick William IV had died at the beginning of 1861. On 18 October his brother, the Regent, was crowned king as William I.

[3] It is a remarkable fact that comparatively little has been written about what are undoubtedly the decisive years in the history of modern Prussia-Germany. The deficiency has recently been remedied at least in part by the publication of E. N. Anderson, *The Social and Political Conflict in Prussia 1858–1864* (University of Nebraska Studies, no. 12, Lincoln, 1954).

Events in Prussia produced a growing estrangement between British liberals and the Prussian government. British criticism of Prussia found vocal expression in connection with the famous 'Macdonald Incident'.[1] In February 1861 Russell in a sharp despatch described Prussia's attitude in the affair as 'in a high degree unfriendly' and 'too clearly evincing a disregard of international goodwill'.[2] Palmerston, in the House of Commons, launched a violent diatribe against the Prussian government.[3] Prussia, Palmerston wrote to Russell, 'sets public opinion in England against her by her aggressive policy against Denmark, by her anti-English policy all over the world, and by the rudeness and roughness of all her people employed either by the Govt or by railroad companies'.[4] Bernstorff, who was still minister in London, described the disappointment produced by Prussia's abandonment of 'liberalism'. This disappointment, he reported, had once again drawn British sympathies to the side of Austria, especially since that country seemed to have returned to the path of constitutional government.[5] Clarendon's attitude, at this time, may be taken as representative of educated British opinion:

All my political sympathies are for Prussia, the greatest Protestant Power in Germany. The marriage of the Crown-Prince with the highly gifted daughter of our Queen has only knitted still closer the old ties between the two countries. Unfortunately, not everything I saw and heard in Berlin[6] tended to strengthen me in my natural sympathies. The King, a man of perfect honour, has no idea of the Duties of a Constitutional Sovereign. Besides, His Majesty has the misfortune not to possess a single statesman in his Kingdom....All Prussian officials overrate themselves and are self-conceited...I am beginning to think that Constitutional Government in Prussia is impossible. Certainly neither the King nor his Ministers have any notion of the volcano seething underneath their feet. I told Lord Russell so plainly on my return....The real difficulty lies in the Prussians overrating themselves.[7]

As the constitutional conflict in Prussia dragged on, fears were expressed in London that the events of 1848 might repeat themselves.[8] Palmerston

---

[1] In September 1860 a somewhat arrogant British traveller found himself involved at Bonn in a dispute with an over-zealous railway official. As the passenger was a personage of some importance, international complications ensued.

[2] Bell, *op. cit.* p. 309.

[3] Bernstorff attributed this outburst to Palmerston's disapproval of the views on Germany held by the Prince Consort (Friese, *op. cit.* p. 244). According to Disraeli, the Prime Minister's friends attributed his outburst to 'the German efforts for unity which, in his view, are bound to provoke an interminable civil war and tend to strengthen the French influence' (Vitzthum, *op. cit.* p. 145).

[4] Palmerston to Russell, 27 October 1861, Bell, *op. cit.* p. 310.

[5] Report of 18 May 1861, Friese, *op. cit.* p. 245.

[6] Clarendon had just attended the coronation of the new king of Prussia as the Queen's chief representative. He had been treated with great courtesy (*ibid.* p. 244) but had been alarmed at the amount of ill-feeling which he had found in Prussia against England (H. Maxwell, *The Life and Letters of the Fourth Earl of Clarendon* (London, 1913), vol. II, pp. 245ff.; Martin, *op. cit.* vol. V, pp. 409f.).

[7] Quoted in Vitzthum, *op. cit.* pp. 201f.

[8] 'Palmerston, full of his belief in constitutionalism, believed that the arbitrary course of the King and Bismarck's defiance of the Prussian Parliament must end in disaster. Public

severely blamed the Prussian government, particularly Bismarck, for the dangers to which the Prussian monarchy was exposed. In 1863, he observed in a memorandum that 'Ct. Bismarck might be privately told that if the King's Life is in Danger, Ct.B. and the unwise and unconstitutional system he is persuading the King to adopt were the true Causes of that Danger'.[1] There was now little prospect of a close understanding between England and Germany led by a liberal Prussia.

When—as a result of Bernstorff's note of 20 December 1861—the question of German reorganization entered a new and more acute phase, the British government adopted an attitude of sceptical aloofness. Russell expressed disapproval of Bernstorff's methods.[2] He explained to a German diplomat

that it would be time for the British Government to interest themselves in the question when a definite scheme for reforming the constitution of the Bund has been brought forward and obtained the full assent of Austria and Prussia. Time was too precious to study one-sided attempts to solve the question.[3]

The Saxon minister in London observed: 'The indifference displayed by Earl Russell with regard to German efforts for reform has struck me on various occasions and I have more than once referred to it in my despatches'.[4] Palmerston, in his turn, felt convinced that real unity in Germany could come about only through a civil war[5] and that such a war could not be fought without provoking the intervention of France.[6] Such a development he contemplated with distaste.

...Perhaps all things considered dualism is the only arrangement possible in Germany. Austria & Prussia are like Caesar & Pompey. Prussia like Caesar will not brook a superior, and Austria like Pompey will not endure an equal. Each might be a centre around which the smaller states might range themselves...and there would be two strong bodies who would unite against a foreign foe.[7]

The Prussians and the smaller German states were 'selfish and foolish', the Austrians blind to their own interests.[8]

opinion would...lead him and his King to abdication, to exile and to the block. Palmerston believed...that the majority of the Prussian Parliament would ultimately reduce Bismarck and the King to submission...Bismarck and his King would be drowned by the rising tide of parliamentarianism' (*Foundations*, pp. 248f.). In 1863, Palmerston was to write in a memorandum: '...I gave Gudin (?) no message for Bismarck but I told him jokingly that as he is a rapid painter he might present the King with two sketches, one representing him sitting on his throne with his crown on his head, the other representing him lying on the ground with his crown on the floor, and that he might leave the King to draw his conclusions' (quoted in Bell, *op. cit.* p. 308).

[1] Rough notes by Palmerston, 27 June 1863, FO 96/27 quoted in *Foundations*, p. 251.
[2] Vitzthum, *op. cit.* p. 144.
[3] *Ibid.* p. 197.
[4] *Ibid.*
[5] *Ibid.* p. 144.
[6] *Ibid.* p. 145.
[7] Palmerston to Russell, 7 September 1863, quoted in Bell, *op. cit.* p. 308.
[8] Palmerston to Russell, 25 December 1860, PRO 30/22, 21.

A further obstacle to British sympathy was German activity in the Duchies. The Federal Diet in the face of popular pressure[1] was endeavouring to wring from the unwilling king of Denmark the faithful execution of his engagements. Palmerston in 1861 spoke of Prussia's 'aggressive policy against Denmark'[2] and expressed the fear that Napoleon would try to profit from a German-Danish quarrel.[3] Two years later, he was still repeating his warning:

...Any aggressive Measure of Germany ag^t Denmark would most likely lead to an aggressive move by France ag^t Germany, and specially ag^t Prussia, the main instigator of such aggression. The Prussian Provinces would at once be occupied by France and in the present state of the Prussian army, its system of drill Formation and movements, the first Serious Encounter between it and the French would be little less disastrous to Prussia than the Battle of Jena.[4]

It was, moreover, Palmerston's opinion that German national enthusiasm about the Duchies was used as a cloak to cover other ambitions:

...There is no use in disguising the fact that what is at the bottom of the German design, and the desire of connecting Schleswig with Holstein, is the dream of a German fleet, and the wish to get Kiel as a German seaport. That may be a good reason why they should wish it; but it is no reason why they should violate the rights and independence of Denmark for an object which, even if accomplished, would not realize the expectation of those who aim at it.[5]

It was for this, the Prime Minister considered, that 'the gentlemen at Frankfurt and the crazy Minister at Berlin'[6] would recklessly run the risk of French intervention in Germany and a major war in Europe. To deter and restrain them, he issued, from his place in the House of Commons, a solemn warning to the German governments.

...I am satisfied with all reasonable men in Europe, including those in France and Russia, in desiring that the independence, integrity and the rights of Denmark may be maintained. We are convinced—I am convinced at least—that if any violent attempt were made to overthrow those rights and interfere with that independence, those who made the attempt would find in the result, that it would not be Denmark alone with which they would have to contend.[7]

The question of the Duchies thus stood between England and Germany. This conflict, together with the swing towards 'authoritarianism' in Berlin, cut across the feeling of sympathy engendered by a common distrust of Napoleon, common Protestantism and close dynastic ties. Prussia as little

[1] The success of the Italian national movement had acted as a great stimulus to German national sentiment. The famous 'Nationalverein' was actively stimulating interest in national concerns all over Germany.
[2] Palmerston to Russell, 27 October 1861, Bell, op. cit. p. 310.
[3] The same to the same, 21 January 1861, Foundations, p. 250.
[4] The same to the same, 27 June 1863, printed ibid. pp. 250f.
[5] Hansard, 3rd ser. 172, 1252, 23 July 1863.
[6] Palmerston to Russell, 27 June 1863, printed in Foundations, p. 250.
[7] Hansard, 3rd ser. 172, 1252, 23 July 1863.

as Austria now seemed cast for the role of England's principal ally. In the great 'ideological' conflict of the age, the two countries stood on opposite sides. Palmerston was 'liberal' at Berlin and 'conservative' in Kiel; the Prussian Government was 'conservative' in Berlin but ready to espouse the 'liberal' cause in the Duchies.

VIII

Napoleon's Italian policy had important effects on relations among the Powers. It made both Alexander II and Palmerston distrustful of his plans and thus contributed to the isolation of France. To replace a system which was evidently in decline, both tried—somewhat half-heartedly—to create new defensive groupings. Both were frustrated by the weakness and 'obstinacy' of Austria. The government in Vienna refused to make the concessions in Germany needed to secure a genuine dualism.[1] It resisted British pressure for the sale of Venetia to Italy. This left Austria, weakened by an unsuccessful war and internal difficulties, exposed to attack from several directions.

The impossibility of counting on Austria induced both England and Russia to seek alternative policies. They could try to strengthen Prussia against France or co-operate with Napoleon in order to restrain him. The first of these courses was dependent, to a large extent, on 'ideological' and internal developments in Prussia. Prussian conservatives looked to Russia, the liberals to England. The two parties were precariously balanced, the first controlling the government, the second the Prussian Diet. The Russian government in its desire to shield Poland from revolutionary 'contagion' had every interest in Bismarck's survival as Prime Minister; the British government, on the other hand, longed for his overthrow by constitutional methods. The constitutional conflict in Prussia, therefore, was more than an internal issue. Its outcome was a matter of European concern.

As regards the policy of 'managing' Napoleon, the British government found itself in a stronger position than that of Russia. Both Gorchakov and Palmerston in turn tried to restrain the emperor, but there was a difference in their methods. Whilst the tsar preached doctrinaire conservatism, the British government merely recommended a policy of moderation in practical questions. Moreover, Palmerston shared with Napoleon the desire to see Venetia pass into the hands of Italy, whilst such a development was anathema to Russia. Palmerston and Napoleon also shared a common distrust of Russian aims in the east. Above all, Napoleon remained faithful to his conviction that the survival of his dynasty was bound up with friendship with England. As long as he

[1] Rechberg's efforts to secure an 'Ausgleich' with Prussia were frustrated by his colleague and rival Schmerling who was determined to maintain Austria's ascendancy in Germany.

remained on the throne of France, his ties with 'liberal' England would outweigh the attraction of 'autocratic' Russia.

The gradual weakening of France's ties with both England and Russia, coupled with the failure to create a defensive league against her, left several of the principal powers in a state approaching isolation. Austria, a paralytic if not a corpse, had not a friend in Europe. England was faced with the prospect of progressive isolation. France no longer possessed a reliable ally. Russia and Prussia alone found in one another a support rendered all the more valuable by the decay of all other groupings. Prussia's position, in particular, had by 1862 become exceedingly advantageous. She was regarded by Russia as her closest ally. Napoleon was openly expressing his sympathy with her desire for federal reform. Relations with the new kingdom of Italy were friendly. England had, in advance, adopted with regard to Germany's future an attitude of neutrality which would favour the stronger party. In fact, before ever Bismarck came to power, Napoleon's policy had cleared the ring for an Italo-Prussian struggle with the disintegrating Habsburg monarchy and the lesser German states. A situation had arisen in which not one of the powers would support an enfeebled Austria or attempt to oppose any reasonable programme of German reorganization under the auspices of Prussia. Times had changed since Olmütz, and Prussia, in her dealings with Austria, could now count on the benevolence or at worst the indifference of Europe.[1]

---

[1] 'So sah sich das preussische Cabinett auf dem ganzen Continent von dem Wohlwollen und der Sympathie der ausserdeutschen Mächte umgeben. Seine einzigen Gegner befanden sich auf deutschem, und leider, wie jetzt zu erzählen ist, auch auf preussischem Boden' (Sybel, *op. cit.* vol. II, p. 449).

CHAPTER 4

NAPOLEON III AND THE BEGINNINGS OF THE SECOND REVOLUTION: ITALY AND POLAND, 1857–63 (*continued*)

THE tendencies which had originated during the Italian national movement were accentuated by the Polish insurrection of 1863. The revolt of the Poles revived—in an acute form—the twin questions of 'western' support for oppressed nationalities and of conservative solidarity in the face of revolutionary nationalism. It increased suspicion of Louis Napoleon and gave rise once again to thoughts of a defensive coalition against him. Moreover, the Polish crisis would force Austria to repeat a fateful choice.[1] Whilst it is difficult to accept the statement that the Polish incident 'foreshadowed a redistribution of forces in Europe'[2] —in fact it merely threw into clearer relief tendencies produced by Italian events—there is yet some justification for describing it as 'the point of departure of the changes accomplished in Europe'.[3] The Polish insurrection together with the diplomatic campaign it provoked, did in effect create the situation which formed the point of departure for Bismarck's early successes. It helped to stabilize and develop the favourable constellation which he had found on assuming office in 1862.

I

By the end of January 1863 it had become clear that the Russian forces in Poland were faced with a large-scale rising which might prove difficult to suppress. The Prussian government thereupon despatched to St Petersburg General Alvensleben with instructions to make arrangements for Prusso-Russian co-operation in pursuing and disarming Polish insurgents along the common frontier. Gorchakov, who considered an agreement of this kind both unnecessary and undignified, was opposed to its conclusion.[4]

---

[1] In fact the Polish rising forced the Austrian government to repeat its choice of 1854. Once again, Austria decided to give half-hearted support to the western powers. The result, as on the previous occasion, was her continued and fateful isolation.

[2] R. W. Seton-Watson, *Britain in Europe 1789–1914* (Cambridge, 1937), p. 437.

[3] '...point de départ des bouleversements accomplis en Europe'. Jomini, *op. cit.* (French ed.), vol. II, p. 416.

[4] This is what Redern, the Prussian minister at St Petersburg, told his Austrian colleague (Thun to Rechberg, 1 March/17 February 1863, no. 5 E, HHSAPAR R[ussie] R[apports], 1863, X 49). Cf. also Friese, *op. cit.* p. 304 and R. H. Lord, 'Bismarck and Russia in 1863', *AHR*, 29 (Oct. 1923—July 1924), p. 40. Lord completely destroys, with the help of material from the Russian archives, the previously held view that the Convention was a master stroke of Bismarckian diplomacy. The older view, however, has persisted, and even Friese is reluctant to jettison this element of the Bismarckian legend (Friese, *op. cit.* pp. 297ff.).

The tsar, however, to spare his uncle's feelings[1] accepted the proposal and told Gorchakov to sign a written agreement.[2] On 8 February, the celebrated Alvensleben Convention was accordingly concluded. In a personal letter to Bismarck, Gorchakov hailed it as a new expression of Russo-Prussian solidarity. It might lead to further developments in which his own co-operation would not be found wanting.[3] In spite of this assurance, however, Gorchakov during the days which followed did everything in his power to prevent the Convention from entering into force.[4]

The news of a Russo-Prussian agreement against the Poles caused excitement in London and Paris. The exact terms of the Convention were unknown in both capitals but there was indignation that the Prussian government should have demonstrated in this manner its solidarity with Poland's 'oppressors'. Cowley reported on 20 February that tempers in Paris were rising.

The feeling in this country is warming again in favor of the Poles. The Empress has taken up their cause.... The public press too, particularly the papers which are supposed to be under Government influence, have not been very mild lately towards Prussia and there has been for the last two days considerable agitation in the political and monied world. Prussia will do well not to go too far, for although I am sure that at this moment war is not in the Emperor's thoughts, there is no saying how soon a warlike feeling with respect to Poland may not be raised, and Prussia would be the first to bear the brunt of it.[5]

Three days later, Cowley repeated his warning. '...The feeling in favor of Poland is becoming stronger every hour here, and the Emperor will be obliged to show that he has done something to satisfy it.'[6]

On 20 February, Cowley told Russell that Napoleon was '...exceedingly desirous to consult with Her Majesty's Government as to

---

[1] This was Gorchakov's explanation to Thun (Thun to Rechberg, 1 March/17 February 1863 no. 5 E, HHSAPARRR, 1863, x 49. Cf. Friese, *op. cit.* p. 304 and Lord, *loc. cit.* pp. 40f.

[2] Bismarck explained to the British ambassador: 'When General Alvensleben arrived at St Petersburg, the Vice-Chancellor finding that the opinions of the Prussian Cabinet were entirely different from his own, met their overtures unfavourably. The Emperor took a different view of the case and when the General saw the Prince again, His Excellency's views had undergone an entire change and he requested him to embody in a Convention any proposals which he might have to make for the co-operation of the troops of the two Governments. As General Alvensleben was unaccustomed to write French, the Convention was drawn up by the Russian Foreign Office' (Buchanan to Russell, 14 March 1863, no. 149, confidential, copy in RA H 50/109).

[3] Friese, *op. cit.* p. 304.

[4] Bismarck told Buchanan: 'It [the Convention] was however no sooner signed than Prince Gortchakov endeavoured to render it unpopular and succeeded in rendering it inoperative so far as the principle of the frontier being crossed by the troops of either Government was in question' (Buchanan to Russell, 14 March 1863, no. 149, confidential, copy in RA H 50/109; cf. also Friese, *op. cit.* p. 304).

[5] Cowley to Russell, private, 20 February 1863, FO 519/230, draft.

[6] The same to the same, private, 23 February 1863, *ibid.* draft.

the propriety of taking some step in common with reference to the St Petersburg convention'.[1] Napoleon had also asked himself whether an attempt should not be made to induce Austria to join with England and France in the remonstrance 'and thus, as it were, to break up the coalition against the liberties of Poland'.[2] The following day, the French ambassador in London called on the Foreign Secretary and declared that his government, although not in possession of the text of the Convention between Russia and Prussia knew enough of its purport 'to form an opinion unfavourable to the prudence and opportuneness of that Convention'. The government of the king of Prussia had 'by their conduct revived the Polish question'. The ambassador wished to know whether these views were shared by the British government. Russell replied that the British Ministers 'entertained precisely the views which he had explained on the part of his Government'.[3] At a meeting of the Cabinet held that day, he advocated 'a policy of intervention in conjunction with France'.[4] Palmerston, on the other hand, 'held cautious language, and agreed that French Policy was dictated by a desire to conciliate Catholic support, and probably by ulterior plans of aggrandizement'.[5]

On the 23rd, Russell submitted to the Queen the draft of a sternly worded dispatch, which he proposed to address to the British ambassador in Berlin.

Upon viewing this Convention in all its respects, therefore, Her Majesty's Government are forced to arrive at the conclusion that it is an Act of Intervention, which is not justified by necessity: which will tend to alienate the affection of the Polish subjects of the King of Prussia: which gives support and countenance to the arbitrary and unjust conscription of Warsaw, and which may be quoted by other Powers of Europe to justify intervention in favour of the Insurgents.

Buchanan was to read this dispatch to Bismarck and to ask for a copy of the Convention.[6] The Queen returned the draft, observing that the question was so serious and likely to lead to such serious consequences that it was her wish to sanction no step that had not received the careful consideration of the Cabinet. She had made some alterations in the margin of Russell's draft and urged strongly that Cowley's advice 'to give Prussia the opportunity of getting out of the difficulty by letting the convention drop' should be followed.[7] The Queen was greatly alarmed[8]

---

[1] The same to the same, 20 February 1863, no. 207, confidential, copy in RA H 50/43.
[2] Ibid.
[3] Russell to Cowley, 21 February 1863, B[ritish] and F[oreign] S[tate] P[apers], vol. 53, p. 788.
[4] Grey to the Queen, ?24 February 1863, RA H 50/58.
[5] Granville to the Queen, 24 February 1863, ibid. H 50/56.
[6] Russell to Buchanan, February 1863, draft, ibid. H 50/50, copy.
[7] The Queen to Russell, 24 February 1863, ibid. H 50/57, copy.
[8] She wrote in a note: 'The Emperor Napoleon is dying for an opportunity to be on the Rhine, and we must take care not to give him a pretence for it' (note by the Queen, 23 February 1863, ibid. H 50/53).

and in her perplexity addressed herself to Granville,[1] her confidant in the Cabinet:

> The Queen is terribly alarmed at the French language and proposals respecting Poland, and thinks *we* must on *no* account let ourselves be dragged into what *may* be a war with Germany! The Queen shudders at the very thought of *what* if we are not *very* careful, and very guarded in our expressions to France, we may find ourselves plunged into! The proposals of France would inevitably bring us into collision with Prussia—and we should have a French army on the Rhine before we could turn round.

She relied upon the Cabinet 'to prevent any imprudent step'.[2] General Grey, the Queen's Private Secretary was despatched in haste from Windsor to London to urge on Granville and Wood[3] '...the evident danger of the position caused by the course adopted by Prussia with regard to the Polish Insurrection, and the desire of the French Government to found on that course a pretence for their own intervention'.[4] The two Ministers 'both saw the danger more clearly than the way of avoiding it' but they and two of their more influential colleagues 'were all quite aware of the necessity of watching lest any incautious or hasty step should involve us in dangerous complications'. The difficulty was increased by the attitude of the Opposition and by 'the feeling generally excited in the country by the conduct of Prussia'.

> It will be hard to avoid making some strong representation to the Prussian Government—and if we do so in conjunction with France, it will not be easy to say to the latter that we shall not go beyond diplomatic pressure.

If war grew up out of the Convention, the French government would declare as it had done in the case of Italy that it was warring for the cause which England professed to have at heart—the freedom and independence of nations and there would probably follow a course of events similar to that which led, after the Italian War, to the annexation of Nice and Savoy.[5]

There was some justification for the Queen's anxiety. At the very moment when she was endeavouring to restrain Russell's ardour, the French ambassador had called at the Foreign Office with a proposal that the two governments should address to Prussia a remonstrance in identical

---

[1] President of the Council.
[2] The Queen to Granville, 23 February 1863, *ibid.* H 50/54, copy.
[3] Sir Charles Wood, Secretary for India.
[4] Grey to the Queen, ?24 February 1863, *ibid.* H 50/58.
[5] *Ibid.* Granville himself had written to the Queen: '...The situation is embarrassing if Lord Palmerston and Lord Russell go warmly into a course of interference. The popular feeling is sure to be roused in favor of the Poles.... The conduct of the Prussian Government is suicidal—and exposes the peace of Europe to the greatest danger. Your Majesty's Government ought to be extremely prudent' (Granville to the Queen, 24 February 1863, *ibid.* H 50/56, copy).

terms in protest against the Convention. The Austrian government had been invited to join in the step. If Russell agreed, all that remained to be done was to decide on the wording. For this purpose, the ambassador transmitted a draft which Drouyn had sent from Paris.[1]

The Cabinet met on the 25th. Russell was nervous in introducing the subject of Poland. He produced his draft to Buchanan, stating that the Queen had desired him to submit it to the Cabinet. The Ministers decided 'to omit everything that savoured of a demand from Prussia, leaving the despatch as a remonstrance against the policy of having made the convention'. Palmerston agreed that '. . .even a remonstrance might give a slight footing to French ambition, and that to make any demand which would probably be rejected would give the Emperor an important advantage'.[2] Russell added to the original draft a paragraph 'which may allow the Prussians to drop the Convention if they choose to do it'.[3] He also read the draft of a despatch to Cowley 'which threw cold water upon any plan of joining France in an interference in Polish matters'. This was approved by the Cabinet.[4] On the 26th Russell learnt that the Austrian government had declined the French invitation.[5] Two days later he in his turn informed the French government that he could not accept the proposal.[6]

In the meantime, anxiety reigned at Berlin. The language of the French

[1] Drouyn to Gros, 21 February 1863 and draft of note to be addressed to the Prussian government BFSP, *loc. cit.* pp. 809ff. On 21 February, Metternich, the Austrian ambassador in Paris, had a conversation with the empress Eugénie and three days later another with Napoleon. During these conversations, the French sovereigns unfolded before Metternich a vast plan of Austro-French alliance. Austria would help in the restoration of Poland both diplomatically and by giving up Cracow and possibly the whole of Galicia. She would cede Venetia to Italy. In return, after a war with Prussia, she would receive Silesia and Lusatia. She would receive unqualified French support in the Balkans. France, after a war with Prussia, would help herself to Prussian territories on the left bank of the Rhine (Metternich to Rechberg, 22 and 26 February 1863, printed in H. Oncken, *Die Rheinpolitik Kaiser Napoleons III von 1863 bis 1870* (Stuttgart, Berlin u. Leipzig, 1926), vol. I, pp. 3ff.).

Queen Victoria's anxiety about Napoleon's motives in proposing a joint protest at Berlin was fully justified by the facts.

[2] Granville to the Queen, 25 February 1863, *ibid.* H 50/64.

[3] Russell to the Queen, 25 February 1863, *ibid.* H 50/66. The paragraph now added to the despatch ran as follows: 'It is possible that the Governments of Prussia and Russia, seeing the inexpediency of their Convention, and aware of the objections to which it has given rise, may be disposed to cancel it or to put an end to its operation. In that case you will inform me what steps have been taken with that view' (Russell to Buchanan, 2 March 1863, no. 48, *ibid.* H 50/89, copy).

[4] Granville to the Queen, 25 February 1863, *ibid.* H 50/64. Russell explained to the Queen that his confidential draft was intended 'to slacken the too rapid movements of the French Government' (Russell to the Queen, 25 February 1863, *ibid.* H 50/66).

[5] Bloomfield to Russell, telegram, 26 February 1863, *ibid.* H 50/69, copy.

[6] The British despatch transmitted a copy of the one which was to be addressed to Berlin. After drawing attention to the 'escape clause' in the latter, Russell continued: 'There is some reason to hope, from communications here and at Paris, that the Prusso-Russian Convention will be set aside, or at all events that it will not be executed; and it is desirable to give Prussia this way of condemning her own act' (Russell to Cowley, February 1863, *ibid.* H 50/70, draft).

and British envoys was severe. It was known that a Franco-British remonstrance was impending.[1] The Austrian government had refused a Prussian invitation to sign a Convention on Polish affairs[2] and was known to be negotiating with England and France. Bismarck's conduct in signing an agreement with Russia was severely criticized in the Prussian Chamber.[3] On the 24th rumours of a ministerial crisis began to circulate in Berlin.[4] Morier, the Secretary of the British Embassy learnt on good authority that Bismarck had offered his resignation.[5] Buchanan also reported a serious misunderstanding between Bismarck and his master. The king, it appeared, considered that the political tendency of the Convention had been concealed from him.[6]

In this situation, the Prussian government took two steps designed to improve its position. On the 27th Buchanan received an assurance that the Convention was unlikely to come into force.[7] On the same day, Bismarck told Oubril, the Russian minister, that Prussia would stand by the Convention if assured of Russian support. At present she was uncertain, not knowing whether Russia was determined and able to accept the struggle. Would Russia, in case of need, come to Prussia's assistance?[8] Informed by the telegraph of this enquiry, Gorchakov replied at once in the sense which Bismarck had undoubtedly anticipated: 'Since Prussia judges it to her interest to renounce the arrangement, the emperor will not oppose.'[9] In a private letter to Oubril approved by the tsar, Gorchakov explained:

The Emperor agrees that the Alvensleben arrangement should be considered *non avenu*. I have never ascribed to this act any practical importance without denying its moral value. They have been very clumsy at the place where you are[10]... but I

[1] Goltz, the Prussian ambassador in Paris had asked Cowley whether the steps contemplated by England and France were directed against Prussia alone or against Russia as well. Cowley replied that they were directed against Prussia only and declared there was a strong feeling 'that public morality had been insulted by the acts of the Prussian Government'. Goltz's conduct, Cowley reported, betrayed great nervousness (Cowley to Russell, 24 February 1863, no. 229 confidential, *ibid.*, H 50/60, copy).

[2] Bloomfield to Russell, telegram, 21 February 1863, *ibid.* H 50/46, copy.

[3] Cf. Lord, *loc cit.* p. 32.

[4] Morier to Russell, telegram, 25 February 1863, RA H 50/61. Lord, who used Russian sources, considers that Bismarck made his offer of resignation presumably on the 23rd. Lord, *loc. cit.* p. 32.

[5] Morier to Russell, telegram, 25 February 1863, RA H 50/60.

[6] Buchanan to Russell, telegram, 26 February 1863, *ibid.* H 50/62.

[7] The same to the same, telegram, 27 February 1863, *ibid.* H 50/75.

[8] Oubril to Gorchakov 17 February/1 March 1863, no. 61 and the same to the same, telegram, 15/27 February 1863, no. 58, quoted in Lord, *loc. cit.* p. 34. Bismarck's language was reported as follows: 'Pouvons-nous compter sur vous et irez-vous avec nous jusqu'au bout?...Si vous voulez marcher avec nous, nous devons en avoir l'assurance' (*ibid.* quoted p. 47, n. 79).

[9] *Ibid.* p. 34.

[10] On an earlier report from Oubril describing Bismarck's difficulties, the tsar wrote the following comment: 'One must admit that our dear Bismarck is a terrible blunderer' (marginal comment on Oubril to Gorchakov, 10/22 February 1863, *ibid.* p. 42).

cannot bear to indulge in any recriminations, for I am in such despair over the humiliation of our friend Bismarck.[1]

In conversation with the Prussian minister at St Petersburg, Gorchakov declared that as far as Russia was concerned, the Convention had always remained a dead letter. She had had no need of it and did not need it now.[2] Respecting Bismarck's inquiry about military assistance, the tsar wrote in the margin of Oubril's report: 'Aid for a war against France and England: no thanks'.[3]

On 3 March Gorchakov finally informed Napier, the British ambassador at St Petersburg, that the Convention had never been ratified, and 'might, as far as he was concerned, be regarded as a dead letter'.[4] On the 4th, Bismarck assured Buchanan that the document was incomplete and that no practical effect had been given to it.[5] On the 9th, Russell told the Queen that: '...the question of the Convention of Prussia and Russia may be considered as set at rest by the despatches from Berlin'.[6] The king of Prussia, saved by the British government from an awkward situation, expressed his gratitude to the Queen. Buchanan was invited

to convey to the Queen His Majesty's thanks for the conciliatory and friendly conduct of Her Majesty's Government during the late discussions at Paris on Polish affairs, and for the moderation with which the French Government under the influence of Her Majesty's Government have hitherto acted. The King said that he entirely understood the remonstrances of Her Majesty's Government and that all would be satisfactorily arranged....[7]

In Paris, great irritation was felt at the policy of England. Cowley wrote to Russell that the emperor and his Ministers were 'bitterly disappointed

---

[1] Gorchakov to Oubril, private, 16/28 February 1863, *ibid.* p. 34.

In fact, the Alvensleben Convention led to a good deal of recrimination between St Petersburg and Berlin. The month following the signature was 'filled with misunderstandings, wranglings and recriminations between the two courts over the meaning, application or abrogation of the "convention", in the midst of which one encounters in the Russian documents plenty of harsh words about Prussia and scarcely a hint of any sense of being under obligation to her' (Lord, *loc. cit.* p. 42).

Gorchakov had some grounds for his anxiety that 'Bismarck's *bévues* should not impair the intimate union between the two courts' (Gorchakov to Oubril 4/16 March 1863, *ibid.*). 'Gorchakov's and Oubril's correspondence is studded with sarcasms and complaints about Bismarck—his rashness, his indiscretions, his mendacity, his fantastic desire to play the part of Frederick the Great etc' (Lord, *loc. cit.* p. 42, n. 6).

It is a tribute to the cordiality of Russo-Prussian relations that the incident of the convention had no lasting ill-effects.

[2] 'Pour nous le papier signé ici est toujours resté une lettre morte; nous n'en avons pas eu besoin, nous n'en avons pas besoin' (Redern to Bismarck, 1 March 1863, quoted in Friese, *op. cit.* p. 307).

[3] Marginal comment by the tsar on Oubril to Gorchakov 17 February/1 March 1863, no. 61, quoted in Lord, *loc. cit.* p. 35.

[4] Napier to Russell, 3 March 1863, no. 121, confidential RA H 50/91, copy.

[5] Buchanan to Russell, telegram, 4 March 1863, *ibid.* H 50/96.

[6] Russell to the Queen, 9 March 1863, *ibid.* H 50/103.

[7] Buchanan to Russell, telegram, 11 March 1863, *ibid.* H 50/105.

at your declining the combined note'.[1] Drouyn regretted the loss of the opportunity afforded by the convention and described it as 'an incident of which we should have taken advantage'.[2] Even he, however, was finally forced to admit that the question had been settled in a manner which enabled the British and French governments to allow it to drop.[3] That was the end of the Alvensleben Convention, Bismarck's début on the stage of European *grande politique*.

II

Palmerston, in the meantime, had come to the conclusion that Russia was 'the real culprit', and that it was 'to her as to the origin of the evil that any real and useful representation ought to be addressed'.[4] He told Russell:

> I am much inclined to think that our communication in conjunction with France ought to be mainly addressed to Russia, the real culprit, rather than to Prussia, an incidental accomplice,...public opinion in this country as well as in France is getting strong upon this subject, and we shall not stand well if we do not do something.[5]

On 27 February a debate showed the House of Commons to be 'unanimously Polish'.[6] Russell, therefore, prepared the draft of a despatch to Napier. He brushed aside misgivings expressed by the Queen.[7] On 2 March, the despatch left the Foreign Office. It called on the tsar to proclaim 'an immediate and unconditional amnesty to his revolted Polish subjects' and to place his kingdom of Poland without delay 'in possession of the political and civil privileges which were granted to it by the Emperor Alexander I in execution of the stipulations of the Treaty of Vienna'.[8]

The French government, spurred on by public opinion, had already made its own representations. On 17 February Drouyn had instructed Montebello, the French ambassador, to recommend 'a policy of reparation and progress' and to sound the Russian government about 'the concessions it might be disposed to make to the general interest'.[9] On the

---

[1] Cowley to Russell, private, 1 March 1863, *ibid.* H 50/84, copy.

[2] 'un incident duquel nous aurions dû profiter' (Grey to Russell, 12 March 1863, no. 19 confidential, *ibid.* H 50/88, copy.

[3] Cowley to Russell, 15 March 1863, no. 299, *ibid.* H 50/113, copy.

[4] Palmerston to Russell, 25 February 1863, PRO 30/22, 22. For a detailed analysis of British policy in the Polish rising cf. W. E. Mosse, 'England and the Polish Insurrection of 1863', *EHR* LXXI, no. 278 (January 1956).

[5] Palmerston to Russell, 26 February 1863, PRO 30/22, 22.

[6] The same to the same, 27 February 1863, *ibid.*

[7] The Queen advised Russell 'to pause with any advice to Russia until the insurrection is quelled' (The Queen to Russell, 27 February 1863, RA H 50/76, copy). The Foreign Secretary replied (in a style of questionable purity): 'A representation to Russia is in the opinion of the Cabinet absolutely necessary to be made' (Russell to the Queen, 28 February 1863, *ibid.* H 50/79).

[8] Russell to Napier, 2 March 1863, no. 53, *ibid.* H 50/85, copy.

[9] F. Charles-Roux, *Alexandre II, Gortchakoff et Napoléon III* (Paris, 1913), p. 337.

following day he had warned the Russian ambassador that the Polish cause was likely to gain great sympathy among all parties in France. The pressure of public opinion in France would grow as events in Poland became more serious. He hoped, therefore, that the Russian government would refrain from all measures likely to exasperate opinion. Should all hopes of concession be disappointed, this would create a painful position for both governments.[1]

Drouyn's despatch struck dismay to the heart of Montebello. He telegraphed on 28 February that if he held the language prescribed to him, it would do serious harm (*portera une atteinte grave*) to Franco-Russian relations. Would it not be desirable, therefore, to modify the tone of the despatch?[2] Drouyn replied that he found nothing to change. 'We do not wish to irritate, but we desire to be sincere.' Napoleon, moreover, had written a letter in a similar sense.[3] With a heavy heart Montebello complied with his instructions. A major step had been taken towards the dissolution of the Franco-Russian *entente*.

On 5 March Russell told Cowley that the next step to be taken should be 'to invite all the chief Powers who signed the Treaty of Vienna to concur in advising Russia to recur to the stipulations and to revert to the policy of the Treaty of Vienna in regard to Poland'.[4] The French government was sulking about the British refusal to make joint representations in Berlin.[5] On 7 March, however, Drouyn agreed in principle to common action provided Austria could be induced to co-operate.[6] On 12 March, in conversation with the British chargé d'affaires, he announced that he favoured the restoration of Poland.[7]

The attitude of Austria now became a matter of importance. On 12 March, Rechberg told Bloomfield that England and Austria had a common interest in restraining Napoleon. Austria wished to co-operate with England in all European questions including that of Poland. Any representations at St Petersburg, however, should be of the mildest kind.[8] Four days later, Apponyi declined on behalf of his government the invitation to joint diplomatic action. 'No one could expect that Austria would embark in an enterprise which in its ultimate result might be to deprive her of a rich and tranquil province. She could not be an accomplice in the work of dismembering her own Dominions.'[9] Yet Austria's co-operation appeared essential: '...without Austria, nothing really

---

[1] Drouyn to Montebello, 18 February 1863. BFSP, *loc. cit.* pp. 827f.
[2] Montebello to Drouyn, telegram, 28 February 1863, Charles-Roux, *op. cit.* p. 337.
[3] Drouyn to Montebello, telegram, 29 February 1863, *ibid.* pp. 337f.
[4] Russell to Cowley, 5 March 1863, BFSP, *loc. cit.* pp. 813f.
[5] Cowley to Russell, private, 1 March 1863, RA H 50/84, copy; and Metternich to Rechberg, 5 March 1863, most secret, Oncken, *op. cit.* p. 13.
[6] Charles-Roux, *op. cit.* p. 341.
[7] Grey to Russell, telegram, 12 March 1863, RA H 50/107.
[8] Bloomfield to Russell, 12 March 1863, no. 135, confidential, *ibid.* H 50/108, copy.
[9] Russell to Cowley and Bloomfield, 17 March 1863, *ibid.* H 50/117, draft.

effective could be done—with her assistance, everything was possible'.[1] On 29 March, the British and French representatives in Vienna again urged Rechberg to join in a collective note. They received the reply that, however desirous the Austrian government might be to act with England and France, its interests in Galicia placed it in a position different from that of the western powers. It would, however, address to St Petersburg a despatch to be delivered simultaneously with those of England and France.[2]

When a copy of the Austrian communication reached Paris, it was found to be 'very piano in tone'.[3] Drouyn considered it 'worse than nothing' (*moins que rien*).[4] Yet Austrian co-operation was considered so important that Drouyn and Russell were ready to accept even the little help that Rechberg was willing to give. The Austrian attitude was, at any rate, more 'western' than that of Prussia. Bismarck, in reply to a question, had stated bluntly that Prussia could not recommend measures tending to re-establish Polish independence and obliging her to add a hundred thousand men to her army. If the Poles got their independence, they would be the allies and soldiers of France.[5] The interests of Prussia, as understood by Prussian conservatives[6] established a solidarity between her and Russia in opposition to western plans for the resurrection of Poland.

When the draft of the French despatch to St Petersburg reached London, Palmerston expressed the view that 'in very measured language', it implied 'a great deal'. He marked some passages which 'put together are a pretty intelligible Threat of War about Poland; and more distinctly hinted at, than it would be advisable for us to join in'. The attitudes of England and France were not identical: 'The French hint Threats which we are not prepared to make and we appeal to the Treaty of Vienna which the French would wish to tear to Tatters.'[7] Palmerston's rival draft, to vary his own expression, in very unmeasured language implied extremely little.[8] The Queen, however, objected to several expressions which Palmerston agreed to modify.[9] Between 10 and 12 April, the three notes, differing considerably in tone, were despatched separately to St Petersburg. In spite of their professed desire to work together, the cabinets of Paris, London and Vienna were pursuing divergent objects.

[1] Cowley to Russell, 21 March 1863, no. 323, confidential, *ibid*. H 50/129, copy.
[2] Bloomfield to Russell, telegram, 29 March 1863, *ibid*. H 50/146, copy.
[3] Cowley to Russell, private, 3 April 1863, FO 519/230, copy.
[4] The same to the same, 3 April 1863, no. 390, RA H 50/159, copy.
[5] Buchanan to Russell, 14 March 1863, no. 146 confidential, *ibid*. H 50/110, copy.
[6] As in 1848, the liberals took up a more sympathetic attitude towards the Polish cause. The Alvensleben Convention was severely criticized in the Prussian Diet.
[7] Palmerston to Russell, 7 April 1863, PRO 30/22, 14.
[8] The original of the first draft, entirely in the hand of Palmerston himself, is to be found in PRO 30/22, 14.
[9] Palmerston to Russell, 8 April 1863, *ibid*.

Since the middle of March, diplomats everywhere had been discussing the prospect of French military intervention. Napoleon was known to be 'on the war-path'. He was reported to have said 'that he had not closed his eyes for four nights, thinking of the wrongs of Poland and he, a Napoleon, unable to redress them'.[1] Wild schemes were known to be floating through his brain. He had visions of Austrian archdukes or Russian grand-dukes on the Polish throne,[2] of French armies on the Rhine,[3] and of a French occupation of an island in the Baltic.[4] His restlessness was such as to convince Metternich that there was 'no other issue to the Polish question than war'.[5]

Alarming news poured into St Petersburg. Budberg reported from Paris that Napoleon's intentions were warlike.[6] Stackelberg wrote that Italy had offered France her military support.[7] Bismarck urged that a Russian gunboat should be sent to the Baltic coast in the region of Polangen. He added that the Prussian authorities in the area had been ordered to keep a strict watch.[8] Oubril warned that the foundations were being laid of an understanding between France, England and Austria.[9]

On 4 April, in a last desperate attempt to appease Napoleon, Budberg called on Drouyn to inquire what Russia could do to meet the wishes of France. Drouyn replied that the French people would be satisfied with nothing less than the independence of Poland. If the tsar felt unable to grant this, he must do the best he could to reconcile the Poles to his rule. When Budberg despairingly asked if this was all the thanks Russia got for repeated acts of friendship, he received a chilling reply.[10] After the interview Budberg expressed the conviction that nothing now remained for Russia except to defend herself as best she could.[11] On the following day the Russian army was placed on a war-footing. Reserve battalions were called out, officers' leave was stopped, the forts at Kronstadt were placed in a posture of defence.[12] Napier reported that the Russians had begun to consider a war with France a not improbable contingency. If France used threats, Russia would resist and fight.[13]

---

[1] Cowley to Russell, private, 14 April 1863, FO 519/230.
[2] The same to the same, 21 March 1863, no. 323, confidential, and 25 March 1863, no. 353 most confidential, RA H 50/129 and H 50/139, copies.
[3] The same to the same, private, 14 April 1863, FO 519/230.
[4] The same to the same, private, 10 April 1863, RA H 50/158, copy.
[5] The same to the same, private, 31 March 1863, FO 519/230.
[6] Napier to Russell, telegram, 5 April 1863, RA H 50/165, copy.
[7] *Ibid.*
[8] Redern to Bismarck, 12 April 1863, no. 55 most confidential, [*Die*] *A*[*uswärtige*] *P*[*olitik*] *P*[*reussens*] *1858–1871*, 10 vols. (Oldenburg, 1932 *et seq.*), vol. III, pp. 467f.
[9] *Ibid.*
[10] Drouyn rejoined: 'C'est vrai, mais vous avez toujours frappé à notre porte après minuit, et lorsqu'il n'y avait personne dans la voiture.'
[11] Cowley to Russell, private, 6 April 1863, FO 519/230.
[12] Napier to Russell, telegram, 5 April 1863, RA H 50/165.
[13] The same to the same 5 April 1863, no. 197, most confidential, *ibid.* H 50/169, copy.

On 17 April, Gorchakov received the notes of the three powers. His expectation of a peaceful outcome dwindled. When asked by the Prussian Minister if he believed in the probability of war, he replied that he did. '"I do" "J'y crois", and it is necessary that we should be prepared. It is evident that France is determined on war unless she is prevented by England, and we do not feel confident that England will do so'.[1] Faced with the threat of war, Russian opinion hardened:

> Great excitement and a general expectation of war continue to prevail in all classes of society here. National patriotic feeling is wound to a high pitch. . . . It is believed that France is secretly bent on war, that overtures have already been made to Italy . . . and that Sweden is entirely at the command of the Cabinet of Paris.[2]

Strong in the support of public opinion, the Russian government would not make concessions to the western powers. Napier explained:

> In my opinion the Government of Russia cannot be urged by external influence to any further concessions in Poland. The nation and the Government are essentially of one heart in this affair. . . . If threatened from abroad the whole Russian people will take up arms and will offer up their fortunes and their lives for their Emperor, their national destiny and their Church. The danger of war will be blindly and boldly met. . . . The Government counts on the neutrality of Germany, hopes for that of England, but will not yield before any combination. . . .[3]

In these circumstances, Gorchakov's reply to the western notes could not be in doubt. Confident of public support his despatches were verbose, polite and completely non-committal.[4] The diplomatic campaign inspired by Palmerston had failed. The resources of diplomacy seemed exhausted. The future, in a large measure, depended on the policy of France.

III

The deadlock between Russia and her opponents lent importance to the attitude of Germany. If Austria, Prussia and the Diet supported the western powers, Russia might be forced to enter without allies a conference on Polish affairs. If, on the other hand they adopted a neutral or pro-Russian attitude, the 'West's' diplomatic campaign against Russia

---

[1] Buchanan to Russell 25 April 1863, no. 234 confidential, FO 64/541. On 28 April Gorchakov received an alarming despatch from Brunnow. 'The Vice-Chancellor has been informed by Brunnow. . . that in his opinion diplomatic action and the hope of peace are nearly exhausted, and Russia should at once prepare against an attack from Europe. France inspires the greatest distrust' (Napier to Russell, telegram, 28 April 1863, RA H 50/214). A copy of Brunnow's warning was forwarded by Napier to London (enclosure in the same to the same 28 April 1863, no. 290 secret and confidential, FO 65/630).

[2] The same to the same 17 April 1863, no. 237, RA H 50/194, copy.

[3] The same to the same, 29 April 1863, no. 305, RA H 50/222, copy.

[4] Clarendon wrote: 'the verbiage leaves matters just where they are and the gist is to complain of the party of disorder and the foreign Governments that protect it' (Clarendon to Cowley, 6 May 1863, FO 519/230, copy). Napoleon spoke of *rigmaroles* of which he could understand nothing and in which he could see no offer of concerting with the other Powers (Cowley to Russell, private, 3 May 1863, FO 519/230, copy).

was doomed to failure and military operations against her would become hazardous in the extreme. Germany once again held the balance between East and West. Would she defend Russia against France and Europe or would she join the western campaign on behalf of Polish nationality?

Palmerston was alarmed at the prospect that a hard-pressed Russia might appeal to Prussia for help. On 24 April Buchanan startled Bismarck with the question whether Prussia, if appealed to, would go to Russia's assistance. Bismarck replied that her attitude would depend on circumstances. It might be 'necessary for our own preservation in the event of a war between France and Russia to become the ally of the latter, as our Rhenish provinces will be the real object of the war on the part of France'. To a further question about Prussia's conduct in the 'possible contingency' of a French landing on the Baltic coast, Bismarck replied that the Prussian government would then concert its attitude with that of Austria. They would take measures for the defence of Posen and Galicia. He did not believe in a French landing. What could thirty thousand men, the largest number that could be conveyed at one time, effect with one flank exposed to the forces of the Germanic Confederation, the other to those of Russia?[1] In any case, Palmerston and Russell would try to prevent a French expedition if they considered that it might lead to war between France and Prussia.[2] In the interest of peace, Prussian diplomacy must hold determined language ('eine wenig friedfertige Sprache') with regard to the possibility of French intervention in Poland.[3]

On the 26th, Palmerston assured the Prussian ambassador that a French descent on the Baltic coast was practicable. He added that, in view of British sympathy for the Poles, he would not be able to oppose such action on Napoleon's part.[4] In addition, King Leopold of the Belgians, widely regarded as an unofficial channel of communications between London and Berlin,[5] warned King William against aligning himself with Russia. Napoleon, he explained, could hardly be blamed for exploiting opportunities offered by the conduct of Prussia. England was not to be relied

[1] Buchanan to Russell, 24 April 1863, no. 234, confidential, FO 64/541.

[2] This was a generally accepted axiom of European diplomacy. Brunnow wrote to Gorchakov: '...j'attache une importance majeure à une entente avec la Prusse et avec l'Autriche. Toutes les deux, à mon avis, nous donnent le meilleur moyen de réagir sur les déterminations finales de l'Angleterre. En effet elle tient avant tout à ne pas exposer la Prusse aux dangers d'un conflit avec la France. Donc notre alliance intime avec la Cour de Berlin est le bouclier qui couvre notre intérêt envers l'Angleterre. Cette vérité vous expliquera...la vivacité avec laquelle la Reine désire personnellement que la crise actuelle parvient à une solution pacifique. Quant à la Cour de Vienne, il nous importe à un égal degré de nous entendre avec Elle sur les affaires de Pologne car le Cabinet Anglais ne se décidera à rien sans l'Autriche' (Brunnow to Gorchakov, 4 May 1863, most secret; extracts in Napier to Russell, 12 May 1863, no. 237 secret, RA H 51/24, copy).

[3] Bismarck to Werther, 24 April 1863, *APP*, vol. III, pp. 507ff.

[4] Bernstorff to Bismarck, telegram, 26 April 1863, *ibid.* p. 513.

[5] Bismarck to Savigny (Brussels), 28 April 1863, no. 60 secret, *ibid.* p. 518.

upon as Palmerston had stated that he would not oppose French measures designed to help the Poles.[1]

After an inconclusive exchange of views with the government in Vienna[2] Bismarck proceeded to explain his attitude to Palmerston and Gorchakov. His reply to the king of the Belgians contained a guarded assurance that for the moment Prussia would maintain a neutral course. She would abandon this policy only in order to resist an unprovoked attack on her frontiers.[3] The Russian government had not, so far, asked for Prussian support in the event of a French attack. However, a French expedition to the Baltic might have repercussions in Posen and Galicia. Austria and Prussia might have to suppress risings in their own provinces and Napoleon might use this as a pretext for an attack on the Rhine. An independent Poland would in any case be a constant threat to Germany. King Leopold should warn British Ministers about the dangers resulting from a permanent French camp on the Vistula.[4]

Bismarck informed Oubril of the advice received from the king of the Belgians. He added that, in the event of a French landing, Prussian hesitations could come only from the hostile attitude of Austria.[5] He personally would advise the king to support Russia, since, in his opinion, an independent Poland would be intolerable for Prussia.[6] Bismarck thus made it clear that he was unwilling to commit himself in advance. He had learnt the lesson of the Alvensleben Convention and was determined to pursue a policy similar to that which Prussia had adopted with success in the Crimean War.

[1] Leopold I to William I, 30 April 1863, *ibid.* pp. 431 f.
[2] Werther to Bismarck, 27 April 1863, no. 136, *ibid.* p. 516. Cf. also Bloomfield to Russell, 30 April 1863, no. 225 secret and confidential, FO 7/652.
[3] 'Und wenn ich zwischen Ihren Zeilen lesen soll so geht Ihre Ansicht dahin, dass Preussen in dem vielleicht in Aussicht stehenden Kampfe zwischen Russland und Frankreich neutral bleiben muss. Dies ist genau die Politik welche ich für jetzt befolge, und ich könnte aus derselben nur gezogen werden, wenn eine absichtliche Feindschaft mir einen ungerechten Angriff auf meine Grenzen brächte' (king of Prussia to king of the Belgians, 5 May 1863, *APP*, vol. III, pp. 543 f.).
[4] '...Denn...ein unabhängiges Polen ist gleich einer französischen Armee von 150,000 Mann in einem Lager an der Weichsel. Diese Ansicht in England klarzulegen und anschaulich in ihrer Gefahr für Europa zu machen, kann wiederum eine erhabene und daher schöne Aufgabe Eurer Majestät sein, zu deren Ausführung ich Sie um so dringender ersuchen muss, als Ihr Postskriptum mit zwei Ausrufungszeichen hinter Palmerston's Ausspruch mir die englische Blindheit in diesem Punkte recht klarmacht' (*ibid.*).
[5] This was a shrewd move by Bismarck to be repeated some weeks later on a more decisive occasion.
[6] Bismarck declared: 'Nos hésitations ne pourraient provenir que de l'Autriche si elle prenait une attitude hostile à notre égard et de nature à nous paralyser. Mais mon opinion est qu'elle ne saurait le faire et que les intérêts de l'Allemagne, ainsi que l'état actuel de la Galicie et du Posen s'opposeraient à notre abstention. La force des choses nous obligerait à prendre part à une lutte pareille...Quoiqu'il en soit, pour ma part je conseillerai au Roi de marcher, car nous ne saurions tolérer sur nos frontières l'établissement d'un état indépendant qui tendrait à nous faire une situation impossible' (Oubril to Gorchakov, 24 April/6 May 1863, no. 165 confidential, *ibid.* pp. 553 f.).

IV

Early in May Palmerston accepted a suggestion from Russell, that to gain time for negotiations an armistice of one year should be concluded between the tsar and the Polish insurgents.[1] Palmerston wrote to Russell:

As things at present stand, your three points seem to be good landmarks for us, namely agreement with Austria, and of course with France as long as possible, the Treaty of Vienna and the Kingdom of Poland according to the limits established by that Treaty.[2]

On 6 May, the British government accordingly invited those of Austria and France to join it in recommending at St Petersburg the suspension of hostilities for one year.[3] The French government accepted the suggestion with alacrity.[4]

The British proposal placed the Austrian government in an embarrassing position. On 19 May a council of Ministers was held under the presidency of the emperor to discuss Austria's future policy. Rechberg declared that the internal state of the monarchy imperatively demanded the preservation of peace. Austria, therefore, could not make recommendations unacceptable to Russia since rejection might be used by Napoleon as a pretext for military action. On the other hand, Napoleon had threatened Austria with dire consequences if she should now separate herself from England and France. Rechberg recommended that a meeting of German princes should be called in co-operation with Prussia to work out a policy of German neutrality. The difficulties likely to be met with in Berlin, however must not be underrated. Schmerling, Rechberg's rival, declared that the restoration of Poland would involve the loss of Galicia without compensation. Austria must not allow her policy to be dictated exclusively by fear of France. Russia also could create serious difficulties.[5] Since Austria was threatened from both sides she must consult only her own interests. An attempt must be made to win the support of Germany. Rechberg interjected that the constellation of the Crimean War appeared

---

[1] Palmerston to Russell, 5 April 1863, PRO 30/22, 22. It is clear from the contents that the correct date is 5 May 1863.
[2] The same to the same, 5 May 1863, *ibid.*
[3] Russell to Cowley, 6 May 1863, no. 619, FO 27/1479 and Russell to Bloomfield, 6 May 1863, no. 92, FO 7/648.
[4] Cowley to Russell, private, 7, 12 and 15 May 1863, FO 519/230. In private, the French ambassador in London described the proposal as 'une idée fabuleuse' (Vitzthum, *op. cit.* p. 225). Bismarck described it as absurd (Bismarck to Goltz, telegram, 9 May 1863, *APP*, vol. iii, p. 547, n. 3). Rechberg 'hardly considered that your Lordship's last suggestions were serious' (Cowley to Russell, 12 May 1863, no. 566, confidential, RA H 51/23, copy).
[5] Gorchakov had already expressed his chagrin at Austria's association with England and France. He had explained to the Austrian chargé d'affaires that, had Austria abstained from this course, 'cela lui aurait paru le meilleur acheminement vers l'entente complète des deux Cours' (G. Thun to Rechberg, 19/7 April 1863, no. 12 A-D, HHSAPARRR, 1863, x, 49).

to have returned. A policy of neutrality would bring Austria into conflict with England and France. It might not prevent the eventual restoration of Poland. The emperor, after some further discussion, ruled that Austria must continue her policy of neutrality and try to strengthen it by a closer understanding with Prussia.[1]

Yet Austria was unable to break her ties with the west. On 10 May Rechberg had listed six points which he was willing to recommend at St Petersburg in conjunction with England and France.[2] Palmerston considered that Austria should, in addition, support his proposal for an armistice.[3] He was informed by Bloomfield that nothing would induce her to do so.[4]

V

French military action was now generally expected. Apponyi felt certain that Palmerston's diplomatic campaign would prove the prelude to war.[5] Rechberg feared that England and France would drag Austria into the conflict.[6] Bernstorff sent alarming reports to his government.[7] Bismarck himself began to consider war as the not improbable outcome.[8] On 27 May Napier warned Gorchakov:

> We were entering upon a new stage of the negotiation. I would ever deeply regret if anything I had said should in the least degree induce the Russian Government to count upon the indifference or neutrality of England in case more serious complications should arise from these discussions.

The Vice-Chancellor replied that this statement occasioned him no surprise:

> For his part he had, he must confess it with regret, never counted with confidence on the neutrality of England in case of a rupture in this cause. He feared that Her Majesty's Government would cast in its lot with that of France, to what extent or for what purpose he was unable to judge.[9]

Five days after this exchange, the tsar addressed a letter to his uncle the king of Prussia. It was impossible, he declared, to ignore how rapidly the situation was deteriorating. War was likely in August. Hostilities would start in the Baltic or on the Vistula and they might easily spread to the Rhine. In what circumstances, then, could Russia count on Prussia's

---

[1] For an account of the meeting cf. Engel-Jánosi, *op. cit.* pp. 102 ff. and H. Wereszycki, 'Great Britain and the Polish Question in 1863', *EHR*, L (January 1935), p. 85.

[2] Bloomfield to Russell, telegram, 10 May 1863, RA H 51/20.

[3] Memorandum by Palmerston, 15 May 1863, PRO 30/22, 22.

[4] Bloomfield to Russell, private, 4 June 1863, RA H 51/62, copy.

[5] Clarendon to Cowley, 3 June 1863, FO 519/179 and Vitzthum, *op. cit.* p. 228.

[6] Bloomfield to Russell, private, 4 June 1863, RA H 51/62, copy.

[7] Bernstorff to Bismarck, 11 May 1863, no. 185 *APP*, vol. III, p. 566.

[8] Oubril to Gorchakov, 17 May 1863, *ibid.* p. 574 n. 1.

[9] Napier to Russell, 27 May 1863, no. 372, RA H 51/44, copy.

active assistance?[1] Not until 17 June did King William reply to this letter. If, he observed, he gave Russia military support without previous agreement with Austria, he would, from the standpoint of the Confederation, commit an act of aggression. This would give Austria and the other members a pretext for disclaiming all obligation under the federal pact. Prussia would lose her right to invoke that pact wherever the war might spread.[2] In any case, the assistance of Prussia alone was of little benefit to Russia.[3] The advanced season of the year, moreover, made a French expedition unlikely. Should one take place none the less, Prussia would try to draw Austria into a policy of neutrality benevolent to Russia. This would be continued until he had succeeded in impressing upon his confederates convictions which were already his own.[4] The tsar replied to his uncle's exposition in a letter less cordial in tone than his earlier appeal. He merely adjured King William to spare no effort to detach Austria from England and France and draw her to the side of the partitioning powers.[5]

VI

In the meantime England, France and Austria had agreed to transmit separately to St Petersburg recommendations tending to the same end. During mid-June notes sent to their representatives in the Russian capital recommended with varying degrees of insistence the Six Points and the conclusion of an armistice. None of the governments entertained hopes of a favourable reply.[6] On 20 June, therefore, Drouyn proposed the signature of a diplomatic document defining the intentions of the three

[1] 'Je Vous demande la confidence du point de vue sous lequel Vous envisagez Vos devoirs et Vos intérêts, ceux de la Prusse et de l'Allemagne en face de cette éventualité.... Je sais que je puis compter sur Vous,—mais dans quelles événtualités et dans quelle mesure Vos intérêts Vous porteront-ils à un concours actif? Ce n'est point une ouverture diplomatique que je Vous addresse, c'est un appel que je fais à Votre loyale amitié' (Alexander II to William I, 20 May/1 June 1863, *APP*, vol. III, p. 597).

[2] 'Si, en suivant de prime abord les inspirations de mon cœur... je voulais, sans une entente préalable avec l'Autriche, Vous prêter un concours actif dès que la Russie serait attaquée, ce procédé constituant au point de vue fédéral une aggression dirigée par la Prusse contre une puissance étrangère, fournirait à l'Autriche et à la Confédération un prétexte spécieux pour se soustraire à toute obligation découlant du pacte fédéral et me priverait du droit d'exiger l'assistance de mes confédérés, quel que fût après le théatre de la guerre' (William I to Alexander II [17 June 1863], *ibid*. pp. 626ff.).

[3] 'En même temps il est difficile de dire si la co-opération de la Prusse seule serait de nature à améliorer les chances d'une guerre contre la France. Sans présager l'influence que l'entrée en guerre de la Prusse pourrait avoir sur les déterminations de l'Angleterre et de l'Autriche, la tâche de la France même devenait plus facile, si au lieu de s'attaquer à des difficultés que lui oppose la situation de la Russie, l'aggression pouvait se diriger dès abord contre mes provinces limitrophes de la France' (*ibid*.).

[4] '...je prendais pour tâche de disposer l'Autriche et l'Allemagne à une entente ayant pour but d'observer une neutralité bienveillante jusqu'au jour où je pourrai amener mes confédérés à la conviction qui dès aujourd'hui est la mienne' (*ibid*.).

[5] Alexander II to William I, 30 June/12 July 1863, *ibid*. p. 652.

[6] Russell to Palmerston, 10 June 1863, PRO 30/22, 22 and Cowley to Russell, 26 June 1863, confidential, no. 735, RA H 51/103, copy.

cabinets in the event of a Russian refusal or an inconclusive conference. Such an act would demonstrate

that the three Governments were quite resolved on their future policy—that while they desired the favourable termination of the Polish question by pacific means, they reserved to themselves, in case of the failure of diplomatic procedure, to have recourse to such other measures, as they might deem advisable.[1]

In conversation with Cowley, Drouyn openly admitted 'that the chance of war was not excluded from his thoughts; though his conviction was that in the present condition of Russia, war was all but impossible'.[2] Cowley felt convinced that, as in 1853, Napoleon meant to drag England into war.[3]

The British government rejected the French proposal.[4] On learning of this decision, Drouyn declared that the emperor's regret would equal his own. He had hoped to define the scope of the alliance. Such a course would have set limits to French acquisitions in the event of war. Now, in the case of the three powers 'admitting their helplessness and each acting within itself...he did not say it would be the case but it might happen that France would be agitated by other desires than those which impelled her now'.[5] Russell's reply defined, for the first time, the British attitude towards French military intervention.

I have to remark that it must not be supposed that in case France were singly to make war for Poland, Great Britain would admit her own helplessness and retire within herself. She would insist on certain conditions in favour of the integrity of Germany and against encroachments on the part of France, before she consented to be neutral.

This need not be said to Drouyn for the time being but a further point must be made clear to him forthwith:

It would be misleading the French government if we were to allow them to suppose that in the present state of things, and in the existing state of feeling and opinion in Parliament and in the Country, Her Majesty's Government would undertake, or would find support in a war against Russia for Poland, however great the sympathy and interest may be which are felt throughout the United Kingdom in favour of the Poles.[6]

On 5 July Cowley accordingly informed Drouyn that, whatever sympathy might be felt for the Poles in Great Britain, 'it would not induce the country to go to war with Russia'. Drouyn agreed with Cowley that without the assistance of Austria it would be difficult if not impossible to

---

[1] *Ibid.*   [2] *Ibid.*
[3] The same to the same, private, 23 June 1863, FO 519/230.
[4] Russell at once circulated the proposal to members of the cabinet dispersed on holiday. He intended, he said, to reject the proposal and asked those who agreed to sign their names. 'Nearly all, including Lord Palmerston, signed' (Russell to the Cabinet, 22 June 1863, PRO 30/22, 27; and Russell to the Queen, 27 June 1863, RA H 51/105).
[5] Cowley to Russell, 26 June 1863, no. 735, confidential, *ibid.* H 51/103, copy.
[6] Russell to Cowley 3 June (this should read July) 1863, FO 27/1480, no. 857, confidential.

go to the aid of the Poles. That either England or France should attempt to do so single-handed would be foolhardy (*insensé*). At the end of the interview Cowley felt able to assure Russell that the French government would now adopt 'whatever line of conduct may be determined on by that of Austria and Great Britain'.[1]

Napoleon could not run the risk of a single-handed war in Europe whilst still deeply involved in his Mexican adventure.[2] The British government, preoccupied with the American Civil War and concerned for the security of Germany more than the independence of Poland, was unwilling to translate diplomatic pressure into military and naval action. England for the second time during the Polish crisis had refused to follow the French lead to war. It was evident that the aims of the two governments conflicted and that Napoleon's ambitions on the Rhine stood in the way of wholehearted co-operation between them. British distrust was increased by Napoleon's evident desire for war; the French government learnt once again that the British alliance was a curb, not a partnership for action.

VII

Gorchakov's reply to the allied communications of June was negative. Russell proposed to end the exchange with a declaration reserving the rights of England and France as signatories of the treaty of Vienna.[3] The French government urged an identic note of the three powers but Palmerston was adamant in his opposition.[4] A continuation of the campaign could now only produce either war or further humiliation.[5] In the end, the cabinets of Paris, London and Vienna addressed to St Petersburg separate communications throwing on Russia the sole responsibility for prolonging the insurrection. In his reply, Gorchakov announced that he considered the discussion closed since, to his regret, it could not produce results.[6]

Gorchakov's rebuff put an end to the diplomatic campaign of the western powers. It did not, however, end either the Polish insurrection or Napoleon's thirst for action. Whilst diplomatic tension continued, complications in the Elbe Duchies helped to usher in a new phase in the national reorganization of Europe.

[1] Cowley to Russell, 6 July 1863, no. 786, confidential, RA H 51/115, copy.
[2] Cowley to Hudson 12 May 1863, FO 519/230 and Goltz to Bismarck, 28 April 1863, no. 130, most confidential, *APP*, vol. III, p. 524; cf. also Vitzthum, *op. cit.* p. 227.
[3] Russell to Cowley, 18 July 1863, PRO 30/22, 105.
[4] Palmerston to Russell, 30 July 1863, PRO 30/22, 22.
[5] The same to the same, 3 August 1863, *ibid.*
[6] Friese, *op. cit.* p. 330.

CHAPTER 5

THE REVIVAL OF THE GERMAN QUESTION AND THE END OF THE ANGLO-FRENCH ALLIANCE, 1863

I N 1848 the question of Poland had, for a time, been linked with that of Germany. Fifteen years later, a new phase of the Polish national struggle coincided once again with an acute crisis in German affairs. In each case, it was the Polish question which gave to German developments much of their European significance. Events in Poland drew attention to the strategic importance of Germany. As long as the Germanic Confederation formed a firm defensive union, France was debarred from active intervention in Poland. A strong Germany, therefore, would effectively protect Russian interests. In a similar manner, a united Germany would promote British objects in the Low Countries. Whilst the Confederation maintained its defensive strength, Napoleon was unlikely to seek adventures on the Rhine or in Belgium. Germany, therefore, seemed destined to protect both Russian interests in Poland and British interests in Belgium. Even if British and Russian policies diverged in the Polish question, the two countries yet had a common stake in Germany's defensive unity. In St Petersburg as in London any weakening of Germany was feared as the prelude to French aggression. As long therefore, as Napoleon continued to be regarded as the principal threat to European peace, British and Russian policies in the German question were likely to follow a parallel course. Both would be favourable to any movement for German consolidation.

I

By the end of 1862 negotiations for the reorganization of Germany which had been going on for over a year, had finally ended in deadlock. A rupture between Austria and Prussia seemed imminent. Bismarck warned Buchanan 'that war within a year or two might be considered certain'.[1]

---

[1] Buchanan had asked Bismarck for an assurance that the bitter exchanges between the cabinets of Berlin and Vienna would not be followed immediately by war. Bismarck replied: 'Immediately—not, at all events Prussia will not provoke war but it was impossible that Austria and Prussia could long remain at peace when their conflicting interests could no longer be treated judicially in the Diet [Prussia was about to withdraw from the Diet in protest against an Austrian proposal for federal reform] and that war within a year or two might be considered certain' (Buchanan to Russell, 3 January 1863, no. 7, RA I 40/6, copy).

The king of Prussia declared that the causes of misunderstanding could not be removed 'until Austria has convinced herself that Prussia is her equal as a European Power and her superior as a German one and can never be forced to hold a subordinate position in the Confederation'.[1] Rechberg in his turn complained that: 'By opposing every measure of reform by which the existing federal institutions might be maintained or improved, Prussia looks to putting forward her own supremacy as the only remedy for an intolerable state of things.'[2] Russell was alarmed: 'Germany in the centre of Europe, ought to be a solid security for European peace and a valuable element in European civilization.'[3] He expressed a hope that the two German powers would by their prudence avert from Europe what would be 'a scandal, a danger and a misfortune'.[4] He also warned the king of Prussia that if he were to rely on the support of France, he would have to pay the price in German territory.[5] Rechberg in his turn was admonished to allow Prussia a position in the Confederation more suitable to her importance, dignity and future welfare than that she now occupied.[6] Prussia should state frankly what she required and Austria should in a spirit of liberality and conciliation declare what she was willing to concede.[7] As a preliminary, she should abandon her recent proposals to the Diet which had given offence in Berlin.[8]

The efforts of Russian diplomacy went parallel with those of Russell and Palmerston. In March, Gorchakov told the Austrian minister that he had repeatedly advised Bismarck to adopt a more conciliatory attitude.[9] The tsar himself, when receiving Thun in a farewell audience, made an urgent plea for an improvement in Austro-Prussian relations. He alluded to the pressing representations to this effect which his government had made in Berlin.[10] The cabinet of St Petersburg observed with pleasure any indication that Bismarck had taken its advice.[11] There prevailed in the Russian capital a profound conviction that the salvation of conserva-

---

[1] The same to the same, 28 January 1863, no. 57, *ibid.* I 40/28, copy.
[2] Russell to Bloomfield, 14 January 1863, *ibid.* I 40/16, draft.
[3] *Ibid.*
[4] *Ibid.*
[5] Russell to Buchanan, 6 January 1863, *ibid.* I 40/8, draft.
[6] Russell to Bloomfield, 14 January 1863, *ibid.* I 40/16, draft.
[7] *Ibid.*
[8] The same to the same, telegram, 6 January 1863, *ibid.* I 40/9.
[9] Thun to Rechberg, 21/9 March 1863, 7F, HHSAPARRR, 1863, x 49.
[10] 'L'Empereur m'a assuré qu'il mettait le plus grand prix à ce que les relations entre l'Autriche et la Prusse reprennent un caractère du plus franc accord, ce qu'il regarde comme une nécessité et en même temps comme la garantie la plus sûre pour la tranquillité et le bienêtre [*sic*] du monde civilisé. Aussi avait-il fait addresser à ce sujet les exhortations les plus pressantes à Berlin et il était heureux de voir par la réponse qu'il en a reçue que Mr de Bismarck paraîssait lui-même sentir cette nécessité et qu'il semblait dans les derniers temps revenir sur les extravagances de sa politique' (the same to the same, 22/10 March 1863, no. 8, *ibid.*).
[11] Guido Thun to Rechberg, 28/16 April 1863, no. 14 A-B, *ibid.*

tive Europe depended on an intimate alliance of the two Germanic powers.[1]

During the spring and summer of 1863 whilst European diplomacy was preoccupied with the affairs of Poland, Austro-Prussian tension relaxed. As soon, however, as it had become tolerably clear that Napoleon would not move against Russia during 1863, the Austrian government returned to the attack.[2] It invited the German princes to meet the Austrian emperor at Frankfurt to discuss federal reform. William I declared that by this act Austria had raised a 'German question' by the side of the Polish one.

II

On 10 August the Austrian chargé d'affaires informed Gorchakov of the Austrian invitation to the German princes. The Vice-Chancellor observed that anything tending to strengthen Germany would give pleasure to the tsar. However, the Austrian initiative would have stood a better chance of success if the invitations had been issued jointly with Prussia.[3] Shortly afterwards, Gorchakov learnt that William I refused to attend the meeting. Oubril, in reporting the fact, expressed regret at this decision. It would, he considered, have been to Russia's interest that the western powers should see Germany strong and united. The absence of Prussia, on the contrary, would advertise the profound division of the German body politic. Austria and Prussia shared the blame for the impasse. The former was, perhaps, the greater culprit for believing that this hasty measure could lead to serious results. If a salutary reform of German institutions was ever to be achieved without external intervention, it could come about only through a sincere understanding of Austria and Prussia.[4]

In face of the Austrian initiative Bismarck—following in the footsteps of Frederick-William IV—appealed to the tsar for support. The way for this appeal was prepared in a letter to Alexander II which Bismarck drafted for King William. The king began by reassuring his nephew about the Polish question. Rechberg and Francis-Joseph, he wrote, had informed him, that Austria would tolerate neither the alienation of a single

---

[1] 'Une alliance intime entre l'Autriche et la Prusse est toujours préconisée dans les cercles de la Cour, qui y voient le salut de l'Europe conservatrice et reviennent de jour en jour d'avantage de l'aveuglement qui leur aurait fait considérer l'Autriche comme une Puissance dont l'alliance n'importait pas à la Russie' (the same to the same, 5 May/23 April 1863, no. 16, réservée, *ibid.*).

[2] The Austrian initiative was the work of Schmerling who considered that Prussia's internal difficulties offered a unique opportunity for reasserting Austrian leadership in Germany. Rechberg, the 'dualist' opposed Schmerling's policy and unsuccessfully offered his resignation to the emperor (Engel-Jánosi, *op. cit.* p. 111). Schmerling's proceedings bear a curious resemblance to those of Schwarzenberg before Olmütz. This time, however, the outcome was very different: an Olmütz in reverse.

[3] Guido Thun to Rechberg, 15/3 August 1863, no. 31 A, HHSAPARRR, 1863, x 49.

[4] Oubril to Gorchakov, 31 July/12 August 1863, *APP, loc. cit.* pp. 717ff. The tsar, in a marginal note, approved of Oubril's conclusions (*ibid.*).

village in Galicia or Posen, nor yet the establishment of an independent Poland.[1] He had, however, declined to discuss with Russia and Prussia the future organization of Poland. In his eagerness to conciliate the western powers he had indeed publicly repudiated the suggestion. Austria was acting under the influence of fear but the calmer attitude now prevailing in London could not fail to influence her policy. All hope, therefore, of leading her back into the conservative fold need not yet be abandoned. If the cabinets of St Petersburg and Berlin continued to work together patiently, they would succeed in either averting war or in renewing their traditional alliance.[2] Prussia must, however, complain strongly of the Austrian invitation to the German princes. This had compelled her to take military precautions which would be explained in detail by the king's personal military attaché.[3]

Late in August, whilst the German princes were deliberating at Frankfurt, the king of Prussia accompanied by Bismarck paid a flying visit to Queen Victoria at Coburg. To the Queen's wish that Austria and Prussia should work together, he replied that this had been made impossible for him by Austria and proceeded to relate in detail what had passed between him and Francis-Joseph at Gastein. The Queen, who was shortly to meet the Austrian emperor, promised to speak to him strongly in favour of full equality for Prussia in federal affairs. King William dwelt on Austria's efforts to increase the power of the Catholic Church,[4] declared that England and Prussia 'being the two great Protestant powers' should keep well together; and ended by appealing for the Queen's support: 'I recommend my interests to your care, to which I replied, he might rely upon me with certainty.'[5] During the visit, Bismarck told Granville that he 'could anticipate nothing but evil from the step which had been taken; one of the most probable results of which would be civil war within six months'. When Granville asked how there could be war, Bismarck talked of the 'pride and sensitiveness of the Prussian people', remarked that 'honour was dearer than life' and quoted the German saying that 'an end with terror is better than terror without end'. Germany would 'drift' into a war which, to him at least, would be a relief rather than otherwise.[6]

Three days later, the Queen met Francis-Joseph. The emperor agreed on the need for German unity in the face of Napoleon but rejected the sug-

---

[1] '...que l'Autriche n'admettrait ni l'aliénation d'un village de la Galicie ou de la Posnanie, ni l'établissement d'une Pologne indépendante' (William I to Alexander II, 12 August 1863, *ibid.* pp. 714 ff.).

[2] '...nous réussirions, soit à maintenir la paix, soit à retrouver en cas de guerre la grande alliance de nos pères' (*ibid.*).　　　　　　　　　　　　　　　　[3] *Ibid.*

[4] '...that swarms of Priests had arrived in the neighbourhood of Frankfurt, trying to influence the lower orders in every direction in favour of Austria' (memorandum by the Queen, 31 August 1863, RA I 40/45, copy).　　　　　　　　[5] *Ibid.*

[6] Memorandum by Granville, 31 August 1863, *ibid.* I 40/43.

gestion that the presidency of the reformed Confederation should alternate between Austria and Prussia. He was reluctant, he declared, to abandon a hereditary prerogative.[1] The Queen's well-meant advice in fact could do little to avert a renewed struggle for supremacy in Germany.

The British government, moreover, was reluctant to take sides in a dispute which was an internal affair of the Germanic Confederation. When on 23 September Russell finally announced the British view,[2] his opinions no longer mattered. Yet another attempt to reorganize the Confederation had been frustrated by the inability of the Germans to agree among themselves.[3]

III

At the beginning of September, Bismarck returned to Berlin[4] enraged at the Austrian proceedings.[5] In conversation with Oubril he observed that Russia and Prussia combined could easily get the better of Austria ('nous pouvions facilement avoir raison de l'Autriche'). Russia must make military preparations. Prussia within four weeks could put 200,000 men into the field. They should act like Frederick the Great in 1756 and strike a sudden and unexpected blow at an unprepared opponent.[6]

The Russian government, however, had decided to adopt in the German conflict an attitude of neutrality and abstention. The tsar was of opinion that the dispute would affect Russia only if it led to a general conflagration.[7] Gorchakov inserted in the official *Journal de St Pétersbourg* a

---

[1] 'This was a great difficulty, the Emperor answered: Austria always had had the presidency and it was quite a new pretension of Prussia to have it also and in Austria they would dislike extremely its being given up' (memorandum by the Queen, 3 September 1863, *ibid.* I 40/52, copy). [2] Russell to Buchanan, 23 September 1863, *ibid.* I 40/79, draft.

[3] Clarendon, who had been sent by Russell to watch the proceedings in Frankfurt, had commented on 'the difficulty of amalgamating so many petty concerts and interests, and making them work harmoniously with the two great and the gradually lessening Powers'. 'In fact they have harnessed together a team of 30 horses—two great dray horses, who must be at wheel, and who are always kicking and biting at each other—then a lot of half-bred shambling vicious beasts of different sizes, and a dozen Shetland Ponies of the smallest dimensions—and how such a team is to be made to look well, or draw evenly, and to have its due share of work assigned to each, with a lumbering coach in a heavy road—is likely to puzzle the raw German Coachmen and Helpers who have undertaken the job' (Clarendon to ?, 27 August 1863, *ibid.* I 40/32, extract, copy).

[4] He had accompanied the king of Prussia to Gastein, Baden-Baden and Coburg.

[5] Oubril reported to Gorchakov on Bismarck's state of mind. '"Dites au Prince", m'a-t-il dit entre autres avant-hier, "que Vous m'avez trouvé froid et calme. En effet, *je rage avec calme*".—Son indignation contre l'Autriche n'a pas de bornes' (Oubril to Gorchakov, private, 3/15 September 1863, secret, *APP, loc. cit.* pp. 791ff.).

[6] 'Mais mon avis serait dans ce cas de procéder comme Frédéric le Grand en 1756, c'est à dire d'agir avec célérité et de frapper un coup avant que l'on ait le temps à Vienne de se prémunir contre un pareil danger' (the same to the same, private, 22 August/3 September 1863, *ibid.* pp. 758ff.). Bismarck complacently quoted the phrase he had recently used to the Saxon Minister Beust: 'Wenn es sich um Niederträchtigkeit handelt, kann der Franz viel—aber der Karl noch mehr' (*ibid.*).

[7] 'Pour nous le différend allemand ne nous intéresse que s'il avait pour résultat une conflagration générale' (tsar's comment on Oubril to Gorchakov, private, 22 August/3 September 1863, most confidential, *ibid.* pp. 760ff.).

declaration favourable to the unity and strength of Germany which was widely considered as approving the Austrian proceedings.[1] Warlike action against Austria the Russian government was unwilling to contemplate. Gorchakov told Oubril that in June Prussia had promised only neutrality in what would have been a purely defensive war against France. Russia would not now, for Prussia's sake, join in a war of aggression against Austria.[2]

On 15 September Bismarck told Oubril that he regarded the Austrian proceedings at Frankfurt as a premeditated attempt to establish Austrian hegemony in Germany. Prussia was determined to avoid a new Olmütz and had made military preparations. Her military leaders considered that she could begin operations against Austria in the spring with certain chance of success. Oubril rejoined that whilst the Prussian government was right in dissociating itself from the proceedings at Frankfurt, it would hardly be justified in resorting to force. A war without allies, as Russia had recently learnt, could be a dangerous matter. The King, moreover, would scarcely wish to push matters to extremes.[3] Bismarck replied that the King was a soldier. Alliances could and would be found.[4] He had always counted on Russia and was the standard bearer of the Russian alliance. If his hopes were disappointed, he would make room for a liberal and even a radical ministry.[5] Gorchakov must understand that neutrality in these conditions was impossible.[6] What advantage would Russia gain from

---

[1] 'En second lieu, notre déclaration favorable aux tendances unitaires de l'Allemagne, a été considérée ici comme un encouragement que nous accordions à la politique allemande de l'Autriche, hostile à la Prusse. "Inde ira".' The representatives of the German states in Berlin had interpreted the Russian declaration in a similar sense. Oubril had explained that it did not refer to the meeting at Frankfurt but to the general trend in favour of German unity (Oubril to Gorchakov, private, 3/15 September 1863, secret, *ibid.* pp. 791 ff.).

[2] Gorchakov to Oubril, quoted in Lord, *loc. cit.* p. 47. Owing to Lord's unfortunate practice of adopting a system of collective references, Gorchakov's remarks may occur in Gorchakov to Oubril 26 August/7 September, 11/23 September or 16/28 September 1863 (*ibid.*).

[3] This reply obtained the full approval of the tsar (marginal comment on Oubril to Gorchakov, 3/15 September 1863, no. 297 most confidential, *APP, loc. cit.* pp. 786 ff.).

[4] Bismarck declared: 'On en trouve, nous en trouverons, dûssions nous nous allier au Diable.' This remark set Oubril speculating on the identity of this devil. Was it Napoleon, Victor-Emmanuel or Mazzini? Interpreting a further remark made by Bismarck, Oubril concluded that Hell was situated on the Seine (the same to the same, private, 3/15 September 1863, secret, *ibid.* pp. 791 ff.). The argument impressed Oubril. It could not but influence the tsar.

[5] '"...Moi-même, je suis ici le représentant de l'alliance Russe—c'est mon drapeau; je serais le premier à céder le pas à un ministère libéral, avancé même, si nous devions faire la triste expérience de nous être trompés sur vous. Voyez de Votre côté si cela peut Vous convenir..."' (the same to the same, 3/15 September 1863, no. 297, most confidential, *ibid.* pp. 786 ff.).

[6] Bismarck asked Oubril to quote to Gorchakov a German ditty:

> Zum hassen oder lieben
> Ist alle Welt getrieben.
> Der Teufel ist neutral

(the same to the same, private, 3/15 September 1863, secret, *ibid.* pp. 791 ff.).

Prussia's disappearance from the map of Europe?[1] To Oubril's remark that Russia's German policy was based on the fear of French intervention, Bismarck replied that the prospect held no terrors for him. Compensation might be found to keep France quiet. For Prussia the line of the Weser was more important than that of the Rhine.[2] A war with Austria would ease the internal situation of the Prussian government.[3] After three months of polemics, the country would march against Austria as one man. What he asked for was Russian pressure at Vienna and on the frontiers to paralyse the actions of the Austrian government.[4]

Oubril expressed alarm at Bismarck's apparent conviction that war would ease the internal problems of the Prussian government.[5] He could well understand, he wrote, that it was not to the interest of Russia to push Bismarck into warlike adventures; but could the Russian government refuse to aid him in his difficulties? Were Prussia to be destroyed by her enemies, the turn of Russia would follow.[6] The attitude now adopted by the Russian government would influence profoundly not only Bismarck's personal position but relations between the two countries. Prussia had assisted Russia to the best of her ability in the Crimean War and during the recent complications in Poland; she now wished to draw on the credit which she believed herself to have accumulated.[7] Bismarck was a dangerous man and one who would stop at nothing but he was the Prussian statesman most devoted to the interests of Russia. Apart from him, Russia would find in the Polish question only lukewarm and timid friends.[8]

---

[1] 'Quel avantage auriez-Vous à laisser la Prusse disparaître de la Carte et nous sommes bien décidés à ne pas subir l'affront qui vient de nous être fait, et qui met notre existence en question' (the same to the same, 3/15 September 1863, no. 297, most confidential, *ibid.* pp. 786ff.).

[2] 'Eh bien...laissez-le s'y ingérer, cela ne nous effraye pas. C'est une chance à courir. N'y a-t-il pas d'ailleurs moyens de désintéresser la France? Il faut se bien rendre compte d'une chose, *c'est que la ligne du Weser est plus important pour nous que celle du Rhin.* Voilà la question en deux mots' (*ibid.*).

[3] 'Du reste une guerre ne pourrait que nous faciliter la situation intérieure. Je l'accepterais donc sans hésitations et sans craintes' (*ibid.*).

[4] 'Mr de Bismarck désire...une attitude prononcée, un langage sévère à Vienne' (*ibid.*). 'Mais entre une guerre et des démonstrations hostiles, destinées à paralyser une partie des forces de l'Autriche, il y a une distance énorme. C'est là évidemment ce que Bismarck voudrait obtenir de nous' (the same to the same, private, 3/15 September 1863, secret, *ibid.* pp. 791ff.).

[5] '...la conviction arrêtée chez Bismarck qu'une guerre faciliterait et allèguerait la position du Gouvernement du Roi à l'intérieur...' (the same to the same, 3/15 September 1863, no. 297, most confidential, *ibid.* pp. 786ff.).

[6] 'Sûr de notre abstention, en cas de complications, on passerait sur le corps de la Prusse écrasée pour diriger tous les efforts contre la Russie rendue à son complexe [*sic*] isolement' (*ibid.*).

[7] 'Après nous avoir assisté de son mieux pendant la guerre de Crimée et durant les récentes complications polonaises, la Prusse...croit avoir dépensé en notre faveur un capital dont elle voudrait toucher aujourd'hui les intérêts' (*ibid.*).

[8] 'Celui des hommes politiques de la Prusse qui nous est le plus dévoué...' (the same to the same, private, 3/15 September 1863, secret, *ibid.* pp. 791ff.). 'En dehors de son individualité...nous ne rencontrerions dans les affaires de Pologne, que des amis plutôt tièdes et

It was a difficult decision to make, but Bismarck, directed and restrained by Russia, appeared to be the lesser evil; such a policy, however, was possible only if the Russian government did not abandon him in Germany.[1] Bismarck's threats, supported by the reflections of Oubril, could not fail to create an impression. The tsar and Gorchakov abandoned their neutral position. They now explained in Vienna and Berlin that they disapproved of proceedings which had sown disunion in Germany instead of promoting unity in the face of France.[2] Thun noted with regret that the failure of Austria's efforts was greeted with satisfaction in the Russian capital.[3]

At the same time the tsar did everything in his power to discourage military adventures. On 21 September, he told the Prussian military attaché that Oubril had inquired on Bismarck's behalf whether Prussia could count on Russian help in a possible war with Austria. Although he supported Prussia in the German question, he was too preoccupied with Poland to give her military assistance. He would, however, spare no pains to 'bring the Austrians to their senses'.[4] On receiving this reply Bismarck telegraphed that his alleged inquiry had been a misunderstanding. All he had asked was that the tsar should admonish Austria to follow a moderate course. She should be given to understand that Russia in her own interest would not permit a weakening of Prussia. A letter from the tsar to the king of Prussia that Russia would be *unable* to help Prussia, would be *most* undesirable.[5] The tsar replied that he would regard the

embarrassants.' This, Oubril added, included both Manteuffel and Goltz, Bismarck's possible successors (the same to the same, 3/15 September 1863, no. 297, most confidential, *ibid.* pp. 786ff.).

[1] '...Bismarck dirigé et enrayé par nous me semble préférable; mais encore faut-il alors ne point l'abandonner sur le terrain allemand' (*ibid.*).

[2] Loën to Bismarck, telegram, 21 September 1863, *ibid.* p. 208; the same to William I, 12/24 September 1863, *ibid.* p. 809. Gorchakov told Redern: 'Ich bedaure aufrichtigst das unüberlegte Vorgehen Oesterreichs im Frankfurter Fürstentage. Statt Einigkeit hat man Uneinigkeit hervorgerufen. Auch habe ich nicht ermangelt, mich darüber in Wien auszusprechen, wo man zu glauben schien, dass Russland dem Wiener Reformprojekt seinen Beifall schenke. Ich habe dem Grafen Rechberg diesen Irrtum benommen und mich gegen ihn dahin erklärt, dass das Wohl und die Kräftigung Deutschlands nur aus dem Einverständnis zwischen Oesterreich und Preussen hervorgehen könne' (Redern to Bismark, 2 October 1863, no. 120, *ibid.* p. 809 n. 1.).

[3] Guido Thun reported: 'on n'a qu'à jeter un regard dans les journaux russes plus qu'inspirés par le Gouvernement, on n'a qu'à causer un instant avec le Vice-Chancelier ou un de ses nombreux acolytes pour reconnaître la satisfaction mal déguisée qu'on éprouve à St Pétersbourg de voir nos efforts paralysés par la Prusse dont la politique ne cesse d'obtenir ce qu'on appelle ici—le suffrage universel' (Guido Thun to Rechberg, 30/18 September 1863, no. 37 B, réservée, HHSAPARRR, 1863, X 49).

[4] 'Wenngleich der Kaiser ganz zu Preussen hält und in der Deutschen Frage Oesterreich Unrecht gibt, so ist er gegenwärtig zu sehr in Polen beschäftigt, um Preussen militärischen Beistand leisten zu können; er wird aber sonst alles tun, um Oesterreich zur Einsicht zu bringen...' (Loën to Bismarck, telegram, 21 September 1863, *APP, loc. cit.* p. 802).

[5] '...Ein Schreiben des Kaisers an den König, das Russland uns in solchem durchaus nicht naheliegenden Falle nicht helfen *könne*, würde ich für *sehr* unerwünscht halten' (Bismarck to Loën, telegram, 22 September 1863, *ibid.* p. 804). Bismarck spoke to Oubril

inquiry as *non avenu*, and would write to the king in the sense desired by Bismarck.[1]

In his letter to the king, the tsar observed that he had noted with profound regret the disagreements between Prussia and Austria. In the immediate dispute, his sympathies were with Prussia. By the very nature of things, no serious reform could take place in Germany without her concurrence.[2] The Austrian attempt, therefore, was doomed to failure and the cabinet of Vienna would be forced to return to a saner policy. He sincerely desired the strength and unity of Germany—but these could be based only on respect for existing rights including those of Prussia.[3] Support for these rights was a tradition of his policy. Without departing from the respect which he had consistently shown for the independence of the Germanic Confederation, he would use all the moral influence at his command to resolve the present differences.[4] He hoped that the king of Prussia in his turn would contribute towards an understanding without which there would be serious dangers for the Confederation and for Europe.[5]

In intimate conversation with Loën, Alexander discussed the European aspect of the German question. A rupture between Prussia and Austria he observed, would be a disaster not only for Germany but for the whole of Europe. Russia needed peace for her internal development and would be unable to intervene. She was tied down in Poland to such an extent that she could throw little weight even into the scales of diplomacy. In the circumstances, the decision might easily fall into the hands of Napoleon. In any case he could not approve of Prussia's present attitude towards France.[6]

of the remark in Loën's report motivating Russia's abstention with the situation in Poland. 'Ce passage produirait à son avis, la plus pénible impression sur l'esprit du Roi, en venant à l'appui de l'opinion des personnes qui ne cessent de représenter à Sa Majesté une alliance avec la Russie comme peu productive pour la Prusse' (Oubril to Gorchakov, 11/23 September 1863, no. 301, confidential, *ibid.* pp. 807 ff.).

[1] Loën to Bismarck, telegram, 23 September 1863, *ibid.* p. 804.

[2] 'La force des choses ne permet pas qu'aucune réforme sérieuse puisse avoir lieu en Allemagne sans l'assentiment de la Prusse' (Alexander II to William I, 11/23 September 1863, *ibid.* pp. 805 ff.).

[3] '...je désire sincèrement la force et l'union de l'Allemagne. Elles ne peuvent se fonder que sur la base du respect de tous les droits, de toutes les positions acquises et en particulier celle de la Prusse, dont le maintien est une de nos traditions en même temps qu'un de mes intérêts personnels les plus chers' (*ibid.*).

[4] '...Vous pouvez être certain que sans m'écarter du respect que j'ai toujours professé pour l'indépendance de la Confédération Germanique, j'emploierai avec un zèle chaleureux toute l'influence morale dont je puis disposer pour concilier les dissentiments actuels' (*ibid.*).

[5] He hoped the king would contribute 'à ramener une entente hors de laquelle je ne vois que dangers sérieux pour la Confédération et pour l'Europe' (*ibid.*).

[6] '...Dabei verhehlte er jedoch nicht, dass er den Ausbruch des Krieges zwischen beiden Staaten als ein grosses Unglück betrachte, nicht nur für Deutschland allein, sondern für die Machtstellung der europäischen Staaten überhaupt. Russland bedürfe seiner inneren Ausbildung wegen durchaus des Friedens, ausserdem sei es durch die Revolution in Polen so gebunden, dass es kein Gewicht in die Wagschale legen könne, die also der Willkür Frank-

The Russian refusal had a sobering effect on Bismarck.[1] By the beginning of October, he was reported to be taking a calmer view of the situation.[2] The Austrian plans were stagnating and he felt that in any case five or six months must now elapse before action could be thought of.[3] The German question—brought to boiling point by Austria's precipitate action—was once again in abeyance. There now existed, however, a real danger that during 1864 the two German powers might come to blows about their respective positions in Germany. Together with the prospect that in the spring Napoleon might attempt a landing in the Baltic, this created an atmosphere of general insecurity and tension.

IV

Anxiety was increased by the evident restlessness of Napoleon. The unsuccessful diplomatic campaign on behalf of the Polish insurgents had left the emperor in a mood of irritation and resentment. None of the grandiose schemes confided to Metternich in February had prospered. His efforts to help the Poles had proved unavailing. He had been severely snubbed by the Russian government. Indeed, a serious estrangement had arisen between Paris and St Petersburg, which was attributed by Napoleon largely to British machinations. England had first encouraged his anti-Russian policy and had ended by 'leaving him in the lurch'. Austria also had proved an unsatisfactory partner and, by her failure to give energetic support to his diplomacy, had helped to bring about his discomfiture.

To restore his damaged prestige, destroy the treaties of 1815 and avenge himself on Austria, Napoleon decided to convoke a congress of the powers. On 4 November he invited the rulers of the principal states to discuss in a congress all questions threatening to disturb the peace of Europe. On the following day he publicly declared that the treaties of 1815 had been so often disregarded that they had, to all intents and purposes, ceased to exist. It had therefore become necessary to review them. Cowley wrote to Russell: 'A Congress or War! Such appears to be the alternative posed by the Emperor's speech. So at least it is understood by the public.'[4]

Russell's first reaction to the proposal was not unfavourable. The question, he thought, required long and careful deliberation. The wishes

---

reichs anheim falle. Dabei äusserte S. M. der Kaiser, er könne mir nicht verschweigen, dass ihm die Haltung Preussens Napoleon gegenüber jetzt wenig gefalle...' (Loën to William I, 12/24 September 1863, *ibid.* p. 809, extract).

[1] Oubril reported to Gorchakov: 'Le télégramme du Colonel Loën a produit...sur lui [Bismarck] l'effet déprimant auquel il fallait s'attendre. Un encouragement de notre part l'aurait jeté dans les aventures les plus hasardées. Un avertissement froid et loyal devait le ramener à des appréciations plus calmes et plus saines' (Oubril to Gorchakov, 11/23 September 1863, no. 301, confidential, *ibid.* pp. 807ff.).

[2] Mohrenheim to Gorchakov, 26 September/8 October 1863, no. 309 most confidential, *ibid.* IV, pp. 60ff.

[3] Oubril to Gorchakov, 11/23 September 1863, no. 301, confidential, *ibid.* III, pp. 807ff.

[4] Cowley to Russell, private, 5 November 1863, RA J 80/7, copy.

of France must 'form an element in the solution'.[1] The Austrian government, on the other hand, was gravely embarrassed by the French proposals.[2] Rechberg expressed the fear that a Congress would lead to general war.[3] In reply to an Austrian inquiry, Russell declared that the reply to Napoleon 'should not be an abrupt refusal'.[4] However, before a congress was accepted, there must be some preliminary understanding between England, Austria and France.

...as Austria, France and Great Britain had hitherto acted in concert on the question of Poland, it seemed to me the most expedient course that Austria and Great Britain should not assent to the proposed Congress unless they could come to a previous understanding with France—both as to the subjects to be treated in the Congress and on the course to be taken finally by the three Powers.[5]

The proposal did not commend itself to Rechberg who feared, not without some reason, that Russell's object was still the independence of Poland.[6] On 10 November the British cabinet decided to inquire in Paris about the questions to be discussed and the powers to be exercised by the congress.[7]

Gorchakov had quickly sensed in Napoleon's proposal an opportunity for destroying the remnants of the Franco-British alliance, isolating France and drawing England into the Russo-Prussian camp. He therefore urged Russell to reject the French proposal: 'Her Majesty's Government being in a more independent position than that of Austria ought to take the initiative and state their resolution without hesitation.' If anyone 'ought to bell the cat (attacher le grelot) the office belonged peculiarly to Her Majesty's Government'. Should the other powers accept the invitation, he would do the same with some conditions and restrictions. He had informed the Austrian government that it should be firm and stand by its own interests, which were 'not inconsistent with those of Russia'. He proposed a frank and confidential exchange of opinions with the British government and asked for an early expression of Russell's views. If there was to be a congress, he did not 'as at present minded' see 'any reason for bringing the state of the East under review'.[8]

The king of Prussia hit on the expedient of accepting the principle of

---

[1] Russell to Cowley, telegram, 7 November 1863, *ibid.* J 80/9.

[2] 'The position of Austria is terrible. Acquiescence implies the loss of Galicia and perhaps Venetia, refusal may induce the Emperor aided by the Italians, to try if he cannot reach Poland through Austria' (Cowley to Russell, private, 8 November 1863, *ibid.* J 80/19).

[3] Bloomfield to Russell, telegram, 8 November 1863, *ibid.* J 80/12.

[4] Russell to the Queen, 9 November 1863, *ibid.* J 80/22.

[5] Russell to Bloomfield, November 1863, *ibid.* J 80/27, draft.

[6] Bloomfield to Russell, telegram, 9 November 1863, *ibid.* J 80/24.

[7] Russell to the Queen, 10 November 1863, *ibid.* J 80/35, draft. The Cabinet strongly reaffirmed the validity of the treaties of 1815. 'It is the conviction of Her Majesty's Government that the main provisions of the Treaty of 1815 are in full force, that the greater number of those provisions have not been in any way disturbed, and that on those foundations rests the balance of power in Europe' (Russell to Cowley, November 1863, *ibid.* J 80/35, draft).

[8] Napier to Russell, 9 November 1863, no. 692, confidential, *ibid.* J 80/23, copy; cf. also the same to the same, telegram, 10 November 1863, *ibid.* J 80/27.

a congress whilst recommending caution in its application. If some of the powers refused to attend, a congress would increase rather than diminish disunion.[1] Bismarck expressed approval of Russell's despatch, requested a copy, and declared that his own reply would follow similar lines. Prussia would insist on the need for unanimity in the acceptance of resolutions. The tsar would reply in the same sense. He hoped that the accord of the five great powers might be preserved. That of the four invited powers was necessary to peace. He would, therefore, follow the lead of England and Russia as long as they acted together.[2] Austria, Russia and Prussia, therefore, although for different reasons, awaited a British lead. None would accept responsibility for killing Napoleon's scheme.[3]

Napoleon, aware that the British attitude would be of decisive importance, expressed to Cowley his readiness to defer, in all matters of detail, to the wishes of the British government.

The emperor adheres to his proposal and states his readiness to come to an understanding with Her Majesty's Government as to the questions to be discussed, observing that if England and France were agreed, it was probable that the other powers would follow in their wake. The only questions he alluded to were the Polish and Italian, but without any definite notion what should or could be done.[4]

In reply to the British inquiry, Drouyn had already suggested that there were four subjects which the congress might discuss: relations between Germany and Denmark, the state of Poland, the Italian question including the problems of Venetia and Rome, and lastly the state of the Danubian Principalities.[5] The French government was entirely disinterested. It was displeased at the British attitude in the Polish question but could not act alone on behalf of Europe in one European question. It had therefore proposed a congress.[6]

On 19 November the Cabinet met to consider the British reply. Palmerston reported to the Queen that

...the Cabinet were entirely of opinion that it would be advisable for Your Majesty to decline the Congress. Such a meeting could only tend to bring out in

---

[1] Buchanan to Russell, telegram, 14 November 1863, *ibid.* J 80/41.

[2] The same to the same, telegram, 15 November 1863, *ibid.* J 80/43.

[3] Francis-Joseph's reply echoed Russell's request for further information (Francis-Joseph to Napoleon III, 17 November 1863, *ibid.* J 80/49, copy). The tsar, whilst accepting in principle, wished to know details of the questions to be discussed and the basis on which the deliberations were to be founded (Napier to Russell, telegram, 20/21 November 1863, *ibid.* J 80/15). William I announced his readiness to join in giving greater stability to the treaties. He added that, in his opinion, the changes since 1815 had not impaired their validity (Buchanan to Russell, telegram, 17 November 1863, *ibid.* J 80/55).

[4] Cowley to Russell, telegram, 18 November 1863, *ibid.* J 80/62.

[5] This programme shows that Napoleon still hankered after a Triple Alliance directed against Russia and Prussia. Austria would be compensated for cessions in Poland and Italy by gains in the Principalities and, *le cas échéant*, in Silesia.

[6] Memorandum of conversation between Russell and Marquis de Cadore, 17 November 1863, *ibid.* J 80/58, copy.

bolder relief all those differences of opinion and conflicts of interest which are at present kept in the background, and the probability is that the Parties who would meet in such a Congress would part upon worse terms with each other than they had been on when the Congress first assembled.[1]

Russell drafted a despatch to Cowley explaining that '...the Congress would probably separate, leaving many of its members on worse terms with each other than they had been when they met'. How, he asked, with a sarcasm scarcely called for by the circumstances, could a congress provide a peaceful solution for the questions of Poland and Italy? '...and if with regard to Poland and Italy no beneficial result is likely to be attained, is it expedient to call together a general Congress of all the states of Europe to find a remedy for the anarchy of Moldo-Wallachia?' Nor would a congress help to solve the dispute about the Duchies.

With regard to Germany and Denmark it is true that several of the Powers have interested themselves in that question, but the addition of Spain, Portugal, Italy and Turkey to the deliberations would scarcely improve the prospect of a satisfactory solution.

For these reasons, the French proposal was unacceptable.

Not being able, therefore, to discover the likelihood of those beneficial consequences which the Emperor of the French promised himself when proposing the Congress, Her Majesty's Government following their own strong convictions...feel themselves unable to accept His Imperial Majesty's invitation.[2]

The despatch was sent to Cowley on the evening of 25 November.[3] It reached Paris the following day.[4] Not until the 28th, however, did the ambassador find an opportunity for transmitting it to Drouyn.[5] In the meantime, the full text had appeared in the London Gazette of 27 November.[6] The French government thus learnt of the British refusal not through diplomatic channels but from an official publication.

In this manner, without perhaps fully realizing the gravity of their decision, British Ministers took the step which ended the French alliance. When Clarendon later questioned his brother[7] about the circumstances of the Cabinet's decision, Charles Villiers

...said that after a little discussion the Cabinet were unanimously of opinion that a Congress must lead to dissension and confusion and probably to war, but they were equally unanimous in thinking that the proposal must be treated with just

---

[1] Palmerston to the Queen, 19 November 1863, ibid. J 80/64, copy.
[2] Russell to Cowley, 25 November 1863, FO 27/1483 no. 1226, draft.
[3] Russell to the Queen, 25 November 1863, RA, J 80/79.
[4] Cowley to Russell, private, 11 December 1863, ibid. J 80/94, copy.
[5] Ibid. Cowley's explanation of the delay is unconvincing and did not impress Napoleon (ibid.).
[6] The London Gazette, 27 November 1863, ibid. J 80/84.
[7] Hon. Charles Villiers, President of the Poor Law Board and a member of the Cabinet.

respect and in the most friendly spirit—that when the declining despatch was read the Cabinet thought only of the argument and not of the form in which it was stated, and that nothing in it struck them as unfriendly, but that since the despatches of other Governments have been published and the tone of [*illegible*] which pervades them all has been observed there has been some regret that a little more soft powder was not used.[1]

Napoleon was furious both at the British decision and the manner in which it was announced. He spoke to Cowley 'in a tone more angry than I have ever known him to assume', saying 'that he conceived he had good reason to complain at the treatment he had received at the hand of Her Majesty's Government'.[2] To a foreign diplomat, the emperor remarked: ' "So it seems we shall have no Congress. Well! I shall have to change my alliances." '[3] Cowley reported: 'The *mot d'ordre* is: let England take the consequences of her refusal. Let her take her own line in the Holstein question. She will soon want us to help her out of her scrape; & *alors nous verrons!*'[4] ' "There will be no more talk now of the beneficent Anglo-French alliance" ', a complacent member of the British cabinet remarked to Vitzthum. That ' "foolish catchword" ' was now ' "put in the lumber room" '.[5] It was the end of the *mariage de convenance*[6] which still united England and France.

The destruction of the Anglo-French alliance was a landmark in the history of European diplomacy. The queen of Holland scarcely exaggerated its importance when she described the British refusal as: '...the deathblow of an alliance which ought to have dominated the world, managed the affairs of the Continent, assured us an era of peace'.[7] The constellation created by the Crimean War was gone, the age of Napoleon had ended. England without the French alliance could play but a modest part in continental affairs; deprived of British support Napoleon ceased

[1] Clarendon to Cowley, 14 December 1863, FO 519/179. Clarendon commented on this explanation: 'The fact is that not one single member of the Cabinet has the sort of instinctive comprehension of the idiosyncrasies of other countries that would lead them to the object in view without giving unnecessary offence. Palmerston's pen is always dipped in gall and the Earl's vision is always obscured by the blue books that stand before him, while the others are indifferent because they are not personally responsible' (*ibid.*).

[2] Cowley to Russell, private, 11 December 1863, RA J 80/94. Recalling a snub publicly administered by Napoleon to the Austrian minister on a memorable occasion in the past, Cowley expressed the opinion that it would be better if he did not attend Napoleon's New Year reception (the same to the same, 20 December 1863, *ibid.* J 80/114, copy). He was overruled by Palmerston and Russell (Palmerston to the Queen, 22 December 1863, *ibid.* J 80/112).

[3] The same to the same, private, 1 December 1863, *ibid.* J 80/89, copy. Ollivier explains that it was an alliance with Prussia which Napoleon had in mind (E. Ollivier, *L'Empire Libéral* (Paris, 1902), vol. VI, p. 490).

[4] Cowley to Russell, private, 1 December 1863, RA J 80/89 copy.

[5] Bell, *op. cit.* p. 352.

[6] In February Napoleon had spoken to Metternich of the '*marriage de raison* qui lie les deux Puissances occidentales dans toutes les grandes questions qui se présentent' (Metternich to Rechberg, 26 February 1863, Oncken, *op. cit.* p. 7).

[7] In a letter to Clarendon: see R. W. Seton-Watson, *op. cit.* p. 347.

to be the arbiter of Europe. British influence would no longer restrain the emperor in his efforts to redraw the map of Europe. The dissolution of the alliance left the friendship of St Petersburg and Berlin as the only stable diplomatic grouping. An event in which Prussian diplomacy had played but a minor part ushered in the age of Bismarck. Europe had reached the watershed between the era dominated by the Congress of Vienna and that of the Congress which would rightly take its name from the Prusso-German capital. Conditions were ripening for a further instalment of the 'new diplomacy' introduced by Napoleon and Cavour.

V

The restlessness shown by Napoleon during 1863 produced an effect similar to that of the French annexation of Nice and Savoy. It deepened the distrust of France felt by the principal cabinets and induced them to draw together in a defensive diplomatic grouping. Napoleon appeared to threaten Russia in Poland, Prussia on the Rhine, Austria in Italy and England in the Low Countries. His revolutionary talk alarmed the Russian ambassador in Paris[1] and convinced the Austrian and Prussian governments that a revolutionary war was to be expected in the spring of 1864.[2] Cowley informed the British government that French Ministers expressed anxiety about the future.[3]

It was the Russian government which took the lead in forming a grouping directed against France. Already during August, William I had noted with pleasure a marked improvement in Anglo-Russian relations.[4] Early in September, Gorchakov had explained to Napier that the breach between St Petersburg and Paris could not be lightly healed. 'It was not a lovers' quarrel—nor was he deaf to the lessons of experience.' 'He attached a high value to a good understanding with Her Majesty's Government, and to that result, which was the object of his wishes, he now saw no obstacle.' Such an understanding would naturally embrace Prussia and he was far from excluding Austria, a power which it was the traditional policy of England to respect. He did not aim at a coalition directed against France. He 'merely proposed such a concert and good understanding between the Powers as would be instrumental to the preservation of peace, and to the prevention of aggressions and disturbances which

---

[1] Budberg 'came away flamergasted [*sic*] at what he called the revolutionary tendency of H.M.'s remarks. Poland, Venetia, Hungary, Gallicia—every thing was to be in a blaze' (Cowley to Russell, private, 1 December 1863, RA J 80/89, copy).

[2] Russell to Cowley, 22 December 1863, *ibid.* J 80/116, copy.

[3] Cowley to Russell, private, 13 December 1863, *ibid.* J 80/99, copy; and the same to the same, 18 December 1863, no. 1179, most confidential, *ibid.* J 80/110, copy. Cowley could not but 'feel apprehensive of what may be the Emperor's next move. He is in one of those dangerous moods fancying that he is distrusted by everyone, which may lead him to some *coup de tête*...' (the same to the same, private, 11 December 1863, *ibid.* J 80/94, copy).

[4] William I to Alexander II, 12 August 1863, *APP, loc. cit.* pp. 714ff.

could only come from a single quarter'.[1] Russell had replied that the present state of affairs in Poland and the cordial agreement of England, France and Austria on the subject ruled out friendly relations with Russia. An Anglo-Russian *rapprochement* would excite jealousy in Paris and Vienna. It might also prove prejudicial to the Polish subjects of the tsar.[2]

Undismayed by Russell's refusal, Gorchakov reckoned up with complacency 'the questions on which Her Majesty's Government and that of Russia are at present going hand in hand'.[3] When Napoleon's proposal for a congress offered a further opportunity for isolating France, he urged the British and Austrian governments to stand firm in the face of French pretensions.[4] He assured the incredulous Napier that in a congress, Russia did not intend to raise the eastern question.[5] On 21 November he renewed his proposal that Russia, England, Austria and Prussia should 'unite in opposing a moral bulwark (*digue morale*) against the dictation and encroachments of France'. They should form 'a moral coalition, a coalition of counsel and political attitude against the French Government'. Gorchakov, Napier reported, '...gave such an emphatic character to these overtures towards Her Majesty's Government that I conceive he will expect some direct response to them on the part of Her Majesty's Government either through Baron Brunnow or through myself'.[6] Russell in conversation with Brunnow repeated 'that there could be no understanding with Russia so long as Poland was not better treated'.[7]

When Napoleon in his anger tried to assemble a congress without British participation, he merely played into Gorchakov's hands. The Vice-Chancellor could now assure the British government that he would in no circumstances adopt an attitude prejudicial to the interests of England.[8] He told the Prussian government that Russia would not consent to the isolation of England, information which Bismarck hastened to transmit to Russell.[9] In claiming credit for the rejection of the French proposal, Gorchakov indicated that he felt entitled in return to an assurance from the British government 'in the event of some serious emergency arising'.[10] The British Ministers, impressed by growing Franco-British tension,[11] at

[1] Napier to Russell, 9 September 1863, no. 607 most confidential, RA H 51/181, copy.
[2] Russell to Napier, 22 September 1863, Wereszycki, *loc. cit.* p. 99.
[3] Napier to Russell, 30 October 1863, no. 683 confidential FO 56/638.
[4] The same to the same, 9 November 1863, no. 692 confidential RA J 80/23, copy.
[5] *Ibid.*
[6] The same to the same, 21 November 1863, no. 712 most confidential, *ibid.* J 80/67, copy.
[7] Cowley to Russell, private, 1 December 1863, *ibid.* J 80/89, copy.
[8] Napier to Russell, telegram, 11 December 1863, *ibid.* J 80/81.
[9] Wodehouse to Russell, telegram, 13 December 1863, *ibid.* J 80/95.
[10] Napier to Russell, 12 December 1863, no. 751 most confidential, *ibid.* J 80/98; and the same to the same, private, 14 December 1863, *ibid.* J 80/102, copy.
[11] Napoleon was refusing to support British efforts to prevent hostilities between Germany and Denmark. Cowley warned that he might even welcome a conflict which might give him an opportunity for action on the Rhine (Cowley to Russell, private, 1 December 1863, *ibid.* J 80/89, copy; and 4 December 1863, *ibid.* J 80/91, copy).

last gave up their resistance and assured Gorchakov of their 'most friendly feelings towards Russia and the German powers'. The interests of those powers and of Europe would be considered in any emergency which might arise. As the tsar well knew, it was contrary to the practice of the British government 'to bind itself beforehand by engagements to any particular course, suited to any future state of affairs', but he might, none the less 'safely rely on the honour and good faith of the British Government in any circumstances, and in any hazards to which the peace of Europe and the Balance of Power may be exposed'.[1] If this assurance had any meaning, it implied that England would not, in any circumstances, lend her support to Napoleonic adventures undertaken on behalf of the Poles. It offered Gorchakov the moral solidarity he sought, and marked a significant change in the direction of British policy.[2] Gorchakov had the satisfaction of witnessing the disintegration of the hateful Crimean alliance.

Austria also was drifting away from France and towards Russia and Prussia. Unrest in Galicia had provoked Austrian precautions which caused displeasure in Paris.[3] Austrian encouragement to Russell to reject Napoleon's invitation to a Congress[4] had increased the emperor's annoyance.[5] At the same time, when the death of Frederick VII of Denmark[6] raised in an acute form the question of the Duchies, Rechberg and his colleagues felt the need for an understanding with Prussia. On 24 November, Austria and Prussia agreed to pursue a joint policy in the Diet.[7] Further precautions in Galicia gave satisfaction in St Petersburg.[8] Rechberg appeared to be steering Austria into the Russo-Prussian camp.

Distrust of Napoleon, therefore, had brought into existence something like the quadruple understanding advocated by Russia. Prussia alone showed a studied reluctance and held out to France some hope of ending her isolation. It was to Bismarck, accordingly, that Napoleon turned in his predicament. In confidential conversation with Goltz he hinted that he was looking for a new alliance and meant to find it in Berlin. A new 'revolutionary' grouping seemed possible. In actual fact, Bismarck was balancing skilfully between France on the one side and the 'moral coalition' on the other. This was a position which greatly strengthened his hand in his dealings with the Danes. Prussia alone now stood between Napoleon and isolation; at the same time, her support was necessary to the 'allies' to check France in Belgium, Italy and the Baltic. In November 1863, therefore, the question of the Duchies entered an acute phase in circumstances widely different from those of 1848.

---

[1] Russell to Napier, 31 December 1863 , no. 287 confidential FO 65/625 draft.
[2] Grey to the Queen, 24 December 1863, RA J 80/118.
[3] Engel-Jánosi, *op. cit.* p. 116.
[4] Bloomfield to Russell, telegram, 17 November 1863, RA J 80/54.
[5] Cowley to Russell, private, 29 November 1863, *ibid.* J 80/86, copy.
[6] On 15 November 1863.
[7] Sybel, *op. cit.* vol. III, p. 163.   [8] Engel-Jánosi, *op. cit.* pp. 119f.

CHAPTER 6

THE POWERS AND THE FUTURE OF THE DUCHIES, 1863–4

IN 1863, as in 1848, the Polish question had been associated almost fortuitously with the reorganization of Germany. That of the Duchies, on the other hand, was closely linked with Germany's national aspirations and had at least some connection with the problem of her future organization. Yet the question of Schleswig-Holstein also was not 'the German question'. It was, in its purely German aspect, simply a violent manifestation of pan-German national sentiment. It was, however, to an equal extent, a 'Danish question' connected with the reorganization of the Danish monarchy on the basis of nationality. Yet both these aspects in 1864 as in 1848 came to be dominated by wider European issues. The fate of the Duchies came to involve the 'sanctity' of treaties and the European balance of power. The struggle for their possession was seen as part of the wider conflict between the upholders of public law embodied in international engagements and revolutionary national movements. At the same time, the area involved was considered to be of strategic importance, affecting the equilibrium of forces in the Baltic. In the eyes of the principal cabinets these wider considerations far outweighed in importance the simple issues of right and wrong in an involved dispute of neighbouring nationalities. The interests of the powers concerned the Rhine, the Vistula and the Sound rather than the humble Eider.

I

The policy of Alexander II and Gorchakov throughout the crisis of 1864, was determined by the Polish insurrection of the preceding year. During the early months of 1864, the insurrectionary movement in Poland remained as yet unsubdued although its final suppression seemed only a matter of time. The one hope of the Polish revolutionaries now lay in French or Franco-Swedish operations in the spring when the Baltic would again be open to navigation. French intervention in Poland was for the cabinet of St Petersburg a practical and dangerous possibility: it was clear that Napoleon had seriously entertained the idea in the preceding year; it was known that he had secured Swedish support for any operations he might choose to undertake. Unpredictable in his immediate actions, Napoleon was known to be obstinate in the support of causes which he had once espoused; his restless energy and ambition, based on the weakness of his personal position in France, might soon require an outlet. The isolation of this dangerous adversary, therefore, had become the first object of Russian diplomacy. Throughout the summer and autumn of 1863 Alexander and Gorchakov had made strenuous efforts to detach England and Austria from France and to draw them closer to the Russo-Prussian grouping. Such a development had been promoted also by the revival of German agitation for an active policy in the Duchies. That agitation had produced an unexpected *rapprochement* between the cabinets of Vienna and Berlin. It had also induced the British government to draw closer to that of Russia in an endeavour to restrain the German powers and prevent Napoleon from fishing in troubled waters. There had thus come into being —albeit in an embryonic form—the quadruple understanding of Gorchakov's dreams. This was to form the basis of Russian policy in the months when the future of the Duchies was being decided and was intended to be the sheet-anchor of Russian security. The quadruple *entente* would keep Napoleon in check and permit the pacification of Poland without foreign intervention. It would give Russia the years of peace desperately needed for internal re-organization,[1] financial recovery[2] and the construction of strategic railways.[3] It would prevent the rebirth of the Franco-British alliance, the constellation most dreaded by Russian diplomacy. It is small wonder that the preservation of a grouping which offered such decisive advantages should become the primary object of Russian diplomacy.

Behind the policy of a quadruple understanding there lay not only Russia's immediate need for peace and security but also a deep-rooted conviction that only the solidarity of the four governments could stem the tide of revolution. A great wave of liberal and national excitement was sweeping Germany. The conservative government in Prussia was engaged in a desperate struggle with the liberal[4] majority in the Diet. A democratic national movement was browbeating the government in Copenhagen. The tide of opposition was beginning to rise in France, the Magyars were in a revolutionary temper and the people of Venetia were awaiting with impatience union with the kingdom of Italy. The events of 1863 had demonstrated

---

[1] The great economic and social transformation following from the liberation of the serfs was far from being completed. In January 1864 the ukaz on the reform of local government setting up the famous all-class zemstvos was published. In December of that year, the great changes in the legal system were announced. The Russian empire was in the midst of a major social upheaval.

[2] The great reforms were to prove extremely costly to the Russian Treasury. The military operations in Poland involved heavy extraordinary expenditure. In 1862 the deficit in the Russian budget had been 34,800,000 roubles. In 1863 it rose to 40,200,000. In 1864 it was no less than 90,300,000. In 1865 it was 54,500,000, in 1866 53,300,000. Thereafter it was to fall rapidly. Between 1869 and 1875 thanks to the efforts of Reutern, the Minister of Finance, there was a small but steady surplus. W. Graf Reutern-Baron Nolcken, *Die finanzielle Sanierung Russlands nach der Katastrophe des Krimkrieges 1862–1878 durch den Finanzminister Michael von Reutern* (Berlin, 1914), pp. 182f.

[3] The first peak period of Russian railway construction was in the years 1868-72.

[4] And polonophile.

the solidarity of European national and democratic movements with the Poles. To the Russian government, the situation seemed fraught with danger. The union of Germany by liberal and democratic methods might have incalculable consequences in Poland, Italy, Scandinavia and France. A weakened Russia could not contemplate with equanimity a repetition of the 'year of revolutions'. In this critical situation there appeared to be but one man capable of holding down the lid of Pandora's box, one man who might still prevent the March of 1864 from becoming a repetition of the memorable spring of 1848. Russia's hopes of preventing a general upheaval seemed bound up with the survival of the conservative government in Prussia. Prussia's 'conservative' Prime Minister was Russia's natural ally.

Bismarck during 1863 had shown himself the bitter enemy of Polish aspirations. He seemed unlikely, except under pressure of dire necessity, to support popular national movements elsewhere. Whilst he remained at the helm Prussia was likely to remain a 'conservative'[1] influence in European affairs. Should he fall, it was more than likely that King William would be forced to yield before the liberal tide. Bismarck alone, therefore, seemed to stand between Europe and a repetition of 1848. It was important to Russia that he should remain in power; to strengthen his position became a major object of Russian diplomacy.

In this situation, Bismarck was able to employ to good purpose a double threat to intimidate the Russian government. In the first place he could threaten resignation. It was practically certain that, in such an event, there could not be found another statesman willing and able to defy the liberals in the Diet. His disappearance would almost certainly be followed by the formation of a liberal ministry which, in the excited state of German opinion, would resume the policies of Arnim and Radowitz. If he did not resign, Bismarck could threaten to reach an understanding with Napoleon and the restive nationalities. The emperor of the French, isolated, restless and embittered, was ready for a small 'pourboire' to become the patron saint of Prussian aggrandizement in Germany. An understanding between Bismarck and Napoleon might destroy Russian influence in Europe. Small wonder that Alexander II and Gorchakov showed extreme nervousness at the slightest sign of a Prusso-French *rapprochement*. Bismarck thus held two trump cards in all his dealings with the Russian government, cards of which he was to make frequent and skilful use. Not only was his continuance in office a matter of vital concern to Russian diplomacy—it was equally important that he should be prevented at all costs from throwing himself into the arms of Napoleon, the Italians and the Magyars.

[1] It was soon realized at St Petersburg that Bismarck was not a true conservative. Neither was Gorchakov. It appeared, however, probable that the sworn foe of the German liberals would not compromise himself more than absolutely necessary through radical and democratic alliances. The conservative security offered by Bismarck was a relative not an absolute one.

These considerations became an axiom of Russian diplomacy. They help in a large measure to explain the attitude adopted by Russia in the German-Danish dispute.

The basic needs of the situation, therefore, dictated to the Russian government an attitude in the Holstein question which would, in the last resort, be not intolerable to Bismarck. The tsar realized the precariousness of Bismarck's position. He knew that German national sentiment both inside and outside Prussia insistently demanded the separation of the Duchies from Denmark. He was aware that, in order to maintain himself in power Bismarck must secure a degree of satisfaction for clamorous national sentiment. He could not but appreciate Bismarck's courage during the early stages of the dispute in acknowledging the agreement of 1852.[1] Bismarck, it was clear, could persevere in his attitude of conservative legality only if the Danes in turn honoured their pledges of 1851. This, in consequence, became the immediate object of Russian diplomacy. The renunciation by the Danish government of the policy of national consolidation at the expense of the German inhabitants of Schleswig would remove the main excuse for the German agitation. It would prevent a European crisis which, although momentarily distracting attention from Poland, might yet produce a host of dangerous complications.

If the Danes proved obstinate a clash with Germany was certain. In that event, it must be the object of Russian diplomacy to circumscribe the conflict and prevent, if possible, the intervention of France. Every attempt must be made to see that the question was finally settled by an arrangement between legitimate governments. It must not become the source of a German movement similar to that which had engulfed Central Italy in 1859. Moreover, in the event of a Danish defeat, Russia must prevent the foundation of a Scandinavian union. A new Scandinavian kingdom under French auspices would be ruled by the russophobe king of Sweden. Two further unpleasant possibilities must, if possible, be forestalled. Serious tension between Germany and England resulting from the German-Danish conflict might drive the British government to seek support in Paris. Again, should the German governments during or after the conflict denounce the arrangements of 1852, Russia would find herself on the horns of a dilemma. She must in that event, either abandon her traditional role as the defender of the Danish monarchy, acquiesce in the tearing up of a treaty to which she was a party and run the risk of a Scandinavian union—or abandon Bismarck and drive him into alliance with Napoleon and revolutionary nationalism. If the dispute about the Duchies produced a European conflict the tsar and his Minister would be placed in an

---

[1] Bismarck's adhesion to the settlement of 1852 was severely criticized among many others by the 'liberal' Prussian Crown Prince. *Kaiser Friedrich III, Tagebücher von 1848–66*, ed. H. O. Meisner (Leipzig, 1929), pp. 229 ff. For Bismarck's defence of his policy see Bismarck to Goltz, 24 December 1863, in Bismarck, *GE*, vol. II, p. 22.

awkward position. It would not be easy to find a solution which did not prejudice one or other of the major objects of Russian diplomacy.

II

Like the policy of Russia that of England during the early months of 1864 was influenced by distrust of Napoleon. With Palmerston, that distrust had become almost an obsession. It appeared, moreover, to be justified by the facts. During 1863 the French emperor had tried to embroil England first with Prussia and later with Russia. He had made no effort to conceal his annoyance at the refusal of British Ministers to 'walk into his trap'. It seemed certain that he would use the first favourable opportunity to alter existing arrangements in Italy, Poland or on the Rhine. The British government therefore no less than the Russian had every interest in preventing the outbreak of hostilities. The Queen and the majority of the Cabinet felt, like the Russian government, that the best means of achieving this was by persuading the Danish king to abandon the projected incorporation of Schleswig in Denmark. Palmerston, on the other hand, considered that the outbreak of hostilities could be prevented by warning the Germans of the danger of extreme measures. The threat of French intervention combined with uncertainty about the course which England would pursue would, in his opinion, deter the German governments from pressing their claims on Denmark. Russell was torn between the views of the majority in the Cabinet and those of Palmerston, between the advantages of firm language at Copenhagen and those of stern warnings at Frankfurt. In the end, he would pursue both policies simultaneously with equal lack of success.

There was disagreement also about the solution to be achieved. Whilst Palmerston was adamant that the treaty of 1852 must be upheld, the majority of his colleagues supported by the Queen, although paying lip-service to the need of maintaining the treaty, were ready to jettison it at the first opportunity. Palmerston, rather paradoxically, took his stand on the sanctity of treaties. His opponents urged the superior claims of legitimate national aspirations and pointed to the lack of consistency in a policy which championed the cause of nationality in Italy and fought it in the Duchies. Russell, as was his wont, wavered between the two opinions. The majority of the Cabinet, Palmerston, Russell and the Queen were, however, agreed that the preservation of an independent Danish state was a major British interest. Denmark must be neither wholly dismembered nor yet become a dependency of the Germanic Confederation.

The execution of any British policy was likely to present considerable difficulties. Since the final breach with France, England was without a powerful ally in Europe. Moreover warnings and admonitions—even when couched in the intemperate language not infrequently adopted by Palmerston and Russell—had lost their weight since the lame and impotent conclusion of the diplomatic campaign on behalf of insurgent Poland. The course of the crisis would soon provide ample proof that Europe refused to take seriously words unlikely to be followed by action. Nor was it in the least likely that Palmerston's favourite policy of collective diplomatic pressure would be either feasible or successful. Since the unsuccessful intervention in Poland, collective diplomatic action had been at a discount. It was, moreover, clear from the very beginning of the Danish crisis that Napoleon had no intention of joining in another campaign of futile diplomatic notes. Nor would he offend German national sentiment 'pour les beaux yeux' of British Ministers whom he held responsible for a series of recent humiliations. Again, in spite of some common objects, there were great ideological differences between the British and Russian points of view. Whilst it had become almost an axiom of Russian policy that nothing must be done to weaken the position of Bismarck, British statesmen were unanimous in the conviction that no effort must be spared to bring about his fall. British opinion feared neither a liberal Prussia nor a liberal Germany, it desired an autonomous Poland and favoured the completion of Italian unity. In spite, therefore, of a common distrust of Napoleon and a common desire to prevent hostilities, preserve the settlement of 1852 and secure the observance by Denmark of the promises of 1851, there was unlikely to be wholehearted co-operation where the future of Bismarck was at stake. The known views of Napoleon and of the Russian government made concerted diplomatic action a virtual impossibility.

The failure of diplomacy would raise the question of military and particularly naval pressure. Would British Ministers be prepared to face the hazards of active intervention and would British opinion sanction such a course? Would Ministers, when the time came, be ready to pay the inevitable price of French military assistance?

In fact both from the British point of view and from that of Russia the situation had changed since the days when Nicholas I and Palmerston had 'settled' the Duchies question. The prestige of both countries had declined since the days of Vilagos and Olmütz, of the Hungarian refugees in Turkey and 'Don Pacifico'. Moreover the rooted distrust felt for Napoleon and the emperor's manifest sympathies for Prussia and nationality seemed to preclude even such limited assistance as France had afforded to the defenders of Danish integrity during the earlier crisis. Austria and Prussia, on the other hand, appeared to be working together. Both were stronger than they had been in 1848 and 1849. Ideologically, their position was strengthened by the fact that neither Rechberg nor Bismarck could easily be denounced as a revolutionary. The Russian government, therefore, had no need to return to the policy of Nicholas. Palmerston, on the other hand, would be prevented from repeating his earlier achievement by the evolution of British opinion and the growing criticism of his policy of the balance of power. The Germans were less likely than in the earlier conflict to be hindered by the Powers in the prosecution of their designs.

III

On 9 July 1863, the German Federal Diet had decided to summon the king of Denmark to revoke within six weeks the Patent of 30 March incorporating Schleswig in the Danish state. Preparations were begun at the same time for the occupation of Holstein by the armed forces of the Confederation.[1] These developments had produced a European reaction. On 19 July, the Swedish Minister of Foreign Affairs informed his agents in London and Paris that in the event of Federal execution—especially if it involved Schleswig as well as Holstein—his government might feel impelled to render assistance to Denmark.[2] England and France should support Denmark and avert the threat of war in northern Europe.[3] Four days later, Palmerston, in the House of Commons, had issued his famous warning

> ...I am satisfied with all reasonable men in Europe, including those in France and Russia, in desiring that the independence, the integrity and the rights of Denmark may be maintained. We are convinced—I am convinced at least—that if any violent attempt were made to overthrow those rights and interfere with that independence, those who made the attempt, would find in the result, that it would not be Denmark alone with which they would have to contend.[4]

On the 29th Russell, in transmitting to Bloomfield a copy of the Swedish despatch observed that Denmark would regard Federal interference in Schleswig as a hostile invasion. It was clear that she would be supported by Sweden. The question of Schleswig, therefore, must be separated from that of Holstein and the Federal Diet limit its activities to the latter province.

> You will communicate these views to Count Rechberg and tell him that if Germany persists in confounding Schleswig with Holstein, other Powers of Europe may confound Holstein with Schleswig and deny the right of Germany to interfere with the one any more than she has with the other except as a European Power.

An invasion of Schleswig, moreover, might provoke the intervention of France. 'Such a pretension might be as dangerous to the independence and integrity of Germany as the invasion of Schleswig might be to the inde-

---

[1] Sybel, *op. cit.* vol. III, pp. 125f.
[2] Manderström to Wachtmeister, 19 July 1863, RA I 90/23, copy. Manderström spoke of a possible conflict 'auquel par la force des choses, nous pourrions facilement être entraînés à ne point rester étrangers puisque nos intérêts les plus chers ne pourraient guère nous permettre de voir d'un œil tranquil écraser nos voisins, sous des prétextes qui plus tard pourraient mettre en danger notre propre indépendance'.
[3] *Ibid.*
[4] *Parl. Debates*, 3rd series, 172, p. 1252.

pendence and integrity of Denmark.'[1] When Bloomfield had accordingly told Rechberg that in Russell's opinion a German invasion of Schleswig was likely to entail the intervention of Sweden and France, the Austrian Minister had replied that his information from Stockholm did not lead him to suppose that Sweden would support Denmark; nor was he aware that there was much feeling on the subject in Paris.[2]

During the month of August, German opinion had been distracted from the Duchies by the 'Fürstentag' at Frankfurt but in September tension between Germany and Denmark had again increased. Russell and Palmerston had thereupon proposed to France that the two countries should jointly offer their good offices.

If however the Government of France would consider such a step as likely to be unavailing, the Powers might warn Austria, Prussia and the German Diet, that any demands or acts on their part, tending to weaken the independence and integrity of Denmark, would be considered by the two Powers as contrary to the Treaty of the 8th of May 1852.[3]

Drouyn had replied that the offer of good offices would, in his opinion, be useless. To remind the German powers of the treaty of 1852 appeared analogous to the course pursued by England and France in the Polish question. He had no intention of putting France in the position—anything but dignified—in relation to Germany, in which the three powers had placed themselves with regard to Russia. If England and France issued such a warning, they must be prepared to go further. He was not indifferent to the maintenance of Danish integrity and had already warned Germany against violent measures with regard to Schleswig. All Russell suggested had been done 'unless it was desired to take a more formal step, such as the presentation of an identic note and to this he most strongly objected, as he desired to preserve entire liberty of action to France in the matter'.[4]

Before he learnt of this reply, Russell was informed by the Swedish government, that it was negotiating with Denmark about an alliance for the defence of the Eider line.[5] Could Sweden and Denmark, if Germany pushed matters to extremes, count on the assistance of England and France?[6]

[1] Russell to Bloomfield, 29 July 1863, confidential, RA I 90/24, draft.
[2] Bloomfield to Russell, no. 400, confidential, 13 August 1863, ibid. I 90/30, copy.
[3] Russell to Cowley, September 1863, ibid. I 90/48, draft. In deference to the Queen's wishes, slight alterations were made in the proposed communication (Palmerston to the Queen, 12 September 1863, ibid. I 90/47).
[4] Grey to Russell, 18 September 1863, ibid. I 90/51, abstract.
[5] The Eider formed the boundary of Holstein and Schleswig. Holstein was tacitly admitted to be a German concern.
[6] Manderström to Wachtmeister, 11 September 1863, ibid. I 90/49 abstract. Some days later, Drouyn asked Russell for his views on the Swedish inquiry which had also been addressed to Paris. He himself expressed a desire for a peaceful settlement (Drouyn to Cadore, 17 September 1863, ibid. I 90/74, abstract).

Russell had replied that the British government was ready to offer its good offices alone or in conjunction with France. Should these fail, its course must be subject to future consideration and decision. Ministers were not prepared to say

that Denmark is altogether in the right, or that Germany has not some grounds of complaint in reference to the German population of Slesvig. But they think these differences should be the subject of negotiation, either in Conferences or otherwise and should not be brought to the issue of war.[1]

In the meantime, the representatives of England, France and Sweden had been urging the Danes to acquiesce in the impending Federal execution in Holstein.[2] It was hoped that this would assist a peaceful settlement.[3] By the end of October, Russell had been able to tell the Queen: 'Prussia is becoming more friendly to England than she has been for many years.'[4]

IV

The *détente* had been of short duration. On 13 November the *Rigsraad* had given a third reading to the new constitution incorporating Schleswig in Denmark. Two days later King Frederick VII died. On the 18th, Christian IX had been proclaimed ruler of the entire monarchy. Two days later, in response to popular pressure in Copenhagen he had given his assent to the new constitution. The majority of German officials in Schleswig had thereupon refused to take the oath of allegiance. Since the traditional order of succession in the Duchies differed from that in the rest of the monarchy, their future position had now become uncertain. The king's decision had raised the spectre of a German rising in the Duchies followed by the intervention of Germany.

The Russian government had tried to prevent Christian IX from signing the constitution but an urgent warning from Gorchakov had remained without effect.[5] All the Vice-Chancellor could do was to express to Plessen, the Danish minister, his disapproval of the action:

You talk to me so often of the necessities of your domestic politics; but I, who am called on to direct the policy of Russia, have to take account also of the domestic

[1] Russell to Wachtmeister, September 1863, *ibid.* I 90/52, draft. To the French inquiry Russell replied that it was 'premature for Sweden to ask Great Britain and France to come to a decision upon a case which has not yet presented itself'. The British government wished 'to remain free to act when the occasion should arise' in accordance with 'the interests and dignity of Great Britain' (Russell to Grey, September 1863 (sent 4 October 1863), *ibid.* I 90/73, draft).
[2] Paget to Russell, 3 September 1863, *ibid.* I 90/38, copy.
[3] Grey to the Queen, 4 October 1863, *ibid.* I 90/75.
[4] Russell to the Queen, 30 October 1863, *ibid.* I 90/159.
[5] For a discussion whether Gorchakov's warning reached King Christian before or after the actual signature cf. Lawrence D. Steefel, *The Schleswig-Holstein Question* (Cambridge, Mass., 1932), pp. 77 and 132.

politics of those with whom you are in conflict. It is impossible for me not to find that by this last act, the Royal Sanction, you have failed to respect your engagements to Germany.[1]

Gorchakov feared that the king of Prussia would now denounce the treaty of 1852.[2] He therefore proposed two steps to meet this danger. The five signatories of the treaty[3] were shortly to send special envoys to Copenhagen to congratulate the new king on his accession. These should state in strong terms that whilst their governments adhered to their engagements respecting the integrity of the monarchy, they expected the Danish government also to fulfil its obligations. This advice, it was hoped, would induce Denmark to abrogate the constitution and enable the five powers to co-operate in preserving her integrity.[4] Moreover, the Danish government had itself suggested that the dispute might be submitted to the congress called by Napoleon. Since the British government had refused to attend, Gorchakov tactfully suggested that a separate ministerial conference might meet in London to consider the future of the Duchies.[5] Care must be taken not to give the Danes undue encouragement by a one-sided anti-German attitude. The British government might try to exercise a restraining influence at Vienna.[6]

Gorchakov's statesmanlike programme commended itself to the British cabinet. Ministers were of opinion that Denmark might well agree to a conference in London and that the authority of the five powers might preserve the peace of Europe.[7] The Queen expressed her delight at the prospect of a peaceful solution.[8]

When, however, it came to implementing such a policy, some difficulty was experienced. On 1 December the Cabinet decided that Lord Wodehouse, a supporter of the Danish cause[9] should represent England at the

[1] Plessen to Hall, 24 November 1863, no. 68, *ibid.* p. 131.
[2] Napier to Russell, telegram, 22/23 November 1863, RA I 91/46.
[3] England, France, Russia, Prussia and Austria.
[4] The same to the same, telegram, 24/25 November 1863, *ibid.* I 91/82.
[5] The same to the same, another telegram, 24/25 November 1863, *ibid.* I 91/81.
[6] The same to the same, 24 November 1863, no. 724, confidential, *ibid.* I 91/78, copy. Similar proposals were being submitted by Gorchakov in Vienna and Berlin and would also be made in Paris (the same to the same, telegram, 24/25 November 1863, *ibid.* I 91/82). It is significant that Gorchakov consulted simultaneously the cabinets of London, Berlin and Vienna but delayed his approach to France.
[7] Russell to the Queen, 25 November 1863, *ibid.* I 91/81. A telegram had already been sent to Copenhagen urging the Danish government to withdraw the Letters Patent of 30 March 1863 which formed the basis of the new constitution (*ibid.*).
[8] The Queen warmly approved of Gorchakov's proposal and rejoiced to see that the cabinet took the same view. 'Denmark could never resist the joint representation of the Five Powers' and if Christian IX withdrew the constitution Prussia would lose every possible pretext for refusing to abide by the treaty of 1852 (Grey to Russell, 25 November 1863, *ibid.* I 91/86, copy).
[9] 'Lord Russell has been accused not only by Lord Derby and Lord Malmesbury, but by Lord Wodehouse and others of the Liberal party, of being unjust to Denmark....' Russell to the Queen, *ibid.* I 91/83 (*QVL*, 2nd series, ed. G. Buckle (London, 1926), vol. I, p. 122).

coronation of Christian IX.[1] His instructions submitted to the Queen by Russell on the following day, were anything but precise:

> The result to be arrived at is the fulfilment of the Treaty of May 1852 and of the engagements entered into by Austria and Prussia and Denmark in 1851–52. The mode for doing this cannot yet be laid down. Patience and impartiality on the part of the great Powers is necessary to do this.[2]

To complicate matters still further, Russell also explained: 'In the view of Her Majesty's Government it is desirable but exceedingly difficult to procure the repeal of a law so recently passed as that of the Dano-Schleswig Constitution'.[3]

The Queen through her private secretary, General Grey, tried to exert pressure on Wodehouse. On 6 December the two men had two separate conversations. After the first Grey reported that he had had 'on the whole, a very satisfactory conversation'. Wodehouse was 'prepared to use the same language to both sides, and on both to avoid any appearance of menace'.[4] He had, however, tried to excuse the actions of the Danish government and had 'attributed motives to Germany which... there was no apparent ground for imputing'.[5] On the Queen's instructions Grey 'impressed upon' Wodehouse in a second interview 'the necessity of using stronger language with Denmark than with Germany—and the mischief that had been done by a contrary course'. Wodehouse, Grey reported, 'does not seem to deny this—but pleads the very strong feeling throughout England, which certainly exists—but exists in utter ignorance of the merits of the question'.[6]

The Queen now turned to the Foreign Secretary. The last paragraph of Wodehouse's secret instructions, she complained, seemed to contain an implied threat to Germany. The same language must be held to both sides. If there was stronger language against one side it must be against Denmark 'for it is the conduct of Denmark that alone makes the German powers hesitate to confirm the arrangement of 1852'.[7] Russell agreed that what was said to Germany 'ought to be no more than what is said to

---

[1] The same to the same, 1 December 1863, RA I 91/118. Russell and Palmerston had originally agreed to send Sir Henry Howard the British minister at Hanover. Howard was well-versed in German affairs and of a 'conciliatory disposition' (the same to the same, 30 November 1863, ibid. I 91/110). The Queen had sanctioned this choice (Grey to Russell, 30 November 1863, ibid. I 91/111). The Cabinet had overruled Palmerston, Russell and the Queen.

[2] Instruction to Wodehouse, 2 December 1863, ibid. I 91/125, draft, abstract.

[3] Instruction to Wodehouse (2) confidential, 2 December 1863, ibid. I 91/124, draft, copy.

[4] Wodehouse had been instructed to go to Copenhagen by way of Berlin. There he was to confer with Buchanan the British Ambassador and, if possible, with Bismarck. He should point out the danger of Federal execution by German troops but not press the point if it appeared inexpedient (ibid.).

[5] Grey to the Queen, 6 December 1863, ibid. I 92/1.

[6] The same to the same (2), 6 December 1863, ibid. I 92/2.

[7] The Queen to Russell, 6 December 1863, ibid. I 92/3, copy.

Denmark'. He had desired the memorandum for Wodehouse to be altered accordingly.[1]

On 26 November, Russell had submitted to the Queen the draft of a despatch he proposed to address to Buchanan. This declared that the treaty of London was 'very clear and explicit'. The British government held Prussia bound 'in honour and good faith' to fulfil its stipulations. It would, on the other hand, urge on Denmark the fulfilment of her obligations.[2] The Queen, in returning the draft, observed that, in her opinion, the Prussian government was more likely to accept the British argument if the reciprocity of the obligations of the two parties was explicitly admitted.[3] The Cabinet, however, declined to adopt this view. On 2 December the Queen sanctioned the despatch as it had been deliberately agreed to by her Ministers. She feared that it would do little good and explained that she did not think it right to disregard, as Russell had done, all connection between the treaty of 1852 and the anterior negotiations between Denmark and the Germanic powers.[4] The Queen's letter, at her request, had been read to the Cabinet. Palmerston, in reply had expounded his own views in a lengthy memorandum to the Queen.[5] Plain sense and good faith, he declared, required that a treaty should be construed 'by its own written text'. That of the treaty of 1852 was clear and unambiguous and the powers parties to it were bound 'by every consideration of honour and good faith' to acknowledge King Christian as King-Duke of all the territories which had owed allegiance to the late king. That done, they would have a responsible sovereign to deal with from whom they might justly claim the fulfilment of any and every engagement taken by his predecessor and not at present made good.[6] The Queen rejoined that it was her only anxiety that the arrangements of 1852 should come into effect and that no pretext should be afforded to Prussia and Austria for setting them aside. She could not, however, treat as lightly as Palmerston had done, the engagements contracted by Denmark in 1851–2. She must earnestly press on the Prime Minister the danger of irritating Prussia and Austria 'by the needlessly dictatorial manner in which she cannot but think the fulfilment of the Treaty has been demanded from them'.[7]

There was thus a difference of opinion whether British pressure should

---

[1] Russell to the Queen, 7 December 1863, *ibid.* I 92/8.
[2] Russell to Buchanan, November 1863, *ibid.* I 91/90, draft, copy.
[3] Grey to Russell, 29 November 1863, *ibid.* I 91/109, copy.
[4] The Queen to Russell, 2 December 1863, *ibid.* I 91/123, copy (*QVL, loc. cit.* pp. 125f.). On the following day, the Queen wrote in a letter to the King of the Belgians: '. . . But I am also almost sure that the Protocol will *not* be tenable, and that it will be necessary to come to some arrangement by which Holstein is given up its *lawful Duke*, after we have recognised the Protocol. . .' RA Y 110/25, copy (*QVL, loc. cit.* p. 130).
[5] Palmerston to the Queen, 3 December 1863, RA I 91/129 (*QVL, loc. cit.* pp. 127ff.).
[6] *Ibid.*
[7] The Queen to Palmerston, 5 December 1863, RA I 91/154, copy.

be applied, in the first place, with greater severity to Denmark or to the German powers. Wodehouse, aware of this difference of views, and personally well-inclined to the Danish cause, was unlikely to show undue severity at Copenhagen. It was doubtful, therefore, whether Gorchakov's plan for concerted pressure on Denmark would be carried into effect in the spirit as well as in the letter.

The Russian government in its instruction to its special envoy Ewers declared that it was far from intending to impose upon King Christian the obligation of revoking a law to which he had given his sanction. It left to the Danish government entire latitude in its choice of means for reassuring the German Confederation. Should the Danish ministry fail, however, to adopt a policy of conciliation the powers must decline all responsibility for the consequences of such a refusal.[1] Wodehouse, who met Ewers in Berlin, gained the impression that Russia appeared 'to go very far on the German side'.[2] On 9 December the tsar himself had explained his views to the Danish Minister. 'Not only from my personal sympathies—they are of long standing and the King knows it', he declared, 'but also from my very sincere interest for Denmark, I will do what I can.'

But you know that already for some time we have found that in your policy towards Germany, you have been drawing the cord too tight. We shall be consistent. ...If unhappily war should break out between you and Germany, I cannot take part in it; you know our situation, you ought to understand....I don't want to say anything painful to you; we are merely consistent; we have often warned you....I admit that the movement against you in Germany has at present in part a revolutionary basis; but on your part, too, there are also—don't take it amiss that I speak of it—symptoms of exaggerated tendencies...All that I can do I will do.[3]

The Russian attitude, therefore, differed from that of England in the determination, expressed from the start, not to join in hostilities on behalf of Denmark or in defence of the treaty of 1852.

On 12 December, Wodehouse learnt from Bismarck that unless the new Danish constitution was declared inapplicable to Schleswig before 1 January, the German powers would hold themselves released from their engagements and from the treaty of 1852.[4] Three days later, in conversation with the Danish Prime Minister, Hall, he expressed the desire of the British government that Denmark should adopt a conciliatory attitude.[5] When he attempted, however, to lend weight to the advice of the special envoys by organizing a joint *démarche* he discovered that their attitudes were far from identical. Ewers indeed was authorized to take part in a joint communication but General Fleury, the French representative, had been instructed to act on his own account. He declared that he had been

[1] Steefel, *op. cit.* p. 137. Ewers' instructions were communicated to the British government (Napier to Russell, telegram, 1 December 1863, RA I 91/126).
[2] Wodehouse to Russell, private, 13 December 1863, *ibid.* I 92/56, copy.
[3] Steefel, *op. cit.* p. 131. [4] *Ibid.* pp. 138f. [5] *Ibid.* pp. 140f.

ordered to make it clear that if Denmark became involved in war with Germany, France would not come to her assistance. He was to advise in general terms moderation and concessions to Germany and to state at the same time that the emperor Napoleon would not consent to any formal negotiation on the question of the Duchies except in a European Congress.[1] Count Hamilton, the Swedish minister, was not authorized to put any pressure whatever on the Danish government.[2]

On 20 December, therefore, Wodehouse and Ewers were jointly received by Hall. At the request of the Russian envoy, the British representative took the lead in presenting the views of the two governments. Wodehouse informed Hall of the substance of his conversation with Bismarck and of the German demand for a repeal of the constitution as it affected Schleswig before 1 January. He added that the British government considered the constitution a violation of Denmark's promise not to incorporate Schleswig with the Danish portion of the kingdom. Ewers expressed his entire agreement with Wodehouse's remarks and urged the revocation of the constitution. The two envoys were followed by Fleury who supported in general terms the advice they had given and put forward the suggestion of a congress.

The Danish government refused to follow the envoys' advice. A royal message closed the session of the *Rigsraad*, the only body which could legally carry out the repeal. The king expressed the hope that in the face of further German schemes, the powers would uphold the undivided inheritance of the Danish monarchy, the preservation of which had been recognized as a European necessity.[3] Paget considered that Hall still hoped for eventual aid from Sweden[4] and France.[5] Reports from London also seemed to indicate that under pressure from public opinion, the British government might yet give help to Denmark.[6]

If the Danish government was unwilling to revoke the constitution, it was ready to follow the advice of the powers in another matter. On 19 December, it decided to withdraw all Danish forces from Holstein.[7] Five days later Saxon and Hanoverian troops began their occupation of the Duchy.[8]

V

Immediately before the execution in Holstein, the question of Schleswig had come to preoccupy the cabinets. On 22 December, the British government learnt that Bismarck had reaffirmed earlier declarations that unless Schleswig was exempted from the operation of the new constitution before

[1] *Ibid.* p. 141.　　　　[2] *Ibid.*　　　　[3] *Ibid.* p. 142.
[4] For the chequered negotiations for the conclusion of a defensive alliance between Denmark and Sweden-Norway, cf. *ibid.* pp. 150 ff.
[5] *Ibid.* pp. 147 f.　　　　[6] *Ibid.* pp. 146 f.
[7] Paget to Russell, telegram, 19 December 1863, RA I 92/84.
[8] Sybel, *op. cit.* p. 192 and Steefel, *op. cit.* p. 101.

1 January, William I would consider himself released from his obligations under the treaty of London.[1] On the following day, the Federal Diet passed a resolution foreshadowing the complete separation of Schleswig as well as Holstein from the rest of the Danish monarchy.[2] On the 28th, it began to discuss the occupation of Schleswig by German forces.[3] The dispute about the Duchies was entering a new phase. With the Prussian threat to abrogate the treaty of 1852 and the discussions in the Diet about the occupation of Schleswig, the question had finally ceased to be mainly Germanic and had become a matter of European concern.

The British government was perturbed. On 24 December, the Queen noted that the reports from Copenhagen and Germany were 'both very alarming'. It was now 'no longer a question of maintaining the treaty of '52 at all hazards' but one of averting war.[4] Russell agreed that there must be some compromise. However, until agreement was reached, the British government could not consent to the German occupation of Schleswig.[5] The majority of the Cabinet 'thought it right to convey in clear terms to the German governments who had signed or adhered to the Treaty of 1852 the sense in which the British Government viewed the obligations of that Treaty'.[6] In accordance with this policy, Russell, on 25 December had instructed Buchanan to ask Bismarck on behalf of the British cabinet 'to point out the Treaty or other document which gives the Diet a right to determine who shall be Duke of Holstein'. The Prussian government should not take precipitate action against Denmark which might prove 'fatal to the peace of Europe and prejudicial to Germany'.[7] On 26 December, the British minister in Frankfurt was instructed to hand to the President of the Diet a copy of the treaty of London. This was to be accompanied by a note explaining that France, England, Russia and Sweden had recognized Christian IX as king of all the component parts of the Danish monarchy. Were the Diet to take a hasty step in opposition to the treaty 'serious complications might ensue'.[8] The British government was prepared to discuss the matter in a conference at which the Diet would be represented.[9] Two days later, the Foreign Secretary submitted the draft of a despatch to Berlin, stating that even the outbreak of war would not relieve

[1] Buchanan to Russell, telegram, 22 December 1863, RA I 92/125.
[2] Sybel, op. cit. p. 201.
[3] Ibid. and Buchanan to Russell, telegram, 26 December 1863, RA I 92/116.
[4] The Queen to Russell, 24 December 1863, ibid. I 92/142, copy (QVL, loc. cit. pp. 131f.). The Queen had been alarmed by a telegram from Buchanan of 15 December discussing the possibility of the fall of Bismarck. Had the government, she inquired, considered what policy to adopt if Prussia and the other German states got new ministries supported by the majorities in the Chambers? (Grey to Russell, 16 December 1863, RA I 92/66, copy).
[5] Russell to the Queen, 26 December 1863, ibid. I 92/177.
[6] The same to the same (2), 26 December 1863, ibid. I 92/118.
[7] Russell to Buchanan, telegram, 25 December 1863, ibid. I 92/62.
[8] The Diet was threatening to proclaim the German candidate Duke Frederick of Augustenburg, Duke of Holstein, and to install him at Kiel.
[9] Russell to Malet, telegram, 26 December 1863, ibid. I 92/113.

Prussia from her obligations under the treaty of 1852 and condemning 'a war of conquest undertaken by Germany'.[1] The Queen demurred[2] and asked the Foreign Secretary to lay her objections before his colleagues. The Cabinet met on 2 January, and the outcome of its deliberations was a note to Malet in Frankfurt. The British government, Russell wrote, understood that the Diet was debating a motion to put the duke of Augustenburg at once in possession of Holstein and, on appeal from him, in possession of Schleswig as well.

> Her Majesty's Government can only say that they would regard the adoption of this plan as equivalent to an attack upon Denmark with a view to its dismemberment, and they would feel bound, in that case, to afford assistance to Denmark in opposing so evident an act of aggression.

They therefore appealed for delay to allow for an impartial consideration of the matter by the signatories of the treaty. Their decision would be communicated to the Diet. Were this proposal rejected, each power would be at liberty to pursue the course its honour and interests dictated.[3] The communication would be made to the Diet only after a similar note had been agreed to at St Petersburg, Stockholm and Paris.[4]

On 6 January, Granville, who represented the Queen's views and led the 'pacific' majority in the Cabinet hurried to Broadlands to tell Palmerston that he objected strongly to 'plunging this country into a war for the maintenance of the Treaty of 1852'. He was assured by the Prime Minister *'that there was no question whatever of England going to war'*.[5]—It was, in fact, the impetuous Foreign Secretary who favoured an energetic policy. Russell urged the Queen that if the courts of Dresden and Stuttgart persisted in agitating and voting against the treaty, the British ministers to those courts should be recalled.[6] He warned Bernstorff, the Prussian envoy:

> But I could not doubt that he [Christian IX] would be assisted by Powers friendly to Denmark in that defence, that as for Great Britain it was no question of war

---

[1] Russell to Buchanan, December 1863, *ibid.* I 92/190, draft, copy.

[2] In a memorandum to Russell she declared that 'under no circumstances will she become a Party in a war undertaken for the purpose of enforcing upon the People of Holstein, against their will, a Sovereign whom they violate no duty or allegiance in rejecting' (the Queen to Russell, 30 December 1863, *ibid.* I 92/215, copy).

[3] Russell to Malet, January 1864, *ibid.* I 92/266, draft.

[4] Russell to the Queen, 2 January 1864, *ibid.* I 92/266; and Grey to Russell, telegram, 3 January 1864, *ibid.* I 92/271.

[5] Phipps to the Queen, 7 January 1863 (?1864), *ibid.* I 92/316 (*QVL, loc. cit.* p. 142). Palmerston hoped to settle the dispute in co-operation with France. In a memorandum of 5 January he outlined the programme for which he hoped to obtain French support. Christian IX should lose no time in taking the proper constitutional steps for exempting Schleswig from the operation of the new constitution. When this was done Federal troops would evacuate Holstein which would be re-entered by the Danes. After the authority of Christian IX had been re-established, he would issue a general amnesty (memorandum by Palmerston, 5 January 1864, RA I 92/291, copy).

[6] Russell to the Queen, ?7 January 1864, *ibid.* I 92/317.

to-morrow or the next day, but that in my opinion she could not consistently with her honour allow Denmark to perish without aiding her in her defence.[1]

On 8 January he submitted to the Queen telegrams which in accordance with the decision reached by the Cabinet on the 2nd he proposed to send to Paris, St Petersburg and Stockholm. In these, he invited the three governments to join that of England in representing to the Diet that the invasion of Schleswig would be 'an act of aggression on non-German territory' which would probably meet resistance. They should add that England had proposed a Conference and that the Germans must not act with precipitation.[2]

The Queen severely criticized the tone adopted by the Foreign Secretary.[3] Palmerston hastened to his defence.[4] Russell himself transmitted to the Queen letters from Bloomfield and Buchanan expressing the view that strong language in Vienna and Berlin would be 'conducive to the maintenance of peace'.[5] It was the general notion that England was not in earnest which had 'tended more than anything else to increase the danger of war just as it tended in 1853–4 to bring on the Crimean War'.[6] The Queen insisted that the draft of Russell's despatch to Bloomfield reporting his language to Bernstorff should be submitted to the Cabinet.[7]

On 12 January, after 'a great tussle' in the Cabinet it was decided to omit altogether any mention of the opinion expressed by Russell about the

---

[1] Russell to Bloomfield and Buchanan, 8 January 1864, ibid. I 93/13, draft. Russell's warning was undoubtedly inspired by information which he had received from Berlin. On 6 January Buchanan had telegraphed: 'I am convinced that he [Bismarck] intends to conquer Schleswig for Germany' (Buchanan to Russell, telegram, 6 January 1864, ibid. I 92/138). Cf. also Morier to Russell, private and confidential, 9 January 1864, ibid. I 93/43, copy).

[2] Proposed telegram to Cowley, Napier and Jerningham, 8 January 1864, ibid. I 93/6.

[3] The Queen to Russell, ?7 January 1864, ibid. I 92/319, and the Queen to Palmerston, 8 January 1864, ibid. I 93/1, copy (QVL, loc. cit. p. 143).

[4] Palmerston to the Queen, 8 January 1864, RA I 93/3 (QVL, loc. cit. pp. 144ff.).

[5] Buchanan had written: 'I think a little decided language on the part of Your Lordship will induce him [William I] to abstain from military operations, on which he is said to be determined' (Buchanan to Russell, private, 9 January 1864, RA I 93/44, copy). Napier similarly urged strong language and the despatch of British warships to the Baltic (Napier to Russell, telegram, 11 January 1864, ibid. I 93/54). Rechberg through Bloomfield also recommended firm language at Berlin and Vienna (Russell to the Queen, 11 January 1864, ibid. I 93/50).

Malet reported from Frankfurt: 'there exists an absolute persuasion that England will not interfere materially, & our counsels are regarded as unfriendly & have no weight' (Malet to Russell, 8 January 1864, FO 30/213, no. 11). Bloomfield wrote from Vienna that the smaller German states did not believe that England was in earnest about the Duchies (Bloomfield to Russell, private, 7 January 1864, RA I 93/51, copy). Napier joined in the chorus. 'The only way to lead Russia on is to take a very decided attitude. They believe here that Her Majesty's Government will do nothing effectual for Denmark. The German representatives believe so too' (Napier to Russell, telegram, 11 January 1864, ibid. I 93/54). 'Palmerstonian bluff' after the unsuccessful Polish 'campaign' was clearly at a discount.

[6] Ibid.

[7] Russell to Palmerston, 12 January 1864, ibid. I 93/67.

course England would pursue if Schleswig were invaded. At the same time, the Ministers unanimously reaffirmed their decision to inquire of the French, Russian and Swedish governments whether, if Denmark cancelled her constitution, they would join England in preventing the invasion of Schleswig and the dismemberment of the monarchy.[1] It was a defeat for Palmerston and Russell.[2]

British Ministers could hardly be in doubt about the reply they would receive from Paris. Already on 3 January, Cowley had reported a conversation in which Drouyn had explained the French attitude. He regretted, he said

the estrangement which circumstances had produced between the British and French governments because he saw no probability of their assuming such an attitude together as could alone conjure the dangers which threatened Europe.[3] The Emperor therefore had resolved upon acting with the greatest prudence and circumspection in the Danish question. There were many reasons which inclined France towards the cause of Denmark. It was the cause of an honest government and of an honorable [sic] people....It was, moreover, a cause sanctioned by a treaty, but a treaty containing no guarantee, in which France had, so to say, but a sixth responsibility.

Whilst therefore the sympathies of the French government might be with Denmark there was nothing which bound them to interfere by arms in her defence.

And France would certainly not interfere alone, particularly if, as might be apprehended, Austria and Prussia were to side with the rest of Germany. When he looked around to see who might be the possible allies of France in defence of Denmark, he found none that could be counted upon. Russia, even supposing that under present circumstances an alliance between Russia and France were possible, had enough on her hands at home and was not likely, moreover, to engage in hostilities with Germany. Sweden might be willing to take up arms...but...could be of but little assistance. The question of Poland had shown that Great Britain could not be relied upon when war was in the distance....France did not wish a collision single-handed with Germany but would wait the development of events.[4]

Napoleon, in fact, would prefer a modification of the treaty to a war

[1] Russell to the Queen, 13 January 1864, *ibid.* I 93/74 and Granville to Phipps, private, 12 January 1864, *ibid.* I 93/65 (*QVL, loc. cit.* p. 150).

[2] Clarendon privately informed his friend Cowley that Russell 'though halting between two opinions, or rather not liking to come down from the height of swagger to which he had climbed, yet had no chance of being allowed by his colleagues to go to war single-handed with Germany' (F. Wellesley, *The Paris Embassy during the Second Empire* (London, 1928), p. 261). Granville reported: '...Lord John was a good deal annoyed, and once or twice alluded to not choosing to go on, if the Cabinet did not approve of his policy. Lord Palmerston supported Lord John strongly, but I got him to repeat before the Cabinet what he had stated to me at Broadlands, viz. that there was no question of our going to war single-handed' (Granville to Phipps, 14 January 1864, RA I 93/90 (*QVL, loc. cit.* p. 153)). Granville confidently foresaw that France and Russia would not agree to the proposed démarche (the same to the same, 12 January 1864, *ibid.* p. 150, I 93/65 (*QVL, loc. cit.* p. 150)).

[3] Drouyn was conservative and sympathetic to Austria.

[4] Cowley to Russell, no. 23, 3 January 1864, Steefel, *op. cit.* pp. 166f.

for its enforcement.[1] Cowley considered the causes of this 'lamentable conduct' to be:

1. A rankling disappointment at the failure of the projected Congress and a desire to justify the project in the eyes of the world by the spectacle of a conflict which might have been avoided had the project been accepted.
2. Anger towards Her Majesty's Government for their imputed abandonment of France in the Polish question.
3. The possibility that out of the complications something may turn up advantageous to France.[2]

The French reply marked an epoch in the history of nineteenth-century Europe. It revealed that during 1863 the Anglo-French alliance, which had survived so many crises, had been struck a mortal blow; that the French and British governments no longer felt even the desire to co-operate in major European questions; that the age of Palmerston and Louis Napoleon was ending and that of Bismarck had begun. The failure of England and France to reach agreement paved the way for the German advance across the Eider. If the responsibility for the break rested in the main with Palmerston and Russell, the '*gran rifiuto*' which might almost be said to have handed over Europe to Bismarck came from the emperor of the French. The French refusal also marked the end of the Palmerstonian age in British foreign policy and the beginning of British isolation. England was left without a sure ally in Europe. Soon Stanley, making a virtue of necessity, would glory in abstention and non-intervention whilst the Germanic Confederation was being destroyed. What the Crimean War had done to Russia in the diplomatic sphere, the defeat of Denmark would presently do to England. Both, after the destruction of their diplomatic systems, withdrew within themselves and almost ceased to act as European powers. In future the energetic Prussian government might well have Austria and France alone to contend with.

The Russian government would not abandon as lightly as the rest of Europe the defence of the treaty and of the established order. Alexander II and Gorchakov had observed with dismay the mounting Anglo-German tension which threatened the very foundations of their cherished quadruple *entente*. To preserve that grouping they were willing to restrain Austria and Prussia and to hold out to the British government the prospect of a joint policy to prevent or circumscribe the threatened conflict.

Provided only that its overriding object of strengthening Bismarck and German conservatism was not jeopardized, the Russian government was willing to co-operate with England in upholding the treaty of

---

[1] The same to the same, 19 and 21 January 1864, RA I 93/128 and I 93/129.
[2] The same to the same, no. 99, 15 January 1864, Steefel, *op. cit.* p. 167. Russell was of the opinion that the policy of Napoleon seemed to be 'by encouraging Denmark and Germany by turns to bring on a war by which France may profit' (Russell to the Queen, 15 January 1864, Gooch, *op. cit.* p. 306).

1852. In a report of 30 December 1863, Napier described Gorchakov's opinions:

Prince Gortchakov affirms that the Imperial Government of France allied with the revolutionary forces in Europe is a constant source of anxiety and disturbance to the other Powers. The bulwark against French ascendancy in the Monarchies of Austria, Prussia and the German Confederation is profoundly shaken and may at any moment be laid in ruins. It therefore behoves England and Russia to lay cautiously and quietly the basis of a common policy the objects of which should be to support the two great German Powers and give them courage to resist the elements of internal dissolution and the menace of foreign aggression. He merely proposes that the four powers should mutually acknowledge their common interests in this matter and avow to each other the formation of a sort of moral coalition against revolutionary conspiracy, Ultra-Democracy, exaggerated nationalism and Military Bonapartist France.[1]

With this object in view Gorchakov, on 24 December, had proposed to the British government a policy of supporting Bismarck as the sole defence against war with Denmark and revolutionary agitation.[2] The Russian government wished to act with that of England but asked, in return, for an explanation of British intentions in the event of complications.[3] Gorchakov did not favour British mediation.[4] He was willing to take part in a conference, even if the Federal Diet refused to be represented.[5] He was reluctant to make on the German powers demands which might be refused[6] but was ready to act with England in warning the Federal Diet about the dangers of a German invasion of Schleswig.[7]

On 15 January, Oubril learnt that the Austrian and Prussian governments were about to present to Denmark an ultimatum summoning her to cancel within forty-eight hours the offending constitution. On 18 January the ultimatum was rejected by the Danish government.[8] Two days later Field-Marshal Wrangel assumed control of the Austro-Prussian forces on the Lower Elbe; on the following day they entered Holstein, already occupied by Saxon and Hanoverian troops.[9]

On hearing of the impending ultimatum, Gorchakov had at once asked the cabinets of Vienna and Berlin to allow more time to Denmark. England and Russia might then employ their good offices. He had earnestly requested Russell to hold similar language in the two German capitals.[10] The Russian minister at Copenhagen received instructions to join with his British colleague in urging the Danes to recall the *Rigsraad*

[1] Napier to Russell, no. 823, most confidential, 30 December 1863, RA I 92/175, copy.
[2] The same to the same, telegram, 24 December 1863, *ibid.* I 92/127.
[3] The same to the same, no. 792, confidential, 22 December 1863, *ibid.* I 92/129, précis.
[4] The same to the same, telegram, 5 January 1864, *ibid.* I 92/188.
[5] The same to the same, telegram, 12 January 1864, *ibid.* I 93/17.
[6] The same to the same, telegram, 10 January 1864, *ibid.* I 93/45.
[7] The same to the same, telegrams, 14 and 15 January 1864, *ibid.* I 93/78 and I 93/97.
[8] *Ibid.* p. 215.　　　　　　　　[9] Steefel, *op. cit.* p. 169.
[10] Napier to Russell, telegram, 16 January 1864, RA I 93/109.

to repeal the Constitution.[1] Brunnow had already been instructed to propose in London that the powers should jointly advise Denmark to accept the occupation of Schleswig[2] in return for the expulsion of Augustenburg from Holstein.[3] It might appear for a moment that Anglo-Russian co-operation was destined to replace that of England and France. Whilst Napoleon sulked and bided his time, England and Russia would speak and act together as the last survivors of the once mighty 'concert of Europe'.[4]

However, Gorchakov soon discovered that Russell's views differed from his own. On 17 January, Brunnow telegraphed that since Prussia's future intentions were unknown, Russell would not recommend the peaceful occupation of Schleswig.[5] On receiving this reply, Gorchakov endeavoured to dispel British mistrust. Prussia's proclamation announcing the impending occupation had stated that she still recognized the treaty of 1852. Gorchakov rightly assumed that Austria also still subscribed to this view. He therefore urged the cabinets of Berlin and Vienna to make a formal declaration in London to this effect. At the same time, he took formal note of the Prussian declaration on behalf of the Russian government.[6]

An exchange of views on this subject now developed between the cabinets of St Petersburg and Berlin. On 19 January, Gorchakov told

[1] The same to the same, telegram, 18 January 1864, *ibid.* I 93/117.

[2] On 15 January, Bismarck informed Oubril that Prussia and Austria would occupy Schleswig as a pledge for the withdrawal of the Danish constitution. The occupation would take place shortly after a forty-eight hour ultimatum. Oubril told Bismarck that such action would create an unfavourable impression. The time allowed to the Danes was too short. This made no impression on Bismarck, from which Oubril concluded that the matter was already settled (Oubril to Gorchakov, 15/3 January 1864, in S. Lesnik, 'Russia and Prussia in the Schleswig-Holstein Question', *Krasny Arkhiv*, 2 (93), (1939), pp. 59ff. (in Russian)). In fact the Austro-Prussian treaty on the occupation of Schleswig was signed on 16 January 1864 (Sybel, *op. cit.* pp. 203ff.).

[3] Napier to Russell, telegram, ? 11 January 1864, RA I 93/56 and Gorchakov to Brunnow, 30 December (O.S.) 1863, Lesnik, *op. cit.* p. 112 n. 15.
In his letter to Brunnow, Gorchakov outlined his future policy. The understanding of the four powers must be maintained. To do so, it was necessary to calm British apprehensions and restrain Prussia from making excessive demands. Apart from this the interest of Russia required the continuance of Bismarck in office. His position in Prussia must be strengthened. Denmark should be induced to accept the occupation of Schleswig in return for the expulsion of the Pretender from Holstein. If England organized a naval demonstration he would hint at Vienna and Berlin that this was directed exclusively against the Diet. In this way, the two powers would be separated from the Diet and 'kept in line' with the other signatories of the treaty (*ibid.*).

[4] Thun told Rechberg: 'Les relations entre les Cabinets de St Pétersbourg et Londres deviennent de jour en jour plus intimes....Le Prince Gortchakov qui, il n'y a pas longtemps, semblait vouloir laisser au Danemarc seul la responsabilité de sa mauvaise foi dans ses rapports avec l'Allemagne, en est maintenant, grâce à l'influence de Lord Napier, à considérer l'intégrité de la Monarchie danoise comme une nécessité européenne, de laquelle il fallait tenir compte n'importe que ce pays remplisse ou non ses engagements internationaux' (Thun to Rechberg, 26/14 January 1864, Steefel, *op. cit.* p. 350).

[5] Gorchakov to Brunnow, 19/7 January 1864, Lesnik, *op. cit.* p. 62.

[6] *Ibid.* Cf. also Thun to Rechberg, telegram, 18 January 1864, Steefel, *op. cit.* p. 350.

Oubril that Russell had rejected a Russian proposal for joint advice to Denmark to accept the occupation of Schleswig. England refused the suggestion because she distrusted the intentions of Prussia and Austria. Both powers must, therefore, without delay give her the necessary assurances. Oubril should explain this to Bismarck.[1] The tsar desired to help Austria and Prussia. He also wished to find a solution capable of reconciling the different interests, thus preserving the understanding of the four powers 'on questions infinitely more important than those now exciting the minds on the banks of the river Eider'.[2]

Gorchakov's despatch crossed a communication from Oubril reporting that Bismarck had expressed anxiety about the eventual attitude of Napoleon.[3] Bismarck had also complained of the silence of England and Russia with regard to the Danish question. He intended to safeguard their interests and would faithfully observe the treaty of London for the sake of four-power agreement. Neither the Russian nor the British government, however, had done anything to help him. He had met only silence on all sides and knew nothing of Russia's intentions. Redern had not written for weeks and Oubril was taciturn. Bismarck, Oubril concluded, was worried by Russian silence. He desired an expression of positive approval for Prussia's continued acceptance of the treaty, couched in language which would commit Russia for the future.[4] On this report the tsar observed: 'We have already said everything it was possible for us to say.' Russia would be neutral in the impending conflict. She would neither encourage Prusso-German adventures nor run the risk of war in defence of the interests of others.[5] In a subsequent conversation reported by Oubril on the 23rd, Bismarck asked even more explicitly that, in view of the correctness of the Prussian attitude, Russia should promise assistance in a possible conflict with France. Oubril replied that as Russia had many internal problems she was reluctant to take an active part in the affairs of others. Prussia, therefore, must not expect material aid. That, Bismarck rejoined, was the view of King William who considered Russia too weak to be an effective ally. He himself had constantly tried to combat this opinion and show that it was unfounded. The Russian government, however, must not itself encourage such beliefs. Could

[1] Thun, Gorchakov added, had been asked to telegraph to Rechberg in this sense. He would also speak to Redern at their next interview.

[2] Gorchakov to Oubril, 19/7 January 1864, Lesnik, *op. cit.* pp. 61f.

[3] Appearances in Paris were peaceful but the French government was evidently reserving its freedom of action supporting neither one side nor the other. Internal difficulties might lead Napoleon to seek diversions abroad. Bismarck considered that Napoleon would first turn to Prussia and take sides against her if his advances were rejected (Oubril to Gorchakov, 20/8 January 1864, *ibid.* pp. 63f.).

[4] *Ibid.*

[5] Thun told Rechberg that Gorchakov had said in his hearing: '"Nous pourrions parler ...plus énergiquement à Copenhague mais comme l'Empereur est décidé à ne faire marcher un homme ou à dépenser un sou ni pour, ni contre le Danemarc, je dois me borner à des conseils"' (Thun to Rechberg, 12/14 January 1864, Steefel, *op. cit.* p. 350).

Russia remain a spectator if French troops occupied Danzig? Oubril, in some embarrassment, replied that, although in his opinion Russia at the moment was very strong, yet internal problems might force her to remain passive. Bismarck, he considered, at the moment of embarking on an active policy in the north, felt uncomfortable between Russian immobility on the one side and French silence on the other.[1] 'As usual, they remember our existence only when they feel themselves threatened', the tsar observed.

On 23 January, Oubril told Bismarck that Russia wished to strengthen his personal position. She had refused a British proposal for mediation by the non-German powers because this would have divided Europe. She had withdrawn from a proposed joint warning to the Diet when it appeared that Drouyn wished to turn it against Austria and Prussia. Russia's main object was the continuance of Austro-Prussian solidarity based on the treaty of 1852 and the satisfaction of Germany's legitimate claims. Gorchakov favoured the Danish proposal for a conference and the peaceful occupation of Schleswig as a pledge for the fulfilment of Danish obligations. Bismarck, Oubril noted, received this communication with satisfaction. He admitted that the idea of a peaceful occupation was new to him but did not deny its advantages. In actual fact, as Oubril observed to Gorchakov, Denmark was unlikely to abandon her defences without a fight. Bismarck did not expect her to do so.[2]

In the meantime, England, Russia and France had finally joined in an effort to prevent the outbreak of war. On 23 January, Napier told Russell that the Russian envoys in Vienna and Berlin would join their British colleagues in advising a six weeks' postponement of all action directed against Denmark.[3] On the following day, Russell invited the co-operation of France. Napoleon agreed to support the Anglo-Russian *démarche*.[4] Representations were accordingly made in Berlin. Buchanan urged the delay of hostilities in writing. Talleyrand made a verbal communication.[5] Oubril read a telegram asking the Prussian government to await at least the arrival of a courier now on his way from St Petersburg.[6] In his reply to Oubril, Bismarck skilfully marshalled the arguments likely to impress the tsar and Gorchakov. He declared that he did not expect fresh developments for another week and was engaged on drafting a note to Russell concerning the integrity of Denmark. For eight days, the king had firmly resisted any declaration on the subject. He had yielded to Bismarck's

[1] Oubril to Gorchakov, private, 23/11 January 1864, Lesnik, *op. cit.* pp. 64f.
[2] The same to the same, 23/11 January 1864, *ibid.* pp. 66f.
[3] Napier to Russell, telegram, 23 January 1864, RA I 93/164.
[4] He did this in the knowledge that the Danish Parliament had already been called to abrogate the constitution of November.
[5] He subsequently told Oubril that Bismarck in his reply had threatened that, if pressed too hard, Prussia would denounce the treaty of 1852 and adopt the principles of the Diet (Oubril to Gorchakov, 25/13 January 1864, Lesnik, *op. cit.* pp. 67f.).
[6] Gorchakov to Oubril, 28/16 January 1864, *ibid.* p. 113 n. 38.

threat of resignation. His opposition was difficult to overcome. Prussia's military honour was at stake. A liberal government might be formed in Berlin and Prussia might be forced to seek the alliance of France. He wished to occupy Schleswig 'on conservative principles', maintain the treaty of 1852 and preserve the Danish monarchy. Was it not the interest of the powers to support him in this policy? Oubril could only express his regret that Denmark's request for a delay had been rejected and point out to Bismarck that France was likely to be found among Prussia's enemies, and that the news from London was alarming.[1]

Russell, in the meantime, had invited the signatories of 1852 to sign a further protocol by which the Danish government agreed to repeal the constitution whilst Austria and Prussia bound themselves to postpone all action in Schleswig.[2] On 27 January, France and Russia 'accepted' the proposal provided Austria and Prussia did the same.[3] Sweden announced her unconditional acceptance.[4] It appeared that some form of European intervention might develop and both Rechberg and Bernstorff expressed alarm at the possibility.[5] William I, bent on war, ordered Russell's proposal to be rejected.[6]

On 31 January, Oubril read to Bismarck a further despatch from St Petersburg. In it, Gorchakov repeated that the tsar desired to facilitate the task of the two German courts by reconciling their international obligations with their internal difficulties and the excitement of spirits in Germany. Napoleon was playing a waiting game. He did not denounce his obligations under the treaty and even promised to support it by diplomatic means. However, when the British government asked for material support, he reserved his freedom of action. Since the moment when the intended occupation of Schleswig and the refusal to delay military action had opened up the prospect of a breach between England and Germany, the cabinet of the Tuileries had become more sympathetic to Denmark.[7] The final attitude of France would depend on relations among the four powers. That was why, in the interest of Prussia, to whom all the tsar's sympathies belonged, as well as in that of general peace, the

---

[1] Oubril to Gorchakov, 28/16 January 1864, *ibid.* pp. 68ff. In fact, Bernstorff was sending alarming reports (Sybel, *op. cit.* p. 222). The *Morning Post*, believed to reflect the views of Palmerston, was thundering against Germany and discussing the possibility of armed assistance to Denmark (Steefel, *op. cit.* p. 165).

[2] Russell to the Queen, 25 January 1864, RA I 93/175 enclosing draft protocol (*ibid.* I 93/176).

[3] Napier to Russell, telegram, 27 January 1864, and Cowley to Russell, 27 January 1864, *ibid.* I 93/198 and I 93/176, copy.

[4] Jerningham to Russell, telegram, 28 January 1864, *ibid.* I 93/202.

[5] Sybel, *op. cit.* p. 222.

[6] Buchanan to Russell, 29 January 1864, RA I 93/205.

[7] Cowley, at this time, wrote to Russell that Drouyn's language was 'very correct'. France would, at the appropriate moment, propose the creation of a Scandinavian kingdom. Napoleon, after a little fighting, would again call for a general Congress (Cowley to Russell, private, 31 January 1864, *ibid.* I 93/218, copy).

Russian government had invariably advocated a solution which would not alienate England from Germany. In the present state of Europe, this consideration must dominate all others.[1] It was doubtful whether the state of public opinion in England, concern for British interests and their own efforts to keep in power would allow the Queen's Ministers to stand idly by whilst the Danish monarchy was being destroyed.[2] If every British proposal was rejected and if, at the same time, the adhesion of the German powers to the settlement of 1852 became doubtful, the British government might be driven against its will to seek agreement with France. Europe would then be divided into two camps: the great interests it was desired to defend would be placed in jeopardy. Already, Russell had inquired of all the signatories whether they were disposed to give Denmark material aid if the Germans attempted to separate the Duchies from the monarchy. Napier, in making this communication, had stated that such action was contemplated only if German demands went beyond the fulfilment of Denmark's international obligations. Gorchakov in reply had invited the British government to describe in greater detail the nature of the help it intended to give to Denmark. He had also asked whether England would help the Danes even if some of the other signatories held back. Since a more detailed despatch was expected from London, Gorchakov had added that he would await its arrival before giving a final reply. In this situation, Gorchakov now appealed to the common sense of the Austrian and Prussian governments. They must reassure England not by ambiguous phrases but in clear and unequivocal terms about their continued adherence to the treaty of 1852 on condition that Denmark fulfilled her obligations. It was impossible with a clear conscience to advise the Danish government to accept passively the occupation of Schleswig without solid guarantees that this act of submission would preserve the integrity of the monarchy. Both Austria and Prussia had solemnly

---

[1] 'We remain firmly of the opinion that in the present state of Europe this consideration must dominate all others' (Gorchakov to Oubril, 28/16 January 1864, Lesnik, *op. cit.* p. 71).

[2] It may be that Gorchakov was not convinced of the likelihood of British intervention and merely used the spectre to frighten Bismarck. Brunnow, at all events, unlike his Prussian colleague in London, did not believe in the British will to act. 'The British fleet', he had written, 'cannot be set in motion without giving France an excuse to move her armies. Palmerston will not decide to cross the Sound for he does not wish Napoleon to cross the Rhine. Therefore both powers will remain immobile' (Brunnow to Gorchakov, undated, *ibid.* p. 113 n. 37). Again on 13 January, he had reported: 'The cabinet decided yesterday to present to the non-Germanic powers the following question: if the Duchies of Schleswig and Holstein should be forcibly separated from Denmark, would they be prepared to defend by material means the integrity of the Danish Monarchy? Russell expects a negative reply without practical result. This is precisely what the majority of the cabinet would prefer in order to justify their inaction, throwing the responsibility on others. Do you not therefore consider it possible, in order to confound their parliamentary calculations, to declare your readiness, together with other powers to consider measures which England might propose in that case?' (the same to the same, 13/1 January 1864, *ibid.* p. 114 n. 43). If Brunnow had hoped, by his suggestion, to promote Anglo-Russian co-operation he failed to achieve his purpose. 'What a pitiful policy!', was Gorchakov's marginal comment (*ibid.*).

declared their intention to occupy Schleswig only as a pledge for the execution of Danish promises. Russia then was merely asking them to repeat formally in London what they had already stated. They were to give to their declarations a practical significance which would contribute to the preservation of peace. They must also consider if it would not be advisable to limit their occupation to a part only of Schleswig without attacking the *Danewerke*, the last defence of Danish independence. The Danish government, in view of public opinion and the uncertainties of the situation, might find it impossible to give up this defensive position.[1]

Bismarck replied that he had used similar arguments with the king but was merely wasting his time. Prussia did not reject the idea of a conference but wanted to 'define the status quo'(!) in the interest of the demands she intended to make on Denmark. Conversations could be held parallel with military events. The king would never agree to the occupation of a part only of Schleswig. Oubril earnestly pressed for firm guarantees to calm British apprehensions. Bismarck again sheltered behind the king who, he claimed, would not agree to a formal guarantee of Danish integrity. Bismarck finally produced the draft of a declaration which was being considered by the Prussian cabinet, but Oubril pointed out that this conditional declaration did not fully meet British wishes. Why, Bismarck then asked, should Prussia be required to give such categorical promises? Could not the powers rely on her 'good faith' and on her confidential assurances?[2]

In fact Gorchakov's efforts to prevent the outbreak of hostilities could no longer affect the course of events. On the very day of Oubril's interview with Bismarck, Wrangel had summoned Meza, the Danish commander, to evacuate Schleswig. In the face of his refusal Austro-Prussian troops crossed the Eider the following morning. On the night of 5–6 February the Danes evacuated the *Danewerke*. The bulk of their forces was concentrated behind entrenched lines in the peninsula of Düppel and on the neighbouring island of Alsen. The rest of the Danish army abandoned Schleswig and retreated into the neighbouring province of Jutland.[3]

When the news of the invasion reached St Petersburg, Gorchakov was unable to conceal his annoyance. The Prussian envoy reported:

'C'est donc la guerre générale que Vous voulez', rief der Fürst. 'Certes' sagte er, 'personne ne peut Vous empêcher de déclarer la guerre au Danemarc, mais personne ne saurait empêcher la France, l'Angleterre et la Suède de venir au secours du

---

[1] Gorchakov to Oubril, 28/16 January, *ibid.* pp. 70ff.
[2] Oubril to Gorchakov, 31/19 January 1864, *ibid.* pp. 72ff. Oubril observed that the British proposals were inconvenient to the Prussian government, which desired to localize but not to prevent the conflict. Bismarck had asked that Prussia should be allowed to exchange a few shots with Denmark. This would clarify the situation. King William particularly desired that his army should see action. Oubril considered that military operations were almost certain. Bismarck refused to name the date but it was certain that they were on the eve of a campaign (*ibid.*).
[3] Steefel, *op. cit.* pp. 169f.

Danemarc. La Russie ne fera amais rien contre la Prusse mais vous aurez les trois autres sur les bras et vous aurez ramené l'entente entre la France et l'Angleterre.'

Gorchakov went on to declare his belief in the value of the treaty of 1852. 'Mais ce n'est pas pour les beaux yeux des Danois', he exclaimed, 'que l'Europe est [*sic*] reconnue de son intégrité, c'est dans un intérêt Européen que le protocol a été signé et cet intérêt prévaut encore aujourd'hui et nous est commun.' During the interview, a messenger arrived with telegrams reporting the first clash of German and Danish forces near Kiel. Gorchakov was profoundly moved[1] and repeatedly exclaimed: 'C'est la guerre générale. Vous aurez la France, l'Angleterre et la Suède contre Vous. La Russie jamais. Jamais elle ne marchera contre la Prusse.'[2] It was fear for Poland as much as concern for Denmark which caused Gorchakov's anxiety. Had not Oubril expressed the belief that Germany would be unable to resist French armies pouring across the Rhine?[3] Had he not told Bismarck that Russia might have to intervene to prevent them from reaching the Vistula?[4] Even if the worst were avoided, would not the invasion destroy the result of months of patient diplomacy? Would there not be a breach between England and the German powers driving one or the other into the arms of France? And with the possible intervention of Sweden as well,[5] would not the dying Polish cause rise like a phoenix from the ashes? There was indeed good reason for Gorchakov's distress.

VI

The unsuccessful Anglo-Russian attempt to prevent the outbreak of war underlined the feebleness of the European concert which had become evident since 1859. United diplomatic action and military preparations were the traditional methods of neutral powers in trying to separate rivals; neither operated effectively during the critical months of December and January, 1863–4. Indeed, Gorchakov had more than once assured the Prussian government that no thought of military intervention would be entertained by Russia. Even without this, Russia's internal situation was known to preclude all possibility of military action not demanded by direct national interests. The British government in its turn, although it spoke of action, was believed almost universally to be unprepared for anything more than words. France alone might be ready to intervene, but it was certain that she would do so in a French, not a European interest. Diplomatic unity among the neutrals was equally far to seek. The tsar's

[1] '...tief erschüttert'.
[2] Redern to Bismarck, 3 February 1864, *ibid.* pp. 349f.
[3] Oubril to Gorchakov, private, 23/11 January 1864, Lesnik, *op. cit.* pp. 65f.
[4] The same to the same, 20/8 January 1864, *ibid.* pp. 63f.
[5] On 4 February Jerningham telegraphed from Stockholm that the king of Sweden had informed the French minister that he could send 20,000 men to Denmark by the end of the month in co-operation with either France or England (Jerningham to Russell, telegram, 4 February 1864, RA I 94/29).

entire policy was based on distrust of Napoleon. Palmerston and Russell heartily shared this sentiment. Napoleon, in his turn, harboured bitter feelings against the British Ministers and watched their embarrassments with pleasure. In addition, the interests of the three governments were incompatible. Russia desired above all the *entente* of the four powers and the strengthening of Bismarck's position. Palmerston and Russell contended for the maintenance of the treaty and the integrity of the Danish monarchy. France stood to gain from hostilities which would destroy the four-power grouping, promote the cause of nationality and offer opportunities for the acquisition of territory. She was consequently unwilling to second wholeheartedly Anglo-Russian efforts to prevent the outbreak of war. No determined opposition to Prussia and Austria was, therefore, to be thought of. Russia was unwilling to back diplomacy by military preparations. The British cabinet was divided. British prestige, moreover, had been sadly shaken by failure to help the Poles. In the circumstances —although Anglo-Russian diplomatic co-operation had become increasingly close—the two powers were unable to prevail over William I's determined desire for war.[1] France, feared and disliked at St Petersburg and deeply distrusted in London, seemed to hold the key to the diplomatic and military situation. Indeed, an energetic policy on her part was likely to have prevented the German occupation of Schleswig. Troop-concentrations on the Rhine carried greater weight than words from St Petersburg and London. Yet both England and Russia would have opposed an active French policy. Their attempts to frighten Bismarck and Rechberg with the empty spectre of hypothetical French intervention in the future were unlikely to be effective. In fact, it was plain for all to see that since the Polish insurrection and the rejection of Napoleon's Congress proposals, France was isolated and not ill-disposed towards Prussia. In the circumstances, such representations as Gorchakov and Russell chose to make could not deflect the German powers from their policy of war and conquest.

[1] The well-informed King of the Belgians wrote to Queen Victoria: 'The poor King of Prussia wanted war, Fritz and Vicky did the same...' (King of the Belgians to the Queen, 2 February 1864, *ibid.* I 94/112 (*QVL, loc. cit.* p. 155)). It is highly significant that King Leopold does not mention Bismarck.

CHAPTER 7

THE POWERS AND THE FUTURE OF THE DUCHIES, 1863–4 (*continued*)

THE German invasion of Schleswig at once made more acute a number of questions hitherto of somewhat academic interest. Would the treaty of 1852 be maintained? Would the Danish monarchy survive the German onslaught? Would Napoleon intervene? Would England afford aid to the Danes? With the outbreak of hostilities decision in these matters was seen to hang in the balance. The initiative of diplomatic action, more clearly than before, appeared to rest with the British government.

I

When Parliament assembled on 4 February the Queen's Speech in the section referring to Denmark ended with the colourless statement that Her Majesty would 'continue Her efforts in the interest of peace'.[1] In the House of Commons Palmerston attempted to show the success of his policy by announcing that

within the last very few hours we have received information from the Austrian and Prussian governments, that they are prepared to declare that they abide by the Treaty of 1852, and will maintain the integrity of the Danish monarchy in accordance with the terms of that treaty.[2]

In the House of Lords, Russell read the text of the Austro-Prussian note of 31 January[3] and his admissions of uncertainty founded on the conditional nature of the undertaking, contrasted strangely with Palmerston's confident assurance.[4] Yet the Foreign Secretary also professed confidence

---

[1] Steefel, *op. cit.* p. 172. A slightly stronger phrase, regarded by the Queen as threatening in tone, had been suppressed at her request (Grey to Granville, 1 February 1864; Lord E. Fitzmaurice, *The Life of Lord Granville* (London, 1905), vol. I, pp. 457f., and the Queen to Palmerston, 2 February 1864, RA I 94/10, copy (*QVL, loc. cit.* pp. 154f.)).

[2] Steefel, *op. cit.* p. 172.

[3] For the genesis of this ambiguous document, cf. Sybel, *op. cit.* pp. 223f.

[4] The cabinets of Berlin and Vienna, Palmerston told the Commons, had now declared 'that they mean as soon as possible to send us a formal declaration that they abide by the treaty of 1852; that they will maintain the integrity of the Danish monarchy; that the invasion of Schleswig, however lamentable it may be and however much to be deplored, is not undertaken for the purpose of dismembering the Danish monarchy; and they are thus committed to evacuate Schleswig whenever the conditions which they attach to the entrance shall have been complied with' (Steefel, *op. cit.* p. 172). Palmerston's confidence in these German assurances appears to have been genuine. Greville, who dined with him on 6 February, found him in 'high feather'. 'He told me', Greville noted in his diary, 'the Danes had evacuated Schleswig, and he supposed the fighting was over. He seemed sanguine that the allies would keep their word and restore to the King of Denmark his dominions,

in Bismarck's promises.[1] The debates in Parliament, in spite of some sharp criticism, did not shake the position of the government. In the Commons, conservative members, led by Disraeli, made it a reproach to Ministers that no material assistance had been given to the Danes. Liberal speakers blamed the Danes for not having done what they ought to have done, but did not much defend the conduct of the Germans.[2] Feeling in the Lords was 'decidedly Danish but against war'. Derby, the leader of the conservatives, made 'a dashing attack' on Russell and his policy of 'meddle and muddle' but deprecated intervention.[3] The hesitant policy of a divided cabinet was shown to represent fully and faithfully the conflicting emotions of Parliament. Neither Derby nor Disraeli could offer an alternative policy to that of Palmerston and Russell.

British representatives abroad, however, warned the government against complacency. From Berlin, Buchanan urged that:

...it is very desirable that the King and all Germany should understand clearly that Great Britain is prepared, in certain eventualities, to give material aid to Denmark. As long as they rest in their present illusion, as to the certainty of our not making any sacrifices...no one is to be trusted.[4]

Napier from St Petersburg echoed the feeling. He recommended the 'presence of an English fleet and Army'. A decided British step 'would probably still lead on the Russians to some extent'. Sympathy for the Danes was rising, although it had not yet reached the Foreign Department. 'I am naturally irritated by the incredulity and sneers of the German Diplomatists and of the Russians, founded on our alleged but misrepresented conduct on the Polish question.'[5] Cowley reported from Paris that the French government still entertained hostile feelings against England and would hold aloof in order to be afterwards master of the situation.[6]

On 10 February, the Cabinet decided to support the proposal for an armistice following the complete evacuation of Schleswig by the Danes. The next day, Austria and Prussia rejected the proposal.[7] On 11 February, the Danish minister in London presented an official appeal for support.

whenever he had revoked the Constitution' (*ibid.* pp. 173f.). It is interesting to note that Gorchakov also continued to affect complete confidence in Austro-Prussian intentions (Napier to Russell, private, 4 February 1864, RA I 94/30, extract copy).

[1] On 2 February, Russell saw Apponyi. 'Lord Russell est enchanté que M. de Bismarck l'ait emporté en définitive sur les idées personnelles du Roi et finit par me faire l'aveu assez piquant dans sa bouche, que dans les circonstances actuelles, Bismarck était le meilleur Ministre qu'on peut avoir en Prusse' (Apponyi to Rechberg, 3 February 1864, Steefel, *op. cit.* p. 173 n. 13).

[2] Palmerston to the Queen, 4 February 1864, RA I 94/21, extract copy.

[3] Granville to the Queen, ?4 February 1864, *ibid.* I 94/22, extract copy.

[4] Buchanan to Russell, private, 6 February 1864, *ibid.* I 94/40, copy.

[5] Napier to Russell, private, 4 February 1864, *ibid.* I 94/30, extract copy.

[6] Cowley to Russell, 5 February 1864, no. 217, confidential, *ibid.* I 94/37, copy.

[7] Russell to the Queen, 11 February 1864, *ibid.* I 94/81 and Bloomfield to Russell, 11 February 1864, no. 106, confidential, *ibid.* I 94/92, copy.

It was probably in consequence of this appeal that Palmerston and Russell gave orders 'to prepare the scheme for an English army to be landed on the shore of Denmark'.[1] On the 12th, Russell telegraphed to Cowley that even if there was a conference it would do little good unless some at least of the non-German powers were agreed on the line they would take. The British government had urged on Austria and Prussia two points: the integrity of the Danish monarchy and the fulfilment by Denmark of her engagements. Would the French, in conference, adhere to these bases and would they agree to confer with the British plenipotentiaries on matters of details and tactics?[2] Drouyn accepted the proposal provided a plenipotentiary of the Diet was invited to the conference and on condition that it was preceded by an armistice.[3] On 13 February, Russell suggested to Palmerston that the British government should invite France to join in an offer of mediation. Moreover

if Austria and Prussia refuse mediation, decline to accept the bases proposed, or insist on terms which are, in the opinion of France and England, inconsistent with the integrity and independence of Denmark, Great Britain will at once despatch a strong squadron to Copenhagen, and France will place a strong corps of troops on the frontiers of the Rhine Provinces of Prussia.[4]

Palmerston raised objections:

I rather doubt however [he replied] the expediency of taking at the present moment the steps proposed. The French government would probably decline it, unless tempted by the suggestion that they should place an armed force on the Rhenish frontier in the event of a refusal by Austria and Prussia—which refusal we ought to reckon upon as nearly certain.

Objections might be urged against the measures suggested as the consequence of a German refusal:

First, that we should not for many weeks to come send a squadron to the Baltic; and that such a step would not have much effect upon the Germans unless it were understood to be a first step towards something more; and I doubt whether the Cabinet or the country are as yet prepared for active interference.

To enter into military conflict with all Germany would be a serious undertaking. If Sweden and Denmark were actively to co-operate with England, 'our 20,000 men might do a good deal'. Austria and Prussia, however, could bring 200,000 or 300,000 into the field and would be joined by the smaller German states.

Secondly, though it is very useful to remind the Austrians and the Prussians privately of the danger they are running at home—Austria in Italy, Hungary and Galicia; Prussia in her Rhenish provinces—yet it might not be advisable nor for our own interest to suggest to France an attack upon the Prussian Rhenish territory.

[1] Steefel, *op. cit.* p. 177.
[2] Russell to Cowley, telegram, 12 February 1864, RA I 94/99.
[3] Cowley to Russell, telegram, 13 February 1864, *ibid.* I 94/106.
[4] Memorandum by Russell, 13 February 1864, Steefel, *op. cit.* pp. 175f.

It would serve Prussia right if such an attack were made and if she remained in the wrong, England could not take part with her against France. 'But the conquest of that territory by France would be an evil for us and would seriously affect the position of Holland and Belgium.' 'On the whole', Palmerston concluded, 'I should say that it would be best for us to wait awhile before taking any strong step in these matters.'[1] Palmerston in this reply had succinctly stated the British dilemma: without the help of Napoleon, no action to restrain the Germans could be effective; to call in the emperor would create dangers on the Rhine and jeopardize British interests. If it was a choice—as it appeared to be—between the Germans in the Duchies and Napoleon on the Rhine, the decision could not be doubted. Had not years of 'Palmerstonian' diplomacy been spent restraining France and Russia and trying to strengthen Germany, Prussia and Austria? To co-operate in a French campaign against Germany would involve a diplomatic revolution which no British government could contemplate in 1864. Russell alone seemed prepared to accept the consequences of French assistance.

Russell's suggested approaches to Russia were likewise vetoed. He had submitted to the Queen the draft of a reply to the Russian inquiry about the nature of possible British assistance to Denmark. Gorchakov, he had written, must understand that for the present it would be premature to enter on matters of detail. The very object of the concert proposed would be 'to settle the nature and extent of the material assistance' to be afforded for maintaining the integrity of Denmark. If the Russian government would 'assent to the principle of giving material aid', the answer to Gorchakov's questions must be 'the result and not the preliminary of the concert to be established'.[2] The Queen objected to the implied proposal for giving material aid to Denmark—which 'she will never, if she can prevent it, allow'—and complained of Napier's 'wild and violent advice'.[3]

On 13 February, there was a meeting of the Cabinet. Granville confidentially reported the proceedings to the Queen: 'Lord Russell announced his adherence to-day to what he believed to be the doctrine of the Cabinet, viz. that there was no question of our going to war single-handed. I believe Palmerston has no wish to go to war at all.' He himself had long come to a fixed determination on the question of war and peace 'which I know is shared by some of my colleagues'. 'On the other hand, I think it would weaken the hands of Lord Russell in negotiation to an injurious degree, if any determination of this sort on the part of the Cabinet, or a portion of it, was allowed to be known.'[4] Wood, another leader of the peace-party gave 'most satisfactory assurances that the

---

[1] Palmerston to Russell, 13 February 1864, *ibid.* pp. 176f.
[2] Russell to Napier, draft, February 1864, RA I 94/9.
[3] The Queen to Russell, 13 February 1864, *ibid.* I 94/127, copy (*QVL, loc. cit.* p. 156).
[4] Granville to Grey, 13 February 1862 (? 1864) confidential, RA I 94/129 (*QVL, loc. cit.* p. 157).

Cabinet is not likely to be dragged into war'. 'It is certain that neither France, Russia nor Sweden will join in giving material aid to Denmark, and even Lord Russell concurs in the resolution adopted by the Cabinet on Sir Charles Wood's proposal, that England could not move alone.' Wood had found Palmerston 'quite as strong against war as he was himself'. The Queen might rest '*perfectly* assured'.[1]

At a further meeting of the Cabinet on 17 February, Russell gave up altogether his proposed despatch to Napier. He also abandoned such portions as the Queen had objected to in his draft reply to the Danish appeal for aid.[2] However, in reporting the proceedings, Wood sounded a warning note:

> It is clear that in present circumstances neither France nor Russia will do anything beyond moral support to her [Denmark]: we also; so Her Majesty may be easy on that score. But it really will require the greatest care in any step that we take for I do not know what may turn up any day....[3]

Gorchakov, in the meantime, was continuing his efforts to save the treaty of 1852. On 11 February, he had addressed yet another despatch to the Russian chargé d'affaires in Berlin. The occupation of Schleswig, he observed, would soon be an accomplished fact. Austria and Prussia would thus achieve the object of their military demonstration. The Russian government for its part had never opposed the Austro-Prussian occupation. The tsar had accepted the explanations offered by the two powers and continued to believe in their loyalty. Indeed, the declaration made by Austria and Prussia in London had helped British Ministers in Parliament.[4] The British cabinet was peace-loving and there could be no doubt of its desire to avoid a conflict with Germany. Nevertheless, it would be unwise to rely on this in all circumstances. The task of the British Ministers must, therefore, be facilitated and they must be reassured about Austro-Prussian intentions. In these circumstances, the tsar hoped that Germany would reject neither the British suggestion of an armistice nor the renewed Danish proposal for a conference.[5] Bismarck replied that the Prussian government supported the integrity of Denmark in the terms of the declaration made in London, that is, conditionally. It considered itself

---

[1] Grey to the Queen, 16 February 1864, RA I 94/148.
[2] In a despatch dated 19 February, Russell announced the intention of the British government not to take any action except after full consideration and communication with France and Russia. In communicating this despatch to the Danish minister in London, the Foreign Secretary added that correspondence exchanged with St Petersburg and Paris afforded no reason for the belief that either Russia or France would join with England in giving material support to Denmark for the defence of her territorial integrity. Steefel, *op. cit.* p. 177.
[3] Wood to Grey, 17 February 1864, RA I 94/150.
[4] Gorchakov added that there had indeed been a shade of difference in the expressions used by Palmerston and those of Russell in describing the declaration. It would have been desirable that the cabinets of Vienna and Berlin should have furnished no cause for this (Gorchakov to Mohrenheim, private, 11 February/30 January 1864, Lesnik, *op. cit.* pp. 74ff.).
[5] *Ibid.*

released from all obligation to Denmark. Should a change become necessary, it would prefer the claims of Duke Peter II of Oldenburg to those of the duke of Augustenburg.[1] Bismarck would agree to a conference provided there were no preliminary conditions; he had no doubt that Austria also would accept.[2] On the previous day, the Danish minister in St Petersburg had addressed to Gorchakov an appeal for aid similar to the one the Danes were making in London. The tsar wrote in the margin: 'We have already done and will continue to do *morally* everything that can be done for the defence of Danish rights. As for material intervention, that is not to be thought of.'[3]

II

On 18 February a Prussian detachment crossed the frontier from Schleswig into Jutland and occupied the town of Kolding.[4] The news of this event created a profound sensation in London and Paris. In conjunction with reports in the newspapers that a squadron of twelve Austrian men-of-war had been ordered to proceed to northern waters,[5] it precipitated the first great crisis of the Schleswig-Holstein dispute. On 20 February, Russell telegraphed to Berlin that the invasion of Jutland of which the British government had never been notified, was 'a very serious affair'.[6] To Vienna, he addressed a telegraphic inquiry. Did Austria intend to send men-of-war into the English Channel? Was it intended that they should attack Copenhagen? The matter was very serious.[7] That day, Palmerston wrote to the duke of Somerset, the First Lord of the Admiralty, to urge the despatch of a British squadron to Copenhagen 'as soon as the season will permit', to 'prevent any invasion or attack upon Zealand and Copenhagen'. Austria and Prussia, 'reckoning upon our passive attitude,

---

[1] The Russian dynasty had distant claims to Holstein and part of Schleswig. In 1762, after the death of Peter III of Russia, Catherine II had renounced these rights on behalf of her son Paul, then a minor. The renunciation had been made conditional on the continuation of the established Danish dynasty. In the event of its disappearance, the claims of the Russian dynasty had been reserved (Lesnik, *op. cit.* p. 53). It was understood—although the formal transfer did not take place until later—that the Russian claims had been transferred to the Oldenburg branch of the house of Holstein-Gottorp in the person of Duke Peter II.

[2] Mohrenheim to Gorchakov, telegram, 14/2 February 1864, *ibid.* p. 115 n. 57.

[3] Remark by the tsar on Plessen to Gorchakov, 13/1 February 1864, *ibid.* p. 77.

[4] The occupation of Kolding appears to have been due to the unauthorized action of a local commander. On 15 February, Field-Marshal Wrangel had been instructed not to cross into Jutland without further orders. The emperor Francis-Joseph had instructed his commanders that they must on no account take part in an invasion of Jutland (Sybel, *op. cit.* pp. 255f.). It appears that the occupation of Kolding came as an unpleasant surprise to Bismarck (Steefel, *op. cit.* p. 201). The Prussian government decided to maintain the occupation but refrain from a further advance into Jutland until agreement with Austria had been reached (Sybel, *op. cit.* pp. 256f.).

[5] Russell to Bloomfield, no. 76, 20 February 1864, FO 7/664, draft.

[6] Russell to Buchanan, telegram, 20 February 1864, RA I 94/189.

[7] Russell to Bloomfield, telegram, 20 February 1864, *ibid.* I 94/185.

contemplate the occupation of Copenhagen...and mean to dictate at the Danish capital their own terms of peace. We should be laughed at if we stood by and allowed this to be done'.[1]

On Sunday, 21 February, Somerset informed the Queen that the Cabinet had decided to recall the Channel squadron to protect British waters and be available in case of unforeseen emergencies.[2] Russell telegraphed to Cowley:

It is in agitation to send the whole or part of our Channel fleet to Copenhagen to watch the enemies of Denmark and act according to circumstances. I have written to tell Brunnow that such a measure has been thought of and I hope both French and Russians will adopt a similar course.[3]

The new determination of the British government coincided with a change in Napoleon's plans. On 19 February, Cowley had reported that the emperor and Drouyn would not sincerely co-operate with England.[4] By the following afternoon, however, the situation had changed. The French government, Cowley now wrote, had watched with alarm Prussian steps to dispose of the Duchies in favour of the duke of Oldenburg and now felt more inclined to act in concert with England.[5] On 21 February, Cowley added that the invasion of Jutland and the Prussian threat to invade Saxony had 'made a great impression here, and we might profit by the moment if we think it advisable. Perhaps co-operation in a naval demonstration might be obtained'.[6]

At six o'clock, on the afternoon of 21 February, La Tour informed Drouyn by telegram of the British proposal for naval action. Russell had just told him that he had intimated in Vienna that if allied troops remained in Jutland, a British squadron would be sent to Copenhagen. Russell considered that the presence of such a squadron in Danish waters would

---

[1] Palmerston to duke of Somerset, 20 February 1864, Ashley, *op. cit.* p. 249.

[2] Duke of Somerset to the Queen, 21 February 1864, RA I 94/203 (*QVL*, *loc. cit.* p. 160).

[3] Russell to Cowley, telegram reported in the same to the same, 21 February 1864, FO 27/1517, no. 189, draft.

[4] Cowley to Russell no. 280, confidential, 19 February 1864, RA I 94/158, copy. Napoleon and Drouyn, Cowley wrote, considered a Scandinavian Union as an ulterior possibility and would not go to war with Germany unless there was a certainty of success.

[5] The same to the same no. 282, confidential, 20 February 1864, *ibid.* I 94/192, copy. Drouyn had expressed a guarded desire for co-operation with England. He had explained that Napoleon's expectant attitude had been dictated 'solely by the feeling of responsibility which would weigh upon him in engaging in a war with Germany, and by the apprehension of the selfish views which would immediately be attributed to him'. That evening Drouyn had telegraphed to Vienna and Berlin to ask whether the troops which had entered Jutland would be withdrawn into Schleswig (Steefel, *op. cit.* p. 187). Goltz sent Bismarck a telegram warning him that France was preparing to assume an attitude unfavourable to Prussia (*ibid.*). The French press had adopted a tone which reminded the Prussian ambassador of the height of the Polish crisis (*ibid.* p. 191).

[6] Cowley to Russell private, telegram, 21 February 1864, RA I 96/196. On the afternoon of 21 February, Drouyn expressed to Goltz his distrust of Prussian policy based on the ambiguity of Prussia's conduct and the lack of proportion between the object professed and the means employed by her (Steefel, *op. cit.* p. 191).

strengthen his hand in the negotiations which were about to open. The squadron would leave in about ten days ('dans une dizaine de jours').[1] Some time after his conversation with La Tour, Russell received from the Prussian ambassador a note explaining and minimizing the German occupation of Kolding. The Austrian government, moreover, disclaimed all intention of sending its vessels into the Baltic.[2] Shortly before midnight, Russell informed La Tour of these developments and explained that they were 'de nature...à suspendre les résolutions' to send a squadron to the Baltic. The ambassador at once apprised his government of the change.[3] When Cowley the next morning broached the subject in Paris, Drouyn informed him that Russell had changed his mind: 'Under these circumstances the proposal which you make to me falls to the ground, and there is no occasion for me to take further notice of it.'[4]

Napoleon's return to a policy of expectancy after his momentary readiness to co-operate with the British government[5] was an event of considerable importance. Bismarck's position at this moment was difficult. He explained to the French ambassador:

> But Austria still refuses her consent to the entry of the allied troops into Jutland. Russia, frightened of a Scandinavian union, urges an armistice, a conference, and the integrity of the Danish Monarchy. England threatens us and, if Prussia has now to face the opposition of France as well, she will have to call a halt, for she cannot alienate the four Great Powers at once.[6]

It was Napoleon's decision to revert to the policy of expectancy which helped Bismarck out of his immediate difficulties.[7]

---

[1] La Tour to Drouyn, telegram, 21 February 1864, 6 p.m., *Les Origines diplomatiques de la guerre de 1870–71* (hereafter quoted as *Origines*), 29 vols. (1910 *et seq*.), vol. I, p. 349.

[2] Rechberg had assured Bloomfield that the report of a meditated attack on Copenhagen was 'absurd'. The vessels that were being despatched were intended to protect Austrian shipping in the Adriatic and Mediterranean although some might 'possibly proceed to the entrance of the British Channel to protect Austrian merchant ships coming from America' from attacks by Danish privateers (Bloomfield to Russell, telegram, 21 February 1864, reported in the same to the same, 21 February 1864, FO 7/667, no. 123).

[3] La Tour to Russell, telegram, 21 February 1864, 11.34 p.m., *Origines, loc. cit.* pp. 349f.

[4] Cowley to Russell, no. 289, 22 February 1864, Steefel, *op. cit.* p. 192.

[5] Under the date of 19 February, Vielcastel had noted in his diary: 'Des renseignements positifs permettent d'affirmer que l'Alliance Anglo-Française est un fait accompli. Cette alliance se combine avec le concours de l'Italie et elle a pour formule la défense de l'intégrité du Danemark' (*ibid.* p. 193 n. 64).

[6] Talleyrand to Drouyn, 23 February 1864, *ibid.* p. 195.

[7] The causes of Napoleon's second *volte face* cannot be established with certainty. Cowley, who was extremely well informed, believed that it was due to the persuasions of the empress, Metternich, and Drouyn, who with the help of La Tour's second telegram were able to persuade Napoleon that the British government was not in earnest (Cowley to Russell, no. 299, most confidential, 23 February 1864, Steefel, *op. cit.* p. 193). Goltz attributed the return to a passive attitude more particularly to the fact that England would not accept the conditions necessary to secure Napoleon's co-operation (Goltz to King William, 24 February 1864, *ibid.* p. 194). Cowley reported yet another reason: 'Rouher told me last night that with patience all would come right—that Metternich had alarmed the

The British government on 22 February was still unaware that Napoleon's attitude had again undergone a change. On that day, a vigorous correspondence took place among those responsible for shaping British policy. The Queen expressed alarm at the tenor of the telegrams sent to her and urged that there should be no change in British policy.

> If indeed there had been any intention to attack Copenhagen, the state of affairs would have been different, and such an eventuality would have required the most serious attention of her Government; but as this is totally out of the question, the Queen expects that there will be no change in our present attitude.[1]

The Queen's letter elicited replies from both the Foreign Secretary and the Prime Minister. Russell in defending the course he had adopted, explained that he was 'obliged when a policy is determined upon, to make enquiries & pursue the line from day to day & almost from hour to hour'. If the German powers were not stopped, they would attack Copenhagen. As long as they did not do so, an attitude of mediation would be best and safest.[2] Palmerston, in his turn, explained in a lengthy letter his views on the European situation:

> ...The French Emperor is holding back to be enabled either to seize the Rhenish provinces of Prussia, or to occupy the Palatinate of Bavaria, or to put himself at the head of a Confederacy of the Rhine, or to co-operate with the Italians against Venetia, or to give countenance and assistance to the Hungarians, or the Galicians, or to support the Moldo-Wallachians and the Servians in a revolt against Turkey, according as one or other of those schemes may in the varying circumstances of the moment seem best adapted to promote the ambitious projects of France; and he feels quite sure that when the proper moment for action arises, he will have a military force sufficient for any purpose, and that he will be backed up in any aggressive action by the general approval of the French nation.

He had hitherto kept himself free from any engagement to co-operate with England

> ...first, because he hoped that England might be led to commit herself by a land operation and thus show to the world the smallness of her military means; and, secondly, because he wished to keep his own hands free to act in any way, and in any place, that might best suit his views, whereas an agreement to concert with

Emperor by stating that a combined movement on the part of England and France would keep Austria and Prussia together, whereas Austria desired to get out of the scrape' (Cowley to Russell, telegram, 24 February 1864, *ibid.* pp. 193f. n. 66). Assurances from Vienna and Berlin as to the accidental character of the advance into Jutland indicated that there was as yet no determination on the part of Austria and Prussia to attack Denmark proper (*ibid.* p. 194). Steefel's surmise that 'the most significant explanation of the restored good humor in Paris' was to be found in certain vague hints from Bismarck, details of which are unknown, is controverted by the dates of the correspondence (*ibid.* pp. 194f.). There seems every reason to believe that the decisive factors in influencing Napoleon's attitude were Russell's hesitations and the advice of the empress and Metternich.

[1] The Queen to Russell, 21 February 1864, RA I 94/193 (*QVL, loc. cit.* p. 161).
[2] Russell to the Queen, 22 February 1864, RA I 94/221.

England would be an inconvenient shackle upon his motions. For these reasons the French Emperor declined our proposal that he should concert and co-operate with us.

When some days ago it was reported that an Austrian fleet was coming to the north,

that seemed to Lord Russell and Viscount Palmerston a favourable occasion for renewing, upon a more limited scale and for a purpose purely naval, and entirely protective, the proposal which, with the consent of the Cabinet and of your Majesty, had been made in the more general and comprehensive terms alluded to above.

It appeared, however, by a telegram from Vienna that the Austrian government entirely disavowed any intention of attacking Zealand or Copenhagen. If any such move were contemplated, it would be 'disgraceful for England' to allow it.

It is quite intelligible and reasonable that the British government should hesitate to send 20,000 British troops, and more could not be got together, to face the hundreds of thousands which Germany, if united, could oppose to us; and even with the co-operation of 30,000 Danes and 20,000 Swedes, our aggregate force would not numerically be a match for the enemy, though possibly in a narrow country like Jutland and Schleswig, the advantage might be on our side. But that England, the first and greatest Naval Power, should allow an Austrian fleet to sail by our shores, and go and conquer and occupy the island capital of a friendly Power, towards which we are bound by national interests and Treaty engagements, would be a national disgrace to which Viscount Palmerston, at least, never would stoop to be a party. It makes one's blood boil even to think of it; and such an affront England, whether acting alone or with Allies, ought never to permit.

There seemed, however, no danger of such an intention on the part of Austria and Prussia at present.[1]

It was against the background of this correspondence that Russell, in ignorance of Napoleon's changed attitude, sent further telegrams to St Petersburg and Paris, inviting the co-operation of the Russian and French governments in a naval demonstration for the protection of Denmark.[2] He informed the Queen that 'in the opinion of the Cabinet the Channel Fleet ought to be sent to Copenhagen. Instructions must be carefully prepared for this purpose and will be submitted to your Majesty.'[3]

[1] Palmerston to the Queen, 22 February 1864, RA I 94/219 (*QVL, loc. cit.* pp. 161 ff.).

[2] To Cowley, Russell telegraphed: 'It is very desirable that if there is naval demonstration it should be by France, Britain, Russia and Sweden. If Russia refuses, the other three might still act together and obtain good terms of peace without leaving the character of mediators. If France and Russia refuse, England must be at liberty to act as she thinks fit' (Russell to Cowley, telegram, 22 February 1864, RA I 94/223). To Napier, Russell sent a similar communication. The British government, he stated, was ready to meet the other powers in conference. To prevent new complications, a British squadron might go to the Baltic. The British government would be glad if France and Russia joined in a naval demonstration to protect the Danish capital. The powers need not go beyond the character of mediators (Russell to Napier, telegram, 22 February 1864, *ibid.* I 94/224).

[3] Russell to the Queen, 22 February 1864, *ibid.* I 94/221.

Russell's telegrams to Paris and St Petersburg had been despatched without the sanction of either Queen or cabinet. When the Queen heard of them, she asked the Foreign Secretary to tell Napier not to act until he received further orders.[1] On 23 February, Russell complied with this request.[2] That day, he learnt from Cowley that the French government was disinclined to engage in hostilities against Germany and had no desire to join in a naval demonstration.[3]

Furthermore at a meeting of the Cabinet on 24 February,

it was generally agreed...that the case not occurring, there is no question of sending the Channel Fleet to the Baltic at present, but in case of a danger to Copenhagen the reason would revive, and that it would be imprudent to withdraw altogether any proposal on the subject.[4]

Russell accordingly sent telegrams to Cowley and Napier saying: 'There is no case at present for sending a fleet to the Baltic, and the question may drop till a fresh danger arises.'[5]

On 23 February before the arrival of the countermanding telegram Napier had made his communication. Gorchakov, who already knew through Brunnow the nature of the British proposal, replied that he must of course refer it to the tsar. For his own part, he could only say that he would not be disinclined to join the British government. However, as the Gulf of Finland would be frozen until May, the Russian squadron could not appear in Danish waters before the middle of that month. To Napier's suggestion that there were Russian vessels in American ports, Gorchakov replied that it would be two months before they could reach the Baltic. They were, moreover, of a class too insignificant for the purpose. If Russia appeared before Copenhagen, she must do so with befitting dignity.[6] In a letter to Brunnow reporting this conversation Gorchakov remarked that he had still to discuss the question with the tsar. From some marginal notes, however, he concluded that the emperor would be prepared to consider the arrangement.[7] He could say no more at present as his master was away hunting; the present letter was merely an expression of good intentions, to keep alive British hope of Russian co-operation. The question itself must be decided during the discussion of details. They must make sure that the prospect of aid, partly material,

---

[1] The Queen to Russell, telegram, ?22 February 1864, *ibid*. I 94/225.

[2] Russell to Napier, telegram, 23 February 1864, reported in Russell to Napier, 23 February 1864, FO 65/655 no. 54, draft.

[3] Cowley to Russell, no. 289, 22 February 1864, *ibid*. I 94/226, copy.

[4] Russell to the Queen, 24 February 1864, *ibid*. I 94/237. [5] *Ibid*.

[6] Napier to Russell, telegram and despatch, 23 February 1864, and telegram, 24 February 1864, Steefel, *op. cit*. pp. 198f.

[7] The evidence only partially supports Gorchakov's assertion. In the margin of a telegram from Brunnow of 9/22 February 1864, Lesnik found written by the hand of the emperor against the passage 'Russell would see with satisfaction our fleet uniting itself (with the British) when the time of the year permits', the words 'I hope that by that time the situation will have improved' (Lesnik, *op. cit*. p. 115 n. 60).

partly moral, did not create dangerous illusions in the mind of the Danish Ministers. The latest news from Copenhagen described them as bellicose, desiring neither conference, armistice nor counsel. However, Anglo-Russian action might calm spirits in Copenhagen. For this it was necessary to make clear to the Danish government the intentions of the friendly courts. Mediation must be a reality not an empty phrase and Russia must not allow herself to be drawn further. On this basis, he would wish to know later on the number and tonnage of the vessels earmarked for the British squadron as well as the reply of the French government to Russell's proposal. The time, however, had not yet come for discussing these questions of detail which presupposed a definite decision. Events might still make such action unnecessary—a fact to which Napier himself had drawn attention. If the Russian government agreed to the demonstration, it would be, above all, to prevent England from throwing herself into the arms of France—thus creating a coalition inevitably directed against Austria and Prussia. A further object would be to acquire influence at Copenhagen to be used for pacific purposes, and to strengthen the Danish government in its struggle with anarchy and local demagogy.[1]

On the afternoon of 25 February, Napier told Gorchakov that, as a result of tranquillizing assurances from Vienna and Berlin, the British government had decided not to send a squadron to the Baltic. Gorchakov expressed his approval of the decision. The invasion of Jutland, he observed, had naturally aroused British apprehensions, and he would have been reluctant to separate himself from England in a naval demonstration. The recent declarations of the Austrian and Prussian governments, however, justified the abandonment of the action previously contemplated.[2]

Napier was disappointed.[3] In a despatch written on 1 March, he repeated the opinion that the appearance of a British squadron before Copenhagen would have a salutary effect. Gorchakov had never stated the views of the tsar on the subject.

I risk nothing, however, in asserting that the sentiments of the Emperor would have been found to be conformable to those of the Minister on this subject and that the Russian flag would not have been wanting eventually if Her Majesty's Government had persevered in their intention to support their mediation by a naval demonstration.[4]

---

[1] Gorchakov to Brunnow, 24/12 February 1864, *ibid.* pp. 79f.
[2] Napier to Russell, no. 132, 25 February 1864, RA I 95/11, copy.
[3] Gorchakov in his correspondence expressed the belief that Napier's reports called for armed intervention and in general for extreme measures. His British pride suffered at the thought that the greatness of his country was being destroyed by the actions of its government. He felt himself humiliated and was dominated by one aim—to free himself from that oppressive feeling. The interest of general peace he relegated to second place (Gorchakov to Brunnow, 24/12 February 1864, Lesnik, *op. cit.* pp. 79f.).
[4] The same view was expressed in even more emphatic terms by Lord Redesdale, who was at this time attached to the British embassy in St Petersburg (Steefel, *op. cit.* p. 200).

Gorchakov declared that the British proposal, although abandoned, had served a useful purpose. 'The Vice-Chancellor thinks that the attitude taken by Her Majesty's Government had a good effect at Vienna and Berlin.'[1]

Thus ended the only serious attempt ever undertaken to bring about some form of armed mediation in the conflicts between Prussia and her successive opponents. Once again a German threat to Denmark had produced the beginnings of a *rapprochement* among powers who had been drifting apart. England had shown a momentary decision, France an unexpected readiness to co-operate. Russia had abandoned her reserve, and although unwilling to take up arms in defence of Denmark, had indicated a strong desire to maintain an understanding with England. Sweden would have joined any move for Scandinavian defence. That the attempt failed was due primarily to Russell's change of language during the course of the critical Sunday. It was this which, when reported to Paris, gave the empress Eugénie and Metternich their chance to convince Napoleon that the time for action had not yet come. The emperor's decision put an end to all serious prospect of mediation even before the Queen and the majority of British Ministers finally killed the proposal. Nor indeed were the circumstances propitious as they had been for the similar concert of 1848-52. Russia was weaker and Alexander II lacked his father's imperious determination. Palmerston who had lost much of his former influence, was effectively restrained by the Queen and his pacific colleagues. The attitude of France was as formerly ambiguous. Last, but not least, Germany was stronger and more united. Bismarck's problem in 1864, therefore, was less difficult than that of his predecessors had been.

Nevertheless, even the threat of armed mediation was not without its effect. Gorchakov remarked to Napier on the salutary impression produced in Berlin and Vienna. On 27 February, Bernstorff notified to Russell Prussia's acceptance of a conference to be attended by the signatories of the treaty and a representative of the Confederation.[2] The powers might yet hope to exercise some influence in shaping the final solution.

III

On 5 March, Austria and Prussia decided to extend hostilities to the whole of Jutland, and to announce at the same time their readiness to conclude an armistice and attend a conference.[3] Confident that 'the love of Peace will prevent either Russia, England or France from stirring'[4] they advanced against their Danish adversary. By 20 March the whole of southern

---

[1] Napier to Russell, no. 137, confidential, 1 March 1864, RA I 95/14, copy.
[2] Bernstorff to Russell, 27 February 1864, *ibid.* I 94/178, copy.
[3] Sybel, *op. cit.* pp. 265ff.
[4] Howard to Russell, no. 147, 14 April 1864, RA I 96/51, copy, summary.

Jutland was in German hands. Bismarck in the meantime was successfully spinning out the preliminary discussions among the powers to enable German troops to take Düppel, Denmark's last fortified line on the mainland of Schleswig, before the opening of the conference. By the end of the month the Germans were ready to open the assault. On 18 April the Danes abandoned the position. Only the waters of the Baltic and the small Danish navy now stood between the islands and immediate invasion. Two days later, the conference opened in London.

In these circumstances the attitude to be adopted by the neutral powers at the forthcoming conference became a matter of importance. Would England, France and Russia, or any two of them agree on a joint policy, re-form the 'concert' and bring about a European settlement of the Danish question? Or would their disunity allow the Germans to dictate terms to a defeated Denmark and impose a German 'solution' of the Schleswig-Holstein dispute?

In anticipation of a conference the French government had on 12 March proposed to the British that they should jointly recommend the division of Schleswig according to nationalities.

> The cause and distinguishing characteristic of this conflict [Drouyn argued] is clearly the rivalry of the populations that make up the Danish Monarchy. There exists in each of them a national sentiment, the strength of which cannot be doubted. What is more natural than, in default of a unanimously accepted principle, to take as a basis the wishes of the populations?[1]

Palmerston and Russell, whilst ready to admit that consultation of the inhabitants might solve the problem of the mixed zones of Schleswig, doubted the wisdom of making it the basis of Franco-British policy before the conference opened. If they did so, other powers would oppose the suggestion which might thus prevent the results to be hoped for from the discussions themselves.[2] There was, moreover, a more fundamental objection to the French proposal: '...the great objection to the proposal of consulting the population of the Duchies as to the choice of their future sovereign is the publicity that was given to it.—It has stimulated revolutionary passions all over Germany....' Fair elections, therefore, would now be almost impossible to organize:

> In fact even the evacuation of the Duchies by the troops of Austria and Prussia and of Denmark also would not now render it possible to have an election of a sovereign fairly conducted, even if the principle were admitted. For German agitators have so disturbed all the elements of peace and order that the population would give their votes under the influence of terror.[3]

Having rejected the French proposal, the British government decided to send to Paris Clarendon, its ablest negotiator, to try and secure Anglo-

---

[1] Steefel, *op. cit.* p. 207.
[2] *Ibid.*
[3] Russell to Cowley, 9 April 1864, FO 27/1518, no. 356, draft.

French agreement on some other basis.[1] A letter from Russell to Clarendon outlined a possible solution.[2] Schleswig, the Foreign Secretary proposed, should be divided. The northern portion should be joined with Denmark but have a local representation of its own, the south should be linked with Holstein. The fate of the mixed districts should be decided by the conference. Holstein and South Schleswig should have a Diet of their own with the exclusive right to legislate and vote taxes. In this way '...the Nationalities might be kept in peace, if not in complete harmony'. If the Danes rejected the proposal, they would be told that they must expect no further help. If the refusal came from Germany, 'it would be desirable to establish a concert between France, England, Russia and Sweden— France, England and Russia, or England and Russia only engaging to defend Zealand, and Sweden engaging to assist in the defence of Jutland and Funen'. In making this suggestion, Russell added, he was going beyond anything the Cabinet had authorized. Clarendon might show his letter to Palmerston and ask him, how far he agreed.[3] Palmerston, in fact, proved unwilling to abandon the settlement of 1852. On the day of Clarendon's departure, Russell wrote:

I quite agree with Palmerston...but I know not how much we shall be able to save out of the fix for Denmark. The thing above all to be depreciated [*sic*] is a plebiscite. It would be conducted by means of terror on both sides and would be an irregular war between German [*illegible*] and a Danish armed force.[4]

These very uncertain instructions augured ill for the success of Clarendon's mission. There were, in fact, three competing British policies: that of the Queen who opposed any understanding with France;[5] that of the Prime Minister, who deluded himself about the possibility of Anglo-French agreement to defend the settlement of 1852; and that of the Foreign Secretary who was working for a compromise based on a modification of Napoleon's proposal. In view of this division, which in fact lead to the absence of any clear policy, the British emissary was faced with an impossible task.

Napoleon received Clarendon with personal distinction but made it clear from the start that he would neither threaten Germany nor go to war for Schleswig. Clarendon reported:

The Emperor seems desirous that his policy with respect to Denmark should not be misunderstood by us. He said that there was no denying that we had received a *gros souflet* with respect to Poland from Russia, and that to get another from Germany without resenting it was more than he could stand, as he would have fallen

[1] Russell to the Queen, 9 April 1864, RA I 96/30.
[2] On 27 March Russell had told the Queen that 'it would be absurd to exclude deliberation on other and better arrangements than those of 1852' (the same to the same, 27 March 1864, *ibid.* J 95/144).
[3] Russell to Clarendon, 12 April 1864, Clarendon MSS.
[4] The same to the same, 13 April 1864 (*ibid.*).
[5] She had expressed misgivings about sending Clarendon to Paris but had been overruled by the Cabinet (Grey to Russell, 10 April 1864, RA I 96/31, copy).

into contempt. He could not therefore join us in strong language to the German Powers, *not being prepared to go to war with them.* The question did not touch the dignity or the interests of France, and caused no excitement here....He was determined not to go to war for another reason, viz. that France would look for some compensation on the Rhine, and that would set all Europe against him. The universal belief that he wanted to extend the French frontier in this direction made him doubly cautious. The policy of nationalities was popular in France and congenial to his own feelings. He could not, therefore, be a party to replacing the Holsteiners under the rule of Denmark, which they detested; and, as his great desire was to see Venetia wrested from Austria and restored to Italy, he could not lay himself open to the charge of pursuing one policy on the Eider and a totally different one on the Po.[1]

In the circumstances there was no possibility of an understanding and Clarendon left Paris empty-handed. British and French policies at the conference would not be identical.

Nor had it proved possible for France and Russia to reach agreement. The Russian government like the British had declined Napoleon's proposal for a plebiscite and the reasons for its refusal had revealed the profound difference between the French and Russian points of view. When the French proposal was first laid before him, Gorchakov replied that he would refrain from arguing against the principle of basing political decisions on the consultation of populations. He must, however, point out that besides the principle of nationality there was another, laid down in a formal treaty which France as well as Russia had signed. This was the principle of Danish integrity which had been recognized by all the powers as an important element in the European balance. Moreover, even were the principle of consultation to be admitted, it would still be necessary to create conditions permitting its application. If a plebiscite was to have even a semblance of expressing popular wishes, the conference would have to restore the situation which existed before the present conflict: German troops must withdraw, the Pretender must be removed, and the authority of the king of Denmark be re-established. It was not in the power of the conference to do this; even if it were, it would be impossible to undo the effects of German occupation and of the excitement created by one-sided moral and material pressure. A plebiscite held in these conditions could offer no hope of a satisfactory solution.[2] In the circumstances, no Franco-Russian understanding was possible.[3]

This left only the possibility of Anglo-Russian agreement. Such agreement was impeded less by differences of approach or a clash of practical interests than by the fact that the British cabinet was profoundly divided and incapable of formulating a policy. Russell, indeed, in his eagerness to find a solution, had privately asked Napier to draw Gorchakov's

[1] Steefel, *op. cit.* pp. 205f.
[2] Gorchakov to Brunnow, 5 April/24 March 1864, no. 81, Lesnik, *op. cit.* p. 86.
[3] For a half-hearted and inconclusive attempt during March to bring about a Franco-Russian *rapprochement*, cf. Steefel, *op. cit.* pp. 209f.

attention to the common interest of England and Russia in defending the freedom of the Sound. Neither could view with equanimity control of the strategic straits by a strong Germany or a united Scandinavia. Napier, however, had thought it best not to alarm Gorchakov's 'excitable imagination' with 'serious contingencies for the future'. He assured Russell that up to the present Gorchakov had acted wisely and fairly. He was probably sincere in his desire to preserve the 'apparent exterior integrity' of Denmark[1] and had sent Oubril for his private guidance a 'secret and severe' despatch about the 'unsteady' course of Prussian policy.[2] The tsar was even better disposed towards the Danes and both he and Gorchakov appeared 'determined for interested motives to keep the peace in the East'.[3] It was, however, a far cry from this to a common Anglo-Russian policy. In fact, the British and Russian governments would decide independently the course to be followed at the conference by their respective representatives.

The policy of Russia was laid down in Gorchakov's instructions to Brunnow, the Russian plenipotentiary. The Russian government, Gorchakov declared, had no illusions about the prospects of the conference; none the less, the mere fact of its assembly would be a step in the direction of peace. Russian policy at the conference could be summarized in the following points: an armistice, if possible, to be the first matter of consideration; the treaty of London as the natural starting point of discussion; maintenance of the stipulations of that treaty—if not absolutely—at least in the spirit, so far as the principles of Danish integrity and the established order of succession were concerned. A purely personal union was admissible if eventually put forward. Within this framework, Brunnow should work for the adoption of the solution most likely to strengthen the links between Schleswig and the Danish monarchy. If the treaty of London was abrogated, Russian rights as they existed before 1851–2 must be formally reasserted. Brunnow should discuss freely with the British plenipotentiaries and those of other neutrals the concessions to be urged on the belligerents to secure a just solution. He should consult confidentially and impartially with the representatives of the two sides and try to find a basis of agreement. Any settlement accepted by both parties, so long as it preserved the European equilibrium, would be approved by the Russian government.[4] If the French proposal for a plebiscite was brought forward Brunnow should oppose it, using the arguments of Gorchakov's original reply.[5]

---

[1] Napier to Russell, private, 13 April 1864, RA I 96/41, copy.
[2] The same to the same, 13 April 1864, no. 201 most confidential, *ibid.* I 96/49, copy. Gorchakov had written that, if Prussia was not careful, she might find Russia 'no longer at her side' (*ibid.*).
[3] The same to the same, private, 13 April 1864, *ibid.* I 96/41, copy.
[4] Gorchakov to Brunnow, 28/16 March 1864, Lesnik, *loc. cit.* pp. 83 ff.
[5] The same to the same, 5 April/24 March 1864, no. 81, *ibid.* p. 86.

The policy finally decided on by the British government hardly deserves the name. When two days before the opening of the conference no decision had been reached, Palmerston and Russell agreed to recommend to the Cabinet that England should simply advise the conclusion of an immediate armistice. If Denmark refused, she would be left to her fate; if the refusal came from Austria and Prussia, Russia, Sweden and perhaps France, should be consulted about a naval demonstration in the Baltic.[1] This substitute for a policy was criticized by the Queen who deprecated threats to Austria and Prussia;[2] it was killed by Clarendon who '. . .forced Ld Palmerston and Ld Russell to give up the implied threat of the fleet in the Baltic, with which they had proposed to press an armistice upon Austria and Prussia, by refusing to be a member of the Conference if such a course was adopted'.[3] Palmerston and Russell could not contemplate a conference without the experienced Clarendon and, on the day before the opening, agreed to withdraw their proposal. In consequence, the British representatives entered the discussions without any plan whatsoever.

In this manner England, Russia and France had proved themselves unable to reach agreement. The principles underlying the policies of Paris and St Petersburg were irreconcilable. The British government, rent by internal divisions and enfeebled by the absence of any firm control, hesitated between the conflicting principles of nationality and treaty rights. It was unable therefore to co-operate wholeheartedly with either France or Russia. This meant that, at least for the moment, the last vestiges of a diplomatic 'concert' had disappeared.

Gorchakov, in pursuit of his policy of a quadruple understanding was trying to reach agreement with Prussia. On 21 April, Oubril read to Bismarck a despatch listing Russian objections to the French proposal for a plebiscite. Bismarck expressed surprise that the Russian government should even consider replacing the Duchies under Danish rule. Plebiscites had taken place in Greece and Belgium and more recently in the Ionian Islands. The population of the Duchies also should be consulted, possibly under the auspices of the conference. Oubril rejoined that the instances quoted by Bismarck referred to vacant thrones or internal problems; the question of the Duchies was of a different nature and Russia's view was shared by England and Austria. Bismarck claimed that the principle must apply also to thrones which had 'vacated themselves'. Prussia's promise to respect the settlement of 1852 had been conditional on an unopposed occupation of Schleswig. If she still upheld the principle of Danish integrity it was of her own free will and not because she was bound to do so. Oubril rejoined that the Prussian government had repeatedly declared

[1] Russell to the Queen, 18 April 1864, RA I 96/62 (*QVL, loc. cit.* p. 173).
[2] The Queen to Russell, 19 April 1864, RA I 96/73 (*QVL. loc. cit.* p. 174).
[3] Grey to the Queen, 23 April 1864, RA I 96/89.
[4] Russell to the Queen, 19 April 1864, *ibid.* I 96/74 (*QVL, loc. cit.* p. 174).

at St Petersburg its intention of respecting the treaty; the Russian government had accepted these declarations; in reliance upon the loyalty of the Prussian cabinet it had in a spirit of conciliation repeated them to other powers. Bismarck then claimed that it was necessary to satisfy King William and the country. Oubril admitted this but added that there must be consideration also for the interests of others. Bismarck expressed particular annoyance at the suggestion that the population of the Duchies might itself ask for the withdrawal of the German troops. The Duchies were occupied by military force and the proposal for their evacuation was simply incomprehensible.[1] Oubril informed Gorchakov by the telegraph that it was urgently necessary to dampen Bismarck's ardour and force him to explain his objects. British dissatisfaction was legitimate; the language held in Berlin concealed an afterthought; excessive demands would be put forward in London.[2] On 26 April, Bismarck told Oubril that the Danish complication was simply a passing incident. A solution satisfactory to Prussia was indispensable, otherwise he would be forced to resign and the king might abdicate. He had not yet made his final choice between personal union, an independent state under Augustenburg or Oldenburg and a policy of annexation to Prussia. What he needed was success. He had accepted the principle of a plebiscite simply because growing British hostility forced him not to reject out of hand a plan which formed the basis of French policy. Oubril rejoined that Gorchakov did not regard the Danish question as a passing incident; it had a European aspect which might produce complications. When acquainted with a letter from Gorchakov appealing for restraint following the capture of Düppel, Bismarck replied that no special moderation was called for. His language convinced Oubril that he was determined to obtain a great triumph. His ambition now clearly extended to annexation of the Duchies to Prussia which had not until then been openly avowed.[3] In the margin of Oubril's report the tsar noted: 'I find Bismarck's language very disquieting.'[4]

Gorchakov replied almost at once. The declaration that Prussia needed success had been repeatedly made at St Petersburg, albeit in general terms. Bismarck should take the Russian cabinet into his confidence and state what advantages he required. He could be assured of absolute secrecy. The Russian government desired to ease his position but to do so it must know his needs. If his aim was annexation there would be strong opposition. The Russian government wished to know what successes—apart from territorial change—would be considered by Bismarck sufficient to strengthen his position. After his own declarations any action in favour of Augustenburg would lay him open to the charge of inconsistency. The question of Schleswig and Holstein was in itself of secondary importance,

---

[1] Oubril to Gorchakov, 21/9 April 1864, no. 18, Lesnik, pp. 87f.
[2] The same to the same, telegram, 11/23 April, *ibid.* p. 116 n. 77.
[3] The same to the same, 26/14 April 1864, no. 18, *ibid.* pp. 88ff.   [4] *Ibid.* p. 90.

but when its further course threatened to divide Europe into two camps, to unite the western against the conservative courts and to sow misunderstanding among the latter, it might become the source of fatal developments. That was why moderation at the coming conference was essential.[1]

Of Prussian moderation, however, there had been little sign. On 26 April, the day following the first full meeting of the conference,[2] Clarendon had expressed the opinion that a rupture was more likely than a settlement.[3] The Prussians seemed determined to push their advantage to the utmost and there was little doubt that they intended to dictate peace at Copenhagen.[4] After the demands put forward by the Prussians at the second meeting on 4 May, Brunnow also noted that Prussia was abusing her victory. Since the capture of Düppel and the occupation of Jutland she no longer recognized even for form's sake, the integrity of the Danish monarchy. She had withdrawn the proposal for personal union and demanded complete separation. The chief Austrian representative was instructed to work with his Prussian colleagues whilst Beust, the spokesman of the Diet was determined to destroy the settlement of 1852. The Danish representatives would not listen to advice and took counsel only from despair.[5] Furthermore, they had no power to negotiate. Could Schleswig and Jutland be taken from Prussia or Holstein from Germany? France was unwilling, England unable to do so. The Prussians were masters of the situation as Bismarck knew only too well. Russia had entered the conference intending to discuss the terms on which the integrity of Denmark could be preserved. Austria and Prussia had repeatedly professed their adherence to this principle: if either now changed her mind, Russia was free to withdraw. This was what Brunnow proposed to do if Bernstorff[6] formally challenged the principle. He would declare that his instructions forbade him to abandon the basis of discussion admitted by both parties. Such a declaration would permit the Russian government to consider whether it should leave the conference rather than participate in discussions involving the sacrifice of its principles without the slightest advantage to Denmark.[7] The tsar observed in the margin: 'should matters take this turn, nothing else will be left for us to do'.[8]

---

[1] Gorchakov to Oubril, 30/18 April 1864, no. 19, *ibid.* pp. 90 ff.

[2] Russell had formally opened the conference on 20 April, but had soon adjourned it as the representative of the Diet had not yet arrived.

[3] Clarendon to Grey, private, 26 April 1864, RA I 96/103.

[4] The same to the same, private, 28 April 1864, *ibid.* I 96/106. Russell told the Queen that it was impossible 'not to see that Prussia is aiming at Prussian supremacy only' (Russell to the Queen, 30 April 1864, *ibid.* I 96/112).

[5] Clarendon reported graphically that 'neither Party was more disposed to yield than two parallel lines are to meet' (Clarendon to the Queen, 4 May 1864, *ibid.* I 97/7).

[6] The chief Prussian representative.

[7] Brunnow to Gorchakov, 4 May/22 April 1864, Lesnik, *op. cit.* pp. 92 ff.

[8] *Ibid.* p. 94.

Brunnow's determination was put to the test almost at once. On 9 May, the belligerents at last agreed on an armistice of four weeks, and the conference was free to consider the substance of the dispute. On the 12th, Bernstorff read a declaration announcing that Prussia and Austria no longer recognized the restrictions 'resulting from engagements which may have existed before the war between their governments and Denmark'. The basis of a new arrangement, therefore, must form the principal object of the coming negotiation.[1] On the following day the British cabinet held a meeting and on the 14th Russell informed Brunnow of an important change in British policy. The Cabinet—the Foreign Secretary explained—had noted that although every power represented at the conference with the sole exception of the Confederation had been a party to the treaty of 1852, none had shown a disposition to maintain its provisions by force. France had expressly declined to do so; Russia had abstained from committing herself; England and Sweden had refused singly to take upon themselves the duty of vindicating by force of arms the interests of peace and the European balance. Austria and Prussia now proposed to find the elements of a solid and permanent peace in a settlement inconsistent with the treaty. A flat rejection of their proposition would serve neither to promote peace nor to preserve the integrity of Denmark. There was no combination of powers prepared to wrest the Duchies from the German invaders. Even were Holstein to be evacuated the Diet would probably insist on its separation from the Danish monarchy. The German powers would never allow Danish troops to re-enter the Duchy and its well-known principles forbade the British government to assist Denmark in crushing the popular will. In this situation the separation of Holstein and the German parts of Schleswig from Denmark ought fairly to be taken into consideration. The neutrals, after hearing Bernstorff, should meet together to discuss their policy. Denmark would secure the great advantage of being freed from interference by the Confederation in her domestic concerns. This would in some way compensate her for the loss of territory. Every step in the proposed arrangement must be carefully watched and particular care should be taken 'that in fulfilling the legitimate desires of the People of Germany, the Conference should not minister to the ambition of a single Power'.[2] To this communication Brunnow could only reply that he would submit the suggestion to Gorchakov. Until he received new instructions, he would continue to devote his efforts to the defence of Danish integrity and the established order of succession.[3]

The sudden and almost simultaneous abandonment of the treaty by Prussia, Austria and England faced the Russian government with the choice of either giving up its principles or accepting complete isolation in

[1] Steefel, *op. cit.* p. 228.
[2] Russell to Brunnow, confidential, 14 May 1864, RA I 97/61, copy.
[3] Brunnow to Russell, confidential, 15 May 1864, *ibid.* I 97/62, copy.

the conference. The decision could hardly be doubtful[1] and, on 25 May, Napier telegraphed that Russia would support Russell's proposal provided Denmark kept a good military frontier and was willing to accept the plan. The British government should make known its views at St Petersburg. The assistance of Russia would depend on the resolution of England.[2] To Napier's inquiry whether the British government could rely on Russian support to secure a defensible frontier for Denmark, Gorchakov had replied that he did not envisage the possibility of armed intervention from any quarter. The Vice-Chancellor, Napier reported, believed that England would accept any terms proposed by Prussia and Austria and would in no circumstances resort to arms; the military frontier would be abandoned as the settlement of 1852 had been. He would not, therefore, take any risk with his German allies by supporting the interests of Denmark. He had, however, warned the Austrian government that it would be dangerous to count too much on British inaction.[3]

When Apponyi on behalf of Austria and Prussia formally proposed on 28 May that the Duchies should be separated from Denmark under the Duke of Augustenburg, Brunnow

in strong language formally protested against the German proposal...denied the right to dispose of territory unless the claims of others had been fully considered and in the name of his government...maintained the existence of the Treaty and declared that all discussion respecting the succession was premature...that until H.M. [the King of Denmark] was prepared to set aside the Treaty, Russia would support it.[4]

Within three days Alexander also had abandoned the treaty of 1852. On 31 May, Napier telegraphed that the tsar had formally ceded his rights in Holstein to the duke of Oldenburg who was warmly recommended as the future ruler of the Duchies.[5] On 2 June, Brunnow officially announced that the tsar's rights had been transferred to the duke.[6] The settlement of 1852 was dead.

[1] A few days earlier Napier had reported on the Russian attitude: 'The interest of Russia on behalf of Denmark is sincere, but it is secondary. The interest of Russia in maintaining an alliance with Austria and Prussia against France on account of Poland is capital and predominant.'

Plessen had discussed with the tsar the possibility of Russian aid to Denmark: 'In reply the Emperor asked him to look around him and then state frankly whether he could advise the Russian government of to-day to act as the government of 1849 had acted....My Danish colleague could not answer conscientiously that he advised it' (Napier to Russell, no. 241, secret and confidential, 11 May 1864, ibid. I 97/48).

[2] The same to the same, telegram, 25 May 1864, ibid. I 79/101, copy.

[3] The same to the same, no. 267, secret and confidential, 24 May 1864, ibid. I 97/128, copy.

[4] Clarendon to the Queen, 28 May 1864, ibid. I 97/142.

[5] Napier to Russell, telegram, 31 May 1864, ibid. I 97/146. Gorchakov informed Napier that in 1862 Alexander II had, in a secret and confidential document, transferred the rights of the house of Gottorp to the Oldenburg branch. Those rights had been conditionally waived under the treaty of 1852, which the Russian government had upheld 'until it was abandoned by all the other signatories'. In present circumstances, Oldenburg would be a more 'conservative' ruler than Augustenburg (the same to the same, no. 282 confidential, 30 May 1864, ibid. I 97/98, copy).

[6] Clarendon to the Queen, 2 June 1864, ibid. I 98/9.

IV

In the meantime, the British government had proposed the division of Schleswig on the basis of nationality and the powers had accepted this 'in principle'.[1] There existed, however, no agreement about the line of division in Schleswig. It was this which was to occupy the conference for the rest of its troubled existence.

On 6 June, Russell privately told Cowley, that if England and France were to propose a line between the one claimed by Germany and that advocated by the Danes, and if they were to tell the German powers that if they refused it, Denmark would receive material aid, the Germans might accept such a line. But, Russell asked, would Napoleon agree to this, would the British cabinet? His proposal was 'almost the only hope left for Denmark'.[2] Cowley replied that if it depended on Drouyn, there would be no difficulty. That Minister quite agreed that without determined language on the part of England and France the conference would effect nothing. He considered Russell's line a fair one[3] but had little hope of prevailing with the emperor. Drouyn believed that there would be little risk of hostilities if England and France announced in advance their support for whichever party accepted the proposal. He asked why England could not act alone, to which Cowley replied that as long as it was supposed that France would on no account interfere but with advice, England would not be listened to. England could prevent single-handed the further advance of the Germans but could not enforce terms of peace without the assistance of France. Moreover, what assurance was there that if England were to declare for Denmark, Napoleon would not openly espouse the German cause?

Drouyn said that he could not deny this, though he was ready to give me the assurance that if Her Majesty's Government were to enter the Baltic, Her Majesty's Government might reckon on the *bienveillante neutralité* of France—nay—the Emperor would pledge his word of honour that if he did not afford us material assistance, he would never afford it to our enemies.

---

[1] Steefel, *op. cit.* pp. 240f.

[2] Russell to Cowley, 6 June 1864, Clarendon MSS. copy. 'Her Majesty's Government entertain very little doubt of the disposition of Denmark to acquiesce in any reasonable line in which France and England concur, if assured of their material support in resisting any further demand of territory' (the same to the same, 8 June 1864, FO 27/1519, no. 491, draft).

[3] The line favoured by Russell was not a strictly ethnographic one but took into consideration the strategic needs of Denmark:
'In the opinion of Her Majesty's Government it would be a step backward in civilization to lay down as a principle that a Sovereign could not rule with justice and fairness subjects of a different race and language from the race and language of the governing nation. Even France could hardly adopt such a principle, and it would not suit Austria, Great Britain, Prussia or Russia to put it forward or support it.'
The German inhabitants of Schleswig had been, on the whole, well-governed and the political institutions of Denmark were 'greatly superior in point of the freedom they confer to those of Prussia' (the same to the same, 11 June 1864, *ibid.* no. 500, draft).

Cowley and Drouyn then examined at length the measures which might be taken. That which according to Drouyn would best suit Napoleon was a declaration by the neutral powers that the line from Flensburg to Husum proposed by Russell ought to be accepted by both parties, and that they would find against whichever might refuse. Should this declaration fail, a combined demonstration might be made by sea.

Drouyn, however, dwells upon the possibility of a naval demonstration on the part of France (supposing the Emperor to agree to one) leading to hostilities by land in which case he says (and it must be admitted that he does but speak the truth) France would never be satisfied to have spent her men and money for no other purpose than to keep half the Duchy of Sleswig under Danish rule—avis au lecteur!

Lastly Drouyn said that there was another formidable difficulty too likely to occur—a protest on the part of the inhabitants of northern Schleswig against separation from the South. In short, he saw no end to the perplexities with which this question was surrounded.[1] Two days later, Cowley telegraphed to Russell that there was nothing to be done with the emperor.[2] He privately told Clarendon:

I am in despair but I can do nothing more. Latour d'Auvergne has written word of the embarrassment of the Government and such is the Emperors and Drouyns [sic] hatred of the Earl [Russell], that if they had before been willing to act more cordially with us, they would not do it now that they see the chance of his going. His appointment to the F.O. was certainly most unfortunate—it is his unpopularity which is killing the government. I hear this on all sides.

Difficulties in Algiers were a further explanation of Napoleon's desire to remain quiet in Europe.[3] To Russell, Cowley reported that the emperor maintained his resolution not to risk a war for the interests of Denmark; he was therefore unwilling to employ menace.

...I am bound to say that the state of public opinion at this moment in France, both with respect to England and Denmark, warrants the Emperor's caution. Then he has his own notions of propitiating Germany and...of founding a Scandinavian Kingdom, which make him look with indifference on the dissolution of the Danish Monarchy.[4]

On 10 June, Russell told the Queen that Napoleon would not accept the British plan, but that it would at least 'shew to Parliament that no effort has been spared to secure French co-operation'.[5]

British attempts to reach agreement with France had caused alarm at St Petersburg and led Russia to redouble her efforts for a compromise

---

[1] Cowley to Russell, private, 7 June 1864, *ibid.* copy.
[2] The same to the same, telegram, 9 June 1864, RA I 98/42.
[3] Cowley to Clarendon, 9 June 1864, Clarendon MSS.
[4] Cowley to Russell, private, 9 June 1864, *ibid.*
[5] Russell to the Queen, 10 June 1864, RA I 98/52.

solution. On 8 June, Brunnow had penned an alarming report: the conference was drawing to a close without the prospect of a settlement; the British government in its anxiety to help the Danes was bidding for French support; an Anglo-French *entente* would alter the entire aspect of European affairs.[1] The tsar received this report at Potsdam where he had stopped on his way to the German spa of Kissingen. He at once told Gorchakov, who accompanied him, to make the fullest use of it in the conversations he was to have with Bismarck and William I.[2] On the evening of 10 June, he himself expressed to Bismarck his earnest wish for the preservation of peace, which in his opinion depended largely upon the Prussian government. Even if the negotiations for a renewal of the armistice should fail,[3] Prussia should confine her occupation to the territory already held. Any attempt to invade Fünen would excite British opinion to a point where the Queen could no longer control it. British vessels would enter the Baltic, the beginning of an intervention incalculable in its consequences. Such a move would give Napoleon a free hand to pursue his doubtful designs. Bismarck replied that an unsatisfactory settlement would be worse than war. It would strengthen the revolutionary party, which was what he wished above all to avoid. The embarrassments which the British government had created for itself must not be removed at the expense of Prussia's internal security. The tsar expressed satisfaction at the reception given by the Prussian government to the candidature of the duke of Oldenburg and declared in strong terms against annexation of the Duchies to Prussia. Bismarck replied that he would not provoke a European war to bring this about but could not refuse if the Duchies were offered to Prussia. Alexander considered this unlikely as he did not see who should offer them. He emphasized the need for Austro-Prussian co-operation and warned against an understanding with France. He was, Bismarck noted, unusually guarded in his language about Napoleon. At the end of the conversation, he repeated his desire for peace and recommended the adoption of a compromise line.[4] Gorchakov, in his turn, expressed his views to both Bismarck and the king. He was ready to admit that a breach with England, the burning of a few ports and seaside towns and the temporary destruction of her trade would not touch Prussia's vital interests; only her financial position, already affected by the present war, would suffer. He did not think, however, that England would be Prussia's only enemy. It was impossible to foresee how the latest British proposals would be received in Paris, but Napoleon might choose to co-operate with England rather than Prussia. When Bismarck and the king disputed this, Gorchakov replied that the idea of the Rhine frontier would electrify all

[1] Summarized in Lesnik, *op. cit.* p. 117 n. 96.
[2] Gorchakov to Brunnow, no. 81, 13/1 July (mistake for June) 1864, *ibid.* pp. 101 ff.
[3] The armistice was about to be extended until 26 June.
[4] Memorandum by Bismarck, 11/13 June 1864, *G[esammelte] W[erke]*, 6 vols. in 8 (Berlin, 1924 *et seq.*), vol. IV, pp. 459 ff.

France. Moreover, provoked by German intransigence, the British government would not hesitate to sanction French expansion on the Rhine. France might not intervene at once but would do so once England and Germany were embroiled. Gorchakov then spoke of the century-old ties between England and Austria and of the Austrian desire to preserve the friendship of England. Was Prussia sure of Austrian support in an Anglo-Prussian war? Or would Austria adopt a doubtful attitude and abandon her old allies in the end? With regard to the attitude of Russia, the position of the emperor would be a difficult one. As long as the present rulers remained, a war between Russia and Prussia would be fratricidal ('Bruder-krieg'). It was unthinkable and Gorchakov excluded this possibility. But in view of the motives which might provoke an Anglo-Prussian rupture, Russia might find it impossible to show her Prussian sympathies openly. Indeed it might happen that were a British squadron to enter the Baltic, the tsar would be unable to remain a passive spectator; the Russian flag, in that event, would not fly among the Prussian vessels. 'At least you will not fire on us', King William of Prussia interjected.

No, your Majesty, Gorchakov replied, but the mere presence of our flag amongst your enemies would be a regrettable proof that from the political point of view, we cannot support the cause you uphold. It would be utterly inconsistent if we acted otherwise.

Having administered this caution, Gorchakov turned to the domestic German scene. The king, he observed, intended to suppress the democratic Opposition in Prussia and to draw all Germany to his side by throwing down the gauntlet to England. He did not reckon with the forces that country could rally to her side and the harm she could do to Prussia's position in Germany. The movement, moreover, which was now sweeping Germany had as its aim not only the acquisition of the Duchies and the destruction of the Danish monarchy—that was merely the prologue to the play. Once this question was settled in accordance with democratic wishes, the king would desire to assert his authority. This might then be a difficult task. Furthermore the united action of England and France would encourage revolutionary elements throughout Europe; it would increase the strength and sympathy Prussian conspirators would find abroad.

If the security, independence or honour of Prussia were at stake, I would be the first to say that for the preservation of such cherished possessions any danger would have to be faced, even in the conviction that the struggle was hopeless.

The tsar would act in a similar manner. But was this really the case of Prussia? She had been completely successful in a military and even in a political sense. Was it worth her while to risk these advantages for a few square miles more or less?

The king knew that the Russian government had always regarded the Danish question as comparatively secondary in itself; it would, however, influence the grouping which could alone for any length of time safeguard the interest of order and the stability of monarchies. The defensive understanding between Russia, Prussia, Austria and England directed against the revolutionary spirit and personal aberrations would be sacrificed since a breach between England and Prussia must necessarily modify the constellation of the powers. As Gorchakov was taking his leave, King William remarked: 'Everything you told me is very serious, I cannot hide this from myself. Be convinced that I shall weigh carefully what should be done.'[1]

Bismarck, treated by Gorchakov to similar arguments, sheltered as usual behind the king. Gorchakov's suggestions could not be entertained on account of the views held by the king and his entourage; if pressed too hard, King William would abdicate; he himself would lose his position; the new ruler would then follow the road of liberalism. Gorchakov could only reply somewhat feebly that Bismarck must not resign as the consequences would be very serious.[2]

Bismarck was able to withstand the Russian pressure because he felt fairly certain that England would not begin a war alone[3] and that Napoleon would not for the moment embark on hostilities.[4] He gave

[1] Gorchakov to Brunnow, no. 81, 13/1 July (mistake for June) 1864, Lesnik, pp. 101 ff.
[2] *Ibid.*
[3] In a highly confidential despatch to Vienna, Bismarck explained that he did not underestimate the gravity of the British symptoms. The British government was guided by public opinion and it was possible that, in order to remain in office, the Ministers would resort to warlike demonstrations. They would try to bring pressure to bear on Germany to secure at least some satisfaction for their public opinion. If, however, this pressure met with a firm attitude on the part of Austria and Prussia, it was doubtful whether this or any other British government would proceed from demonstrations to warlike action. The peace party in England was not to be underestimated. England, moreover, would not decide on war unless France took a direct part. For France, however, the present situation did not offer direct inducements for a war against Germany. It seemed neither the interest nor the desire of Napoleon to provoke such a war and produce a European conflagration of incalculable consequences.
Even if British opinion forced the government to take action, Prussia would fear this less than the consequences of a yielding attitude. 'Wir dürfen die grossen konservativen Interessen, welche wir verteidigen, nicht um eines augenblicklichen guten Verhältnisses zu England willen aufs Spiel setzen....' If Austria and Prussia were united, they would have nothing to fear from England in spite of her maritime supremacy. British interference would unite all Germany around its Princes and would rob the German Liberals of many illusions. On account of the unifying effect which such a war would have on Germany, France also was unlikely to start hostilities.
He had recently explained to the tsar these 'deeper motives' of Prussian policy. He had assured him that Prussia sincerely desired peace but did not fear war if that was necessary to defend the great conservative interests (Bismarck to Werther, confidential, 14 June 1864, draft, *GW*, pp. 462 ff.).
[4] Bismarck admitted that there were internal difficulties in France, but these did not seem strong enough to overcome the desire for peace which for the present undoubtedly existed among many Frenchmen and was shared by Napoleon himself. There were no external circumstances to force him into action at the moment, and it could not be his intention to

Gorchakov the impression that he would welcome a war with England to strengthen his internal position. Both he and the king appeared to rely on anti-British feeling throughout Germany and considered that national sentiment would unanimously support them in the event of a breach.[1] In these circumstances Gorchakov's advocacy of a compromise line could make little impression on Bismarck.[2]

Russian diplomacy, however, had another string to its bow. From Berlin, Gorchakov informed the Russian minister in Vienna that the British cabinet had made overtures to France for a common stand against the German demands. England was being driven to make Napoleon the arbiter of the situation. The emperor would be able to re-establish the Anglo-French alliance 'sur la base qui lui convient le mieux'. The only hope of saving Europe from the humiliation of having its fate decided by Napoleon now lay in the return of the German powers to a policy of moderation. Gorchakov counted above all on the Austrian cabinet, less likely than any other to overlook the dangers of a grouping which Germany's attitude had rendered imminent. These considerations must be presented to Rechberg.[3] Gorchakov was as little successful in Vienna as he had been in Berlin. Russian diplomacy could do no more.

After the failure of the tsar and Gorchakov, nothing could save the conference. At a meeting on 18 June, Bernstorff proposed that the population of Schleswig should be consulted in whole or in part about its desire to belong either to Germany or Denmark. The Danish plenipotentiaries objected that since Schleswig was an integral part of the Danish monarchy, the whole of Denmark should be consulted.

Baron Brunnow, on principle and in the strongest terms, protested against the Prussian proposal as being at variance with public law and having for its object to depose the King of Denmark by his own people under the pretext of tracing a frontier.

provoke a coalition against himself—even if assured of British support. The dangers of such a war would have to be borne by France alone. Napoleon could not doubt that a coalition would be the outcome of an attack on Germany. Austria and Prussia would stand together and even Russia could not remain inactive if French troops advanced into Germany. Napoleon knew this and was not inclined to provoke complications.

In any case, he himself would prefer a resumption of hostilities to an unsatisfactory agreement, even at the risk of British warlike action and an Anglo-French alliance (the same to the same, most confidential, 14 June 1864, draft, *ibid.* pp. 464f.).

[1] Gorchakov to Brunnow, 13/1 July (mistake for June) 1864, Lesnik, pp. 101 ff.

[2] Gorchakov himself recorded that Bismarck had made no objection to his proposals for a compromise line, the king only one, Prussia's 'honour'. Gorchakov had reasonably pointed out several times that Prussia had won great military and diplomatic victories and that the king himself was the judge of Prussian honour (*ibid.*). Bismarck, on the other hand, considered that Gorchakov had carried away the conviction that the king and his cabinet were unwilling to make concessions. In their last conversation he did not, as Bismarck had expected, resume either his earlier pressure or his warning about the dangers from England (Bismarck, Aufzeichnung, 11/13 June 1864, *GW*, pp. 459ff.).

[3] Knorring to Rechberg, 14 June 1864, Steefel, *op. cit.* pp. 352f.

Apponyi accepted the proposal with modifications. Bernstorff then read another declaration recording the reasons why his government considered itself absolved from the obligations of the treaty of London 'upon which a long discussion took place as to the new and subversive principles that Prussia seemed disposed to introduce into the public law of Europe. It was acrimonious and unsatisfactory....' Russell then suggested that the belligerent powers should accept the good offices of a friendly power. The proposal was cordially supported by the Russian, French and Swedish representatives. It was objected to by Beust who said that the Confederation would not refuse mediation but would reject any form of arbitration. Since some of the plenipotentiaries were without instructions on the subject it was decided to postpone the next meeting until 22 June.[1]

On that day the representatives of Austria and Prussia accepted the mediation of a neutral power not represented at the conference, on condition that an armistice of long duration was agreed on. They reserved the right to veto any line which might be proposed. The Danish representatives declined to accept any reference to another power. All that could now be done was to arrange a final meeting to wind up the unsuccessful conference.[2]

When the difficulties of the conference had become apparent, the British government had tried to adjust its policy to the altered circumstances. There had been 'a very long discussion' in the Cabinet on 11 June. Granville had subsequently told the Queen that '...the majority of the Cabinet is not as compact as it was, on the question of what part England should take in the case of the conference being broken up and the war renewed'.[3] There had been 'much desultory and conflicting discussion on this point, but nothing was decided'. Russell had been urged to see more of the different plenipotentiaries in private to see if they could be brought to agree either to an appeal to the inhabitants or to an arbitration.[4] Russell himself informed the Queen of the Cabinet's decision to support 'the plan of arbitration for a line to be traced between the German and Danish proposals'. 'That, in case this plan should be accepted by the Danes and

---

[1] Clarendon to the Queen, 18 June 1864, RA I 98/90 (*QVL, loc. cit.* pp. 221ff.).

[2] Clarendon to the Queen, 22 June 1864, RA I 98/126 (*QVL, loc. cit.* pp. 224f.).

[3] Granville to the Queen, 13 June 1864, RA I 98/63. Gladstone noted on 11 June 'Cabinet. Very stiff on the Danish question, but went well' (John Morley, *The Life of William Ewart Gladstone* (London, 1903), vol. II, p. 118). Already on 7 May, Gladstone had recorded: 'Cabinet. The war "party" as it might be called—Lord Palmerston, Lord Russell, Lord Stanley of Alderley, and the chancellor (Lord Westbury). All went well' (*ibid.*). The pacific group in the Cabinet was led by Sir Charles Wood, Gladstone and Granville who, through General Grey, was in regular communication with the Queen. For the views of the Duke of Argyll, cf. his letter to the Queen of 1 June 1864 forwarding a memorandum on the Dano-German dispute (RA I 98/1 and 98/2).

[4] Granville to the Queen, 13 June 1864, *ibid.* I 98/63. Palmerston had been 'much opposed at first to the latter alternative, but finally came to the opinion that it would be the best arrangement' (*ibid.*).

rejected by the German Powers, in the event of the resumption of hostilities, material aid should be afforded by Great Britain to Denmark.'[1] The Queen in reply expressed her disapproval of the decision 'that if the Danes accept and Germany refuses the offer of arbitration, England will be pledged to declare war against Germany!' This appeared 'to be *too important* a decision to be arrived at without the *fullest consideration*'. She therefore wished the Cabinet to discuss her remonstrance before further action was taken.[2] On 13 June, Granville and Wood declared that Russell had misrepresented the views of his colleagues.[3] On the 15th the Cabinet had met again. There was 'much desultory conversation on war and peace'. Russell had been anxious to obtain an explicit declaration as to his colleagues' future intentions 'but Lord Palmerston, supported by the Cabinet, declared that this question was not yet ripe for decision'.[4] Bernstorff in a letter had offered to make concessions on the line in Schleswig and Russell and Clarendon had been told to meet him before the question of active intervention was considered.[5]

The hope of a more conciliatory Prussian attitude had proved short-lived. After the meeting of the conference on the 18th, Clarendon expressed the view 'that at this moment the intentions of Prussia are *not* pacific'.[6] Buchanan reported that Bismarck's language was 'unsatisfactory'. He had stated that if he was to believe his own agents and the press, Prussia and England would be at war within a fortnight. He was ready to accept this eventuality as preferable to the evils which concessions to Denmark would entail.[7] On 19 June, Russell told the Queen that Bismarck appeared to court rather than to avoid war with England.[8]

It was whilst the British government was wrestling with the problem of its future policy that Napoleon emerged once more from his expectant attitude. On the night of 16 June the British embassy received a note from Drouyn together with the copy of a letter from the emperor himself. The tenor of these documents is revealed by Cowley's comment: 'The pertinacity with which His Majesty urges us to action, shows how much he desires to see us engaged, but we shall wait long enough before we obtain more than words from him, except on his own conditions, in the way of

[1] Russell to the Queen, 12 June 1864 (*ibid.* I 98/54 (*QVL, loc. cit.* p. 215)).
[2] The Queen to Russell 12 June 1864, RA I 98/57, copy (*QVL, loc. cit.* pp. 216f.).
[3] Wood wrote: 'I do not consider myself pledged to go to war' (Wood to Granville, 13 June 1864, and Granville's note on this letter in forwarding it to the Queen. RA I 98/64 and 65, (*QVL, loc. cit.* p. 217)).
[4] Granville to the Queen, 15 June 1864, RA I 98/75. Granville felt convinced that Palmerston 'although he may talk big, is quite aware of the folly of going to war' (*ibid.*). Wood reported that the tone of the cabinet had been pacific 'Palmerston very right, Clarendon too' (Wood to Grey, 15 June 1864, RA I 98/76).
[5] Palmerston to the Queen, 15 June 1864, *ibid.* I 98/74. Wood considered that Bernstorff's letter held out the hope of a solution (Wood to Grey, 15 June 1864, *ibid.* I 98/76).
[6] Clarendon to the Queen, 18 June 1864, *ibid.* I 98/90.
[7] Buchanan to Russell, telegram, 18 June 1864, *ibid.* I 98/93.
[8] Russell to the Queen, 19 June 1864, *ibid.* I 98/97.

assistance.'[1] On the afternoon of 20 June, Drouyn 'evidently very uneasy at these meetings of the Northern Potentates'[2] returned to the charge. He explained to Cowley 'that there was but one alliance worth anything—an alliance between France and England...together they could govern the world'. When Cowley replied that this was what he had preached for the past six months, Drouyn continued 'Yes...we do not know our own interests. What an incomplete business we have made of Italy because we were alone. How paralysed you are in the Danish question, because you are alone. *Why can't we come to an understanding?*' Cowley, to sound Drouyn further, said that it would doubtless be difficult for England single-handed to bring Germany to reason. If they were to give material assistance to Denmark, they would probably be unable to stay in the Baltic during the winter. If indeed the Baltic were the Adriatic, it would be a different matter. Drouyn interrupted:

'Oh, then we may do something together—in the Adriatic.' 'Yes', I rejoined, 'and set the world on fire.' 'Oh', said he, 'but we shall be masters and can control the movement.' 'Well', I replied, 'unfortunately the Adriatic is not the Baltic and the assistance we could give the Danes in the former sea would only be auxiliary. The greatest culprits would go unpunished.'

Drouyn replied that Napoleon was under no engagements whatever to Prussia. He was free even to insist on the fulfilment of the treaty of 1852; '*if we had any proposals to make* that would tend to a better understanding with this Government they would meet with every consideration'. Drouyn, Cowley added, would not have gone so far without the emperor's approval. 'The upshot is that His Majesty wishes to turn present circumstances to account 1° to turn the Austrians out of Venetia 2° to get a bit of the Rhine.' When Cowley left Drouyn, the latter repeated: 'let us forget past jealousies and rancours and come to an understanding that is necessary to us both'.[3]

The following day, Drouyn asked Cowley's opinion of the proposal that the neutral powers should constitute themselves mediators and insist on whatever line they might propose being adopted by both parties. Cowley asked whether Napoleon would agree to this.

'Ma foi', he replied, 'the Emperor is getting so sick of the question and so disgusted with the proceedings of the Germans that I think he would consent, provided the line was a fair division of the German and the Danish element.'

Intelligence reaching Cowley convinced him that something was 'at work in the Emperor's mind'. The interchanges of the northern monarchs might

---

[1] Cowley to Russell, private, 17 June 1864, Clarendon MSS. copy.

[2] The Russo-Prussian conversations in Potsdam and Berlin were about to be followed by a meeting of Francis-Joseph, William I, Rechberg and Bismarck.

[3] The same to the same, private, 20 June 1864, *ibid*. copy. Morny, who had seen Napoleon the previous day, had sent a message that 'if Her Majesty's Government wanted the co-operation of the Emperor, they must send a fleet into the Adriatic' (*ibid*.).

have something to do with the matter. England must make the most of this.[1] His personal views Cowley had already explained in a letter to his friend Clarendon:

It is clear, I think, that the French alliance is to be bought, but the price will be perhaps more than it is worth. The [*illegible*] destruction of Austria is a high price to pay. As to the Rhine, as I do not think Belgium to be asked for, I confess I should not care.[2]

The decision now lay with the British government. On 21 June the Queen found Palmerston 'very sensible, wonderfully clear-headed, and fully alive to the extreme dangers of the situation'.

He did not apprehend the great danger of the whole of Germany being united as one man against us, though he thought matters most serious. The greatest danger he saw from France joining us was dragging us into a war, in which she would claim the Rhine, and possibly revolutionize the whole of Italy. He also entirely agreed... that it was very doubtful whether we could do anything, for nothing but naval assistance could be given and that only for three months.[3]

On the following day Clarendon assured the Queen that he did not think there was 'any fear of the Emperor's overtures for a bribe being favourably entertained'. He feared, however, that after the resumption of hostilities, the Germans would renew their advance and try to dictate peace at Copenhagen itself. In consequence, 'exasperated public opinion' might compel the Queen's Ministers 'or those who in a few days may succeed them', 'to take some rash measures if there is a conviction that the blotting out of Denmark from the map of Europe will be tamely witnessed and submitted to by England'. The problem was how to prevent Bismarck from making a clash inevitable and the British public from rushing headlong into an unnecessary conflict.

...if the fleet is not sent for the protection of Copenhagen public indignation will be irresistible.—This measure however which should simply be one of precaution ought not to entail war or even imply any intention of making war. The duty of the fleet should be strictly defined...Lord C. under present circumstances considers that it would be dangerous to do more than this but not safe to do less.[4]

That day, Cowley telegraphed that his hopes of co-operation on the part of Napoleon were strengthened.[5] A decision had to be made.

Russell's report to the Queen of 23 June betrayed his perplexity:

The more Lord Russell reflects on the present position of affairs, the more difficult does it appear to him not to assist Denmark in her extremity, and the more evident does it become that that assistance will be inefficient unless France joins in.

But then comes the question, what will France require as the price of her alliance

[1] The same to the same, private, 21 June 1864, *ibid.* copy.
[2] Cowley to Clarendon, private, 20 June 1864, *ibid.*
[3] Extract from the Queen's Journal, 21 June 1864, RA (*QVL, loc. cit.* pp. 223f.).
[4] Clarendon to the Queen, 22 June 1864, *ibid.* I 98/126.
[5] Cowley to Russell, private, 23 June 1864, Clarendon MSS., copy.

with England in checking the ambition of Germany, and is it the interest of England to pay that price?

Such are the momentous questions which must be considered at the Cabinet of to-morrow, and, until the Cabinet has considered them, discretion commands the greatest caution.[1]

The Cabinet, on the 24th, decided against war either single-handed or in conjunction with France. Then came the question whether 'we should be quiet, reserving to ourselves to act or not if the existence of Denmark was threatened', or 'should intimate to Austria that her fleet should not enter the Baltic;[2] and as a variety of this should send our fleet to the Cattegat'. The last, Wood reported, was very much disliked as leading to complications which might end in war. The opinion against sending the fleet gained ground during the discussion. The Cabinet, in fact, was very evenly divided. Gladstone, Granville and Wood had taken 'the decided peace line', as did Milner Gibson. Wood thought the peace side was 'the heaviest' but no decision was taken.[3] On the following day, the Queen sent Grey to 'lobby' the Ministers[4] but her intervention was probably no longer needed. That night, Russell reported: 'That the Government do not propose to engage in a war for the settlement of the present dispute, so far as the Duchies of Schleswig and Holstein are concerned.'[5] Clarendon in his account of the meeting recorded that Ministers had been 'united and pacific'.[6] No proposal for sending the fleet to the Baltic would at present be submitted to the Queen. Opinion both inside Parliament and without seemed increasingly to favour a policy of peace.[7] Even Russell now expressed his belief that a pacific policy would suit the House of

[1] Russell to the Queen, 23 June 1864, RA I 98/130 (QVL, loc. cit. pp. 227f.).

[2] On 11 June the British Minister at the Hague had telegraphed that six Austrian men-of-war, including a vessel of 91 guns, had arrived at the Texel (Milbanke to Russell, telegram, 11 June 1864, RA I 98/58).

[3] Wood to Grey, 24 June 1864, ibid. I 98/142 (QVL, loc. cit. pp. 228f.). Russell reported that the Ministers were 'entirely averse to any immediate hostilities in behalf of Denmark; and to any attempt to form a combination with France against Austria and Prussia'. He himself favoured a warning to Austria. 'But some wished to take an entirely new line and to shew a total indifference to the fate of Denmark.' The majority were not disposed to adopt this attitude. The decision was postponed until the following day. (Russell to the Queen 24 June 1864, RA I 98/139.) Gladstone noted after the meeting: 'Cabinet. A grave issue well discussed' (Morley, op. cit. vol. 2, p. 118).

[4] Grey to the Queen, 25 June 1864, ibid. I 98/140.

[5] Russell to the Queen, 25 June 1864, ibid. I 98/143 (QVL, loc. cit. pp. 229f.).

[6] In fact, a difference of opinion had arisen whether the resolution to be adopted should contain a remark to the effect that the Cabinet would reconsider its attitude in the event of a threat to the security of Copenhagen. Eight members of the Cabinet voted for the reference, seven against. Those in favour were Palmerston, Russell, Lord Westbury, the dukes of Argyll and Somerset, Lords de Grey and Stanley of Alderley and Sir George Grey. The opponents were Granville, Clarendon, Cardwell, Milner Gibson, Gladstone, Villiers and Wood (cf. Erik Møller, 'Det engelske Kabinet og den dansk-tyske Strid 1863-64', Historisk Tidsskrift 11 IV [Kobenhavn, 1954], p. 298). Gladstone, the leader of the 'peace party' wrote after the meeting: 'Cabinet. We divided, and came to a tolerable, not the best, conclusion' (Morley, op. cit. vol. II, p. 118).

[7] Clarendon to the Queen, 25 June 1864, RA I 98/144.

Commons and the country better than any other.[1] On 27 June, both Russell and Palmerston made statements in Parliament. The Foreign Secretary wound up his account of the dispute by announcing the government's view 'that we should maintain the position that we have occupied, and that we should be neutral in this war'.[2] Palmerston in the House of Commons, after some observations strongly favourable to Denmark, explained: 'We had also to consider what really was the matter in dispute for which hostilities were to be begun, and it did not appear to us to be one of very great importance.'[3]

In accordance with this policy, a cool reply was sent to the emperor of the French. The government, Russell wrote, were very sensible of the confidence reposed in them by the offer of moral support in an attempt to give material assistance to Denmark. They were however of opinion 'that with only a naval force and no other ally but Sweden it would be useless to attempt to recover Schleswig for Denmark'. At the same time, it was to be hoped that it would not be necessary to use force in order to preserve Denmark as an independent state.[4]

The British decision to reject Napoleon's overtures[5] and abandon Schleswig to its fate marked the end of the European crisis. Denmark now stood alone without hope of foreign assistance. On 29 June the Prussians succeeded in crossing to the island of Alsen. On 8 July the warlike ministry in Copenhagen resigned. Four days later, its successor asked for an armistice. This came into force on 20 July and before the end of the month negotiations for peace were opened.[6]

V

On 4 July, Disraeli, in the House of Commons, moved a vote of censure on Russell's conduct of British policy during the recent crisis. The grand inquest which followed foreshadowed important changes in the British attitude towards European affairs. Disraeli severely blamed the govern-

---

[1] Russell to the Queen, 26 June 1864, *ibid.* I 98/161.

[2] *Parl. Debates*, 3rd series, 176, cc. 322f.

[3] *Ibid.* cc. 349f.

[4] Russell to Cowley, 29 June 1864, FO 27/1519, no. 563, draft. Russell had told the Queen that 'it is well we should not embark in a perilous undertaking in reliance upon his [Napoleon's] assistance....A war for Venetia is his aim, and will probably occur before long. But it is not for us to stir the coals' (Russell to the Queen, 26 June 1864, RA I 98/161).

[5] To the last, Napoleon had hoped that England would become involved in hostilities. On 1 July, Cowley told Clarendon: 'The disappointment at our pacific resolution is very great here, and proves how glad they would have been, had they been able to involve us in difficulties.' The end of Palmerston's speech was much criticized. Napoleon was now more determined than ever to avoid war. 'He told Nigra who has just returned from Fontainebleau that nothing would induce him to stir, and that Italy *must* remain quiet' (Cowley to Clarendon, private, 1 July 1864, Clarendon MSS.).

[6] By the treaty of peace signed at Vienna on 30 October 1864, Christian IX ceded to Austria and Prussia his rights to the three Duchies of Schleswig, Holstein and Lauenburg (Steefel, *op. cit.* p. 250).

ment for failing to evolve and make known a definite policy in the question. They had neither declared in advance that they would keep out of a war, nor had they defined the circumstances in which they would help Denmark.[1] Stanley soon to be Foreign Secretary in a conservative administration, observed: 'I do not believe there has been at any time on their part a deliberate determination to adopt a policy either of war or of peace.'[2] Lord Robert Cecil, another Foreign Secretary of the future, declared that the policy pursued by the Ministers was 'founded upon no definite principle…oscillating, vague and fluctuating in its course'.[3] Russell's methods also were severely criticized. 'Nature intended him for a schoolmaster; and Fortune made him a statesman.'[4] 'The noble Lord's method of practising the *suaviter in modo* may be ascertained by his treatment of the German Powers; and what his ideas of *fortiter in re* are, I leave unfortunate Denmark to decide.'[5]

It was widely recognized that British intervention had been completely ineffective. Disraeli declared:

Within twelve months we have been twice repulsed at St Petersburg. Twice have we supplicated in vain at Paris. We have menaced Austria and Austria has allowed our menaces to pass her like idle wind. We have threatened Prussia, and Prussia has defied us. Our objurgations have rattled over the head of the German Diet, and the German Diet has treated them with contempt.[6]

General Peel considered that Russell might say:

From the first moment I entered office, I have constantly and systematically interfered in the affairs of other nations. Notwithstanding all the rebuffs which I have received and the humiliations to which I have been subjected,[7] I have persevered in that course of moral interference…You will therefore perceive that my system of moral interference has been a complete failure.[8]

The conclusion from these facts was drawn both by conservatives and by the followers of Cobden. Lord Robert Cecil declared:

If we did not intend to carry out by arms our threats and measures, we must abstain from the luxury of indulging in them. That is the only policy for the future which I believe is involved in the censure of the government for the past.[9]

---

[1] Disraeli, *Parl. Debates, loc. cit.*, cc. 711 ff.

[2] *Ibid.* cc. 813 ff.

[3] *Ibid.* cc. 843 ff.

[4] Roebuck, *ibid.* cc. 892 f. Cogan declared: 'It was a cruel kindness of the Prime Minister to have placed the noble Earl in a position for which he was constitutionally unfitted' (*ibid.* c. 1039).

[5] General Peel, *ibid.* cc. 795 ff. [6] *Ibid.* cc. 711 ff.

[7] Horsman considered that the events now taking place in Denmark 'and the humiliation of England arising from those events, are naturally and logically the results of the inconsistency and crookedness of our proceedings last session with respect to Poland' (*ibid.* c. 902).

[8] *Ibid.* cc. 795 ff.

[9] *Ibid.* cc. 843 ff. General Peel declared: 'If you choose to set yourselves up as the champions of the world, and to constitute yourselves the arbiter of other people's affairs, you must be prepared to fight for your position' (*ibid.* cc. 795 ff.).

Stanley announced: 'I believe that a policy of neutrality and non-intervention may be not only a safe but a respectable and an honourable position.'[1] General Peel told the House: 'I am opposed to all treaties and guarantees that render it necessary to interfere in the affairs of others.'[2] Cobden in his turn observed: '...why do we trouble ourselves with these continental politics? We have no territorial interests on the continent. We gain nothing there by our diplomatic meddling.'[3] W. E. Forster called for 'a change in our foreign policy, and for replacing that meddling, dishonest system of apparent intervention, but which was really non-intervention, ...by an honest, dignified and plain-spoken system of non-intervention'.[4]

The agreement between conservatives and liberal radicals was startlingly revealed by Cecil's observation that England would be in a happier position if Cobden had been Foreign Secretary in the place of Lord John Russell.[5] In fact Cobden's assertion that a new system of foreign policy was needed as the old one was now totally discredited[6] contained a large element of truth. Palmerston and Russell finally obtained a surprise majority of eighteen in the House of Commons[7] and were left in a minority in the Lords. They might thus continue in office, but after Poland and Schleswig-Holstein, the Whig policy of 'intervention' of which they had been the chief exponents was thoroughly discredited with public and Parliament alike. A turning-point in British diplomacy had been reached. Two years later, the future Marquis of Salisbury would write to the Danish minister in London:

> The policy that was pursued in 1864 has undoubtedly had the effect of severing her [England] in a great measure from the course of continental politics: & the declared principles of non-intervention, which it was the effect of the policy of that year to establish have necessarily diminished her influence in the decision of Continental questions. The general feeling in this country is in favour of abandoning the position which England held for so many years in the councils of Europe.[8]

In fact, for years to come, the doctrine of non-intervention would strongly influence the course of British foreign policy.

---

[1] *Ibid.* cc. 813 ff.　　　　　　　　　　　　　[2] *Ibid.* cc. 795 ff.

[3] *Ibid.* cc. 829 ff. Lord Robert Montagu pithily remarked :'It is meddling which costs money and necessitates armaments' (*ibid.* c. 880).

[4] *Ibid.* cc. 859 f.　　　　　　　　　　　　　[5] *Ibid.* cc. 843 ff.

[6] 'Eight gentlemen met in London about the celebrated round table to settle the destinies of a million people, who were never consulted on the matter at issue. Let us take note of this event. It is the last page in the long history of diplomatic action. It will not be repeated again' (*ibid.* cc. 829 ff.). It is interesting to note that neither the population of Schleswig nor that of Lorraine would be consulted in the disposal of those provinces.

[7] 'This was a much larger majority than was expected; four was the calculation yesterday, and from six to eight to-day. Several conservative members went or stayed away' (Palmerston to the Queen, 8 July 1864, RA A 33/8 (*QVL, loc. cit.* p. 240)).

[8] Cranborne to Torben Bille, private, 4 July 1866, in the Rigsarkivet, Copenhagen, P. Vedel Papers VII Breve fra andre Brevskrivere. I owe the communication of this interesting document to the kindness of Dr Erik Møller of Copenhagen.

VI

The question of Schleswig-Holstein was not 'the German question'. In consequence, the views of the powers on the future of the Duchies were distinct from those on the future of the Confederation. In fact, in the question of the Duchies, the policies of the powers were determined by their mutual relations and by extra-German considerations.

Russian policy throughout the crisis was dominated by concern for Poland, distrust of Napoleon and fear of revolution. It was this which accounted for the desire to strengthen the hand of Bismarck, the policy of the quadruple *entente*, and the eagerness to preserve the settlement of 1852. In actual practice, these aims proved difficult to reconcile. It was all but impossible to strengthen Bismarck and, at the same time, preserve the integrity of Denmark. It was scarcely less difficult to keep on friendly terms with both the German powers and the British government. By dint of skilful diplomacy, however, Gorchakov succeeded in the end in attaining several of his objectives. There was no revolutionary outbreak, Bismarck was strengthened, and friendly relations with Prussia, Austria and England were maintained. Napoleon was given no opportunity to start a general upheaval. These were no mean achievements but they were bought at the price of Danish integrity. Much as the tsar and Gorchakov would have liked to do so, it proved impossible to achieve the major aims of Russian policy, and, in addition, preserve the settlement of 1852. The Russian government had made it clear from the start that it could not take up arms in defence of the Danish monarchy. Short of this, however, Alexander and Gorchakov were ready to do everything in their power to uphold the Danish cause. From the beginning of the conflict down to their visit to Prussia in the summer of 1864 they consistently and indefatigably preached moderation in Berlin, Vienna—and Copenhagen as well. Almost to the end, the Russian government formally took its stand on the London Protocol and Gorchakov could declare with justifiable satisfaction that it had not abandoned the settlement of 1852 until every other signatory had done so. Thus, contrary to a widespread belief, Russian diplomacy during the Schleswig-Holstein dispute did not play Bismarck's game. In the last resort, indeed, the tsar and Gorchakov were determined that Bismarck should not be driven into resignation or a French alliance, but, short of pushing matters to extremes they did their utmost to restrain the ambition of Prussia. Their steady pressure caused irritation in Berlin. Russian policy, which was fundamentally conservative and European was incompatible both with the liberal nationalism of Germany and the Prussian ambitions of William I and Bismarck. Yet fear of France and revolution made acquiescence in Bismarck's designs the lesser evil from the Russian point of view. Bismarck was 'authoritarian' in his outlook and 'Russian' in his sympathies and professions—the

Prussian liberals were neither. It might well appear that Bismarck alone stood between Germany and a repetition of the 'year of revolutions'. This fact, together with Russia's internal state, made acceptance of a *fait accompli* which could not be altered by peaceful means a practical necessity.

British policy was inspired in almost equal measure by distrust of Napoleon and sympathy for Denmark. There was a general desire to help the Danes without affording the emperor an opportunity to carry out his plans. The two objects were mutually exclusive. Without French support, British policy in the Duchies was doomed to be ineffective, yet any agreement with France involved the probability of a war accompanied by territorial changes in Italy and on the Rhine. Compared to this prospect, the abandonment of Schleswig-Holstein to Germany appeared the lesser evil. The actual aim of British policy—conducted with an incredible lack of skill and consistency—was to reach an agreement with France and utilize French prestige—without paying the price demanded by Napoleon. Such a policy was doomed to failure for the emperor was too shrewd to abandon a promising position 'pour les beaux yeux de l'Angleterre'. In addition, he had old scores to settle with Palmerston and Russell and saw no reason for strengthening their position. Bismarck in his turn knew only too well that England would not pay the price demanded by Napoleon and that he had little to fear from isolated British action. British policy, even in hands more competent than those of Russell and the aged Palmerston, had little chance of success. It could indeed prevent the outbreak of a war of nationalities but only at the price of sacrificing the Duchies to Germany.

It was Napoleon who appeared to hold the key to the diplomatic situation created by Anglo-German tension. A policy of masterly inaction seemed well-calculated to promote the objects of his diplomacy. There is every reason to believe that he planned—eventually—to join the British government in warlike action. However—warned by his experience in the Polish crisis—he was determined that, before he intervened, England should be committed beyond recall. The price of his support would be nothing less than a *remaniement de la carte de l'Europe*, with benefits for Italy, perhaps for Poland and last, but not least, for France. It was, therefore, with growing disappointment that the emperor watched British hesitations and the refusal of Palmerston and Russell to embark on a policy of active intervention. Incautious encouragement was certain to increase British distrust but the prospect of British acquiescence in the dismemberment of Denmark finally forced Napoleon to show his hand. The result was the British decision to leave the Duchies to their fate. Another of Napoleon's 'combinazioni' had been wrecked by the distrust his personality and ambitions had come to inspire.

Distrust of Napoleon in fact, formed the meeting ground of British and

Russian diplomacy. This feeling, shared by Palmerston and Alexander II, was responsible for their joint desire to prevent the outbreak of war and to limit its scope once it had begun. The greatest evil in the eyes of both the British and Russian governments was a situation which would allow Napoleon to embark on a policy of action. To avoid this danger, they first co-operated in the attempt to find a solution and later acquiesced in the dismemberment of Denmark.

The Schleswig-Holstein dispute exercised little influence on the evolution of the German question or the Austro-Prussian struggle. Its indirect consequences, however, were to prove of far-reaching importance. Perhaps the most important was a revulsion in England against the policy of Palmerston and Russell. It might be said with little exaggeration that Poland and Schleswig did for British diplomacy what the Crimean War had done for Russia. Home affairs became for a time the principal preoccupation of the British public. Palmerston's death in 1865 symbolized the end of an era which had in fact been closed by Russell's 'meddle and muddle'. With Russia not yet restored to her old position, the partial withdrawal of England left Prussia and Austria face to face, with Napoleon holding the balance between them.

A further indirect result of the Duchies crisis was the strengthening of Bismarck's position in Prussia and of Prussian prestige in Germany. It was Bismarck who had presided over Germany's first military and diplomatic successes since the Congress of Vienna, and who had reversed the verdict of 1850 and 1852. It was clear that the Cabinet in Vienna, in spite of its espousal of the Augustenburg candidature, had been lukewarm in defending the 'interests of Germany'. For geographical reasons, if for no others, the 'liberation' of the Germans in the Duchies had been mainly the work of Prussia. Rechberg in his co-operation with Bismarck had laboured less to increase Austrian popularity in Germany than 'pour le roi de Prusse'.

Within the Germanic Confederation, therefore, the struggle for the Duchies had improved the standing of Prussia and of Bismarck. In the international sphere, it had still further reduced the probability of effective British intervention in future continental disputes. The British withdrawal —as long as Austro-Prussian rivalry continued—appeared to leave Napoleon the arbiter of Europe.

CHAPTER 8

THE STRUGGLE FOR SUPREMACY IN GERMANY, 1866

THE Danish surrender of Schleswig-Holstein failed to clear the European atmosphere. A new outburst of Austro-Prussian rivalry prevented both federal reform in Germany and the final disposal of the captured Duchies. Indeed by the spring of 1865 the Schleswig-Holstein question had again become—in a new form—the most burning issue in Europe. Other problems, at the same time, continued to claim attention: Italy coveted Venetia, the Magyars were clamouring for autonomy and opposition to Prince Couza was rising in Bucharest. Napoleon, as was his wont, eagerly awaited an opportunity to restore his battered prestige.

The central issue in the impending conflict was, once again, the future of the Habsburg monarchy. Austria, threatened by Prussia, Italy, the Magyars and, potentially, Romania, faced the coming crisis without the active sympathy—let alone support—of a single European government. She could, indeed, have bought the benevolence of the tsar by supporting the Oldenburg candidature in the Duchies and Russian policy in the Principalities. Such a course, however, would give mortal offence alike to liberal public opinion in Germany and to Napoleon, the champion of Romanian nationality. Equally, the friendship of France and England could be won—at the price of selling Venetia to Italy. Not only, however, was such an action repugnant to the patriotic pride of Austrian statesmen, but it also involved the danger of serious external complications. The proposal was linked with a plan to compensate Austria in the Principalities and had in consequence incurred the bitter hostility of Russia.[1] The policy of buying Russian sympathy, therefore, would almost automatically provoke a revolutionary coalition of France, Prussia, Italy, the Magyars and probably Romania; that of appeasing Napoleon was certain to bring about a Russo-Prussian alliance. Moreover no concession could win Austria active support. Faced with this predicament, the Austrian government hesitated before it finally promised Napoleon to surrender Venetia to Italy.[2] This concession secured the neutrality of France; it could no longer buy that of Italy who wished to win Venetia by force of arms and had, with

---

[1] The tsar considered the proposal 'inadmissible jusqu'à la guerre'; Gorchakov observed: 'if I had the nature *of a sheep*, I should revolt at the very idea' (Taylor, *Struggle for Mastery*, p. 160 n. 1).

[2] It was agreed that Austria should seek compensation in Silesia after a victorious war against Prussia. The latter might be compensated in northern Germany. These changes might be brought about as a result of the impending conflict.

Napoleon's blessing, already linked her national aspirations with those of Prussia.

The national movements of 1848, revived since 1856 with the active support of Napoleon, were about to challenge once more what was left of the system of Vienna. National ambitions in Germany, Hungary, Italy and Romania, championed by France and Prussia,[1] the leading military powers of the continent, clamoured for satisfaction. The 'conservative' bulwark now formed by strife-torn Austria, weakened and preoccupied Russia, abstentionist England[2] and the lesser German governments

[1] Bismarck's domestic conservatism partly disguised the purely revolutionary character of his foreign policy.

[2] In March 1864, Sir Robert Morier had lucidly analysed the position of England in relation to the ideological struggle in progress on the continent:

'Now in seeking for a general or first principle which should rule our foreign policy, I think that the first fact to be realised is *that England stands outside the circle of organic changes now going on in Europe*...there is no real *solidarity* of political interests between ourselves and any of the great political parties contending for the soul of Europe. There may be any amount of sympathy, but there are no common interests, in the sense that the victory or defeat of the one or other party would affect our well-being in any appreciable degree.'

'The next fact that requires to be realised is that the organic changes going on are very *real* changes, and that the parties concerned, both the attacking and defending forces, are very much in earnest, and that it is childish to throw mere words at them and entreat them in God's name to be quiet.'

'...I think the deduction which naturally follows is that it is no business of ours to step across the channel and enter the lists on one side or the other—that standing as it were on vantage ground above the two parties it is no business of ours either to assist or retard the work of transformation going on—that it is not our vocation to compete with the Emperor Napoleon in his professional pursuits as surgeon accoucheur to the ideas of the nineteenth century or, on the other hand, to put ourselves forward as the champions of the *status quo*, and to spend our capital in maintaining the arrangements made at the Congress of Vienna as if they were the final forms into which Europe was to be moulded.'

'If once public opinion fairly seizes the principle that to effect any practical purpose in Europe and to avoid the repetition of the reiterated fiascos of late years it would be necessary for England to embark her fortunes definitely either with the Holy Alliance or with the party of the rectifiers of the European map, it will (from the total impossibility of getting British tax-payers to adopt either course) come logically and by a sound process of reasoning to the conclusion which vaguely and not upon any definite principle it has already more than half come to viz. that non-intervention is the true policy for England and...that the task which will devolve upon any Ministry that desires to merit well of the country will be to follow a policy of systematic non-intervention based on a definite *principle* instead of the unsystematic policy which, proclaiming in theory that it will not intervene, does practically meddle in every question, now on one principle now on another the most opposed to it. Dignified, intelligent non-intervention *versus* undignified, unintelligent non-intervention, that is the change we require, and for this purpose it is absolutely necessary that our Foreign Secretary should...be thoroughly able to grasp and comprehend the organic changes out of whose sphere it would be his duty to keep England' (Morier to Lady Salisbury, 15 March 1864, Mrs Rosslyn Wemyss, *Memoirs and Letters of Sir Robert Morier* (London, 1911), vol. I, pp. 401 ff.).

It is interesting to compare Morier's analysis with Disraeli's almost contemporary definition of England's role in the affairs of Europe:

'The position of England in the councils of Europe is essentially that of a moderating and mediatorial power. Her interest and her policy are, when changes are inevitable and necessary, to assist so that these changes, if possible, may be accomplished without war; or, if war occurs, that its duration and its asperity may be lessened' (Disraeli in House of Commons on 4 July 1864, *Parl. Debates, loc. cit.* cc. 711 ff.).

seemed unlikely to withstand the coming attack.[1] The restoration settlement laboriously created by Nicholas I and Schwarzenberg now stood in dire peril.

I

On 22 August 1864 Francis-Joseph, William I, Rechberg and Bismarck discussed at Schönbrunn the future fate of the Duchies. They failed to find a solution but Bismarck and Rechberg agreed to continue their collaboration in German affairs. Bismarck, however, soon showed his true temper when during the negotiations for a renewal of the *Zollverein* he refused Rechberg's modest requests. This enabled the latter's enemies to convince Francis-Joseph that there was nothing further to be gained from the policy of co-operation with Prussia. On 27 October 1864, Rechberg resigned and was succeeded by an honest, and well-intentioned but inexperienced soldier, Alexander Mensdorff-Pouilly. The real control of foreign policy soon fell into the hands of Maurice Esterházy an ardent opponent of Prussia who hoped to revive the glories of Schwarzenberg. The Austrian government now proposed that Prussia should annex the Duchies in exchange for the county of Glatz. Neither William I nor Bismarck would consider this arrangement. On 22 February 1865, Bismarck announced the terms on which Prussia would consent to the setting up in the Duchies of an independent state: they amounted to disguised annexation to Prussia. The Austrian government rejected this proposal. As a result, tension rapidly mounted. On 29 May a Prussian Crown Council discussed the possibility of war. After prolonged negotiations, however, agreement was finally reached and embodied in the Convention of Gastein. Francis-Joseph sold to Prussia his rights in the Duchy of Lauenburg and took over the administration of Holstein. That of Schleswig was awarded to Prussia. In spite of the Convention, however, friction persisted. In November, Bismarck proposed without success that Austria should give up Holstein in return for an indemnity. On 28 February 1866 the Prussian government finally resolved that since Austria would not yield, the matter must be settled by war. King William was advised to begin diplomatic and military preparations.[2]

In the face of these developments the Russian government had continued in its policy of conservative solidarity coupled with almost complete abstention. In September 1864, during a conversation with Revertera, the newly appointed Austrian minister, the tsar had expressed the hope that

---

[1] The parallel between the events of 1848 and 1850 and those of 1863–7—in spite of the difference in the outcome—is striking and was noted by more than one participant in the second crisis. Poland, the Duchies, Italy, Hungary and Austro-Prussian rivalry came to the fore in each of the two great crises in almost the same chronological order. It may be that this parallelism is not accidental. Moreover, each of the two 'settlements' was followed by an—apparently fortuitous—eastern crisis.

[2] For the above, cf. Steefel, *op. cit.* pp. 256ff.

peace would soon be signed at Vienna and would strengthen the conservative ministry in Copenhagen. He had criticized Bismarck's conduct and announced his intention of appealing to William I to show greater generosity in his dealings with Denmark.[1] He hoped that the duke of Oldenburg's claims to the Duchies would finally be admitted[2] and had stressed the need for an understanding of the three conservative powers in the face of Bonapartist threats.[3] He regretted that Bismarck's proceedings appeared to have alienated England.[4] Finally, he had disclaimed all ambition in the east. Russia, he declared, was led by her interest and principles alike to attempt the preservation of the Ottoman empire. The distrust, of which he himself had for so long been the object, was singularly misplaced. '"On a peur du Panslavisme" the tsar exclaimed, "quant à moi, je suis Russe avant d'être Slave".'[5] Turkey had nothing to fear from Russia, who regarded her '"…comme un triste nécessité", ajoutai-je en complétant la pensée de l'Empereur et voyant qu'il hésitait à prononcer cette parole. Il accepta de grand cœur mon interprétation à laquelle il ne trouvait rien à ajouter ni à retrancher.'[6]

Some weeks later Gorchakov in his turn assured Revertera that, as far as he was concerned, past grudges had been banished. Nowhere was there a clash between the interests of Russia and those of Austria. In consequence, 'une entente parfaite pourrait avoir lieu entre les deux cabinets'. Revertera believed that some nervousness was felt at St Petersburg about the possibility of a *rapprochement* between Austria and France.

Cette inquiétude, je devrais plutôt dire ce malaise, se traduit par une indifférence apparente pour ce qui se passe en Europe. La Russie, me dit Mr le Ministre des affaires étrangères, est moins intéressée à la plupart des questions, elle en a moins

---

[1] 'Il déplora le caractère fougueux de ce Ministre qui n'avait toujours en vue que de tirer le plus grand avantage des premiers succès de sa politique. Sa Majesté a l'intention de faire à cet égard des remontrances au Roi de Prusse et de l'engager à un peu plus de clémence vis-à-vis du Danemarc.'

[2] 'Il a vivement insisté sur les intérêts conservateurs qu'on sacrificierait en installant ce dernier prétendant [Augustenburg] avec tout son cortège de démagogues.'

[3] 'L'Empereur semblait se complaire dans l'idée d'une alliance des principes conservateurs à opposer aux envahissements de la révolution. Selon Lui, la Puissance toujours croissante de cette dernière, concentrée pour ainsi dire dans les mains du Bonapartisme, n'aura de contrepoids que dans une alliance solide des trois élémens dont se composait jadis la Sainte Alliance. "Ce n'est cependant pas la Sainte-Alliance que je voudrais faire revivre", continua l'Empereur, "elle n'était qu'une idée sublime, trop sublime pour des hommes, et par laquelle on n'aurait pu gouverner qu'un monde peuplé d'anges".'

[4] 'Sa Majesté me témoignant le regret que la guerre de Danemarc avait contrecarré l'entente à quatre qui était en très bonne voie de se former, la conduite de Mr de Bismarck fut à cette occasion de nouveau l'objet d'une critique sévère.…l'Empereur avoue que les étranges illusions de Mr de Bismarck lui inspirent des inquiétudes. Il est décidé d'en parler sérieusement au Roi de Prusse.'

[5] Alexander was of course almost purely Germanic by race and hardly a drop of Slav blood flowed in his veins. Throughout his reign he was a consistent opponent of Panslavism and his assurances to Revertera were probably sincere.

[6] Revertera to Rechberg, 3 September/22 August 1864, HHSAPARRR, 1864, x 51, no. 1 A-B.

à souffrir que l'Autriche qui sera toujours exposée en première ligne, en cas de guerre. La Russie pourra se contenter de vivre en paix avec tout le monde, sans s'engager avec personne.[1]

In a subsequent conversation Gorchakov returned to a favourite topic, the relative unimportance for the time being of foreign policy for Russia: '...le Prince Gorchakov dit lui-même que la politique extérieure n'est maintenant...que d'une importance secondaire, toute l'attention du Gouvernement étant absorbée par les grandes questions de réforme intérieure'.[2] That this attitude was not a simple pose is shown by a memorandum on Russia's diplomatic relations which Gorchakov drew up for the tsar in September 1865. Relations with foreign powers, the Vice-Chancellor observed, had assumed their present form at the time of the Polish rebellion. It had then been demonstrated that in spite of the value for both countries of a Franco-Russian understanding, Napoleon's wish for friendship with the tsar had not shaken his predilection for the revolutionary principle of nationality. It had also been made clear that other powers desired to break up the Franco-Russian understanding. The *rapprochement* with France, therefore, gave Russia enemies without providing true friends. At the same time, the Polish crisis had created problems which demanded immediate decisions and far-reaching action in the future. These considerations must determine the policy of Russia: to complete her task in Poland, she must, above all, preserve the general peace. For ten years, this principle had guided the imperial cabinet, the only object of whose policy had been to remove all external obstacles to the transformation of the empire. Useful and wise when Russia had no direct interest in the affairs of Europe, that policy had become an absolute necessity since the Polish rebellion. Any general conflict was bound to extend to Poland.

Apart from this, Russia's relations with her neighbours had a two-fold significance: the Polish partitions had created a solidarity of interests among the partitioning powers and, in addition, Germany was the road to Poland.[3] Russia therefore must wish that the understanding between Austria and Prussia should continue. She could not side with either without driving the other into the arms of her enemies. Her interest also required that the Germanic Confederation should remain undisturbed. Civil war in Germany would open the door to foreign intervention which might extend to Poland. It was these considerations which had guided Russian policy in the conflict about the Duchies. Russia had done everything in her power to preserve the understanding of Prussia and Austria and had welcomed their decision to remove the question from the hands of the lesser states with their democratic tendencies. After the defeat of the

---

[1] Revertera to Mensdorff, 12 November/31 October 1864, *ibid.* no. 7 A-D.
[2] The same to the same, 30/18 March 1865, *ibid.* 1865–6, x 52, no. 7 B réservé.
[3] '...Germanija—eto doroga Pol'shi'. «Германия—это дорога Польши».

Danes, Russia had continued her cautious policy. As the tsar had transferred his rights to the duke of Oldenburg, she no longer had a direct interest in the future fate of the Duchies; all she required was that the question should be examined in accordance with the principles of dynastic law. Above all else, Schleswig-Holstein must not cause a rift in the Germanic Confederation. Apart from this, Russia was aware of a possible change in the balance of naval power in northern Europe. Its importance, however, must not be overrated: a new naval power would not be born in a day, nor could it be created by order. Although the probable outcome of the crisis would be contrary to the true interests of Russia, the considerations which had induced her to acquiesce in the destruction of the Danish monarchy still suggested a policy of caution. Such a policy, moreover, reflected the fundamental attitude of the imperial cabinet: in the present state of the empire and of Europe, the Russian government must concentrate on internal development—all matters of foreign policy must be subordinated to this imperative need.

The Convention of Gastein had not altered the Russian point of view. Russia would have regretted a break between Austria and Prussia but this now appeared unlikely. Austria would make concessions. She would abandon her position in northern Germany in exchange for a Prussian guarantee of her Italian possessions. In all probability, she intended to use Holstein merely as a bargaining counter. Since the solution adopted was provisional, the Russian government need not express an opinion on the Convention. The tsar preserved his freedom of action and would be guided by Russian interest alone. His policy would be based on two principles: the avoidance of anything which might interfere with the process of internal reform, and the prevention—as far as this fundamental need permitted—of changes likely to modify the political situation to Russia's disadvantage. Russia's relations with the two great powers in Germany would be kept within these limits. Relations with Prussia were friendly but her objectives as well as the ruthlessness of her methods made a closer understanding impossible. With Austria, there was an agreement on principles, but in practice her policy was dictated to such an extent by the momentary needs of her internal and external situation that no reliance could be placed on her. Even in the Principalities where the views and interests of the two governments appeared to be identical,[1] Russia

[1] Colonel Alexander Couza, Prince of Moldavia and Wallachia since 1859, had incurred the hostility of the boyars and the Orthodox Church by his policy of liberating the peasants and confiscating ecclesiastical property. On 2 May 1864 he had carried out a *coup d'état* to overcome the 'parliamentary' opposition of the feudal and military groups. In August 1865 during the Prince's absence in Germany, a counter-coup was attempted in Bucharest. Couza had hurried back to face growing opposition to his dictatorship. An association of influential men from various parties was formed with the object of replacing Couza by a foreign Prince. An emissary (John Bratianu) was sent abroad to find a suitable candidate. Finally on 23 February 1866 a nocturnal palace revolution forced Couza to abdicate.
The treaty of Paris had placed the Principalities under the general supervision of the

had received little support. The experiment about to be tried in Hungary which, it appeared, was to be extended to Galicia as well,[1] would not contribute to a *rapprochement*.

Friendly relations with France had been interrupted by the Polish crisis; Napoleon's conduct since that time had shown that he was conscious of his failure, but had not understood the nature of his mistake. Wherever the two countries met, France manifested a hostility justified neither by differences of principle nor by a conflict of interests. In the east in particular, France adopted on all questions an attitude openly hostile to Russia. It was difficult to say how far the French government was to blame. The entire French diplomatic service was traditionally anti-Russian and its hostility had been strengthened by the recent Polish crisis. Polish agents among the lower ranks of French officialdom perpetuated this feeling, which the French government did nothing to remove. Napoleon's position was similar to that in 1852. Coming to power without allies, he then discovered in the east a field for shifting on to Russia the distrust and hostility of Europe. The manner in which Europe welcomed any weakening of Russia's position in the east encouraged and would continue to promote Napoleon's designs. It was impossible to say what were the ultimate objects of his policy or how long it would continue. It was, however, so deeply ingrained in French diplomatic traditions that a return to a sincere Franco-Russian understanding appeared impossible. None the less, the door must be kept open and Russia's attitude must everywhere be cautious and defensive. The uncertainties of a situation where England was showing indulgence to France whilst Austria and Prussia alike were bidding for French support forced Russia to be watchful.

With England, there existed fundamental agreement on all European questions. Both countries desired peace based on the preservation of the European equilibrium and the *status quo* in the east. Both desired the calming of passions through a general pacification and the development of material well-being. Yet this community of interests existed mainly in theory. In practice, the British cabinet did everything in its power to conciliate France. British Ministers preferred to co-operate with

signatory powers. The representatives of the powers, therefore, had met in Paris to consider the state of the two provinces. Russia and France took opposing views of the question. Russia stood alone in her support of the *status quo* and the Russian government felt deeply its isolation at the conference. Russia's prestige among the Balkan nations was at stake.

[1] In the spring of 1864 the Austrian government had gained Russian approval by proclaiming a state of emergency in Galicia. Early in 1865 the state of siege was raised which caused ill-humour at St Petersburg. Gorchakov told Revertera that he had received information that new risings were planned in Poland and Hungary. He also read a report about agitation in the Principalities (the same to the same, 7 February/26 January 1865, *ibid.* no. 3 B, confidential). In reply to the Russian complaint, Mensdorff observed that Austria had the right to do what she liked in her own territory (the same to the same, 1 March/ 17 February 1865, *ibid.* no. 5 A-C, reporting the transmission of Mensdorff's reply).

Napoleon and thus make him respect their interests, rather than provoke his enmity—the wars of the first Napoleon had left bitter memories. This determination put a strain on Russo-British relations and paralysed the beneficial influence the two countries might jointly exert. It would be even more regrettable if events in Central Asia[1] were to cause misunderstandings which would have an adverse effect on Russia's political situation.[2]

In the circumstances, almost complete abstention appeared to be the order of the day. In December, Revertera reported to his government:

La politique extérieure de la Russie est à peu près nulle aujourd'hui vis-à-vis de l'Europe, et toutes les forces dont cet empire peut disposer pour maintenir au dehors le prestige de son nom semblent devoir être portées du côté de l'Asie où de nouvelles expéditions se préparent tranquillement.

A part cette préoccupation lointaine, la diplomatie russe ne se donne pour le moment d'autre mission que de vivre en paix avec tout le monde. Le Prince Gortchacow dit qu'un Ministre des Affaires Etrangères n'est actuellement qu'un objet de luxe pour Son Souverain, la Russie ayant le bonheur d'être au mieux avec tout le monde et de n'avoir d'affaires avec personne.[3]

Gorchakov could not, however, but cast a melancholy glance at the active policy pursued by his colleague in Berlin.

Dans ses épanchements intimes, le Prince Gortchacow ne se cache pas cependant de la fascination qu'exerce sur son esprit la politique entreprenante de Mr Bismarck. Il m'a avoué, il n'y a pas longtems que, s'il en avait les moyens et l'occasion, il aimerait bien aussi faire de la politique à la Bismarck; mais comme la Russie n'a de besoins plus impérieux que la paix, la première règle de sa conduite sera de s'abstenir dans les questions qui ne touchent aux intérêts vitaux de son existence.[4]

Russia, it was clear, would react to events in Germany only if direct Russian interest appeared to be at stake.

England and France, on the other hand, had been less ready to accept in silence the arrangements made at Gastein. Cowley reported that Drouyn was indignant at the cynicism with which the victors had divided the spoils:

It was the first time, he said, that an arrangement of that nature had been made without some attempt at justification on the part of those who had made it. In the

---

[1] It was at this time that the Russians embarked on the conquest of the khanates of Central Asia. In 1864 General Chernyaev took the towns of Chimkent and Turkestan. Tashkent fell in 1865 and Samarkand in 1868. In a circular note to the powers of 21 November 1864, Gorchakov had justified Russian policy by the need to secure Russia's boundaries. As he pointed out, the subjugation of one tribe brought the civilizing power into contact with fresh tribes. To defend the new boundaries it was necessary to crush new raiders. So the boundary continually expanded. Gorchakov quoted the experience of England and the U.S.A. to show that this must happen whenever a civilized state comes into contact with barbarous peoples. Cf. H. Seton-Watson, *The Decline of Imperial Russia* (London, 1952), p. 86.
[2] Gorchakov to Alexander II, 3 September 1865, Lesnik, pp. 107ff.
[3] Revertera to Mensdorff, 16/4 December 1865, HHSAPARRR, 1865–6, X 52, no. 20 A-B.
[4] The same to the same, 17/5 January 1866, *ibid.* 1866, X 53, no. 3 E.

present instance, every principle of justice, right and equity had been set aside to meet the exigencies of violence and convenience. There was really no other excuse for the conduct of the two great German Powers than that, having possessed themselves of the Duchies by force, they now thought fit to treat them as suited the political requirements of the moment without reference to past declarations and engagements, to the wishes of the Duchies themselves, or to the voice of Germany.[1]

The French government had indulged in a formal protest likely to remain purely platonic.

Queen Victoria, indignant at Prussia's conduct,[2] wished her government to follow the French example: '...if we do not take some means, without unnecessarily mixing ourselves up in the question, of letting the German Powers, and especially Prussia, know what we think of their conduct...we shall lower ourselves in the opinion of the world'. When Napier[3] had received without a word of reprobation the communication made 'with such effrontery' by Bismarck he had made himself 'in some sort a Party to this iniquity'.[4] Palmerston, apprised of the Queen's opinion, wrote a letter to Russell which was to prove his swan-song on the German question. He agreed indeed in condemning the Convention of Gastein, but considered the Queen's indignation to be unjustified.[5] It was right to record disapproval of the 'selfish and unprincipled conduct which Prussia has pursued and contemplates pursuing' and sorrow at 'the participation of Austria in those proceedings'. There was, however, a future as well as a present and a past to be considered. It was dishonest and unjust to deprive Denmark of Schleswig and Holstein; it was another matter how those two Duchies, once separated from Denmark, were to be disposed of in the best interests of Europe.

I should say that, with that view, it is better that they should go to increase the power of Prussia than that they should form another little state to be added to the

---

[1] Cowley to Russell, 29 August 1865, quoted in Grey to Russell, 9 September 1865 (RA I 100/157 (*QVL, loc. cit.* pp. 276f.)).

[2] Prussia seemed 'inclined to behave as atrociously as possible, and as she *always has done!* Odious people the Prussians are, *that* I *must* say' (the Queen to the King of the Belgians, 3 August 1865, RA Y 114/25 (*QVL, loc. cit.* p. 271)).

[3] In August 1864, Napier and Buchanan had exchanged posts, the former becoming ambassador in Berlin, the latter in St Petersburg.

[4] Grey to Russell, 9 September 1865 (RA I 100/157 (*QVL, loc. cit.* pp. 276f.)).

[5] 'But it seems to me rather late for the Queen and Drouyn to have opened their eyes as to the injustice of the two German Powers, and the falsity of the allegations in which they have guarded their proceedings. What they are doing now is quite of a piece with what they did in the beginning of their quarrel with the King of Denmark about the Duchies. It was the Wolf and the Lamb from the beginning, and no wonder that two wolves were too much for one lamb, however pugnacious that lamb showed himself, and the two wolves having grabbed up what they wanted would hardly be expected to give up their prey out of a mere sense of what may be called posthumous justice.'

'The fact is, as far as the Queen is concerned, that so long as the injustice committed appeared calculated to benefit Germany and the Germans it was all right and proper; but now that an example is about to be set of extinguishing petty states like Coburgh [*sic*], her sense of right and wrong has become wonderfully keen, and her mind revolts at the idea of consequences which grow naturally from the proceedings she approved of.'

cluster of small bodies politic which encumber Germany, and render it of less force than it ought to be in the general balance of power in the world. Prussia is so weak as she now is ever to be honest or independent in her action; and, with a view to the future, it is desirable that Germany, in the aggregate, should be strong, in order to control those two ambitious and aggressive powers, France and Russia, that press upon her west and east.

As to France, they knew how restless and aggressive she was 'and how ready to break loose for Belgium, for the Rhine, for anything she would be likely to get without too great an exertion'. As regards Russia, she would, in due time 'become a power almost as great as the old Roman Empire'. She could become mistress of all Asia, except British India, whenever she chose to do so. When enlightened arrangements would have made her revenue proportionate to her territory and railways should have abridged distances, her command of men would become enormous, her pecuniary means gigantic and her power of transporting her armies over great distances most formidable.

Germany ought to be strong in order to resist Russian aggression, and a strong Prussia is essential to German strength. Therefore, though I heartily condemn the whole proceedings of Austria and Prussia about the Duchies, I own that I should rather see them incorporated with Prussia than converted into an additional asteroid in the system of Europe.[1]

Within five weeks of writing these words Palmerston was dead. After a short illness, he died on 18 October. Eleven days later, at the age of seventy-three, Russell kissed hands as First Secretary. Clarendon, trained in the Palmerstonian school but experienced in diplomacy and not unsympathetic to the liberal view of foreign policy, resumed his post at the Foreign Office. He believed in the operation of the concert, the value of diplomacy and the advantages of an understanding with France. Like Gorchakov, he wished to preserve peace and the *status quo*. Under his guidance, England was unlikely to play an active part in a possible German conflict.

With England and Russia likely to remain passive spectators, Austria and Prussia were left face to face. Napoleon, for the last time, appeared to be the arbiter of Europe. The diplomatic pattern created by the abstention of England and Russia was a novel one: the ring was cleared for Bismarck, Esterházy and Napoleon.

II

When towards the end of February the Prussian attitude became increasingly menacing, Mensdorff applied to London and St Petersburg for diplomatic support. On 1 March he told Apponyi: 'Nous verrions avec une vive satisfaction que l'Angleterre fît entendre sa voix aussi bien à

---

[1] Palmerston to Russell, 13 September 1865, printed in Gooch, *op. cit.* pp. 314f. and Ashley, *op. cit.* pp. 270f.

Berlin qu'à Florence pour y donner des conseils de modération et y calmer les velléités belliqueuses qu'on nourrit à notre endroit'. This would be of real service to Austria and would help the cause of peace. It was unlikely that in a dispute with which it had no immediate concern, the British government would agree to oppose the aggressor. In fact, British neutrality would work in favour of Prussia: '...en déclarant trés haut sa volonté de maintenir en tous cas une stricte neutralité entre l'Autriche et la Prusse, l'Angleterre fait déjà pencher la balance en faveur de cette dernière'.

The aggressor could feel assured that no attempt would be made to frustrate his evil designs. Was it, in any case, true, that no British interest was at stake? 'Nous comprenons que l'Angleterre ait le désir de se maintenir neutre entre les deux Grandes Puissances Allemandes mais elle a pourtant grand intérêt à ne pas mettre en péril l'équilibre politique de l'Allemagne et de l'Europe.' It was Austria who defended that equilibrium: 'Notre défaite amènerait des complications et des calamités qu'on se répentirait de n'avoir pas prévenues comme il aurait été aisé de le faire en nous accordant à temps quelque soutien.' The decision rested with the powers 'dont l'attitude peut précipiter ou retenir les événements et nous devons les inviter à méditer mûrement leurs résolutions'. In view of the crisis in the Principalities it could not be a matter of indifference to England in particular that Austrian forces should be absorbed in Germany and Italy.

Si le Gouvernement Anglais compte toujours trouver dans le Cabinet Impérial un auxiliaire qui le seconde dans ses efforts pour maintenir l'Empire Ottoman, il faut que l'Angleterre nous aide de son côté à écarter des périls dont l'approche peut paralyser notre influence en Orient ou y donner une autre direction à notre politique.[1]

Clarendon replied

...that reference to the past was useless and...that the advice of England having unfortunately been disregarded two years ago, we had ceased to take a concern in the Schleswig-Holstein question and had remained passive spectators of the process by which Prussia was carrying out her intention to annex the Duchies....

He need not assure Apponyi of the British government's earnest desire to prevent the outbreak of war and of the readiness with which its good offices would be employed to that end, 'but that we know by experience of how little avail such good offices were with the German Governments if we acted singly and had not the support of other Powers'.

Should Prussia push matters to extremes, the Austrian government was right in assuming that

England would preserve a strict neutrality but that in desiring that we should address something in the nature of a threat to Prussia the Austrian government

[1] Mensdorff to Apponyi, 1 March 1866, copy in Murray (for Clarendon) to Buchanan, 7 March 1866, FO 181/440, no. 81, confidential.

sought to make us partizans in the war, and that I could hold out no expectation that after adopting a policy of neutrality we should depart from our duty as neutrals, although it would be a part of that duty to hold the balance as equally as possible between the Belligerents.[1]

Gorchakov's first reaction to the Austrian request resembled Clarendon's.

'La Russie' continua-t-il d'une façon assez dramatique, 'ne parle que quand elle a la volonté et les moyens de se faire écouter. Elle a bien conseillé la prudence et la modération de tous les côtés; aujourd'hui elle ne conserve plus l'espoir que de pareils conseils soient écoutés. Que lui reste-t-il à faire que d'attendre les événemens?'

Revertera rejoined that Russia had acted differently in 1850 'et que la situation d'alors présentait une ressemblance frappante avec ce qui se passe à présent'. Revertera must have known in advance the answer he would receive. Gorchakov agreed that the situation was indeed similar:

...mais il ajouta que ce que l'Empereur Nicolas a fait alors, l'Empereur Alexandre ne le ferait plus. D'abord les circonstances ne sont plus les mêmes et ensuite l'Empereur a renoncé à l'habitude qu'avait Son père d'intervenir personnellement dans les affaires de la diplomatie.

He would, however, consult the tsar who would himself decide 'de l'opportunité d'une démarche privée et confidentielle auprès du Roi de Prusse' For the rest, Gorchakov remarked more than once 'que la Russie n'aurait au premier moment aucun intérêt de prendre part au conflit, et que par conséquent elle resterait neutre aussi longtemps que les circonstances le lui permettraient'. Her neutrality was 'réelle et parfaite' and no assurances of any kind had been given to Prussia. At the same time, Russia would neither condemn the policy of Bismarck nor exercise official pressure at Berlin. Gorchakov had even carried his neutrality to the length of saying that he would refuse to decide which party was the aggressor.[2]

Both Clarendon and Gorchakov had thus, in almost identical terms, declined the Austrian request. Yet the traditions of European diplomacy died hard and the attitude of Napoleon suggested to both England and Russia the prudence of averting hostilities. On 9 March, Revertera reported that he had again asked Gorchakov whether he would not use his moral influence at Berlin. 'Je lui ai demandé enfin, si lui et l'Empereur son Maître pensaient se renfermer dans un silence absolu, ce qui laisserait les événemens s'échapper complètement de leurs mains.' Gorchakov's reply showed that official neutrality did not rule out private admonition:

'Non', répondit-il, 'nous continuerons, comme par le passé, à donner des conseils de modération, et à ranimer les dispositions pacifiques du Roi de Prusse. Nous ne pouvons pas cependant, comme vous semblez le désirer, exprimer une désapproba-

---

[1] Clarendon to Bloomfield, 7 March 1866, no. 62, confidential, copy in Murray (for Clarendon) to Buchanan, 7 March 1866, FO 181/441, no. 81, confidential.
[2] Revertera to Mensdorff, 8 March/24 February, no. 7 B. HHSAPARRR, 1866, x 53.

tion ou un blâme à l'endroit de la politique prussienne. Ce serait sortir de la neutralité que nous nous imposons. Et tant que nous sommes neutres, nous ne voyons que deux adversaires dont chacun peut être l'aggresseur.'[1]

Five days later Gorchakov's sentiments appeared to have swung further to the side of Austria when he tried to get England to intervene on her behalf. He pointed out to Buchanan that the Austro-Prussian dispute might lead to war and that, in view of this, British inaction was to be deplored. He believed 'that if Prussia had reason to fear that Austria would be supported by Great Britain, she would not attempt to realize her ambitious projects by violence'. Buchanan replied that England had only adopted the policy of isolation after her discovery in 1864 that if she wished to defend Denmark she would have to do so alone.[2]

Towards the end of the month, Russia made a further attempt to secure the preservation of peace. On the 27th, Gorchakov, after seeing the tsar, told Revertera 'à titre de confidence (indiscrète comme il l'appelait)' that Alexander some days before had written a personal letter to William I who had replied at once by telegraph and in 'excessively cordial' terms ('dans des termes excessivement chaleureux'). This proved '...la sollicitude avec laquelle la Cour de Russie, sans faire du bruit, s'attachait au maintien de la paix générale'. Bismarck's conduct, Revertera reported, caused growing irritation at the Russian Court.

On y est vivement contrarié des allures indépendantes qu'il se donne, du peu d'égards qu'il témoigne envers des conseils de prudence qui lui sont donnés et aussi ...du mépris avec lequel il a écarté les prétentions du Grand Duc d'Oldenburg, au moment où il se croyait assez fort pour avouer le but de l'annexion des Duchés à la Prusse.

Russia had recently proposed the candidature of the duke under the patronage of the three neutral powers, but the British government had refused its assent. Gorchakov had stated that if his proposal had been accepted, he would have counted on Austria to have sacrificed the duke of Augustenburg. The Oldenburg candidature could then, if necessary, have been imposed on Prussia. 'C'est ainsi que la Russie était une première fois sur le point de sortir de son abstention et elle l'aurait fait sans se préoccuper des intérêts prussiens.' The Russian government, in this instance, would have acted only for a definite Russian interest. 'Mais ce qui est arrivé une fois pourra encore arriver dans des conditions différentes, et j'en conclue que la position de l'Autriche est devenue pour le moins aussi bonne à St Pétersbourg que celle de la Prusse. Libre à nous d'en profiter.'[3] Russian support was probably to be bought.

Il est positif que nous avons gagné beaucoup de terrain à St Pétersbourg. La neutralité russe, avant qu'il y ait guerre, commence déjà à pencher de notre côté.

---

[1] The same to the same, 9 March/25 February, no. 8, *ibid.*
[2] Buchanan to Clarendon, 14 March 1866, FO 65/698, no. 113.
[3] The same to the same, 27/15 March 1866, no. 10 B, confidential, *ibid.*

Je crois que des efforts pas trop violens suffiraient pour attirer l'Empereur Alexandre dans notre camp. Point d'illusions cependant! La Russie ne se donne pas gratis. Elle accepterait un marché qui lui assurât certains avantages....Le prix que nous devrions offrir serait une entente cordiale dans l'affaire des Principautés.

Another means of gaining Russian sympathy would have been support for the Oldenburg candidature. 'Mais cet expédient n'offrirait pas les mêmes facilités et me parait inconciliable avec la politique allemande du Gouvernement Impérial. J'en reviens donc toujours aux Conférences de Paris.'[1] As to the neutrality of Russia, that was assured 'pour quelque temps du moins'. The value of a Russian alliance for Austria had sometimes been discussed:

Je ne veux nullement dissimuler les faiblesses d'une pareille alliance. Les sympathies naturelles du pays ne sont pas pour nous, ses ressources ne sont pas abondantes, ses finances sont épuisées &c. Ces raisons et bien d'autres sont de nature à affaiblir l'importance des progrès que nous pourrions faire sur le terrain de St Pétersbourg.[2]

Mensdorff replied that Austria could not support Russian policy in the Principalities. Such a course would be useless and might lead to a breach with England and France which must be avoided at all cost. Nor could the candidature of the duke of Oldenburg be considered at the moment. Discussion of an alliance would be premature 'et...ce serait aujourd'hui s'exposer à de fâcheux mécomptes que de vouloir modifier notre attitude à Paris dans l'espoir (fort hasardé) d'améliorer notre position à St Pétersbourg'. An understanding was not, indeed, impossible. 'Il faut pour qu'une pareille éventualité puisse se réaliser que les événemens marchent et que la Russie se voie conduite dans notre camp par le soin de ses propres intérêts.' For the moment, Gorchakov's sole object was to secure Austrian support in Paris, and perhaps later for the Oldenburg candidature. In neither question could Austria at present support the Russian view.[3]

In the meantime, the British government also had made an effort to prevent the outbreak of war. In a memorandum of 12 March, Russell had expressed alarm at the prospect of hostilities. Austria, as a result, would, in all probability be seriously crippled in her finances and exhausted in her resources, particularly if Italy were to take part against her. It was not the policy of England 'either to put Prussia in possession of territories in the North of Germany not now belonging to her, or to look with favour on her humiliation'. It appeared to him 'that a war would be prevented and Holstein might continue in tranquillity if the Grand-Duke of Oldenburg were suggested as Duke of Holstein and of Schleswig'. He proposed to state this view at the next meeting of the Cabinet and to

---

[1] On the future of the Principalities.
[2] The same to the same, 27/15 March 1866, no. 10 C, confidential, *ibid.*
[3] Mensdorff to Revertera, no. 3, 5 April 1866, *ibid.* draft.

suggest that it might be put forward 'as a matter for consideration of the German Powers'.[1]

Russell's proposal appeared to offer a possible solution of the question that was threatening the peace of Europe. The Grand-Duke's candidature had the enthusiastic support of the Russian government; Bismarck, although without enthusiasm, seemed ready to accept it.[2] With England, Russia and Prussia agreed, Napoleon would have little choice. Russell's proposal, therefore, might have paved the way for a novel diplomatic grouping and postponed the war in Germany.

The Queen, however, strongly opposed the suggestion. She told Clarendon 'that the claims of the duke of Augustenburg are the only claims which accord with the wishes of the People of the Duchies' and that it would be 'impossible for her to consent to any step, such as that suggested by Lord Russell, for setting them aside'.[3] After an interview with Clarendon, Russell abandoned his proposal.[4]

Clarendon himself, however, had already taken action designed to avert a conflict.[5] In a private letter of 7 March he had instructed Loftus to seek

an opportunity of saying to M. de Bismarck that we purposely abstain from making any official communication upon the present state of affairs, but that we earnestly beg of him to pause before he embarks in a war of which no man can foresee the results or the termination.

It was impossible that any 'well-founded' complaints which Prussia might have against Austria should not be capable of being settled by negotiation; and if ever there was a case calling for the sort of reference to a friendly power which was agreed upon at Paris in 1856, it was the case which had arisen between the two great German powers. It would reflect great credit upon Prussia if she 'volunteered to place herself in the hands of seconds upon whose impartiality she could rely and with whom her honour would be in safe-keeping'. He did not know upon what means of resistance Austria could reckon but felt sure that any grievous injury to her 'such as would destroy the present equilibrium of power', would be a misfortune to the rest of Europe and as such would be resented. The more the question was considered, the more certain it seemed that Prussia would array

---

[1] Russell to the Queen, 12 March 1866, RA I 43/59.

[2] On 11 March after a conversation with Bismarck Loftus, who had succeeded Napier as British ambassador, telegraphed from Berlin that the Prussian Minister 'spoke strongly against Prince Frederick [Augustenburg] but would accept Grand-Duke of Oldenburg' (Loftus to Clarendon, telegram, private, 11 March 1866, *ibid*. I 43/58).

[3] The Queen to Clarendon, 13 March 1866, *ibid*. I 43/70; cf. also the Queen to Russell, 12 March 1866, and Grey to Clarendon, private, 12 March 1866, *ibid*. I 43, nos. 60 and 68, copies.

[4] Russell to the Queen, 13 March 1866, and Clarendon to the Queen, 13 March 1866, *ibid*. I 43, nos. 71 and 72.

[5] 'Of course it would be useless for us to make an official remonstrance against Bismarck's peace-breaking proclivities, but I wrote Loftus a private letter...' (Clarendon to Cowley, private, 12 March 1866, Clarendon MSS., copy).

against herself the public opinion of Europe 'as an aggressive and unreasonable power' and they had no wish for that.

Setting aside family ties, Prussia is the great Protestant Power of Europe, with which we naturally have kindred feelings, and it would be with deep regret that we should see her regarded as a common enemy, because a wilful disturber of the peace of Europe; and still more if, in the course of events, we found ourselves compelled to take any part against her.

Such were the considerations to be submitted to Bismarck 'as friendly and confidential, and offered without intention to interfere with the policy of Prussia' but without concealing from him 'our opinion upon the disastrous consequences to ourselves, as well as to others, which may ensue from that policy being carried beyond the limits of absolute necessity'.[1]

If Clarendon's intervention was infinitely more tactful than had been that of Palmerston and Russell in the affair of the Duchies, its success was equally problematical. Bismarck, informed of Clarendon's views, 'made no reply'[2] and disclaimed all violent intentions on the part of Prussia.[3] Some days later, William I in conversation alluded to Clarendon's letter and Loftus used the opportunity to repeat the British proposal. The king, still hesitating between war and conciliation, surprisingly replied that he was 'well-disposed to accept the good offices of England'.[4] Bismarck confirmed this, adding that he would 'write a private letter to Bernstorff in this sense'.[5] On the following day, King William invited the Crown Prince 'to write in the same sense to the Queen'.[6]

On 17 March, Crown Prince Frederick, therefore, wrote to Queen Victoria that Prussia was ready to accept the proffered mediation. The king asked the British cabinet to invite Austria to lay aside her jealousy of Prussia. Speaking for himself, the Crown Prince suggested that Clarendon should begin by asking both parties to state their grievances and then try to effect a reconciliation. It was with the greatest reluctance that King William was slowly beginning to reconcile himself to the idea of a conflict of incalculable consequences. It depended on the Queen and her government to prevent a dreadful calamity.[7] On 21 March, the Cabinet duly decided that if the Prussian government desired it, 'good offices should be tender'd it, and in conformity with the sensible views of the Crown Prince, Prussia and Austria should be ask'd what complaints they have to make'.[8]

---

[1] Clarendon to Loftus, private, 7 March 1866, *The Diplomatic Reminiscences of Lord Augustus Loftus 1863–1878* (London, 1894), 2nd series, vol. II, pp. 43 ff.
[2] Loftus to Clarendon, telegram, private, 11 March 1866, RA I 43/58.
[3] Loftus, *op. cit.* p. 45.
[4] The same to the same, telegram, 17 March 1866, FO 64/591, no. 48.
[5] The same to the same, 17 March 1866, FO 64/591, no. 55, confidential.
[6] The same to the same, 17 March 1866, FO 64/591, no. 54, most confidential.
[7] Crown Prince of Prussia to the Queen, 17 March 1866, RA I 43/95.
[8] Russell to the Queen, 22 March 1866, *ibid.* I 43/110.

British mediation, however, was the last thing Bismarck desired. The 'wicked man', the Crown-Princess wrote to her mother, was *'frantic that the K. shd have desired F. to write to you'*, and would now do everything in his power 'to pin the K. to *his* politics and paralyse any intervention from elsewhere'.[1] On 20 March, Bismarck in fact telegraphed to Bernstorff that the Crown Prince had, without his knowledge, written to Queen Victoria. Bernstorff should ignore all communications in the matter until he had received a private letter from Berlin.[2] On the morning of 22 March, Bernstorff read Clarendon 'an enormous long letter' from Bismarck which contained

...a long catalogue of grievances in general terms and of a frivolous nature against Austria,—in the midst of them however jumped out the real Prussian cat viz. that Austria was opposed to the annexation of the Duchies which was politically and militarily indispensable to Prussia.

Clarendon thereupon told Bernstorff 'very shortly' that as for England 'helping directly or indirectly Prussia in acquiring those Duchies, it was not to be thought of for a moment'.[3] Two days later, Clarendon and Bernstorff agreed that since Bismarck had made it known that Prussia stood in no need of good offices 'the question was...at an end, and...the relations between our respective governments remained as before'.[4]

On 26 March, Queen Victoria who had received from the Queen of Prussia a letter stating that, if anything could still be done to avert war, there was no time to lose,[5] addressed herself to Clarendon. The Foreign Secretary agreed 'that something ought to be done' to 'avoid a dreadful complication'. The only action likely to preserve peace was for France to join with England 'in telling Prussia we shd not see with indifference the accomplishment of her unjust designs'.[6] On 30 March, therefore, the Queen wrote a memorandum 'showing the absolute necessity of our attempting to do something, in conjunction with France, to arrest the misfortunes a war would entail'.[7] This memorandum, Russell told Clarendon, clearly proposed 'an interference by force against Prussian designs in the Duchies'. He could not acquiesce in the policy suggested. England might have intervened in 1863 to defend Denmark against both Prussia and Austria, but the government and Parliament had then decided against undertaking such a war. England had 'spoken in defence of right', she could not interfere 'in the division of the spoil'. It would be nothing less than an injustice to the people of England to employ

[1] Crown Princess of Prussia to the Queen, 20 March 1866 (*ibid.* I 43/105 (*QVL, loc. cit.* pp. 305f.)).

[2] Bismarck to Bernstorff, telegram, 20 March 1866, Bismarck, *GW*, vol. v, p. 407.

[3] Clarendon to Loftus, 22 March 1866, FO 244/208, no. 30.

[4] Clarendon to the Queen, 24 March 1866, RA I 43/120.

[5] Grey to Russell, private and confidential, 26 March 1866, *ibid.* I 43/124.

[6] Clarendon to the Queen, 29 March 1866, *ibid.* I 43/144.

[7] Extract from the Queen's Journal (*QVL, loc. cit.* p. 314).

their military and pecuniary resources in a quarrel in which neither English honour nor English interests were involved. The Ministers who had attended the Cabinet the previous day were 'decidedly against interference'. An amicable mediation, however, might be agreed to in conjunction with France and Russia if asked for by both parties.[1] In accordance with Russell's views Clarendon informed the Queen that some time ago he had consulted Cowley about the possibility of 'a joint representation being made by England and France against the unjust and high-handed proceedings of Prussia'.[2] He had been told in reply 'that the prospects of war in Germany were by no means displeasing to the Emperor'.[3] It was quite clear that the good offices of England alone would not be accepted by Prussia; they had been offered indirectly and confidentially and declined. If offered officially, England would merely incur 'an insolent refusal'. Even in conjunction with France, England would be unable to use 'the language of menace which might entail the necessity of action'. Moreover, both on account of the 'menacing aspect' of relations with the United States and of the present state of Ireland, 'the military and pecuniary resources of England must be husbanded with the utmost care'. The country, therefore, would not tolerate 'any direct interference in a quarrel with which we had no concern'. The Ministers who attended the last cabinet 'expressed themselves in the strongest terms against it'.[4] Russell in his turn, after repeating Clarendon's arguments,[5] expressed the opinion that the British government 'ought not alone to give any advice, or interfere in any way with Prussia, while Count Bismarck is the Minister of the King'.[6] The Queen, with a heavy heart, abandoned her proposal.[7]

As a last resource, she now decided to use her dynastic ties with the

[1] Russell to Clarendon, 30 March 1866, Maxwell, op. cit. p. 311.

[2] This had been done on 12 March (Cowley to Clarendon, private, 13 March 1866, Cowley MSS. in the Public Record Office, London, copy).

[3] Cowley wrote: 'My impression is that a war between them [Austria and Prussia] would be nuts here and the Emperor might say that as his good offices have not been asked for by either belligerent, and as he has latterly studiously kept out of the question of the Duchies, he will not interfere now' (ibid.). Ten days later, Cowley reported: 'I am more and more convinced that they will do nothing here to prevent hostilities between the German Powers. Some of the Ministers openly avow that it is in the interest of France that they should fight and the Emperor perhaps will not be sorry that there should be some event abroad to divert the public mind from thinking too much of internal affairs, which are not over bright, and then who knows but what favourable opportunity may offer to assert the supremacy of France abroad, if matters get worse at home' (the same to the same, 23 March 1866, ibid. copy).

[4] Clarendon to the Queen, 31 March 1866 (RA I 43/154 (QVL, loc. cit. pp. 314ff.)).

[5] The two Ministers were not in full agreement. Clarendon wrote: 'He thinks it quite right that Prussia should have the military disposal of the North of Germany—I cannot say I agree with him, though we of course should not interfere to prevent such an arrangement...' (Clarendon to Cowley, private, 11 April 1866, Clarendon MSS. copy).

[6] Russell to the Queen, 1 April 1866, RA I 43/161.

[7] On 6 April Clarendon recorded: '...The Missus is in an awful state about German affairs' (Maxwell, op. cit. p. 310).

house of Hohenzollern. On 10 April, without consulting her Ministers, she wrote to William I adjuring him in the name of everything he held sacred to renounce the thought of war. One man alone was responsible for all this evil.[1] The king himself, however, would bear the ultimate responsibility for a dreadful war. She could not believe that he would abandon the principles of a true Christian.[2] It was a forlorn hope. In his reply, William I expressed his complete solidarity with the policy of Bismarck.[3]

The British government had for some time resigned itself to the probability of war. Clarendon expressed his indignation at Bismarck's policy.[4] He was aware that the war would be not unwelcome to Napoleon and told Cowley that the security of Belgium must be England's main concern:

> Except for reasons of humanity, which must weigh lightly enough with him, he [Napoleon] can't see with displeasure the prospects of war in Germany, for the abatement of the military means of Austria and Prussia will relatively increase the military Power of France, and out of such a shindy as those two might get up and into which they will draw all the Minor States it is impossible to say that France will not reap some advantage, and I believe that territorial extension will be a good basis for his son's throne. Our great care must be for Belgium and our resources of all kinds must be husbanded for fulfilling our Treaty engagements respecting that Country.—Russell is very anxious that I should impress this on you and beg that you will miss no opportunity of giving the Emperor to understand it [sic]. He will probably admit our position and not try to embarrass us by meddling with Belgium.[5]

In anticipation of hostilities Clarendon was privately supporting a French proposal that Austria should cede Venetia to Italy in exchange for the Principalities, financial compensation or, if she could get it, Silesia.[6] On the last day of March, the Foreign Secretary confided to Cowley: 'Prince Napoleon's advice to the Italians was very wise and sound, and all Europe would rejoice if they got Venetia, and Austria Silesia, and Prussia a licking'. Napoleon should press this proposal on Metternich. He 'would gain great popularity in Europe by helping to take the shine out of Prussia and by getting a fresh guarantee for peace by the cession

---

[1] '...ein Mann allein trägt die Schuld an diesem Unheil'.

[2] The Queen to the king of Prussia, 10 April 1866, translation (RA I 44/5 (*QVL, loc. cit.* pp. 317f.)).

[3] The reply bore the date of 12 April but was not despatched until the 21st (king of Prussia to Queen Victoria, 12 and 21 April 1866, RA I 44/20).

[4] 'I know of no parallel to Bismarck or any precedent for such a war as he is determined upon except some of those of Napoleon. He told Loftus that Attila was a much greater man than John Bright [the Germans appear to have had an unfortunate *penchant* for Hunnish analogies] and had handed himself down to history, that the Duke of Wellington would be remembered as a great warrior and not as a pacific statesman—and that he meant to be remembered also by making his country great and stamping out all opposition to her supremacy in Germany...' (Clarendon to Cowley, private, 9 April 1866, Clarendon MSS. copy).

[5] The same to the same, private, 11 April 1866, *ibid.* copy.

[6] The first French soundings had taken place as early as 8 March (the same to the same, private, 8 March 1866, *ibid.* copy).

of Venetia, and Austria would get the money she wants'.[1] Cowley himself should present these views to Metternich who might have some influence with his government 'from his position at Paris—the supreme Umpire's court'. There was no time to be lost. If Italy once entered an offensive and defensive alliance with Prussia they must attack Austria and run the chance of 'being well-licked' if they did not obtain Venetia at enormous cost instead of securing it by amicable negotiation.[2]

On 16 April, Russell, in his turn in a private letter to Apponyi, proposed the cession of Venetia. If Austria was disposed 'to listen to arguments founded on her own interests in the question and to admit the possibility of ceding Venetia to Italy', he would say 'strongly and decidedly' that she should avail herself of the present moment. A cession made now would have the grace of a voluntary surrender to national aspirations, would satisfy the wishes of France and England, and might 'form a lasting friendship with Italy'. Were Austria to wait until Venetia was wrested from her, the claims of victorious Italy might extend to parts of the Dalmatian coast. By making the cession now, Austria could determine its extent.[3] Mensdorff replied that the cession of Venetia was impossible:

Ce n'est pas une rancune mesquine contre les Italiens, ce n'est même pas l'importance extrême de la Vénétie pour l'Autriche qui nous dicte notre politique actuelle à l'égard de l'Italie. C'est notre existence même qui est mise en question par le principe sur lequel se fond l'unité Italienne. Nous pouvons à la rigueur nous accomoder de tout arrangement territorial reposant sur des combinaisons politiques. Mais si l'Europe doit être reconstruite d'après le système des nationalités je ne vois pas la place que l'Autriche peut y occuper, et nous ne sommes pas encore résignés à donner le signal de notre démembrement pour complaire à un entraînement qui ne sera, je l'espère, que passager.[4]

Mensdorff's arguments impressed Clarendon[5] and for a time the matter

[1] The same to the same, private, 31 March 1866, *ibid.* copy. Two weeks later Clarendon wrote: 'The whole thing might be *déjoué* at once by the cession of Venetia, but I expect that as usual the Austrians will be 24 hours too late and that the sacrifice, evidently contemplated, will not be made until it is useless' (the same to the same, 14 April 1866, *ibid.* copy).

[2] *Ibid.* Clarendon was, of course, unaware of the fact that after prolonged hesitation the Italian government had on 8 April, with the consent of Napoleon, signed an offensive and defensive alliance with Prussia.

[3] Russell to Apponyi, 16 April 1866, RA.I 44/35, copy. Two days later, Clarendon wrote to Cowley: 'Metternich like Apponyi does not seem bold enough to broach the Venetian subject with his Govt. and from all I hear the Emperor [of Austria] is unapproachable upon it but I wish he could be made to see that the cession of Venetia would be the most effectual means of rendering himself independent of France and of her assistance, or neutrality, or hostility in a war with Prussia, and that an alliance with Italy would set the hands of Austria so completely free that she might chastise Prussia and help herself if she chose to some of her old Silesian territory' (Clàrendon to Cowley, 18 April 1866, Clarendon MSS. copy).

[4] Mensdorff to Apponyi, 26 April 1866, RA I 44/78, copy.

[5] He told Cowley that Russell's recommendation had 'brought an answer from Mensdorff, so well-argued and so conclusive' that he could not believe Metternich had been authorized to broach the question in Paris (Clarendon to Cowley, private, 5 May 1866, Clarendon MSS. copy).

was allowed to drop. British diplomacy had virtually reached the limit of its resources.

The Russian government, in the meantime, had not been idle. On 2 April the tsar had handed to Schweinitz, the king of Prussia's military attaché,[1] a letter to be delivered personally to William I. Schweinitz was to recommend to the king the installation of the duke of Oldenburg. Thereafter, Prussia should secure from the duke the concessions her interests required.[2]—At the same time, the tsar had addressed a letter to Francis-Joseph to be delivered in person by the Russian general Richter. Alexander wrote that some time ago Francis-Joseph through Revertera had expressed the desire that Russia should counsel conciliation at Berlin. He had done this on the first suitable occasion. 'J'ai profité de l'anniversaire de la naissance de mon Oncle pour faire un appel direct à sa sagesse, à son caractère chevaleresque, à ses sentiments de Souverain Allemand.' The king in his reply had disclaimed all desire for war but had complained of Austrian armaments which forced him in his turn to make military preparations.

Permets moi, mon cher ami, [the tsar continued] d'appeler toute Ton attention sur cet état de choses. Je suis convaincu que, pas plus que le Roi de Prusse, Tu ne désires une rupture. Ce serait jouer le jeu des ennemis de l'Autriche comme de ceux de la Prusse et de l'indépendance de l'Allemagne. Mais la pente où Tu T'es placé et où le Roi se croit obligé de se placer à son tour, peut conduire d'armements en armements, de démonstrations en démonstrations, à une de ces situations où les canons parlent tout seuls, et alors, sans le vouloir, le cœur saignant à la pensée de cette lutte fratricide, Vous arriveriez néanmoins à l'affaiblissement de cette Allemagne qui Vous est chère à tous deux.

He therefore appealed to Francis-Joseph to withdraw his troops from their advanced positions. A step of this kind 'détendrait les rapports et rendrait possible la reprise des négociations'. He had addressed a similar appeal to William I.

Tu sais, mon cher ami, [Alexander concluded] que mes vœux sont pour le maintien de l'accord entre les deux grandes Puissances Allemandes. Je suis sûr que Tu apprécieras l'appel que je fais en toute franchise à Ta sagesse, après avoir invoqué celle de mon Oncle.—Je prie Dieu d'éclairer Vos résolutions, car la paix du monde peut en dépendre et ce serait une bien lourde responsabilité.[3]

Schweinitz reached Berlin on 5 April and soon realized that the

---

[1] Schweinitz was treated at the Russian court as the direct personal representative of William I. He was completely in the tsar's confidence. This, together with his transparent honesty and independence of character renders his reminiscences an invaluable source for the study of Russian policy during the Austro-Prussian war (*Denkwürdigkeiten des Botschafters General v. Schweinitz* (Berlin, 1927), containing extensive extracts from Schweinitz's diaries).

[2] *Ibid.* vol. I, p. 201.

[3] Alexander II to Francis-Joseph, 21 mars/2 avril 1866, HHSAPARRR, 1866, x 53.

atmosphere was warlike and the tsar's effort at mediation hopeless.[1] He was, moreover, detained in Berlin until 17 April before being allowed to return to Russia. In the meantime, Francis-Joseph had replied to the tsar's letter. He had protested his peaceful intentions and outlined the development of the dispute since the Convention of Gastein. Prussia had expressed the desire to annex the Duchies, he had taken some small military precautions.[2] This had been done to offset the greater speed of Prussian mobilization. He felt deeply the evils of a fratricidal war. Could any country desire peace more earnestly than Austria? 'Je puis me dispenser de te parler de nos difficultés intérieures, de nos embarras financiers. Ils ne sont que trop connus et il est clair qu'aucun pays n'a plus besoin de la paix que l'Autriche.'[3] Francis-Joseph's letter by its moderate and dignified tone created a favourable impression.[4] Buchanan reported to Clarendon: 'Whatever other consequences result from this correspondence, it has for the present caused the Russian Court to look more favourably on the proceedings of Austria than those of Prussia.'[5]

---

[1] This became clear to Schweinitz more particularly after a conversation with Abeken, Bismarck's trusted assistant. The Crown Prince confirmed that Bismarck was bent on war. 'Jedenfalls wusste ich nun, woran ich war, und vermied es, mich zum Don Quixote einer aussichtslosen Friedensvermittlung zu machen' (Schweinitz, op. cit. p. 203).

[2] During a visit to the General Staff in Berlin Schweinitz made the discovery that the movements of Austrian troops, of which Bismarck was loudly complaining, were no threat whatever to Prussia. The honest general noted, in speaking of the Austrians: 'die Aermsten wurden wirklich verleumdet' (ibid. p. 205).

[3] Francis-Joseph to Alexander II, 7 April 1866, HHSAPARRR, 1866, x 53, draft.

[4] Revertera to Mendsorff no. 12 D, 10 April/29 March 1866, with postscript of the following day (ibid.).

[5] Buchanan to Clarendon, 11 April 1866, FO 65/698, no. 173. Queen Olga of Württemberg, the tsar's favourite sister, told Revertera 'que les anciennes rancunes contre l'Autriche étaient enterrées, oubliées à la Cour de Russie...' (Revertera to Mendsorff, no. 11 C, 7 April/26 March 1866, HHSAPARRR, 1866, x 53). Alexander was being influenced every day and every hour in an anti-Prussian sense by the Empress, Queen Olga of Württemberg, Grand-Duke and Grand-Duchess Constantine and the Duke of Mecklenburg-Strelitz. The only supporter of Prussia among influential members of the imperial family was the Grand-Duchess Helen (Schweinitz, op. cit. p. 211). The tsarevich and future Alexander III, about to be married to a Danish princess, was violently anti-Prussian. One day, he interrupted an argument between two ladies of the imperial family one of whom favoured Austria, the other Prussia, with the words: 'Laissez-faire ces ennuyeux Prussiens, et vous verrez comme ils seront rossés par les Autrichiens' (Revertera to Mendsorff, no. 12 A-D, 10 April/29 March 1866, HHSAPARRR, x 53). It is interesting to note that all members of the imperial family were either Germans or half-Germans. The connections of the emperor himself were with Prussia for his mother had been a Hohenzollern princess. Schweinitz considered that these Prussian associations influenced the tsar's conduct: '...der Vizekanzler war gegen uns, ebenso die russischen Gesandten in Berlin und Paris; nur einen Bundesgenossen hatte ich, einen mächtigen, im Herzen jenes edlen Monarchen. ...Seine Pietät für das Andenken seiner Mutter, die Erinnerung an seine Kindheit und Jugend, die so innig mit preussischen Dingen verknüpft waren, und sein bewundernswertes Verständnis für die Tugenden unseres Heeres erwiesen sich stärker als alle feindlichen Einflüsterungen und wie die wohlbegründeten Mahnungen politischer Ratgeber' (Schweinitz, op. cit. p. 221). Unlike those of the emperor himself, the dynastic associations of the rest of the imperial family led by Queen Olga and Grand-Duke Constantine, were with the secondary German states, particularly Württemberg and Hanover.

Gorchakov claimed credit for the emperor's efforts to prevent the outbreak of war.[1]

Whatever hopes of peace might have been felt at St Petersburg, however, were destined to be short-lived. Duke George of Mecklenburg, a guest at the silver wedding of Alexander II, reported that, on passing through Berlin, he had found the king completely under the domination of Bismarck. Any attempt to control events would be useless. In the face of this news, the tsar abandoned all serious hope of preserving peace. He expressed his distrust of Napoleon: '"Notre bon ami de Paris...est aux aguets, et si la guerre éclate, il ne tardera pas d'en faire son profit."' He regretted the passing of the Holy Alliance: ' "La Sainte Alliance...qu'on a tant attaquée a cependant donné à l'Europe 50 ans de paix. Ne nous attachons pas au nom, mais le système offrait des garanties, et je regrette qu'on ne puisse y revenir..."'[2]

Events were now moving rapidly. On 8 April Bismarck had concluded his alliance with Italy. On the following day the Prussian representative at the Federal Diet proposed the creation of a German Parliament with a lower house elected by universal suffrage.[3] The tsar did not conceal his indignation at the revolutionary proposal. Bismarck, he declared, had: 'à jamais perdu la confiance qu'il semblait mériter comme champion de la légitimité'.[4] Gorchakov, whilst critical of Bismarck,[5] considered that this was a German matter in which Russia could not take part.[6] He did, however, write to Berlin that even his personal friendship for King William would never induce Alexander II to become an accomplice in Prussia's subversive designs.[7] On the evening of 19 April the tsar gave an audience to Schweinitz who had returned from Berlin. He read to the general the reply he had received from Francis-Joseph. From time to time he interrupted his reading with the remark: 'Il a raison; ceci est vrai; c'est encore vrai.' The tsar accepted the view that the Convention of Gastein marked the limit of Austrian concession. With regard to the proposal for federal reform, he repeated what Gorchakov had written to Oubril. He added that he would write again to William I. When Schweinitz—against his own innermost convictions—defended the Prussian proceedings, Alexander repeated that the calling of a Parliament was revolutionary and dangerous.

[1] Gorchakov proudly remarked to Revertera: 'que la Russie fesait [sic] des efforts réels pour le maintien de la paix....De tous les Souverains de l'Europe, l'Empereur Alexandre seul a pris la résolution d'intervenir personnellement et s'il y a une chance de prévenir la guerre, c'est Lui qui l'aura créée' (Revertera to Mensdorff, no. 11 C, 7 April/26 March 1866, HHSAPARRR, 1866, X 53).

[2] The same to the same, no. 12 A-D, 10 April/29 March 1866, *ibid.*

[3] For details of the Prussian proposals, cf. Sybel, *op. cit.* vol. IV, pp. 323 ff.

[4] Revertera to Mensdorff, no. 13 B, 11 April/30 March 1866, HHSAPARRR, 1866, X 53.

[5] ' "Das ist nicht mehr Politik", sagte er zu mir, "das ist Revolution"' (Graf F. Revertera, 'Erinnerungen eines Diplomaten in St Petersburg 1864 bis 1868', *Deutsche Revue*, Stuttgart u. Leipzig, 1904, 29 Jahrg. p. 130).

[6] Revertera to Mensdorff, no. 13 B, 11 April/30 March 1866, HHSAPARRR, 1866, X 53.

[7] The same to the same, no. 16 A-B, 25/13 April 1866, *ibid.* and Revertera, *loc. cit.* p. 130.

He was pressed on all sides; 'c'est un haro général contre Bismarck; on le croit capable de tout'. In imagination, the German princes already saw themselves mediatized. Napoleon appeared to be working for war and was trying to create incidents between Austria and Prussia. He would write about this to King William. There followed the now inevitable eulogy of the Holy Alliance.[1] On the following day, Schweinitz found Gorchakov in a mood of irritation less about universal suffrage than about the creation of a German Parliament which would force the secondary states to make concessions to a central power.[2] At a Court Ball on 30 April, the tsar expressed to Revertera his satisfaction at Francis-Joseph's letter. He strongly condemned the Prusso-Italian alliance, the existence of which he could no longer doubt.[3] In reply to Revertera's expression of gratitude for his efforts at Berlin, Alexander remarked: '"Et je le ferai encore...je ferai tout mon possible pour détourner le Roi de la guerre vers laquelle on cherche à l'entraîner".'[4]

On 2 May, the tsar again sent Schweinitz to Berlin with a further letter to William I.[5] It was a hopeless mission. When Schweinitz reached Berlin on 4 May, he found Prussian mobilization in full progress. On the evening of 10 May, he left Berlin empty-handed.[6]

The British government, in the meantime, had shown less concern about the impending conflict.[7] When invited by Drouyn to state his views on the Prussian proposal for federal reform, Clarendon had given a feeble and ambiguous reply:

> Prince La Tour has more than once asked me what we thought of Federal reform and the new Constitution for Germany but I declined giving an answer till I had consulted my colleagues. They all look upon it as a European question and think the Emperor [Napoleon] right in making his reserves.—We probably shall take no part in the matter actively but we shall not be indifferent spectators to so great a change in the arrangements made at Vienna.[8]

The Queen alone refused to accept the inevitable. On 6 May she again asked Clarendon whether England and France could not act together

---

[1] Schweinitz, *op. cit.* pp. 208f.

[2] After his interview with Gorchakov, Schweinitz noted with regret 'dass ihm das deutsche Parlament höchst widerwärtig, dagegen das allgemeine Stimmrecht ganz nebensächlich erschien' (*ibid.* p. 209).

[3] Revertera, *loc. cit.* p. 133.

[4] Revertera to Mensdorff, no. 18 B, 7 May/25 April 1866, HHSAPARRR, 1866, x 53 and the same to the same, telegram, 1 May 1866, *ibid.*

[5] Schweinitz, *op. cit.* p. 214.

[6] *Ibid.* p. 215.

[7] On 9 April, Clarendon had informed the British ministers at the secondary German courts: 'However much this country may regret to see Germany a prey to civil war, yet so long as the war is confined to Germany there is no British interest of sufficient magnitude to render imperative the tender of British good offices' (Clarendon to the British ministers at Stuttgart, Frankfurt, Hanover and Dresden, 9 April 1866, copy in Clarendon to Buchanan, 18 April 1866, FO 181/422, no. 124, most confidential).

[8] Clarendon to Cowley, private, 14 April 1866, Clarendon MSS. copy.

'positively to prevent such an awful misfortune as this war in Germany'. Clarendon replied that nothing could be done as Napoleon declined to interfere. When the Queen asked whether the British government could not threaten or remonstrate, the Foreign Secretary replied that he feared 'that would *not* do'. He had prepared a draft proposing that England should do alone what it had been intended to do together with France, that is, to 'make an *appeal* to the conflicting Powers'. The Cabinet had decided against this since it would clearly demonstrate that France and England were not agreed. A naval demonstration by England alone would be equally unprofitable. Such action would not be sufficient by itself 'and we had weakened ourselves so much by a threatening policy without its being supported by deeds'. The Queen offered, 'if it would be any use' to write to Napoleon herself, but Clarendon did not encourage the idea.[1] There was, in his opinion, only too much reason to believe that the time for appeals had passed and that 'a groundless and therefore horrible and unjustifiable war' was about to commence.[2]

When Schweinitz returned to St Petersburg empty-handed on 12 May, he found the tsar still hopeful about the possibility of preserving peace.[3] The Austrian government was ready for a compromise;[4] Gorchakov still urged a direct Austro-Prussian understanding on federal reform and the future of the Duchies. It was a scandal, he declared, that Germany should go to war when her territory was threatened by France.[5] On 17 May, Schweinitz found the emperor in a bad humour after reading despatches from Berlin; he was beginning to realize that Bismarck would frustrate every well-meant effort to prevent the outbreak of war.[6] On 23 May, Gorchakov denied rumours that Russia contemplated intervention in the impending conflict; only a direct national interest would induce her to abandon the policy of neutrality.[7]

During the last week of May, there appeared a last remote prospect that the powers might meet in congress. On 24 May, England, France and Russia invited Prussia, Austria and Italy to a meeting in Paris for the discussion of European problems. On 29 May, Prussia notified her grudging acceptance.[8] The Austrian government, however, announced that it would enter a conference only if assured in advance that no

---

[1] Memorandum by Queen Victoria, 6 May 1866 (RA I 44/144 (*QVL, loc. cit.* pp. 325f.)).
[2] Clarendon to the Queen, 6 May 1866, RA I 44/145.
[3] Schweinitz, *op. cit.* p. 216.
[4] *Ibid.*
[5] Revertera to Mensdorff, no. 19 B, 16/4 May 1866 HHSAPARRR, 1866, x 53, confidential. Revertera remarked: '...la grandeur de l'Allemagne n'est pas ce qui intéresse si vivement le Vice-Chancelier russe. Il sent que l'antagonisme entre l'Autriche et la Prusse ouvre la porte à une foule de combinaisons inconnues et peut-être incommodes à la Russie' (*ibid.*).
[6] Schweinitz, *op. cit.* p. 217.
[7] Revertera to Mensdorff, no. 20 A-C, 23/11 May 1866, HHSAPARRR, 1866, x 53.
[8] Schweinitz *op. cit.* p. 219.

territorial changes would be discussed. This put an immediate end to the possibility of a meeting. In London and St Petersburg alike it was at last admitted that all hope of preserving peace had disappeared.[1]

III

On 14 June the Federal Diet accepted an Austrian proposal to mobilize the federal contingents. The Prussian delegate thereupon announced that, in the opinion of his government, the Federation was dissolved. He would bring forward proposals for the reorganization of Germany.[2] This denunciation made the question of Germany's future an international issue.

The British government, on learning of the Prussian action, adopted the view

that the Confederation owing its existence to the general assent of all the Powers of Europe and having been accepted as a substantive European Institution by all the states of Germany, it is not in the power of a single state...to dissolve the Confederacy without the concurrence of the other non-German Powers, who were Parties to its Institution.[3]

Clarendon, therefore, decided to consult the French and Russian governments. Napoleon's reply revealed that he was not inclined to shed tears at the possible demise of the Confederation associated with the hated treaties of 1815.[4] Gorchakov, on the other hand, agreed with the British view. They were, he lamented, 'returning to the chaos of savage life'. Right was replaced by force and cunning. In these circumstances '...the Powers who look upon right and legality as the best guarantee of the interests of society should come to an understanding and declare their intentions'.[5] The question of legality, however, had by this time become secondary to decisions in the field; the future of Germany would be decided not by paper remonstrances but by military force.

Russian sympathies in the impending war were unequivocally on the side of Austria. Revertera reported:

Les allures de plus en plus audacieuses de la politique prussienne rencontrent ici une réprobation générale....L'indignation se mêle à l'étonnement qu'on en éprouve et les sympathies se tournent plus que jamais de notre côté.[6]

---

[1] Clarendon to the Queen, 31 May 1866, RA I 87/11 and Schweinitz, *op. cit.* pp. 219f. One word from Napoleon, even at this late stage, would probably have prevented the outbreak of war. The emperor remained silent. Aware that the coming struggle would be essentially a war for nationality and that a new 'Nice and Savoy' might be the reward of France, he tacitly promoted the outbreak of a conflict which, in its effects was to destroy the equilibrium first of Germany and eventually of Europe. He did this, of course, in the mistaken belief that the contestants would be evenly matched.

[2] Sybel, *op. cit.* pp. 442ff.

[3] Clarendon to Buchanan, 21 June 1866, FO 181/443, no. 193.

[4] Napoleon to Drouyn, 11 June 1866, *Origines*, vol. x, p. 122 and Drouyn to La Tour, 26 June 1866, *ibid.* pp. 277f.

[5] Buchanan to Clarendon, 23 June 1866, FO 65/700, no. 300.

[6] Revertera to Mensdorff, no. 22 A-B, 20/8 June 1866, HHSAPARRR, 1866, x 53.

Gorchakov received with delight the news of an Austrian victory in Italy:

Victoire en Italie chaleureusement accueillie par le Prince Gortchacow qui l'a aussitôt télégraphiée à l'Empereur. Il dit qu'il est *très* nécessaire d'avoir bientôt un succès contre la Prusse où l'esprit militaire s'est accru par les succès inespérés.[1]

Gorchakov's joy was short-lived. On 30 June official despatches from Berlin reported great Prussian victories. 'Ici grande consternation', Revertera reported to Mensdorff.[2]

On 4 July, Gorchakov proposed to Buchanan that England, France and Russia should reply in identical terms to Prussia's notification of her withdrawal from the Confederation. The three powers should jointly declare that no single member state could either leave or dissolve the Germanic Confederation. Nor could it arrogate to itself the right of forming a new Confederation on a basis 'which might affect the balance of Power in Europe'. Identical notes setting out these principles would serve as a warning to Prussia; they would encourage the lesser states, and afford the neutral powers a firm basis in a possible future congress. If the matter was left in its present state, Prussia might later claim the tacit acquiescence of the neutrals. Should the British government accept the proposal, Brunnow would invite Clarendon to sound the French government. The drafting of the notes, which should be made public, would be left to England and France. If Clarendon agreed, he must act without delay.[3]

Gorchakov's proposal had already been overtaken by events. On 2 July, Austria had appealed to Napoleon to arrange an armistice in Italy. The following day the Austrian armies in Bohemia had been routed at Königgrätz. Napoleon had agreed to mediate and to bring about an armistice with Prussia and Italy on condition that Venetia was surrendered to him. On 4 July the Austrian government agreed to this.[4] When Napoleon invited the Russian government to support his proposals for an armistice, Gorchakov replied that he must wait until that situation was more clearly defined. He added that in his opinion 'where the general interests of Europe are at stake, peace negotiations could not properly be carried on under the mediation of a single Power, and that the three great Powers should take an equal part in them'.[5] In fact, the Austrian decision to make Napoleon the sole mediator was severely criticized at St Petersburg. Revertera reported:

On est très étonné qu'en demandant la médiation française l'Autriche n'ait pas même jugé à propos d'en prévenir le Gouvernement russe. Prince Gortchacow m'a

---

[1] The same to the same, telegram, 26 June 1866, *ibid.*
[2] The same to the same, telegram, 30 June 1866, *ibid.*
[3] Buchanan to Clarendon, 4 July 1866, FO 65/700, no. 317.
[4] H. Friedjung, *Der Kampf um die Vorherrschaft in Deutschland* (9th ed. Berlin, 1913), vol. II, pp. 336f.
[5] Buchanan to Clarendon, 7 July 1866, FO 65/700, nos. 321 and 321A.

fait observer avec une certaine amertume que toutes les sympathies de la Russie jusqu'à présent étaient pour nous.[1]

Mensdorff replied that Austria had been unable to decline the mediation offered by France but counted on Russia's good offices in the coming negotiations.[2] This answer pacified Gorchakov only in part. The cession of Venetia, he declared, put France in a special position. Russia must now wait until the situation was clearer. Had Austria indicated earlier that she counted on Russia's good offices, this would have helped to maintain the tsar's friendly dispositions. The cession of Venetia combined with the intervention of France, however, had created a bad impression. Russia reserved the right to take part in the settlement of all European questions.[3]

Mensdorff's belated appeal to St Petersburg had coincided with an invitation to the British government to use its good offices in the coming negotiations. When this request reached London, Clarendon's place at the Foreign Office had just been taken by Stanley, Foreign Secretary in Derby's conservative ministry. On 9 July the new Prime Minister in his declaration of policy had announced as the object of his administration:

...above all to endeavour not to interfere needlessly and vexatiously with the internal affairs of any foreign country, nor to volunteer to them unasked advice with regard to the conduct of their affairs....Above all, I hold that it is the duty of a Government to abstain from menace if they do not intend to follow that menace by action.

The war now raging was one '...in the objects of which the honour of this country is in no degree involved and a war in which the interests of this country are very remotely, if at all, involved'. The policy of strict neutrality would be maintained:

...the conduct of the Government with regard to such a war as that now raging is studiously to maintain a strict and impartial neutrality between all the contending parties, only ready at any time to offer their good offices, if there should appear to be the slightest gleam of hope that, combined with other neutral Powers such as France and Russia, they might lead to a termination of this bloody struggle.[4]

Stanley in his turn had informed Cowley of the anxiety of the new Ministers 'not to be drawn further into this entanglement than they can help'. If Prussia refused the armistice proposed by France, the latter could either swallow the rebuff or join the fighting. If the armistice was accepted, difficulties would arise. England could hardly refuse to join in a congress, 'yet a Congress under such circumstances is one in which our practical power will be exceedingly small'. The simplest solution for all parties would be to avoid a congress altogether.[5] He could do little to

[1] Revertera to Mensdorff, telegram, 11 July 1866, HHSAPARRR, 1866, x 53.
[2] Mensdorff to Revertera, telegram, 12 July 1866, *ibid.*
[3] Revertera to Mensdorff, telegram, 13 July 1866, *ibid.*
[4] *Parl. Debates*, 3rd series, 184, cc. 736f.
[5] Stanley to Cowley, private, 7 July 1866, Cowley MSS.

help Napoleon in the difficulties in which he had involved himself whilst trying to extricate Austria.[1] He would preach moderation to Bernstorff 'but without anticipating that it will be of any use. The Prussians know their strength and Europe knows it too.'

...we must be very cautious how we interfere. I have not the slightest faith in Prussia being stopped by words. We certainly will not fight: the Emperor must choose whether to risk a war or to submit to the terms of peace being dictated by Prussia.[2]

Napoleon had placed himself in an awkward position:

In 1859, he encouraged an Italian war, hoping to establish an Italian confederacy dependent on France. Instead of that he has created a strong united Italy, not even friendly to France. In 1866 he has allowed a German war to begin, hoping various results none of which have been attained. He has created by the side of France a strong compact German empire fully the equal of France in military power. Was ever man so over-reached twice? It must be his chief object to get out of the affair, even at some sacrifice of prestige.

He would advise his colleagues to help Napoleon by recommending Austria to accept the Prussian terms.

I do not doubt but that I shall be authorized by my colleagues to express publicly and in their names the strong conviction at which I have personally arrived—that we ought to support France in inducing Austria to accept the Prussian terms.

A congress would be useless for Napoleon as well as for England.

It strikes me that it will be neither his nor our interest, under all the circumstances, that a congress should take place. What can a congress do but ratify the decrees of Prussia? Is it not better that the combatants should make peace on their own account....As to the terms, I regard them as being dictated by events, rather than by the choice of any of the neutral powers.[3]

There was nothing to stop the Prussians from entering Vienna within ten days. The negotiations for an armistice might therefore end in failure. Austria's only hope was for her rulers to submit 'before even worse terms are imposed than those now talked of'. Neither Napoleon nor the British government could do anything to help her. 'We must make up our minds to consider Prussia as a leading—perhaps as the leading—military power of Europe.' Austria, although excluded from Germany, might still have a great future if, for a generation, she would attend to internal improvement. Prussia, on the other hand, might find her very victories embarrassing. Northern Germany was homogeneous and would easily amalgamate with her, but the case might be different with Bavaria and the adjoining states.[4]

---

[1] Whilst Prussian armies were pursuing the defeated Austrians, the Prussian government in spite of Napoleon's efforts at mediation was refusing both an armistice and information about its terms.
[2] Stanley to Cowley, private, 12 July 1866, *ibid.*
[3] The same to the same, 13 July 1866, *ibid.*
[4] The same to the same, private, 14 July 1866, *ibid.*

On 17 July, Bismarck at last informed the cabinets of the terms he meant to impose. Austria was to leave the Confederation; Electoral Hesse, Hanover, Frankfurt, Nassau and part of Hesse-Darmstadt were to be annexed to Prussia.[1] Stanley considered the Prussian terms 'moderate under the circumstances' and felt certain that Austria would accept them.[2] The tsar received them in a calmer spirit than Schweinitz at least had feared and merely expressed the wish that Austria should be given in southern Germany a position similar to that of Prussia in the north.[3]

On 21 July, Brunnow read to Stanley a despatch explaining that in the Russian view the questions to be decided were 'too important in themselves to be adjusted under the mediation of a single Power, and that any such mediation ought to be conducted by the three Neutral Powers'. It was not fitting that England and Russia should act 'merely as assistants to France'. Any application for their intervention should come from the belligerents and not 'emanate solely from the French Government'.[4] Stanley, confirmed in his 'abstentionist' convictions by a debate in the House of Commons,[5] forebore to reply to the Russian communication.[6]

That day Apponyi, on behalf of Mensdorff, expressed the wish 'that England and Russia which have hitherto stood aloof, should exercise their right of interfering in order to check the aggressive pretensions of Prussia'. Mensdorff hoped that if French mediation led to an armistice, the other neutrals would join in the peace negotiations. In conversation, Apponyi referred to what had passed the previous night in the House of Commons. He stated 'in very courteous terms' his dissent from the opinion expressed by Stanley as to the formation of a strong and compact Power in the North of Germany being neither injurious nor inconvenient to England'. The existence of such a power would involve the risk of future war since neither Russia nor France 'were likely to remain long on good terms with a neighbour so powerful and so ambitious'. 'I said that I could not agree in this opinion, that I thought on the contrary, that the danger of disturbance to the peace of Europe lay in the weakness rather than in the strength of Germany.' Apponyi mentioned the treaties of Vienna: 'An allusion having been made to the Treaties of 1815, I did not hesitate to express my belief that in the actual state of Europe, it was useless to appeal to those

---

[1] Schweinitz, *op. cit.* p. 239.

[2] Stanley to Cowley, private, 17 July 1866, Cowley MSS.

[3] Schweinitz, *op. cit.* p. 241.

[4] Stanley to Cowley, no. 52, 21 July 1866, copy in Stanley to Buchanan, 21 July 1866, FO 181/444, no. 9 confidential.

[5] 'In the H. of C. debate of last night, it was remarkable that not a voice was raised in favour of Austria, except that of Sir. G. Bowyer..."Keep us out of the quarrel" seemed to be the universal feeling of the House' (Stanley to Cowley, private, 21 July 1866, Cowley MSS.).

[6] 'I have also seen Brunnow, who is evidently annoyed at the mediation not being in the hands of the three neutral Powers, but in those of France only....I gave no opinion, indeed he did not seem to expect it' (*ibid.*).

Treaties as being still binding.' England was reluctant to interfere. 'I said that we should not in any case interfere willingly, and certainly we would not do so unless we knew first on what basis Austria was prepared to treat.' France and Prussia would insist on Austria's exclusion from the Confederation and it would be useless for the Austrian government 'to attempt to treat on other terms'.[1]

Two days later Brunnow repeated 'at some length and with considerable earnestness' Gorchakov's arguments about 'the inexpediency of an European question...being decided by the combatants alone, or by the mediation of a single Power'. It was a slight on England and Russia as great powers 'if they were not consulted'. 'The precedent would be a bad and dangerous one for the future...and...England might regret having sanctioned it.' Stanley replied that it was 'premature to express an opinion at a time when the question had not actually arisen'.[2]

At noon on 22 July an armistice of five days had at last come into force. Four days later preliminaries of peace between Prussia and Austria were signed at Nikolsburg. If the new settlement was to receive the sanction of Europe, it was time for the neutrals to speak. On 24 July, Gorchakov had told the French ambassador: 'Les grandes puissances neutres...sont en devoir de revendiquer dès à présent une part dans les arrangements préliminaires qui doivent précéder la réunion d'un congrès.'[3] After learning that the preliminaries had been signed, he vented his ill-humour on Revertera:

Permettez-moi de Vous dire en toute franchise [he observed] que Votre Cour nous rend la tâche très difficile. Principale partie intéressée,—Vous avez consenti d'avance à tous les arrangements territoriaux et à la modification des institutions en Allemagne telles que les demandait la Prusse.

Russia, however, had not accepted the *fait accompli.*

Nonobstant, l'Empereur m'a ordonné hier de télégraphier à Vienne, Berlin, Paris, Londres et Florence que Sa Majesté ne saurait consentir à ce que la carte de l'Europe fût modifiée sans la participation directe des trois grandes Cours neutres. Nous convions le Cabinet Anglais à une déclaration semblable et nous savons déjà que l'Empereur Napoléon est disposé à la soutenir.[4]

On 28 July, Brunnow called on Stanley to draw his attention once again to 'the inconvenience of a great European negotiation being conducted under the mediation of a single Power'. The tsar

---

[1] Stanley to Bloomfield, no. 12, 21 July 1866, copy in Stanley to Buchanan, 21 July 1866, FO 181/444, no. 9, confidential. Apponyi thanked Stanley 'for the frankness with which I had spoken, adding that it was better for his Government to understand the situation distinctly than to be encouraged in delusive expectations of support' (*ibid.*).

[2] Stanley to Buchanan, 23 July 1866, FO 181/444, no. 11.

[3] Talleyrand to Drouyn, 24 July 1866, Charles-Roux, *Alexandre II, Gortchakoff et Napoléon III*, p. 388.

[4] Gorchakov to Revertera, 18(30) July 1866, in Revertera to Mensdorff, no. 23, 2 August/21 July, HHSAPARRR, 1866, x 53.

would take amiss the extinction of the small German States, several of whose Princes were connected by ties of kindred with the Imperial family of Russia:...the total exclusion of Austria from Germany seemed to his Government to be an exorbitant demand on the part of the Prussian and Italian Governments,...a peace concluded on terms too unfavourable for Austria would probably be only a truce: and...although his Government desired peace as much as any Government, they wished for a lasting peace and not for a settlement which should be liable to be disturbed again in a year or two.

Brunnow added confidentially that Budberg had made to Napoleon a communication 'somewhat in the sense of what he had been saying to me, and that the effect of that communication remained to be seen'.[1] On the afternoon of 31 July, Brunnow inquired of Stanley whether he was now prepared to state the views of the British government 'as to the expediency of holding a congress to decide on the various International questions raised by the late War'. Stanley's qualified approval of a congress amounted to a rejection of the idea.[2] He afterwards told Cowley:

> Under these circumstances it seemed to me that a conditional consent was safe: the conditions being all but impossible of fulfilment. If the Emperor [Napoleon] sees it in the same point of view, the thing is done. Prussia will take the responsibility of a refusal: and we shall not press her to reconsider it.[3]

In the meantime, Russian diplomacy had been active in Berlin. On 27 July, Bismarck at Nikolsburg was informed that Oubril had formally proposed the calling of a congress.[4] The tsar informed Schweinitz that he had taken the initiative and that Napoleon had already accepted the invitation. He could not allow Austria and Prussia to destroy the settlement of 1815 without the participation of Europe. Whilst admitting the need for the territorial consolidation of Prussia, he would prefer this to take place without Prussian annexations.[5] King William had expressed the wish that Russia should abstain from further action until she had reached an understanding with Prussia. He desired nothing better but it was difficult to arrange such matters in writing. He would, therefore, receive with alacrity any person possessing the king's confidence who could explain to him the intimate views of the Prussian government.[6] On

[1] Stanley to Buchanan, 28 July 1866, FO 181/444, no. 21.

[2] The same to the same, 31 July 1866, FO 181/444, no. 22. Stanley declared that the proposition for a congress had not originated with the British government; nor were they 'interested in one being held' (*ibid.*). Already on 26 July, Stanley had spoken of 'Brunnow's great anxiety for a Congress, which to my mind is another reason against it, as it is not likely that the English and Russian view of the situation will be the same' (Stanley to Cowley, private, 26 July 1866, Cowley MSS.).

[3] The same to the same, private, 31 July 1866, *ibid.* Gorchakov's object, Stanley considered, was clearly 'to delay not to assist, a solution. He wants to save the small Princes· and gain time, thinking that perhaps another year may find France and Russia better prepared to check Prussian aggrandisement. This at least is the only construction I can put on his language' (*ibid.*).   [4] Sybel, *op. cit.* p. 356.

[5] Schweinitz, *op. cit.* p. 241. The tsar's remarks appear illogical.

[6] Sybel, *op. cit.* p. 360.

3 August, William I consequently decided to send to St Petersburg General von Manteuffel who had commanded the Prussian forces in southern Germany. On the 6th, the tsar expressed his pleasure at the impending mission.[1]

The announcement of Manteuffel's visit did nothing to diminish Gorchakov's eagerness for a 'European' settlement. On 5 August a leading article in the official *Journal de St Pétersbourg* condemned the attitude of the neutrals: '...nous verrons l'Europe suivre dans l'ordre politique le plan qui a si merveilleusement réussi au maréchal Benedek;[2] laisser venir la Prusse et lui permettre de réunir toutes ses forces.'[3] On 6 August, Brunnow once more told Stanley

that the territorial arrangements resulting from the preliminaries of peace which had just been signed would have the effect of putting an end to the actual existence of the Germanic Confederation, of determining the fate of the Elbe Duchies and lastly of impairing the independence and integrity of several states in the centre of Europe.

The changes 'in as much as they altered the lawfully established order of things in Germany would involve a departure from the Treaties which had been signed by Great Britain and Russia'. By right 'no Treaty could be modified without the participation of all the Contracting Parties'. The Russian government adhered to this principle and wished to know 'whether the British government had the same intention as Russia in order to maintain and to reserve its right to take part, as a signing party to the Treaties which it is proposed to modify'. Stanley replied that he must have time to consider the matter and to consult his colleagues.[4]

As the result of a similar Russian communication in Paris, the French *chargé* was instructed to ask for the British view. On 8 August he was informed by Stanley that 'with regard to the Treaties of Vienna, the present is not the first instance in which they have been violated without any protest being made on the part of the Powers by whom they were signed'.

If Russia merely wished to reserve her freedom of action, 'that end could be obtained simply by abstaining from an active adhesion to the new arrangements'. England would not join 'in any such declaration as may have the appearance of a protest against what is passing in Germany'. The British government reserved their entire freedom of action with regard to the future and 'while on the one hand they are not responsible for the steps that Prussia has taken to increase her power at the cost of other States, they have on the other hand no cause to object to such increase of

---

[1] *Ibid.* and Schweinitz, *op. cit.* p. 242. Queen Olga of Württemberg had recently acknowledged the General's honourable conduct.
[2] The Austrian commander in Bohemia.
[3] Buchanan to Hammond, private, 5 August 1866, FO 65/700.
[4] Stanley to Buchanan, 6 August 1866, FO 181/444, no. 29.

power on her part'.[1] That was the official British verdict on the settlement of Nikolsburg which on 11 August the Foreign Secretary communicated also to the Russian ambassador. Brunnow, in replying to this declaration, made a statement which foreshadowed a reversal of Russian policy. He concurred in the views expressed by Stanley adding 'that Russia had no intention of protesting against what Prussia, with whom she had always been on the most friendly terms, was doing'.[2] Since the 'European' policy had once again proved a failure, Russia also would come to terms with 'reality'.

IV

On 7 August, Manteuffel had received his instructions. He was to stress the excitement of public opinion in Prussia and the need of some reward for the sacrifices which had been made. To disregard this need would be to hazard the vital interests of the Prussian monarchy. With regard to details, everything possible had been done to take no more than the situation demanded.[3] Similar arguments were contained in a letter from the king to his nephew which Manteuffel was to deliver.[4]

The General reached the Russian capital on 9 August. That same night, he was received by the tsar who showed satisfaction at the mission which bore witness to Russia's importance in Europe. Alexander then expressed his painful surprise at the terms which the Prussian government intended to impose. He could not but recognize the consideration shown to Württemberg and Hesse-Darmstadt,[5] but did not conceal his horror at the deposition of entire dynasties.[6] These, he declared, rested on the same foundations of divine right as his own house or that of Prussia. Moreover, the tsar expressed his deep disquiet at the proclamations which, during the war, the Prussian government had addressed to the Czechs and which were designed to arouse subjects against their rulers. Nor did the democratic character of the future North German Parliament inspire confidence. Finally Alexander felt anxiety about the fate of the south German states. Left without support, they would either succumb to revolutionary movements or fall under the influence of France. Bavaria, especially after her conduct during the war, could not be a substitute for Austria which, to his regret, was now to be excluded from Germany.[7]

[1] Stanley to Cowley, 8 August 1866, copy in Stanley to Buchanan, 8 August 1866 FO 181/444, no. 28.
[2] The same to the same, 11 August 1866, *ibid.* no. 31 (reporting telegram).
[3] Sybel, *op. cit.* pp. 385f.
[4] *Ibid.* p. 386.
[5] And therefore to himself. His favourite sister, Olga, was Queen of Württemberg, his wife came from the ruling family of Hesse-Darmstadt.
[6] Manteuffel reported that the deposition of entire dynasties 'erschreckte ihn complett' (Stählin, *op. cit.* p. 257).
[7] *Ibid.*

Gorchakov, on the following day, reinforced these arguments. After expressing the tsar's pleasure at Prussia's victories, he added that if she now forebore to depose entire dynasties, left Saxony her military sovereignty and assured the independence of southern Germany, she would secure a strong position and avoid a conflict with France. If, by safeguarding dynastic rights, Prussia found herself in agreement with 'old Europe', Napoleon would not dare to claim compensation. As for Russia, she coveted neither the Principalities, where conditions seemed to be improving, nor Galicia. Nor did she desire the immediate abolition of the Black Sea Clauses; these must indeed disappear one day, but they would wither away by themselves. When the time should come to bury them, the tsar counted on Prussian support.[1]

When Bismarck received Manteuffel's report of this conversation, he addressed an angry despatch to St Petersburg. Prussia, he explained, had practically reached agreement with Württemberg and Hesse-Darmstadt; the terms were moderate, mainly from consideration for Russia. If this was not sufficient to secure her acquiescence in the annexation of Hanover, Electoral Hesse and Nassau, no treaties would be concluded with Württemberg and Hesse-Darmstadt. Prussia would be driven to proclaim the Constitution of 1849 and embark on a revolutionary policy.[2] If the Russian government required more than a courteous notification, its objections would be ignored.[3]

Manteuffel therefore informed Gorchakov and the tsar that, driven to desperation, Bismarck would stop at nothing. The warning did not at once achieve its object. In spite of some minor Prussian concessions,[4] the emperor and empress continued to deplore the Prussian terms.[5]

---

[1] Sybel, *op. cit.* p. 388. Before the war, when a conference was still expected, Bismarck had inquired of Russia whether, in the event of war, she wished to extend her influence in Poland by annexing certain portions and incorporating Galicia in the Polish kingdom. Gorchakov had replied that all Russia desired was the preservation of peace. (Buchanan to Stanley, 31 July 1866, FO 65/700, no. 349.) On the other hand in a telegram to Oubril of 2 August, Gorchakov had explained that in a congress he would agree to a modification of the treaty of Vienna in exchange for the consent of Prussia, England and France to the abrogation of the Black Sea Clauses (Gorchakov to Oubril, telegram, 21 July (2 August) 1866, in C. W. Clark, 'Prince Gorchakov and the Black Sea Question 1866', *AHR*, XLVIII, no. 1 (New York, 1942), p. 54). When Bismarck realized that Prussia's peace terms were causing irritation at St Petersburg, he informed Manteuffel that Prussia had no interest in the perpetuation of the Black Sea Clauses. Should the tsar and Gorchakov express a desire to abolish them, Manteuffel should show a favourable disposition (Sybel, *op. cit.* p. 386).

[2] 'Pression des Auslands wird uns zur Proclamirung der Reichsverfassung von 1849 und zu wirklich revolutionären Massregeln treiben. Soll Revolution sein, so wollen wir sie lieber machen, als erleiden' (*ibid.* p. 389).

[3] *Ibid.*

[4] Contrary to the original plan, the Grand-Duchy of Hesse would be allowed to keep Upper Hesse and lose only Homburg. The duke of Cumberland, Crown-Prince of Hanover was offered the succession in Brunswick. The negotiation eventually failed because the Prince refused to renounce his rights to the Hanoverian throne.

[5] Manteuffel reported: 'Das Fürstentum sitzt tief', Stählin, *op. cit.* p. 258.

Bismarck's threat that he might be forced to resort to revolution was resented at St Petersburg.[1] In the end, however, the tsar decided to subordinate his personal feelings to his faithful friendship for Prussia, and accept the *fait accompli*. In a letter of 24 August, after repeating his conviction that Prussia's conduct had struck a severe blow at monarchic principles, he told his uncle that Russia and Prussia must 'remain in future what they had been in the past: old and faithful allies'.[2] He hoped that Russia's relations with a strengthened Prussia would become even closer than before.[3] With this, the Russian government finally gave up its objections to the Prussian reorganization of northern Germany.

Already on 13 August, Gorchakov in conversation with Talleyrand had made it clear that he had abandoned all serious idea of a protest or a Congress:

'Si je n'ai pas réussi, j'ai du moins la conscience d'avoir rempli le devoir de grande Puissance qui revenait à la Russie. Puisque nous n'avons pas été écoutés, il ne nous reste plus, sans nous désintéresser de ce qui se passe en Europe, qu'à nous renfermer dans une politique *purement russe*.'[4]

Two days later Buchanan reported a similar change of tone. Gorchakov now declared that he was satisfied to leave matters as they were. Russia had made the proposals which she considered the circumstances required of her. Having fulfilled this duty, she had nothing further to say, and was ready to accept the new order of things.[5] Indeed, as early as 11 August, Stanley had told Cowley: 'Brunnow has quite changed his tone and assures me that nothing was further from his thoughts than to protest against the acts of Prussia! If this is true, words don't carry the same meaning to him as to me.'[6] Oubril also changed his tone. 'From the period...of General Manteuffel's return to Berlin, a change was apparent in the language and bearing of M. d'Oubril, and this has become more striking since his own visit to St Petersburg.' Bismarck's North German Confederation was accepted without a murmur:

The former sympathy for Prussia appears to have returned, no expression of disapproval of Prussian annexation is heard. 'Les faits accomplis' no longer find a murmur. The only Legation of a neutral state which illuminated (altho' very

[1] According to Manteuffel, everyone in the Russian capital was 'kopfscheu und verletzt' at the threat (*ibid.*).

[2] *Ibid.* p. 259. Bismarck was so encouraged by this change of tone that in a last telegram he instructed Manteuffel to sound the Russian government about its willingness, in a possible Franco-Prussian conflict, to neutralize Austria 'schwach wie es gegenwärtig ist'. Prussia, in her turn, would in that event accept certain obligations. Manteuffel's soundings, however, met with no success (*ibid.*).

[3] *Ibid.* Alexander added that, even if his advice at the present juncture were to be disregarded, he would never join the enemies of Prussia (Sybel, *op. cit.* pp. 389f.).

[4] Talleyrand to Drouyn, 14 August 1866, *Origines*, vol. 12, p. 104.

[5] Buchanan to Stanley, 15 August 1866, FO 65/700, no. 363.

[6] Stanley to Cowley, private, 11 August 1866, Cowley MSS.

modestly) on the eve of the entry of the victorious Prussian Army was that of Russia. In short, the attitude of M d'Oubril is no longer one of jealous disquietude but has become one of passive and calm satisfaction.[1]

Stanley in London had accepted the reorganization of Germany with even greater complacency, but viewed the future with alarm:

> The growing jealousy of Russia, and, I suspect, of France also, against Prussia is natural. We should feel the same in their position. But to us there is no loss, rather a gain, in the interposition of a solid barrier between the two great aggressive powers of the Continent.[2]

Complications between Prussia and France need not involve England: 'Our line is plain: let German and Frenchman fight, or divide the plunder as they please: but speak out strongly for Belgium if it should be necessary. I hope the necessity will not arise.'[3] They now appeared safe for the winter and the only danger in the actual situation was for the emperor of the French:[4]

> I begin to suspect that the German revolution may go farther and faster than its authors intend. Bismarck wants a new German federation. Napoleon wanted an Italian federation. We know what came of that: may not the precedent be followed? In any case the southern states will not long endure exclusion: and then will be seen, whether France and Russia will tolerate a German empire. But, as I think you said in one of your letters, it is a question for '68 rather than for '66.[5]

V

The treaty of Prague which put an end to the war between Prussia and Austria completed the destruction of the political order established by the Congress of Vienna. That order, shaken when a Bonaparte first returned to the throne of France, had been demolished first in Italy and then in Germany. Napoleon III had played a leading part in bringing about this result. Indeed it might almost be said that first Cavour and later Bismarck had been his chosen instrument in the campaign to avenge Waterloo and Vienna. Sadowa, in a manner, was the posthumous revenge of Napoleon I.

The destruction of the system established at Vienna signalled the triumph of national revolution in several parts of Europe. The Romanians with the tacit support of Bismarck and Napoleon had secured a foreign

---

[1] Loftus to Stanley, 6 October 1866, copy, in Stanley to Gould, 12 October 1866, FO 181/445, no. 12, confidential.

[2] Stanley to Cowley, private, 7 August 1866, Cowley MSS.

[3] The same to the same, private, 11 August 1866, *ibid.* Stanley's sentiments accurately foreshadow the British attitude during the Franco-Prussian war of 1870.

[4] 'We do not want Napoleon upset, nor do we want a new war' (the same to the same, private, 15 August 1866, *ibid.*). This also foreshadows the efforts of four years of unavailing British diplomacy.

[5] The same to the same, private, 18 August, 1866, *ibid.*

prince as ruler of the united Principalities.[1] Venetia, after a plebiscite, was finally united to Italy. Early in 1867 the *Ausgleich* gave the Magyars equality—and more than equality—with the Austrian portion of the Habsburg monarchy. Last but not least, Bismarck during 1867 constituted his North German Confederation linked by customs unions and military agreements with the states of southern Germany. These triumphs of nationality everywhere reversed the decisions of 1849. The election on purely Romanian initiative of Charles of Hohenzollern-Sigmaringen and its acceptance by the powers contrasted strikingly with the Russo-Turkish occupation which, seventeen years before, had followed the convention of Balta Liman. The treaty of Prague undid the effects of Olmütz, the *Ausgleich* those of Vilagos; the plebiscite in Venetia wiped out the defeat of Manin. The victories of Prussia had gone far to create a 'new order' based on the principle of nationality.

Yet this 'new order' was precarious and liable to disturbance. It might not matter for some time to come that the triumph of nationality was incomplete as long as Germany remained divided politically along the Main and Italy deprived of her national capital. Of more immediate importance was the fact that Prussia's rapid successes had disturbed her three principal neighbours and aroused in their statesmen a desire for further change. Beust, Mensdorff's successor, dreamt of reversing the verdict of Sadowa; Napoleon III demanded territorial compensation; Gorchakov also longed for some success to balance his rival's achievements. The changes of 1866–7 therefore left behind unsatisfied ambitions; observers considered that the new settlement would not long remain unchallenged.

[1] On 30 March 1866 a provisional offer of the throne to Prince Charles of Hohenzollern-Sigmaringen had been made by John Bratianu. It had been confirmed by a plebiscite in April. On 22 May the Prince had entered Bucharest. His election, contrary alike to the treaty of Paris and the wishes of the conference assembled in that city, was presently accepted by the sultan and the powers.

PART III

THE REVOLUTION COMPLETED, 1867–71

CHAPTER 9

THE EASTERN QUESTION AND THE RE-GROUPING OF THE POWERS, AUGUST 1866–MARCH 1868

O N the morrow of the Austro-Prussian war, each of the major powers found itself in a state of relative isolation. Whilst prostrate Austria was left without a friend in Europe, victorious Prussia also had to face her growing unpopularity without a reliable ally. Napoleon, conscious that the unexpected rapidity of the Prussian triumph had changed the situation to his disadvantage, was brooding over his defeat. The relations of Russia with the other powers had become uncertain; England appeared to have withdrawn from all serious participation in European affairs. Whilst the powers were thus in a state of diplomatic 'disorientation', new problems were beginning to loom on the horizon. Napoleon's prestige had suffered a catastrophic decline and his search for 'compensations' rendered his actions more unpredictable than ever. The future of the south German states was uncertain. The Roman question was awaiting solution. Austria, after her expulsion from Italy and Germany seemed likely to look in the Balkans for a new sphere of action at a moment when the Cretan revolt against the Turks had already reopened the 'eastern question'. In this unsettled state of affairs, prudent statesmen were taking stock of national needs: the possibility of new alignments was submitted to earnest study. The groping for new policies was symbolized by two changes of diplomatic personnel. Early in September 1866, Drouyn was replaced by Moustier, the French ambassador at Constantinople. In October, Mensdorff was relieved of his unsought duties and replaced by Beust, until recently Minister of the king of Saxony. The new Ministers were faced at once with a revival of the eastern question. The unstable equilibrium within the Ottoman empire (already shaken by the installation of a new ruler in Bucharest and a Serbo-Turkish dispute) threatened to collapse under the impact of the Cretan rising supported by the active sympathy of Greece.[1] From this time the eastern question and the western—represented principally by Beust's plans for revenge and Napoleon's quest for 'compensations'— repeatedly interacted. The Turkish and German questions became the crystallizing points for new diplomatic groupings.

[1] For the genesis of the Cretan insurrection see *Origines, loc. cit.* p. 72 n. 1.

I

It was at the end of August 1866 that the Russian government—having finally acquiesced in the Prussian reorganization of northern Germany—began with some reluctance[1] to turn its attention to the east. Researches in the Russian archives revealed that when Crete had been restored to Turkey after the fighting of 1823, the Porte had entered into certain engagements towards the Christian inhabitants. These it had failed to observe—a fact which, to Gorchakov at least, appeared to call for a remonstrance by the three protecting powers.[2] In conversation with Talleyrand the Vice-Chancellor proposed that the cabinets of Paris, St Petersburg and London should combine to remind the Turkish government of its engagements with regard to internal reform in Crete.[3] Talleyrand found Gorchakov disturbed about the state of Europe and anxious for a *rapprochement* with France:

> L'état des choses actuel ne saurait être que provisoire, et c'est en se plaçant dans cet ordre d'idées qu'il m'a exprimé de nouveau l'espoir d'une entente entre la France et la Russie. 'Il nous faut, m'a-t-il dit, des bases et une occasion.—Trouvons les bases, lui ai-je répondu, l'occasion viendra à nous.'[4]

The following day Gorchakov officially proposed as a matter of urgency joint remonstrances at Constantinople by the representatives of France, Russia and England and the despatch to Cretan waters of naval vessels of the three powers.[5]

The Russian proposal reached Paris at an unpropitious moment. On 31 August, Drouyn had announced his resignation and the appointment of Moustier to succeed him.[6] Whilst continuing to conduct affairs until his successor's arrival, he now informed Talleyrand that, as the sultan had sent a new governor to Crete, the result of this measure should be awaited. If there was no improvement in the situation, France might consult with Russia on a joint policy.[7] This reply gave little satisfaction at St Petersburg. Moustier's appointment also had not been well-received in the Russian capital, as the new Minister, who at Constantinople had lived in constant rivalry with his Russian colleague, was considered to be turcophil and

---

[1] '...Der orientalischen Frage beginnt man hier', wenn auch anscheinend mit Widerstreben, einige Aufmerksamkeit zu widmen....Sowohl der Fürst Vizekanzler als seine vertraute Umgebung nehmen vorläufig die Miene an, als ob die Beschäftigung mit der orientalischen Frage eine wenig befriedigende Entschädigung für die verminderte Befugnis ihrer Teilnahme an deutschen Angelegenheiten sei, seitdem Preussen so mächtig zu werden beginne' (Keyserling to Bismarck, 29 August 1866, *APP*, vol. 8, pp. 48f.).
[2] *Ibid.*
[3] Talleyrand to Drouyn, 30 August 1866, Charles-Roux, *op. cit.* p. 398.
[4] The same to the same, 31 August 1866 (misdated by Charles-Roux 21 August 1866), *ibid.* p. 399.
[5] Gorchakov to Budberg, 20 August/1 September 1866, *Origines, op. cit.* pp. 249ff.
[6] Cowley to Stanley, private, 31 August 1866, Cowley MSS. copy.
[7] Drouyn to Talleyrand, 6 September 1866, Charles-Roux, *op. cit.* p. 399.

anti-Russian. Furthermore, Russian jealousy of France was aroused when the Serbian envoy attending the wedding of the tsarevich remarked that France might prove a better friend than Russia, which did little to help the Serbs.[1] Gorchakov felt impelled to complain to the Turkish *chargé d'affaires* of French calumnies at Constantinople.[2]

Russian disquiet was increased by the policy of Austria. Early in October, Count Goluchowski, a Pole, became Governor of Galicia. This measure—at a time when Russia was forcibly russianizing her Polish provinces—gave great offence at St Petersburg.[3] Beust's appointment as Foreign Minister increased the Russian alarm. Gorchakov complained to Buchanan that Beust would attempt to establish an understanding between Austria and France 'through which the peace of Europe might ere long be again disturbed'.[4] Revertera reported that Russia feared an Austro-French *rapprochement* over Turkish affairs.[5]

It was in these circumstances that the Russian government became aware of a new development in the Balkans. As early as the beginning of October the Prussian minister at Athens had drawn Bismarck's attention to a significant change in Austrian policy:

Un fait digne d'attention se produit depuis la dernière guerre en Allemagne. L'Autriche, l'ancienne amie de la Sublime Porte, fait par la presse et même par le langage de ses agents de la propagande libérale, je dirais même révolutionnaire en Orient, elle se pose comme protectrice de la religion et de la nationalité des populations chrétiennes. On ne voit pas encore bien où l'Autriche veut en venir. Aurait-elle compris enfin que son avenir n'est point en Allemagne mais en Orient?[6]

The shift in Austrian policy might pave the way for an Austro-Russian understanding in the eastern question; it might equally, however, inaugurate a period of intensified rivalry between the two countries. On 7 November, Revertera reported to Beust that the excitement caused by the appointment of Goluchowski appeared to be dying down. If the cabinet of Vienna were to propose a confidential exchange of views on the eastern question, friendly relations between Austria and Russia might be re-established.[7] Even a cordial understanding was possible if Austria

---

[1] Buchanan to Stanley, 12 and 28 November 1866, FO 65/702, nos. 414 and 443.
[2] The same to the same, 7 November 1866, *ibid.* no. 399.
[3] Brenner to Mensdorff, 10 October/28 September 1866, HHSAPARRR, 1866, X 53. The appointment had 'given the greatest offence to the Imperial Government, which it is at no pains to disguise' (Gould to Stanley, 9 October 1866, FO 65/701, no. 30).
[4] Buchanan to Stanley, 7 November 1866, FO 65/702, no. 401.
[5] Revertera to Beust, 7 November/26 October 1866, HHSAPARRR, 1866, X 53, no. 30 C.
[6] Wagner to Bismarck, 6 October 1866, *APP, loc. cit.* p. 106. On 10 December, Werther (Vienna) reported to Bismarck: '...sagte mir der Minister von Beust, er habe für das Kaiserliche Kabinett in diesen Gegenständen eine neue Aera inauguriert. Bisher hätte nämlich Oesterreich stets als seine Richtschnur angesehen, in allen diesen Fragen sich ausschliesslich auf den Standpunkt der Pforte zu stellen. Er habe dies nicht mehr unbedingt den Interessen Oesterreichs entsprechend gefunden' (Werther to Bismarck, 10 December 1866, *ibid.* p. 208).
[7] Revertera to Beust, 7 November/26 October 1866, HHSAPARRR, 1866, no. 30 C.

recovered rapidly and if agreement could be reached on a joint policy in the Balkans. The Austrian government might give Russia a formal assurance that in the event of a Turkish collapse it would seek no influence in the Principalities; Russia, in exchange, might recognize Austrian interests in the western Balkans.[1] Gorchakov, moreover, had not concealed his pleasure at the change in Austrian policy. He had congratulated himself on finding in Vienna 'des dispositions favorables aux Chrétiens; ce qu'il considère comme l'abandon d'une tradition funeste qui établissait pour règle de soutenir l'autorité de la Sublime Porte'.[2] Beust, more far-sighted than his Russian colleague, felt that the new Austrian policy contained the germ of future jealousies. He explained to Werther that, much as he would welcome a good understanding with Russia, he had some reason to believe that the Russian government would prefer to keep a monopoly of protecting the Christians in Turkey.[3] His reply to St Petersburg was cautious. After explaining the appointment of Goluchowski, he drew attention to Austria's need for peace and complained of Slav agitation in the Austrian empire. In vague terms he accepted the possibility of consultations about the Balkans but his tone was cautious and distrustful.[4]

The uncertainty of her relations with France and Austria made Russia aware once again of the value of Prussian friendship. Late in September Gorchakov surprised Keyserling—accustomed to critical comment on Prussia's conduct in Germany—by singing the praises of Russo-Prussian friendship.

'L'alliance entre la Russie et la Prusse', he naïvely declared, 'repose bien sur les liens de parenté et d'amitié des Souverains, mais aussi...sur l'honnêteté et l'honorabilité parfaite du caractère allemand vers lequel on se sent toujours attiré. Avec l'Autriche, ça n'a jamais été ainsi, ce n'est plus du sang allemand pur, il y a déjà de la fausseté italienne en eux.'

He did not wish to hamper Prussia in Germany. '"Vous voyez bien que ce n'est pas de nous que vous viennent des difficultés dans vos affaires allemandes, au contraire, nous vous souhaitons forts et unis. Quant à la France, vous avez tout lieu de vous en méfier, ce me semble."'[5] A few days later Gorchakov addressed a personal note to Bismarck. After expressing a touching concern for the latter's health, he declared:

...Veuillez conserver *inébranlablement* la conviction de notre détermination d'entretenir avec la Prusse les relations les plus intimes. La divergence de quelques

---

[1] The same to the same, 19/7 November 1866, *ibid.* no. 32 A-C.
[2] The same to the same, 3 December/21 November 1866, *ibid.* no. 33 A-D.
[3] Werther to Bismarck, 10 December 1866, *APP, loc. cit.* p. 208.
[4] Beust to Revertera, 1 December 1866, HHSAPARRR, 1866, x 53, draft.
[5] Keyserling to Bismarck, no. 96, confidential, 26 September 1866, *APP, loc. cit.* pp. 96f. It seems probable that Gorchakov's exuberant friendliness was not unconnected with the Russian plan to denounce the Black Sea Clauses. In fact, during the second half of September he had drafted notes to the signatories of the treaty of Paris, announcing that Russia no

nuances d'appréciation n'a ni affaibli cette résolution, ni nous fera devier de cette ligne principale de notre politique. Ein Mann, ein Wort....[1]

Growing preoccupation with the eastern question had shown the Russians the full value of Prussian support.

II

Whilst Gorchakov was still seeking support for Russian policy in the east, the Russian government was alarmed by an unexpected development. The Greek and Serbian envoys to the wedding of the tsarevich declared categorically that during the following spring the Balkan Christians would rise against the Turks.[2] A struggle in the east seemed imminent;[3] to avert a general conflict, the Russian government must try once again to secure some measure of agreement among the powers.[4]

longer considered herself bound by these clauses, but was willing to discuss with the powers a satisfactory settlement of the eastern question (cf. Clark, *loc. cit.* pp. 52ff.).

This plan probably explains the curious language which, on 26 September, Gorchakov held to the British *chargé d'affaires*. He told Gould that the dismemberment of Turkey appeared imminent. It was the result not only of Turkish maladministration but of two other causes. The conference in Paris had allowed Prince Charles of Hohenzollern to assume the government of the Principalities in defiance of the treaties and the unanimous decision of the guaranteeing powers; a precedent had thus been set for the rule of a foreign prince over part of the sultan's dominions. Moreover, the great territorial changes lately accomplished in Europe by violent means had met with no opposition from the three great neutral powers (Gould to Stanley, 26 September 1866, FO 65/701, no. 14).

Gorchakov's plan miscarried. His drafts—previously approved by the tsar—were discussed in a Council presided over by Alexander himself and composed of Constantine Nicolaevich and the Ministers of War, Finance and Foreign Affairs. The Grand Duke and Gorchakov's two colleagues opposed the plan 'commᴇ dangereuse dans les circonstances politiques du moment'. Reutern, the Minister of Finance, observed 'que toute agitation politique qui surgirait en ce moment serait funeste pour notre crédit'. Gorchakov persisted in urging his proposal. The tsar declared that he personally favoured it. However, Alexander and Gorchakov finally abandoned the suggestion. The date of the Council cannot be established with accuracy. Clark marshals the evidence for believing that the incident took place during the last week of September (Clark, *loc. cit.* p. 58). Information of the meeting comes from a memorandum in a secretarial hand signed by Gorchakov and dated 16 May 1868 (*ibid.* p. 52).

Gorchakov had to console himself with the reflection that he would be able to achieve his object during a Franco-German war which he confidently anticipated (Gorchakov to Oubril, confidential, 5 (17) November 1866, *ibid.* p. 57). In fact, with a few corrections and additions, Gorchakov's drafts were to be used for the Russian denunciation of the Black Sea Clauses in October 1870 (*ibid.* p. 55).

[1] Gorchakov to Bismarck, 3/15 October 1866, *APP, loc. cit.* pp. 130f.

[2] Revertera to Beust, 3 December/21 November 1866, HHSAPARRR, 1866, x 53, no. 33 C, secret. Revertera had obtained this information from a member of the imperial family (*ibid.*).

[3] 'La question d'Orient parait être mûre. Au printemps prochain il y aura guerre entre la S. Porte et les populations chrétiennes qui sont prêtes à se soulever. Cela n'est plus maintenant une simple supposition; ce que je dis est un fait constant, indubitable, qui se produira d'ici à quelques mois au plus tard' (*ibid.*).

[4] Russia was arming to be prepared for any eventuality. She had promised the Balkan Christians benevolent armed neutrality but would intervene actively only if other powers took part. 'La Russie arme non point pour intervenir, mais bien pour empêcher les autres d'intervenir'. Gorchakov desired an alliance with Prussia 'auquel l'Empereur répugne'. Alexander would accept such an alliance only if Austria could be included as well (*ibid.*).

Approaches were made to both Austria and France. Gorchakov told Revertera that a crisis was approaching in Turkish affairs: nobody would lament the collapse of Ottoman power. When Revertera in reply drew attention to Austria's special interests in the western Balkans, Gorchakov at first was unsympathetic. He expressed the hope that Austria would follow the example of Russia, who cared only for the well-being of the Christians. The powers should renounce all territorial ambitions: Russia would content herself with the retrocession of southern Bessarabia, which would be a restitution rather than a new acquisition. Revertera insisted that Austria's special interests must be considered and casually mentioned Herzegovina. Gorchakov expressed doubts whether the populations bordering on the Habsburg empire wished to become Austrian and favoured a policy of securing for them the administrative autonomy to which they aspired.[1] On the following day Revertera submitted to Gorchakov a minute of the conversation which contained the following passage: '"J'ai essayé de sonder à cet égard les dispositions du Prince Gortchacow, mais j'ai le regret de dire à Votre Excellence [Beust] que je n'ai trouvé de son côté aucun encouragement."' Gorchakov interrupted: '"C'est trop péremptoire...aucun encouragement est presque capable de produire du découragement."' At the Vice-Chancellor's request, Revertera then drafted 'en sa présence, je puis dire sous sa dictée', the following exposition of the Russian attitude:

> Le Prince Gortchacow croit que dans le cas d'une dissolution de l'empire ottoman, que la Russie ne désire d'amener d'aucune façon, mais qui néanmoins entre dans le calcul des probabilités, le Gouvernement russe qui, pour sa part, ne désire aucune acquisition territoriale, pense que les populations chrétiennes aujourd'hui sous la domination turque auraient à se constituer en états autonomes sous telle forme qui répondrait à leurs mœurs et à leurs habitudes, et que l'Autriche et la Russie, Puissances limitrophes et amies leur prêteraient leurs conseils pour leur faciliter ce premier essai d'une existence autonome.

For the benefit of Beust, Gorchakov added

qu'il ne fait qu'effleurer aujourd'hui cette question, mais qu'il sera charmé d'entrer dans des développements ultérieures avec M. le Baron de Beust, à la haute intelligence et à l'élévation des vues duquel, appliquées à l'Orient, il rend la plus entiére justice.[2]

Parallel with this approach to Austria went an attempt to reach an understanding with France. The tsar addressed himself to Talleyrand

...quant à moi, je veux continuer comme par le passé à entretenir avec vous de

[1] The same to the same, 10 December/28 November 1866, *ibid.* no. 34C, secret.
[2] *Ibid.* When Revertera observed to Gorchakov 'qu'on le croyait généralement partisan de l'alliance prussienne', the latter frankly replied: 'que les intérêts de la Russie et particulièrement la réparation qu'elle poursuit en Orient lui sembleraient le mieux assurées par une entente avec la Prusse et avec le Prince de Hohenzollern. Il m'insinua ensuite que la tension prolongée de nos rapports avec la Prusse lui paraissait très regrettable' (the same to the same, 10 December/28 November 1866, *ibid.* no. 34D, secret). It is clear that Gorchakov wished Austria to become a junior partner in a revived alliance of the eastern monarchies.

bonnes relations. Elles nous sont mutuellement nécessaires, dans ce moment surtout où la question d'Orient semble devoir s'ouvrir d'un moment à l'autre. Je n'ai aucune convoitise...et je prie l'empereur de bien vouloir se rappeler nos entretiens à Stuttgart à ce sujet; mes idées sont restées les mêmes.[1]

Gorchakov in his turn, after alluding to the critical situation in the east, asked whether the two governments could not agree on a joint policy:

Puisque la Russie en particulier ne poursuit aucune augmentation de territoire, ne pourrions-nous pas nous entendre sur la conduite à tenir pour sauvegarder les intérêts chrétiens en souffrance et prévenir de plus grands troubles comme de plus grands désordres?[2]

In accordance with these views, Budberg some days later submitted detailed proposals to Moustier. Crete should be transformed into an autonomous state similar to Romania. In addition, Russia and France should jointly proclaim the principle of non-intervention in Turkish affairs to prevent all outside interference with the free development of Romanians, Serbs, Bulgarians and Greeks.[3]

In his reply, Moustier proceeded to state the price which France would expect for her complaisance: 'J'ai dit au baron de Budberg que notre adhésion à cette entente...supposait avant tout l'adhésion préalable du cabinet de Pétersbourg à la politique que les circonstances pourraient nous amener à suivre en Occident.'[4] He was ready to urge the Porte to reach agreement with Serbia and to give Crete a semi-independent administration. He also wished to know what should, if necessary, take the place of Turkey in Europe.[5] Gorchakov expressed his delight at Moustier's attitude and seemed to consider agreement within reach.[6]

In the meantime, an exchange of views had taken place between the cabinets of Vienna and Paris. Moustier had invited Metternich to tell Beust

que le moment était venu de s'occuper sérieusement de l'Orient et de l'attitude assez inquiétante de la Russie tendant à préparer pour le printemps prochain une explosion générale qu'il serait de la plus haute importance d'empêcher à temps.

Moustier therefore wished Beust 'd'amener une entente réelle et loyale entre l'Autriche et la France sur un point aussi important pour les deux pays'.[7] In response to this invitation and to the soundings from St Petersburg, Beust had devised a plan to settle the eastern question. The treaty of Paris, he told Metternich, had been repeatedly violated

---

[1] Charles-Roux, op. cit. p. 401.
[2] Talleyrand to Moustier, 11 December 1866, ibid. p. 402.
[3] Moustier to Talleyrand, 24 December 1866, ibid. pp. 402f.
[4] Budberg, wrote Moustier, 'n'a pas fait d'objections à un accord favorable à nos vues ultérieures en Occident, quand nous serions en mesure de les formuler' (ibid.).
[5] That Moustier fully understood the implications of Gorchakov's proposal is shown in Metternich to Beust, 8 January 1867, HHSAPAR, IX 86, France 1867, no. 3B.
[6] Talleyrand to Moustier, 25 December 1866, Charles-Roux, op. cit. p. 405.
[7] Metternich to Beust, 10 December 1866, APP, loc. cit. p. 223 n. 1.

in relation to the Principalities and had come to be out of date. Had not the time arrived for its revision by a conference of the signatories? Their first task would be to dispel all uncertainty about the rights of Turkey's Christian subjects. Any plan agreed on should be presented to the Porte —which would be excluded from the deliberations—as the joint decision of Europe. In addition, in order to secure the loyal co-operation of Russia, the restrictions on her sovereignty in the Black Sea should be lifted.[1] These proposals were ill-received in Paris. Moustier feared too close an understanding between Austria and Russia and told Metternich that whilst ready to adopt many of Beust's suggestions, 'il ne céderait jamais sur les restrictions concernant la marine Russe dans la mer Noire'.[2] Napoleon disliked the idea of a general congress on the eastern question[3] and favoured instead a conference in Vienna to consider the immediate problems of Serbia and Crete.[4] In general, he desired a triple understanding of France, Austria and Russia.[5]

When Beust received the French reply, he had the unwisdom to inform Gorchakov of his action,[6] inviting him at the same time to work for a general conference on Turkish affairs.[7] Gorchakov, intent on his private negotiations with Moustier, regretted the Austrian intervention. In particular, he considered the mention of the Black Sea Clauses inopportune. He told Revertera 'que cette manière d'agir était précipitée, qu'elle a éveillé sans nécessité la méfiance du Cabinet des Tuileries et qu'il aurait mieux valu attendre un moment plus propice'. He also disliked the

[1] Beust to Metternich, 1 January 1867, HHSAPAR, IX 86, France 1867, no. 1, draft. Beust declared:
'A notre avis, il y a lieu de tenir compte...du rôle naturel qu'assure à la Russie, en Orient, la communauté des institutions réligieuses et de se ménager par une attitude conciliante, le concours sincère de cette puissance dans les affaires du Levant.'
'...on ne saurait se dissimuler que c'est aller contre la nature des choses que d'interdire à un état d'une étendue et d'une population aussi immense sa liberté d'allures dans le cercle de son action légitime' (*ibid.*).
[2] Metternich to Beust, telegram, 5 January 1867, *ibid.* no. 4. Moustier added that England, Turkey and French opinion would oppose the abolition of the Black Sea Clauses (the same to the same, 8 January 1867, *ibid.* no. 3 B). Napoleon doubted whether England and Russia would accept Beust's proposals. He asked: '...Comment pensez-Vous qu'une révision radicale du traité de Paris puisse s'effectuer sans que j'en subisse un nouvel échec?' (the same to the same, 7 January 1867, *ibid.* no. 2).
[3] '...des conférences sur l'ensemble de la question orientale, welche eine sogleiche Revision des Pariser Vertrages voraussetzen und einschliessen würden, lui semblent inopportunes' (the same to the same, 12 January 1867, *ibid.* no. 4 A-G).
[4] The same to the same, telegram, 11 January 1867, *ibid.* no. 8.
[5] 'Sogleiche Anbahnung eines Einverständnisses zwischen uns, Frankreich und Russland wünschenswerth, entente qui pourra mener à une alliance dont les avantages seraient immenses en face de toutes les prévisions' (*ibid.*).
[6] 'Si la démarche faite par nous...a rencontré au premier moment quelque difficultés à Paris, il n'y a certainement pas à s'en étonner. Mais nous sommes persuadés que la Cour de Russie saura apprécier ce qu'il y a de bienveillant pour elle dans une initiative...qui a été dictée par une conviction sincère' (Beust to Revertera, 22 January 1867, *ibid.* X 54, Russie 1867, no. 1).
[7] *Ibid.*

suggestion of a conference: results would be slow and the Christians in Turkey were indifferent to the idea. Only pressure at Constantinople could produce early results and a joint policy must be found by negotiations between the powers.[1] This was a severe snub to Beust. Gorchakov, in fact, had been forced to recognize that his attempt to reach a working agreement with Austria was not likely to succeed.

This made success in the negotiations with France all the more important. Agreement appeared to have come nearer when Moustier on 23 January submitted a new proposal to the Russian government. France would join Russia in urging the sultan to abandon the Serbian fortresses, enlarge the frontiers of Greece and sanction the union of Crete with the latter country. This would involve serious sacrifices by Turkey, for which she must be offered adequate compensation.

Nous ne doutons pas que le cabinet de St Pétersbourg, dans les vues duquel nous entrons si largement, ne s'entende avec nous pour offrir et garantir au gouvernement ottoman toutes les conditions de sécurité et de vitalité qui lui sont indispensables. Notre intention en effet n'est pas de rouvrir la question d'Orient mais de la fermer résolument de concert avec la Russie.[2]

In reply to further inquiries from Gorchakov, Moustier re-stated the terms of the proposed bargain: 'l'accord établi avec la Russie sur ces concessions importantes a pour corollaire indispensable dans notre pensée 1° une attitude franchement sympathique vis-à-vis de nos intérêts en Occident; 2° une entente dans le but de fermer la question d'Orient....'[3] Gorchakov considered Moustier's references to the interests of France in the west to be excessively vague.[4] The same was true of the guarantees to be given to Turkey, which were unlikely in his opinion to produce even a temporary solution.[5] Gorchakov's inquiry about French plans in the west was, at the same time, embarrassing to Napoleon who, whilst negotiating secretly for the acquisition of Luxemburg and coveting the larger prize of Belgium, was unwilling to avow openly either of these objectives. Moustier's reply, therefore, was once again evasive.[6] Furthermore, the French government now produced a plan for extensive administrative reforms in the Ottoman empire to benefit the Muslims as well as the Christian populations.[7] These elaborate proposals were unwelcome to Gorchakov, who was impatient for quick results.[8] Agreement between Russia and France on a common policy was becoming increasingly doubtful.

[1] Revertera to Beust, 29/17 January 1867, *ibid.* no. 3 A-I.
[2] Moustier to Talleyrand, 23 January 1867, Charles-Roux, *op. cit.* p. 406.
[3] Moustier to Talleyrand, 30 January 1867, *ibid.* p. 407.
[4] '...Vous parlez de vos intérêts en Occident; dites-moi en quoi ils consistent, quels sont les désirs et les projets de votre empereur. Plus d'une fois cette question s'est trouvée posée et il ne nous a jamais été fait de réponse catégorique' (Talleyrand to Moustier, 1 February 1867, *ibid.* pp. 407ff.). [5] *Ibid.*
[6] Moustier to Talleyrand, 18 February 1867, *ibid.* pp. 414f.
[7] The same to the same, 22 February 1867, *ibid.* p. 415.
[8] Talleyrand to Moustier, 4 March 1867, *ibid.* p. 416.

Lack of success in the negotiations with the cabinets of Vienna and Paris again turned Russian attention to Prussia. Early in March, the tsar unburdened himself to Reuss, the representative of the North German Confederation. It was necessary, he explained, to take steps to forestall a major conflict in the east. A small result was preferable to none and he would be satisfied if certain territories were placed under Christian rule. His friendship for King William was loyal and sincere. '"Je vous prie cependant de dire au roi qu'en échange j'espère pouvoir compter sur son puissant appui dans cette question qui m'intéresse au plus haut degré."' Gorchakov held similar language but Reuss replied that the Prussian government could hardly take the initiative and had to consider also the views of its western neighbours.[1] The tsar and Gorchakov had to take note of the fact that the road to the Balkans continued to lie through Paris.

Negotiations with France, however, were advancing at snail's pace. When Gorchakov proposed an immediate demand to Turkey for the cession of Crete to Greece, Moustier rejoined that Russia should hasten the conclusion of a general agreement with France 'avant de nous pousser dans les voies d'exécution'.[2] Gorchakov was reluctant to commit himself to the extent demanded by Moustier. It was whilst the negotiations were dragging on that the tsar learnt of the proposed sale of Luxemburg to France.[3] A development of this nature, which at any moment might provoke a flare-up of the 'western question', could not but increase Russian unwillingness to give the pledges demanded by Napoleon. On 1 April the Luxemburg question became public property with the result that the attention of Europe was, for a time, diverted from eastern affairs. The first stage of Gorchakov's attempt to protect Russian interests in the east had ended without result.

III

Whilst Russia continued to seek support for her eastern policy and a general rising of the Christians in Turkey remained a dangerous possibility, the attention of Europe was dramatically diverted to the west. On 1 April the impending sale of Luxemburg to France was attacked in the North German Parliament; public opinion in Germany began to protest against the alienation of territory which had belonged to the Germanic Confederation. Napoleon, on the other hand, could hardly afford yet another diplomatic defeat. In consequence, a Franco-Prussian war became, for a time, a dangerous possibility. Yet neither of the protagonists was ready for open hostilities whilst the neutrals, for a variety of reasons, wished to

[1] Reuss to William I, 9 March 1867, *APP, loc. cit.* pp. 451 ff.
[2] Charles-Roux, *op. cit.* p. 421.
[3] Revertera to Beust, telegram, 15/3 March 1867, HHSAPARRR, 1867, x 54.

prevent a new conflict. The neutral governments intervened and, under their auspices, the dangerous dispute was settled.

The Luxemburg crisis—although without permanent effect on the alignment of the powers—is significant because it forced neutral governments for the first time to face the prospect of a Franco-Prussian war. By drawing attention to the unresolved conflict in the heart of Europe it emphasized the connection between the eastern and western questions: Gorchakov was made aware of the difficulty of uniting France and Prussia to serve Russian interests in the east. In fact, the crisis revealed the insuperable difficulties in the way of a *rapprochement* between Russia and France. More than ever, French attention now came to be concentrated on the affairs of the west. At the same time, the dress-rehearsal for the crisis of 1870 raised the question of England's casting vote. Whichever party could obtain British support, would be almost certain of victory: active British diplomacy would make a Franco-Prussian war all but impossible.[1] In fact, not only England but also Russia and Austria were vitally concerned in the conflict, and since, for once, neither of the principals desired the outbreak of war, neutral diplomacy was able to save the peace of Europe.

On the last day of March, Bernstorff read Stanley two telegrams from Berlin. The first of these stated that a danger of war between Prussia and France now existed, and invited the British government in the interest of peace to prevent the sale of Luxemburg by the king of Holland. The second telegram contained a declaration that the Prussian government considered Luxemburg to be covered by the treaty on Belgian neutrality of 1839. Did the British government share this view?—Stanley's first reaction was that England was not concerned with the matter and that, in the interest of peace, Napoleon should be allowed to gain this modest success.

> I certainly did not consider that the arrangement whatever might be its precise character, was one of a nature to call for the intervention of England. Though the principle involved in it might be questionable, yet if by so small a re-arrangement of territory the irritation now undoubtedly existing in France could be allayed and the peace of Europe thereby secured, I should have thought so great an advantage cheaply purchased.[2]

Two days later Stanley replied to the second of Bismarck's questions:

> I did not...see in whose interest Her Majesty's Government was asked to interfere. The guarantee...was meant for the protection of the King of Holland, but if

---

[1] Bismarck had recently expressed the view that the combination most dangerous to Prussia would be one between England and France. 'Wir würden schon die.... Tripelallianz zwischen Frankreich, Italien und Österreich... [als] eine Gefahr erblicken, eine noch grössere aber in einer engeren Verbindung Frankreichs mit England, dessen überwiegende Seemacht in einem solchen Falle unseren Handel vernichten und den Landoperationen Frankreichs eine Stütze geben würde' (Bismarck to Goltz, 15 February 1867, no. 117, secret, *APP, loc. cit.* pp. 392f.).

[2] Stanley to Cowley, 1 April 1867, RA I 71/20, draft.

the King were an assenting party to the transfer, the question of protecting his interests could not arise. The Prussian Government appeared to regard it as a question affecting the integrity of the German territory... but it had certainly never been contemplated by England to guarantee the integrity of Germany. The only question, therefore, that remained, was how far the transfer... would affect the security of Belgium.... It did not seem... that the possession of Luxemburg would materially affect the future of Belgium.

The Foreign Secretary reserved his final reply but did not conceal from Bernstorff his strong conviction 'that it would not be the duty of Her Majesty's government to interfere in the matter which seemed to be one entirely between France and Germany'.[1] On the following day, Bernstorff presented himself with a further inquiry:

He did not see how a war could be avoided, and in the event of its taking place, and of France obtaining any success, the position of Belgium would become exceedingly precarious. He was anxious therefore to know whether, in the event of war being forced on Prussia by France, Her Majesty's Government would take part in it and to what extent they would give their co-operation to Prussia?

Stanley's reply may well have delayed by three years the clash between Prussia and France:

I said that was a question which I could answer without hesitation. England was on the most friendly terms with both France and Prussia; with the causes of their quarrel, if unfortunately a quarrel were to break out, she had absolutely nothing to do and I felt sure that no Minister, whatever his political connection or tendency might be, would venture to propose to Parliament, nor would public opinion sanction, an armed interference on either side.

As to Belgium, that was a different question. England was pledged in the strongest manner to assist in maintaining the independence of that country and those pledges it would be her duty to redeem.

But there was a wide distinction between taking up arms in case of necessity for the protection of Belgium, in fulfilment of promises solemnly and repeatedly given, and joining in a war between France and Germany, in which no English interest was involved and with regard to which we stood absolutely free and unpledged.[2]

Whilst thus rebuffing Bismarck, the Foreign Secretary unofficially notified Napoleon

that it would be a great satisfaction to Her Majesty's Government to receive in some formal and authentic shape an assurance that whatever may be the issue of a war between France and Prussia on account of Luxemburg, if war should unfortunately break out, the Independence and Territorial Integrity of Belgium as now constituted, will be respected by France.

It would not be expedient, Stanley told Cowley,

by formally inviting any declaration to that effect to seem to imply a doubt that France might under any circumstances be disposed to depart from her engagements

---

[1] The same to the same, 2 April 1867, *ibid.* I 71/27, draft.
[2] The same to the same, 3 April 1867, *ibid.* I 71/31, draft.

in regard to Belgium by which equally with the other Great Powers of Europe she is now bound....

Cowley would do well, however, 'to encourage any disposition which may be shewn on the part of the Emperor or of His Government spontaneously to renounce views of aggrandizement at the expense of Belgium'.[1] Stanley, who understood perfectly the true cause of the Franco-Prussian impasse,[2] had thus done his utmost to reduce for both parties the temptation to go to war. The Queen, who believed in the probability of war, entirely approved his attitude

both as regards the non-interference of England in a quarrel between France and Prussia respecting the possession of Luxemburg—and the determination of England to resist any attempt against either the Independence or Integrity of Belgium.[3]

By 5 April it appeared that the crisis had passed, for the king of Holland had withdrawn his consent to the sale of Luxemburg. Stanley, somewhat prematurely, wrote:

I fear the state of things is not improved by this unsuccessful negotiation. Luxemburg would have been a small price to pay for a reconciliation between France and Prussia. As matters stand, the feeling of exasperation in France will be aggravated by this fresh failure—and the prospect of permanent peace seems to me very gloomy. If the affair had gone on, I certainly would have left untried no means... for bringing about a friendly arrangement: but all that is unnecessary now....[4]

Both parties to the conflict indeed were showing a desire for compromise. On the morning of 6 April, Bernstorff read a despatch from Bismarck inviting the British government to urge restraint in Paris and hinting at a willingness to discuss the future of Luxemburg in conference.[5] That same day an important French diplomat spoke to Cowley of France's desire for the preservation of peace. A war in the west would enable Russia to do as she pleased in the east whilst Italy would settle the Roman question. Napoleon hesitated.

However the question was what satisfaction could now be obtained for France, for otherwise the spirit of the country would be roused and all hope of maintaining peace would be at an end. Could I under these circumstances give him any advice?[6]

On the afternoon of 7 April, Napoleon himself followed up this overture:

He was most desirous to maintain the peace of Europe and if the Great Powers could prevail on Prussia to give him satisfaction, or suggest any mode of settling this question, he would be only too glad to adopt it.

[1] The same to the same, 3 April 1867, *ibid.* I 71/32, draft.
[2] '...The danger of a war between France and Germany...seems to me increased by this Luxemburg difficulty: of which I believe the explanation to be, that Bismarck has held out hopes to the Emperor, of Prussia giving her consent to the transfer, which hopes will be disappointed by the general feeling of Germany being too strong for any Prussian minister to disregard' (Stanley to Grey, private, 3 April 1867, *ibid.* I 71/33).
[3] Grey to Stanley, private, 3 April 1867, *ibid.* I 71/34, copy.
[4] Stanley to Grey, private, 5 April 1867, *ibid.* I 71/40.
[5] Stanley to Cowley and Loftus, 6 April 1867, *ibid.* I 71/46, draft.
[6] Cowley to Stanley, private, 7 April 1867, *ibid.* I 71/53, copy.

Cowley asked what it was the emperor actually wanted and 'after a great deal of questioning it came to this: "that Luxemburg should be made over to the Grand Duke, Prussia withdrawing the garrison from the fortress"'. Cowley considered that some such plan might form the basis of a compromise:

> Would it not be wcrth while to sound the ground at Berlin to see what Prussia will now accept? Would she agree to give up Luxemburg to the Grand Duke provided an agreement was to be made that it would not be made over at any time afterwards to France?

Cowley concluded: 'If you can do any thing in the matter, you will confer a great favor here and I firmly believe will have the satisfaction of preventing a war, *tho*' perhaps only for a time—which is otherwise inevitable.'[1] That night Niel, the Minister of War, informed Napoleon

> that it was out of the question he should engage in war with Germany at present, and that it would take eight months to get ready; but he promised His Majesty then to be prepared with an Army in a state to take the field. The Emperor was wavering all Sunday [the 7th] what he should do and this probably determined him.[2]

On the morning of 8 April, at an extraordinary Council of Ministers

> it was decided that a pacific declaration should be made to the Chambers to-day. The Emperor will say that Prussia having appealed to the Powers who signed the Treaty of 1839, His Majesty is ready to abide by their decision and has no doubt that the solution will be a peaceable one.[3]

Napoleon, Cowley observed, 'had a bad choice to make either way, but of two evils he has, I think, chosen the least. The present check may be forgotten or atoned. A reverse in the field must have been fatal to him.'[4] On 11 April the ambassador reported that public opinion in France was becoming more pacific: 'le jeu ne vaut pas la chandelle'. One of Napoleon's intimates had suggested that the matter could be settled by the destruction of the fortress and the neutralization of the country.[5] On the following day the French ambassador appealed to Stanley to do everything in his power to preserve peace. France did not absolutely reject any

---

[1] *Ibid.*

[2] The same to the same, private, 9 April 1867, *ibid.* I 71/58, copy.

[3] The same to the same, telegram, 8 April 1867, *ibid.* I 71/54. It is impossible not to contrast this declaration with the one made, in not dissimilar circumstances, by Gramont on 6 July 1870. The present pacific declaration was not a matter of choice. Whilst France was completely unprepared for a campaign, Loftus reported from Berlin that reports of mobilization and military preparations in Prussia were unfounded. 'Nothing has been done, and for the best of reasons viz: that everything is so organized that in 14 days the Army could be put in motion' (Loftus to Stanley, private 20 April 1867, *ibid.* I 71/115, copy). Cowley reported: 'It looks as if the object here was now to gain time until France is better prepared. Raison de plus for the Neutral Powers to be active at Berlin' (Cowley to Stanley, private, 23 April 1867, *ibid.* I 71/126, copy).

[4] The same to the same, private, 9 April 1867, *ibid.* I 71/58, copy.

[5] The same to the same, private, 11 April 1867, *ibid.* I 71/69, copy.

of the combinations which had been informally canvassed.[1] On 13 April, Stanley summed up the situation:

> ...I take the matter to stand thus. France will waive all claim of her own to Luxemburg, and accept almost any arrangement that can be made, provided only that arrangement includes the removal of the Prussian garrison. The point therefore now is, will the King of Prussia (or rather Bismarck) consent to this? and if so, on what conditions? If he will, all may go straight. If he will not, a war must probably follow. The decision is to be made at Berlin. The Emperor has been moderate in his language, the French are daily less and less disposed for war, but having asked for a great deal, they must have something to show as the result of their demand. I do not think there is any need of haste. France will not be armed, at the earliest, till the autumn: probably too late to begin a campaign.[2]

On the afternoon of 15 April, Bernstorff called on Stanley with a message from Bismarck that Prussia would not, and could not, evacuate Luxemburg. It would be better for her to fight France rather than lose the confidence of Germany.[3] Stanley replied that Prussia had every interest in finding a peaceful solution. Her coast was exposed to French attack; her maritime commerce might be destroyed; her influence over her Confederates might be weakened. He merely threw out these suggestions without wishing to pronounce an opinion on the merits of the question.[4] Warnings of this kind were unlikely to influence Bismarck, supported as he was by German public opinion. Stronger action at Berlin was needed. The King of the Belgians urged from Paris that England should formally advise Prussia to evacuate Luxemburg.[5] Moustier called for British intervention.[6] Cowley pressed for action.[7] On 19 April, Stanley finally informed the Prussian government that, in his opinion, the solution of the question without war depended on the withdrawal of the Prussian garrison. It was deserving of the consideration of Prussia 'whether she should not make so small a sacrifice since her hesitation to do so would seem to countenance the notion that she wishes to keep Luxemburg for aggressive purposes against France'. The British government would see with deep regret the outbreak of war for an object apparently so trifling 'which could not but retard the consolidation of Germany'.[8] Three days later, the Queen reinforced this plea. In a private letter to William I she

---

[1] Stanley to Cowley, 12 April 1867, *ibid.* I 71/73, draft.

[2] Stanley to Grey, 13 April 1867, *ibid.* I 71/76. It is interesting to note that Stanley seems to consider France as the only possible aggressor.

[3] Stanley to Cowley and Loftus, 15 April 1867, *ibid.* I 71/81, draft. Bismarck at the beginning of the crisis had remarked to a friend, probably sincerely: 'It is a question of existence both to the Emperor Napoleon and to me' (Loftus to Stanley, private, 6 April 1867, *ibid.* I 71/48, copy).

[4] Stanley to Loftus, 17 April 1867, *ibid.* I 71/96, draft.

[5] Leopold II to the Queen, 16 and 18 April 1867, *ibid.* I 71/94 and I 71/105.

[6] Cowley to Stanley, private, 18 April 1867, *ibid.* I 71/107.

[7] 'It is not for me to say more than I have already done on previous occasions, but surely it must be worth while to make the attempt' (*ibid.*).

[8] Stanley to Loftus, telegram, 19 April 1867, *ibid.* I 71/109.

declared that the withdrawal of the Prussian garrison would be a small sacrifice compared to Napoleon's renunciation of his plan to acquire the Duchy. If this concession was refused, world opinion would hold Prussia responsible for desiring a war.[1]

Whilst the British government was working for a peaceful solution, Russian diplomacy also had not been idle. Gorchakov's first reaction to the proposed sale of Luxemburg had been unfavourable:

Je ne puis vous cacher [he told Talleyrand] que j'éprouve les plus sérieuses inquiétudes pour le maintien de la paix. L'irritation à Berlin est grande et générale; elle se propagera, croyez-le bien, dans toute l'Allemagne et l'Autriche ne pourra pas se mettre de votre côté. M. de Bismarck se trouvera placé dans la terrible extrémité de voir sa popularité et son œuvre crouler devant une condescendance de sa part ou abandonnées à la merci d'une guerre formidable.

The French government had been wrong to raise the question.[2] In a private letter to Talleyrand, Moustier expressed his disappointment at the Russian attitude:

Le Prince Gortchakoff, en nous proposant de nous entendre sur la question d'Orient, savait bien la nature du prix que nous mettions à notre concours...On nous a promis une attitude franchement sympathique pour nos intérêts en Occident. Cela s'accorde peu avec l'attitude apparente du cabinet de Saint-Pétersbourg.[3]

In an official despatch, Moustier tried to gain Russian sympathy by holding out hopes of closer co-operation at Constantinople:

Il me paraît chaque jour plus nécessaire de préciser notre entente avec la Russie sur toutes les questions aussi bien occidentales qu'orientales. Nous lui avons donné des preuves suffisantes de notre disposition d'agir avec elle dans toute chose dans un concert cordial et loyal.

Russia had accepted his suggestion for an international inquiry into the affairs of Crete. They must now decide how to raise the matter at Constantinople and approach the other powers.[4] Moustier's despatch was well-received by Gorchakov who urged again the need for concerted action to end the bloodshed in Crete.[5] He also repeated an earlier assurance that he had not expressed to Prussia any opinion on the merits of the Luxemburg dispute.[6] Moustier replied with an undertaking that France would renounce all plans of acquiring the Duchy in exchange for evacuation of the fortress by Prussia.[7] He also urged the sultan to make concessions in Crete.[8] This action finally produced the result desired in

---

[1] The Queen to William I, 22 April 1867, *ibid.* I 71/122, draft. Stanley wrote: '...the Queen's personal appeal will be of more use...than a dozen despatches' (Stanley to Grey, 23 April 1867, *ibid.* I 71/124).
[2] Talleyrand to Moustier, 3 April 1867, Charles-Roux, *op. cit.* pp. 423ff.
[3] Moustier to Talleyrand, private, 8 April 1867, *ibid.* p. 426.
[4] The same to the same, 8 April 1867, no. 21, *Origines, loc. cit.* pp. 326ff.
[5] Talleyrand to Moustier, telegram, 14 April 1867, *ibid.* vol. 16, p. 7.
[6] The same to the same, telegram, 17 April 1867, *ibid.* pp. 33f.
[7] Moustier to Talleyrand, telegram, 18 April 1867, *ibid.* p. 34.
[8] Moustier to Bourrée, 19 April 1867, *ibid.* pp. 57ff.

Paris. On 21 April, Gorchakov informed Talleyrand that the tsar had written a personal letter to William I, whose reply was 'de nature à nous laisser quelque espoir de réussite'.[1]

In fact, in the face of neutral pressure, the Prussian government was beginning to yield. On 25 April the King of the Belgians reported from Berlin that there was a wish to avoid war 'but great indecision as to the means of doing so'.[2] On the 26th, Loftus transmitted to Bismarck, Stanley's advice in favour of evacuation. Bismarck replied that Prussia would agree to a conference. She would make to Holland[3] and Europe concessions she could not make to France alone. She was unable to accept a preconcerted basis for the meeting but Loftus might confidentially inform Stanley that she would be disposed in conference to consent to the neutralization of the Grand-Duchy and the withdrawal of the Prussian garrison provided the fortress was placed under a European guarantee. She would use her influence to secure German acceptance for the plan.[4] Stanley remained distrustful,[5] but by 29 April, even he no longer anticipated any difficulty.[6] He remained anxious about the 'very stringent guarantee' which Prussia would try to obtain[7] but pressed by the Queen,[8] agreed to give way 'rather than break up the conference'.[9] On 9 May the agreement was finally initialled. Three days later, Stanley recorded:

> From all I can learn, the feeling in France is one of real gratitude to this country for our having helped to extricate the Emperor from his troubles. What is thought in Prussia I have no means of knowing.[10] I am told there is no wish for war there, but an intense feeling of distrust, which is fully reciprocated in France.[11]

[1] Talleyrand to Moustier, 21 April 1867, Charles-Roux, *op. cit.* p. 429. The Russian government was proposing at Berlin the assembly of a diplomatic conference in London. '...elle avait dit nettement à Berlin que le droit de la Prusse d'occuper la forteresse de Luxembourg lui paraissait très contestable; qu'il ne pouvait y avoir atteinte pour son honneur à déférer au conseil de l'évacuer, s'il lui était unanimement donné par les grandes puissances, et qu'enfin on lui avait fait envisager tous les inconvénients de la situation où elle se placerait, en refusant de souscrire à un arrangement qui paraissait acceptable à chaque cabinet' (the same to the same, 27 April 1867, *ibid.*).

[2] Loftus to Stanley, telegram, 25 April 1867, RA I 71/140.

[3] Beust had proposed that Luxemburg should be left to Holland and the Prussian garrison withdrawn.

[4] Loftus to Stanley, telegram, 26 April 1867, *ibid.* I 71/151. On the same day Gorchakov informed Talleyrand that Prussia had agreed to a conference in London at which Luxemburg would be neutralized under a European guarantee. Prussian evacuation of the fortress would follow (Charles-Roux, *op. cit.* p. 230).

[5] 'The fact is one cannot trust Bismarck, even if he had given a promise, unless it were in a form that could be made public' (Stanley to Grey, private, 27 April 1867, RA I 71/175).

[6] The same to the same, private, 29 April 1867, *ibid.* I 71/187.

[7] The same to the same, private, 3 May 1867, *ibid.* I 71/227.

[8] The Queen to Stanley, 5 May 1867, *ibid.* I 71/248, copy.

[9] Stanley to Grey, private, 7 May 1867, *ibid.* I 71/261.

[10] The aggrieved tone in which the king of Prussia had replied to the letter from Queen Victoria might have enlightened Stanley on this subject (king of Prussia to Queen, 27 and 28 April 1867, *ibid.* I 71/167).

[11] Stanley to Grey, private, 12 May 1867, *ibid.* I 71/268.

Whilst Stanley was reflecting on the doubtful future of Franco-Prussian relations, Gorchakov, his fellow peace-maker, was turning once more to the east. When complimented by Reuss on his part in bringing about a peaceful solution, he replied that when Buchanan had congratulated him in a written note, he (Gorchakov) had expressed the hope that having gained this success in the west, British Ministers would now feel more inclined to allow others to obtain some successes in the east.[1] It was from France rather than England, however, that Gorchakov hoped to claim the reward for his contribution to the preservation of peace.

IV

The possibility of the tsar's visit to Paris during the exhibition of 1867 had been discussed, on Bismarck's initiative,[2] before the Luxemburg dispute. Alexander, who had strong personal reasons for the journey,[3] had wished his stay to coincide with that of his uncle, the king of Prussia,[4] but when Napoleon expressed displeasure at the suggestion[5] it was finally agreed that the tsar should arrive forty-eight hours before the king.[6] On the evening of 28 May, Alexander and Gorchakov departed for Berlin and Paris.[7]

[1] 'Er habe dem englischen Botschafter, welcher ihm heute früh in einem Billett zu diesem Resultate gratuliert habe, geantwortet, er hoffe dass die englischen Minister nach diesem Erfolg, den sie auf dem Terrain des Okzidents errungen, nunmehr auch geneigt sein dürften, andern ähnliche Erfolge auf dem des Orients zu gönnen' (Reuss to Bismarck, 10 May 1867, APP, loc. cit. p. 825).

[2] On 22 February, Bismarck had informed Benedetti that King William would be 'not unwilling' to come to Paris during the exhibition. On 22 March, Benedetti had transmitted an official invitation from Napoleon. Bismarck had then inquired at St Petersburg, whether the tsar would also visit the exhibition. He received the reply that if his uncle went to Paris, Alexander would be glad to do the same (ibid. vol. 9, pp. 5ff.).

[3] He intended to meet in Paris, Princess Catherine Dolgoruky who had recently become his mistress. The fact was well known to foreign diplomats (Revertera to Beust, 8 May/ 26 April 1867, HHSAPARRR 1867, x 54, no. 22 A-G; and Reuss to Bismarck, 22 May 1867, APP, loc. cit. vol. 9, pp. 67ff.).

[4] Bismarck expressed the hope that the joint visit would help to preserve peace and reduce tension (Bismarck to Reuss, 25 March 1867, GW, loc. cit. vol. 6, p. 311 n. 717).

[5] He wrote to Moustier: 'Je vois par la dépêche de ce soir que l'empereur de Russie doit venir à Paris avec le roi de Prusse. Il faut tâcher d'éviter que ces deux souverains viennent ensemble, si on ne peut empêcher complètement le voyage du roi de Prusse. Je vous prie de ne pas perdre un instant pour dire à M. de Budberg qu'autant l'empereur de Russie sera bien reçu en France s'il y vient seul, autant son arrivée avec le roi de Prusse fera mauvais effet; que d'ailleurs cela nous gênerait beaucoup de les recevoir en même temps. Tâchez qu'il écrive immédiatement par le télegraphe à Saint-Pétersbourg. Tâchez enfin de faire de la diplomatie pour atteindre le but que je désire' (Napoleon III to Moustier, 11 May 1867, Charles-Roux, op. cit. p. 433).

[6] On 14 May, Schweinitz telegraphed from St Petersburg that the tsar would prefer not to arrive in Paris together with his uncle. King William remarked on his report: 'I, too. I shall therefore arrive 48 hours later' (Schweinitz to William I, telegram, 14 May 1867, APP, loc. cit. vol 9, p. 69 n. 2).

[7] Brenner to Beust, 28/16 May 1867, HHSAPARRR, 1867, x 54, no. 26.

The tsar's visit to France began under unfavourable auspices. Gorchakov from the start had expressed misgivings about its value.[1] Shortly before leaving, he had told Reuss that the Prussian cabinet was the only one to be trusted. The intrigues of Austria[2] and France would finally lead to the result least desired in Paris, a still closer *rapprochement* between Russia and Prussia.[3] He would be very cautious in Paris. The tsar's open and honest nature did not know distrust, but the empress had undertaken to warn him to be careful.[4]

On 30 and 31 May the tsar and Gorchakov met William I and Bismarck at Potsdam. The king afterwards recorded that both visitors were completely agreed in their views: 'la paix, la paix, et encore une fois la paix'. They had, however, expressed doubts whether it would prove possible to secure guarantees from France, the only country which threatened the peace of Europe. The danger sprang less from Napoleon himself than from national sentiment which might drive him into a war for the sake of his dynasty. Gorchakov wished to explore in Paris what guarantees could be obtained by Prussia for the Rhine and by Russia in the east.[5]

[1] Early in April, he had told Reuss: 'Ja wenn man die Sache so vorbereiten könnte, dass die drei mächtigsten Souveräne eine Art von Garantievertrag in Paris abschlössen, welcher der Welt den Frieden zu erhalten imstande wäre, dann wäre es eine andere Sache; dazu gehörte aber eine in Paris sehr geschickt geführte Negoziation und vor allen Dingen eine Persönlichkeit von grösserer Sicherheit als die des Kaisers Napoleon, der uns durch den letzten Handel von neuem einen Beweis dafür gegeben hätte, wie wenig man sich auf ihn verlassen könnte' (Reuss to Bismarck, 5 April 1867, *APP, loc. cit.* vol. 8, p. 545 n. 6). Somewhat later Gorchakov told Reuss that he had opposed the journey from the beginning. He had not been consulted about the original arrangements. 'Wenn der Kaiser durchaus reisen wollte, so hätte man dies recht gut so einrichten können, dass man diesen Besuch den Franzosen als einnen hohen Preis für gute Aufführung hingehalten hätte. Leider sei dies nicht geschehen' (the same to the same, 22 May 1867, *APP, loc. cit.* vol. 9, pp. 67 ff.).
[2] On 18 May, Gorchakov expressed 'le plus vif déplaisir' at the news that the Austrian government would not join the collective action at Constantinople proposed by Russia. He had spoken to Revertera 'dans des termes qui trahissaient un profond désappointement' (Revertera to Beust, 18/6 May 1867, HHSAPARRR, 1867, X 54, no. 23 A-C).
[3] 'Das Königliche Kabinett sei das einzige, auf welches man sich wirklich verlassen könnte, und die französischen und österreichischen Ränke würden gerade dahin führen, wohin man weder in Paris noch in Wien gelangen wollte, nämlich zu einem noch intimeren Verhältnis zwischen dem preussischen und dem russischen Hofe' (Reuss to Bismarck, 22 Mai 1867, *APP, loc. cit.* p. 53 n. 3).
Stremouchov, the influential head of the Asiatic Department in the Russian Foreign Ministry criticized the tsar's journey. He expressed the hope that full Russo-Prussian agreement would previously be reached during the tsar's stay in Berlin. This should be clearly demonstrated in Paris.
'Ein solches Einverständnis könne sehr leicht dadurch erzielt werden, dass Preussen in den orientalischen Angelegenheiten womöglich noch entschiedener, als dies sehr anerkennenswerterweise bereits geschehen, die russische Politik zu unterstützen sich verpflichte. Wäre man dessen ganz sicher, so könnten wir mit Entschiedenheit darauf rechnen, dass russischerseits in Paris kein Wort gesprochen werden würde, welches sich nicht mit den preussischen Interessen vereinigen liesse' (the same to the same, 15 May 1867, *ibid.* vol. 9, pp. 52 ff.).
[4] *Ibid.*
[5] '...*wir* für den Rhein, *er* für den Orient.' William I to Queen Augusta, 2 June 1867 *APP, loc. cit.* pp. 102 f. n. 4.

Bismarck afterwards explained to Loftus:

that the visit of the Emperor of Russia had not been popular in Russia and that Prince Gortchakov was therefore anxious on his return to have some favourable result from it in order to reconcile it to the Russian nation. Count Bismarck further remarked that Prince Gortchakov entertained some ideas which he hoped to utilize in Paris for the maintenance of peace. These...were of a very vague nature and appeared chiefly to consist of a guarantee to be given by France that she would not attack Germany. Count Bismarck appeared to attach no importance to them and to think their practical realization impossible.[1]

Gorchakov, however, had by this time persuaded himself that results might be obtained. On reaching the French frontier he informed General Lebœuf who had been attached to the person of the tsar—'J'arrive avec une chancellerie pour faire des affaires'; he also asked the general to arrange for him a private interview with Napoleon.[2] Gorchakov and his master were rapidly disillusioned. Napoleon had little desire for political talks which could not produce results. He therefore tried to avoid all serious discussion with his guests.[3] When he finally granted a private audience to Gorchakov, their exchange of views was of a general nature. Moustier in his turn had a private audience with the tsar which was cut short by Napoleon's arrival at the very moment when the interesting subject of Turkey had been reached. Only a conversation between Gorchakov and Moustier seriously touched on the subject the Russians had at heart. When Gorchakov urged the despatch of identical notes to Constantinople, the French Minister agreed. What, however, was to be done, if the Porte ignored the wishes of Russia and France? Gorchakov also proposed the despatch of warships to evacuate the old, women and children from Crete. Moustier reluctantly consented to submit the matter to Napoleon. When Gorchakov recommended the union of Crete with Greece, he received little encouragement:

la force des choses [said Moustier] tendait certainement à séparer ce pays de l'empire ottoman; mais la manière de procéder à tous égards la plus sage était de laisser le fruit se détacher de l'arbre lui-même en quelque sorte sans y porter la main.

Nor could Gorchakov persuade Moustier that the reforms to be recommended to the Porte should be limited to the Christians. Moustier merely promised to draw up a programme for subsequent discussion. With regard to the west, the conversation was even less productive. Gorchakov rather

---

[1] Loftus to Stanley, 7 June 1867, *ibid*. Cf. also Wimpffen to Beust, 1 June 1867, *ibid*. pp. 101 ff.

[2] For this, and the following, see Charles-Roux, *op. cit.* pp. 434 ff.

[3] Alexander before the first dinner given to him at the Tuileries had let it be known that he would arrive early to have the opportunity of a private conversation with his host. He had hardly entered Napoleon's study when the empress Eugénie appeared and the talk turned to trivialities.

naïvely summed up his impression to Montebello: 'Votre ministre aime à pérorer; mais il ne conclut pas. J'aime des hommes d'action.' The hour of departure sounded for the Russian guests without either the emperors or their Ministers having resumed political discussions.

Nor had the visit been a social success. On the drive from the station to the Tuileries there had been cries of 'Vive la Pologne!'—too few, perhaps to reach the ears of the tsar. Yet Alexander could not but notice the coolness of the crowds lining the streets. During a subsequent visit to the Palais de Justice mutterings about Poland were heard from a group of lawyers. On 6 July, returning in an open carriage from a military review, the tsar was fired on twice by Berezowski, a Pole. He bore himself bravely but his stay in Paris was poisoned. If, on arrival, his demeanour had been grave, it now became haughty and reserved. The failure of the visit was complete and matters were not improved by the fact that as Alexander was about to leave Paris, he could watch preparations for the reception of the sultan who was also to visit the exhibition. He returned to St Petersburg 'fatigué, vieilli et sérieux'.[1]

Gorchakov, although he tried valiantly to minimize the extent of his failure,[2] could not conceal the fact that the visit marked a turning point in Russo-French relations.[3] Ten years earlier, at Stuttgart, Napoleon had first held out to the Russians a hope that he would support their policy in the east. Since that time, France had reaped solid advantages from her understanding with Russia—the tsar had gained little in exchange. All hope of effective French support in the eastern question now seemed to have vanished for many years to come; in consequence the Russian government no longer had any interest in supporting France in the west. The friendship of the two countries—badly shaken at the time of the Polish insurrection —had reached its natural term. The reason for the failure of the Russo-

---

[1] Brenner to Beust, 3 July/22 June 1867, HHSAPARRR, 1867, x 54, no. 32B.

[2] Charles-Roux, *op. cit.* pp. 440ff.

[3] Six years later he would give Chaudordy, the French minister in Bern, a highly coloured and inaccurate account of the tsar's visit to Paris:

'Lorsqu'en 1867 j'ai eu l'honneur d'accompagner à votre exposition mon auguste maître, il était animé des dispositions les plus favorables à un rapprochement. Il souhaitait ardemment à causer avec votre empereur et, à plusieurs reprises, il en a cherché l'occasion. Mais celui-ci se dérobait sans cesse, et quelque fois avec si peu de ménagements que nous étions amenés à nous demander s'il avait toute sa tête et si ses facultés n'étaient pas dérangées. Puis, ce fut l'injure personnelle que fit à mon souverain M. Floquet [the lawyer who had spoken about Poland], et enfin l'attentat Berezowski. Alexandre quittait Paris le cœur ulcéré. Il était encore dans cet état quand la Prusse est venue nous faire des propositions. Nous n'avions plus aucun motif pour les décliner. Nous avions pris des engagements envers elle et nous sommes liés' (E. Daudet, *Histoire Diplomatique de l'Alliance Franco-Russe 1873–1893* (Paris, 1894), p. 63).

Gorchakov forebore to mention that his conversation with Moustier had clearly shown that there did not exist the slightest basis for a Russo-French understanding in either east or west. His reference to alleged Prussian offers after the visit shows that he was either deceived by his memory or trying to mislead Chaudordy. His remarks, however, do show clearly that, in retrospect, he regarded the visit to Paris as a turning-point in Russo-French relations.

French understanding are clear: Russia, in her own interest, could not afford to sacrifice Prussia to France even in exchange for active support in the east;[1] France had no interest in a grouping which would antagonize England without providing compensation for Prussia's increased importance.[2] In Germany and in the east, no less than in Poland, the interests of the two countries clashed, a fact which no amount of talk about 'natural alliances' could conceal.

The failure of the Franco-Russian talks had important effects on the diplomatic situation of both countries. It placed the Russian government in an unenviable position. England, in the east, was passively hostile. Relations with Austria had reached their lowest ebb since 1863.[3] No support could now be looked for from France. The sultan's visits to London and Paris boded ill for the future of Gorchakov's plans. Even Bismarck was showing understandable restraint when it came to supporting Russia in the east. Whilst he might have gone a long way with France and Russia combined, he could not afford to antagonize the western powers for the sake of fair words and 'moral support' which was all the tsar and Gorchakov were likely to offer. Yet, in spite of this, it was Prussia alone which now stood between Russia and complete diplomatic isolation. There was a distinct possibility that the Crimean coalition might be renewed to oppose Russian plans at Constantinople. Gorchakov profoundly distrusted both Beust and Moustier, and watched with disquiet the steady *rapprochement* between the cabinets of Vienna and Paris. Would not the British government be tempted to side with France and Austria? However little Bismarck might be willing to promote the designs of Russia, he remained her only friend. Should he, as at times he seemed inclined, settle his differences with Austria and perhaps with France as well, Russia would stand alone.[4] Gorchakov justly observed at this time to an agent of the dispossessed king of Hanover, who criticized his support of Prussia: 'What else can we do? Nobody can rely on France or England; Austria is weak and not well-disposed towards us. If we break with Prussia, we

[1] Bismarck was fully aware of this fact which formed an important element in his calculations (Bismarck to Goltz, 15 February 1867, *APP*, vol. 8, pp. 392f.).

[2] It is, however, interesting to speculate what would have happened if Russia and Prussia had offered to support France in an attempt to acquire Belgium. This alone could have formed the basis of an understanding among the three powers, directed against England. This possibility explains persistent British anxiety about Prussia's attitude in the 'Belgian question'.

[3] The state of relations between the two countries was typified by a severe snub which, on passing through Warsaw, the tsar had administered to an Austrian Field Marshal come to deliver a personal letter from Francis-Joseph (Field-Marshal-Lieutenant Count St Quentin to First Adjutant-General Feldzeugmeister Count Crenneville, 19 June 1867, HHSAPARRR, 1867, x 54).

[4] Already in November 1866 in the course of a general analysis of Russian policy, Revertera had shrewdly remarked that the day Prussia settled her differences with Austria and France, Russia would stand alone (Revertera to Beust, 19/7 November 1866, *ibid.* x 53, no. 32 A-C).

stand alone.'[1] The failure of the visit to Paris made Russia—for good or ill—dependent upon Berlin.

For France also the failure of the negotiations—symbolized by the joint Russo-Prussian visit—was a decisive event. A conflict with Prussia was considered probable. The tsar's conduct had shown that in such a conflict he would not side with France. If, therefore, Napoleon wanted allies, he must look for them elsewhere. England, although seemingly well-disposed, was unlikely in her present mood, to afford France active support. Anxiety about the future of Belgium might even induce her to throw the weight of her diplomatic influence into the Prussian scales. One possible ally remained. Austria might be weak and Beust unreliable, but as long as her government dreamt either of regaining its influence in Germany or of strengthening its position in the Balkans, she seemed the 'natural ally' of France. This fact was understood at Vienna as well as in Paris. As the relations of the two countries with Russia and Prussia deteriorated, their *rapprochement* became more pronounced. Austrian weakness—now that the Magyar problem was set at rest—might be only temporary; within a few years, the Dual Monarchy might become a valued ally. The failure of the Franco-Russian 'negotiations' drove Napoleon into the arms of Austria. The breakdown of the Russo-French exchanges, therefore, accentuated the division of Europe into two hostile camps—Russia and Prussia on the one side, Austria and France on the other. This constellation was the joint product of the eastern and the western questions, of tensions in the Balkans and Franco-Prussian rivalry. England—with a foreign policy directed by the most realistic and at the same time the most self-willed Foreign Secretary since Palmerston—held, in a manner, the casting vote between the rival groups. All but eliminated since 1863 from the affairs of Europe, she was beginning to assume a new importance. It was becoming a matter of concern whether, influenced by anxiety about the future of Turkey, she would throw her diplomatic weight into the scales of Austria and France, or whether, from fear for the security of Belgium and a desire to prevent war, she would join Bismarck and Alexander II in their 'moral coalition' against Napoleon and Beust.

V

It was the astute Bismarck who made the first attempt to draw Stanley from his policy of cautious neutrality. Bismarck was conscious of the hostility felt for Prussia in Paris and Vienna. He had no illusions about the efficacy of Russian aid in the event of a future conflict. Further-

---

[1] 'Was können wir sonst machen? Auf Frankreich kann sich niemand verlassen, u. auch nicht auf England, u. Oesterreich ist schwach u. uns nicht hold. Verfeinden wir uns mit Preussen, so stehen wir allein da' (Memorandum by the Rev. H. Douglas, *Bemerkungen über die inneren Zustände Russlands und sein Verhältnis zu Oesterreich 1867* (n.d. but written from internal evidence after the tsar's visit to Paris), *ibid.* x 54, Russie 1867).

more, exclusive reliance on Russia would make Prussia dependent on St Petersburg. It would force Bismarck to pay Russia's price in the east and would, in the upshot, tend to promote an alliance he feared above all others, that between France and England. In spite, therefore, of the rebuff which he had received from Stanley early in the Luxemburg dispute, Bismarck resumed his advances.

Late in June, whilst on a visit to Queen Victoria, the Queen of Prussia received a letter from the king.

The Luxemburg question [he wrote] has only been settled by the greatest modera-tion shown on all sides, and by the timely intervention of England by proposing the Conference. It is not necessary to dwell on the danger which the most disastrous of all wars would have had for the whole of civilized Europe, but it is well to point to the necessity of doing all in one's power in order to protect the friendly relations [die friedlichen Beziehungen (sic)] from new dangers, and to establish them for the future. If England together with the 30 millions of the North German Confederation sincerely wishes for peace, and in proper time removes all causes which eventually might lead to war, that is to say if she keeps a watchful eye on France, and if she does not desert Germany whenever that country has a natural right to expect at least the moral support of England, then France neither under the present nor under any future form of Government will be able to provoke a conflict.[1]

The king's letter, a copy of which was handed to Queen Victoria, was by her duly passed on to the Foreign Secretary.[2]

Her Majesty thinks it an important letter. . . . The desire he [William I] manifests to be on the best of terms with England, and the belief he expresses that while England and North Germany are united, it will not be in the power of France to disturb the peace of the world, deserves, Her Majesty thinks, the most friendly consideration.[3]

Stanley's reply was cautious:

The King of Prussia [he wrote] may be assured that England can have no wish except the maintenance of peace, and that we shall continue to do what is in our power for that object: without leaning (in the event of future disputes) to either side, but endeavouring to hold fairly and impartially the balance between them.[4]

On 10 July, therefore, Queen Victoria wrote to the Queen of Prussia· Stanley, she explained, had said that England could have no wish but the maintenance of peace. She would continue to do what was in her power for effecting that object without making herself a party to any future conflict that might arise, endeavouring as she had done hitherto, to hold an even balance and to soothe animosities on either side.

More perhaps he could not say. In all her dealings with England, France has shown a scrupulous good faith and an earnest desire for our friendship, which must

---

[1] William I to Queen Augusta, 26 June 1867 abstract, translation (RA I 48/14 (QVL, loc. cit. pp. 437ff.)).
[2] Grey told the Queen that the letter 'certainly ought to be communicated, as was probably expected when it was written, to the Government' (Grey to the Queen, 3 July 1867, RA I 48/16). [3] Grey to Stanley, 5 July 1867, ibid. I 48/17, copy.
[4] Stanley to Grey, 5 July 1867, ibid. I 48/18.

prevent our doing or saying anything which would seem to imply distrust of her, or consequently excite her jealousy or suspicion.[1]

Stanley, to whom the public part of the Queen's letter was shown, declared that he agreed with every word she had written.[2] Bismarck's attempt to draw England from her neutral course had failed.

VI

Gorchakov, in the meantime, was persevering in his efforts to help the Cretan insurgents. His anxiety about the policy of Austria was increased in August by a meeting between Francis-Joseph and Napoleon at Salzburg.[3] Relations with France were far from cordial,[4] but it was in

[1] Queen Victoria to Queen Augusta, 10 July 1867, *ibid.* I 48/12, extract copy.

[2] Stanley to Grey, 11 July 1867, *ibid.* I 48/22. Some days later, Stanley amplified his views: 'It is perhaps a circumstance inseparable from the feeling of mutual distrust which still exists between France and Prussia, that the Prussian government should consider England as an ally against France, regarding the latter as the probable disturber of the peace of Europe: Lord Stanley however feels sure that your Majesty will think with him that—closely bound as England is to both these countries by ties of alliance and friendship—it is the duty of your Majesty's government to observe an attitude of strict and impartial neutrality between them in the event of any difference unfortunately arising. Such an attitude is that which gives the best guarantee for the preservation of peace: for it is only the reputation for impartiality that can give weight to the advice of a mediator' (Stanley to the Queen, 20 July 1867, *ibid.* B 23/92).

The Queen advised by Grey continued to urge the need for some defensive assurance to Prussia in face of the aggressive disposition of France (Grey to the Queen, 28 July 1867, *ibid.* I 48/27; Grey to Stanley, private, 8 and 18 August 1867, *ibid.* I 48/34 and 48/37). She tried to enlist the support of Disraeli (Grey to the Queen, 17 July 1867, *ibid.* 48/23 and Grey to Disraeli, private, 29 July and 5 August 1867, *ibid.* I 48/28 and I 48/32, copies). Disraeli assured the Queen that 'the general bias' of Stanley's mind was 'to lean towards Prussia'. He himself had always encouraged and enforced that tendency (Disraeli to Grey, confidential, 31 July 1867, *ibid.* I 48/30). Grey considered this answer 'not *quite* so satisfactory as it might have been. He hardly seems to see that it was the *principle* of a good understanding with Germany, a country with which we have no clashing interests...that it was sought to enforce, as the foundation on which English Foreign Policy should rest.' However, as he said he agreed in the Queen's views and hinted that he had already directed his attention to foreign affairs, it might be best to leave the matter as it was (Grey to the Queen, 1 August 1867, *ibid.* I 48/29). Stanley, however, refused to budge. 'If war does break out, we have only one course, that of rigidly impartial neutrality' (Stanley to Grey, private, 9 August 1867, *ibid.* I 48/36).

[3] The official occasion for the meeting was the wish of Napoleon to express to Francis-Joseph his condolences on the tragic death of his brother Maximilian in Mexico. In fact, an Austro-French alliance was discussed. It proved impossible to reach agreement because the aims of the two parties differed. Beust pressed by Magyar opinion was looking for an ally against Russia in the Balkans, whilst Napoleon sought support against Prussia.—The Russian government was alarmed at the possible effects of the meeting on Austrian policy in the Balkans. In particular, the subsequent despatch of an Austrian naval squadron into Turkish waters was regarded with distrust (Keyserling to Bismarck, 7 September 1867, *APP*, vol. 9, pp. 219f; and Revertera to Beust, 20/8 November 1867, HHSAPARRR, 1867, x 54, no. 40 A-E). The unveiling in Vienna of a monument to John Sobieski added fuel to the flames (Seiller to Beust, 25/13 September 1867, *ibid.* no. 36B).

[4] Russo-French relations had not improved since the tsar's return from Paris. At the trial of Berezowski, counsel for the defence had launched into a violent attack on Russian policy in Poland. The Procurator General, even whilst demanding the death penalty, had disclaimed any desire to justify Russian policy. Berezowski, in the end was sentenced, not

Gorchakov's interest to preserve at least a semblance of Russo-French co-operation.[1] Indeed, towards the end of the month, he was able at last to register some progress at Constantinople. The representatives of Russia and France in the Turkish capital were instructed to urge the suspension of hostilities in Crete and an international inquiry to determine the wishes of the Cretans.[2] Bismarck considered it safe to associate Prussia with this advice,[3] and the Italian government decided to follow suit. The concert at Constantinople was weakened however, both by the demonstrative absence of England and Austria and by the evident reluctance of the French and Prussian government to press the matter with vigour. The Porte rightly concluded that it could safely ignore the unwelcome advice of the powers. On 10 September, Ignatiev himself hastened to St Petersburg to inform Gorchakov of the fact.[4] Gorchakov wrote to Budberg:

Si, en dehors des assurances qui nous ont été données quant aux bonnes intentions du sultan, on extrait la substance pratique des décisions finales de la Porte, on y trouve: refus positif de la cession de Candie et de toute enquête européenne sur le terrain politique; proclamation d'une amnistie à terme avec expulsion des volontaires, autorisation aux indigènes de s'expatrier en aliénant leurs biens, maintien du blocus et des positions militaires, c'est à dire une invitation aux Crétois de se livrer, désarmés et privés de leurs auxiliaires volontaires, à la merci des Turcs, aucune garantie ni pour leur sécurité présente, ni pour leur avenir; sous ce dernier rapport, rien de précis, des assurances vagues; enfin, quant aux réformes organiques générales pour le reste des chrétiens, on les dit encore à l'étude.[5]

Was Gorchakov aware that the closest of parallels existed between the Turkish reply and the one he had himself given to the powers in 1863? At all events, the Turkish refusal confronted Russia with the prospect of diplomatic defeat:

Le Prince Gortchakow est très mécontent de la tournure que les affaires d'Orient et la question de Candie en particulier ont prise [sic] dans ces derniers tems [sic].... Cette campagne si brillamment commencée par le Gouvernement russe et sur la réussite de laquelle des millions avaient mis leur espoir, a donc complètement échoué. Nous sommes ici en pleine retraite et il est facile a comprendre qu'un tel échec doit vivement blesser l'amour propre d'un homme d'Etat tel que Mr le Chancelier.[6] Que va-t-on faire maintenant?[7]

to death, but to forced labour for life.—In a debate on foreign policy in the Chamber, Jules Favre attacked Russian policy in Poland. Two other speakers criticized the tsar's conduct during his stay in Paris. Russian public opinion seized on these incidents and expressed indignation at the French attitude (Charles-Roux, *op. cit.* pp. 444ff.).

[1] Keyserling to Bismarck, 7 September 1867, *APP, loc. cit.* pp. 219f.

[2] Moustier to Talleyrand, 17 August 1867, and Talleyrand to Moustier, 26 August 1867, Charles-Roux, *op. cit.* p. 450.

[3] For Prussia's recommendation to the Porte to suspend hostilities in Crete and consent to a European commision of inquiry see *APP, loc. cit.* p. 219 n. 5.

[4] Charles-Roux, *op. cit.* p. 451.

[5] Gorchakov to Budberg, 21 September 1867, *ibid.*

[6] Gorchakov had been appointed Chancellor of the Empire immediately after the tsar's return from the visit to Paris.

[7] Seiller to Beust, 25/13 September 1867, HHSAPARRR, 1867, X 54, no. 36 A-B.

In fact, Gorchakov's only hope now lay in a diplomatic retreat similar in some respects to that which he had himself helped to arrange for Napoleon in the spring. On 21 September, he addressed himself to Paris with a proposal, designed to help him out of his difficulties:

Nous sommes arrivés à la conviction que les efforts de persuasion morale de la diplomatie sont épuisés. Les puissances se trouvent dans l'alternative ou d'une acceptation de cette fin de non-recevoir, ou de l'emploi de mesures de coercition. La première est incompatible avec leur dignité; la seconde a été exclue de leurs prévisions. Il ne leur reste donc plus qu'à prendre une attitude qui dégage leur responsabilité. Les cabinets pourraient adresser à la Porte une déclaration conçue dans cet esprit. Si le gouvernment français adhère à cette proposition, les autres gouvernements pourraient être invités à s'y associer.[1]

Moustier replied that he would support any declaration acceptable to the other powers, including Austria; he would take no initiative in the matter.[2] Nothing now remained for Gorchakov except to draft his declaration, which was accepted in Paris with some alterations. The Prussian and Italian governments also found the declaration acceptable; those of Austria and England demurred. It even seemed that—in consequence of hesitations in Vienna—the French government would withdraw its support. However, in response to a pressing appeal from the tsar and Gorchakov, the French ambassador at Constantinople received instructions to read the document to the Porte. On being informed of the fact, Gorchakov heaved a sigh of relief. The tsar remarked to Talleyrand '"Je suis fort heureux de la bonne nouvelle venue de Paris. Depuis longtemps, rien ne m'a fait autant de plaisir."'[3] The face of the Russian government had indeed been saved but the Cretans had little cause for rejoicing: the diplomatic campaign undertaken by Russia on their behalf had ended in abject failure. It was difficult, Revertera observed, to understand Gorchakov's extreme satisfaction at the delivery of the joint note: 'C'était ...l'acte final d'une pièce montée à grands frais et dont le succès laissait fort à désirer.'[4]

VII

The failure of Russian diplomacy was soon underlined by a new development in the east. Napoleon, who had reaped nothing but defeat and humiliation from his policy of half-hearted co-operation with Russia, decided to subordinate his conduct to the needs of his newly found

---

[1] Gorchakov to Budberg, 21 September 1867, Charles-Roux, *op. cit.* p. 452.
[2] Moustier to Talleyrand, 2 October 1867, *ibid.* In a postscript to Talleyrand, Moustier added: 'En ce qui concerne l'affaire de Crète, il me semble...que la Russie est assez disposée à ne pas troubler la période d'apaisement où entre en ce moment l'affaire de Crète [*sic*]. Au fond, nous désirons la voir se calmer et, sans trop le laisser voir, dirigez-vous dans ce sens' (*ibid.*).
[3] *Ibid.* p. 454.
[4] Revertera to Beust, 20/8 November 1867, HHSAPARRR, 1867, x 54, no. 40C

friendship with Austria. French and Austrian diplomatic agents began to co-operate in every part of the Turkish empire and especially at Constantinople. Brassier de St Simon, the Prussian minister, reported to Bismarck:

Le nouveau revirement de la politique française dans la question de Candie et qui, au fond, n'est que la clôture d'une farce jouée comme entr'acte, s'est simultanément dessiné ici....Ce désaccord entre la France et la Russie se manifestant aujourd'hui au grand jour....La France, l'Angleterre et l'Autriche forment aujourd'hui un groupe compact, en face se trouve la Russie. Ce fait me paraît indubitable....[1]

Prince Charles of Romania told a Prussian agent that France had asked him not to disturb Austria in the event of an Austro-Prussian war in the coming spring.[2] Gorchakov, acquainted by Bismarck with these reports,[3] remarked that Ignatiev's correspondence confirmed the existence of an Austro-French understanding.[4] It might, however, be doubted whether the British government had yet formally associated itself with Russia's enemies.[5]

The *rapprochement* between France and Austria in the eastern question placed Russia in an embarrassing position. A war, whether in western Europe or the Balkans, was now widely expected for the coming spring. The Serbs were hastening their military preparations. Arms were being supplied to the Bosnians and Bulgarians.[6] Austria was taking military precautions on her southern border.[7] Excitement prevailed at Constantinople.[8] The Prussian representative in Belgrade reported that if present

[1] Brassier de St Simon to Bismarck, 18 November 1867, *APP, loc. cit.* p. 412.

[2] Keyserling to Bismarck, telegram, 19 November 1867, *ibid.* pp. 456f.

[3] Bismarck to Reuss, telegram, 4 December 1867, *ibid.* p. 479, and the same to the same, 11 December 1867, *ibid.* p. 523.

[4] The Russian government had suspected the existence of such an understanding at least since the end of November (Reuss to Bismarck, 29 November 1867, *ibid.* p. 461). Early in January 1868 during a conversation with Beust, Ignatiev finally convinced himself that a complete understanding on the eastern question existed between Austria and France (Werther to Bismarck, 8 January 1868, *ibid.* p. 600).

[5] Reuss to Bismarck, 18 December 1867, *ibid.* pp. 500ff.

[6] Meetings were being held each morning at the residence of the Serbian Minister of War attended, besides Serbian staff officers, also by a Russian officer, who had been in Belgrade for some months. A Greek major had had several conversations with the Prince of Serbia. Seventy-two drawn guns had reached Belgrade. It was said that 9000 needle guns had also arrived. Military supplies on a considerable scale had been ordered from a Viennese firm (Thile to the Prussian Missions at St Petersburg and Vienna, 1 October 1867, *ibid.* pp. 260f.). On 5 November the Serbian government applied to Prussia for the sale of 50–60,000 rifles of French or British manufacture. The Bosnians had already been supplied with 100,000 rifles; it was now the turn of the Bulgarians to be armed (Rosen to Bismarck, telegram, 5 November 1867, *ibid.* p. 583 n. 2).

[7] Brandt to Bismarck, 6 December 1867, *ibid.* p. 523 n. 1.

[8] Alarm was felt both at Russian armaments and at the ferment in Serbia, Greece and Montenegro. It was feared that a Franco-Prussian war in the spring would be the signal for a general rising of the Christians. Friendly powers would be preoccupied and unable to assist Turkey. The Porte, therefore, was quietly mobilizing its forces and concentrating troops in Roumelia (Brassier de St Simon to Bismarck, 11 and 19 December 1867, *ibid.* p. 523).

developments continued, the southern Slav question would, within a few months, become the most burning in Europe.[1] Early in February, the tsar discussed the situation with Reuss. Beust, he observed, who had at first appeared to pursue in the east a policy less hostile to Russia, now seemed to have returned to the traditions of the Austrian Foreign Office.[2] Russia was trying in vain to dispel the Austrian belief that she was preparing a rising in the Balkans. This was not, in fact, the case.[3] On the contrary, his

[1] 'Wenn in den Donau- und Saveländer die Dinge so fortgehen, wie sich jetzt anlässt, so ist zu vermuten, dass binnen weniger Monate die südslawische Frage die brennendste unseres Erdteils ist' (Memorandum by Consul-General Rosen, 23 November 1867, *ibid.* pp. 485 ff.).

[2] During the summer of 1867 Beust had explained to the Hessian Minister Dalwigk that he intended in co-operation with France to make war on Prussia and possibly Russia. The war should develop out of the eastern—or Polish—not the German question (W. Vogel, *Die Tagebücher des Freiherrn Reinhard von Dalwigk zu Lichtenfels als Geschichtsquelle, Historische Studien*, Heft 234 (Berlin 1933), p. 61).

[3] The Russian government believing that a Franco-Prussian war in the spring would be the signal for a rising in the Balkans had at first favoured the Serbian preparations. Late in November, it demanded in Bucharest the free passage of arms destined for the Serbs. (Keyserling to Bismarck, telegram, 29 November 1867, *APP, loc. cit.* pp. 456 f.). Supplies were being collected in southern Russia (Keyserling to Bismarck, 1 October 1867, *ibid.* p. 264). A high official in the Russian Ministry of Finance early in January expressed to the British *chargé d'affaires* the opinion

'...that the Russian government are making ready for certain eventualities in Bulgaria and Servia and that with that view troops have been moved towards the Galician frontier. He likewise connects the purchase of specie by the State Bank, at a premium, with the preparatory or precautionary measures which are being taken in this country, in view of further complications in the East' (Michell to Stuart, 6 January 1868, no. 13 secret, enclosed in Stuart to Stanley, 14 January 1868, FO 65/747, no. 10).

When during the course of January it became clear that an immediate clash in the west was unlikely, the Russian government decided to discourage the ardour of the Balkan Christians:

'Die französischen, österreichischen, englischen und türkischen Nachrichten bestätigen, dass Russland seit dem Monat Januar d. J. von dem Moment an, wo es sich überzeugte, dass es für jetzt nicht zum Kriege zwischen Preussen und Frankreich kommen werde, abgewiegelt und die Parole ausgegeben hat, sich vorläufig ruhig zu verhalten' (Goltz to Bismarck, no. 90 secret, 27 March 1868, *APP, loc. cit.* p. 777 n.1). Cf. also Stuart to Stanley, 15 January 1868, FO 65/747, no. 13 and Loftus to Stanley, no. 121, 21 February 1868, RA H 2/29, précis.

In fact, Russia was not yet ready for a radical 'solution' of the eastern question. A British agent reported:

'I have been confidentially informed by an official of high rank in the Ministry of Finance whose statements I have always found accurate, that in June or July last, he read a Memorandum drawn up by the Minister of War in answer to His Imperial Majesty's inquiry by what date and at what cost the Russian army could be placed on a war-footing.

'General Miliutin undertook to concentrate 600,000 men in the Kingdom of Poland and the old Polish Provinces and to place a Corps d'Armée on the Danube by the month of March next at an expense of twenty two million Roubles (about three million sterling).

'The Memorandum having been referred to the Minister of Finance the latter declared his inability to meet such an additional expenditure and the project of placing the army on a war-footing was accordingly abandoned' (Michell to Stuart, 6 January 1868, copy, in Stuart to Stanley, 15 January 1868, FO 65/747, no. 13, secret).

Stuart, in transmitting the information, added:

'Mr Michell tells me that the above information has since been confirmed to him in its most important points by a person holding a high confidential position, who, however, described the sum mentioned as representing the cost of collecting a sufficient supply of *matériel* and provisions, together with the means of transport required for placing the army

government was warning the Christians against foolhardy attempts. The king of Greece had been told not to expect Russian aid in a war to acquire neighbouring provinces. Serbia no longer showed much inclination to seek full independence by force of arms. Only a rising against oppression in the other Christian provinces remained a danger. Should Austria use such risings in Bosnia and Herzegovina as a pretext for intervention, Russia would do the same.[1]—Nor was the possibility of an Austrian occupation of Bosnia and Herzegovina the only source of Russian anxiety. Beust openly favoured the Poles and secret reports from Vienna even suggested that the coronation of Francis-Joseph as king of Poland was under consideration.[2] The evident *rapprochement* between Vienna and Paris lent colour to Russian suspicions. In these circumstances it was with alarm that the tsar and Gorchakov discovered symptoms of a Prussian desire to seek a *rapprochement* with Austria.

On 10 January 1868 the *Kreuzzeitung*, influential organ of the Prussian conservatives, published an article advocating an Austro-Prussian understanding. The article criticized the Pan-Slav agitation directed against Austria, and spoke of her 'German Mission' in the east.[3] The publication attracted the attention of Gorchakov, who spoke to Reuss 'with some ill-humour'.[4] He had, he declared, been somewhat 'peeved' ('verschnupft') at the appearance of such views in a paper normally friendly to Russia. The article would provoke replies in the Russian press. It was in any case not easy to keep within bounds Katkov's anti-Prussian *Moscow News*; the present article would add fuel to the flames. He did not doubt Prussia's

on a war-footing. Both Mr Michell's informants connect the recent purchase of specie at a premium by the State Bank with the desire of the Imperial Government to be prepared for any contingencies in the East...' (Stuart to Stanley, 15 January 1868, FO 65/747, no. 13, secret).

The Russians now found it more difficult to damp the ardour of the Christians than it had been to give it modest encouragement. Reports continued to circulate that irregular bands of Serbian militiamen would invade Bosnia in March. They would try to create 'Cretan' conditions by guerilla warfare against the Turks. It was hoped to drive the Serbian government into action and to start risings in Bulgaria and among the Greeks under Turkish rule (Promemoria Keudells, 16 January 1868, *APP, loc. cit.* p. 614).

The Turkish government, to meet the threat, continued its military preparations. It appeared ready to summon its Muslim subjects to a war of extermination against the Christians (Brassier de St Simon to Bismarck, 23 January 1868, *ibid.* p. 631).

[1] Reuss to Bismarck, no. 19, most confidential, 5 February 1868, *ibid.* pp. 670ff. In a subsequent conversation, the tsar expressed a fear that in the event of disturbances in Bosnia and Herzegovina the Porte might invite Austria to occupy the two provinces (the same to the same, no. 57, most confidential, 27 March 1868, *ibid.* pp. 816ff.).

[2] Schweinitz to William I, sent on 19 March 1868, *ibid.* p. 760 n. 6.

[3] 'Auch wir wünschen Frieden mit Oesterreich, und zwar nicht einen bloss äusserlichen Frieden, wie wir ihn z.B. auch mit Frankreich wünschen, sondern positive und inhaltsvolle Freundschaft, weil eine solche Freunschaft die Garantie für den Frieden Deutschlands in sich trägt, aber auch zugleich für den Frieden Mitteleuropas. Die panslawistische Propaganda, wir können vom preussischen Standpunkt aus wahrlich nicht den Sieg derselben wünschen. Und was endlich den Orient anlangt, so können wir nur von ganzem Herzen wünschen dass Oesterreich dort seinen deutschen Beruf im vollsten Masse erfüllen möge' (*ibid.* pp. 616f. n. 1.) [4] Reuss to Bismarck, 11 January 1868 (*ibid.* p. 617 n. 2).

loyalty in the eastern question, but regretted the prospect of press polemics likely to follow the article in the *Kreuzzeitung*.[1] On 23 January, Schweinitz reported speculation among journalists and amateur politicians about an alleged change in Prussia's eastern policy.[2] Reuss was asked confidentially whether Prussian policy was changing.[3] A high official at the Foreign Ministry noted that French and Austrian papers had altered their tone about Prussia.... This coincided with the withdrawal of Prussia and Italy from the efforts to evacuate Cretan families. The Russian cabinet was beginning to doubt the sincerity of Prussian support in the east.[4] Had Bismarck really abandoned a plan attributed to him of placing Austria at the head of a Danubian Confederation to compensate her for losses in Italy and Germany?[5] Stremouchov inquired whether it was true that Prussia was turning towards Austria in the east and proposed a bargain by which Prussian support in the Balkans would be paid for by Russian assistance in the west.[6] Reuss avoided detailed discussion.[7] William I, in a marginal note, declared that his government could not take a prominent part in the eastern question.[8] Bismarck promptly instructed Reuss to contradict categorically all rumours about a Prussian *rapprochement* with Austria and France.[9]

On the night of 5–6 February, the tsar during a railway journey engaged Reuss in a long and confidential conversation. He spoke more fully than

[1] The same to the same, 17 January 1868, *ibid.* pp. 616ff.

[2] Schweinitz to William I, 23 January 1868, *ibid.* p. 631.

[3] '...Von verschiedener Seite bin ich sowohl wie andere mir näherstehende Personen gefragt worden, ob es wahr sei, dass Preussen sich mit Frankreich und Oesterreich zu verständigen anfinge, nicht allein über die Behandlung der römischen, sondern auch der orientalischen Angelegenheiten....'

[4] In any case, the support Russia was likely to obtain from Prussia was strictly limited. When Brassier informed Bismarck that the French, British and Austrian representatives at Constantinople were co-operating against Ignatiev, and asked for instructions about his own conduct, Bismarck wrote in the margin of the report: 'abstenez-vous!' (Brassier de St Simon to Bismarck, 18 November 1867, *ibid.* p. 412).

[5] Reuss to Bismarck, no. 12 confidential, 23 January 1868, *ibid.* pp. 631ff.

[6] '...und kam zuletzt darauf hinaus, dass es für beide Regierungen das beste wäre, ein Geschäft abzuschliessen. Wir sollten der Kaiserlichen Regierung offen sagen, dies oder das können wir Euch zur Unterstützung Euerer orientalischen Politik leisten, dafür würde sich Russland dann uns gegenüber wiederum verpflichten, uns in gewissen Eventualitäten zur Seite zu Stehen...' (*ibid.*).

[7] '...Ich bin weit entfernt davon zu glauben, dass man eine aktive Politik im Orient vorhat, die Besorgnis aber, seit der Trennung von Frankreich auf diesem Gebiete völlig isoliert zu sein, ist so gross, dass das Bedürfnis nach einer Stütze täglich mächtiger wird. Daher dies Drängen nach bindender Annäherung an Preussen und dieses Zurschautragen eines wirklich empfundenen oder nur fingierten Schmollens über unser angebliches Einverständnis mit Frankreich und Oesterreich' (*ibid.*).

[8] 'In der orient(alischen) Frage bleibt Preussens Politik in 2 Linie stehen; also kann es keine bindende Stellung nach keiner Seite einnehmen. Russland sollte aber sich erinnern, dass der *kranke Mann* 1853–56 *Aerzte* gefunden hat, deren Kur Russland einen nicht zu vergessenden Aderlass verursachte, woran est gut wäre, dasselbe zu *erinnern*, um es von Uebereilungen wie 1853 zu *warnen*! W(ilhelm)' (the same to the same, 27 January 1868, *ibid.* pp. 638ff.).

[9] Bismarck to Reuss, telegram, 4 February 1868, *ibid.* p. 657.

he had done for some time about the state of Russo-Prussian relations and expressed his pleasure at the assurances which Oubril had received from Bismarck and William I.[1] He then dwelt on his distrust of Beust and his fear that Austria might profit from disturbances to occupy Bosnia and Herzegovina. This Russia would not tolerate. The tsar continued:

> Let us hope this does not happen; let us hope also that France will not attack Germany. If, however, contrary to expectation, these events should occur, the King can rely on me to paralyse Austria just as I count on his aid. An army placed on the Austrian frontier would secure this object in the one case as in the other.[2]

These eventualities were unlikely to occur, but it was necessary to be prepared.[3] His confidence in William I was unshakable: '"Tell the King that he can count on me just as I count on him."'[4] In a personal letter to his uncle, moreover, the tsar some days later recalled historic memories of the Russo-Prussian alliance: 'Il est doublement à désirer à voir se perpétuer entre nous l'entente sur laquelle elle reposait. Elle a ses racines dans les gloires du passé, sa sanction dans les intérêts présents et à venir des deux pays, elle peut se passer d'actes écrits.'[5] Bismarck's reaction to the Russian approach was cautious. He told Reuss that, as far as Prussia needed friends—in view of the complete British withdrawal from Europe—an understanding with Russia was the only acceptable one.[6] William I in his turn replied to his nephew's effusion in a carefully worded letter:

> ...espérons que de notre temps aussi nos efforts réunis en se basant sur l'intérêt commun que nous avons à la consolidation de la paix, parviendront à en assurer le maintien. Nos rapports personnels et les sentiments d'amitié qui nous unissent, ne peuvent que nous faciliter cette tâche....[7]

In neither reply was there a mention of the proposed understanding against Austria.

The tsar decided to try again.[8] On 4 March he told Reuss that Oubril's

---

[1] Reuss to William I, 5 February 1868, *ibid.* pp. 669f.
[2] 'Hoffen wir, dass dies nicht eintreten wird, hoffen wir auch, dass Frankreich Deutschland nicht angreifen wird. Sollten aber wider Erwarten beide Fälle eintreten, so kann der König ebenso auf mich rechnen, um Oesterreich lahmzulegen, wie ich seine Hilfe in Anspruch nehmen würde. Die Aufstellung einer Armee an der österreichischen Grenze würde im einen wie im anderen Falle genügen, um diesen Zweck zu erreichen.'
[3] The same to the same, no. 19, most confidential, 5 February 1868, *ibid.* pp. 670ff.
[4] The same to the same, 5 February 1868, *ibid.* pp. 669f.
[5] Alexander II to William I, 2/14 February 1868, *ibid.* pp. 701f.
[6] 'Bei der vollständigen Enthaltung, die England in neuerer Zeit in der europäischen Politik beobachtet, bleibt uns daher soweit wir einer Anlehnung bedürfen, die an Russland die einzig annehmbare' (Bismarck to Reuss, no. 51, most confidential, 16 February 1868, *ibid.* pp. 706f.).
[7] William I to Alexander II, end of February 1868, *ibid.* pp. 744f.
[8] At the end of February news reached St Petersburg that Prince Napoleon, the stormy petrel of the Second Empire, was about to visit Berlin. Bismarck—probably truthfully—disclaimed all knowledge of his object (Bismarck to Reuss, telegram, 28 February 1868,

reports spoke of important conversations with Bismarck and Moltke about a Russo-Prussian *entente*. He was glad to find that there was agreement between the Prussian views and his own. He now repeated that he was ready to keep Austria in check should Prussia be involved in war with either her or France. He would do this on the understanding that should Russia become involved in war with Austria, Prussia would act in a similar manner. In the first case he would concentrate an army of 100,000 on the Austrian frontier;[1] he expected similar Prussian action in the second.[2] The tsar expressed the hope that the contingency he had envisaged would not arise. Napoleon at present desired war as little as Prussia but the state of affairs in Paris was unsettled. His own government had no desire to provoke an outbreak in the east, even though he was convinced that it must come sooner or later. He would prefer to delay for some years the reopening of the eastern question but the policy of Austria was so unpredictable that she might at any moment set the match to the powder-keg.[3] Three days later in conversation with Schweinitz, Alexander repeated his offer to keep Austria in check with an army of 100,000 in the event of a Franco-German war. He asked in return that if Austrian troops were to enter Bosnia, Prussia should concentrate a similar force on the Austrian border. He expressed deep distrust of Beust, but agreed with Schweinitz that Austria would hardly move without the support of France. He added that in Vienna the coronation of Francis-Joseph in Warsaw had already been spoken of, and expressed the hope that in the Polish question he could rely on the absolute solidarity of Prussia.[4]

Bismarck in reply instructed Reuss to avoid discussions of detail which might involve Prussia in precise obligations. He should, at the same time, be bountiful in assurances of friendship and emphasize the similarity of Russian and Prussian interests.[5] Privately, Bismarck recommended an

---

ibid. p. 749). The tsar and Gorchakov, on hearing of the visit, expressed their confidence in the sagacity of William I (Reuss to Bismarck, telegram, 29 February 1868, *ibid.*). The visit, none the less, could not but increase their desire for a firm understanding with Prussia.

[1] Reuss considered that the figure of 100,000 repeated by the tsar in a second conversation, proved that this was a carefully considered proposal. Such a force could be moved at very short notice. A higher figure would have been a delusion. The figure chosen proved that the Russian government knew what it could do and was honest in its intentions. The tsar seemed to wish to know whether this figure was acceptable to the Prussian government (Reuss to William I, no. 38 most confidential, 4 March 1868, *ibid.* pp. 759f.).

[2] 'Er wiederhole mir...dass er...bereit sei, Oesterreich im Schach zu halten, wenn Preussen in einen Krieg mit Frankreich oder Oesterreich verwickelt werden sollte, vorausgesetzt, dass Eure Majestät ebenso ihm hilfreiche Hand leisten würden, wenn Russland mit Oesterreich kriegerische Verwicklungen haben sollte. Er wolle für ersteren Fall sich verpflichten, eine Armee von 100,000 Mann an der russisch-oesterreichischen Grenze aufzustellen und erwarte das gleiche von Preussen.' [3] *Ibid.*

[4] Alexander II expressed the hope that he could assume 'dass die Solidarität Preussens und Russlands in Bezug auf Polen unerschütterlich sei, wie ein Naturgesetz, und dass, wenn Oesterreich wirklich dort vorginge, Ew. Königliche Majestät Armee gewiss neben der russischen stehen werde' (Schweinitz to the King, sent on 19 March 1868, *ibid.* p. 760, no. 6).

[5] Bismarck to Reuss, no. 100, confidential, 12 March 1868, *ibid.* pp. 778f.

expectant attitude, particularly as Gorchakov himself had not yet raised the matter.[1]

On 20 March, however, Oubril read to Bismarck extracts from a despatch in which Budberg expressed the view that, as soon as Austria was ready, France would attack Prussia. In that event, Oubril now officially offered the concentration of 100,000 Russians on the frontiers of Austria to prevent her from joining France. It was assumed that if Russia was threatened by Austria, Prussia would take similar action.[2] Bismarck replied that the king of Prussia accepted the principle of mutual assistance.[3] However, Prussia felt confident that she could deal with France alone as long as Russia protected her rear. He assumed that, in a similar manner, Russia could deal with Austria alone as long as Prussia prevented the intervention of France. As soon, however, as either country was attacked by two powers, the solidarity of their interests would oblige the other to come to its assistance.[4] The difference between his own proposal and that of Gorchakov was unlikely to be of practical importance: however reckless Beust might be, he would not begin a war without the previous promise of active French support.[5] Oubril had given formal assurances that the Russian government had no intention of provoking a

[1] The same to the same, private, 14 March 1868, *ibid.* pp. 780f.

[2] '...bot nun Herr von Oubril...die Aufstellung von 100,000 Mann an der österreichischen Grenze an, um Oesterreich im Schach und von einer aktiven Teilnahme am Kampfe abzuhalten, unter der bestimmten Voraussetzung, dass, wenn Russland bedroht wäre, preussischerseits ein Gleiches geschehen werde.'

[3] '...es sind die eigenen Worte Seiner Majestät "dass Preussen ebensowenig einem gefährlichen Angriff gegen Russland wie Russland einer Vergewaltigung Preussens neutral zusehen könne und dass es eine unkluge und kurzsichtige Politik wäre, eine sukzessive Kriegführung gegen die einzelnen Mächte ruhig hinzunehmen. Preussen dürfe im Interesse seiner eigenen Sicherheit Russland nicht im Stiche lassen und Russland könne nicht zugeben, dass Preussen in einem Kampfe gegen die Uebermacht einer Koalition unterliegend, in eine Abhängigkeit geriete, welche die französische Grenze gegen Russland gleichsam bis nach Schlesien vorrückte".'

[4] 'Ich habe Herrn von Oubril...gesagt, dass wir einem Kriege gegen Frankreich *allein* gewachsen zu sein glaubten und kein Bedürfnis hätten, den Krieg zu verallgemeinern, wenn Russland uns nur den Rücken gegen Oesterreich decke. Dasselbe setzten wir von Russland voraus, wenn es in einen Krieg mit Oesterreich verwickelt würde und wir ihm die Sicherheit gegen eine Unterstützung dieser Macht durch Frankreich gewährten. Sobald aber einer von uns beiden...von einer Koalition von zwei Mächten angegriffen werde, nötige die Solidarität der Interessen jede von beiden Mächten zur Unterstützung der andern.'

In a passage omitted from the final despatch, Bismarck had summed up his proposals: 'Ich kann hiernach die Bedeutung unserer gemeinsamen Politik und der gegenwärtig beabsichtigten Verabredungen kurz dahin zusammenfassen: im Falle eines österreichisch-russischen Krieges decken wir Russland gegen Frankreich; im Falle eines französisch-deutschen Krieges deckt Russland uns gegen Oesterreich; im Falle eines Krieges von Frankreich und Oesterreich gegen eine der beiden Mächte ist letztere der Unterstützung der andern gewiss.'

[5] 'Ich glaube aber allerdings nicht, dass der Unterschied zwischen diesen Auffassungen von praktischer Bedeutung werden wird. Denn ich halte es nicht fur möglich, dass Oesterreich allein Krieg mit Russland wagen sollte. Wie kühn auch die Politik des Freiherrn von Beust sein möge, so wird er doch Anstand nehmen, Oesterreich in einen Krieg mit Russland zu verwickeln ohne ein Bündnis mit Frankreich, welches ihm dessen aktive Teilnahme zusichert.'

conflict. Similarly, nothing was further from the mind of King William; the solidarity of the two countries, therefore, would be essentially defensive.[1] In a private letter to Reuss, Bismarck added that the king would be reluctant to sign a formal document; his views on the matter, however, were clear and unambiguous. It would be foolish of Russia and Prussia in the present situation to trust to the lies of Vienna and Paris instead of supporting each other.[2]

Both the tsar and Gorchakov expressed to Reuss their satisfaction at Bismarck's reply.[3] The fact that they had failed to secure a written engagement did not cause them anxiety. Gorchakov declared that his master placed absolute confidence in the king of Prussia's word.[4] More serious from the Russian point of view was the fact that the Prussian government had refused to promise military support if Austrian troops entered Bosnia and Herzegovina.[5] Gorchakov consoled himself with the reflection that Beust was unlikely to act without French assistance. He did not, however, conceal his disappointment[6] and Reuss reported that it was the danger of

[1] The original draft declared it to be a mutual assumption ('gegenseitige Voraussetzung') of the agreement 'dass die gegenwärtigen Verabredungen einen rein defensiven Charakter tragen und jedes aggressive Vorgehen ausschliessen'. He altered this to 'dass die Solidarität der Politik beider Mächte einen wesentlich defensiven Charakter tragen wird', which was considerably weaker (Bismarck to Reuss, no. 114, secret, 22 March 1868, *ibid.* pp. 799ff.).

[2] The same to the same, private, 23 March 1868, *ibid.* pp. 806f.

[3] Reuss to Bismarck, nos. 56 confidential, and 57 most confidential, 25 and 27 March 1868, *ibid.* pp. 814f. and 816ff.

[4] 'Er setzte hinzu, es bedürfe *keiner schriftlichen Abmachung*: es sei ihm nicht darum zu tun, die Archive des Auswärtigen Amtes um einen neuen Vertrag zu vermehren; solche Verträge könnten nicht leicht geheim bleiben, und das Bekanntwerden ihrer Existenz würde ohne Zweifel die Absicht der preussisch-russischen Allianz entstellen. Der Kaiser setzt ein solches Vertrauen in Seine Majestät und in Eure Exzellenz, dass er einen unterzeichneten Vertrag für überflüssig halte, und dass ihm der jetzige Gedankenaustausch vollkommen genügend erscheine....'

[5] It was this eventuality which the Russian government feared above all others. Gorchakov had read to Reuss a report from Stackelberg in Vienna about an interview with Beust, showing that the Austrian government refused to accept the principle of non-intervention in Turkish affairs. Reuss reported Gorchakov's language:
'Daraus gehe hervor, dass sich Oesterreich eine Tür offen halten wolle, um seinen alten Plan auf die Herzegowina und Bosnien nicht aufzugeben, und gegebenenfalls durch die türkische Regierung gerufen, dort einrücken zu können. Russland könne dies nicht zugeben, und wenn Eure Exzellenz an Herrn von Oubril gesagt hätten, es sei die Sache des russischen Kabinetts, eine solche Eventualität dadurch zu verhindern, dass man in Wien diesen Fall entschieden als einen Kriegsfall bezeichne, so sei diesem Rat bereits entsprochen worden....'

[6] Gorchakov considered '...dass das Wiener Kabinett sich nicht in einen Krieg mit Russland verwickeln werde, ohne eines aktiven Bündnisses mit Frankreich gewiss zu sein. Aus diesem Grunde sei es eigentlich auch nicht nötig, von Preussen noch bestimmtere Versicherungen über den angegebenen Fall zu erhalten. Eins würde dem andern selbstverständlich folgen, und der Fall eines Einrückens Oesterreichs in die Türkei könne sich nicht isolirt zeigen. Deshalb bäte er mich, wenn er mir auch gesagt hätte: "es wäre ihm lieb gewesen" entschiedenere Erklärungen seitens der Königlichen Regierung über diesen Fall zu erhalten, Eurer Exzellenz zu schreiben, dass er hierauf kein so grosses Gewicht lege, und dass sein Vertrauen gewiss deswegen nicht geringer sei. Er habe an Oubril geschrieben— "de se montrer relativement à ce point ni mécontent ni impatient."—man könne die Ereignisse ruhig abwarten und dann zusehen, was am besten zu machen sein würde.'

Austrian intervention in the two provinces which, above all else, occupied the mind of the tsar.[1] In a conversation with Schweinitz on 10 April, Alexander finally summed up the results of the negotiation. He formally repeated his assurance that if Prussia were threatened by two powers, Russia would concentrate an army.[2] Schweinitz replied that in analogous circumstances Prussia would do the same.[3] Gorchakov, in his turn, confirmed the tsar's declaration.[4]

Russia's growing dependence on Prussian support in the east had involved as a necessary corollary her acceptance of German unity. In this respect, the Russian government had completely changed its attitude since the days when it had protested against Prussian annexations in northern Germany. Sympathy for the lesser German dynasties was not indeed extinct, but it was now subordinated to wholehearted acceptance of the principle of German unification. The Russian government merely hoped that this would be brought about by peaceful means through the slow operation of historical necessity. In June 1867, when criticizing French opposition to an extension of the *Zollverein*, Gorchakov had explained his views:

La réunion douanière consentie pouvait offrir un dérivatif à la pression que le parti libéral surtout exerce sur les gouvernements. Elle établissait un lien sans amener de fusion au moins immédiate. Nous ne disconvenons pas que ce résultat peut être amené forcément plus tard mais, dans les circonstances données, il était essentiel de gagner du temps et de l'utiliser pour calmer les défiances réciproques.[5]

In July the tsar, in conversation with his sister Olga, had criticized the anti-Prussian attitude adopted by the government of Württemberg. He had indicated to the Russian minister in Stuttgart that if he wished to keep his post he must renounce his anti-Prussian views.[6] In October, Gorchakov had told a German diplomat that the tsar favoured the unification of Germany. He wished to see the dynasties preserved, but would refrain from even a semblance of intervention in Germany's

---

[1] Reuss told Bismarck that he had endeavoured to reassure Gorchakov about Austrian designs in Bosnia and Herzegovina. 'Ich mache aber darauf aufmerksam...dass diese Eventualität hier sehr präokkupiert und wahrscheinlich noch oft wieder ans Tageslicht kommen wird. Dass der Kaiser persönlich einen grossen Wert auf diesen Punkt legt, hat Oberst von Schweinitz seiner Zeit an Seine Majestät den König berichtet' (Reuss to Bismarck, no. 57, most confidential, 27 March 1868, *ibid.* pp. 816ff.).

[2] 'Bestimmter als sonst drückte sich der Kaiser diesmal aus, dass er eine Armee aufstellen wolle, wenn Preussen von zwei Mächten bedroht würde' (Schweinitz to William I, 10 April 1868, *ibid.* p. 844).

[3] *Ibid.*

[4] The same to the same, 14 April 1868, *ibid.* n. 1.

[5] Gorchakov to Budberg, private, 25 June 1867, *ibid.* pp. 144ff.

[6] '...und ist dem dortigen russischen Gesandten in sehr entschiedener Weise eröffnet worden, dass er sich in seinen anti-preussischen Agitationen durchaus nicht in Uebereinstimmung mit seiner Regierung befände und sich in Zukunft, falls er seinen Posten behalten wolle, einer anderen Haltung zu befleissigen hätte' (Reuss to Bismarck, no. 111 confidential, *ibid.* pp. 106f.). The tsar's action was the result of a complaint made to him in May by Reuss on behalf of Bismarck (*ibid.*).

internal affairs.[1] This resolve, however, had not prevented him from making further confidential representations in Stuttgart after Bismarck had complained of the anti-Prussian attitude adopted by the government and press of Württemberg.[2] Bismarck expressed his appreciation and claimed to note a change of tone at Stuttgart;[3] Gorchakov congratulated himself on the fact that Russian intervention had produced the desired result.[4] The Russian government—in return for services in the Balkans[5]— was helping Bismarck to neutralize the principal centre of anti-Prussian resistance in southern Germany.

VIII

The Russo-Prussian agreement of March 1868 completed the realignment of the powers following the war of 1866. Manteuffel's mission to St Petersburg, the tsar's visit to Paris, the meeting between Napoleon and Francis-Joseph at Salzburg and finally the Russo-Prussian *entente* had been the principal landmarks in the creation of a constellation opposing Austria and France to Russia and Prussia. The trends first revealed by the Austro-French agreement on the future of Venetia and the Manteuffel mission had culminated in recognized diplomatic alignments. The groupings which had been formed could become the basis of military and diplomatic calculation. The period of international anarchy which had followed the Polish insurrection was at an end.

The new alignments which had emerged from the crisis of 1866–7 seemed likely to determine the course of future events.[6] Should a conflict

[1] '"Mein Kaiser", sagte er, "ist der Einigung Gesamtdeutschlands nicht nur nicht entgegen, sondern *er wünscht dieselbe*, wünscht jedoch nicht minder lebhaft die Erhaltung der Dynastien. Uebrigens hält der Kaiser an dem Satze, auch den entferntesten Schein einer Einmischung in die inneren Angelegenheiten Deutschlands zu vermeiden, unbedingt fest"' (Tauffkirchen to Hohenlohe, 5/17 October 1867, *ibid.* p. 298).

[2] Bismarck to Reuss, no. 18, confidential, 18 January 1868, *ibid.* pp. 619f. and Reuss to Bismarck, 7 and 15 February 1868, *ibid.* pp. 620ff. n. 6.

[3] Bismarck to Reuss, most confidential, 15 February 1868, *ibid.* p. 622 no. 6.

[4] Reuss to Bismarck, 10 March 1868, *ibid.*

[5] The Prussian government had indicated its willingness to meet the Serbian request for the sale of arms (Bismark to Reuss, telegram, 3 January 1868, *ibid.* p. 583; Reuss to Bismarck, telegram, 4 January 1868, *ibid.* n. 3; Thile to Reuss, 19 January 1868, *ibid.* pp. 624f.; Reuss to Bismarck, 24 January 1868, *ibid.* p. 625 n. 3).

[6] It is an interesting fact that from the crisis of 1866–7 there emerged the principal issues which were to trouble the repose of Europe for the following fifty years. The Prussian victory over Austria, the Luxemburg dispute and the failure of Napoleon to find 'compensations' originated the modern phase of that Franco-German rivalry which would lead to Sedan and the Somme, and the treaties of Frankfurt and Versailles. Similarly the events of 1866 and 1867 mark the emergence of the 'eastern question' in its 'modern' form. Beust's eastern policy underlined Austria's newborn interest in the Balkans and accentuated Austro-Russian rivalry. At the same time, the recognition of Charles of Hohenzollern as Prince of Romania shifted that rivalry from the Principalities to the western Balkans. It is no accident that at this moment the fatal names of Bosnia and Herzegovina began to occupy the chanceries. Except for Anglo-German naval rivalry, therefore, the elements of the great war of 1914 go back to the crisis of 1866–7. The events of 1914 were the direct consequence of the war of 1866.

break out in the east, Russia could not count on Prussian support as long as she was opposed to Austria alone; on the other hand, the tsar was freed from the nightmare of having to face single-handed the revived Crimean coalition. Should the anticipated conflict begin in the west, Bismarck seemed assured of a free hand against France; should Austria attempt to intervene, the Russians would keep her in check.[1] Even though the Russo-Prussian understanding remained a close secret, its effects were widely anticipated. As early as January 1868, Revertera had reported:

> Un de mes collègues, qui a beaucoup de sagacité, m'a communiqué le résultat des observations auxquelles il s'était livré sur les intentions du Gouvernement russe. 'En cas de guerre entre la France et la Prusse', me dit-il, 'l'attitude de la Russie dépendra probablement de celle de l'Autriche. Si l'Autriche bouge, elle se mettra aussi en campagne; mais si l'Autriche s'abstient, la Russie s'abstiendra également.'

Yet whilst the future was slowly becoming predictable, there still remained one element of uncertainty in the diplomatic situation: England, passive and uncommitted, stood aloof, sympathetic to Austria and France in the east as well as to France in the west, but unwilling to bind herself. The British attitude also was not entirely unpredictable: it was certain that in any conflict England would remain a neutral spectator unless a direct threat developed to either the Straits or Belgium. The effects of British diplomacy, however, during the troubled period which was seen to lie ahead, were less easy to foresee. In diplomacy at least, England held the casting vote: any serious threat of intervention on her part—unlikely but not impossible—might prevent the outbreak of war in either east or west. France and Prussia, therefore, had every reason to cultivate British sympathy.

The formation of the new 'balance' raised a number of issues for the future. To what extent would British diplomacy be able to restrain the rival groupings and delay—if not perhaps prevent—the outbreak of hostilities? If there was a conflict, would it arise in the east or the west? Would one necessarily involve the other? Last, but not least, how would the incomplete and limited alliances stand up to the strain of diplomatic conflict? How long would it be possible to maintain the new and unstable equilibrium among the powers?

[1] Bismarck by his handling of the Russian proposal had shown diplomatic skill of the very highest order. He had achieved the seemingly impossible in partly dissociating the eastern and western questions. His insistence on the 'double threat' meant that an Austro-Russian clash in the Balkans need not necessarily involve the west; it meant equally that a Franco-German war need not automatically revive the 'eastern question'. It may be largely thanks to this that the war of 1870 did not become a European war. In 1914 there was no possibility of separating the two issues, and a general war resulted. Bismarck's effort, naturally, was not disinterested. The refusal to commit Prussia to the support of Russian policy in the Balkans—even for the price of direct Russian support in the event of a French attack—anticipates in its effects the celebrated dictum about the Pomeranian grenadier. In any case, Russian help in a Prusso-French war could hardly have been effective.

CHAPTER 10

THE STRUGGLE FOR SUPREMACY IN EUROPE, 1870

THE excitement and diplomatic activity of 1867 was succeeded by a prolonged lull in European affairs. The groupings born from the crisis remained in being, but none of the powers was ready to face the risk of war. In Russia, the construction of arterial railways together with Miliutin's military reforms was absorbing all available resources; the Austrian government was preoccupied with internal problems arising from the *Ausgleich* of 1867 and the *Nagoda* of the following year; Bismarck was busy organizing the North German Confederation and 'digesting'[1] Prussia's recent gains. The Luxemburg crisis had shown that France was unready for war; Napoleon, ill, unsure of himself and faced with growing internal opposition, shrank from provoking a conflict. England, now pacific and passive, was preoccupied with questions of parliamentary reform and the beginnings of the rivalry between Disraeli and Gladstone. In consequence, an age of war and diplomatic activity was succeeded by a period of comparative calm. Yet the reduction in international tensions was more apparent than real. The two great issues of the preceding crisis, Franco-German rivalry in the west and unrest among the Balkan Christians aggravated by Austro-Russian distrust in the east, were ever present on the horizon to cloud the Indian summer of 1868 and 1869. It had become almost an axiom of diplomacy that sooner or later there must be a clash between France and Prussia: the great armaments race on which the two countries had embarked boded ill for the future of peace; it was equally clear that the eastern question was only in abeyance and that sooner or later Russia, Austria and the Balkan Christians would attempt its final solution. It was, therefore, clearly understood in all the chanceries that the 'appeasement' of 1868 and 1869 was merely a lull to be followed by further storms both in the west and the east.

I

Early in 1868 Gorchakov's feverish activity on behalf of the Cretans had been succeeded by complete diplomatic calm. In mid-February, Revertera had told Beust: 'La situation dont j'ai à rendre compte aujourd'hui se résume dans le mot "Apaisement". C'est dans ce sens que s'énoncent Mr. le Chancelier de l'Empire et les hauts fonctionnaires auxquels il

---

[1] The expression is Disraeli's (A. Bernstorff, *Im Kampf für Preussens Ehre*, ed. K. Ringhoffer (Berlin, 1906), p. 609).

communique ses inspirations.'[1] In April Gorchakov expressed his belief in the continuation of peace 'si le Cabinet autrichien seul ne persistait dans son refus de reconnaître le principe de Non-intervention dans les affaires de l'Orient'.[2] On 18 July the tsar in emphatic terms assured Vetsera, the Austrian *chargé d'affaires*, of his peaceful intentions.[3] Early in November Vetsera reported that the keynote of Russian policy was peace, conservatism and internal development.[4] When in December a breach between Greece and the Porte was imminent, Gorchakov refused to be drawn into the conflict.[5] The tsar shared his views: Russia must not do Austria[6] and France the favour of getting involved in the quarrel. Peace for Russia was 'more important than the fate of a handful of Greeks.'[7] Gorchakov did not hesitate to describe the Greek cabinet as 'un Ministère d'harlequins'.[8] He proposed in the end that the Greco-Turkish dispute should be submitted to a conference[9] and loyally co-operated in imposing a solution unfavourable to Greece.[10] In September

[1] Revertera to Beust, 12 February/31 January 1868, HHSAPARRR, 1868, X 55, no. 3 B.

[2] The same to the same, 22/10 April 1868, *ibid.* no. 9 A–B.

[3] '…Ich will die Türkei an mich reissen, ruft man von allen Seiten; was immer vorfalle …überall habe *ich* meine Hand im Spiele. Ich aber gebe Ihnen mein Wort darauf, das solche Verdächtigungen grobe Verleumdungen sind. Russland ist gross genug für mich, ich will nichts von meinem Nachbar. Es ist wohl eine Partei in meinem Reiche, die mir ihre Pläne aufdringen möchte, doch so lange *ich* regiere, biete ich meine Hand nicht dazu und für meinen Sohn stehe ich auch ein. Dass ich für die Christen im Orient Sympathien habe, das habe ich nie geläugnet [*sic*] und glaube auch keinen Grund zu haben es zu verbergen. …Ich wiederhole es und sagen Sie es dem Kaiser, dass ich kein Begehren nach des Nachbars Land in mir trage. Kann ich jedoch überzeugt sein, dass auch er keine Convoitisen hat? Denn auch gegen ihn liegen Verdächtigungen vor…' (Vetsera to Beust, 19 July 1868, *ibid.* no. 17B, confidential).

[4] 'Die Haltung der russischen Politik ist gegenwärtig deutlich als eine friedliche und conservative accentuirt…die der Kaiser entschieden vorgezeichnet hat….Um die gegenwärtige Situation kurz zu zeichnen, wiederhole ich: die Losung ist Friede und ruhiger Fortschritt. Der Kaiser hat sich von den "Moskowitern" abgewendet; das Ministerium ergreift zuweilen Repressiv-Massregeln gegen deren Ausschreitungen; Fürst Gortchacow persönlich steht zwischen den Parteien, die Wagschalen beobachtend, wie sie steigen oder sinken' (the same to the same, 4 November/23 October 1868, *ibid.* no. 31B).

[5] Reuss to Bismarck, telegram, 11 December 1868, in H. Michael, *Bismarck, England und Europa* (München, 1930), p. 191. Cf. Vetsera to Beust, two telegrams, 6 December 1868, HHSAPARRR, 1868, X 55.

[6] On 14 November 1868 the Habsburg empire had officially become the 'Austro-Hungarian monarchy'. The term 'Austria' will continue to be used to describe the entire monarchy.

[7] 'Der Friede sei für Russland wichtiger als das Schicksal einer Handvoll Griechen' (Reuss to Bismarck, 10 December 1868, Michael, *op. cit.* p. 191).

[8] Vetsera to Beust, telegram, 8 December/26 November 1868, HHSAPARRR, X 55.

[9] The same to the same, telegram, 20 December 1868, *ibid.*

[10] Vetsera told Beust: 'Sowohl der französische als englische Botschafter, die Gesandten Preussens und Italiens sind überzeugt, und ich theile diese Ueberzeugung ganz, dass der Kaiser und Fürst Gortchacow entschlossen sind jetzt im Orient ernstes Zerwürfnis nicht aufkommen zu lassen. Die Mächte, die sich an der Beilegung des gegenwärtigen Conflictes betheiligen, können in der Wesenheit die aufrichtige Mitarbeit des russischen Cabinets erwarten, in der Form dürfte es wohl die Wahrung seines Prestiges gegenüber den Griechen nicht ganz vergessen' (the same to the same, 25/13 December 1868, *ibid.* no. 44 A–C). It proved an accurate forecast.

1869 Vetsera again reported complete calm and stagnation ('Windstille und Stagnation') at St Petersburg. There was no European issue of sufficient importance to stir Russia from her attitude of reserve. The German question had not assumed a form sufficiently precise to call for a Russian reaction; internal developments in Spain were remote; the dispute of Egypt and Turkey was considered a 'querelle de ménage'.[1]

In November Talleyrand, who was personally unpopular at St Petersburg,[2] was recalled. He was replaced by Fleury, one of Napoleon's intimates, who had orders to warn the tsar against the 'German menace'.[3] His mission was unlikely to be successful. There had indeed been some friction between Russia and Prussia over matters of secondary importance,[4] but the basic friendship of the two countries had remained unshaken. As Talleyrand had earlier reported, a close understanding with Prussia was for the Russian government an absolute necessity.[5] Fleury did indeed create a favourable impression, but the only success he obtained in the political sphere was an ineffectual Russian appeal to William I to carry out Article V of the treaty of Prague.[6] 'La Russie', Fleury was forced to admit, 'veut rester en termes affectueux avec la Prusse, en même temps qu'en relations courtoises avec la France.'[7] In December the tsar demonstratively conferred on the king of Prussia the Grand-Cross of the Order of St George, the highest Russian decoration, evoking memories of Russo-Prussian victories over France.[8] The event created a painful impression in Paris and demonstrated the futility of any attempt to weaken the Russo-Prussian understanding.

At the beginning of 1870 the 'eastern question' once more attracted attention: a conflict threatened between Montenegro and the Porte; at Bucharest, Prince Charles was getting ready to assert the complete independence of Romania; there was unrest also in Dalmatia. In these circumstances the tsar took the opportunity of explaining to Chotek, the new Austrian minister, his views on matters of common interest to Austria

---

[1] 'Die deutsche Frage und die preussischen Bestrebungen haben keinen genug prägnanten Charakter angenommen um das Petersburger Cabinet zu einer Meinungsäusserung zu veranlassen;...' (the same to the same, 25/13 September 1869, *ibid.* x 56, no. 35).

[2] The same to the same, telegram, 20 November 1869, *ibid.*

[3] Fleury's private instructions from Napoleon contained the following passage: 'Le général Fleury...fera comprendre le danger que fait courir à l'Europe l'idée germanique, qui, si elle continue à grandir, doit naturellement englober dans sa sphère d'action tous les pays qui parlent allemand, depuis la Courlande jusqu'à l'Alsace' (Charles-Roux, *op. cit.* p. 474).

[4] The most serious of these was the Prussian refusal to renew a Convention for the mutual extradition of deserters (*ibid.* p. 463).

[5] Talleyrand observed: 'Si, à Saint-Pétersbourg, on professe peu de sympathie pour l'Allemagne, si le développement de sa marine dans la Baltique inspire de la crainte, chacun comprend cependant que l'alliance prussienne est une nécessité dont on ne saurait s'affranchir actuellement, parce qu'elle est imposée par l'état des relations de la Russie avec les grandes puissances. Le danger de se trouver isolée en Europe lui conseille souvent la condescendance...' (Talleyrand to La Valette, 12 July 1869, *ibid.*).

[6] *Ibid.* pp. 467f.   [7] *Ibid.* p. 468.   [8] *Ibid.* p. 469.

and Russia. In the east, Alexander declared, he believed in the possibility of agreement:

...pour les questions orientales il ne serait pas si difficile de nous entendre, car nous partons du même principe, le maintien de l'intégrité et de l'indépendance de l'Empire Ottoman. Ce n'est que sur la manière d'arriver à ce but que Mon Gouvernement s'est souvent trouvé en désaccord avec le vôtre, mais plus souvent encore avec les Cabinets de Paris et de Londres. Les populations chrétiennes soumises à la domination turque ont des aspirations de liberté et d'autonomie et nos conseils à la Porte devraient porter, selon nous, sur ces concessions dans l'intérêt bien-entendu de l'Empire Ottoman. Ne serait-il pas possible de se rencontrer sur ce même terrain?[1]

With regard to Poland, he could only warn against encouraging revolutionary tendencies. On Germany the tsar's language was completely 'Prussian'. Chotek told Beust: '...je fus frappé d'entendre la manière de laquelle l'Empereur parla des pays du sud de l'Allemagne. C'était le langage pur et simple des diplomates prussiens ou des journaux subventionnés à Berlin.'[2] Events soon proved once again that there was no basis for an Austro-Russian *entente*. When the Russian government submitted plans for a settlement of the dispute between the Porte and Montenegro, Beust put forward counter-proposals unacceptable to Gorchakov. 'Mais pourquoi', asked the Chancellor, 'le comte Beust se fait-il si châleureusement le porte-voix des Turcs; qu'il les laisse donc se défendre eux-mêmes; —c'est un passage bien peu satisfaisant!'[3] And he pointedly added: 'le Cabinet de Berlin naturellement ne nous fait part que d'un acquiescement plein et entier à notre proposition.'[4] Nor could the two governments agree about Romania. In May Chotek read a despatch from Beust which did not find favour with Gorchakov:

...l'invocation fréquente et accentuée du traité de 1856—que nous ne sommes pas (vous le savez) payés pour aimer—ne me paraît point heureusement choisi pour servir d'appui principal aux déductions que fait valoir le comte Beust. Il n'y a pas une seule question...pour laquelle ce traité se trouve plus entamé, et dès lors, plus imparfait, que celle relative à la Roumanie.

Gorchakov added:

Je dois Vous avouer de plus que les sentiments de reconnaissance que j'ai éprouvés pour les intentions bienveillantes que le comte Beust nous a manifestées lors de ma dernière entrevue avec lui, précisément par rapport au traité de 1856,[5] se trouvent, en quelque sorte, atténuées par l'impression que viennent de me faire Vos paroles.[6]

---

[1] Chotek to Beust, 12 January/31 December 1870/1869, HHSAPARRR, January–June 1870, x 57, no. 2 A–B, G.

[2] The same to the same, 12 January/31 December 1870/1869, *ibid.* no. 2 C.

[3] The same to the same, 10 February/29 January 1870, *ibid.* no. 10 A–B.

[4] The same to the same, 10 February/29 January 1870, *ibid.* no. 10 B.

[5] During the summer of 1869 Gorchakov had met Beust at Ouchy and had agreed with him to keep the eastern question quiet. Beust had declared that the Austrian government was not interested in the maintenance of the Black Sea Clauses of the treaty of Paris.

[6] The same to the same, 18/6 May 1870, *ibid.* no. 26 C, confidential. Gorchakov had held similar language to Fleury: 'l'invocation du traité de 1856 pour les affaires des Principautés me fait l'effet comme si, pour se protéger contre les courants d'air, l'on choisissait entre plusieurs paravents le plus troué' (the same to the same, 21/9 May 1870, *ibid.* no. 28 A–C).

Thus, if the French government had been unable to detach Russia from Prussia, it had proved equally impossible for Russia to detach Austria from France.

II

Under the conservative administration British policy, like that of Russia, was pacific and favourable to the further consolidation of Germany under Prussian leadership. Disraeli, who in February 1868 succeeded Derby as Prime Minister, had replied to a remark by Bernstorff that Prussia desired only to be left in peace: 'Yes, certainly, we do not wish Prussia to be disturbed in her digestion...tell Count Bismarck, that we don't wish her to be disturbed in her digestion.'[1] Stanley, in an election speech in November, had publicly welcomed the eventual unification of Germany by Prussia.[2] The days of the conservative government were, however, numbered. A liberal majority was returned and the Queen invited Gladstone to form an administration.

The post of Foreign Secretary in the coming liberal cabinet had been earmarked for some time for the veteran Clarendon. At the last moment, however, an unexpected obstacle had arisen: the Queen had objected strongly to his known views on Prussia and Germany, and expressed doubts of his fitness for the post.[3] In fact, when it had become certain that a change of government was at hand, the Queen had sent her Private Secretary to plead with Lord Halifax[4] against Clarendon's appointment. General Grey represented to Halifax that a good excuse might be found on grounds of health for selecting a younger man. The Queen would not object to Granville, Kimberley or Lyons.[5] Halifax promised to discuss the matter with Gladstone.[6] Some days later Grey, in delivering to Gladstone the official invitation to form a government, re-stated the Queen's objections:

...As regards Lord Clarendon it seems enough to say, that the two years and a half he has spent in Opposition, have completely changed the opinion your Majesty

---

[1] Bernstorff to Bismarck, private, Bernstorff, *op. cit.* pp. 609f.

[2] Valentin, *op. cit.* p. 385. Stanley's views appear from a letter addressed to him by Morier: '...I entirely agree with you in believing that the great springtide of the nineteenth century is moving irresistibly forward towards huge centralised social agglomerations' (Morier, *op. cit.* vol. II, p. 108).

[3] 'It is not only that...it would not be personally agreeable to your Majesty that Lord Clarendon should be that Minister; but that his feelings and opinions about Germany and Prussia, which have been almost offensively expressed, make him the most unfit Person, in your Majesty's opinion, to conduct the foreign Relations of this Country, at a moment when it is most essential that we should preserve a good understanding with Germany.—The Crown Princess [of Prussia] thinks his return to the Foreign Office would have a bad effect at Berlin, where his opinions are well known as hostile to Germany' (Grey to the Queen, undated, RA C 32/129).

[4] Formerly Sir Charles Wood, now a widely respected 'elder statesman', high in the Liberal counsels.

[5] *Ibid.*

[6] The same to the same, 26 November 1868, *ibid.* C 32/136.

entertained in 1866 of his fitness for the Foreign Office.—His language during that time has been very indiscreet, and has created an impression abroad and especially in Germany, as to his present views and feelings, which it is most undesirable, in the present state of the Continent, should be entertained of the English Foreign Secretary. This, added to your Majesty's personal grounds of complaint, which Mr Gladstone must not ignore, though he should not put them unnecessarily forward, is a sufficient ground for placing someone else at the Foreign Office.

Gladstone replied that Clarendon was one of the two or three people with whom, some six months before, he had discussed a possible change of government. He had then expressed to him a hope that he would return to the Foreign Office. Moreover, public opinion had 'pointed, unhesitatingly, to Clarendon as the future Foreign Minister'. In speaking to Clarendon, Gladstone had acted in the belief 'that he was the person who would be most acceptable to your Majesty in that situation'. It was to be feared that, were Clarendon now to be set aside, it would be ascribed directly to the Queen.[1] In these circumstances, and after the failure of an attempt by Gladstone to interest Clarendon in another post, the Queen had reluctantly accepted the latter's appointment.

Clarendon's return to the Foreign Office was soon seen to involve—as the Queen had feared—a distinct *rapprochement* with France.[2] In his first private letter to Lyons, who had succeeded Cowley as ambassador in Paris, Clarendon wrote: 'Pray present my respects to M. de Moustier and to M. Rouher. They well know with what cordiality I desire to maintain the best relations with France.'[3] Within a few days La Valette had succeeded Moustier: '...pray congratulate him from me on his accession to office and say how glad I shall be if we succeed in together extinguishing this Eastern fire[4] and not allowing it to become a conflagration'.[5] In fact, there was full co-operation between the representatives of England and France during the Paris conference on the Greco-Turkish dispute. Clarendon observed: 'The perfect understanding between France and England at the Conference is thoroughly felt in Europe as far as I can judge.'[6] When the conference had finally concluded its labours Clarendon, in congratulating Lyons on the result, declared: '...the intimate and co-

---

[1] The same to the same, 1 December 1868, *ibid.* C 32/142.

[2] In actual fact, the change in British policy was one of emphasis rather than direction. Stanley, Clarendon's son-in-law, had been right when he privately told Loftus: '...Lord Clarendon, I know, will follow in the track which events and public opinion have marked out for every English Minister—that is, of assisting, if possible, to keep the peace of Europe without compromising our own' (quoted in Loftus, *op. cit.* pp. 239f.).

[3] Clarendon to Lyons, private, 10 December 1868, Clarendon MSS. copy.

[4] The Greco-Turkish conflict.

[5] The same to the same, private, 18 December 1868, *ibid.* copy.

[6] The same to the same, private, 26 January 1869, *ibid.* copy. Some days later Clarendon wrote: 'I am glad that the revision of our blue book has gone on so smoothly and that such a complete partnership exists between the two Governments. The identity of views and action which will be made manifest by comparing the blue and yellow [books] cannot be without its effect in Europe...' (the same to the same, 30 January 1869, *ibid.* copy).

partnership relations established between you [Lyons and La Valette] are not one of the least good effects of the Conference.'[1]

Whilst working with France to end hostilities in the east, Clarendon had not for one moment lost sight of the 'western question'. He had in fact spared no effort to bring about a Franco-Prussian *détente*. Shortly after his return to the Foreign Office he had had 'an interesting conversation' with the Crown-Prince of Prussia:

He is even more pacific than his Father and unlike his Father would be glad to put the army on something more like a peace footing.—The King however is unapproachable on this subject, but the Prince says that in a year or two he will have to yield to the outcry of the people against the increased taxation that such monster armaments entail.

The Crown-Prince was more reassuring on the subject of union with the South:

I urged strongly upon him the necessity of maintaining the status quo and particularly warned him against the incorporation of the Grand Duchy of Baden into the Northern Confederation. He quite entered into the reasons for this and said it would probably be a long time before the interests of the South would necessitate a junction with the North although it would ultimately be inevitable.[2]

Some weeks later Clarendon had been able to transmit to Paris further encouraging news. He had, he explained, 'at various times prescribed caution at Berlin as to not offending France by hastening the incorporation of the South with the North'. Loftus had recently had a conversation with the king of Prussia, who had repeated the view '...that *time* must work on the completion of German unity without force...it would be reserved for his son or even perhaps his grandson to accomplish'. Lyons was to transmit these remarks to La Valette in confidence.[3] At the same time, the French government must reconcile itself to the inevitable:

The King [of Prussia] is right—and La Valette is wrong in persisting to say that the 'inevitable' is a menace, and in not trying to educate the Public into regarding it with indifference. In reality the complete unification of Germany could not be one bit more dangerous to France than the actual state of things, when Bavaria and Wurtemburg [*sic*] are bound by Treaty to place her [*sic*] armies under Prussian command in the event of war.[4]

Clarendon's efforts to bring about a *détente* were complicated by an unexpected crisis. A French company had made arrangements to acquire one of Belgium's major railways and the Belgian government, fearing for the independence of the country, had passed a law forbidding the transaction. Clarendon was alarmed: 'I cannot exaggerate the anxiety I feel

---

[1] The same to the same, private, 20 February 1869, *ibid.* copy.
[2] The same to the same, private, 18 December 1868, *ibid.* copy.
[3] The same to the same, private, 25 January 1869, *ibid.* copy.
[4] The same to the same, private, 27 January 1869, *ibid.* copy.

about this Belgian business as it is the only one that can produce an estrangement between England and France.' Bismarck would not be sorry to see a Franco-Belgian quarrel and perhaps one between England and France as well.[1] Clarendon therefore issued a friendly warning:

> Both for family relations and political interests this country does take a special interest in Belgium and I am sure that if it was absorbed by France the thing would produce a most painful impression here. I don't mean to say that the misunderstanding would be of a hostile character, but there would no longer exist the confidence which is now felt in the Emperor and I ardently hope that the French government will not insist on concessions that would threaten Belgian independence and her guaranteed neutrality.[2]

There was a further reflection, which Lyons should place before the French government: 'I believe nothing could be more agreeable to Prussia than that the intimacy between the 2 Countries should be disturbed by a territorial encroachment that would run on all fours with Prussian aggrandizement.'[3] On 10 March Clarendon wrote that he had heard enough from good judges of public opinion to feel sure that there would be a tremendous explosion if an attempt was made to crush or annex Belgium. Gladstone had written 'that the day when this nation seriously suspects France of meaning ill to Belgian independence will be the last day of friendship with that Country and that then a future will open for which no man can answer'. Why should Napoleon, Clarendon asked, 'create hornets' nests for himself'?[4] Three days later Clarendon had to confess his growing conviction that Napoleon had evil designs on Belgium and that the railway was merely a pretext.

> I think it to the last degree impolitic on the part of the Emperor, the moment some turmoil is over straitway [sic] to bring another on the tapis and never to allow mankind to be at ease respecting the maintenance of peace. If there is one thing however that more than another would gladden his enemies in general and Prussia in particular it is a misunderstanding between France and England, and the misunderstanding would be most serious if he were to annex Belgium or threaten her independence.

Then followed a double warning: '... there is already some evidence here to shew that public opinion would be roused to an extent not perhaps suspected in France—at all events the relations between the two Countries

---

[1] The same to the same, private, 17 February 1869, *ibid.* copy.

[2] The same to the same, private, 2 March 1869, *ibid.* copy.

[3] The same to the same, private, 6 March 1869, *ibid.* copy. 'Bismarck is biding his time quietly. If France annexes Belgium and we take no part he will be delighted as France could no longer complain of Prussian aggrandizement.—If we do take part he would be delighted at the rupture between England and France and would come to our assistance.—Either way he thinks Prussia would gain. Why should the Emperor assist him? A quarrel between France and England or even a coolness is the great German desideratum' (the same to the same, private, 8 March 1869, *ibid.* copy).

[4] The same to the same, private, 10 March 1869, *ibid.* copy.

would be most seriously damaged'. England might even be drawn into hostilities against France:

> Prussia seems to be quiet and prudent and any influence we can use has been exerted to keep her so, but supposing that it suited her to go to the aid of Belgium in defence of her Treaty obligations and that she called upon us to do the same, I believe that the call would be responded to because the English people would think that they couldn't hold aloof without dishonour. Of course it is the furthest from our intention to hold the language of menace but it is our duty to look out for eventualities and to guard by every means in our power against any disturbance of the French alliance which we prize so highly and which has always been productive of advantage to both countries.[1]

When private admonition failed, a more formal warning was issued:

> We are very anxious about the Belgian business [Clarendon wrote on the 16th], because more and more convinced that the Emperor is meaning mischief and intending to establish unfriendly relations with Belgium preparatory to ulterior designs. —It is very imprudent on his part and he will only reap disappointment for even if he meditates war with Prussia he could not undertake it upon a worse pretext or one less likely to win public opinion to his side, as it would wantonly obtain an interruption, to use a mild term, of friendly relations with England.

As the Cabinet attached extreme importance to the maintenance of friendly relations, they would spare no effort to avert a breach:

> I have accordingly by the unanimous desire of the Cabinet written you a dispatch calling the serious attention of the French government to the dangerous eventualities that we see looming in the distance, but the mode of dealing with that dispatch may be delicate and difficult and we therefore leave the decision on that point to your discretion.[2]

By the following day the immediate crisis had passed and Napoleon's attitude towards Belgium had become more conciliatory: 'I am of course prepared', Clarendon told Lyons, 'for your not making use of my dispatch of yesterday as things have assumed a smoother aspect, but it may be of use if you hear that too much pressure is put upon M. Frère Orban.'[3] Clarendon's anxiety was only partly allayed. The peace of Europe, he informed the Queen, might at any moment be threatened by causes independent of Belgium.

> Prussia and France both believe that an attack upon Belgium would not be viewed with indifference by England and that is a proper state of things, but extreme caution is necessary in our dealings with those two Powers.—Lord Clarendon does not feel the slightest confidence in Prussia, and thinks that Count Bismarck is quite as likely to support France in annexing Belgium as he would be to support England in resisting it—we must not therefore promise support or hold out expectations that we may be unable to fulfill, and this policy of caution is all the more needed now with

---

[1] The same to the same, private, 13 March 1869, *ibid.* copy.
[2] The same to the same, private, 16 March 1869, *ibid.* copy.
[3] The same to the same, private, 17 March 1869, *ibid.* copy. Orban was the Belgian First Minister.

reference to the state of our relations with America and the disloyal feeling in Ireland.

What he had to complain of in the policy of the Belgian government was 'a fixed purpose to rely upon England alone, to ask our advice, and then to make us responsible for it'. British policy must aim at avoiding commitments: 'All that Lord Clarendon desires is to secure the most perfect freedom of action for Your Majesty's Government in any contingency that may arise.'[1]

Clarendon's nervousness was aggravated by the general state of tension prevailing in Germany. Howard in Munich spoke of continuous Prussian pressure to hasten Bavaria's military preparations.[2] Loftus reported from Berlin that an early conflict was expected.[3] When Clarendon invited the Prussian government to assure Napoleon that it was not actively pursuing the unification of Germany,[4] Bismarck countered with a proposal for a defensive alliance between England and Prussia:

'This abstention of England', continued Count Bismarck, 'forces us into almost a State of Vassalage to Russia, and the only way we can recompense Russia is by supporting her interests in the East. This is not congenial to our interests—but we have no choice. It acts also prejudicially to Europe for it prevents the consolidation of a firm and lasting Peace.' 'If', said Count Bismarck, 'you will only declare that whatever Power should wilfully break the Peace of Europe, would be looked upon by you as a common enemy—we will readily adhere to, and join you in that declaration—and such a course, if supported by other Powers, would be the surest guarantee for the Peace of Europe.'[5]

Clarendon was unlikely to listen to an overture of this nature, but the persistence of Franco-Belgian tension made it desirable to improve relations with Prussia: a British warship was therefore sent to join in a naval review at Wilhelmshaven. William I in a letter to Queen Victoria expressed his pleasure at this gesture. The recent elections in France, he added, appeared to presage a more peaceful future. There existed, moreover, a gratifying similarity in the Prussian and British views on the Franco-Belgian dispute.[6] Clarendon expressed satisfaction at the letter,

but it must not be forgotten that the aim of Prussian policy is to produce misunderstanding between England and France and that Count Bismarck before the late war

---

[1] Clarendon to the Queen, 19 March 1869, RA Q 3/70.
[2] Howard to Clarendon, no. 21, 13 February 1869, RA I 48/106, abstract.
[3] Loftus to Clarendon, private, 27 March 1869, *ibid*. I 48/112, copy.
[4] The same to the same, no. 198, most confidential, 17 April 1869, *ibid*. I 48/115, précis.
[5] Valentin, *op. cit.* p. 544.
[6] 'In der politischen Welt scheint ja nach dem Ausfall der Wahlen in Frankreich, wirklich ein Friedensgefühl durch die Welt dringen zu wollen, wenn nicht in jenem so ganz unterwühlten Staate alle [*illegible*] nur zu oft scheitern.... Sehr glücklich bin ich, dass ich mit Dir und Deinem Gouvernement in so grosser Uebereinstimmung in der franco-belgischen Frage mich befunden habe und gewiss auch ferner bleiben werde' (King William to the Queen, 20 June 1869, RA I 48/118).

recommended the Emperor to take Belgium. He would do so again if it did not suit Prussia to go to war with France.[1]

Grey might express regret that Clarendon should persist 'in always attributing sinister objects to Prussia',[2] but the Foreign Secretary's distrust was ineradicable. When early in July the Franco-Belgian dispute was finally settled, he observed: 'I fancy that it will be a disappointment to the Prussians which ought to make La Valette more glad of the dénouement.'[3]

If the Greco-Turkish dispute had been the last flicker of the eastern crisis touched off by the Cretan rebellion, the Franco-Belgian quarrel marked the end of Napoleon's quest for compensations. By the summer of 1869, therefore, although an atmosphere of tension persisted, there remained no acute problems likely to cause a conflict. The diplomatic situation had been modified by the appointment of Clarendon who had cautiously aligned England with France and Austria. He had virtually restored the Crimean coalition in the east and the policy of restraining Napoleon through friendship and alliance in the west. He did indeed accept as 'inevitable' the ultimate unification of Germany, but meant to assure that this came about by slow and peaceful methods. Under his guidance England had, to a limited extent, returned to the European scene, in order to forestall possible threats to Constantinople and Belgium. It was fitting that the heir of a modified Palmerstonian tradition should preside over this return.

III

During the rest of 1869 little happened to affect the relations between the major powers. In December Bismarck complained to Clarendon about the activities of the British minister in Munich. Howard, he declared, was Austrian and ultramontane in his sympathies, and was working against the union of the states of southern Germany with the North German Confederation. Clarendon refused to entertain the complaint. If Howard defended the *status quo* in Germany, he rejoined, that was the policy prescribed by his instructions.[4] Clarendon received with greater sympathy a French request to recommend in Berlin a policy of disarmament. Even though he feared 'that failure is certain with the King', he agreed to make the attempt.[5] The Prussian reaction was as expected,[6] but undaunted

---

[1] Clarendon to the Queen, 21 June 1869, *ibid.* Q 3/197.
[2] Grey to the Queen, 22 June 1869, *ibid.* Q 3/198.
[3] Clarendon to Lyons, private, 3 July 1869, Clarendon MSS. copy. On 26 June the Foreign Secretary had written: 'It is clear to me that Prussia hopes the matter will not be settled and that *offers* of cooperation with us will not be wanting' (the same to the same, private, 26 June 1869, *ibid.* copy).
[4] Valentin, *op. cit.* p. 402.
[5] Clarendon to the Queen, 26 January 1870, RA I 48/142 (*QVL*, vol. 2, p. 5).
[6] Loftus to Clarendon, private and confidential, 5 February 1870, RA I 48/148, copy.

by a first rebuff Clarendon persevered. In a private letter to Loftus he wrote:

The question then to my mind appears quite simple—the military forces of the great Continental Powers have a certain proportion to each other—in order to maintain that proportion very heavy burdens are imposed upon each country but if by common agreement each reduces its army by a certain number of men the same proportion will be maintained while the burthens which are fast becoming intolerable will be alleviated.

A query of Bismarck's as to guarantees for Prussia's security if her forces were reduced, Clarendon tried to evade by unconvincing arguments. Even in return for some measure of disarmament he was still unwilling to pay Bismarck's price of a defensive alliance.[1] Bismarck's reply was realistic and left no hope of agreement.[2] 'It entirely puts an end to all question of disarmament and Lord Clarendon has told Count Bernstorff, with thanks to Count Bismarck for the frankness with which the matter had been discussed by him, that he should not revert to it again.'[3]

Clarendon's inquiry about disarmament coincided with one from Berlin on a very different subject. On 12 March the Crown Princess of Prussia, at the request of her husband, consulted Queen Victoria about a matter which was to be treated as '*Most profoundly secret*'. It appeared that General Prim, the dictator of Spain, had sent a messenger to Berlin with several autograph letters to Leopold Hohenzollern, urging him most earnestly to accept the Spanish Crown. The Princess continued:

They do *not* wish the French to know it, but the King, Prince Hohenzollern,[4] Leopold and Fritz, wish to know *your opinion* in private, as it is so great a secret, there is no way of communicating with Lord Clarendon on the subject,—except your speaking to him confidentially. Neither the King, nor Prince Hohenzollern, nor Antoinette and Leopold, nor Fritz are in favour of the idea, thinking it painful and unpleasant to accept a position which has legitimate claimants.

General Prim, however, had made his invitation very pressing. 'Will you please let me have an answer which I can show the persons mentioned, *perhaps* you could write it *in German* to Fritz, as it is particularly disagreeable to *me* to be a medium of communication in things so important and serious.'[5] The Queen at once informed Clarendon, who expressed the view 'that it would not be expedient for Your Majesty to give any advice upon a matter in which no British interest is concerned, and which can only be decided according to the feelings and the interests of the Family'.

---

[1] Clarendon to Loftus, private, 9 March 1870, *ibid.* I 48/166, copy.
[2] 'Würde Lord Clarendon', Bismarck aptly asked, 'in den friedlichen Gesinnungen des Kaisers der Franzosen und seines gegenwärtigen constitutionellen Gouvernements ein hinreichendes Motiv finden, um in der englischen Marine irgendwelche Veränderungen oder Reductionen vorzunehmen, die er nicht in der Sache selbst, aus inneren Gründen angezeigt erachtet?' (Bismarck to Bernstorff, private and most confidential, 25 March 1870, *ibid.* I 48/182, extract copy).   [3] Clarendon to the Queen, 7 April 1870, *ibid.* I 48/181.
[4] He was the father of the candidate for the Spanish throne.
[5] Princess Royal to the Queen, 12 March 1870, *ibid.* Z 24/38 (*QVL, loc. cit.* p. 10).

He had, however, little doubt 'that the proposed arrangement would produce an unfavourable impression in France'.[1] On 16 March, accordingly, the Queen in replying to the Prussian inquiry repeated Clarendon's arguments.[2] The Hohenzollern family now knew that the Foreign Secretary saw no objection to the candidature of Prince Leopold.

British attention was soon distracted by other matters. During April there were rumours that Bismarck intended to proclaim the king of Prussia emperor of Germany.[3] The question was shelved,[4] but Clarendon noted that there were clouds on the horizon.

> The eventuality looming in the distance and which may be of great importance is the incorporation of the Grand-Duchy of Baden and possibly that of Hesse-Darmstadt into the North German Confederation. This might and probably would lead to war with France.[5]

In fact, Clarendon was not to see the outbreak of the conflict. He had been ailing during February and March;[6] on 21 June he finally took to his bed; six days later the last active British survivor of the Palmerstonian era had passed away. Bismarck heaved a sigh of relief. Clarendon, he later confessed, was the one man who might have prevented the outbreak of war;[7] such was also the opinion of Loftus.[8] Clarendon's death, therefore, was an event of some importance in the affairs of Europe.

[1] The same to the same, 14 March 1870, RA I 63/2 (*QVL, loc. cit.* pp. 10f.). Clarendon's almost incomprehensible negligence had thus not a little to do with the outbreak of the Franco-Prussian war.

[2] 'Wegen der Briefe von General Prim an den Fürsten von Hohenzollern habe ich ganz im Vertrauen mit Lord Clarendon gesprochen, und wir stimmen beide darin überein, dass ich keine Meinung äussern, weder zu- noch abrathen kann, da es sich um eine Entscheidung handelt, welche allein der Fürst und sein Sohn zu treffen haben und auf welche ich nicht die geringste Einwirkung ausüben möchte' (Memorandum by the Queen, 16 March 1870, RA I 63/3, copy. Printed in R. Fester, *Briefe, Aktenstücke und Regesten zur Geschichte der hohenzollernschen Thronkandidatur in Spanien* (Leipzig, 1913), vol. I, pp. 63f.).

[3] Loftus to Clarendon, 30 April 1870, Valentin, *op. cit.* pp. 411f.

[4] Morier to Clarendon, 25 and 27 April 1870, Morier, *op. cit.* vol. II, pp. 150f.

[5] Clarendon to the Queen, 26 April 1870, RA I 48/184.

[6] Granville to the Queen, 14 February 1870, *ibid.* B 25/124 and Clarendon to the Queen, 9 March 1870, *ibid.* I 48/168.

[7] 'In 1871, after Odo Russell succeeded Lord Augustus Loftus as ambassador at Berlin, he and Lady Emily attended a party where they met Count Bismarck. Lady Emily was sitting beside the great man, when he suddenly said to her—"Never in my life was I more glad to hear of anything than I was to hear of your father's death." Lady Emily was naturally taken aback by such an extraordinary speech, and showed it; whereupon Bismarck, patting her hand, said, "Ach, dear lady, you must not take it like that. What I mean is that, if your father had lived, he would have prevented the war"' (Maxwell, *op. cit.* p. 366). For a somewhat different version of the incident see Dora Neill Raymond, *British Policy and Opinion during the Franco-Prussian War* (New York, 1921), p. 36, quoting from Lord Algernon Freeman-Mitford Redesdale, *Memories* (London, 1915), vol. II, pp. 525f., which places the incident in London and makes Bismarck say simply: 'Madam, nothing ever gave me so much pleasure as your father's death.'

[8] Loftus, *op. cit.* p. 265. During the Franco-Prussian war Queen Victoria in a letter to the Queen of Prussia wrote: 'People (in Germany)...are also very unfair to the good Lord Granville, for he has been particularly cautious and unbiased, much more than Lord Clarendon would have been!' (the Queen to the Queen of Prussia, 10 August 1870, *Further Letters of Queen Victoria*, ed. H. Bolitho (London, 1938), pp. 172f.).

IV

On 3 July 1870 it became known in Paris that the Spanish government intended to assemble the Cortes to proclaim Leopold of Hohenzollern king of Spain. Three days later Gramont, the Foreign Minister, read a declaration in the *Corps Législatif* which seemed to foreshadow military action on the part of France unless the plan was abandoned.[1] The spectre of a Franco-Prussian conflict had raised its head once again.

News of the crisis reached London at the very moment when Granville was about to accept the seals of office.[2] The new Foreign Secretary lacked both the diplomatic experience of Clarendon and the clear-cut views of Stanley. A courtier rather than a statesman, he seemed made for the conduct of affairs in times of peace and quiet. On 7 July he told Bernstorff that he disapproved of Gramont's language; he desired the preservation of peace and would do everything in his power to find a settlement compatible with the honour of the two protagonists. He severely criticized the candidature of the Prince of Hohenzollern and hoped that the king of Prussia would refuse his consent. French irritation was understandable, especially in view of the suddenness with which the Spanish candidature had been sprung on Europe[3].

Gorchakov like Granville disapproved of Gramont's language,[4] but urged the Prussian government to be careful.[5] On 12 July at Berlin he learnt that Karl-Anton of Hohenzollern-Sigmaringen had, on his son's behalf, abandoned the candidature.[6] Gorchakov informed the tsar: '...Quant à la Prusse, il me semble qu'on ne peut guère lui demander plus qu'elle n'a fait....La France a certainement tout fait pour amener la guerre et cette conviction est celle des diplomates qui sont venus me voir.'[7] The king of Prussia had rendered a service to

---

[1] The declaration, although moderate in its earlier portions, ended with a challenge: 'But we do not believe that respect for the rights of a neighbouring people obliges us to permit a foreign power, by placing one of its princes on the throne of Charles V, to disturb to our detriment the present equilibrium in Europe and to place the interests and the honor of France in peril. This eventuality, we firmly hope, will not be realized....But if it should be otherwise, strong in your support, gentlemen, and in that of the nation, we should know how to do our duty without hesitation and without weakness' (R. H. Lord, *The Origins of the War of 1870* (Cambridge, Mass., 1924), p. 42).

[2] Bernstorff to King William, telegram, 6 July 1870, *ibid.* pp. 135f.

[3] The same to the same, telegram, 7 July 1870, *ibid.* p. 140.

[4] Chotek to Beust, telegram, 8 July 1870, HHSAPARRR, July–December 1870, x 58. Gorchakov criticized the policy pursued by France in 1866 and added: 'Ils veulent rattraper cela, mais sur quel mauvais terrain! *Je ne dis pas si c'était encore sur la question du Schleswig.*' He blamed the inexperience of those in charge of French policy (the same to the same, 11 July/29 June 1870, *ibid.* no. 32D).

[5] *Ibid.* and Buchanan to Granville, 11 July 1870, FO 65/803, no. 242, reporting telegram of same date. Gorchakov was stopping at Berlin on his way to Wildbad.

[6] Prince Leopold himself was on a walking tour in Switzerland and all efforts to reach him had proved unsuccessful.

[7] 'et la mienne', the tsar wrote in the margin.

peace.[1] Gorchakov had suggested that the powers should officially thank him for his conciliatory attitude and Bismarck had accepted the idea.[2]

By 13 July the European cabinets knew that the French government would not content itself with the 'informal' renunciation of the previous day[3] but demanded in addition an undertaking from the king of Prussia that the candidature would never be renewed. In fact, Napoleon had almost made up his mind to provoke Prussia to war.[4] Bismarck also, at least from 12 July, was actively working for war.[5] In consequence, the French demand for further guarantees made a conflict all but inevitable. On the night of the 13th Bismarck edited the celebrated 'Ems telegram' from which Europe learnt on the following morning of the rebuff which William I was supposed to have administered to Benedetti.[6] A British proposal for a peaceful solution, made on the afternoon of the 14th,[7] came too late to appease French indignation; that night the French government finally decided to call out the reserves. On the following day war became certain.[8]

---

[1] It was due almost exclusively to the personal pressure of King William that the Hohenzollern candidature was abandoned. It appears that advice from London and St Petersburg did little to influence the decision of the King, whose object was to avoid war with France (Lord, *op. cit.* pp. 49ff.).

[2] Gorchakov to Alexander II, 1/13 July 1870, printed in Chester W. Clark, 'Bismarck, Russia and the War of 1870', *The Journal of Modern History*, XIV, 2 (June 1942), pp. 195ff.

[3] The renunciation, made on behalf of the absent Prince by his father, was contained in a letter to General Prim of which a copy had been sent to the Spanish minister in Paris. Since the renunciation was made neither by the Prince himself nor by the Prussian government, the French government had some ground for distrust. Four years earlier, in somewhat similar circumstances, Prince Charles of Hohenzollern-Sigmaringen, brother of the present pretender, had suddenly appeared in Bucharest.

[4] Metternich, who through his relations with the Empress was informed about Napoleon's intentions, reported to Beust on the 12th:
'Il [Napoleon] décrétera demain, mardi, la mobilisation au premier degré sans changer l'état de la question et croit que cela rendra la guerre inévitable. Vous voyez que l'on désire marcher, pensant avec raison...ne jamais trouver une meilleure occasion, vu que la question allemande n'est pas touchée et qu'on a dix jours d'avance sur la Prusse' (Metternich to Beust, telegram, 12 July 1870, HHSAPAR, X 92, France Rapports 1870, no. 78).
Napoleon, however, had not taken a final decision. There were still prolonged hesitations as late as the afternoon and evening of 14 July. The final decision to mobilize was not taken until 11 p.m. on the 14th (Lord, *op. cit.* pp. 113ff.).

[5] *Ibid.* pp. 70ff.

[6] In view of the attitudes adopted by Gramont and Bismarck on 12 and 13 July the importance of the telegram in provoking the war is not perhaps as great as has sometimes been supposed.

[7] Granville proposed that France should waive her demand for a guarantee in exchange for an official declaration by the king of Prussia that he consented to Prince Leopold's renunciation (Bernstorff to William I, telegram, 14 July 1870, *ibid.* pp. 244f.).
For a detailed discussion of whether the British government could, at any stage of the crisis, have prevented the outbreak of war, see appendix B.

[8] Lord, *op. cit.* pp. 113ff.

V

Once it was clear that France and Germany would fight, interest began to centre on the policy of Austria. Although there was no written alliance between Austria and France, their understanding was a close one and they had repeatedly discussed contingencies similar to the one which had arisen. On 14 July, therefore, Bismarck inquired of Oubril whether, if Austria joined the war, Russia would permit the destruction of Prussia at the risk of seeing French armies in Berlin and Posen.[1] Two days later he received the reply that if Austria declared war on Prussia, the tsar would concentrate an army of 300,000 to paralyse the Austrian forces. If military events made it necessary he would occupy Galicia. The Russian guns at Krupp's Russia would cede to Prussia.[2] On 18 July, in reply to letters from Berlin, the tsar telegraphed to William I: 'Heureux d'avoir Vous donné nouvelle preuve de l'amitié qui nous lie. Que Dieu bénisse Votre juste cause!'[3]

The further course of events would now depend on Austria. On 18 July the Council of Ministers met in Vienna under the presidency of Francis-Joseph. Beust in an introductory survey explained rather vaguely that the Russian attitude, which had remained uncertain, had become clearer in the last few days.[4] There was now every reason to believe that Russia and Prussia had reached agreement.[5] Russian public opinion appeared to

---

[1] 'Cette éventualité ne pouvait nous être indifférente...et il serait heureux d'être rassuré sur nos intentions à l'égard de l'Autriche, dans le cas où cette Puissance voudrait entrer effectivement en lice' (Oubril to Westmann, no. 138, 2/14 July 1870, Clark, *loc. cit.* pp. 204f.).

[2] 'Kaiser lässt seiner Majestät dem Könige sagen, dass im Falle einer Kriegserklärung Oesterreichs an Preussen der Kaiser die Paralysierung der österreichischen Streitkräfte durch eine Armee von 300,000 Mann übernehmen würde. Sollten die kriegerischen Verhältnisse es nötig machen, würde der Kaiser eventuell zur Besetzung von Galizien schreiten. Der Kaiser ist damit einverstanden, dass die bei Krupp befindlichen russischen Geschütze an Preussen abgetreten werden' (Pfuel [*chargé d'affaires*] to Bismarck, 16 July 1870, *GW*, p. 389). On the following day Bismarck communicated the news to Munich for confidential information of the Bavarian government (Bismarck to Werthern, telegram, 17 July 1870, *ibid.*). Immediately afterwards it was sent to Schweinitz, the Prussian minister in Vienna, for his personal information (*ibid.* n. 1). In view of these facts, Taylor's assertion that Bismarck 'used the story that Russia had placed 300,000 men in Galicia in order to frighten Austria-Hungary and the south German states; it had no solid foundation, not even a Russian promise' (Taylor, *op. cit.* p. 207 n. 3), is, to say the least, curious.

[3] Alexander II to William I, telegram, 18 July 1870, *GW*, p. 422.

[4] 'Die Haltung Russlands, welches bisher noch nicht Farbe bekannte, sei gleichwohl in den letzten Tagen aczentuirter [*sic*] geworden.'

[5] It seems clear from Beust's language that he did not, at this moment, know the details of the tsar's offer to hold Austria in check with 300,000 men. The contrary is asserted in Bismarck's collected works (*GW, loc. cit.* p. 389 n. 1) on the strength of an assertion by Stern (*op. cit.* vol. x, p. 359 n. 1) and a remark in Schweinitz's memoirs (Schweinitz, *op. cit.* p. 265). Stern's assertion is based on an alleged private letter addressed on 16 July to Beust by Wimpffen, the Austrian minister in Berlin. This letter is not to be found in the Austrian archives. These do, however, contain another letter sent to Beust from Berlin on 16 July. Münch, the writer, expresses a [mistaken] conviction that during Gorchakov's recent visit a written agreement had been signed. Moreover, a south German diplomat had confidentially informed him of two utterances by Bismarck: 'wir wissen durch eine uns befreundete Macht und auf eine hohe Autorität hin, dass Oesterreich eine für uns sympathische

incline to the side of France rather than Prussia,[1] a phenomenon which might become important if Russia joined in the war.[2] Austria had until now pursued a passive policy. Should this be continued, more particularly in view of Russian dispositions, or should there be preparations for an emergency? This was an internal matter on which those more directly concerned must now express an opinion. Andrássy, the representative of Hungary, declared himself in favour of neutrality accompanied by military precautions.[3] Prussia might be given assurances that these had regard only to eventualities in the east and that, as long as Russia kept out of the war, Austria would do the same. Should Russia, however, intervene, Austria also would be forced to abandon her policy of 'expectant neutrality' ('zuwartende Neutralität').[4] Potocki, the Pole who in April had become Prime Minister of the Austrian half of the monarchy, impressed with the difficulty of military preparations, recommended purely diplomatic activity. When Andrássy explained that the preparations he advocated were of a limited nature ('eine partielle Truppenaufstellung'), the emperor drew attention to the technical difficulties: there must be either complete preparation or inaction ('vollständige Armeeausrüstung oder Passivität'). After the Minister of War had expressed his conviction that Austria could not escape war, Archduke Albrecht raised the question of timing. Between 27 and 30 July, he considered, French troops would cross the Rhine. Prussia would be ready between 1 and 4 August. At the beginning of September a decisive battle might be expected which would call for Austrian decisions.[5] Russia would require two months to purchase

Neutralität bewahrt' and 'durch Russlands moralischen Druck sind wir der österreichischen Neutralität sicher' (Münch to Beust, 16 July 1870, HHSAPAR, III 104, Prusse, Varia confidential unnumbered). There is, in this report, no mention of Russian military concentrations. Schweinitz in his turn merely records in his memoirs, written after the event: 'Graf Beust aber wusste auch ohne Choteks Berichte und ohne Andeutung von mir, dass Russland nicht untätig bleiben würde, wenn Oesterreich sich rührte' (Schweinitz, op. cit. p. 265). There is, therefore, no direct evidence that at the Council of 18 July Beust knew of the Russian promise to Prussia. Both the evidence and his own language at the meeting suggest that he merely had general reasons for believing—what was indeed hardly a secret —that Austrian intervention might lead to that of Russia.

[1] For the evolution of Russian nationalist opinion as expressed in the Russian press see appendix C.

[2] 'und dies sei jedenfalls eine merkwürdige Erscheinung, welche bei einer Theilname Russlands am Kriege nicht übersehen werden dürfe.'

[3] 'Wenn nun aber Oesterreich-Ungarn nicht zum Spielballe seiner Nachbarn werden solle, und dies sei ein Standpunkt, welchen er mit Hinweisung auf Russland nicht nur in Ungarn begreiflich zu machen können hoffe'..., it was necessary to adopt a form of neutrality which would allow the monarchy 'gewisse militärische Vorbereitungen zu treffen, um von den Ereignissen nicht überrascht zu werden'.

[4] 'Nur wenn Russland sich einmenge, bliebe uns keine Wahl' (this forms a curious parallel to the attitude adopted at the same time by Russia with regard to Austria. In the event, as neither Austria nor Russia were committed to their partners to the extent of active intervention, it proved possible to separate the eastern and 'western' questions).

[5] 'Anfangs September könne also die entscheidende Schlacht stattfinden, die uns zur That ruft.' The archduke's chronology was to prove more accurate than his geography: he expected the fateful battle on the borders of Saxony!

horses for her armies in Poland; she would then be ready for a winter campaign, which Austria was not. If, therefore, Austria either would not or could not intervene before 15 September, she should not make military preparations; if it was decided to be ready by that date, measures taken now must be prompt and energetic. Beust then argued that the war would be prolonged and that Austria ran no risk of being 'too late'.[1] Whatever the name given to her neutrality, she must prepare against emergencies. There was not only an enemy, Russia, but peaceful mediation also must be based on armed preparedness.[2] This would be understood by the Delegations and public opinion. After prolonged discussion, Francis-Joseph decided that Austria whilst adopting a neutral attitude for the time being, should begin military preparations, particularly the construction of fortifications and the purchase of horses.[3] She should announce her neutrality but accompany the declaration with a statement explaining her military precautions. The armaments should begin on the day of the proclamation; Potocki should hasten his explanations to the Council of Ministers for Cisleithania so that the declaration could be issued at once.[4] Two days later Beust in a Circular announced the neutrality of the Dual monarchy.[5]

Whilst Austria had thus decided on military preparations, Russia also had taken up her position. On 22 July Chotek reported that the Russian declaration of neutrality would be published on the 24th. Russia would observe a strict neutrality 'tant que des événements imprévus jusqu'à présent et venant du dehors n'apporteraient une modification dans l'état actuel des choses'. Two drafts, making the future conduct of Russia depend on 'celle de l'Autriche' or 'des puissances limitrophes de la Russie', had been abandoned. The tsar had observed to an Austrian diplomat: 'il faut que nous restions strictement neutres tous les deux pour circonscrire le temps et l'étendue de la lutte, car dans le cas contraire, ce ne serait que la révolution qui en profiterait.'[6] On 23 July Chotek transmitted by the telegraph a personal message from the tsar:

'Priez Votre Auguste Maître', Alexander had said, 'de rester comme moi dans une *stricte* neutralité. Je n'ai rien augmenté militairement. Moment pour marcher tous deux d'accord venu spécialement; soyons francs amis bons voisins.' L'Empereur nous met en garde contre des entraînements français et m'a dit: '*Je vous donne ma parole qu'au nom du Roi de Prusse je me porte garant de la sécurité des frontières de l'Autriche si elle reste tranquille.*'[7]

[1] This had been Napoleon's miscalculation in 1866.

[2] 'Uebrigens hätten wir nicht nur einen sich immer mehr dessinierenden Feind, nehmlich [*sic*] Russland vor uns, sondern es sey [*sic*] auch, wenn wir friedlich vermittelnd eintreten wollen, nöthig bewaffnet zu sein....'

[3] '...dass vorläufig Neutralität beobachtet zugleich aber mit der, bei der Sachlage nöthigen Armirung, und zwar zunächst mit den zeitraubenden Vorbereitungen nehmlich Befestigungsarbeiten und Pferde-Einkäufen begonnen werden solle.'

[4] HHSA [xxxx 275] P[räsid.] S[ektion] D[ep.] 1 RM P[rotokoll] [1869-71] M[inisterrats-protokoll], meeting of 18 July 1870.   [5] *Ibid.* meeting of 20 July 1870.

[6] Chotek to Beust, telegram, 22 July 1870, *ibid.* HHSAPARRR, July to December 1870, x 58.   [7] The same to the same, telegram, 23 July 1870, *ibid.*

In a long despatch, Chotek amplified his report on Alexander's language:

'Je désire rester complètement en dehors de la guerre qui s'engage; je veux observer une *stricte* neutralité *non-armée*. Je resterai ainsi tant qu'un intérêt direct de la Russie ne sera pas touché. J'appelle un intérêt direct la question de la Pologne sur laquelle je ne puis pas transiger. Du moment que Vous prendriez une position armée et menaçante, elle se soulèverait et moi, quoique bien à contrecœur je devrais transformer mon attitude en une neutralité armée et diriger mes dispositions militaires contre Votre frontière. Cette position pourrait devenir une pente inclinée des plus dangereuses.'[1]

In spite of official assurances that France would not raise the Polish question,

'...je reçois déjà à présent des informations qui me prouvent qu'on relève la tête dans ces provinces. Je pense que ces déclarations françaises leur sont encore inconnues et quoique je les aie accueillies avec reconnaissance, je ne m'y fie pas entièrement.'[2]

The tsar had then launched into an impassioned plea for an understanding between Russia and Austria:

'Dites à Votre Auguste Maître que le moment et les circonstances actuelles me font ressentir...le désir que nous soyons de bons voisins et de francs amis, ayant les mêmes vues d'abstention désintéressées, le même désir pour le prompt rétablissement de la paix, la même pensée de rétrécir autant que possible la durée et l'extension de cette lutte.

'Il est désirable que nous nous entendions de jour en jour, car la situation est tellement grave que nous devons cela à nos pays et à la sécurité de l'Europe. Je Vous mets en garde contre les instigations de la France qui voudra Vous entraîner dans la guerre; j'ai des raisons pour le croire.

'Il est vrai que vous vous trouvez en face de la Prusse vis-à-vis de laquelle vous avez si non une revanche à prendre, du moins une rancune à garder, sentiment que je trouve fort naturel. Cependant ce ne serait pas...d'une bonne politique pour l'Autriche dans le moment actuel que de se laisser entraîner par un sentiment de vengeance.'

[1] The tsar's disquiet about Poland had been stimulated by recent Austrian actions. The appointment of Potocki as Austrian Prime Minister in April had been followed by a series of measures designed to satisfy Polish national aspirations in Galicia. Officials in Galicia were to be Poles by preference; all officials must have a knowledge of the Polish language; Polish professors were appointed at Cracow and Lvov. The creation of a Polish Academy of Science was authorized (P. Renouvin, *L'Empire d'Autriche et l'Autriche Hongrie (de 1860 à 1914)*, (Paris, 1938), vol. II, pp. 69f.). This Austrian policy contrasted sharply with the Russian attempt since 1864 to obliterate the Polish nationality. The Russian reaction to Austria's new policy is typified by a violent attack on Potocki in the *Gazette* of 12 June 1870 (Chotek to Beust, 29/17 June 1870, HHSAPARRR, January–June 1870, X 57, no. 31 E).

[2] The tsar's nervousness about Poland and France shows that he expected—at the very least—great French successes in the early stages of the war. In this he was not alone. Archduke Albrecht of Austria anticipated a decisive battle on the borders of Saxony (HHSAPSDıRMPM, Protocol of meeting of 18 July 1870). On 19 July the Crown Princess of Prussia wrote to Queen Victoria: '...the odds are fearfully against us in the awful struggle which is about to commence and which we are forced into against our will, *knowing* that our existence is at stake' (Crown Princess of Prussia to Queen Victoria, 19 July 1870, RA I 63/124 (*QVL, loc. cit.* pp. 42f.)).

When Chotek observed that a victorious Prussia might form an irresistible attraction for the German populations of Austria, the tsar replied that, as long as the Dual Monarchy remained neutral, he would formally guarantee its territorial integrity.

'...Veuillez dire à l'Empereur Votre Maître que *Moi* avec ma parole d'honnête homme et au nom du Roi de Prusse, je me porte garant de la sécurité des frontières de la Monarchie Autrichienne.[1]

'...ma parole vous est donnée aussi longtems que votre neutralité reste non armée et que vous ne faites pas de démonstrations ni de fortes concentrations militaires. J'espère que vos suspicions [*sic*] du côté de la Prusse pour votre sécurité doivent être écartées par mes assurances et les garanties qu'elles vous donnent.'

The emperor spoke of the south German states and expressed the view that having joined northern Germany in the war they might obtain, even in the event of a Prussian victory, 'un mode d'existence plus supportable que celui d'avant guerre'. Moreover:

'...si l'Empereur d'Autriche et moi nous trouvant d'accord, nous disons hautement comme j'ai l'intention de le faire pour ma part, notre opinion sur cette question, nous trouverons toujours moyen de nous faire entendre même vis-à-vis d'une Prusse victorieuse.'

Alexander added, and his remark gains a special significance from the fact that throughout his career he was absolutely straightforward in his dealings: '...quant à moi, je serais pour donner le protectorat du Sud de l'Allemagne à l'Autriche et je tiens pour cette combinaison l'assentiment de l'Empereur Napoléon en main'. Speaking of Romania, he said: 'oh! oui il faudra bien aussi faire tout au monde pour que les populations chrétiennes en Orient ne bougent pas.' In addition, he appeared to contemplate at some future date joint Austro-Russian mediation in the Franco-German conflict: 'Tâchons de garder la paix pour nous-mêmes et de la rendre à l'Europe par notre concours étroitement lié.' If Chotek had anything to ask, 'demandez à me voir et je vous recevrai à toute heure avec plaisir car c'est une époque sérieuse que nous allons traverser et chaque jour peut avoir sa tâche'.

'Pour moi je n'ai augmenté mes troupes ni d'un seul homme ni d'un cheval, je vous l'affirme; les concentrations ordinaires à Varsovie, quelques petites mesures de sécurité intérieure, voilà tout. Priez l'Empereur en mon nom de faire de même.'

---

[1] The tsar gave this assurance without having consulted the Prussian government. 'Dès que je me suis résolu à Vous tenir le langage que vous venez d'entendre, j'ai écrit au Roi de Prusse que je vous ferai cette déclaration en mon nom et au sien. Je ne m'attends pas à ce qu'il me donne un démenti; quant à moi—c'est égal, ma parole vous est donnée aussi longtems que votre neutralité reste non armée' (the same to the same, 23/11 July 1870, *ibid.* no. 35 B, confidential). In a letter to William I he repeated his promise to concentrate 300,000 men on the Austrian border in the event of Austrian military preparations. He added that to counteract Fleury's insinuations he had undertaken to guarantee that Prussia would take no steps against Austria. On 25 and 26 July, Bismarck submitted to King William the draft of a telegram and a letter accepting the Russian guarantee to Austria (Bismarck, *GW*, p. 422).

Alexander's plea concluded: 'Répétez tout ce que je vous ai dit à Vienne, je n'ai pas de secrets devant vous, et faites-le vite.'[1]

It soon became apparent that the policies of Russia and Austria were not identical. On 24 July Russia formally declared her strict neutrality as long as her interests remained untouched by the vicissitudes of war.[2] Three days later Chotek transmitted the Austrian declaration of neutrality. When Westmann, the acting Russian Minister of Foreign Affairs, remarked that the two pronouncements were similar in character, Chotek drew attention to the fact that whilst the Russian declaration spoke of 'des chances de la guerre', that of Austria stressed 'la sauvegarde de notre sécurité'.[3] In fact, the Austrian government was continuing its policy of military precautions. Between 22 and 24 July no fewer than three meetings of the Council of Ministers discussed the financial measures made necessary by military preparations. On 30 July a further meeting presided over by the emperor himself[4] resolved that the financial needs of the Minister of War ('Geldbedarf des Kriegsministers') should be met by the immediate authorization of essential expenditure and subsequent grants voted by constitutional methods.[5] On 2 August Beust gave a discouraging reply to Alexander's appeal for unarmed neutrality:

Le fin mot [sic] est ceci. La Russie d'après tout ce qui nous revient militairement très faible, craint d'être mise en demeure de tenir ses engagemens envers la Prusse. De là les câlineries et les menaces. J'ai fait observer à Wassilchikoff, que je ne l'ai jamais interrogé et que je ne Vous ai jamais chargé d'interpeller qui que ce soit, et que je suis d'avis que chaque gouvernement est juge des conditions de sa sécurité. Une dépêche partant avec courrier d'après demain Vous expliquera la différence des positions géographiques des deux Empires, excluant une complète identité de position pour neutralité. Parlez-en à l'Empereur. Son offre de nous garantir contre une attaque de la Prusse, que nous saurions bien repousser nous-mêmes, a beaucoup froissé. Vous ne lui en direz pas moins les choses les plus aimables de la part de l'Empereur. Ajoutez que dans tout ce que nous faisons il n'y a rien d'hostile ni d'agressif et que notre seule devise est la défense de notre indépendance.[6]

Military preparations, therefore, continued. On 3 August the Council of Ministers discussed the accelerated construction of certain strategic railways ('Rascherer Ausbau einiger Eisenbahnen').[7] The following day it considered among other matters army orders for the purchase of horses and the partial recall of reservists.[8]

[1] Chotek to Beust, 23/11 July 1870, HHSAPARRR, July–December 1870, x 58, no. 35 B, confidential. The interview is particularly interesting as revealing the tsar's views uninfluenced by the absent Gorchakov.
[2] The same to the same, telegram, 24 July 1870, *ibid.*
[3] The same to the same, 30/18 July 1870, *ibid.* no. 38 A–D.
[4] At the three previous meetings Beust had assumed the presidency.
[5] *Ibid.* PSDiRMPM, protocols of meetings of 22, 23, 24 and 30 July 1870.
[6] Beust to Chotek, telegram, 2 August 1870, HHSAPARRR, 1864–70, x 58.
[7] These were strategic lines linking Hungary and Galicia.
[8] HHSAPSDiRMPM, 3 and 4 August 1870.

In the meantime the tsar was inquiring anxiously about the truth of rumours that Austria was arming the Poles in Galicia;[1] he also awaited with impatience the Austrian reply to his original proposals.[2] On 7 August Chotek notified Beust that the reply had arrived: he would transmit it to the tsar, emphasizing Austria's desire to preserve her independence. He asked at the same time that Austrian troop-concentrations should be delayed for eight days and requested permission to visit Vienna for a personal report.[3] Beust replied that there were as yet no military concentrations.[4] Chotek might leave for Vienna at once. He should, in the meantime, emphasize the defensive character of the Austrian preparations and explain that Austria harboured no aggressive designs against Russia.[5]

VI

Whilst the tsar was trying, without conspicuous success, to prevent Austrian military preparations, the British government had devoted its attention to the security of Belgium. At first, indeed, it had appeared that this would not be endangered. On 16 July Napoleon had formally assured Leopold II of his intention to respect Belgian neutrality 'd'accord avec mes devoirs internationaux'. He trusted that Prussia would give similar assurances and that Belgium's neutrality would therefore be secured.[6] King Leopold had at once transmitted the news to Queen Victoria.[7] On 18 July, moreover, Lyons had reported a formal assurance from Gramont that, provided Prussia did the same, France would scrupulously respect the neutrality of Holland and Luxemburg as well as that of Belgium.[8] On the 19th, Lumley announced from Brussels the receipt of a formal assurance that Prussia would respect the neutrality of Belgium as long as France did the same.[9] It therefore appeared that the primary object of British diplomacy had been successfully attained.

On the 20th, however, Loftus reported that Bismarck had privately informed him of a French proposal, which he claimed to have indignantly rejected, for exchanging Belgium against the states of southern Germany.[10]

---

[1] On 27 July, by order of the emperor, Westmann officially requested from Chotek an explanation of the alleged distribution of arms in Galicia (Buchanan to Granville, 27 July 1870, FO 65/803, no. 276). Beust, in a telegraphic reply, denied the report from the Governor of Podolia that arms had been issued to the Poles in Galicia (the same to the same, 29 July 1870, *ibid.* no. 282, most confidential reporting telegram).

[2] Chotek to Beust, telegram, 2 August 1870, *ibid.* PARRR, July–December 1870, x 58.

[3] The same to the same, telegram, 7 August 1870, *ibid.* Chotek reported: 'Expedition mit Dank erhalten; Ablehnung wird besorgt; Devise: Wahrung unserer Unabhängigkeit von mir entschieden hervorgehoben. . . .'

[4] Beust to Chotek, telegram, 8 August 1870, *ibid.* PAR, x 8, Russie 1864–70, Protokoll.

[5] The same to the same, telegram, 9 August 1870.

[6] Napoleon III to King of the Belgians, 16 July 1870, RA I 63/100, copy.

[7] King of the Belgians to Queen Victoria, 17 July 1870, *ibid.* I 63/99.

[8] Lyons to Granville, telegram, 18 July 1870, *ibid.* I 63/113.

[9] Lumley to Granville, telegram, 19 July 1870, *ibid.* I 63/120.

[10] Loftus to Granville, telegram, most confidential, 20 July 1870, *ibid.* I 63/126.

On Bismarck's instructions, moreover, Bernstorff privately informed Gladstone and Granville of the existence of a draft treaty in the hand-writing of Benedetti:

> This communication was made to them personally, in strict secrecy. Probably the object of the Prussian Government was to prompt them to become the agents for making it known to the world. This Lord Granville and Mr Gladstone thought no part of their duty. They entered into no compact respecting the intelligence, but determined to take time to consider it: with an expectation...that it would find its way into print by some other agency.[1]

Bismarck had also shown the draft 'dans le sceau du plus grand secret' to the Belgian minister in Berlin, accompanying his 'revelation' with 'une déclaration des plus satisfaisantes, signée de lui, pour le respect de notre neutralité'.[2] On 25 July, as the climax of his campaign, Bismarck had the text of the draft treaty published in *The Times*. The measure only partially achieved its purpose: 'A large portion of the public put down this document as a forgery, and indeed a hoax; Mr Gladstone fears it is neither.'[3] Granville had the perspicacity to see that the draft was, at any rate, not simply the outcome of a proposal made by Benedetti.

> Bernstorff, who I believe sent the treaty to *The Times*, says it exists in Benedetti's writing at Berlin, but there are some odd circumstances about it.

> It gives the precedence to the King of Prussia, which a French draft treaty would not do.

> It is impossible that it should have been proposed without preliminary *pourparlers*.

In fact, Granville concluded, Napoleon and Bismarck had been exchanging views on what it was better not to put on paper.[4]

Even if the origin of the draft was doubtful, however, it created disquiet, and the Queen, on 29 July, urged Gladstone 'that a decided expression on the part of England not to allow Belgium to be attacked would have the best effect and would prevent a greater extension of this wicked war'.[5] The following day the matter was considered by the Cabinet.

> They feel that the explanations which have thus far appeared in regard to the notorious project of Treaty are unsatisfactory: and that the best method of dealing with the subject...is to find a new point of departure, from which new securities if possible may be taken for the safety of Belgium, and against the possibility of any combination of the two belligerents for the purpose of its destruction as a neutral and independent state.

---

[1] Gladstone to the Queen, 25 July 1870, *ibid.* I 63/163 (*QVL, loc. cit.* pp. 46f.).
[2] King of the Belgians to Queen Victoria, 24 July 1870, RA I 63/159 (*QVL, loc. cit.* pp. 45f.).
[3] Gladstone to the Queen, 25 July 1870, RA I 63/163 (*QVL, loc. cit.* pp. 46f.).
[4] Granville to Ponsonby (the Queen's private secretary), 26 July 1870. RA I 63/773 (*QVL, loc. cit.* pp. 52f.). In fact the draft had been written down by Benedetti in Bismarck's presence and perhaps in part at his dictation in the course of their conversations in August 1866.
[5] The Queen to Gladstone, 29 July 1870, RA I 64/7, copy (*QVL, loc. cit.* p. 58).

It was impossible to exaggerate the value of time in this matter as a great battle might radically alter the situation.

But it seems to them that a great public and European advantage might be gained if at this time both France and Prussia could be brought to enter into engagements respecting Belgium which would fill up what is wanting or uncertain in their declarations of neutrality.

The Cabinet, therefore, had decided that Granville should ask separately each of the belligerents 'whether it is willing not only to respect the neutrality of Belgium, but to join in upholding it if it should be invaded by another Power'. Austria and Russia 'should be invited to adhere to each of the two arrangements if completed'.[1]

Whilst the British government was thus endeavouring to obtain additional safeguards for the security of Belgium, its attention was suddenly drawn to the position of another small country. On 27 July Buchanan telegraphed from St Petersburg:

The Russian government fear that if French troops occupy Sleswig, and Denmark were to accept the Duchy from France, the consequences might be disastrous in the event of Prussia being victorious in the war. The Russian government have therefore made serious representations on the subject at Copenhagen and hope Her Majesty's Government may do the same.[2]

The Russians considered that Prussia was 'likely to prove very weak in the North' and that it was 'far from improbable' that a French force might succeed in occupying at all events North Schleswig.[3] On 31 July Brunnow was instructed by the telegraph to request Granville to

make a joint appeal with Russia to France not to urge Denmark to become a party to the war, on the ground that while England and Russia consider the existence of Denmark necessary to the freedom of the Baltic, she might as a belligerent be conquered by Prussia if France be not successful in the war.[4]

On the following day Buchanan reported: 'the expediency is under consideration here of proposing that the neutral great powers should come to some understanding with a view by a common action to localize the war and give support to the neutrality of the smaller States'.[5] In reply to Westmann's remarks on this subject Buchanan observed that Prussia might remove all risk of a Franco-Danish alliance[6] by undertaking to

[1] Gladstone to the Queen, 30 July 1870, RA A 40/54 (*QVL, loc. cit.* pp. 53 ff.).
[2] Buchanan to Granville, 27 July 1870, FO 65/803, no. 274, reporting telegram of same date.
[3] The same to the same, 27 July 1870, *ibid.* no. 279.
[4] The same to the same, 1 August 1870, *ibid.* no. 286, reporting telegram.
[5] *Ibid.*
[6] On 3 August the Prince of Wales, who had just returned from Copenhagen, reported to the Queen: 'The position of Denmark is just now a very critical one. She has proclaimed her neutrality and is most anxious to adhere strictly to it—at least the King and Government are—but they don't know how long that neutrality may last—unless the Great Neutral

execute after the war the stipulations of the treaty of Prague. Westmann replied 'that the wisdom of such a course was so evident, he intended to recommend it, through Prince Reuss, to the serious consideration of the Prussian Government'.[1] For the rest, he spoke 'with some asperity' of the danger Europe might incur from an extension of the war through the influence of France on other states. The tsar, he said, desired an understanding among the neutral powers 'under whatever name it might be designated,...as a support to the independence and neutrality of the smaller States, and in checking a spirit of adventure on the part of France'. The question would be examined on Gorchakov's return from Germany.[2]

On 3 August the tsar in person expressed to Buchanan his earnest wish that England should join Russia in representations at Paris to prevent Denmark from being drawn into the war. He attached great importance to this 'and to some concert being established between England, Russia and Austria for localizing the war and acting together with a view to the restoration of peace'.[3]

When, in return, Buchanan invited the Russian government to associate itself with a new guarantee for Belgium, Westmann declared this unnecessary as Belgian neutrality was already guaranteed by existing treaties. The tsar, on the other hand, raised no objection 'but wished Her Majesty's Government would make a similar one with respect to Denmark whose existence he considers is now at stake'.[4]

On the night of 4 August the tsar told Buchanan that although Fleury had expressed a hope that Russia would not associate herself with the British proposal to guarantee Belgian neutrality and although he himself 'thought a protocol such as proposed unnecessary' he wished to act in concert with England.

He said the two Powers by maintaining a strict neutrality and holding identic language might localize the war, and he attached the greatest importance to the influence which their common action might have on the arrangements for peace.

With regard to Denmark he had informed Fleury that if her territory was necessary to France for strategic purposes, 'he would prefer its occupation by force, so that the Danish Government might protest, to Denmark

Powers use a strong pressure on France to observe the neutrality—as the French are doing their utmost to drag Denmark into the war—and if they are forced to go with France—then later I feel sure Germany will "swallow them up". If only Prussia would give them North Schleswig as they promised in the Treaty of Prague—that might alter matters, but the people are very strong for a French alliance and the Government may not be able to resist. I saw Lord Granville and Mr Gladstone to-day and pointed this out to them' (Prince of Wales to the Queen, 3 August 1870, RA I 64/38).

[1] Buchanan to Granville, 1 August 1870, FO 65/803, no. 290 confidential.
[2] The same to the same, 1 August 1870, *ibid.* no. 291, most confidential.
[3] The same to the same, 3 August 1870, *ibid.* no. 292, reporting telegram.
[4] The same to the same, 4 August 1870, *ibid.* no. 294, confidential reporting telegram.

becoming a belligerent'.[1] The British Government, however, was unwilling to act in Paris. Granville informed Brunnow that:

...it seems to Her Majesty's Government that the most effectual inducement that could be held out to Denmark to maintain her neutrality is one which would render her unassailable to temptation on the part of France, and this could alone be brought about by obtaining for Denmark as a neutral state that concession which she would seek to obtain as a Belligerent State from Prussia.

Brunnow, therefore, should ascertain from his government

whether it would not be better to endeavour to obtain from Prussia a fair settlement of the Danish question as preliminary to any attempt being made to dissuade France from attempting to induce her to depart from her neutrality.[2]

Gorchakov[3] replied with a refusal to associate Russia with the treaties on Belgian neutrality signed by England on 6 August with the governments of France and Prussia.[4] He observed:

...while Her Majesty's Government appear unwilling to adopt any means for protecting the independence and perhaps the very existence of Denmark, which Russia considers to be in imminent danger, Russia cannot be expected to enter into new engagements, to protect the independence and neutrality of Belgium which she believes to be in no danger, and more especially because, if England has any apprehensions on the subject, a declaration in Parliament or a few ironclads sent to Antwerp would as effectually secure Belgian neutrality as an engagement entered into by Treaty.

The tsar, to meet the wishes of the British government, might 'have joined in a protocol or convention, recording the declaration of Russia to maintain the neutrality of Belgium, which was in no danger'. He (Gorchakov) could not, however, advise his master

to enter into engagements of which the object was to change in certain eventualities his present position of neutrality into that of a Belligerent,...the people of Russia would have a right to disapprove of the Government engaging to send troops to Belgium which might be required to defend Russian interests nearer home.

The question of Belgium was 'an isolated question in which England alone could be said to have any immediate or material interest'. For the rest,

---

[1] The same to the same, 5 August 1870, *ibid.* no. 294, reporting telegram.

[2] Granville to Brunnow, 4 August 1870, copy in Buchanan to Granville, 10 August 1870, *ibid.* note. On 2 August Gladstone had written to Granville: 'The difficulty in the case of Denmark seems to be that though neuter she has an unsettled controversy of territory with Prussia. It seems difficult therefore to do more than join Russia in urging France not to drive Denmark from neutrality by pressure: and to urge Prussia to remove the cause of danger on the side of Denmark by making a fair arrangement of the matter as to territory now in difference. I do not know whether this would satisfy Russia. It is desirable no doubt that we should do any thing in reason for the sake of working with Russia at the present juncture' (Gladstone to Granville, 2 August 1870, *The Political Correspondence of Mr Gladstone and Lord Granville*, ed. A. Ramm (London, 1952), vol. I, p. 119).

[3] Gorchakov had resumed his functions after returning from his holiday in Germany.

[4] Whilst the Prussian government had readily accepted the proposed engagement, that of France had requested some amendments before it finally agreed to sign.

he had every wish to reach an understanding with England and, if possible, with Austria

that the three Powers should act in concert and hold identic language to the belligerents in all incidents affecting the interests of Europe, which might arise out of the war, and for the purpose of promoting the restoration of peace.[1]

During the course of these exchanges matters had moved on the field of battle. On 4 August the French suffered a reverse near Weissenburg and two days later a major defeat near Wörth. The superiority of the German armies stood revealed[2] and their victory became a probability. Gladstone readily accepted the prospect:

Perhaps, he said, it might all be for the best for Europe, for, though he was always very fond of the French, he thought a Bonaparte on the throne had always an element of uncertainty and danger. The management of this war, and the boasting and bragging had been most unfortunate, as well as the haggling about this Treaty [on Belgian neutrality].[3]

In fact, having secured a promise by both sides to respect the neutrality of Belgium, the British government could afford to observe with some equanimity the future course of events.[4]

VII

The Russian government, in the meantime, had continued its discussions with Vienna. On 9 August at a Court ball Chotek in accordance with his instructions had explained to the tsar the different geographical situation of the two empires and Austria's need for special precautions. Alexander replied somewhat impatiently that he could not see this need. France could not attack Austria now and was unlikely to do so later on; Austro-Italian relations were friendly; in the east he had himself preached quiet;

---

[1] Buchanan to Granville, 8 August 1870, *ibid.* no. 301.

[2] '...The losses of the unfortunate French seem to be greater and greater, 12,000 killed and wounded and 4,000 prisoners. They are quite disorganised. Dreadful excitement at Paris. The anger and panic great.' Extracts from the Queen's Journal, 9 August 1870, RA (*QVL, loc. cit.* pp. 55f.).

[3] *Ibid.*

[4] Morier, on the other hand, was unhappy. He was alarmed at the British export of ammunitions to France which was causing bitter feeling in Germany. He wrote:
'Oh, the fools, the fools! Can they not see that Germany *must* beat France, that forty millions of Teutons sending forth the whole of their *citizen* manhood must beat an army of Pretorian guards? Can they for one moment believe that *Germany* (mind you, not Bismarck and not Prussia) would trample on the public conscience of Europe by giving away Belgium to the foe they had conquered?...Can they not for one moment realise what the real issues at stake are? France draws the sword to assert her political preponderance over Europe. Germany draws the sword to assert her national existence. But the result will be that the preponderance of Germany over Europe for centuries to come will take the place of French preponderance. We sit by like a bloated Quaker, too holy to fight, but rubbing our hands at the roaring trade we are driving in cartridges and ammunition. We are heaping up to ourselves the undying hatred of the German race that will henceforth rule the world, because we cannot muster up courage to prevent a few cursed Brummagem manufacturers from driving their unholy trade' (Morier to Malet, 9 August 1870, Morier, *op. cit.* vol. 2, pp. 164f.).

against Prussia, he had guaranteed the Austrian frontiers.[1] The tsar spoke with some irritation[2] and his remarks concluded with a warning. If Austria armed or concentrated her forces, Russia must do the same; there would be recriminations; a spark might be lit from outside; and relations between the two countries might be seriously disturbed.[3] Chotek telegraphed to Vienna: '...On tient tellement empêcher grand armement ou concentration de notre part que nous pourrions à présent extorquer concessions et garanties diverses à la Russie dans la voie "de l'échange d'idées..."'.'[4]

Before leaving for Vienna, Chotek was received by both Gorchakov and the tsar. The Chancellor invited the Austrian government to indicate the measures which would remove its present distrust of Russia. When Chotek remarked that in the interest of a good understanding he should not go to

[1] '...ja, welche Gefahren? Frankreich kann sie jetzt nicht u. wird sie später nicht angreifen; mit Italien sind sie ja auf dem besten Fusse; im Orient habe ich Ruhe gepredigt und gegen Preussen die Sicherheit ihrer Grenzen mit meinem Ehrenworte verbürgt.'

[2] There existed a feeling of irritation on both sides. Earlier during the ball Westmann had told Chotek that the Russian chargé d'affaires in Paris had reported a French attempt to induce Austria to concentrate 100,000 men in Bohemia 'pour gêner la Prusse'. Chotek had given Westmann a curt reply but the tsar himself had later raised another delicate question, the alleged formation of a revolutionary committee at Leopol in Galicia. Chotek had replied with firmness: 'Je prie Votre Majesté instamment de croire et de Vous tenir assuré que nous saurons maintenir l'ordre et l'autorité chez nous, à nous tous seuls.'

[3] 'Aber, wenn sie rüsten oder concentriren...muss ich dasselbe thun; wir werden uns darüber in einen Austausch recriminirender Bemerkungen einlassen,—es kommt von ungefähr ein Funke dazu und unsere Beziehungen können ernstlich gestört werden' (Chotek to Beust, 9 August/28 July 1870, HHSAPARRR, July–December 1870, x 58, no. 42 A–B).

[4] The same to the same, telegram, 10 August 1870, ibid. This conviction was based in part, at least, on a conversation with D. Miliutin, the influential Minister of War. Miliutin explained that he did not desire the decisive victory of either side 'was bei einem russischen Generale so viel heisst, als: stark anti-preussisch, und eher etwas französisch'.
Miliutin had readily admitted the divergences of policy between Austria and Russia arising from their different geographical positions.
'Nichtsdestoweniger...würde es ihm vollkommen unbegreiflich sein, vorausgesetzt das wir weder durch ein bindendes Engagement an Frankreich gekettet, noch entschlossen seien, überhaupt die Initiative ergreifen zu wollen um in eine kriegerische Aktion einzutreten,— warum Oesterreich den ihm von Kaiser Alexander gemachten Antrag nicht annehemen sollte.'
The continued existence of the Habsburg monarchy in its entirety was a political necessity not only for Europe but for Russia. When Chotek complained of Russian Pan-Slavism, Miliutin replied that the Austrian government should not pay too much attention to the Russian press.
Miliutin admitted that an Austro-Russian rapprochement was not a question of general principles 'sondern dass es sich um die praktische und faktische Abstellung der thatsächlich bestehenden einzelnen Gravamina, Punkt für Punkt, handle. Die Vorbedingungen dazu seien gegenseitige Offenheit, guter Wille zur Abstellung...' and disregard of all elements trying to prevent an Austro-Russian understanding.
Chotek believed that Miliutin's language was inspired by hatred of Prussia and Germany, by his conviction that France would be defeated and the Napoleonic dynasty disappear, and by the wave of German patriotism sweeping the Baltic provinces.
The initiative for the conversation had come from Miliutin, who had actually called on Chotek. It was now, Chotek considered, for the Austrian government to decide whether it wished to pass from polite phrases to concrete negotiations. If Beust desired it, Chotek could have a more serious and practical exchange of views with Miliutin, perhaps the tsar's most influential adviser (the same to the same, 9 August/28 July 1870, ibid. no. 42B).

Vienna empty-handed, Gorchakov rejoined that his offer to discuss any points the Austrian government wished to raise was a far-reaching one. Moreover, a *rapprochement* with Russia would contribute to the internal consolidation of the monarchy.[1] Regarding the subject of the greatest interest to Beust—though not to his rival Andrássy—Gorchakov's language was unlikely to give satisfaction. In speaking of the future of south Germany, the Chancellor remarked that the Germans of the south had from the beginning rejected without a moment's hesitation all thought of a neutral or expectant attitude.[2] The preservation of the southern states, threatened with absorption by Prussia since 1866, now seemed assured for the future. Prussia would demand from them only a common military organization. Public opinion, moreover, would force her to reduce her armies. Again, the new order of things would create internal difficulties for Prussia and north Germany. The prospect of this, Chotek reflected, seemed to allay Gorchakov's fears of an excessive increase in Prussian strength.[3]

The tsar in his turn repeated to Chotek his desire for an understanding on armaments. Austrian neutrality should remain unarmed like that of Russia. By preserving her forces through a neutral policy, Austria would strengthen her position for the future and for the restoration of peace. He did not ask her to give up her freedom of action but merely wished to preserve her 'entière autorité pacifiante'. Austria as a great power was an indispensable necessity for the equilibrium of Europe. She would be strongest by pursuing a policy as similar as possible ('aussi *semblable* que possible') to that of Russia. He commended the British proposals for agreements among the neutral powers:[4] 'Il faudra bien se resserrer les uns avec les autres, être bien uni, car du train que va la Prusse il faudra nous en mêler tous pour empêcher qu'elle ne règle les affaires à elle seule et exclusivement à son gré.' A league of neutrals should interpose. 'Je serai impartial dans tous les cas et je voudrais utiliser dans le but d'abréger la durée de la guerre l'interposition de l'alliance des Etats neutres.' He would try to protect the vital interests of France: '...je ne donnerai mon consentement que pour un arrangement de paix durable, pas pour des conditions *impossibles* à la France, préjudiciables à l'équilibre européen et n'étant dès lors qu'une trêve non une paix réelle.'

[1] The same to the same, 13/1 August 1870, *ibid.* no. 44 A–C, secret.

[2] '"Unwiderstehlichkeit" mit welcher der Süden—*vor seinen Augen*—jeden Gedanken einer zurückhaltenden neutralen Stellung vom ersten Augenblick an zurückgewiesen hat.'

[3] The same to the same, 13/1 August 1870, *ibid.* no. 44B.

[4] On 10 August, Granville had proposed to Russia an understanding on neutrality among the great neutral powers and between them and the lesser states. No power party to the understanding would abandon its neutrality without communication with all the others. England and Italy had already agreed on this. The Austrian government had suggested a similar agreement. (Buchanan to Granville, 11 August 1870, FO 65/803 no. 307.) Gorchakov in his turn had welcomed the proposal.

Sooner or later, a Congress must be convened: 'Ce sera un congrès auquel il faudra venir et à des efforts tâchant de trouver pour longtems au moins des solutions définitives et des bases stables.' He desired more specifically to improve Austro-Russian relations, but there were two obstacles to this. The first was Poland, 'c'est une question sur laquelle je ne puis pas transiger'. Chotek replied that Austria could be conciliatory on matters of detail, 'Mais des concessions de *principe*, de système de gouvernement intérieur, l'Autriche ne saurait les concéder.' The tsar, Chotek considered, accepted this point of view.

'Oui, je crois que Vous avez raison. Si nous nous parlons honnêtement sur les questions de détail qui peuvent mettre du fiel dans nos relations, si nous tâchons de les résoudre d'une manière réciproquement complaisante, j'admets, que si en outre nous sommes plus intimement liés sur les grandes questions européennes, qu'il pourrait que l'effet décourageant sur le parti révolutionnaire polonais qu'aurait cette situation ferait qu'il ne serait plus question de mon côté de revenir sur mes désidérata vis-à-vis de Vous, sur un changement de Votre système politique intérieur.'

Chotek commented on these words:

Cette parole Impériale une fois recueillie, nous resterons enfin tranquils sous ce rapport du côté de St Pétersbourg, d'autant plus que le Prince Gorchacow est dans des dispositions encore meilleures si possible sous ce rapport.

The second difficulty, the tsar continued, lay in the Balkans. 'Là, je n'ai aucune convoitise, nous sommes assez grands. Plus de territoire serait un affaiblissement...pour la Russie.' He desired to preserve the Ottoman Empire, 'un chiffre connu'. Other arrangements would be an unknown quantity. Relations with the Porte were, at present, good.

'Mais si en dehors de notre pouvoir, ou malgré nous, la Turquie venait à se dissoudre, l'idée que nous avons est: Constantinople ville libre et centre d'une Confédération d'Etats souverains du Balkan. Il serait le mieux que nous concertions à nous deux et les conditions de la transformation et de l'existence de cet ensemble en faisant participer plus tard l'Europe à la création de cette œuvre.'

Russia would remain quiet. 'Je ne bougerai pas pour l'Orient tant que Vous ne montrerez pas de convoitises d'agrandissement territorial, que je ne pourrai pas admettre.'

'Le plus sage serait de prendre comme base de la politique russe et autrichienne pour l'Orient, la dépêche que le Comte de Beust a écrit à ce propos quand il a pris la direction du Ministère des affaires étrangères....Ce serait le meilleur moyen de nous rapprocher aussi sur ce terrain.'

The Black Sea Clauses the tsar forebore to mention: 'Ni le Chancelier', Chotek noted, 'ni l'Empereur ne parlèrent un mot de la mer Noire, du traité de 1856. Comme je ne faisais qu'écouter, ces sujets n'ont donc pas été touchés.' The tsar had been less hopeful than Gorchakov about the possibility of maintaining the Napoleonic regime in France: 'Si la république arrive, raison de plus pour nous rapprocher et nous prémunir contre les dangers de *cette* éventualité.' Alexander concluded with a solemn assurance that Russia had no intention whatever of attacking Austria. No extraordinary preparations had taken place:

'Apportez aussi à l'Empereur ma promesse que ce ne sera pas moi qui commencerai avec des armemens et des concentrations, je ne puis en faire que de grands et je ne voudrais absolument pas commencer pour des raisons d'économies nécessaires, à moins qu'on ne m'y force.'

Finally, the tsar proposed a personal correspondence between Francis-Joseph and himself.[1]

That day, Chotek had another conversation with Gorchakov. The Chancellor's language was, in certain respects, even more precise and outspoken than the tsar's. Gorchakov also wished Austria to accept the British proposal for agreements among the neutrals. The best hope of peace, he considered, lay in Napoleon rather than Prussia. The more compact the neutrals, the more weight they would carry with the less pacific of the two belligerents:

Il ne faudrait pas laisser à la Prusse la possibilité d'une initiative même pour l'interruption de la guerre, il faudrait la lui imposer les premiers. L'action des Puissances une action unie et *n'ayant pas de cocarde*.[2]

Suite de l'interposition des neutres un grand Congrès, ou siègeraient les chefs des Cabinets.

This Congress would have to settle as far as possible all questions connected directly or indirectly with the war such as the future of southern Germany and Article V of the treaty of Prague. Russia would enter the Congress in an impartial spirit. Peace not a truce was the aim; hence the terms finally agreed on must be not totally unacceptable to France.

Une indemnité de guerre même considérable est admissible, ainsi que le désarmement des forteresses françaises situées spécialement sur la frontière, mais les prétentions d'une cession de l'Alsace et de la Lorraine ainsi que d'autres demandes exorbitantes (p.e. pour la flotte) ne pourraient pas être prises en considération.

Détacher l'Alsace et en former avec le Luxembourg un pays indépendant neutre sous la garantie des Puissances serait possible, peut-être utile comme un "tampon" mais à concéder à la Prusse que dans le cas le plus extrême [*sic*] de sa victoire absolue et donc dans la supposition de grandes difficultés de traiter avec elle.

Échange d'idées entre l'Autriche et la Russie en cas d'une bataille décisive pour l'un des belligérants, également dans le cas d'une déchéance de la Monarchie Buonaparte en France.

Then Gorchakov turned to the question of Austrian armaments. 'Tâcher d'obtenir des affirmations renforcées par des faits sur la non-existence

---

[1] Minutes of Conversation of Chotek with Alexander II at Peterhof on 14 August 1870, handed personally by Chotek to Beust on 22 August 1870. HHSAPARRR, July-December 1870, x 58.

[2] Chotek simply recorded the main points raised by the tsar and Gorchakov—not always in complete sentences.

d'armements considérables et augmentants de la part de l'Autriche.' After this Gorchakov alluded briefly to a point developed in more detail by the tsar: 'Échange d'idées sur les relations spéciales entre la Russie et l'Autriche (communication franche de griefs respectifs)'. The Russian government would do everything in its power to influence Bismarck in a sense favourable to Austria:

La Russie prête à conseiller à la Prusse une politique prévenante envers l'Autriche, tâchant d'abord à empêcher le Comte Bismarck de continuer les mauvaises voies suivies jusqu'ici. Si l'Autriche apportait des preuves suffisantes pour prouver la continuation d'une pareille conduite hostile, la Russie donnerait de sérieux conseils à Berlin; si cette conduite continuait malgré ces exhortations russes, on prendrait à St Pétersbourg fait et cause pour l'Autriche dans un intérêt conservateur si des intimités et menées du Comte Bismarck perséveraient de lier le Cabinet prussien avec des éléments subversifs.

Then followed a revealing observation on the Polish question:

Déclaration du Prince Gortchacow qu'il n'envisageait pas *lui* personnellement la question polonaise comme aussi dangereuse que ne la considère l'Empereur et que cette question polonaise ou galicienne n'étant point si importante ne devrait d'après son opinion *personnelle* (un peu contraire à celle de Sa Majesté) ne [sic] pas être mise en avant par la Russie vis-à-vis de l'Autriche.

The two empires would co-operate 'contre la révolution internationale'. 'Nous voulons contenir la Prusse vis-à-vis de Vous. Vous gagner pour nous d'abord et puis pour le concert strictement neutre du reste de l'Europe.' A further object of the understanding was described by Gorchakov as: 'Empêcher trop grande prépondérance prussienne suivant l'esprit public russe très vif dans le Pays depuis 8 jours, partial pour la France, inquiet vis-à-vis de la Prusse.' Austria had nothing to fear from Russia:

Nous n'armons pas, nous ne ferons *rien* contre Vous et nous espérons seulement que Vous voudrez nous croire. 'Vous apportez à Vienne la vérité vraie.'

Nous n'avons *aucune* convoitise territoriale et nous désirons l'accroissement de la force et de l'influence de la Monarchie Austro-Hongroise en Europe.

One of the principal reasons why Russia desired unarmed neutrality: 'Épargnons nous des millions par l'identité de nos attitudes.' In conclusion, Gorchakov passed to the eastern question. Russia in face of the Franco-Prussian war, had strongly urged calm, particularly at Athens and Cetinje. Chotek should note the remarkable quiet in those parts in spite of the conflict in the west. Russia's relations with the Turkish government, moreover, were excellent.[1]

Parallel with their approaches to Austria, Gorchakov and the tsar had

---

[1] Minutes of conversation between Chotek and Gorchakov at Peterhof on 14 August 1870, handed personally by Chotek to Beust on 22 August 1870, *ibid.*

tried to enlist the support of the British government. Buchanan, entirely in sympathy with their ideas, reported on 15 August:

Every prospect of a satisfactory understanding being come to between Austria and Russia. The Austrian Minister after an audience with the Emperor yesterday leaves to-day for Vienna to confer with Count Beust.

The Emperor proposes entire assimilation of attitude of the two Empires and the early convocation in concert with England of a Congress with a view to the restoration of peace on the basis of entire impartiality between the Belligerents and the maintenance of the Balance of Power in Europe.[1]

Gorchakov believed

that Prussia does not wish an immediate termination of the war and that France cannot accept mediation yet, but he has told the Prussian Minister that Europe requires the establishment of peace on a just and durable basis and that if one neutral power makes a practical proposal for that object, Russia will immediately adhere to it.[2]

Gorchakov had explained

that he meant by a just and durable basis arrangements which both parties could accept without an intention of disturbing them as soon as they might be strong enough to do so; and he considered that humiliating concessions extorted from France would be quite inconsistent with such a peace as is essential to the permanent interests and welfare of Europe. It was premature... to speak of the terms on which a satisfactory settlement might be made,[3] but when conferences took place, Russia would doubtless be represented by a person, who could be trusted by the Emperor to conciliate the opinions of the Russian government with those of other Powers,[4] and that as to the place where the conference should be held, Paris and Berlin were the only capitals, to which the Emperor would object.[5]

As a first step, Gorchakov desired

that Her Majesty's Government should take steps without delay to carry out the suggestion... as to a common arrangement among the Neutral Powers in support of their Neutrality! Russia's adhesion to such an arrangement had already been notified to Italy, Sweden, Austria, Denmark, Holland, Spain, Turkey and Portugal.[6]

Such was the policy by means of which the tsar and Gorchakov hoped to counter-balance the increased power of Germany, soften the consequences of French defeat and bring about a settlement which might

---

[1] Buchanan to Granville, 15 August 1870, FO 65/803 no. 313, confidential, reporting telegram. Buchanan had earlier told Granville that Chotek was convinced of the tsar's sincerity in seeking agreement with Austria. Buchanan made himself the advocate of Chotek's views and urged Granville to try and dispel Beust's distrust of Russia. (The same to the same, 29 July 1870, *ibid.* no 283, most confidential.) He warned, however, that, although it was possible that in a future congress the Russian government might propose a revision of the Black Sea Clauses of the treaty of Paris. (The same to the same, 15 August 1870, *ibid.* no. 313, confidential, reporting telegram.)

[2] The same to the same, 16 August 1870, *ibid.* no. 314, reporting telegram.

[3] It is interesting to note that, in his conversation with Chotek, he had not found this impossible.

[4] Could this be Gorchakov himself?

[5] The same to the same, 16 August 1870, *ibid.* no. 314A, confidential.

[6] The same to the same, 16 August 1870, *ibid.* no. 314, reporting telegram.

develop into a peace rather than a truce. Perhaps the most striking feature of the programme was its openly anti-Prussian character, reflecting the widespread Russian anxiety at the sweeping nature of the German victories.[1] In fact, Gorchakov's overtures to Chotek and Buchanan mark a significant change in Russian policy. Whereas at the beginning of the war the main object of Russian diplomacy had been to prevent Austrian armaments and a violation of Danish neutrality, it now sought an understanding with Austria and England to organize neutral intervention and stop the victors in their course. In following the new policy, the tsar was acting in a European as much as a purely Russian interest. His was an eleventh hour effort to redress the European balance imperilled by the impending collapse of France, and to save that country from the consequences of Napoleon's folly and incompetence.

On 22 August, Chotek handed to Beust the memoranda of his conversations with Alexander and Gorchakov. His report faced the Austrian government with a fateful and urgent decision. The Russian proposals by themselves could do little to dispel the deep-seated Magyar distrust of Russia. They offered no striking or immediate advantages to the Dual Monarchy. The tsar's concrete offers were limited to a promise to discourage Panslav propaganda and to prevent anti-Austrian articles in the Russian press.[2] In addition, Alexander had unilaterally guaranteed the integrity of the Monarchy in face of the possible consequences of a Prussian victory and had undertaken, in a future congress, to demand the execution of the treaty of Prague. In the Balkans, he had declared his readiness to consent to any arrangement other than a one-sided extension of Austrian influence. The direct advantages offered to Austria by these proposals were thus limited in scope. On the other hand, the proffered understanding might enable the cabinet in Vienna to help its French friends in their predicament and to create, to some extent, a counter-weight to the increased importance of Prussia.

---

[1] The leading Russian journals, *Moscow Gazette* and *Golos* considered Russian interests to be seriously compromised by Germany's growing power. They expressed the view that, if Russia was to exercise any influence on the future settlement, she must begin to arm. The *Gazette* demanded that, in the remodelling of Europe, Russia must play a part befitting her importance. Whatever was done without her, would be done against her. *Golos* predicted the 'dictation of Prussia to Europe' resulting from the successes of the *Landwehr*. It added that whether victory went to Prussia or France, either the Baltic provinces or Poland would be threatened. (The same to the same, 12 August 1870, *ibid.* no. 310 enclosure.) Chotek translated, for the benefit of Beust, part of an article in *Golos*: 'Wir wollen nicht Preussens Ruin, doch liegt dessen *weitere* Vergrösserung nicht in unserem Interesse; das Gebot der Selbsterhaltung erlaubt uns nicht zu gestatten, dass ganz Deutschland unter dem Scepter eines Hauses vereinigt werde, das nach den Traditionen Friedrichs des Grossen regiert.... Würde Frankreich unterliegen, so würde vielleicht nach einigen Jahren an uns die Reihe kommen, wegen irgendeiner neuen hohenzollernschen Kandidatur uns in einen Krieg zu stürzen, um einem unleidlichen Zustand ein Ende zu machen' (Chotek to Beust, 30/18 July 1870, HHSAPARRR, July–December 1870, x 58 no. 38 D).

[2] *Ibid.*, and the same to the same, 13/1 August 1870, *ibid.* no. 44 A–C secret.

On 22 August, the Austrian council of ministers met under the presidency of the emperor to consider the future policy of the Monarchy. Beust opened the proceedings with a review of Austrian policy since 1867.[1] The problem now was what could be done to avert the consequences to Austria of Prussian victories. For the moment, there could be no question of armed intervention but only of diplomatic mediation. There was a proposal about neutrality from Italy, England and Russia to which Austria had been invited to adhere. The agreement meant little and an Austrian refusal would arouse distrust. He therefore favoured the acceptance with the proviso that the neutrals must bind themselves to refrain from single-handed mediation.[2] The tsar, in repeated conversations with Chotek had expressed the desire that Austria should not intervene in the war so that Russia need not do so either. Austria's reply had been at first evasive. Recently, however, the Russian approaches had become so persistent that Chotek had come to Vienna in order to report in person. According to Chotek, there was as yet no positive proposal for an agreement[3] but the Russian advances were none the less of such a nature that they should not be rejected. Only the united action of the powers could influence the decisions of Prussia; and Austria must avoid isolation. Gorchakov had given assurances about the Balkans. The tsar had discussed Poland in a reasonable spirit. If in addition Russia were to disavow the Czech agitation, this would be a distinct gain to Austria. To test her friendly dispositions she should be invited to make a public pronouncement against the Czechs. In conclusion, he recommended acceptance both of the British proposal for exchanging declarations of neutrality and of the Russian one for joint mediation to preserve the integrity of France. In addition, Austria should confine herself for the time being to the military preparations which had already been made. Beust's rival Andrássy

---

[1] In 1866 Austria had been isolated. Efforts to improve relations with Prussia had been frustrated by Prussian hostility. Agreement on some parts of the eastern question might have improved relations with Russia but here also Austrian advances had been repulsed. This left only the possibility of a *rapprochement* with France. Since 1867 relations between the two countries had become increasingly friendly. They had culminated in negotiations for an alliance of Austria, France and Italy. These had failed in the late summer of 1869 because France was unable to meet Italian wishes with regard to Rome. They had, however, produced a promise of French support for Austria if she was attacked. France had pursued a mistaken policy in the matter of the Spanish candidature and had played into the hands of Prussia. Whilst diplomatic action still had a purpose, Austria had spoken for France in Madrid and Berlin. When Leopold announced his renunciation Austria had advised restraint in Paris because her own unreadiness would not allow assistance to France in time ('mit Hinsicht auf unsere eigene Unfertigkeit, die uns die rechtzeitige Mithilfe nicht gestatte'). Had Austria joined in the war, Russia would have done so on the side of Prussia. If Austria had not been able to prevent the subsequent Prussian successes the question remained of what could be done to mitigate the consequences of Prussia's victories.
[2] This, presumably, was intended to prevent the tsar from playing the role assumed by Napoleon in 1866.
[3] The statement was perhaps misleading but Beust's intention was undoubtedly to allay the suspicions of Andrássy.

expressed doubts about the sincerity of the Russian desire for a *rapprochement* with Austria.[1] Even he, however, finally agreed that Russian influence might be used unofficially[2] to calm agitation in the Balkans and even within the Monarchy. Military preparations must be continued.[3] Potocki, the next speaker, favoured co-operation with Russia to increase Austria's weight in European affairs,[4] whilst the Ministers of War and Finance also considered that collaboration with England and Russia would strengthen Austria's position. After a curious speech by the emperor,[5] Beust made a final plea for accepting the Russian advances.[6]

Two days later, Francis-Joseph in a letter to Alexander expressed his readiness to continue the exchange of views:

Tendons nous donc la main sans arrière-pensée, et compte sur mon ancien amitié comme je compte sur la tienne. Qu'un échange de loyales explications prévienne entre nous tout malentendu et nous permette d'agir de concert afin de rendre à l'Europe le calme et la sécurité.[7]

On the following day, Beust translated these words into more concrete terms. He accepted wholeheartedly Gorchakov's formula 'd'une action aussi étroitement unie que possible des Puissances neutres', and invited

---

[1] He was unable to believe in the permanence of Russia's friendly dispositions. Whilst he accepted the peaceful intentions of the tsar and Gorchakov, he was certain that no good could come to Austria from Miliutin and his supporters. If they also favoured a *rapprochement* it was merely because Russian railway construction and military reforms were incomplete. Perhaps Russia wanted merely to push Austria forward against Prussia. The Russian proposal was a tactical move which must be viewed with caution.

[2] No pretext must be offered to Russia to interest herself in Austria's internal affairs. This regarded the Polish, Czech and Southern Slav questions and the construction of strategic railways.

[3] Austria could not disarm simply on the strength of a temporary improvement in her relations with Russia. The present state of affairs was transitory: it remained the task of the Monarchy to form a bulwark against Russia: only whilst she fulfilled this function was Austria a European necessity. The present negotiation, therefore, should be continued only on the understanding that military preparations would go on.

[4] Austria might soon have to express her views on the terms of peace and the co-operation of Russia would then be an advantage.

[5] Francis-Joseph voiced the extraordinary suspicion that both the British and Russian proposals might be inspired by Prussia. He then asked whether, in the coming peace negotiations, Austria should wholeheartedly defend the integrity of France or allow Prussia to acquire territory which she would not enjoy in peace.—Andrássy replied that common decency obliged Austria to defend French integrity. However, should Prussia overrule the Austrian plea, this would be advantageous: Alsace-Lorraine would keep Prussia occupied for a long time to come and would keep alive French desire for revenge. Beust added that Prince Latour had received a formal promise before he left Vienna that in case of need Austria would try by diplomatic means to defend the Napoleonic dynasty and the integrity of France. He did not believe that either the British or Russian proposals had originated in Berlin.

[6] HHSAPSDiRM, Protokoll 1869–71, protocol of meeting of Council of Ministers on 22 Ausgut 1870.

[7] Francis-Joseph to Alexander II, 24 August 1870, HHSAPAR x 59, Russie Expéditions, Varia 1870, draft.

the Russian government to formulate its proposals.[1] He transmitted memoranda explaining the nature of Austria's military preparations and defending their necessity.[2] The Russian government was invited to disavow Panslav agitation in Austria[3] and to restrain the Prince of Montenegro.[4] In return, the Austrian government formally disclaimed all intention of favouring subversive movements in Poland[5] and invited Russia to take a more active part in Roumelian railway construction.[6]

The Austrian reply, delivered by Chotek on 29 August, was ill-received at St Petersburg. The tsar expressed his displeasure at the continuance of Austrian military preparations. Gorchakov took up the cue. He warned Chotek: 'Deux puissances voisines armant et concentrant leurs forces dans un but qui ne serait pas *identique* se placeraient sur une pente qui entraîne l'une et l'autre dans une direction qui n'est ni dans les vœux ni dans les intérêts d'aucune d'elles.' He therefore called upon the Austrian government to end its military activities: 'Je vous propose donc de signaler à Votre Cour la gravité des conséquences que pourraient produire une contradiction à nos desseins et une persistance de Votre Gouvernement dans les armemens projetés.'[7]

The difference of views about Austrian armaments was not the only difficulty encountered by Chotek. On his arrival in the Russian capital, he had noticed a change in the political atmosphere. Severe but indecisive actions along the Châlons road fought on 16 and 18 August had greatly reduced French military prospects; indeed reports from the theatre of war suggested the possibility of a French collapse. In consequence, the Russian press had begun to change its tone and was now advocating a policy of abstention and self-interest.[8] The new attitude was reflected in Gorchakov's language: '...nous nous tenons à l'écart parce que nous savons tout récemment que depuis quelques jours surtout les Prusses ne veulent plus écouter ni qui que ce soit, ni quoi que ce soit.'[9] Indeed the Chancellor

---

[1] How did the Russian government envisage the method of neutral intervention? What bases of peace should be proposed to the belligerents? What action should be taken if they were rejected? 'Nous abandonnons *l'initiative à prendre pour un congrés à la Russie;* nous ne ferons aucune difficulté pour le choix de l'endroit où il se réunirait' (Beust to Chotek, 25 August 1870, *ibid.* x 8, Russie 1864–70, Protokoll, draft no. 1).

[2] The same to the same, 25 August 1870, *ibid.* draft no. 2.

[3] 'Nous désirons que le gouvernement russe répudie hautement le semblant de solidarité qu'on essaye d'établir entre lui et certaines *menées* panslavistes en Autriche' (the same to the same, 25 August 1870, *ibid.* draft no. 3).

[4] The same to the same, 25 August 1870 *ibid.* draft no. 4.

[5] '...nous déclarons que rien ne peut être plus éloigné des intentions de notre Auguste Maître, que d'encourager en quoi que ce soit les élémens révolutionnaires en Pologne ou de favoriser des entreprises subversives, qui seraient dirigées contre la Russie' (the same to the same, 25 August 1870, *ibid.* draft no. 3).

[6] The same to the same, 25 August 1870, *ibid.* draft no. 4.

[7] Chotek to Beust, 4 September/23 August 1870, *ibid.* PARRR, July–December 1870, x 58 no. 46.

[8] The same to the same, telegram, 29 August 1870, *ibid.*

[9] The same to the same, telegram, 3 September 1870, *ibid.*

frankly explained that after the unhappy turn events had taken during the past week, the interposition of the neutrals no longer seemed practicable; Prussia, he feared, would now refuse to listen to anyone.[1] The Russian government still preferred the preservation of the Napoleonic dynasty and the principle of French integrity, but he was afraid that both would remain pious hopes. As Russia was determined to avoid military pressure on either belligerent and unwilling to invite a certain rebuff, she would now support only proposals which were sure to be accepted.[2]

At the moment when the news of Napoleon's surrender at Sedan reached St Petersburg, Chotek in a private letter to Gorchakov was giving a résumé of the unsuccessful negotiation.[3] Further exchanges, now mainly retrospective in character, were finally closed on 18 September by a letter from the tsar to the Austrian emperor. He had read with great pleasure, Alexander declared, Francis-Joseph's letter of 24 August.

Si j'ai tardé à y répondre, c'est que j'ai cru trouver dans les communications que le Comte Chotek m'a apportées de Ta part, quelques malentendus qu'il était urgent d'éclaircir. Je les lui ai franchement signalés et je vois avec satisfaction qu'actuellement ils sont ecartés et que Tu Te places avec moi sur le terrain d'une stricte et absolue neutralité.—Cette attitude me paraît la plus sage dans les conjonctures actuelles. Elle donnera aux Puissances qui n'ont pas pris part à la guerre une autorité morale qu'elles pourront d'autant mieux faire valoir en faveur d'une paix juste et durable qu'elles se seront abstenues d'apporter à la crise présente de nouveaux éléments de complications.[4]

In fact, Russia's attempt to bring about a 'European' solution had been prudently abandoned in the face of Prussia's overwhelming victories; the tsar had no wish to play the part acted with such conspicuous lack of success by Napoleon after the battle of Königgrätz.

[1] 'Die Möglichkeit einer "Interposition" neutraler Mächte "wie eben die Sachen sich *leider* in den letzten 8 Tagen gestaltet haben", fügte er achselzuckend hinzu, halte er für kaum mehr wahrscheinlich und ausführbar, weil er fürchte, dass die Preussen gar nichts mehr und von gar niemandem würden etwas anhören wollen.'

[2] 'Da man hier entschlossen sei eine materielle militairische [*sic*] Pression auf einen Kriegführenden unter gar keinen Umständen eintreten zu lassen, man sich aber dem mit Sicherheit vorauszusehenden refus nicht aussetzen will, so müssten eben nur solche Propositionen überhaupt vorgebracht werden, deren Annehmbarkeit evident vorauszusetzen wäre' (the same to the same, 4 September/23 August 1870, *ibid.* no. 46).

[3] Chotek to Gorchakov, confidential, 22 August/3 September 1870, copy (in Chotek to Beust, 4 September/23 August 1870, *ibid.* no. 46).

[4] Alexander II to Francis-Joseph, 6/18 September 1870, *ibid.* x 59, Russie Expéditions, Varia 1870.

VIII

British diplomacy, in the meantime, had been almost completely passive. With the independence of Belgium seemingly assured and the auspices for neutral mediation clearly unpropitious,[1] there was little to do but watch the course of events. The Prince of Wales, indeed, from the wilds of Aberdeenshire, had written imploringly to his mother:

> If only something could be done to stop this terrible war. Could not England backed up by the other neutral powers now step in, to try and induce the belligerants [sic] to come to terms—How I wish you could send me with letters to the Emperor and the King of Prussia with friendly advice even if it ultimately failed—I would gladly go any distance—as I cannot help feeling restless.[2]

The Queen had prudently replied that the time had not yet come when anything could be done: '...any attempt to interfere would only be refused and make matters worse, for that we should be asked to bind ourselves for future contingencies'.[3] Granville shared the Queen's opinion: '...we have no reason to suppose that Prussia would consent to our mediation and there is some doubt whether she will ever do so—and as to France, we have been distinctly informed by the Prince de Latour d'Auvergne that the time is not come'. The Queen and Prince of Wales might rely on Her Majesty's Ministers 'seriously watching for an opportunity to be of use, but a premature attempt would be fatal to our influence, and harmful for the object'.[4] The collapse of the Second Empire merely emphasized the need for caution. Gladstone told the Duke of Argyll: 'I would not say a word ever so gently. I believe it would do great mischief. As at present advised, I see but two really safe grounds for mediation, (1) a drawn battle; (2) the request of both parties.'[5] To a young Frenchman 'now in a private station', but who was 'probably in communication with persons in authority',[6] Gladstone defended his policy of non-intervention:

> '...I do not see that it is an offence on our part not to interfere when the belligerents differ so widely, when we have not the hope of bringing them

[1] On 17 August Granville told Buchanan that the latter's telegrams of the two preceding days seemed to indicate a disposition on the part of the Russian government to prepare for an offer of mediation. Gorchakov seemed conscious of the fact that the time for such a step had not yet come and the British government 'fully coincide in that opinion'. Any offer now would be disregarded by the belligerents (Granville to Buchanan, telegram, 17 August 1870, RA I 64/129). The following day the ambassador replied that Gorchakov entirely concurred in the opinion expressed 'as to inexpediency of offering mediation at present to belligerents' (Buchanan to Granville, 18 August 1870, FO 65/803, no. 315, reporting telegram).
[2] Prince of Wales to Queen, ? 19 August 1870, RA I 64/135.
[3] Queen to Granville, 22 August 1870, ibid. I 64/149, extract, copy.
[4] Granville to the Queen, 23 August 1870, ibid. I 64/157.
[5] Gladstone to Argyll, 6 September 1870, Lord Morley, Life of Gladstone (London, 1903), vol. II, p. 344.
[6] Gladstone to the Queen, 8 September 1870, RA I 65/59.

together, and when we cannot adopt without reserve the language and claims of either.'[1]

In the meantime, Granville had been severely attacked in Germany as being partial to France. Halifax, the 'elder statesman' of the Liberal Party, defended the Foreign Secretary. Granville, he told the Queen, had

truly represented the opinion of your Majesty's Government that in order to have the power, if an opportunity should offer itself, of successfully mediating with a view to the restoration of peace, it was essential to preserve the most impartial neutrality between the contending parties.

Neutral conduct was always liable to be misconstrued.

...the party which at the time considers itself in the worst position naturally complains. At first, the Prussians were discontented with the attitude of England, when they thought France had an advantage. Now that the French have suffered reverses, they are the complaining party.

Neither complaint affected 'the wisdom of the conduct of this country'. Granville's policy, it was hoped, would enable the Queen 'to take a prominent part in putting an end to this sad war on terms not degrading to any one, and most advantageous to the future welfare of Europe'. With regard to the future, Halifax pinned his hopes on the liberal Crown Prince of Prussia.

The sovereigns of Germany and its people will have every reason to be grateful to him, and England in common with all Europe will benefit by the creation of such a power, ruled in such a spirit, as will, by God's blessing, arise out of the present confusion.[2]

Morier expressed similar views from Darmstadt:

...You will know without my telling you, how heart and soul I am with Germany at this great turning-point, not of her history only but of that of mankind. What untold heights of civilisation may not the world attain with a German Empire preponderant over the destinies of Europe—if only there is as much wisdom in the upper stories of the building as there has been valour and self-sacrifice in the lower. I confess, however, that I have all along feared rather the possible consequences of victory than the probability of defeat.

The source of Morier's anxiety was the possible annexation of Alsace-Lorraine.

What I meant by saying that I have feared the possible result of victory, is that I have all along feared the demand for Alsace and Lorraine...a hostile occupation of this kind means more or less the continuance of armed peace and the impossibility of disarmament.[3]

---

[1] Gladstone to Michel Chevalier, September 1870, Morley, *op. cit.* p. 344. Cf. also the same to the same, 6 September 1870, copy RA I 65/61, enclosed in Gladstone to the Queen, 8 September 1870, *ibid.* I 65/59.
[2] Halifax to the Queen, 29 August 1870, *ibid.* I 64/175.
[3] Morier to Stockmar, 21 August 1870, Morier, *op. cit.* p. 165.

Goschen, who had welcomed the German victories, yet expressed misgivings at their possible consequences:

...What I have been opposed to, in common I believe with all the Cabinet, is the giving of advice, the offering mediation, the useless attempt of bringing people together who won't be brought together. And I should be most jealous of every action based on any idea of Prussia becoming too strong or France too weak. On the whole I have cordially sympathised with the German victories and quite think the downfall of the military prestige of France will be of incalculable benefit. But I confess I see great danger ahead in the unbounded success not only of the German arms, but of Bismarck's unscrupulous, cynical and cruel policy. I do not know that anything actually occurred which gave us any actual *locus standi* for showing our cards one way or another, and therefore, though beginning to feel most uneasy at the unchecked progress of Bismarckism, I still considered you were perfectly right in preserving absolute silence.[1]

The Queen rejoiced at the triumph of Germany. She completely identified herself with the German people, who had been united by French boasting and insults to other nations:

It is this which has united those millions of Germans (whose conduct is admirable) as One Man, who look on it as a holy war to obtain once and for all the means of living at peace. They take it in the most serious light and they suffer fearfully—but it is the cause of civilization, of liberty, of order and of unity, which triumphs over despotism, corruption, immorality and aggression! They consider this as the continuation of the war of liberation of 1813![2]

The Earl of Lytton saw the Teutons as glorious and 'juvenescent', whilst France had been rotted by lies in every fibre till there remained to her nothing but her native ferocity.[3] George Eliot considered the war as one between two civilizations and believed that with the German victory the world had entered a better period which would be 'marked in future histories and charts as the "period of German ascendancy"'.[4] Carlyle's enthusiasm over the German victories is well known and the 'Sage' felt impelled to inform the Prussian ambassador: 'that whatever our newspapers may say, the great body of solid English Opinion on the subject is in agreement with my own'.[5] Such was the British reaction to events by which Germany replaced France as the leading European power. Soon Gladstone would reply to a French warning about the possible consequences for England of the collapse of France:

...il ne faut pas oublier, en tout cas, que la Russie a des provinces allemandes, et qu'elle est plus menacée par la Prusse que nous. D'ailleurs, nous sommes à l'abri des attaques de la Prusse par la situation naturelle de notre pays. Elle ne pourrait pas encore prendre la petite île de Helgoland contre notre volonté.[6]

---

[1] Goschen to Granville on 30 September 1870 (Hon. A. D. Elliot, *Life of Goschen* (London, 1911), vol. I, p. 131).

[2] Queen to Mr A. Helps, 29 August 1870, RA I 64/176, copy.

[3] Quoted in Raymond, *op. cit.* p. 131.   [4] *Ibid.*

[5] Carlyle to Bernstorff, 26 November 1870, Bernstorff, *op. cit.* p. 641.

[6] F. Reitlinger, *Une Mission Diplomatique en Octobre 1870* (Paris, 1899), p. 156.

England, as well as Russia, thus accepted the verdict of Sedan. Both took the view that mediation by the neutrals would be practicable only if accepted by both sides which meant, above all, by Bismarck. However, German peace terms, although the subject of surmise, were not yet officially known; the French, even after Sedan, continued a desperate resistance. The situation remained fluid; unexpected developments were still within the realm of possibility.

CHAPTER II

ALSACE-LORRAINE, THE BLACK SEA CLAUSES AND THE ESTABLISHMENT OF THE GERMAN EMPIRE, SEPTEMBER 1870–MARCH 1871

ALTHOUGH history does not repeat itself in detail, similar situations sometimes recur as the result of similar circumstances. During the summer of 1866, Russia had tried to organize a concert of neutrals to supervise the reorganization of Germany; four years later, she had again attempted to create a neutral bloc to preserve the threatened equilibrium of Europe. Both attempts had come to an abrupt conclusion. Russian failure in the one case as in the other had been due, primarily, to decisive Prussian victory in the field. In addition Prussia in 1866 had offered support for a revision of the Black Sea Clauses as the price of Russian acquiescence. Four years later, almost to the day, Bismarck again employed the abrogation of these clauses as a bait to disarm Russian opposition. Yet the outcome of the two incidents differed: in September 1866, Gorchakov's declaration denouncing the Black Sea Clauses was pigeon-holed in face of opposition from the Ministers of War and Finance; in 1870 it was taken out of the drawer and after some alterations of detail was presented—not unexpectedly—to an embattled Europe.

Another parallel between the two crises may be found in the motives for neutral opposition to Prussian policy. In 1866 the tsar had attempted to rally European opinion in the name of the treaties of 1815, of legitimacy and of dynastic rights. In 1870–1 Gladstone supported by some of his colleagues would 'protest' against the annexation of Alsace and Lorraine in the name of the rights of the inhabitants. Both protests were doctrinaire[1] since England would no more go to war for the rights of the Lorrainers[2] than would the tsar for those of the king of Hanover. In each case academic 'idealism' yielded readily to the dictates of political expediency: a promise of support for treaty revision induced the Russian government to abandon the cause of the German dynasties; British Ministers accepted German annexations in exchange for Bismarck's assist-

---

[1] In 1864, Palmerston and the Russian government had similarly taken their stand on the 'sanctity of treaties', Napoleon and Queen Victoria on the right of populations to determine national allegiance and the person of their ruler. Bismarck's strength lay in his freedom from ideology: some would say, his lack of political principles.

[2] It was an entirely different matter when it came to the Russian denunciation of the Black Sea Clauses which immediately aroused bellicose sentiments in the British press and public.

ance in the settlement of the Black Sea question. In 1870–1 Bismarck was able to pay both England and Russia for their acquiescence in German supremacy by means of a single diplomatic transaction in which, moreover, their interests were opposed. The settlement of the Black Sea question marks the beginning of Bismarck's ascendancy in Europe.

I

On 10 August 1870, Reuss told Bismarck on behalf of the Grand-Duchess Helen[1] that, if Gorchakov could be persuaded to denounce the treaty of Paris, this would prevent him from making awkward proposals for neutral mediation in the Franco-German war. Prussia might then assure him that, as long as he refrained from intervention, he could count on her benevolence.[2] The Duchess intended to press her views on Gorchakov and the tsar. As the former refused to receive her on the plea of ill-health, she submitted her ideas in writing. In his reply, the Chancellor ignored the suggestion.[3] The Grand-Duchess felt increasingly convinced that he was planning a neutral intervention to deprive Prussia of the fruits of her victory.[4] She therefore invited Prince August of Württemberg to discuss with the king of Prussia the expediency of a direct appeal to the tsar.[5] At this point, Bismarck decided to act. On 24 August he told Reuss to inform the tsar either personally or through the Grand-Duchess, that Prussia would not make peace without the acquisition of territory to protect southern Germany. If Russia in her turn had wishes concerning the treaty of Paris, Prussia would make them her own.[6] Reuss replied that caution was necessary in broaching the subject: the initiative should come

---

[1] The Grand-Duchess, a former Württemberg Princess, was the widow of one of the tsar's uncles, Michael Pavlovich. Fanatically pro-German, she had for years headed the German faction in the imperial Russian family.
'Die Haltung der Frau Grossfürstin ist über alles Lob erhaben. Sie nimmt sich unserer Sache mit einem wahren Feuereifer an und bringt dabei ihrer persönlichen Bequemlichkeit wirkliche Opfer. Die grosse Klugheit, mit der sie dabei die Menschen zu nehmen weiss, und der feine Takt, den sie in der Beurteilung der Sache zeigt, ist bewundernswürdig. Alle ihre Deduktionen haben immer den Vorteil Russlands zum Zielpunkt, welchen sie mit patriotischer Wärme herauszustreichen versteht, wo es nötig ist' (Reuss to Bismarck, 31 August 1870, GW, loc. cit. pp. 145 ff.).
[2] The same to the same, 10 August 1870, Rheindorf, op. cit. p. 143.
[3] 'In dem Antwortbillet, welches ich gesehen habe, übergeht der Kanzler zum Erstaunen und Missfallen der Grossfürstin diesen Gedanken vollständig mit Stillschweigen. Dies bestärkt sie in der Ansicht, dass er sich in Tripotagen mit den Neutralen eingelassen hat, die ihr nicht gefallen dürften, und deshalb sowohl eine Begegnung als auch einen schriftlichen Gedankenaustausch vermeidet.'—In fact, on 14 August the tsar and Gorchakov had made the 'Peterhof' proposals to Chotek.
[4] 'Die Grossfürstin ist nun durch diese Beobachtungen immer besorgter, dass sich Russland hinreissen lassen möchte, im Verein mit den anderen Neutralen uns in unserem Siegeslauf aufzuhalten und dadurch die Früchte der einmütigen Erhebung Deutschlands zu kompromittieren.'
[5] The same to the same, 16 August 1870, most confidential, ibid. pp. 143 f.
[6] Bismarck to Reuss, telegram, 24 August 1870, GW, loc. cit. pp. 457 f.

from St Petersburg and Russia's appetite must first be whetted. However, the Russian press was already beginning to show an interest in the matter.[1] Six days later, in conversation with Gorchakov, Reuss complained that the Chancellor had constantly preached 'moderation' and spoken of a European congress. Gorchakov insisted that the war was changing the face of Europe, that a variety of interests was involved, and that powers other than the belligerents must play a part in the settlement.[2] In alluding to the treaty of 1856, Reuss then found an opportunity to observe that individual states might have wishes and needs to which the Prussian government would not be insensitive.[3]

Reuss's ally, the Grand Duchess, had in the meantime tried to influence the tsar. Alexander had facilitated this by reading to her a letter in which he had recalled to the king of Prussia that only 'une paix honorable et juste, sanctionnée par l'Europe' held out the prospect of security for the future. The Grand-Duchess thereupon observed that this would not please King William. Peace would not be safe without German annexations. Only if France now lost Alsace would she give up her dreams of the Rhine. Moreover, in the present state of German opinion, Prussia could not make peace without territorial gains. Russia would obtain advantages if she now sought agreement with Germany instead of calling for a congress. Participation of other powers would merely hinder the attainment of her objects.[4] Finally, a peace unsatisfactory to Germany conjured up the prospect of revolution.[5] Gorchakov in his turn was informed by the Grand-Duchess that he must extricate Russia from the position in which he had placed her. He had made the mistake of talking to the neutrals and must atone for this by preventing Russia's hands from being tied.[6]

---

[1] 'Der russische Appetit nach Revision muss erst noch mehr gereizt werden, und fängt die russische Presse schon an, dieses Geschäft zu betreiben' (Reuss to Bismarck, 26 August 1870, Rheindorf, *op. cit.* pp. 144f.).

[2] 'Europa werde durch die jetzigen Kämpfe aus den Angeln gehoben, es kämen zu viel Interessen zur Sprache und müssten daher auch die anderen dabei mithelfen; er machte dabei eine Andeutung auf den 56er Frieden.'

[3] 'Ich gab ihm zu, dass einzelne Staaten auch Interessen und Wünsche haben könnten, und gab ihm zu verstehen, dass wir uns solchen Wünschen nicht verschliessen würden' (the same to the same, 30 August 1870, *ibid.* p. 145).

[4] Russian interests, the Grand Duchess told Reuss, concerned not only the Black Sea but also North Schleswig. She strongly urged the Prussian government to pay attention to this point to which the tsar attached great importance.

[5] Reuss had previously alluded to this point in conversation with the tsar. The Grand-Duchess noted that this infallible bogey had once again done its work with Alexander. Gorchakov had complained to her that the tsar had been frightened ('dass man dem Kaiser Angst gemacht habe'). She had, therefore, made the most of this argument. On the following day, she had received a note from the empress saying that no agreement had been reached between Russia and the neutrals, 'es bestehe kein Vertrag und man könnte sich die andern abschütteln, wenn sie es zu bunt machten'.

[6] 'Sie hat dem Kanzler gesagt, seine Aufgabe sei es nun, Russland aus dieser schwierigen Stellung herauszulotsen; er habe den Fehler begangen, sich zu weit mit den Neutralen einzulassen, das müsse er wieder gut machen und dafür sorgen, dass sich Russland nicht die Hände binden lasse.'

Having thus prepared the ground, Reuss decided to strike. The Grand-Duchess must tell the tsar that Prussia neither could nor would make peace without annexing French territory. In return, the king of Prussia would be willing to support possible Russian wishes. There would be the added advantage of the most cordial relations between the two neighbouring states.[1]

Impressed by the overwhelming German victory at Sedan, Gorchakov had abandoned his plans for neutral mediation. There now seemed little hope, he told Buchanan,

of England and Russia being able to prevent the dismemberment of France, should the Prussian Government have decided not to relinquish their conquests of Alsace and Lorraine; and he fears that the Neutral Powers can only look on with regret, if Prussia should commit so great an error as to annex territory which cannot fail to be a constant source of weakness and embarrassment to Germany, and a germ of future wars.[2]

The Russian government had finally resigned itself to French territorial losses and German supremacy in Europe. It now remained—after the failure of a 'European' policy—to see what advantages could be gained from a separate agreement with Germany.

On 8 September, Gorchakov for the first time mentioned treaty revision to Reuss. He had, he declared, stood by quietly whilst the treaty had been violated and ignored ('verletzt und durchlöchert') by all the other powers. However, he would now abandon this silence and at an early opportunity denounce arrangements which were offensive to Russia.[3] He had no wish to reverse the unimportant territorial cession in Bessarabia; what mattered was the article restricting Russian sovereignty in the Black Sea.[4] Reuss replied that Russia could count on Prussian support.[5]

Bismarck in Berlin, promptly submitted the matter to the King and the Crown-Prince, both of whom repeated their already well-known readiness to support the Russian wishes, not only against France but against all other powers. If the Russian requirements could be met without a

---

[1] The same to the same, 31 August 1870, most confidential, *ibid.* pp. 145ff.
[2] Buchanan to Granville, 5 September 1870, FO 65/804, no. 337, confidential.
[3] 'Sobald die Zeit gekommen sein werde, würde er aus diesem Schweigen heraustreten und die für Russland verletzenden Klauseln umwerfen.'
[4] Stremouchov had already explained to Reuss that Russia wished to end the closing of the Bosphorus and Dardanelles and throw open the Black Sea to the ships of all nations. This would not need a congress. Russia would simply inform the powers that in her opinion the provisions of the much ignored treaty of Paris had ceased to operate. With Prussian support, she need fear no opposition. British protests would probably remain platonic ('Englands Protestationen würden wohl nunmehr nur noch platonischer Natur sein'). It was improbable that Russia would either rebuild Sevastopol or maintain a strong fleet in the Black Sea. She would be satisfied if she regained her freedom of navigation and removed the stain of 1856.
[5] 'Ich sagte dem Fürsten, dass, wie ich ihm bereits angedeutet hätte, Russland auf das freundschaftlichste Entgegenkommen des Kabinetts Seiner Majestät des Königs würde rechnen können' (the same to the same, 9 September 1870, Rheindorf, *op. cit.* pp. 148f.).

congress, this would facilitate matters. Reuss must be cautious but leave no doubt whatever about the support of Prussia.[1]

On 12 September 1870 the *Kölnische Zeitung* published a letter 'from a reliable source', dated from Berlin on the previous day. This declared that with the sole exception of Russia, the neutral powers had 'certainly not manifested any good will towards us'. Except for Russia, therefore, no neutral power need be considered in future peace negotiations.

It will be easy for the Government of Germany to come to a friendly accord with Russia respecting the conditions of peace. We even think that it would be possible on the part of Germany, in the course of the negotiations, to take Russian interests into consideration and to defend them, should it be desired at St Petersburg.[2]

Buchanan, in transmitting a translation of the letter, observed that its language was

nearly identical with the assurances which I have reason to believe Count Schouvaloff, the Minister of the Secret Police, on passing through Berlin about a fortnight ago, was charged by Queen Augusta to convey to the Emperor, that the King of Prussia and the people of Germany will not forget the services for which they are indebted to Russia, and that they will be ready to give their support to any question raised in Europe of interest to Russia, if a wish to that effect is expressed from St Petersburgh.

Buchanan added that he had frequently stated in his correspondence that the Russian government would avail itself of the first favourable opportunity to bring the question under consideration. Gorchakov's desire for a congress might have originated in the hope of raising the issue there.

Prussia has however as yet shewn no disposition to gratify this wish for a Congress, but she may not, nevertheless, be unwilling to support a proposal made some other way for a revision of the Treaty and to repay by such support the services rendered to her by Russia during the present war.[3]

On 25 September, Bismarck informed Reuss that he was prepared to warn the Turkish government against speculating on any change in the friendly

---

[1] '...dem König in Gegenwart des Kronprinzen vorgetragen und wiederholt die Ew. Durchlaucht bekannte Bereitwilligkeit gefunden, die Wünsche Russlands in Bezug auf das Schwarze Meer, die wir für berechtigt halten, zu unterstützen und nicht nur Frankreich, sondern auch den andern Mächten gegenüber zu vertreten. Werden sie in dem Umfange gehalten, wie sie ohne Kongress faktisch durchführbar sind, ist es um so leichter. Aeussern Sie sich mit der Vorsicht, die Ihnen angemessen erscheint; über unsere Bereitwilligkeit aber zur Unterstützung lassen Sie keinen Zweifel' (Bismarck to Reuss, telegram, 16 September 1870, *ibid.* pp. 149f.). Cf., also, the same to the same, 20/9 September 1870, a telegraphic despatch of which a copy found its way into the Russian archives, (1870 Prusse, Légation, rec. 22/10 September 1870, Goriainov, *op. cit.* p. 154). This leads Potemkin to write: 'le 20 Septembre, Bismarck exécuta la promesse qu'il avait contractée en 1866 de prêter son entier concours à la Russie dans une question de grande importance: la suppression des clauses du traité de Paris...' (Potiemkine, *op. cit.* p. 523).

[2] Translation in Buchanan to Granville, 21 September 1870, FO 65/804, no. 354, confidential.

[3] Buchanan to Granville, 21 September 1870, FO 65/804, no. 354, confidential.

relations between Prussia and Russia.[1] In return, however, he needed a precise explanation from Gorchakov about his attitude towards the peace negotiations between Prussia and France. Reuss must confidentially explain that arrangements of this kind required a measure of reciprocity.[2] As this hint suggested, the question of German annexations had become the issue of the moment.

II

On 13 September, Bismarck in a circular despatch announced that the annexation of Alsace and Lorraine to Prussia was an indispensable necessity. On the 22nd, Bernstorff communicated this despatch to Granville.[3] It was a challenge to the British government to explain its views on the terms of peace. Four days later Gladstone wrote to Granville that perhaps the inhabitants should be consulted: 'There is very great difficulty in seeing how to obtain an unbiassed expression of their wishes: but is not anything better than simply handing them over as Chattels? This is for rumination only.'[4] When Granville questioned the wisdom of an official declaration, Gladstone embodied his view in an elaborate memorandum. He wrote to Granville:

I am much oppressed with the idea that this transfer of human beings like chattels should go forward without any voice from collective Europe if it be disposed to speak.[5]

He felt that:

...A matter of this kind cannot be regarded as in principle a question between the two belligerents only, but involves considerations of legitimate interest to all the Powers of Europe. It appears to bear on the Belgian question in particular. It is also a principle likely to be of great consequence in the eventual settlement of the Eastern question. Quite apart from the subject of mediation, it cannot be right that the neutral Powers should remain silent, while this principle of consulting the wishes of the population is trampled down, should the actual sentiment of Alsace and Lorraine be such as to render that language applicable. The mode of expressing any view on this matter is doubtless a question requiring much consideration.[6]

Goschen, Gladstone's principal supporter, explained to Granville why he agreed with the Prime Minister:

...I was anxious to say a word in favour of a course which seemed to me to combine the advantages of:

(1) being right and just in itself;

[1] Bismarck to Reuss, 26 September 1870, Rheindorf, *op. cit.* p. 150. In fact the Turkish government in anticipation of a Russian move had proposed an engagement between England, Austria and Italy that in any possible Congress they would not allow the revision of the treaty to be discussed. Musurus, the Turkish ambassador, made his proposal to Granville on 6 October 1870 (Granville to Elliot, 6 October 1870, FO 195/959, no. 207).
[2] Bismarck to Reuss, 26 September 1870, Rheindorf, *op. cit.* p. 150.
[3] Ramm, *op. cit.* p. 130, n. 3.
[4] Gladstone to Granville, 26 September 1870, *ibid.*
[5] The same to the same, 30 September 1870, *ibid.* p. 135.
[6] Gladstone to Bright, 1 October 1870, Morley, *op. cit.* p. 339.

(2) opening a moral campaign in Europe against Bismarckism [*sic*], militarism and retrograde political morality;

(3) giving a lead to opinion in this country at a moment when everybody is at sea and grounding our action and our sympathies not on preference for one of the combatants, but on political truth.[1]

Granville demurred on grounds of expediency:

It would be a difficult matter for an impartial person at this moment to say what would be reasonable conditions of peace for Germany to demand after her great victories, and accompanying loss of men and treasure. Lord Granville feels sure that your Majesty will approve of his being as reticent as possible on the subject, until the moment, if it ever comes, when he may be empowered by your Majesty to give advice.[2]

To Gladstone, he explained:

My objection to doing at present what you propose is, that it is impossible according to my views to do so, without being considered to throw our weight into the French scale against Germany, with consequent encouragement on one side and irritation on the other.

Palmerston 'wasted the strength derived by England from the great war, by his brag'. 'I am afraid of our wasting that which we at present derive from moral causes by laying down general principles, when nobody will attend to them, and when in all probability they will be disregarded.'[3]

On 30 September a severe tussle took place in the Cabinet, Gladstone and Goschen being supported by Forster. After the meeting, Granville wrote to his wife:

Quite exhausted after the longest fight I ever had against Gladstone. The losses were great; the killed and wounded innumerable; but I remained in possession of the field and the Cabinet. He wanted to declare our views on the conditions of peace; I was against doing so.[4]

Granville afterwards wrote to Gladstone:

We have reserved our full liberty of action, and can protest whenever we like. But there are symptoms of both sides wearying of the war, they may come to us at last, and it is not at all clear that we may not be glad to arrange a peace which would include a cession of some thousands of my 'intellectual' Strasburgians, and the inhabitants of a narrow strategical line, without much reference to their wishes.[5]

[1] Goschen to Granville, 3 October 1870, PRO G[ifts and] D[eposits] 29/54. With their attitude towards the annexation of Alsace and Lorraine, Gladstone and his supporters initiated the theory of 'moral intervention' pointing to the campaign about 'Bulgarian atrocities' and other demonstrations of moral indignation. The new 'interventionism' was as ineffective as that of Russell had been but differed from it in being dissociated from treaty rights and based on moral considerations alone.—In opposition to this Granville, supported by the majority of the Cabinet, adhered to the principle of non-intervention on grounds of political expediency.
[2] Granville to the Queen, 21 September 1870, RA I 65/157.
[3] Granville to Gladstone, 7 October 1870, Ramm, *op. cit.* pp. 138f.
[4] Granville to Lady Granville, 30 September 1870, Fitzmaurice, *op. cit.* vol. II, p. 62.
[5] Granville to Gladstone, 7 October 1870, Ramm, *op. cit.* pp. 138f.

Gladstone reported to the delighted Queen:

As far as he can judge, the Cabinet is duly determined to shun all sole action on the part of this country with reference to the war now raging, and not to encourage any act of partisanship, or any attempt at mediation under present circumstances except with the assent of both parties.

He still maintained his former opinion:

The matter stands over, at any rate for the present: freedom has, however, been expressly reserved by Lord Granville to comment hereafter on the circular of Count Bismarck if he should see cause. Doubtless the great difficulty of declaring an opinion is to do so without seeming to depart from impartiality as between the two Powers at war.[1]

Public opinion seemed to support the decision of the Cabinet:

The general feeling throughout England seems to be in favour of non-intervention and the decision of the Cabinet is approved by *The Times* and *Daily News* and *Morning Post*, but opposed by the *Standard* which does not point out in what way any interference at present could be of the slightest use.[2]

Undaunted by his defeat, Gladstone on 11 October wrote to Granville:

But would it not be well that you should endeavour to ascertain the views of Russia as to the terms of peace, and especially as to the transfer of Alsace and Lorraine? Undoubtedly the decision of the Cabinet on the 30th was in some degree governed by the belief strongly declared by you that Russia would adhere to inviolability of soil but would not commit herself to any objection founded on the sense of the inhabitants. When that decision comes to be questioned, as it may, I think it will be very important that we should be able to show something about the actual views of Russia at this juncture. If you verify your opinion by communication with Brunnow, it will powerfully support the decision of the 30th ult. But considering that Russia is the only *substantive* among the Neutral Powers (besides ourselves) I think we ought not voluntarily to remain in the dark, but to learn all we can. I had a vague idea that this had been understood between us....[3]

The following day, Granville in a private and most confidential note to Brunnow, proposed an Anglo-Russian understanding on 'reasonable' terms of peace.[4] Brunnow in reply recommended an effort to protect Paris

---

[1] Gladstone to the Queen, 5 October 1870, RA I 66/47 (*QVL, loc. cit.* pp. 73 ff.).

[2] Ponsonby to the Queen, 2 October 1870, RA I 66/40. Individual members of Parliament, however, spoke publicly against German annexations and letters to *The Times* urged the danger of the Prussian demands. The *Edinburgh Review* published anonymously an article 'Germany, France and England' generally and rightly attributed to Gladstone—the issue ran to a second edition, unusual in a quarterly. The *Quarterly Review* in its turn set out the case for France. A public meeting was held at Blackfriars to enlist sympathy for the French Republic (Raymond, *op. cit.* pp. 219 ff.).

[3] Gladstone to Granville, 11 October 1870, Ramm, *op. cit.* pp. 143 f.

[4] '...if we found there was any agreement between us as to what was to be done, we might then consider whether there was any practicable mode of attempting to stop the horrors of the Seige [*sic*] at Paris—All the Neutrals would gladly follow in the wake of Russia and England, but what that course should be is one of the greatest difficulty and delicacy. Please ruin yourself in telegraphs' (Granville to Brunnow, 12 October 1870, GD 29/115, draft).

and another to discover the 'strictly necessary' conditions of peace.[1]
Gladstone and Granville then exchanged opinions about an official
approach to the Russian government.[2] In the course of their correspondence, Gladstone explained:

I quite agreed that Russia and we may co-operate in endeavouring to save Alsace
and Lorraine from actual severance, while we should perhaps do it on different
grounds, but I thought the closing words[3] might be held to involve *some* absolute
severance and I think it would be premature to commit ourselves to this, particularly
as what we desire is to give Germany security in another form.[4]

On 16 October therefore, encouraged by a leader in *The Times* advocating
neutral intervention[5] Granville told Buchanan to ask Gorchakov confidentially 'whether we could agree generally as to acceptable terms of
peace and if so, whether there would be any probability of stopping the
siege of Paris?'[6] On 17 October, Buchanan handed the Russian Chancellor
a memorandum embodying Granville's inquiry. He received a discouraging reply:

His Excellency seems to consider that nothing but a change in the events of the
war will modify the Prussian terms and that Alsace, at all events, is the least concession they will accept. He thinks the mere opinion of the Neutral Powers without
any intention to support it by arms would be disregarded and would have no
influence on the military operations against Paris. He said that Russia had gone
further than other Powers, the Emperor having expressed an opinion privately to the
King of Prussia against the annexation of French Territory, but the King considers
himself obliged to adopt the views of his allies and of Germany. His Excellency
therefore thinks it would be useless for England and Russia to enter into any.
confidential consideration of the question.

If the British government could make any proposals which they thought
might be accepted, they should address them on their own behalf to

---

[1] Brunnow suggested that Granville should send a telegram to Buchanan of which he
enclosed a draft (!). It was stated in this draft that the British government wished to reach
an understanding with that of Russia on a direct appeal to the humane sentiments of the
king of Prussia to spare Paris. The two governments, moreover, should 'approfondir les
conditions jugées strictement nécessaires, dans la pensée du Roi, pour rétablir la paix sur une
base durable, afin de mettre à couvert la sûreté des frontières de l'Allemagne, sans porter
atteinte au maintien de l'équilibre de l'Europe' (Brunnow to Granville, 14 October 1870,
confidential, GD 29/98).
[2] Two letters from Gladstone to Granville, 15 October 1870, Ramm, *op. cit.* p. 148 and
the same to the same, 16 October 1870, *ibid.* pp. 149f. Granville in the course of the
correspondence, wrote: 'If Russia agrees to do something, it is a serious matter acting
without the consent of our colleagues. On the other hand that communication ought to be
made with as little ostentation as possible' (Granville to Gladstone, 16 October 1870, *ibid.*
p. 150).   [3] Of Granville's draft to Buchanan.
[4] Gladstone to Granville, 16 October 1870, *ibid.* pp. 149f.
[5] Ponsonby regretted 'that the *Times* in its leading article advocates intervention and that
we should offer to guarantee that no fortresses are built in Alsace or Lorraine which should
remain French....The suggestion will produce feeling on the Continent. The Times is said
still to be much influenced by the Rothschilds' (Ponsonby to the Queen, 16 October 1870,
RA I 66/70).
[6] Granville to the Queen, telegram, 17 October 1870, *ibid.* I 66/71.

Prussian headquarters.[1] The tsar in his turn suggested that England should try to induce the Provisional government in Paris to accept an armistice. He had reason to believe

that a proposal for that object would be favourably received at Prussian Headquarters, and that an armistice for forty days would be granted on the condition that some second-rate fortresses should be placed in the hands of the Prussians, and the investment of Paris continued, while every facility would be afforded for a free vote being given for the Constituent Assembly in the districts occupied by the Prussian troops.[2]

On 20 October, accordingly, the Cabinet agreed on a telegram to Lyons urging the Provisional government to accept an armistice.[3] The Russian government, however, would not even support the British move. Gorchakov merely declared that he had already instructed the Russian *chargé d'affaires* at Bordeaux[4] to support Lyons's recommendations.

On my expressing a hope that he would also make urgent representations in support of those of Her Majesty's Government to the Government of Prussia, he said that the Emperor could not speak more earnestly than he had already done in his correspondence with the King; and he did not believe more could be said.[5]

On 24 October, Gorchakov finally told Buchanan that any Russo-Prussian correspondence about the peace would be carried on directly 'between the Emperor and the King'.[6] In fact, by this time, the Russian government was preoccupied with matters other than an armistice or the future of Alsace-Lorraine.

III

On 27 October a Council of Ministers met under the presidency of the tsar. Alexander, having demanded the strictest secrecy, then announced his intention of denouncing the Black Sea Clauses. All present supported the proposal with enthusiasm; no one raised any objections. Only when the Council was breaking up did some of the Ministers ask themselves whether a decision which might have serious consequences had not been too lightly taken.—The matter, however, was too popular and of too national a character for any of those present to express their misgivings.—The tsar had explained in detail the reasons for his decision.[7] He relied above all on the Prussian promise of support.

---

[1] Buchanan to Granville, 17 October 1870, FO 65/804, no. 400, reporting telegram.
[2] The same to the same, 18 October 1870, *ibid.* no. 402, reporting telegram.
[3] Ramm, *op. cit.* p. 151 n. 2.
[4] The Provisional government had moved to that city from Paris.
[5] Buchanan to Granville, 21 October 1870, FO 65/804, no. 412, reporting telegram.
[6] The same to the same, 24 October 1870, *ibid.* no. 418, reporting telegram.
[7] Buchanan later learnt that the tsar himself had submitted the proposed repudiation to the Council of Ministers 'in an address during which, pale with emotion, He declared He could not die in peace, until he had wiped out the stain with which the neutralization of the Black Sea had sullied the honour of Russia, and that the time had now come for doing so, as France was crippled, Austria had already twice proposed the abrogation of the obnoxious

The moment seemed favourable for throwing off a yoke which weighed heavily on himself and the Russian nation. France had been laid low; Austria had declared more than once that she would not oppose Russian wishes and might even lend them support; Italy was preoccupied with her own internal affairs. Serious opposition would come from England alone. However, even this would be a war of pen and ink. England was dangerous through her navy and her money. The former, at this time of the year, was not a threat in the Baltic; in the Black Sea, it would find nothing to destroy. England might indeed subsidize an Austro-Turkish army but he doubted whether Austria would allow herself to be drawn into hostilities. Turkey alone was no danger. If England, deprived of her French ally, stuck to simple protests, the Porte also would finally acquiesce.[1]

The denunciation was to be effected in three distinct stages. The first was a notification to the king of Prussia inviting him to afford Russia the support which he had repeatedly promised. The tsar's letter bore the date of 31 October. After announcing his decision, Alexander reminded his uncle

qu'en 1866, le lieutenant-général Manteuffel était venu à Saint-Pétersbourg lui porter de sa part des assurances de ce qu'il reconnaissait l'impossibilité pour la Russie, comme grand puissance, de tolérer indéfiniment des clauses qui la blessaient dans sa dignité et sa sécurité. C'est pourquoi l'empereur Alexandre exprimait l'espoir que non seulement le vote du roi lui serait favorable, mais encore qu'il emploierait son influence auprès des autres cabinets pour leur faire comprendre ses intentions tout à fait pacifiques et les déterminer à prendre son parti.[2]

On 2 November, Annenkov, one of the tsar's adjutants left for Versailles to deliver the letter to the king.[3] That same day, Alexander read the text to Reuss, asking him not to transmit the news by the telegraph. He added the most formal assurances that although he demanded the restoration of Russian sovereignty in the Black Sea, he was far from nursing ambitious projects in the east. His policy would not change and it would remain pacific. Reuss was to emphasize this in his report. Asked whether he intended to claim the strip of Bessarabian territory ceded in 1856, the tsar replied that for the moment his interest was limited to the Black Sea; the other matter might perhaps be redressed on some future occasion.[4]

The second step was to communicate the decision to the powers. For this the circular prepared by Gorchakov in the autumn of 1866 lay

stipulations, and Great Britain would not make such a question a cause of war' (Buchanan to Granville, 22 November 1870, FO 65/805 no. 484, confidential). On receiving the telegram reporting the surrender of the French army at Sedan, the tsar was reported to have signed himself with the cross and exclaimed: 'Thank God, Sebastopol is now avenged!' (the same to the same, 16 November 1870, *ibid.* no. 466, confidential).
[1] Reuss to Bismarck, 2 November 1870 confidential; Rheindorf, *op. cit.* pp. 151ff. Reuss got his information from one of the Ministers who had attended the meeting.
[2] Alexander II to William I, 19/31 October 1870, paraphrase in Goriainov, *op. cit.* p. 162.
[3] Buchanan to Granville, 2 November 1870, FO 65/805 no. 425, confidential.
[4] Reuss to Bismarck, 2 November 1870, confidential, Rheindorf, *op. cit.* pp. 151ff.

ready to hand.[1] With some slight alterations, it was now despatched to Russia's principal missions abroad. Buchanan, indeed, had already learnt the news from Reuss. On 9 November he had informed Granville of his belief that despatches had been or were about to be sent notifying the great courts that Russia no longer acknowledged her obligations under the Treaty of 1856—an announcement to that effect would be made at St Petersburg the day before the despatches were delivered.[2] On receiving confirmation of the news from Reuss, Buchanan had addressed to Gorchakov a private letter stating that 'if the course is followed with respect to this question which has been described to me, I have the most serious apprehensions as to the light in which it may be looked upon by her Majesty's Government'.[3]

On 9 November, Brunnow handed Granville a despatch and a circular 'denouncing on the part of Russia the limits put on her fleet in the Black Sea'.[4] The following day, the Cabinet unanimously approved a firm protest against the Russian proceedings 'with a doquet [sic] open at the end to friendly discussion'.[5] Granville reflected that it was difficult to know how far the agreement between Russia and Prussia had gone, 'and much will depend upon this'.[6]

Before the British reply reached St Petersburg, the Russian government had taken the final and irrevocable step of publishing its intention. On the morning of 15 November, Gorchakov's circular appeared in the *Journal de St Pétersbourg*. It met with a mixed reception. Persons attached to the Foreign Office spoke of it as 'an impotent attempt of Prince Gorchakov's which will not be supported by action, and will end in failure if it meets with decided opposition from England'.[7] The general opinion seemed to be that Gorchakov had opened the question 'clumsily and indiscreetly'.[8] The press of St Petersburg, however was 'unanimous in favour of the declaration which the Country, if necessary, will support by arms'.[9]

On 16 November the British reply was communicated at St Petersburg. Buchanan, who had gained much of his diplomatic experience in tussles with Bismarck, noted with satisfaction that during the reading Gorchakov's feet and legs shook with a nervous tremor. Gorchakov defended his proceedings by saying that whilst the British government would never have made concessions to diplomatic requests, it was too prudent and desirous

[1] Clark, *loc. cit.* pp. 55f.
[2] Buchanan to Granville, 9 November 1870, FO 65/805 no. 444, reporting telegram.
[3] *Ibid.*
[4] Granville to the Queen, telegram, 10 November 1870, RA H 4/160.
[5] The same to the same, telegram, 11 November 1870, *ibid.* H 4/162.
[6] The same to the same, 12 November 1870, *ibid.* H 4/167 (*QVL, loc. cit.* pp. 182f.).
[7] Buchanan to Granville, 14 November 1870, FO 65/805 no. 458, reporting telegram.
[8] The same to the same, 15 November 1870, *ibid.* no. 462, reporting telegram.
[9] The same to the same, 16 November 1870, *ibid.* no. 464, reporting telegram.

of peace not to accept a *fait accompli*.[1] Russia had not added a single man to her armies and desired an arrangement which would secure the peace of the east. However, 'if the Porte spontaneously or by the advice of other Powers resents the declaration, all the Christian populations hitherto kept quiet by the influence of Russia will avail themselves of the opportunity to rise against the Turks'. Whatever happened, the tsar would no longer submit to stipulations dishonourable to Russia and his decision was irrevocable. There was, however, no objection to a discussion of the question in all its bearings among the other powers. 'I said Her Majesty's Government consider the declaration precludes discussion and he answered that they had made no objection to abrogation of Treaties respecting Hanover and the German Confederation.'[2]

In view of the Anglo-Russian deadlock much would depend on the attitude of Prussia. On 7 November, Annenkov had delivered the tsar's letter, as well as one from Gorchakov to Bismarck and a copy of the Russian circular. Bismarck, although he considered the Russian move inopportune, was determined to keep his promise. He informed Reuss that Prussia would support the Russian step.[3] On the following day, however, he suggested a postponement of the Russian declaration if that was possible; if not, Prussia would support it.[4] Gorchakov replied that action could not be delayed. All necessary measures had been taken 'et le moment est venu de mettre à l'œuvre les bonnes dispositions que Vous nous avez manifestées à diverses reprises sur cette question de dignité et d'honneur national—et dont je puis dire Vous avez même pris l'initiative'. Against which Bismarck remarked in the margin: 'In *this* form certainly not' ('In *dieser* Form sicher nicht'). Reuss explained that he had repeatedly asked to be informed of the *modus procedendi* and that Gorchakov, when he realized that Prussia would not support his proposal for a congress, had replied with commonplaces. King William observed in a marginal note that he had always thought of the question as one to be considered by a congress after the conclusion of peace. He had never contemplated a denunciation without the previous consent of the signatories.[5] Bismarck, however, was determined to keep his promise, however awkward might be

---

[1] The same to the same, private and most confidential, 16 November 1870, RA H 4/175, abstract.
[2] The same to the same, 16 November 1870, FO 65/805 no. 464, reporting telegram.
[3] Bismarck to Reuss, telegram, 7 November 1870, *GW, loc. cit.* p. 590.
[4] The same to the same, telegram, 8 November 1870, *ibid.* Bismarck telegraphed: 'Ist es unwiderruflich, dass der durch Annenkov angekündigte Schritt schon in diesem Augenblick geschieht? Einige Wochen später würde unsere Russland günstige Stellung zur Sache voraussichtlich bei den übrigen Neutralen stärker ins Gewicht fallen. Ist Aufschub untunlich, so ändert das die diesseitige Auffassung nicht, aber das Gewicht unserer Stimme bei England wird heute geringer sein als vielleicht in einigen Wochen.'
[5] 'Ich habe aber immer diese Frage als vor einen Kongress gehörig nach unserem Frieden mit Frankreich betrachtet. Jedenfalls habe ich nie daran gedacht, dass eine *Kündigung* ohne vorhergegangene *Verständigung* mit den Unterzeichnern möglich sei' (Reuss to Bismarck, 9 November 1870, Rheindorf, *op. cit.* pp. 153 f.).

the method chosen by the Russian government.[1] He therefore asked Thile, to arrange for the publication in unofficial papers ('durch indifferente Blätter') of Beust's despatches of 1867 and other documents suggesting that the Russian step had the approval of Austria,[2] and to assure Oubril that in no circumstances would Prussia join an anti-Russian coalition.[3]

In spite of Prussian support, however, matters were developing awkwardly from the Russian point of view. Not only was the British attitude stiffer than had been expected,[4] but the Austrian reaction also, which had at first been favourable,[5] had soon become ominously hostile.[6] Nor was Gorchakov pleased at Bismarck's freely publicized declaration that Prussia had been taken by surprise. This, he considered, encouraged Austrian opposition.[7] Reuss, moreover, was pressing for a conciliatory

[1] Bismarck telegraphed to the Foreign Office in Berlin: '...Die russische Form ist nicht geschickt, aber wir können gegen die Sache nicht auftreten. Europa hat Frankreichs Angriff auf uns nicht gehindert, und England seiner Neutralität einen für uns ungünstigen Charakter verliehen. Dass Oesterreich nicht dasselbe tat, hinderte nur Kaiser Alexander. Der König ist letzterem dankbar, wir haben an dem Vertrag von 56 wenig Interesse und nur einen äusserlichen, von England damals bekämpften Anteil...' (Bismarck to Foreign Office, telegram, 18 November 1870, *ibid.* p. 154).

[2] Bismarck to Thile, telegram, 14 November 1870, *ibid.*

[3] Bismarck to Foreign Office, telegram, 18 November 1870, *ibid.*

[4] Chotek to Beust, telegram, 17 November 1870, HHSAPARRR, July–December 1870, x 58.

[5] The Austrian Council of Ministers had discussed the Russian note on 14 November. Beust had opened proceedings by remarking that Austria had for some time admitted the possibility of a revision of the treaty of 1856. The Russian note, none the less, was both a surprise and a challenge. He had told Novikov verbally that Austria could not accept such unilateral action and that he would reserve his final observations for a later reply.—Andrássy then analysed Granville's reply which had been communicated to Austria. England, he said, rejected the Russian demand and denied Russia's right of unilateral denunciation. He thought that this might form the basis of a collective step. He proposed that the Austrian reply should be analogous to the British and recommended an approach to the other signatories. England could not refuse to support collective action; Italy, Turkey and perhaps France would join. Even Prussia could hardly refuse.—Beust rejoined that if England had formally protested, Austria would have had to do the same; England had not done so, therefore Austria must make her own declaration. She must not go further than other states. The British reply left open the possibility of negotiation; that of Austria must do the same. An Austrian proposal for collective action would end in failure but the British government might be approached confidentially.—Andrássy replied that he feared the effect of Russia's action on the Slavs; this would be weakened by a collective protest. He felt sure that Prussia was not committed to Russia in this question. Beust disagreed and declared that no measure directed against Russia would find the support of Prussia. The opinion of the Porte would have to be heard. Francis-Joseph then remarked that Turkey must not be encouraged to ask for a congress: an anti-Russian majority was not assured. Potocki proposed a reply similar to that of England and further steps in co-operation with Turkey. The Minister of War prudently pointed out that unless Austria was prepared to go to war she must not utter threats. The emperor finally decided that Austria must act strictly according to legality: she must not take her stand on ground where other powers might be disinclined to follow her (*ibid.* PSDiRMPM, 1869–71, protocol of meeting of 14 November 1870). In fact the Austrian reply of 16 November closely followed that of England (Beust to Chotek, 16 November 1870, *ibid.* x 8, Russie 1864—70 Protokoll, nos. 1 and 2). Gorchakov's reaction to the reply is described in Chotek to Beust, 21/9 November 1870, *ibid.* x 58, Russie Rapports, July–December 1870, no. 66B).

[6] Chotek to Beust, telegram, 19 November 1870, *ibid.* PARRR, July–December 1870, x 58.

[7] Reuss to Bismarck, telegram, 17 November 1870, *GW, loc. cit.* p. 590.

attitude. Gorchakov, surprisingly, was now placed in the position in which Napoleon had found himself during the Luxemburg dispute; he was seeking a way to appease unexpected opposition without suffering a major diplomatic defeat. In fact, he was looking for a way of escape. On 19 November the fiery Buchanan telegraphed:

I venture to recommend that no armed demonstration should take place till next week....I am not without hopes that an answer will be given to your note stating that it was not intended to carry out the declaration without the assent of the Powers and expressing a desire to negotiate in a conference or otherwise.[1]

On the 23rd, Buchanan reported that, when shown by Reuss the text of Gorchakov's reply, he had stated that it would fail to satisfy the British government. Gorchakov's note had already left but was likely to be amended, especially since Brunnow had urgently requested that no reply be sent before the arrival of his own despatches. He (Buchanan) had recommended that before Gorchakov's note was finally delivered in London, Brunnow and Granville should agree on a formula acceptable to England.[2] Gorchakov had explained that if he could ascertain confidentially that the claims of Russia would be admitted, he would do what he could to remove British objections to the manner in which they had been raised.[3] The Russian public, however, was less conciliatory. On 23 November, Buchanan noted that the news from Constantinople had 'greatly increased the arrogance of the official class of Russians'. They did not believe England to be in earnest, and he feared that unless the British government insisted firmly 'upon satisfaction being given to them for the present disregard of a solemn engagement to Great Britain', they might have to deal ere long with some other question in which serious consequences would be inevitable.[4]

The British Ministers, placed between official Russian arrogance and inflamed opinion at home, found themselves in a difficult position. Granville on 21 November had told the First Lord of the Admiralty

that it is impossible to say that we may not be driven into it [war] by Russia, or by other foreign powers, or by our own people; that we must take care of our dignity; but if there ever was a cabinet which is bound not to drift into an unnecessary war, it is ours.[5]

Gladstone, on the other hand, deprecated military preparations:

I will frankly own [he wrote] that I am much disgusted with a good deal of the language that I have read in the newspapers within the last few days about immediate

---

[1] Buchanan to Granville, 19 November 1870, FO 65/805, no. 472, reporting telegram. The following day Chotek reported to Beust that the Russian government seemed to have a strong desire to avoid complications. It was willing to offer additional guarantees to Turkey and awaited proposals from the powers (Chotek to Beust, telegram, 20 November 1870, HHSAPARRR, July-December 1870, x 58).
[2] Buchanan to Granville, 22 November 1870, FO 65/805, no. 481, reporting telegram.
[3] The same to the same, 22 November 1870, *ibid.* no. 482, reporting a further telegram.
[4] The same to the same, 23 November 1870, *ibid.* no. 489, reporting telegram.
[5] Granville to Gladstone, 21 November 1870, Morley, *op. cit.* p. 351.

war with Russia. I try to put a check on myself to prevent the reaction it engenders. Your observation on drifting into war is most just: though I always thought Clarendon's epithet in this one case inapplicable as well as unadvisable. I know, however, nothing more like drifting into war than would be a resort to any military measures whatever, except with reference either to some actual fact or some well-defined contingency....[1]

In the meantime, it was hoped that Odo Russell's visit to Prussian headquarters in Versailles would 'have a good effect'.[2] That mission had been decided upon before the Russian action[3] but after Gorchakov's circular it had assumed a new importance.[4] Indeed Bismarck was awaiting Russell's arrival before committing himself to a final course of action.[5] On 21 November, Russell had his first interview with the formidable Prussian:

I...must frankly confess...that I felt very shy when I first met the great man face to face.—However I soon recovered under the influence of his marvellous powers of conversation, which he carried on in English, French and German changing from one to another according to the fancy of the moment but dwelling most in his own which is evidently the favourite and in which his originality, quaintness and sudden flashes of genius remind one of Shakespeare's most powerful writing.

He 'kept me talking over three hours and I left him much discouraged'.[6] In fact, as Russell reported by the telegraph, Bismarck had received him with great cordiality and had explained that the Russian circular had taken him by surprise. He regretted it but could not interfere or answer officially at present. He recommended conferences at Constantinople before hostilities were opened and was anxious to prevent the outbreak of war.[7]

Undaunted by Bismarck's attitude Russell returned to the charge:

...on returning to him in the evening when we had two hours and a half's more talk I felt that I knew him better and could express more easily all that I had determined to say to convince him that unless he could get Russia to withdraw the circular we

---

[1] Gladstone to Granville, 22 November 1870, *ibid.* pp. 351f.
[2] Granville to the Queen, 14 November 1870, RA I 67/30 (*QVL, loc. cit.* pp. 84f.)).
[3] On 15 October, Granville had written to Gladstone: 'How would it do to invent some excuse (such as getting the residue of the Embassy out of Paris or anything else) to send Odo to Head Quarters. His knowledge of Germany and Germans would enable him to ascertain a little of what was going on, and certainly have influence with the Crown Prince, who I think I remember to have heard, was very fond of him' (Granville to Gladstone, private, 15 October 1870, Ramm, *op. cit.* pp. 147f.)).
[4] On 12 November, Granville told the Queen that 'it was proposed merely to send Bismarck the British answer to Gorchakov's circular and to tell him that Russell would give him all further explanations he might require' (Granville to the Queen, 12 November 1870, RA H 4/167 (*QVL, loc. cit.* pp. 82f.)).
[5] 'Sagen Sie den Diplomaten, die fragen sollten, dass wir uns erst nach Russells Herkunft äussern würden...' (Bismarck to the Foreign Office in Berlin, telegram, 18 November 1870, Rheindorf, *op. cit.* p. 154).
[6] Odo Russell to Granville, private, 30 November 1870, RA I 67/54, copy.
[7] The same to the same, telegram, 21 November 1870, FO 65/807.

should be compelled with or without allies to go to war.—He was long obstinate and would not believe we could ever be roused to action—but as he gradually admitted the truth of the consequences to which a pacific acceptance of the Russian kick must inevitably lead, he came round to our standpoint and felt that in your place he could not recede.

In fact, Russell had been able to convince Bismarck that in her own interest Prussia must intervene.

The evil consequences to Germany of a European War before Paris was taken, the moral support the Tours Government might get from a renewal of the old Anglo-French Alliance, the opportunities war might give Beust to play a more important part in European questions and the increasing difficulty of bringing the Franco-Prussian conflict to a speedy and satisfactory close, together with the stern fact that England *must* fight and that he *Bismarck* alone could prevent it which I endeavoured to bring as forcibly as I could before his mind, gradually worked the change in his mind which has led him to support the cause of Peace and England against Gortschakoff and his circular.

When Bismarck realized that he must—to use a later phrase—act as the 'honest broker' between England and Russia, he tried to drive a bargain:

Before I could convince Bismarck that Her Majesty's Government were in earnest and would *really* go to war if Russia would not recede from her present attitude, he strove hard to drive a bargain with me evidently thinking that I had secret instructions in my pocket, to offer him, if absolutely necessary, some political advantages in exchange for the moral support I asked for.

He repeatedly said that in his opinion in politics 'one hand should wash the other' (dass eine Hand die andere waschen muss) and seemed to wait anxiously and attentively for my reply. Of course I took no notice and turned a deaf ear to his insinuations and dealt with the question on its own merits only, without offering him any other advantage for Germany but the choice between Peace or War with Russia on our part.[1]

What Russell could not know was that even before his arrival at Versailles, Bismarck had taken steps to ensure a peaceful solution. Already on the 18th, Bernstorff had reported from London that the situation there was grave. Granville's language was firm: Disraeli considered the position to be very serious ('sehr ernst') and thought the country might pronounce for war. The final decision would rest with Parliament; its attitude would show whether the country was as warlike as the capital appeared to be.[2] There was moreover a general belief that Russia would abandon her position if Prussia expressed disapproval. An understanding with Prussia, therefore, was eagerly desired.[3] At the same time, a conviction was gaining ground that Russian intransigence would provoke a

---

[1] Odo Russell to Granville, private, 30 November 1870, RA I 67/54, copy.
[2] '...es wird sich dann zeigen, ob die Meinung des Landes wirklich so kriegerisch ist, wie die der Hauptstadt in diesem Augenblick'.
[3] Bernstorff to Bismarck, confidential, 18 November 1870, [Die] G[rosse] P[olitik der europäischen Kabinette], vol. II (Berlin, 1922), p. 12.

conflict in which England would find herself on the side of Prussia's enemies.[1]

Bernstorff's reports could not fail to impress Bismarck and on the 20th he had inquired at St Petersburg whether Russia would agree to a conference of ambassadors at Constantinople or elsewhere to seek a peaceful solution.[2] On the following day Gorchakov had accepted a conference in principle whilst expressing the wish that it should be held at St Petersburg.[3] In consequence, when Russell made his famous threat, Bismarck and Gorchakov were already agreed on the possibility of a conference. Bismarck's delay in suggesting it to Russell sprang from his desire to drive a bargain with England. Russell's language finally convinced him that the British government would not pay for Prussian mediation. In his own interest therefore, Bismarck now had to pull out of his hat the rabbit he had concealed. On 22nd November he telegraphed to Bernstorff that the Russian government had agreed to submit the question to a conference.[4]

That day also, Gorchakov informed Buchanan that he would himself represent Russia if a conference was to meet. Buchanan later told Reuss that the Chancellor presumably wished to hold the conference at St Petersburg; other governments, however, might object.[5] News of Gorchakov's conciliatory attitude reached Granville on the afternoon of 24 November. The following day the Foreign Office received the Russian reply to the British protest. Gladstone thought it 'silky in manner and expression' but 'not satisfactory in substance'.[6] An answer, in the meantime, had been sent to a telegram from Russell reporting Bismarck's proposal for a conference:

> In this answer, the Government express their willingness to enter into Conference, but not at St Petersburg, nor with any foregone conclusion as to the result; the subject of deliberation to be any proposal which Russia might put forward for the modification of the Treaty of 1856.[7]

That same night, at St Petersburg, Reuss asked Buchanan to acquaint Granville with a communication which he had received from Gorchakov: the Chancellor stated that if the Conference met it would not, as the

---

[1] 'Man sieht mit äusserster Spannung der Entscheidung in Versailles entgegen, wovon, wie man überzeugt ist, die ganze Wendung der Dinge abhängt. Wenn wir mit den anderen Vertragsmächten die einseitige Aufkündigung Russlands für unzulässig erklären und jedes Einverständnis mit ihm verleugnen, so glaubt man, dass Russland sich besinnen wird. Wo nicht, hält man den Krieg für unvermeidlich, welcher sich fast über ganz Europa erstrecken dürfte, und worin England jedenfalls tatsächlich der Bundesgenosse unserer Feinde sein würde' (the same to the same, telegram, 19 November 1870, ibid. p. 13).
[2] Bismarck, GW, loc. cit. p. 604.
[3] Ibid.
[4] Bismarck to Bernstorff, telegram, 22 November 1870, GP, loc. cit. pp. 16f.
[5] Buchanan to Granville, 24 November 1870, FO 65/805, no. 492, reporting telegram.
[6] Gladstone to the Queen, 25 November 1870, RA A 40/80 (QVL. loc. cit. pp. 86f.).
[7] Ibid.

Foreign Secretary appeared to think, simply register the Russian declaration. Its object would be to place the peace of the east and the independence of the Porte upon a more secure basis than at present, and Russia would willingly contribute to this result. If the choice of St Petersburg as the venue of the conference was repugnant to Granville, he would not object to London to satisfy British national feeling. 'The Prussian Minister says this concession made at his instance, costs His Excellency much.'[1] This information reached London on the morning of 26 November. Early on the 28th, a further assurance was received. Bismarck had told Russell that a conference would be useless without a clear understanding that it was subject to no previous assumptions as to its result. The king of Prussia had spoken in a similar sense.[2] Two days later, Granville received another message from Buchanan:

> The Prussian Minister said to me today that the Russian Plenipotentiaries if not unfairly pressed at the opening of the Conference will be instructed to offer explanations which should satisfy the national susceptibilities of the Powers parties to the treaty of 1856.

In addition, a telegram[3] from Russell announced on Bismarck's behalf that Russia, Turkey and Italy had agreed to meet in conference in London. Austria alone hesitated. Granville should fix the date of the meeting and arrange all other details to suit his own convenience.[4] A final telegram brought the assurance from Bismarck that Russia accepted the invitation on the distinct understanding that the conference was to meet without any assumption of a foregone conclusion.[5] On 7 December, Granville expressed his pleasure at Bismarck's efforts and added that the British government would 'much value any intimation of Count Bismarck's views on the course of proceedings in conference'. They wished to hear also his views on the new arrangements to be made, as they desired an Anglo-German understanding before the conference opened.[6] Moreover, Prussia should associate herself with the policy of containing Russia in the east:

> It is desirable [Granville told Russell] that you should avail yourself of any opportunity which may present itself for sounding Count Bismarck but as entirely from yourself whether Prussia would be disposed to accede to the Tripartite Treaty between England, Austria and France of 15 April 1856 by which those powers specially guaranteed between themselves the independence and integrity of the Ottoman Empire.—Such accession on the part of Prussia you might suggest would afford an additional guarantee of the most valuable kind for the maintenance of peace in the Levant.[7]

---

[1] Buchanan to Granville, 25 November 1870, FO 65/805, no. 496.
[2] Odo Russell to Granville, telegram, 27 November 1870, RA H 4/213.
[3] Buchanan to Granville, 29 November 1870, FO 65/805, no. 503, most confidential.
[4] Odo Russell to Granville, telegram, 30 November 1870, RA H 4/224.
[5] The same to the same, telegram, 1 December, 1870 *ibid.* H 5/1.
[6] Granville to Odo Russell, telegram, 7 December 1870, *ibid.* H 5/26.
[7] The same to the same, telegram, 7 December 1870, *ibid.* H 5/27.

Russell, therefore, had further discussions with Bismarck:

...In the course of two long conversations about the conferences he threw out the course of proceeding reported in my despatch no. 25 of 14 December[1] which he had evidently settled telegraphically with Prince Gortschakoff and Bernstorff—but he would not commit himself to any mode of adjustment saying he had no particular opinions on the subject and no interest in the matter, but the maintenance of peace. He condemned the Russian circular but he sympathised with their wish for a Revision of the Treaty and would support any scheme likely to satisfy all parties.

Bismarck finally asked for a British suggestion. Russell replied that it would please the British government if, without prejudging the conference, they found that there was a general harmony in the views of Prussia and England as to the objects to be attained.

'Very well' he said 'the object to be attained is peace–what would you do in my place?' 'In your Excellency's place', I said, 'I would at once accede to the Tripartite Treaty between England, Austria and France of the 15 April 1856 which guarantees the independence and integrity of Turkey and I should invite Italy to do the same so as to prove to the world that the secret understanding you are accused of having established with Russia respecting Turkey is really a myth, as your Excellency was pleased to assure me yourself the other day. Such accession would afford the most valuable guarantee for the maintenance of peace in the Levant you could give and would facilitate the revision of the separate convention.'

Bismarck reflected for some time and said he did not think the German Parliament would ratify an engagement of this kind which in the present temper of the German people would be very unpopular.

I said that if for the sake of peace he put his name to it it would become popular. 'No' Count Bismarck replied, 'the Germans will now be solely employed in organizing their political strength at home and will resist any engagements to fight for other nations abroad, and having no conquests to make for themselves, will only care to resist invasion while the conquests made by others will be indifferent to them'. 'But', I asked, 'would Germany not for instance object to Russia having the naval command of the mouths of the Danube?'

Bismarck replied that this would be 'a matter of perfect indifference' to Germany so long as her commerce on the Danube was not interfered with; she would make commercial treaties with any power which conquered the shores of the Black Sea. Russell then asked whether it would be equally indifferent to Germany who held the Principalities and Bismarck replied that it would.

Germany would not care to go to war if Russia or Austria took possession of Roumania although he personally would prefer to see them in the hands of Austria because the German element would be more civilizing than the Russian. Meanwhile

---

[1] On 17 December, Russell informed Granville: 'If you agree Count Bismarck will support in conference the sovereign right of the Sultan to shut or open the Bosphorus and Dardanelles at his own pleasure. His Excellency thinks Russia will agree' (Odo Russell to Granville, telegram, 17 December 1870, *ibid.* H 5/56).

he hoped they would remain as they were and he had advised Prince Charles to throw himself entirely under the Protectorate of Turkey and the Guaranteeing Powers.

Bismarck then repeated that after the present war 'Germany would care for nothing but peace and would be very unwilling to follow any but a policy of strict non-intervention and neutrality'.

I observed that from all he had said I concluded that he not only declined to join the Tripartite Treaty—but was indifferent to the maintenance and independence of the Ottoman Empire.

Personally he replied he was far from indifferent, but he felt sure that no German Parliament would support a Minister who proposed to go to war for Turkey—on the other hand he could assure me that Russia could not bribe Germany to acquiesce in the dismemberment of the Ottoman Empire.

This gave Russell his cue:

'Granted', I said, 'but could England, Austria, France and Italy not bribe Germany into guaranteeing the integrity of Turkey by acceding to the Tripartite Treaty?'—'If you put it in that form', Count Bismarck replied, 'I cannot answer without much reflection—for England and Austria are the natural allies of Germany and their alliance would offer advantages to Germany she could not prudently neglect even at the cost of sacrifices of friendship.'[1] 'Very well,' I said, 'I leave your Excellency to reflect and shall consider your first refusal as non avenu like the Russian circular.'

Russell then asked how Prussia proposed to deal with the Black Sea question. After a great deal of conversation Bismarck finally expressed the belief that Turkey would prefer to keep her sovereign rights over the Bosphorus so as to let in or exclude the ships of other nations at her will and pleasure. However he could and would give no positive opinion until he knew what Turkey really wanted and what Granville advised. He would support none but a peace policy in the conference and would seek to conciliate all parties.

The sympathies of Germany and of the Royal Family were with Russia and the Imperial Family, and Prussia would have to support the reasonable wishes of Russia —but he would resist any exaggerated demands on her part if she put forward any, as he had resisted the ill-advised and ill-timed circular. More than that he could not say till he had become acquainted with the views and respective positions of the Powers in conference assembled but he had no preconceived opinions and was open to conviction.

In the course of the conversation Bismarck inquired whether England wished to acquire a naval station in the Black Sea. He saw no objection to this. In conclusion he committed himself to no positive opinion beyond

[1] In an earlier telegram, Russell had already reported: 'Last night after dinner Count Bismarck told me confidentially that his ambition for Germany was an alliance with England and Austria in preference to a Russian alliance but he did not see his way to it yet' (the same to the same, telegram, 1 December 1870, *ibid.* I 67/55).

the oft repeated conviction that the sooner the conference met the better, so that their labours might be pacifically completed before the various parliaments of Europe met again.

Russell after the conversations outlined to Granville his impressions:

I am inclined to believe in the truth of his oft repeated assertion that no *secret understanding* exists between him and Russia—but on the other hand I see that there is an open avowed unconcealed alliance between them which he not only does not attempt to deny but openly declares to be a national and family alliance of friendship and gratitude for past services and which it is his duty to Germany to maintain until future events bring about more advantageous alliances.

The personality of Bismarck must not be underestimated:

It should not be forgotten that he has devoted and will devote his whole life to the creation of an all-powerful Germany and that he will shrink from nothing (like Cavour) to accomplish his object.—Now that I know him I shall no longer be surprised to see him change the map of Europe far more than the Emperor Napoleon was expected to do and we must be prepared for many disagreeable surprises.

Bismarck did not like England: 'He has no love for England because he feels we stand in the way of his ambitious plans and he hates Count Beust because he stands between him and an alliance with Austria which he ardently desires.'[1] Bismarck had also spoken of the vexed question of annexations.

I said I was very sorry to hear him speak again of annexations which would render friendly feelings between us more and more distant. He said he was very sorry for it but after the sacrifices Germany and more especially Southern Germany had made, a safe frontier was the least they had a right to expect.

Germany would take Alsace and a part of Lorraine, including Thionville and Metz; she would occupy Champagne, perhaps for some years. All Russell could do was to express his regret at what Bismarck had told him.[2]

---

[1] Some days later, Russell reported that there was good reason to believe that Bismarck earnestly desired an alliance with Austria and that, to gain it, he would throw over Russia. He and his friends thought that England was the only impediment to the realization of these wishes (the same to the same, private, 22–7 December 1870, *ibid.* I 67/111, abstract). Shortly afterwards, the Prussian Crown Prince in a letter to Queen Victoria expressed a hope for the realization of '...the natural alliance that, binding England and Germany, will also embrace Austria'. When these three mighty empires stood firm together, they might enjoin peace to the world (Crown-Prince of Prussia to the Queen, 3 January 1871, RA I 68/6 (*QVL, loc. cit.* pp. 101 ff.)).

[2] Odo Russell to Granville, private, 18 December 1870, RA I 67/104, copy. On 8 December Russell had telegraphed: 'I am convinced that the position of Prussia is now so strong that no peace negotiation short of unconditional surrender will be entertained by Count Bismarck' (the same to the same, telegram, 8 December 1870, *ibid.* I 67/76). In reply, he had been told not to commit himself without further instructions regarding the terms of peace. Granville had 'not yet given any opinion'. 'As to mediation and good offices, I have only said that I should not offer them unless they were acceptable to both Belligerents, as likely to be effective. I have not restricted myself as to advice' (Granville to Odo Russell, telegram, 10 December 1870, *ibid.* I 67/81).

If Bismarck was adamant about annexations, he was doing everything in his power to meet British wishes about the conferences. On
21 December, Buchanan reported that he had proposed a declaration to
be signed by the powers in conference that no treaty should henceforth be
denounced without the prior consent of all the contracting parties.
Brunnow would be told to accept this.[1] Bernstorff in his turn would
suggest 'any text or wording calculated to obtain the consent of all parties
and ensure a speedy and pacific solution to the Conference'.[2]

IV

Although, as a result of desperate French efforts to escape the inevitable,
the final dénouement was to be delayed for over two months, Granville,
Gorchakov and Bismarck had clearly laid down the bases of the coming
settlement. It merely remained to embody them in formally binding
engagements. On 17 January 1871 the London conference on the Black
Sea took the first step by a solemn declaration 'that it is an essential
principle of the law of nations that no Power can liberate itself from the
engagements of a treaty, nor modify the stipulations thereof, unless with
the consent of the contracting Powers, by means of an amicable arrangement'.[3] On the following day William I was proclaimed emperor of
Germany.[4] On 26 February, preliminaries of peace between Germany and
France provided for the annexation to the former of Alsace and Lorraine.
In announcing this event to the tsar, the German emperor declared:
'. . .jamais la Prusse n'oubliera que c'est à Vous qu'elle doit que la guerre
n'a pas pris des dimensions extrêmes. Que Dieu Vous en bénisse.'[5] The
tsar, without consulting his Minister of Foreign Affairs,[6] replied:

Vous remercie pour détails des préliminaires de paix et partage Votre joie. Dieu
donne qu'une paix solide en soit la conséquence. Suis heureux d'avoir pu Vous
prouver mes sympathies en ami dévoué. Puisse l'amitié qui nous lie assurer le
bonheur et la gloire de nos deux pays.[7]

[1] The same to the same, telegram, 21 December 1870, *ibid.* H 5/59.
[2] The same to the same, telegram, 3 January 1871, *ibid.* H 5/90.
[3] Fitzmaurice, *op. cit.* p. 76.
[4] The same European crisis which culminated in the creation of the German empire had
brought about the national consolidation of Italy. On 20 September 1870, Italian troops
had entered Rome. On 2 October the inhabitants of the city, in a plebiscite, had declared
for union with Italy.
[5] Chotek to Beust, telegram, 5 March 1871, HHSAPARRR, 1871, x 60, quoting from
Journal de St Pétersbourg.
[6] The British *chargé d'affaires* learnt from a source 'which it is impossible for me to
doubt' that the tsar on receiving the emperor's message had replied without consulting
Gorchakov (Rumbold to Granville, 5 March 1871, FO 65/820, no. 19, confidential).
[7] Chotek to Beust, telegram, 5 March 1871, HHSAPARRR, 1871, x 60, quoting from
Journal de St Pétersbourg.

The publication of the two telegrams in the official *Journal de St Péters-bourg*[1] created a sensation.[2] Chotek viewed it 'in a very serious light, understanding the language of the Emperor of Russia to convey an indirect threat to Austria'.[3] Gorchakov also attached importance to the telegrams:

It is certain that the 'mot d'ordre' on this occasion—as usual here implicitly obeyed in official circles—is to represent Prussia as having 'agreed to honour a certain bill of exchange on presentation'—which promise has, for precaution's sake, been publicly registered here.[4]

Whatever might be Russia's expectations for the future, the tsar was about to achieve at least one cherished object of his ambition. On 13 March, a treaty signed in London finally removed the hated limitations on Russian sovereignty in the Black Sea. The sultan, in exchange, was authorized

to open the said Straits in time of Peace to the Vessels of War of friendly and allied Powers, in case the Sublime Porte should judge it necessary in order to secure the execution of the stipulations of the Treaty of Paris of the 30th March 1856.[5]

The tsar expressed his delight at the agreement:

The Emperor is said to be personally overjoyed at the success of his policy and is reported to have ordered a 'Te Deum' to be sung in the Chapel of the Winter Palace in honour of the conclusion of the Treaty, after which he publicly embraced the Chancellor of the Empire.—I cannot vouch for the accuracy of this report, but I hear from a thoroughly trustworthy source that His Majesty went to the Cathedral of St Peter and St Paul in the fortress, which contains the tombs of the Emperors, and there prayed for some time with signs of deep emotion at the grave of His Father, saying to his attendants as he left, that he trusted the shade of the Emperor Nicholas would now be appeased.[6]

---

[1] After he had sent off his own reply, the tsar in the evening had sent the two telegrams to the Foreign Office with an inquiry whether there was any objection to their publication. Gorchakov, having looked at them rather hurriedly, 'was principally struck by the pledge of gratitude taken by the Emperor William in his telegram, and considered that a positive political advantage would be gained by holding His Majesty to the engagement he had taken'. The telegrams, therefore, were ordered to be published. Not until the following morning was Gorchakov's attention drawn to certain passages in the tsar's reply:
'It was pointed out to the Chancellor that such an open departure from neutral feeling as the words: "Suis heureux d'avoir pu Vous prouver mes sympathies en ami dévoué" must create surprise and resentment in the numerous party who in this Country have been opposed to Prussia throughout the struggle, while it was urged that even impartial persons have been of late so led by compassion for the sufferings of France that they could not but be struck by the inconsistency of the Emperor in rejoicing at terms of peace so far removed from the moderation His Majesty is understood to have counselled.'
Gorchakov had fully admitted the cogency of these arguments and regretted the publication (Rumbold to Granville, 5 March 1871, FO 65/820, no. 19, confidential).
[2] Chotek to Beust, 7 March/23 February 1871, HHSAPARRR, 1871, x 60, no. 10B.
[3] Rumbold to Granville, telegram, 2 March 1871, FO 65/820.
[4] The same to the same, 5 March 1871, *ibid.* no. 19, confidential.
[5] Oakes and Mowat, *op. cit.* p. 330.
[6] Rumbold to Granville, 19 March 1871, FO 65/820, no. 28.

On 16 March a notice appeared in the *Journal de St Pétersbourg*:

La Russie est restée pendant quinze ans scrupuleusement fidèle au traité de 1856. Livrée à ses grands travaux intérieurs, elle a regagné en force et en prospérité bien au delà de ce que la guerre de Crimée lui avait fait perdre....

Son abstention temporaire dans les affaires de l'Europe a démontré jusqu'à l'évidence la place considérable qui lui appartient dans le concert européen et le rôle éminent conservateur qu'elle y joue.[1]

That was the Russian epitaph on fifteen eventful years during which a new great power had taken its place in Europe. Official Russia professed to consider that it had no reason to regret this development; such misgivings as might still be felt were quietened by the hope of future rewards and by diplomatic dependence on the new Germany.[2] France—employed for so long to balance Prussian aggrandisement—had proved a broken reed. Westmann—from the Russian point of view—delivered her funeral oration. He had taken the initiative in conversation with Rumbold to discuss the 'fall of France' and amazed the British diplomat 'by the severity of his language respecting the French nation and the future of France'.

After saying...that the Paris elections gave mortifying proof of the unchanged spirit of the Paris population, he went on to say that he well nigh despaired of the future of France; that the French nation shewed such indiscipline and such impatience of authority that they could only be compared to the Poles.—That France had long played a leading part in Europe and had wielded great power; but that she had made such bad use of her advantages that it was not to be regretted that the preponderance to which she had held so much should now pass to a Power which shewed so much greater 'sens politique' and that the final eclipse of France would be no European calamity.

Westmann, in fact, 'pronounced a complete funeral oration over that unhappy country—leaving out the expressions of regret which are customary on such occasions'.[3] A similar oration was pronounced—in writing —by the one British diplomat who had reflected deeply on the movements underlying the events of his age. Morier wrote to Lady Derby:

There remained, therefore, nothing for it but a trial of strength between the two big neighbours. That this trial of strength should have resulted in the consolidation

---

[1] The same to the same, 16 March 1871, *ibid.* no. 24.

[2] It was with serious alarm that the Russian government during February had noted Bismarck's evident desire to establish close relations with Austria. An Austro-German *rapprochement* threatened Russia with isolation. Her relations with England and Austria were strained. France inspired aversion and contempt (Chotek to Beust, 22/10 February 1871, HHSAPARRR, 1871, x 60, no. 9B and Rumbold to Granville, 22 February 1871, FO 65/820, no. 6, most confidential). A serious *rapprochement* of Germany, Austria and England would restore a 'Crimean coalition' in a form disastrous to Russian plans in the Balkans. When early in March a rumour circulated at St Petersburg that such an alliance had in fact been concluded, the tsar expressed his disbelief and declared the story to be a slander on his uncle (Chotek to Beust, 7 March/23 February 1871, HHSAPARRR, 1871, x 60, nos. 10B and 10C, confidential. Cf. also W. Platzhoff *Die Anfänge des Dreikaiserbundes* (Berlin, 1922), pp. 298 ff.).

[3] The same to the same, 22 February 1871, *ibid.* no. 6, most confidential.

of Germany, i.e. the fulfilment of a natural law (which until fulfilled would have necessarily kept Europe in a state of fever and turmoil) and in the rooting up, once for all, of the pretension of France to a privileged and exceptional position in Europe, seems to me so desirable an event that I confess myself totally incapable from the political point of view to understand anyone in his senses wishing the result to have been otherwise. It seems to me, in order to establish the positive proof of the beneficence of this result, sufficient to consider for one moment what would have been the result of French victory: the re-establishment of the divisions and impotence of Germany from which every European war for the last three centuries has arisen, and a new lease of Napoleonism, i.e. the establishment thenceforth on a tolerably firm basis by Napoléon le Petit of the ideas of Napoléon le Grand....I come back, therefore, to the thesis from which I started, that, *putting the emotional aspect of the war aside*, I must continue to declare that I consider its political results as beneficial.[1]

Neither conservative Russian nor liberal British diplomat saw cause to regret the eclipse of Napoleonic France and the triumph of Bismarckian Germany.

[1] Morier to Lady Derby, 5 January 1871, Morier, *op. cit.* pp. 213 ff.

CHAPTER 12

CONCLUSIONS

I

THE story of European diplomacy in the various phases of the German question between 1848 and 1871 shows the dangers of generalization. A detailed study of the facts makes untenable two plausible and widely accepted views. The first of these, which may be described as the 'German', is that the German nation had to fight its way to unification by 'blood and iron' against the opposition of a jealous and hostile Europe. The second, which might be described as 'Austro-French', is that, next to her armies, Prussia–Germany owed her success to unwavering Russian support. Both views, in their simple form, are unacceptable. In reality, no simple explanation fits the facts because not one of the leading powers between 1848 and 1871 pursued a consistent policy with regard to German affairs. It is possible, indeed, to detect in the actions of the powers certain unvarying 'principles' but these, in their application, were constantly modified by internal developments in the different countries and even more by completely extraneous issues in no wise connected with Germany. It is from the interplay of the 'basic principles' of the different governments and the various 'modifying factors' that the final attitudes of the powers to the German question emerge.

The 'principles' underlying British policy in the German question were of a threefold nature, political, ideological and dynastic. British statesmen regardless of party sincerely desired—in the abstract—the emergence of a strong German power capable of checking the ambitious designs attributed to France and Russia. A strong Germany would be the best safeguard against any repetition of the Napoleonic nightmare.[1] Germany, moreover, having no interest in the eastern question conflicting with those of England, might prove willing to oppose the encroachments of Russia. The new Germany, therefore, would assist in the defence of Belgium and the Straits. She would also free England from too exclusive a dependence on the French alliance which was popular on neither side of the Channel and ran counter to time-honoured historical traditions. Whereas a French *entente* must always be precarious on account of French restlessness and political instability, the new Germany, especially if grouped around the Prussian monarchy, would prove a solid and reliable partner. Such was the political, 'Palmerstonian', basis of British policy.

[1] No one, at the time, appears to have considered seriously the possibility that Germany herself might one day become a menace of 'Napoleonic' dimensions.

359

Superimposed on the idea of a natural community of political interests was the liberal concept of an ideological alliance propagated by the Prince-Consort and accepted by a large body of British liberal opinion. Both England and Germany would be Protestant,[1] teuton and liberal and would defend common values against Paris, St Petersburg and Rome. If this common liberalism remained largely a dream, the idea had yet some justification in fact. The German national movement—whatever its later history—sprang from liberal roots and a liberal tradition persisted. Even the hard fact of successful Prussian conservatism could not destroy the vision of an idealized 'other Germany'. The hopes of British liberals were kept alive by the Parliament in the *Paulskirche*, the 'liberalism' of two successive heirs-apparent in Prussia, by the 'New Era', the British marriage of the Prussian Crown-Prince and the struggle of the Prussian Parliament against Roon's military reforms. Confidence was felt in the known strength of liberal sentiment in western and south-western Germany. Even after a large part of the German liberal movement had made its peace with Bismarck, hopes were placed in the Prussian Crown-Prince and his Anglo-liberal wife.

The Anglo-German community of interests and ideals would be cemented by close dynastic ties. The Prince Consort was a German liberal and several of his daughters had married into German princely families. There was reason to believe that a free and unreserved exchange of views between the Queen and the Hohenzollerns would facilitate agreement on common policies and the settlement of possible disputes. As a result of these various considerations the basic British attitude was entirely favourable to the consolidation of Germany. It was felt that, together with her 'natural' ally, a 'new Germany', England would impose peace on east and west and decide the affairs of Europe.

Like the basic British ideas on the German question, those underlying Russian diplomacy were political, ideological and dynastic. In the first place, Russian views on German affairs were determined by concern for the security of Poland. The solidarity of the three partitioning powers in the face of Polish national aspirations was a cardinal principle of Russian policy. As long as Prussia and Austria were ready to co-operate in the fight against the Poles they could count on Russian sympathy. In addition, Germany was regarded in Russia as 'the road to Poland' and for this reason anything which promoted her defensive consolidation was welcomed. A strong Germany including Austria would form the protective glacis of the Russian fortress against the armies of France advancing towards the Vistula. It would, in addition, protect the Russian land

---

[1] It is curious that in all British discussion of Germany's future she should figure as the second great Protestant power. Even disregarding Austria, the rest of Germany still contained almost as many Catholics as Protestants; even 'Protestant' Prussia contained large Catholic populations in the Rhineland, the former Polish provinces and parts of Silesia.

frontier between the Baltic and the Black Sea in the event of a clash with England and France in the eastern question. A strong and stable Germany–Austria, therefore, was generally recognized to be a Russian necessity. Moreover, united under Russian leadership, the three 'eastern monarchies' would dominate the affairs of central and eastern Europe and defend the peace of the continent.

Both Austria and Prussia were monarchical states with traditions of bureaucratic and authoritarian government. They would 'naturally' support Russia in the fight against subversion whether of Poles, liberals or democrats. Both the powerful military party in Vienna and the Prussian conservatives looked to St Petersburg under Nicholas I and continued to do so under his successor. It must, therefore, be the aim of Russian diplomacy to strengthen the 'Russian' parties in the two capitals in their struggles with 'western' liberal groups. Only the rock of German conservatism could break the waves of Anglo-French subversion.

The community of interests and ideology among the three 'eastern monarchies' was strengthened by dynastic ties. Thus the Russo-Prussian alliance against the first Napoleon had led to the marriage of the tsarevich to a Hohenzollern princess. Nicholas Pavlovich by his marriage with princess Charlotte (Alexandra Feodorovna) linked the house of Holstein-Gottorp—misnamed Romanov—with that of Hohenzollern. Their offspring—more than half a German—would treasure the family heritage of Russo-Prussian friendship. No such links could be established with the proud Habsburgs in Vienna. Indeed his failure to bring about a marriage alliance between the two dynasties was one of the major disappointments in the life of Nicholas. None the less, after the final 'defection' of his brother-in-law, 'the dreamer', the tsar eagerly transferred his patronage to young Francis-Joseph, whose heritage he was defending in Hungary. Russia like England, therefore, was essentially well disposed towards the political and military consolidation of Germany. This basic disposition, however, did not imply identical objectives and was, in practice, subject to modification by a variety of causes not directly connected with German affairs.

II

The basic attitudes of the powers underwent some modifications during the revolutions of 1848 and the counter-revolution which followed. British opinion became aware of the fact that German liberals might claim —at least in theory—that all German-speaking populations should be ruled by one political authority. German nationalism—however liberal in its ideology—was seen to have implications fatal to the order established by the treaties of Vienna. The clash between revolutionary nationalism and existing treaty rights faced British diplomacy with a dilemma —especially where national claims conflicted with British interests. In consequence, the problem of Schleswig-Holstein modified British approval of German consolidation. In defence of treaty rights and the 'balance of power' in the Baltic, England, a theoretical protagonist of German unity, became in practice a leading opponent of Germany's most urgent national demand. Furthermore, British opinion soon came to realize that, owing to internal divisions and the weakness of German liberalism, the peaceful establishment of a constitutional German state was all but impossible. The reaction which followed the early revolutionary successes deepened British disillusionment. The triumph of counter-revolution in Vienna and Berlin, the Punctuation of Olmütz brought about under Russian auspices and finally the Manteuffel era in Prussia with its conservative and 'russianizing' tendencies confirmed earlier doubts about the possibility of a liberal unification of Germany. Any other, however, would fall short of British ideals.

Like England, Russia between 1848 and 1851 made the discovery that the German national movement might assume unwelcome forms. During the year of revolutions, the tsar observed with grief the weakness of the German dynasties and the strength of liberal, national and democratic movements throughout Germany and the Habsburg dominions. The explosive force of liberal-nationalism, moreover, directly touched Russian interests through Posen in Poland and the 'western provinces' and also in Schleswig-Holstein. Furthermore, during the period of 'counter-revolution' the threat of civil war in Germany again placed in jeopardy the vital interests of Russia. It was therefore natural for Nicholas I, to try and prevent the unification of Germany under liberal auspices and to avert the threatened civil war. The powerful weight of Russian diplomacy and prestige backed by some military preparations was thrown into the scale of conservative restoration. Similarly Russian pressure was brought to bear in favour of a 'conservative' settlement of the Danish question. Largely through the force of circumstances and without Russian military intervention in Germany, counter-revolution triumphed; the Russian concept of a conservative and dualist Confederation finally prevailed.

The Crimean War reacted on the German question mainly indirectly through the altered position of Russia. After the war, the exhausted Russian empire urgently required a prolonged period of peace for internal reconstruction. The necessary consequence was a period of reduced diplomatic activity. This, whilst it did not alter Russia's basic attitude to the German question, meant that she had in fact lost the sanction of force in her dealings with Germany. In consequence, she ceased to be the arbiter of Germany and was reduced to defending her interests by diplomatic means alone.

Moreover, Russia's defeat had produced certain modifications in her policy. Her traditional system in Germany had been destroyed by the occupation of the Principalities which had driven Austria into the ranks of her enemies. The events of the war had earned for Austria the lasting resentment of the Russian nation. Ties with Prussia, on the other hand, had been significantly strengthened. Buol's policy, in fact, had undermined the basis of the restoration settlement. It had destroyed the solidarity of the eastern monarchies, driven a wedge between Russia and Austria, and, as a result, upset the Austro-Prussian equilibrium in Germany. Gorchakov, under the influence of his recent experiences, professed to inaugurate with the tsar's support a 'national' Russian policy. Nicholas and Nesselrode were accused of having sacrificed the 'national' interest of Russia for the benefit of Germany without securing either gratitude or tangible results. Gorchakov and diplomats like Oubril and Brunnow were less well disposed towards even a conservative Germany than Nesselrode and Meyendorff had been. Moreover, the treaty of Paris distracted Russian attention from the affairs of Germany. It was considered a national disgrace and seemed to prescribe to Russian diplomacy a specific 'national' task to which the affairs of central Europe must, if necessary, be subordinated. Russia's preoccupation with the 'eastern question' would now offer an adventurous statesman in Berlin or Vienna a lever for destroying the equilibrium on which the 'Russian' system in Germany reposed. In this Bismarck, whose task was the easier of the two, was to prove himself more adept than his blundering rival Beust. The Crimean War, therefore, had reduced alike the ability and the inclination of Russia to defend the *status quo* in Germany. Alexander II would not repeat the conduct of his predecessor between 1848 and 1850.

The progress of the Italian national movement provided yet another occasion for modifications in the Russian attitude. Russia's *rapprochement* with France and Sardinia after the Crimean War aggravated the strain in Russo-German relations. During Napoleon's Italian campaign, Russia and Austria found themselves on opposite sides with Prussia and the lesser German states threatening to join Austria. Russia's 'aberration' in supporting Napoleon and Cavour placed her for four years in opposition alike to her own principles and to the German states. The further progress of the Italian national movement, however, drove her back into the 'conservative' anti-national camp. Conservative reform in Germany, in conformity with Russian needs, appeared once again a practical possibility. References to the alliance of the three eastern monarchies, to common conservative sentiments and interests and to the need for joint vigilance in the face of Napoleon and the Poles were multiplied. The Polish insurrection of 1863 revealed that—in her own interest—Prussia was prepared, albeit clumsily, to play the part assigned to her in Russian diplomatic strategy. Austrian policy, on the other hand, revealed itself as ambiguous and incompatible with the alleged solidarity of the three partitioning powers.

The dispute about the Duchies faced both England and Russia with a conflict between their desire for the consolidation of Germany and the wish to defend strategic positions and secure the observance of treaties. In England, there now arose a division of opinion. The Queen, Granville and the majority of the Cabinet sympathized with the claim of the Germans in Schleswig-Holstein to join the Germanic Confederation under a liberal Duke related by marriage to the British royal family. Palmerston, supported by a minority of his colleagues, on the other hand, saw no occasion to sacrifice to the claims of German nationalism the Protocol of 1852 and the integrity of the Danish monarchy. In this clash of opinions, it was the liberal 'German' view which finally prevailed, the Whig 'European' one which was defeated. The victory was a narrow one, but it sufficed to allow Prussia followed by Austria to present Europe with the first great *fait accompli* of the German question.

The Russian attitude, traditionally pro-Danish and hostile to German aspirations in the Duchies, was modified under the impact of Polish events. The Polish insurrection of 1863 placed a severe strain on an economy which had not yet recovered fully from the effects of the Crimean War. Peace at almost any price became Russia's basic need. In addition, the Polish rising had drawn attention once more to the similarity between the interests of Russia and those of Prussian conservatives. They had, at the same time, focused attention on the clash—actual or potential— between these interests and those of Catholic Austria and the polono-phile German liberals. To support Bismarck, the 'symbol' of Prussian conservatism, had thus become for Russia an act of self-defence. In these circumstances, the German sympathies of the tsar founded on dynastic and anti-Polish sentiments were able to assert themselves against the francophile tendencies of Gorchakov. Finally the dispute about the Duchies did not, from the Russian point of view, appear to involve the German question—so long, at least, as the matter remained in the hands of legitimate governments. Indeed the governments of Prussia and Austria must be given some measure of support precisely to prevent the dispute from raising the German question in its popular and 'democratic' form. The events of 1859 and 1860 in the Italian peninsula afforded a warning example. In consequence, the Russian government was willing to tolerate the Austro-Prussian *fait accompli*—whilst showing at the same time an almost 'schizophrenic' desire for a 'European' solution based, at least in form, on the observation of existing agreements. Russian diplomacy, in fact, was torn between a clear recognition of military and political realities and the longing for a conservative, 'legitimate' solution. In the end, internal weakness, Poland, distrust of Napoleon and fear of a German revolution led Russia to acquiesce—albeit reluctantly—in the 'dismemberment' of the Danish monarchy.

The Danish crisis and its aftermath had a profound effect on the British attitude to German affairs. Prussia's evident unwillingness to hand over the Duchies to the liberal duke of Augustenburg, her ill-concealed intention to annex them herself, and the cruel reality of Bismarckian *Realpolitik* shook the faith of British liberals in German 'idealism'. The Queen, Clarendon and Russell came to share the anti-Bismarckian sentiments of Napier, Buchanan and Cowley. Henceforward only 'realists' like Palmerston or 'fatalists' like Morier would applaud the strengthening of Germany through 'prussianization'. However, the feeling against Bismarck and Prussia was counteracted by a yet more potent sentiment, the desire for withdrawal from Europe. The repeated failures of 'Palmerstonian' diplomacy and the 'meddle and muddle' of Russell had produced in Parliament and the country a profound distaste for 'unnecessary' interference in the affairs of the continent . As a result, even the great German crisis of 1866 found England largely indifferent. The lone voices of a few surviving Whigs and the later Marquis of Salisbury were powerless against the prevailing sentiment faithfully reflected by Stanley. No British statesman was prepared to put up for the Federal Acts of 1815 even part of the struggle which Palmerston had waged for the Protocol of 1852. There was now an almost universal readiness to accept any *fait accompli* not directly hurtful to British interests. The laments for Austria or the Hanoverian dynasty indulged in by the Queen or Clarendon did not reflect a strong movement of opinion but merely a nostalgic recognition that with the decision of 1866 an age of German history had passed away.

The tsar, on the other hand, showed a genuine reluctance to accept the 'revolutionary' settlement of 1866. The outbreak of a fratricidal war—forestalled in 1850—showed that Russia's traditional 'system' in Germany had broken down. The second shock administered to the Russian government was Prussia's attack on the dynastic principle through the dispossession of dynasties and the promise of a democratic parliament. Both were resented at St Petersburg. For a moment, the Russian 'national' party and conservative opinion led by the tsar himself were united in disapproval. The attempt, however, to retrieve the situation by organizing a European congress was forestalled by Bismarck's hurried peace with Austria, whilst Russian irritation was finally appeased by the Manteuffel mission and the promise of Prussian support in revising the treaty of Paris. Three reasons explain Russia's willingness to sacrifice the German 'system' of Alexander I and Nicholas I. Russia was too weak in the diplomatic as well as the military sphere to prevent single-handed the Bismarckian settlement in North Germany. England was passive, Napoleon adopted an ambiguous attitude, and Russian diplomacy had to make a virtue of necessity. Moreover, whilst denying France effective 'compensations' at the expense of Germany, Bismarck was able to offer Russia a 'reward' mainly at British expense. Finally, the new settlement formally maintained the existing system: Prussia was supreme north of the Main whilst Austria might be held to have retained her position in the south.

Even Nicholas I would have been prepared to accept an arrangement of this kind in 1849. So long as the tsar's influence remained powerful at Stuttgart, it might be held that the sacrifice of Russian interests had been small.

It was another non-German issue—the eastern question—which facilitated the final destruction of the system established at Vienna. Gorchakov's attempt to raise the question 'prematurely' in 1867 gave hostages to fortune and made Russia dependent on Prussian diplomatic support. The revival of Austro-Russian rivalry in the Balkans, moreover, together with tension between Russia and France, destroyed any 'European' motive the Russian government might have had for defending the settlement of 1866. It was the eastern question together with that of Poland which finally induced Alexander II to accept in principle the union of Germany under the leadership of Prussia.

Even in the years immediately preceding 1870, when Europe was conscious of the possibility of a Franco-German war, eastern issues were not without influence on the attitudes of England and Russia. Prussia–Germany had no direct interest in the fate of Turkey in Europe and might therefore lend her support to either England or Russia. She had, in the past, tended on grounds of expediency to give cautious support to Russia. French interests in the east also—although greater than those of Prussia —were of secondary importance. In spite of repeated 'flirtations' with Russia, France at decisive points had tended to adopt the British point of view. Russian interests, therefore, might seem to be best served by a Prusso-German victory, whilst those of England in the east appeared bound up with the victory of France.

The alignment resulting from the eastern question, however, was checked by other issues. England's second major concern in Europe, the security of Belgium, was threatened by a French victory but would be safe in the hands of victorious Prussia–Germany. On the other hand, whilst the Russian national party feared the effect of triumphant Germanism on Russia's Baltic provinces, no such danger need be apprehended from France. The latter consideration, however, might again be balanced by the possible repercussions of a French victory on the Poles. Whatever the outcome of the conflict, therefore, both England and Russia seemed likely to pay for increased security in certain areas by growing danger in others.

Sympathies like interests were divided. In England francophiles like Clarendon and Granville had since 1867 succeeded to a large extent in reviving the old Anglo-French *entente*. Napoleon III, whatever the vagaries of his policy, was seen to have proved himself a consistent friend of England. It was the breakdown of the Anglo-French alliance in 1863 which had opened the door to many calamities. Moreover, British policy had on more than one occasion been successful in restraining the emperor of the French. As long, therefore, as Napoleon remained in control, it might appear that British interests as well as British sympathies must be on the side of France. Against this, it was pointed out that France was the home of revolutions, that the Napoleonic dynasty was insecure, that the French were excitable and aggressive. The 'natural' alliance of England and Germany, on the other hand, would be a stabilizing influence in Europe. The future appeared to belong to the liberal Crown Prince. Repeated messages from the Court and even from Bismarck himself suggested that it was a British alliance which Prussia–Germany desired. If England helped Germany against France, Germany would repay her services by support against Russia in the east. Bismarck, moreover, had promised military support in defending the independence of Belgium as the price of an alliance against France. British Ministers had consistently refused this bargain, but it was clear, none the less, that the triumph of Germany was likely to prove compatible with England's vital interests.

In fact, when the God of battles had finally declared for Germany, England had no difficulty in accepting the verdict. The 'fall of France' was greeted by British opinion with satisfaction, indifference or at best philosophic regret. Moreover, during the crisis produced by Gorchakov's circular, Bismarck had played the role of 'the honest broker'—for the first time if not the last—and had thereby acquired some claim to British gratitude. It was England which favoured the maintenance of the *status quo* in the east: a peaceful and disinterested Germany—even whilst adopting a 'neutral' attitude—would, in fact, help England rather than Russia. There was, moreover, some hope that the new Germany with its liberal public opinion and a government eagerly courting the anti-Russian Magyars, would one day be ranged against Russia. The evident growth of anti-German sentiment in Russia would tend to separate the two empires —to the great advantage of England. In consequence, even if certain illusions about common liberalism had been shattered by the stern reality of Bismarck, there yet remained a sufficient community of interests to justify the view that the replacement of France by Germany as the strongest continental power was not a British loss. That the new Germany would one day be England's principal rival was hidden alike from British opinion and governments. Cowley alone, aged, embittered and anti-Prussian, warned against the possible danger of German naval power. His was a lonely voice.

In Russia also, the Franco-German struggle for supremacy produced a divided opinion. After 1866 the Russian 'national' party through Katkov's influential *Moscow Gazette* persistently drew attention to the alleged menace of a powerful German empire. What was especially feared was the attraction of German strength and prestige for the Baltic Germans whom Russian 'patriots' wished to 'denationalize'. Moreover, the creation of a state embracing all Germans would spell the dissolution of the Habsburg empire. Such a development, though not in itself a cause for regret, might yet have unfortunate repercussions. Russian nationalists,

367

therefore, advocated an understanding with France to 'contain' the new German power. They were willing even to bolster up unpopular Austria to maintain a 'balance' of power. In opposition to this view 'conservatives' led by the tsar himself welcomed the rise of Prussia–Germany. They were ready to accept and even to welcome the ascendancy of 'conservative' Prussia within a 'conservative' Germany, and the substitution of Germany for France as the leading power in Europe. Russia needed a powerful ally to achieve the objects of her national policy. Even Russian conservatives were forced to recognize that the age of Napoleon, Cavour and Bismarck was one of *Realpolitik* rather than conservative sentiment. *Realpolitik*, however, suggested a partnership with the powerful German empire rather than the Habsburg 'corpse' or unstable 'polonophile' France. If Russia was ever to achieve her objects in the east, it could only be with the goodwill of Prussia–Germany. Without at least Germany's benevolent neutrality a conflict in the east was unthinkable. German assistance in the east must be bought with Russian support in the west. In fact, the tsar placed his trust in the 'gratitude' publicly proclaimed by the Emperor William after the Preliminaries of 1871.[1] The liberation of Russia—with Prussian support—from the hated Black Sea Clauses seemed an earnest of benefits to come.

Neither England nor Russia, therefore, saw reason to regret the outcome of the Franco-German struggle. In London it was felt that the new Germany would restrain, and, if necessary, oppose Russia in the east, whilst in St Petersburg it was hoped that she would, on the contrary, tip the scales against Austria and England. If neither calculation in the end proved completely correct, neither was utterly falsified by the event. Owing to the success of Bismarck's statecraft, neither England nor Russia had serious cause to regret the eclipse of France. Bismarck, in fact, tried to hold the scales evenly between them, allowing small and carefully balanced advantages to each in turn. It is difficult to deny that at least from the British and perhaps even from the Russian point of view, he proved himself a more reliable and disinterested arbiter than Napoleon had ever been.

The attitudes of England and Russia towards the unification of Germany thus underwent between 1848 and 1871 important modifications. At no time, however, was there a determined and consistent opposition to German national aspirations either at St Petersburg or London. This was true even though German policy in the Elbe Duchies, the 'fratricidal' war of 1866, the dispossession of German dynasties, anxiety about the Baltic provinces, and finally the annexation of Alsace-Lorraine, caused, at different times, apprehensions and even indignation in the two 'peripheral' capitals.

[1] After the Congress of Berlin he would, in a bitter letter to his uncle, tax Germany with ingratitude.

III

Although the German national movement repeatedly touched the interests of other powers, little attempt was made—except by paper notes—to interfere in the conduct of German affairs. It seems possible that in certain circumstances Nicholas I might have intervened between 1848 and 1850, Palmerston and Russell would have liked to do so in 1864 and Napoleon vaguely toyed with the idea in 1866. In the first case intervention proved 'unnecessary', in the other two impracticable. Moreover, in the first two instances, interference would have been concerned with Denmark as much as with Germany. Austrian intervention, if it had come about in 1870 under the inspiration of Beust, would have been essentially 'internal' and Germanic.

If intervention by armed force was rarely a serious possibility, diplomatic intervention was possible but not in practice very effective. The powers frequently expressed their views through 'diplomatic channels' but their advice was rarely taken. This is true both of official diplomacy and of the stream of correspondence addressed without avail to the king of Prussia by the tsar and Queen Victoria. There were, however, some notable exceptions. Nicholas I intervened with considerable effect to prevent a German civil war and bring about the Punctuation of Olmütz. In 1866 Napoleon's intervention may have influenced the terms proposed to Austria at Nikolsburg whilst the tsar's intercession may have lightened the fate of some lesser German dynasties. Odo Russell's threat of an Anglo-Russian war strengthened Bismarck's determination to find a peaceful solution for the 'marginal' Black Sea crisis. It is impossible to say to what extent Russian warnings influenced the course of Austrian policy before Sedan. The total effect, therefore, of diplomatic intervention by individual powers was small; it affected details rather than major issues.

Diplomatic intervention by the concert was hardly more productive of results. 'European' diplomacy was responsible for the Protocol of 1852 and the abortive London conference of 1864. It may be held to have contributed to the peaceful settlement of the Luxemburg dispute and helped to find a solution for the question raised by Gorchakov's Circular. It is interesting to note that concerted diplomatic action was confined to 'marginal' issues like those of the Duchies, the neutrality of Luxemburg and the Black Sea Clauses.[1]

Between 1848 and 1850 concerted diplomatic action had been confined to the affairs of the Duchies; it might have developed also in opposition to Schwarzenberg's proposals for the inclusion of the entire Habsburg monarchy in Germany, but the issue never became acute. The London Protocol of 1852 was the last major achievement of the European concert.

[1] The list might be extended to include the affairs of the Principalities and the Greco-Turkish dispute.

After the Crimean war, the 'new diplomacy' of Napoleon and Cavour all but destroyed the older conception of 'international' settlements. The idea of the concert, however, died hard. In 1864 both England and Russia strongly favoured a 'European' solution of the Danish question—but did not persist in the face of German hostility and French indifference. It is interesting to note that the Russian government was the last to abandon the Protocol of 1852 and the concept of international legality. Indeed the tradition of settlement by conference—discredited by the failure of the London conference on the Duchies—survived in the cabinet of St Petersburg. In 1866 the Russian government tried, unsuccessfully, to mobilize the powers against Prussia's unilateral abrogation of the Federal Acts of 1815. Again, in 1870, it attempted to secure agreement with Austria and England to impose a settlement on the belligerents. Neither attempt was persevered in in the face of Prussia-Germany's military triumphs. Both after Königgrätz, and again after Sedan, the Russian government precipitately abandoned its efforts to secure a European solution and tried to reach agreement with the victors. The military strength of Prussia threw into relief the feebleness of the concert. The powers by their joint efforts might still settle, albeit inefficiently, the affairs of the Principalities, Crete or Greece; they could discuss in conference the future of the Duchies or legalize the abrogation of the Black Sea Clauses. For the rest, whenever the interests of a major power were concerned, the concert could neither prevent the outbreak of war nor influence the terms of peace. Except indirectly during the Schleswig-Holstein crisis of 1848–1850, it at no time seriously impeded the progress of the German national movement.

If the weakness of the concert created conditions favourable to the consolidation of Germany, so also did repeated shifts in the diplomatic alignment of the powers. Four possible 'basic' groupings emerge at different times either fully grown or in embryonic form. The ideas of the Holy Alliance died hard and a league of the three 'eastern monarchies' remained an ever-present possibility. This, almost inevitably, would be counter-balanced by an understanding of England and France. Another constellation emerging on more than one occasion is that in which England, France and Austria were opposed to Russia and Prussia. A Franco-Russian understanding directed mainly against Austria and supported by Prussia or Italy is another possibility. Finally, a Catholic alliance of Austria, France and Italy in opposition to Prussia (and Russia) seriously entered the calculations of Bismarck.[1]

Within the framework of these possibilities the situation changed with almost kaleidoscopic rapidity. The crisis of 1848–50 revived the solidarity of the 'eastern monarchies' and produced, as its counterpart, an Anglo-

[1] It is significant that neither Russia and Prussia nor England and France ever figure on opposite sides.

French *entente*. During the Crimean war, Austria detached herself from the eastern alliance and joined the western powers. After the war, Russia and France reached an understanding on a joint policy in east and west and agreed to support Sardinia against Austria. The 'violence' of the Italian national movement provoked an attempt to reconstitute the 'eastern bloc' in opposition to France. After the annexation of Nice and Savoy, England appeared to draw closer to this conservative grouping. The Polish crisis for a moment revived the Crimean alliance. After the failure of tripartite diplomacy, however, England once again drifted into the orbit of the 'eastern powers'. In 1863, with the end of both the Anglo-French *entente* and the Franco-Russian understanding, Europe was left without a stable combination beyond the general solidarity of interests between Russia and Prussian conservatives. It was only the eastern crisis of 1866–7 which produced a new constellation. Austria and France drew together; Russia and Prussia did the same. England held aloof. In the end, the rise of the German empire on the ruins of defeated France tended to restore a semblance of co-operation among the 'eastern powers' under German leadership. This also failed to produce a stable equilibrium.[1]

The repeated changes in the alignment of the powers were doubly favourable to the cause of German consolidation. In the first place, the general absence of stability impeded the defence of the *status quo*. More specifically, recurrent European crises either dissolved or frustrated combinations inimical to German progress. A clash of interests in the Balkans followed by Buol's 'westernizing' diplomacy destroyed the Austro-Russian *entente* which formed the sole protection of the restored Germanic Confederation. The annexation to France of Nice and Savoy shook the Anglo-French alliance, feared by Bismarck above all others; the unsuccessful western attempt to help the Poles, followed by the British refusal to attend Napoleon's Congress, finally destroyed it. Events in the Principalities, Italy and Poland therefore, dissolved, without active Prusso-German participation, the alignments potentially most dangerous to Prussia's future progress. Nor was this all. Differences over Italy permanently blocked the road to an Austro-French alliance, whilst fear for the future of Bosnia and Herzegovina finally drove Russia into the arms of Prussia. In this manner, events unconnected with German affairs consistently favoured the cause of Prussia and Bismarck.

[1] In fact, in so far as a 'balance' may be said to have existed between 1848 and 1871, it is to be sought in a general tendency to oppose first the Russia of Nicholas I, then the France of Napoleon and, finally, the Germany of Bismarck. This desire to restrain an 'overmighty' power—although rarely effective as a political force—may be held to have contributed to the outbreak of the Crimean war and to have promoted the policy of 'containing' Napoleon III. It might, however, be noted that this feeling did not lead the powers to prevent the outbreak of the Franco-Prussian war, which seemed certain to upset such 'equilibrium' as might exist, and in which a French victory was, in the beginning, widely expected. Nor did the feeling—at least at this time—seriously impede the progress of Bismarck's Germany.

IV

Bismarck's task, therefore, was made easier by circumstances. If he played his hand with great skill, it was a good one in the first place. Neither British nor Russian statesmen felt the interests of their countries threatened by the consolidation of Germany. Moreover, developments in the 1850's and 1860's made them less able or less inclined to interfere in European affairs. In essence, therefore, the crucial questions concerning the future of Germany could be settled within the 'little Europe' of Prussia, Austria, Italy and France. Given Prussia's military strength, this meant that the struggle for German 'unification' reduced itself in fact to a duel between Prussia and France. Here, too, Bismarck was favoured: an Austro-French alliance, the only grouping which he feared within 'little Europe', was prevented between 1856 and 1866 by the Italian question and by disagreement in the Principalities; even after 1866, Italian issues remained to obstruct its conclusion.

In these circumstances, the moves made by Bismarck were, on the whole, such as would have suggested themselves to any 'conservative-minded' Prussian statesman. Thus it was obvious that any German and especially Prussian 'conservative' must in 1863 have taken the part of Russia against the Poles and their western backers—and have thereby gained such 'gratitude' as could be obtained from the tsar. Indeed, in analogous circumstances, Manteuffel had pursued a very similar policy during the Crimean war. Again, it was known to every cabinet in Europe that Russian sympathy could be bought for support in the eastern question. England, however, felt no need to buy such sympathy and preferred to defend the only tangible gain of the Crimean war. Napoleon did not dare to pay the Russian price for fear of offending England and was, moreover, opposed in any case to an extension of Russian influence in the east. Rechberg and Beust, although willing enough to pay for Russian support by the abrogation of the Black Sea Clauses, were prevented from striking a bargain by the weakness of the Habsburg monarchy. In any case, it was all but impossible to remove the sources of Austro-Russian distrust and rivalry in the Balkans. Prussia–Germany alone combined a lack of interest in the neutralization of the Black Sea with the ability to paralyse British or Anglo-French opposition to a revision of the treaty. Prussia alone, therefore, was both able and willing to make the promises which would secure the benevolence of Russia. The Manteuffel Mission to St Petersburg in 1866 was an obvious expedient of Prussian diplomacy: the bargain struck was the natural bargain. It was by an uncovenanted stroke of luck that Bismarck was able to make the same concession twice over and to be twice paid for the same service to Russia. Finally, it was again self-evident that any 'conservative' Prussian government must do everything in its power to confirm

Alexander II in his German sympathies—another gratuitously favourable factor.

Bismarck, moreover, found himself in the happy position of being able to 'dole out' his assistance to Russia in the knowledge that, in the last resort, the tsar depended on Prussia to save him from isolation. The basic antagonism of Russia and England could not be bridged; the distrust between St Petersburg and Vienna proved ineradicable; Poland and the personality of Napoleon stood between Russia and France. The success of Russian policy, therefore, depended in the last resort upon the goodwill of Berlin, a fact which gave Bismarck a powerful lever in his dealings with the Russian government. In addition, whilst Prussia was herself disinterested in the eastern question, her position enabled her to hold the balance between England, Russia and Austria. It was this circumstance which forced Russia to accept Bismarck's 'arbitration' as Prussia had once accepted that of Nicholas I at Olmütz.

Where circumstances were less favourable—as in his dealings with England—Bismarck's success was less spectacular. British neutrality of course was assured without much effort on his part. When, however, he tried to obtain more active British support, he was unable to make headway. In theory, at least, he held two invaluable cards, the French threat to Belgium and the Russian threat to Constantinople, and he persistently tried to use these to draw England into a defensive alliance. All he ever obtained was an informal understanding that, in return for Prussian efforts to restrain France and Russia, England would forbear from joining—even diplomatically—a coalition of Prussia's enemies. More than this he could not gain: England would throw over France as little as Prussia would give up her understanding with Russia. Isolationist sentiment and the known aversion of British statesmen to binding agreements further increased Bismarck's difficulties. If, as he claimed, no German parliament would sanction Germany's adhesion to the Treaty of 15 April, it was equally certain that no British Parliament would ratify an Anglo-German alliance.

As to Bismarck's policy in the eastern question, it was that which any Prusso-German statesman[1] would naturally pursue. Once feelers in London had established that England would not join Prussia in a defensive alliance, there was no reason why, by supporting her in the east, Prussia should antagonize Russia. Similarly, it was clear that, in her own interest, Prussia must not support Russian policies likely to revive the Crimean coalition. There was, in fact, no visible reason why any Prusso-German government should act in the eastern question as anything but the 'honest broker'. Bismarck conducted in the east—albeit with

[1] That of an Austrian would have been different.

373

uncommon tactical skill—the policy any sensible Prusso-German Minister would have followed.[1]

V

Bismarck's achievement, therefore, was great but not 'superhuman'. Twice Austria and France failed to combine against him and he was able to defeat them in isolation, thanks to Prussia–Germany's military superiority. That he was able to do so without 'European' intervention was due mainly to the policies of England and Russia. Both these powers repeatedly changed their attitudes towards events in Germany but neither was opposed—on principle—to German consolidation. Whatever view they might take of the various methods adopted, both powers considered that they stood to gain from the strengthening of Germany. In fact, neither was to see the complete fulfilment of its hopes: the new Germany did not become England's 'faithful ally' against Russia, nor yet did it justify Russia's high hopes of unstinted support in the Balkans. By 1878 British and Russian statesmen alike knew that, like their predecessors, they had, in part, miscalculated. Nor was opinion in London and St Petersburg unaware of the problems created by the rise of the new Germany. Ever since 1866 forebodings had been expressed in Russia about the 'inevitable' future struggle of Slav and Teuton, whilst the German annexation of Alsace and Lorraine was held, almost universally, to foreshadow future strife. Moreover, those who still believed in the theory of a European equilibrium were conscious that the European 'balance' had been upset by the decisive defeat of France. Yet in 1871— as generally during the previous twenty years—neither England nor Russia saw serious reason to fear, or experienced the urge to prevent, the emergence of a unified German state.

[1] There is no evidence that Bismarck's eastern policy in those years ever became the subject of controversy. The nearest approach was Liberal criticism of the Alvensleben Convention. In this case, it was Bismarck who had momentarily departed from the dictates of sound sense. The Liberals, although inspired largely by doctrinaire motives, were proved right by the event. Threatened with a possible revival of the Crimean coalition, Bismarck had to abandon the Convention.

GERMAN HISTORIOGRAPHY AND THE GERMAN QUESTION

I

The views of German historians on the attitude of foreign powers towards the German question have a curious and significant history. The earliest accounts of Germany's consolidation tended to concentrate on the purely Germanic aspects of the process and to pay comparatively little attention to its European repercussions. Thus Sybel, in his monumental work, emphasized the struggle for supremacy between Austria and Prussia. Austria represented the historic tradition of Habsburg leadership in Germany whilst Prussia embodied the modern force of nationality.[1] Friedjung's classic work lent further weight to the view that the most prominent aspect of German consolidation was internal. Austrian statesmen could not abandon without a struggle their country's time-honoured leadership in Germany. Against their will, they were forced to take up the Prussian challenge and to fight a civil war which they deplored.[2] Bismarck himself in his memoirs dwells on the importance of eliminating the historical dualism from the German body politic.[3]

There were several reasons why Sybel and Friedjung tended to concentrate on the internal history of the 'Reichsgründung'. It was natural for German historians to begin their work in German archives. Moreover, as Sybel noted, they would have found it difficult to obtain access to foreign ones.[4] There was, however, a deeper reason for focusing attention on

---

[1] 'Die Kämpfe von 1866 waren nicht ein willkürlich gemachtes Ergebnis persönlicher Leidenschaften: sie entsprangen vielmehr aus dem unvermeidlichen Conflicte alter durch Jahrhunderte herangewachsener Rechte mit den immer stärker drängenden nationalen Bedürfnissen. Der hierdurch erzeugte Krankheitszustand wurde zuletzt unerträglich, und nur eine heftige Krisis konnte die dauernde Genesung herbeiführen' (Sybel, *op. cit.* vol. I, p. xi).

[2] 'Für Oesterreich gab es überhaupt keinen Preis, um den es freiwillig auf den Primat in Deutschland verzichten mochte: so dachte jeder österreichische Staatsmann, und so musste er denken. Denn eine europäische Grossmacht gibt sich selbst auf, wenn sie ein so grosses Ding ohne Waffengang fahren lässt' (H. Friedjung, *Der Kampf um die Vorherrschaft in Deutschland* (Berlin, 1896), vol. I, p. 12).

[3] 'Der gordische Knoten deutscher Zustände liess sich nicht in Liebe dualistisch lösen, nur militärisch zerhauen; es kam darauf an, den König von Preussen, bewusst oder unbewusst, und damit das preussische Heer für den Dienst der nationalen Sache zu gewinnen, mochte man vom borussischen Standpunkt die Führung Preussens oder auf dem nationalen die Einigung Deutschlands als die Hauptsache betrachten; beide Ziele deckten einander' (*GE*, vol. I, pp. 317f.).

[4] 'Um die Benutzung anderer Archive habe ich mich aus dem einfachen Grunde nicht bemüht, dass für die Gewährung eines solchen Gesuchs nicht die mindeste Aussicht vorhanden war' (Sybel, *op. cit.* p. x).

Austro-Prussian rivalry and the events of 1866. Sybel and Friedjung wrote whilst Germany was at the height of her power. The shadow of 'Einkreisung' which was to give Germans a morbid awareness of the outside world had hardly begun to fall. It was therefore natural for German historiography to be 'self-centred'.

The situation was radically changed when England, France and Russia formed an 'unholy alliance' to destroy the German powers and ruin 'the work of Bismarck'. After a four-year struggle against a 'world in arms', German opinion, obsessed by the historical parallel between the World War and the Seven Years War, began to develop the myth of the implacable hostility invariably shown by the outside world towards Germany and everything German. This myth was faithfully reflected in German historiography. It now appeared that for a long time Germany's neighbours had conspired together to deprive her of her rightful 'place in the sun' and that Germans had always been forced to fight for their just 'rights'. The legend was applied in retrospect to the years between 1848 and 1871. It was now asserted that the failure of the movement for 'unification' between 1848 and 1851 was due principally to foreign intervention. French ill-will and Russian arrogance combined with the hypocritical meddling of England to destroy Germany's chance of creating for herself a stable political organization. It needed Bismarck, the German 'superman', to bring about this result by 'blood and iron' in the face of a hostile Europe.

Moreover, foreign archives were gradually being opened to historians and some of the revelations seemed to confirm the theory of European hostility.[1] In addition, an anti-Bismarckian legend was being developed outside Germany. Both these developments tended to reinforce the interest of German historians in the European aspects of German consolidation. The age dominated by Sybel and Friedjung gave way to that of Marcks, Oncken, Meinecke and Srbik. The attitude of the European powers towards the German national movement underwent a critical reappraisal: the study of 1848–51 tended to replace that of 1866.

On 30 January 1930, Erich Marcks read to the Prussian Academy of Sciences a paper[2] marking the transition to the 'neo-nationalist' interpretation. Whilst admitting that the German failure of 1848–51 was due primarily to the hesitations of Frederick-William IV, Austro-Prussian rivalry and the internal divisions of Germany, Marcks asserted that even a united German movement would have been stifled by hostility from without:

Once again: there cannot be the slightest suggestion of the good-will of Europe, of a toleration of German national aspirations. The veto was never pronounced because

---

[1] This applies particularly to the documents published in Oncken's one-sided work on the German policy of Napoleon III.

[2] Printed in *Historische Zeitschrift*, Band 142 (Berlin, 1930), pp. 73ff., as 'Die europäischen Mächte und die 48er Revolution'.

—as we have seen—German action never became effective: otherwise a little sooner or a little later a reaction would have been inevitable. A furtive counter-action persisted.[1]

From this it was only one step to the assertion that in 1848–9 the powers had in fact vetoed the unification of Germany. The step was taken by Friese who, in his admirable study of Russo-Prussian relations,[2] unequivocally accused Nicholas I of having been the grave-digger of German unity. Faced with German national aspirations, the tsar forgot his legitimist scruples and linked hands with the revolutionary French Republic. When it came to a possible strengthening of Germany their interests were the same.[3]

The view that Europe had prevented German consolidation found its most extreme exponent in Alexander Scharff.[4] Even though he did not completely disregard the internal obstacles to German union, Scharff asserted in unmistakable terms the 'primacy' of external opposition:

> Above all, not one of the great European powers was willing to tolerate the joining together of the German people in a unified state and the consolidation of the European centre. England, who in the name of 'the balance of power' tried to exploit the rivalries of the nations for her own advantage, France, who could not forget her diplomatic traditions hostile to German unity, Russia, clothing her brutal 'Machtpolitik' under the guise of legitimist ideology—finally, the collaboration between the liberal western powers and the autocratic empire of the tsars—these counter-forces were not the least in destroying all-German hopes and ambitions.[5]

This view did not pass unchallenged. The collapse of Hitler's Third Reich led to a re-opening of the discussion among German historians. Some, indeed, adhered to the older view. Ritter wrote in 1948:

> The German revolution of 1848 on the other hand succumbed to the pressure of a constellation of powers which became increasingly unfavourable as the first shock of the risings in Paris, Berlin and Vienna receded. What remained was an increasing

---

[1] 'Nochmals: von gutem Willen des Erdteils, von einer Duldung des deutschen nationalen Willens kann nie die Rede sein. Das Verbot wurde nie akut, weil, so sahen wir, die deutsche Tat nie akut geworden ist: andernfalls wäre die Gegentat, etwas früher oder später, unvermeidlich gewesen. Schleichend blieb die Gegenwirkung stets' (Marcks, *loc. cit.* pp. 86f.).

[2] Friese, *op. cit.*

[3] 'Als die immerhin doch massvolle deutsche Revolution die Gefahr einer Einigung und damit die einer Erstarkung Deutschlands heraufbeschwor, da hat Nikolaj alle seine legitimistischen Bedenken zurückgestellt und sich darauf besonnen, dass demgegenüber Russlands Interessen mit denen Frankreichs, auch des republikanischen, identisch seien' (*ibid.* p. 40).

[4] Scharff, *op. cit.*

[5] 'Vor allem war keine der europäischen Grossmächte gewillt, die Zusammenfügung des deutschen Volkes zu staatlicher Einheit und die Festigung der Mitte Europas zu dulden. Grossbritannien, das unter der Parole des "europäischen Gleichgewichts" die Gegensätze der Völker zu eigenem Gewinn auszubeuten suchte, Frankreich, das sich nicht lösen konnte von den der deutschen Einheit feindlichen Traditionen seiner Aussenpolitik, Russland, das mit dem Mantel legitimistischer Ideologie seine brutale Machtpolitik umkleidete, schliesslich das Zusammenspiel der liberalen Westmächte mit dem autokratischen Zarenreich—diese Gegenkräfte haben nicht zum letzten die Zerstörung gesamtdeutscher Hoffnungen und Zielsetzungen herbeigeführt' (*ibid.* pp. 296f.).

resentment on the part of the German national movement against Germany's European neighbours: against Russia, whose threatening veto had stifled Prussia's last attempts at union; also against France, who had so bitterly disappointed liberal hopes and revealed herself once again as the 'hereditary enemy' of the German nation.[1]

Schnabel extended the theory to the entire process of German consolidation:

All the evidence we have supports the position that the powers accepted only unwillingly the formation of a new national state in the heart of Europe. Either, like Napoleon III, they wished for 'compensations', or they were surprised by Bismarck's procedure and did not have time to prepare themselves spiritually and materially to counter it....It was not alone the extension of Prussian power which the other states disliked. They did see with misgivings that the traditions of Frederick the Great had been taken up again, that the old policy of rounding off the borders of Prussia and conquering new territories...now led to the annexation of Schleswig-Holstein and the kingdom of Hanover. But the programme of establishing a national state...gave the powers no less reason for anxiety and interference.[2]

The opposite view was defended by Stadelmann, a younger German historian, who pointed out that

if the Germans had shown moderation and restraint in the Schleswig-Holstein controversy in 1848, Britain would have been willing to help create a German nation-state in conformity with the prevailing liberal attitude of the nineteenth century and not in opposition to the *Zeitgeist*.[3]

If the German movement of 1848–51 ended in failure, the causes must be sought in German conditions rather than in European intervention.[4]

[1] 'Die deutsche Revolution von 1848 dagegen erlag dem Druck einer Mächtekonstellation, die immer ungünstiger wurde, je mehr der erste Schock der Aufstände in Paris, Berlin und Wien in seiner Nachwirkung verebbte. Was blieb war ein verstärktes Ressentiment der deutschen Nationalbewegung gegen die europäischen Nachbarmächte: gegen Russland, dessen drohender Einspruch die letzten Unionsversuche Preussens erstickt...hatte; aber auch gegen Frankreich, das die liberalen Hoffnungen so schwer enttäuschte und nun erst recht wieder als der "Erbfeind" deutscher Nation erschien' (G. Ritter, *Europa und die Deutsche Frage* (München, 1948), p. 77).

This view echoes that expressed three years earlier by a British historian:

'Tsar Nicholas did not much care whether schemes for German unification were liberal or monarchist. He was opposed to German unification of any kind.'

'Both France and Russia had made the maintenance of German disunity the cardinal principle of their policy, France since the time of Richelieu, Russia since the peace of Teschen in 1778 and as recently as the agreement of Olmütz' (A. J. P. Taylor, *The Course of German History* (London, 1945), p. 91).

Taylor has since changed his view:

'It is now widely held that France or Russia or both of them would have forbidden national unification in 1848. There seems little evidence of this' (A. J. P. Taylor, 'Bismarck and Europe' in *Rumours of Wars* (London, 1952), p. 52).

[2] F. Schnabel, 'The Bismarck Problem' in *German History: some new views*, ed. H. Kohn (London, 1954), pp. 70f. Schnabel's article first appeared in the Munich periodical *Hochland* in October 1949.

[3] H. Kohn, 'Rethinking of recent German History' in *German History: some new views*, ed. H. Kohn (London, 1954), p. 36.

[4] 'Die äusseren politischen Voraussetzungen für einen massvollen deutschen Verfassungs-staat waren also nicht ungünstig, und wenn dieser deutsche Nationalstaat nicht geboren

Attempts were also made to reconcile the two views. Bühler, returning to the earlier 'Marcksist' standpoint, whilst attributing the failure of the German national movement to internal dissensions, adds that, even had these been overcome, the powers would hardly have permitted the consolidation of Germany.[1] Griewank, in a summing up so judicious that it fails to reach a conclusion, agrees with Stadelmann that it might have been possible, in reliance on British sympathy, to achieve a 'little German' solution. This, however, would have presupposed the abandonment by Germany of at least a part of Schleswig-Holstein, which German opinion would not tolerate.[2] For the rest, the powers were hostile. Nicholas I was bitterly anti-revolutionary. The cabinets were interested in maintaining an equilibrium established by the Congress of Vienna which presupposed the political division of the German nation.[3] All discussion of the matter must, in any case, be based on an assessment of probabilities. External resistance did not, in 1848, become a decisive factor because the attempts to reorganize Germany were wrecked by German dissensions.[4] Such is the state reached by German historiography in its discussion of the relations between the powers and the German national movement of 1848–51.

II

The views of German historians on the European attitude towards the German revolution of 1848 have coloured their assessment of Bismarck and his achievement. If an 'Unholy Alliance' of hostile powers had stifled the 'pacific' and idealistic beginnings of the German national movement,

wurde, so werden wir die Ursachen nicht in feindlichen europäischen Voraussetzungen, sondern im Innern der Revolution selbst zu suchen haben' (R. Stadelmann, *Soziale und Politische Geschichte der Revolution von 1848* (München, 1948), p. 115).

Scharff also has now reached the conclusion that the primary cause of German failure in 1848 was the egotism of thirty-eight separate states and dynasties aggravated by Austro-Prussian dualism (A. Scharff, 'Die Revolution und Reichsgründungsversuche. 1848–1851' in *Deutsche Geschichte im Ueberblick*, ed. P. Rassow (Stuttgart, 1953), pp. 430ff.).

[1] 'Mehr als Augenblickserfolge mit höchstwahrscheinlich gefährlichen Rückschlägen wären indes damals nicht zu erreichen gewesen, selbst wenn ein Mann wie Cavour oder Bismarck zu jener Zeit die preussische Politik geleitet hätte' (J. Bühler, *Deutsche Geschichte* (Berlin, 1954), vol. 5, p. 316).

[2] 'Eine Chance bestand immerhin, worauf Stadelmann mit Nachdruck hingewiesen hat, in der Anlehnung an England; sie hätte aber den Verzicht wenigstens auf einen Teil von Schleswig-Holstein zur Voraussetzung gehabt, und diesem Verzicht stand jenes Denken in geschlossenen Landeseinheiten gegenüber, das die deutschen ebenso wie andere Nationen nicht aufgeben wollten, wenn es zu ihren Gunsten sprach' (K. Griewank, 'Ursachen und Folgen des Scheiterns der Deutschen Revolution von 1848' in *Historische Zeitschrift*, Band 170 (1950), p. 517).

[3] '...Aber auch die anderen europäischen Grossmächte verfochten jede in ihrer Weise, ihr Interesse an der Gleichgewichtsordnung des Wiener Kongresses, die ein geteiltes Staatensystem in Deutschland voraussetzte' (*ibid.* p. 516).

[4] 'Jede Erörterung dieser Frage sieht sich freilich mehr oder weniger auf Wahrscheinlichkeitsberechnungen angewiesen. Denn zum eigentlichen entscheidenden Faktor ist dieser Widerstand der europäischen Mächte im Jahre 1848 nicht geworden, weil das deutsche Einigungswerk schon an den innerdeutschen Gegensätzen, vor allem an dem Widerstand der deutschen Einzelstaaten zerbrach' (*ibid.*).

then the German question could be settled only by power politics of 'blood and iron'. If the powers would not tolerate the peaceful emergence of a new Germany, they must be forced to recognize her rights. There must be power ('Macht') and there must be a man to apply it at the proper moment.[1] The hostile forces with which Bismarck had to contend were essentially the same as those which had prevented German consolidation in 1848–51,[2] and it required all the great man's skill and daring to achieve the aims of the German national movement.[3] Only 'the deed' could free Germany from her 'provisional' state and only the great leader with his wide political views and sense of European responsibility could burst the barriers blocking the nation's road to unity. By his achievement Bismarck helped to lay the foundations of a new and healthier order in Europe.[4]

Bismarck's achievement—in the eyes of German historians—made him the central figure of the age to such an extent that no event in the diplomatic history of the period could be legitimately studied from a point of view other than his:

Therefore, whoever describes the diplomacy of his age without regarding it from the point of view of the centre of all political movement runs the risk of being, in the event, confounded by Bismarck. Whoever follows him from the start finds himself in an easier position; if, however, he proves right in the end, this is without any merit of his own.[5]

In retrospect European history appeared to have been dominated by Bismarck even before he had come to power in Prussia. The observations of one German historian on this point defy translation and only the original German can do them justice:

...Im Zeitalter *Bismarcks* war der Mann, dessen Namen es füglich trägt, die *Tat*, die verkörperte Idee, nach der sich die politischen Kräfte fügten; im Geiste zunächst,

---

[1] 'Insbesondere aber zeigt der Verlauf der deutschen Revolution dass es nicht allein des idealistischen Willens bedurfte, um das Reich aller Deutschen zu gründen, sondern auch der Kraft, sich nach Aussen zu behaupten, der *Macht* um die hohen Ziele auch gegen eine oft feindliche, der Erstärkung der deutschen Mitte widerstrebende europäische Umwelt zu erreichen—wie auch der staatsmännischen Kunst und der überragenden Führerpersönlichkeit, um die Macht am rechten Ort und zur rechten Zeit zu benutzen' (Scharff, *op. cit.* p. 6). 'Die deutsche Frage konnte nur gelöst werden, wenn Preussen eine neue machtpolitische Stellung in Deutschland und Europa erlangte' (Hubertus Prinz zu Löwenstein, *Deutsche Geschichte* (Frankfurt a.M. 1950), p. 330).
[2] Marcks, *loc. cit.* p. 87.
[3] 'All the virtuosity of Bismarck's manipulation of the rival powers, his skill in the handling of men and his daring as well, were required to achieve this goal' (Schnabel, *loc. cit.* p. 71).
[4] 'Nur die Tat konnte Deutschland aus seinem Zustande des "Provisoriums" erlösen, nur der grosse politische Führer mit der weiten Sicht europäischer Verantwortung konnte die Pforten zersprengen, die der Nation den Weg zur Einheit versperrten, und damit zugleich den Grund zu einer neuen und gesünderen Ordnung des gesamten Erdteils legen' (Scharff, *op. cit.* p. 295).
[5] 'Wer daher aus seinem Zeitalter einen Gegenstand der auswärtigen Politik beschreibt, ohne dass er ihn zugleich auch immer aus dem nun einmal gegebenen Zentrum der politischen Bewegung her betrachtet, der begibt sich in Gefahr, von Bismarck hernach korrigiert zu werden. Wer sich von vornherein ihm anschliesst, hat es leichter; und bekommt er recht, so geschieht es ohne eigenes Verdienst' (H. Michael, *op. cit.* p. xv).

als *Bismarck* noch in Frankfurt und auf andern Posten beobachtend, erkennend nur, den Ereignissen folgte, aber doch schon innerlich die Dinge auf sich lud; in voller Wirklichkeit, als er dann die Führung Preussens selbst ergriff.[1]

Small wonder, therefore, that in discussing Anglo-German relations during the 'Bismarckian age', Michael felt that only Bismarck's point of view was of interest or importance. England's right to a foreign policy of her own was—by implication—denied.[2] Similarly Oncken, in what professed to be a study of Napoleon's foreign policy, concerned himself almost exclusively with the difficulties facing Bismarck from the side of France.[3] It never occurred to Oncken that France might legitimately pursue a policy of national self-interest.[4] Michael and Oncken are extreme cases, but their attitude, as recognized by Ritter,[5] was symptomatic of the views expressed by German historians. Bismarck was infallible and always right by definition: it was therefore inadmissible, not to say immoral, for others to have policies and interests of their own, especially when these conflicted with the designs of Prussia-Germany.[6] The legend about Prussia-Germany's relations with the European powers between 1848 and 1871 forms an extreme instance of the 'Whig interpretation' of history.

[1] *Ibid.*

[2] 'Die folgende Arbeit hat den Staatsmann und Diplomaten *Bismarck* zum Gegenstand. England ist jeweils nur der Beziehungspunkt, nicht Selbstzweck der Betrachtung' (*ibid.* p. ix).

[3] Oncken, in his own words, set out to show 'unter welchen europäischen Bedingungen dieses Reich zu seiner Einheit aufgestiegen ist, im besonderen, gegen welches Gegenspiel einer feindlichen Politik es den steilen Pfad zu seiner Begründung hat zurücklegen müssen. Dieses Gegenspiel, der eigentliche Gegenstand dieser Publikation, ist die Wiederaufnahme der historischen Rheinpolitik und Interventionspolitik in die deutschen Angelegenheiten durch Kaiser Napoleon III' (Oncken, *op. cit.* p. ix).

[4] 'Aber auch in den deutschen Darstellungen und Quellenveröffentlichungen ruht das Schwergewicht in der Regel mehr auf dem eindrucksvollsten Vorgang dieser Jahre, dem Aufbau des Deutschen Reiches, als auf den Motiven und Zielen der französischen Politik, die den Aufbau zu stören versuchte' (*ibid.* p. viii).

[5] 'Niemand wird diese Aufgabe ernster zu nehmen haben als der Vertreter deutscher Fachhistorie, die...über ein halbes Jahrhundert lang vom Geiste Bismarcks überschattet worden ist, von ihm ihr politisches Denken weithin hat bestimmen lassen, ja bis auf wenige Ausnahmen an die Unfehlbarkeit wenigstens seiner Aussenpolitik geglaubt hat' (Ritter, *op. cit.* p. 79).

[6] Bismarck himself was free from moralizing delusions. 'Wir haben kein Recht eine gemüthliche Hingebung für Preussen in der französischen Politik vorauszusetzen, wie auch unsere Politik von derartigen Gefühlen für irgendeine fremde Macht frei ist. Wir beklagen uns daher nicht über die vorliegenden Thatsachen' (Bismarck to Goltz, 20 February 1865, Sybel, *op. cit.* vol. 4, p. 75).

BRITISH DIPLOMACY AND THE OUTBREAK OF THE FRANCO-PRUSSIAN WAR

In July 1870 it was widely believed in Germany that determined British intervention could have prevented the outbreak of war. The Crown Princess of Prussia wrote to her mother: 'The feeling is very general here that England would have had it in her power to prevent this awful war, had she in concert with Russia, Austria and Italy, declared she would take arms against the aggressor.'[1] This view was echoed in England. At a dinner party on 15 July 1870 Morier observed: 'The war could have been prevented if for twenty-four hours the British people could have been furnished with a backbone. . . .' Some days later, he was asked to explain his remarks:

> What I meant was that there were certain moves on the political chess-board which necessarily led to checkmate, and that good players did not go on playing after these were executed. There was one thing known positively to everyone who had to do with European politics during the last fifteen years, which was that Louis Napoleon would *never face* a coalition between England and Germany, consequently all that would have been necessary would have been to indicate the move. But for such a coalition even *in posse*, a backbone was necessary, as mere dolls filled with bran are not taken into account.[2]

The question whether England could have prevented the outbreak of the Franco-Prussian war is one of historical speculation. Before it is possible to give even a tentative answer, it is indispensable to examine the course followed by British diplomacy during the crisis.

At 2.40 p.m. on 5 July, Lyons reported to Granville by the telegraph that Gramont had informed the Prussian ambassador that France would not tolerate the establishment of the Prince of Hohenzollern on the throne of Spain. The French government hoped for British assistance 'in averting a measure so fraught with danger to the peace of Europe'.[3] That evening Ollivier told Lyons of French indignation at the candidature: 'Public opinion in France. . .would never tolerate it. Any Cabinet, any Government which acquiesced in it would be at once overthrown. . . .he felt this proceeding to be an insult and fully shared the indignation of the public.'[4]

---

[1] Crown Princess of Prussia to Queen Victoria, 25 July 1870, RA I 63/167 (*QVL, loc. cit.* pp. 48f.). Bismarck shared this opinion. He told Loftus that England 'should have forbidden France to enter the war. She was in a position to do so, and her interests and those of Europe demanded it of her' (Loftus, *op. cit.* 2nd series, vol. I, p. 283).

[2] Morier, *op. cit.* pp. 153f.

[3] Lyons to Granville, 5 July 1870, FO 27/1805, no. 684, reporting telegram.

[4] The same to the same, 7 July 1870, *ibid.* no. 697.

The following day Gramont made his celebrated declaration to the *Corps Législatif*. He afterwards defended the strong language he had used:

His speech was in fact, as regarded the Interior of France, absolutely necessary and Your Lordship would...as Minister in a constitutional country, understand perfectly the impossibility of contending with public opinion. The nation was, he said, so strongly roused upon this question, that its will could not be resisted or trifled with....Diplomatic considerations must yield to public safety at home.[1]

On the afternoon of 8 July, Lyons telegraphed to London that Gramont had told him that Prussian silence would compel France to begin military preparations 'in earnest' on the 9th.[2] '...On my manifesting some surprise and regret at the rapid pace at which the French Government seemed to be proceeding, M. de Gramont insisted that it was impossible for them to delay any longer.'[3] On 9 July, Gramont told Lyons that no answer had yet been received from Prussia. Benedetti was to see King William that afternoon. In the meantime, France would continue her military preparations 'in all that is real and essential'. She would postpone 'apparent preparations' for twenty-four hours longer.[4]

The news from Paris convinced Granville and Gladstone of the need to counsel caution. On the morning of 10 July, Lyons received two dispatches written by Granville the previous day. That afternoon he called on Gramont:

I thanked His Excellency in Your Lordship's name for the frankness of his communications to me and for the friendly confidence he had shown in Her Majesty's Government. I observed that Her Majesty's Government hardly understood that the selection of a Prince of Hohenzollern for King of Spain was a matter of so much importance to a great nation like France, as to warrant extreme measures. Making every allowance for the resentment which the secrecy with which this choice had been matured, was calculated to arouse in France, still...Her Majesty's Government trusted that the Government of the Emperor would act with moderation and forbearance in the further conduct of the discussion. They could not but regret the strong language used by the Government and the Press in France. They were still more disquieted by the military preparations which were in progress and they could not but ask themselves whether in this state of things it would be judicious to persevere in efforts to bring about an amicable settlement. Her Majesty's Government had...used every endeavour to effect such a settlement, but they could not help fearing that the precipitation of the French Government might render all their exertions nugatory.[5]

Gramont, in reply, explained

that in this matter the French Ministers were following not leading the Nation. Public opinion would not admit of their doing less than they had done. As regarded

---

[1] The same to the same, 7 July 1870, *ibid*. no. 698.
[2] The same to the same, 8 July 1870, *ibid*. no. 707, reporting telegram.
[3] The same to the same, 8 July 1870, *ibid*. no. 708.
[4] The same to the same, 9 July 1870, *ibid*. no. 715, reporting telegram.
[5] The same to the same, 10 July 1870, *ibid*. no. 726.

military preparations, common prudence required that they should not be behind hand.[1]

Lyons reported by the telegraph that the situation remained unchanged.

The King of Prussia has told M. Benedetti that having given his consent to Prince Hohenzollern's accepting the Crown, it would be difficult to withdraw it, but that he would confer with the Prince and give the French government an answer as soon as he had done so.

In the circumstances, the French government was continuing its military measures but was postponing the 'great ostensible preparations' for a further twenty-four hours. Moreover, Gramont had said 'that if the King induces the Prince to retire, the affair may be regarded as over'.[2] Such was the information received at the Foreign Office at 10 p.m. on Sunday, 10 July.

Earlier that evening Granville had learnt from Madrid that the candidature might be withdrawn. He at once communicated the news to Lyons. Next day the ambassador reported:

I have very strongly urged the French government not to be precipitate. Duc de Gramont tells me that they have no answer from the King of Prussia and that they will wait another day for one, although this sacrifice to peace will make the Ministry very unpopular with the Chamber and the Country.

To this information Lyons added a warning:

Your Lordship is aware that it is a question of hours, because the French think they have got the start of the Prussians in preparations and they consider it to be of the utmost importance not to allow the Prussians time to overtake them.[3]

The following day, 12 July, was likely to prove decisive. Early in the afternoon, Lyons reported that the Prussian ambassador had returned to Paris empty-handed.

Baron Werther is returned. I am told on good though not official authority that the King sends no answer by him on the plea that the Prince of Hohenzollern cannot be found. If the information thus given me be correct, there can be little or no hope of any further delay of war.[4]

At 7.55 p.m. Lyons sent further news:

The renunciation of the Spanish Crown by the Prince of Hohenzollern in the name of his son has been received. The French Government hold that it puts an end to all dispute with Spain but they do not at present admit that in the form in which it

[1] The same to the same, 10 July 1870, *ibid.* no. 726.
[2] The same to the same, 10 July 1870, *ibid.* no. 725, reporting telegram.
[3] The same to the same, 11 July 1870, *ibid.* no. 733, reporting telegram. In a despatch of the same date, which did not, however, reach the Foreign Office until 13 July, Lyons gave the first indication of another serious development:
'It is quite true that the Nation is extremely impatient, and as time goes on the War Party becomes more exacting. It has in fact already raised a cry that the settlement of the Hohenzollern question will not be sufficient, and that France must demand satisfaction on the subject of the Treaty of Prague...' (the same to the same, 11 July 1870, *ibid.* no. 735).
[4] The same to the same, 12 July 1870, FO 27/1806, no. 737, reporting telegram.

has been given, it removes their complaint against Prussia. They are dissatisfied with the communication they have received from the King. They will determine at a Council to-morrow what course to take and announce it to the Chamber immediately afterwards. I have urged in the strongest possible manner that they are bound to accept the renunciation as completely putting an end to the dispute with Prussia as well as with Spain.[1]

This telegram reached London during the night. At 11.30 p.m. Gladstone wrote to Granville:

...It seems to me that Lyons should be supplied with an urgent instruction by telegram before the council of ministers to-morrow. France appealed to our support at the outset. She received it so far as the immediate object was concerned. It was immediately and energetically given....Under these circumstances it is our duty to represent the immense responsibility which will rest upon France, if she does not at once accept as satisfactory and conclusive the withdrawal of the candidature of Prince Leopold.[2]

Granville immediately wrote to the Foreign Office that a telegram should be sent to Lyons instructing him to 'make urgent representations' before the Council met on the following day. Granville then repeated Gladstone's arguments.

It is therefore our duty to represent the immense responsibility which will rest upon France, if she enlarges the ground of quarrel and does not at once accept as satisfactory renunciation of the candidature of Prince Leopold.[3]

His words were converted into a telegram despatched to Lyons at 2.30 a.m. on the morning of 13 July.[4] At 9.30 a.m. it was received in Paris.[5]

Lyons, however, had not waited for instructions from London to express the British misgivings. On the previous afternoon, when informed by Gramont that the Prussian answer was neither courteous nor satisfactory, he had warned against the consequences of picking a further quarrel.

I did not conceal from M. de Gramont my surprise and regret that the French Government should hesitate for a moment to accept the renunciation of the Prince as a settlement of the affair. I reminded him pointedly of the assurance which he had formally authorized me to give to Her Majesty's Government that if the Prince withdrew his candidature, the affair would be at an end. I urged as strongly as I could all the reasons which would render a withdrawal, on his part, from this assurance, painful and disquieting to Her Majesty's Government....I pointed out, moreover, that the renunciation wholly changed the position of France....In fact, I said that France would have public opinion throughout the world against her and her antagonist would have all the advantage of being manifestly forced into war, in self-defence, to repel attack....the Ministry would, in a very short time, stand better

---

[1] The same to the same, 12 July 1870, *ibid.* unnumbered reporting telegram.
[2] Gladstone to Granville, 12 July 1870, Morley, *op. cit.* p. 328.
[3] Granville to the Foreign Office, undated, FO 27/1791.
[4] Granville to Lyons, 13 July 1870, telegram, *ibid.*
[5] Lyons to Granville, 13 July 1870, FO 27/1806, no. 749, reporting telegram.

with both [the Chambers and the Country] if it contented itself with the diplomatic triumph it had achieved, and abstained from plunging the country into war for which there was certainly no avoidable [*sic*] motive.

Gramont's reply had not been encouraging:

> After some discussion M. de Gramont said that he was himself not very far from agreeing with me—but still he did not know how the Ministry could face the country. He could not tell what pressure might be brought to bear upon himself and his colleagues during the night.[1]

When Lyons received Granville's telegram on the morning of 13 July, the French Council of Ministers was already in session at St Cloud. The ambassador therefore embodied the substance of Granville's message in a letter[2] which was handed to Gramont at the council board whilst the Council was sitting in the presence of the Emperor.[3] At 3 p.m. Lyons telegraphed to London:

> Minister for Foreign Affairs has just announced to the *Corps Législatif* that he has been officially informed by the Spanish ambassador that Prince Leopold has withdrawn his candidature. He added that the negotiations with Prussia not being concluded, he could give no information respecting them.[4]

Later, Gramont asked Lyons whether France could count on the good offices of England in obtaining the prohibition of any future candidature. He promised in writing that this would terminate the incident. Lyons, unable to give a reply, asked Granville for instructions. On receiving this inquiry, Gladstone hastily summoned the Cabinet to meet at noon on 14 July.[5]

In the meantime, a different chain of events had already been set in motion.[6] On the afternoon of 12 July—after the renunciation of Leopold was unofficially known in Paris—Gramont had asked the Prussian ambassador to procure a written assurance from William I that the candidature would not be renewed. At 7 p.m. that evening he further instructed Benedetti, who was with the king at Ems, to demand such an undertaking. On the following morning Benedetti duly approached King William, who refused the assurance but indicated that he would see the ambassador again in the afternoon. Later that morning the king informed Benedetti through an *aide de camp* that he had now received in writing Prince Leopold's renunciation and regarded the incident as closed. Benedetti persisted in his attempt to extract a further undertaking, which met with no success.

[1] Lyons to Granville, 12 July 1870, FO 27/1806, no. 738.
[2] The same to the same, 13 July 1870, *ibid.* no. 751, enclosure.
[3] The same to the same, 13 July 1870, *ibid.* no. 749, reporting telegram.
[4] The same to the same, 13 July 1870, *ibid.* no. 750, reporting telegram.
[5] Morley, *op. cit.* p. 330.
[6] Except where otherwise stated, the account here given follows that of Lord.

At 3.50 p.m. a telegram despatched on King William's orders by a high Prussian official informed Bismarck at Berlin of what had occurred. Bismarck was authorized to communicate the contents of the telegram to the public and to Prussia's missions abroad. That night, he produced his famous 'shortened version' which, on the following morning, appeared in the ministerial *North German Gazette*.

In consequence, when the British cabinet met at noon on 14 July, the 'Ems telegram' had already been published. Unaware of this fact, the Ministers decided to propose a compromise to both parties. William I should notify the French government in writing that he approved of the renunciation; France, in return, should waive her demand about assurances for the future. On the evening of 14 July, Lyons received telegrams from Granville containing the Cabinet's proposals. The ambassador went at once to the Quai d'Orsay, where, in the absence of Gramont, he saw Count de Faverney, his *chef de cabinet*. Lyons now learnt that the substance of the Ems telegram had been officially communicated to the Prussian missions abroad. Early next morning, he made an unsuccessful attempt to see Gramont before the meeting of the Chambers. He told Granville:

> If however I had been able to speak to him I could have found nothing to add to the arguments I had already so pertinaciously urged in favour of peace nor could I have hoped to shake a resolution already deliberately adopted by the Emperor and his Ministers.[1]

In fact, at 11 p.m. on the previous night, the French government had finally reached the decision to call out the reserves.[2] On the following day 'At twenty minutes past one the Duc de Gramont stated in the Senate that the negotiations with Prussia having failed, the reserves would be called out and steps would be taken to maintain the honour and glory of France'.[3]

During the course of the crisis, the British government had at least three 'opportunities' of warning France that England might side with Prussia. The first of these was afforded by Granville's despatches to Lyons on 9 July. It must, however, be remembered that at this moment France still had a legitimate grievance and that Granville's sympathies were on her side. Granville had assumed the seals of office only three days before. The 9th, moreover, was a Saturday, and Ministers were dispersed. In

---

[1] Lyons to Granville, 15 July 1870, FO 27/1806, no. 767.
[2] At about 4 p.m. on 14 July the French Council of Ministers reached the decision to call out the reserves. Nevertheless, the matter was still discussed intermittently until 11 p.m. when it was finally resolved that the earlier resolution should stand (Morley, *op. cit.* p. 334, following A. Sorel, *Histoire diplomatique de la guerre franco-allemande* (Paris, 1875), vol. 1, pp. 169ff.).
[3] Lyons to Granville, 15 July 1870, FO 27/1806, no. 768, reporting telegram. Gramont told Lyons that what finally ruined the chances of an accommodation was the publication of the Ems refusal after the rest of the negotiation had been conducted in secret (the same to the same, 15 July 1870, *ibid.* no. 778).

the circumstances, a threat to go to war with France was hardly a practical possibility. The second 'opportunity' occurred on the night of 12/13 July when Gladstone and Granville learnt that the French government might not content itself with Leopold's renunciation. The news was received shortly before midnight. Gladstone considered that a British warning must reach Paris before next morning's meeting of the French Council of Ministers. It is difficult to see how the two Ministers could, on their own authority, have instructed Lyons to utter a threat of war. The third 'opportunity' was offered by the Cabinet meeting on 14 July. However, the pacific liberal majority in Gladstone's first Cabinet was little likely to run the risk of having to interfere directly in a quarrel with which England had little concern.[1] Moreover, it is doubtful whether, after the publication of the Ems telegram, even a British ultimatum to France could have averted the outbreak of hostilities.[2] The conclusion, therefore, is difficult to escape that no action psychologically or constitutionally open to British Ministers could have prevented the outbreak of the Franco-Prussian war.

[1] The situation would be altered only by a serious threat to Belgium. Moreover Granville considered that a British threat to France 'would in all probability have resulted in Russia and England taking the part of Prussia; and Austria and Italy that of France, and thus precipitating a European war' (Ponsonby to the Queen, 5 August 1870, RA I 64/50).

[2] The war-party had been in the ascendant in Paris at least since 12 July. In Berlin, it had assumed the initiative on the night of 13 July. Thereafter, the chances of a peaceful solution were remote.

THE RUSSIAN NATIONAL PRESS AND THE 'GERMAN PERIL', 1870-1

It is well known that after the Polish Insurrection of 1863 the *Moscow Gazette* (*Moskovskie Viedomosti*), edited by Michael Katkov, became the principal organ of independent nationalist opinion. Only *The Voice* (*Golos*), the other great nationalist newspaper, exercised any influence even remotely comparable.[1] Both publications were frequently quoted (in translation) in the correspondence of British and Austrian diplomats. Both frequently criticized Russian official policy and Gorchakov at least was sensitive to their criticism. Both papers faithfully reflected the growth of anti-Prussian and anti-German sentiment among Russian nationalists and their strong desire for a *rapprochement* with France.

The Prussian victories of 1866 alarmed Russian nationalist opinion: during the years which followed, the *Gazette* became notorious for its anti-German polemics.[2] Russian nationalists feared for the future of the Baltic provinces.[3] The *Golos* also expressed alarm at German progress in Europe. In its issue of 18 February 1870 the paper discussed the king of Prussia's Speech from the Throne which foreshadowed the union of southern Germany with the north. Such a union, *Golos* declared, would be a clear breach of the Treaty of Prague. If the king of Prussia had

---

[1] Katkov 'le rédacteur du journal le plus répandu de Moscou' (Revertera to Mensdorff, 18/6 January 1865, HHSAPARRR, x 52, no. 1 C). '...sowohl "Golos" als "Moskauer Nachrichten"—diese beiden Hauptorgane der hierländigen Presse' (Chotek to Beust, 8 March/24 February 1870, *ibid.* Jan.–June 1870, x 57, no. 14 A–B).

[2] '...Der bekannte Katkoff hat in sein politisches Programm auch die Bekämpfung der freundlichen Beziehungen des russischen Hofes zu Berlin aufgenommen. Dieser heftige und mächtige Vorkämpfer der demokratisch-moskowitischen Partei vertritt in seinem Blatte mit Leidenschaftlichkeit die Ansicht, dass Preussen seit den grossen Ereignissen in Deutschland, seit es eine Flotte gegründet, der offene und gefährlichste Nebenbuhler Russlands geworden ist.'

'...Ich weiss dass der Kaiser selbst wiederholt auf Katkoff einzuwirken gesucht hat um dessen Sprache gegen Preussen zu mildern; doch dieser antwortet, die Regierung könne sein Blatt, wie andere gleicher Richtung, unterdrücken; doch nie seine Ueberzeugung. Katkoff ist eine Macht, man wagt es nicht an ihn zu rühren...' (Vetsera to Beust, private, 15 December 1869, *ibid.* x 56, Russie 1869, Varia).

[3] An Austrian agent, who had met Katkov and his staff and tried to dispose them in favour of Austria, reported:

'Es ist ein Characteristicum der Moskauer Zeitung, dass sie den gründlichsten Hass gegen die Deutschen, oder was jetzt gleichbedeutend geworden ist—gegen die Preussen predigt....'

'Aber *verständlich* ist mir dieser Hass—denn die Verbreitung preussischer Ideen, die ganz entschieden in den Ostseeprovinzen angefangen hat, droht den Umsturz aller russischen Institutionen.'

(Confidential memorandum by the Rev. H. Douglas, 1867, no date, *ibid.* x 54, Russie, Rapports, 1867.)

emphasized the matter so strongly, that merely proved that the European situation was favourable to his designs.[1] France, preoccupied with the death-throes of the Second Empire, could not fully devote her energies to foreign affairs. If the Austrian government viewed with dislike the progress of Prussia in Germany, its Hungarian partner welcomed it. The union of Germany, which might include the German portions of the dual monarchy, would leave the Magyars the unchallenged masters in the non-German lands. No Hungarian minister, therefore, would raise a hand against Prussia. This left only Russia, but what could she do by herself to oppose the advance of Prussia? She must certainly not repeat the thankless task of 1813–15. She was under no obligation to save Europe from Bismarck as she had done from Napoleon I. Russia also would come to feel in time the proximity of a colossus like the united German fatherland; but it would be unwise to plunge at once into a calamitous preventive war at a time when the wounds of the Crimean war were not yet fully healed. It was no secret that Russia did not possess the means for offensive war against a power like Prussia; her military strength lay chiefly in the defensive; that advantage would be lost as soon as the theatre of war was moved beyond her borders. An alliance with Austria and France in their present state would be hardly more advantageous than the accepted policy of *laissez-faire* with regard to Prussian expansion. Matters might be different if such an alliance allowed Russia to revise the Treaty of Paris and solve the eastern question in a sense favourable to the Christians. For this, even heavy sacrifices would be justified. In any case, Russia could afford to wait—with every year, her strength increased and her political stituation became more favourable. Delay, therefore, would hasten the achievement of the desired goal.[2]

[1] 'dass wenn die preussische Thronrede die deutsche Einigung so scharf betone, hierin nur der Beweis liege, dass die allgemeine Weltlage einer so kühnen Sprache günstig sei.' (Article in *Golos* of 18 February 1870, reported in Chotek to Beust, 22/10 February 1870, *ibid*. Jan–June 1870, X 57, no. 12C.)

[2] 'Es bleibt daher nur Russland übrig. Was kann aber Russland allein thun, um neue Uebergriffe Preussens zu verhindern? Gewiss nicht die undankbare Rolle der Jahre 1813, 14 und 15 wieder aufnehmen. Europa vor Bismarck zu erretten, wie einst vor Napoleon I —dazu ist Russland keineswegs verpflichtet. Ohne Zweifel wird die Nachbarschaft eines so colossalen Reichs, wie es das *einige deutsche Vaterland* einst sein wird, sich mit der Zeit auch uns fühlbar machen; nichts desto weniger wäre es nicht rathsam zur Verhütung möglicher Verwicklungen, uns schon jetzt in die *unvermeidlichen* Kalamitäten eines Krieges zu stürzen, wo noch die Wunden des Krim-Feldzuges nicht ganz verheilt sind. Es ist für Niemanden ein Geheimnis, dass wir zu einem Offensivkriege gegen eine Macht wie Preussen nicht über hinreichende Mittel verfügen; unsere ganze militärische Stärke liegt hauptsächlich in der Defensive, deren Vortheile verloren gehen, sobald das Kriegstheater über unsere Westgrenze gerückt wird. Ein Bündnis mit Oesterreich und Frankreich in ihrer jetzigen Verfassung dürfte uns aber kaum mehr Nutzen bringen, als die Politik des *laissez-faire* Preussen gegenüber. Eine andere Sache wäre es freilich, wenn sich uns darin die Möglichkeit bieten würde, eine Revision des Pariser Friedens von 1856 und eine Lösung der orientalischen Frage zu Gunsten der christlichen Völkerschaften des Orients zu erlangen:—für ein solches Zugeständnis würde es sich lohnen mit einem, selbst mit schweren Opfern verbundenen Gegendienste zu antworten. In keinem Falle brauchen wir uns zu beeilen, denn mit jedem

In February 1870, Möller, a former collaborator of the *Gazette*, published an anonymous pamphlet advocating a *rapprochement* between Russia and France. Its appearance caused some sensation as it was believed to have been written under official inspiration. Both the *Gazette* and the *Golos* supported the pamphlet's main thesis, although Katkov's paper observed that the alliance of France was asked for in a needlessly pressing and undignified manner. The official *Journal de St Pétersbourg* after disclaiming official authorship for the pamphlet expressed its agreement with the author's general views:

> Ces réserves faites, nous n'avons rien à objecter contre le fond. Les considérations qui militent en faveur d'un rapprochement entre la Russie et la France, ne sont pas nouvelles. La brochure en question les expose avec netteté, en les appuyant d'arguments d'une grande vigueur de logique. Et ce qu'il y a de mieux, c'est qu'elle donne à cette entente un but précis de paix, de concorde et d'équilibre....[1]

Gorchakov, as always, felt the need to placate the growing feeling in favour of a defensive understanding with France.[2]

In June the *Augsburger Allgemeine Zeitung* published an article 'Russland und die Ostseeprovinzen' which offered the *Gazette* an excuse for a violent tirade against the entire German press.[3] Russian public opinion, on the eve of the Franco-Prussian war, was far from favourable to Germany.

Early Prussian successes alarmed the Russian nationalists. The *Gazette* declared that in the re-modelling of Europe Russia must play a part befitting her importance. Everything done without Russia would be done against her. She must assume an attitude of armed neutrality. *Golos* in its turn foresaw the 'dictation of Prussia to Europe' resulting from the successes of the *Landwehr*. There was danger for Russia whoever won the war: in the one case to the Baltic provinces, in the other to Poland. According to a member of the British embassy staff both *Gazette* and

---

Jahre kräftigt sich unser staatliche [*sic*] Organismus und gestalten sich die Konstellationen des politischen Horizontes für uns immer günstiger; in dieser Frage zögern, heisst für uns —die Erreichung des gewünschten Zieles beschleunigen' (*ibid.*).

[1] The same to the same, 23/11 February 1870, *ibid.* no. 13.

[2] 'Es ist...hier etwas in der Luft, was einem unwillkürlich sagt: das Ueberwiegen und noch weitere Fortschreiten Preussens ist hier verhasst, ein Gefühl welches der wachsende slawische Antigermanismus verstärkt. Es hat den Anschein, als ob Russland's öffentliche Meinung zur Intimität mit Frankreich drängte. General Fleury gestand mir neulich ein, das Gefühl der Nixe zu haben, "halb zog sie ihn, halb sank er hin"' (the same to the same, 16/4 March 1870, *ibid.* no. 17).

[3] The *Gazette* accused the German papers of opening their columns to all 'junkerliche Correspondenzen von der Ostsee'. (Baltic Germans were complaining in the German press about the policy of russification pursued in the Baltic provinces.) They should remember 'das derartig freche Auslassungen mit der Zeit eine ernstliche Erbitterung in den internationalen Beziehungen hervorbringen müssen, deren Folge nur die stete Erhöhung des Militärbüdgets sein wird.... Die deutsche Presse bietet in ihren Beziehungen zu Russland ein unwürdiges Schauspiel. Die unsinnigsten Forderungen und Erfindungen unserer baltischen Feodalen...finden in den grössten deutschen Blättern Mitgefühl und Aufmunterung' (quoted in the same to the same, 29/17 June 1870, *ibid.* no. 31 F).

Golos considered 'the interests of Russia to be seriously compromised by the increasing power of Germany' and expressed the view that Russia must arm to influence future territorial arrangements.[1] After Sedan, the nationalist press became more insistent; the *Gazette* called for the intervention of the neutral powers:

Can Europe remain indifferent [it asked] while one of the great Powers is being crushed and almost abolished? Can her right to participate in the settlement of the fate of so important a member of her system be disputed? No, if Europe is a reality, one cannot remain indifferent at the sight of a catastrophe of such importance and she cannot abdicate a right without which she becomes a mere empty name.

The *Golos* likewise considered that the neutral powers must intervene to put an end to the bloodshed. Russian newspapers in general drew attention to the danger of revolutionary outbreaks in Spain, Italy, and the Slavonic provinces of Turkey. 'The Prussians', said Golos, 'have stirred up this revolutionary ant-hill with their bayonets and no one can tell what the consequences may be to them.' The *Exchange Gazette* considered that Bismarck might even attempt to restore Poland.

In general the tone of the Russian press is one of great alarm at the success of Germany and at the prospect of a dismemberment of France, whose republican form of Government is at the same time a new source of disquietude to the Imperial Government.[2]

The inability of 'Europe' to restrain Germany led the Russian nationalist press to cast around for some force to balance the new power.

The fear of Germany entertained by the National Russian Party can hardly be better illustrated than by the bold bid made by the *Moscow Gazette* for an alliance with Austria based on the common Slavonic interests of the two Empires.

Katkov's paper declared:

The professed friendship of Germany for Austria is like the friendship of the savage for the prey which he tightly holds. If the Empire of the Habsburgs desires to retain its independence and integrity, that friendship cannot be sincere; it will, on the contrary, be a secret enmity, a poison that will bring about the dissolution of the Empire that has been modelled by Counts Bismarck and Beust.

There is however another policy which presents itself naturally to Austria, namely that Slav policy which is preached by the Czechs whom Count Beust persecutes.... The Slavonic element is a source of regeneration for Austria, and the basis of a '*rapprochement*' with Russia.

If an unrestrainable and natural tendency impels Germany on the path of conquest, Russia's law of existence forbids her to pursue a similar policy particularly in Europe.

[1] Memorandum on the attitude of the Russian press transmitted in Buchanan to Granville, 12 August 1870, FO 65/802, no. 310.
[2] The same to the same, 7 September 1870, FO 65/804, no. 336, transmitting a further memorandum on the attitude of the Russian press.

The interests of Europe required an Austro-Russian understanding:

After the fall of France, and when the friendship of Germany shall have wiped away Austria and swallowed up her Slav population, the European system will have completely disappeared. A Slavonic Austria, independent of Germany, while saving herself will at the same time save the Balance of Europe.

In a similar vein a leading article in *Golos* urged Austria to 'cast off Germany and become a Slavonian power'. Beust was warned against alienating Russia as well as Germany 'under the influence of a pitiful delusion respecting the pretensions of Russia to the Slavonic subjects of the House of Habsburg'.[1]

The alarms of the Russian national press—in spite of Gorchakov's susceptibility—had little influence on the policy of the imperial government. The tsar—although almost completely alone even at Court in his Prussian sympathies[2]—successfully withstood the pressure of public

[1] The same to the same, 7 March 1871, FO 65/820, no. 22, transmitting a further memorandum on the attitude of the Russian press.

[2] The Court made no secret of its anti-Prussian sentiments:

'...In dieser Hinsicht scheint es mir nicht ohne Interesse die Veränderung zu erwähnen, welche in den wechselseitigen persönlichen Gefühlen der Höfe von Berlin und St Petersburg durch den dänischen Krieg und durch die Ereignisse des Sommers 1866 herbeigeführt worden ist. Kaiser Alexander, der mit einer gewissen Zähigkeit an Neigungen und Ueberlieferungen hängt, hat in seinem Innern vielleicht am wenigsten dem schrillen Eindruck Raum gegeben, den die Unternehmungen Seines Königl. Oheims und die Art wie er diese ausbeutete, auf seine Anschauungen und Empfindungen hervorgebracht haben. Doch alle andern Glieder der Kaiserlichen Familie stehen mehr oder weniger unter der Einwirkung des tiefen Risses, welchen die Bande verwandtschaftlicher Zuneigung in den letzten Jahren erlitten. Diese Stimmung ist auch zum Durchbruch gekommen, als der Prinz von Preussen zur Vermählungsfeier des Thronfolgers hierhergekommen war; so sehr der Hof auch bemüht war bei diesem Anlasse die wahre Gesinnung durch äussere Höflichkeit zu decken, so gab es doch Symptome, die den Schleier momentan hoben und die dänische Königstochter insbesondere verwand ihre verletzten Gefühle nicht. Und so schied der künftige König von Preussen mit der Aeusserung: Ich bin wohl der letzte preussische Prinz, der mit der Gesinnung verwandtschaftlicher Freundschaft nach Russland gekommen.'

The young princess was profoundly opposed to the German element:

'...so glaubt in weiterer Verfolgung dieses Ideenganges die Partei der "Moskoviter" in dem Palaste Anitschkov, welchen der Thronfolger bewohnt, ein geneigteres Ohr zu haben, als beim Kaiser selbst und deshalb hofft sie von der Zukunft, mehr als von der Gegenwart, die Verwirklichung ihrer Gedanken und ihrer Wünsche' (Vetsera to Beust, 24/12 March 1869, HHSAPARRR, 1869, x 56, no. 9B, confidential).

A year later Chotek in his turn reported:

'Was den Wunsch der Forterhaltung freundlicher Beziehungen zu Preussen betrifft, so hat derselbe ganz besonders und beinahe ausschliesslich bei dem Kaiser Alexander seine Stütze. Die Tradition, der Eindruck der Erfolge, persönliche Familienbeziehungen, eine gewisse Abneigung gegen den hier immer stärker werdenden, *besonders* gegen Preussen abstossenden "slawischen Nationalismus", dann keine Divergenz im Oriente und Harmonie bezüglich Polens, endlich eine ähnliche Geistesrichtung, die sich gerne mit formelvollen [*sic*] Parade—und Uniformwesen befasst und in einer stramm sein sollenden militärischen Aussenseite sich gefällt. Fürst Gortschakoff, der nächste für Preussen noch halbwegs gut gesinnte Staatsmann, beschränkt sich darauf, General Fleury und mir von seiner Ueberzeugung zu sprechen, dass Preussen gemässigter als je auftreten, abwiegeln und nichts gegen den Prager Frieden unternehmen werde. Hiermit endet aber die Propensität des russischen Reichskanzlers für den Berliner Hof. Er belobt sich der Sprache der russischen Presse, welche Preussen bei jeder Gelegenheit angreift...' (Chotek to Beust, 16/4 March 1870, *ibid.* Jan.–June 1870, x 57, no. 17).

opinion. Gorchakov spoke only the truth when he warned Thiers—come to St Petersburg to plead for Russian intervention—against attaching importance to the language of the national press:

I am told [Buchanan reported] that, on his speaking of the public sympathy expressed by the Russian Press in favour of France, Prince Gortchakoff warned him against adopting the illusion of General Fleury as to the influence of the Press in Russia,—for it had no power whatever, and the policy of the Government was entirely dependent upon the will of the Emperor.[1]

The foreign policy of Russia was still the autocrat's alone.

[1] Buchanan to Granville, 30 September 1870, FO 65/804, no. 374, confidential.

BIBLIOGRAPHY

This book is based principally on documentary material, archival and printed. The following are among the more important sources:

I ARCHIVES

(A) THE ROYAL ARCHIVES, WINDSOR CASTLE

A 40, B 23, H 50, I 40–8, 63–8, 90–8, and Q 3. These volumes contain correspondence on foreign affairs between Queen Victoria and her Ministers together with drafts and copies of despatches for the period 1863–71. They convey a comprehensive picture of the formulation of British policy during the period.

(B) THE PUBLIC RECORD OFFICE, LONDON

FO 7 (reports from Vienna), 486–90, May–September 1856
FO 27 (reports from Paris), 1612–22, February–August 1866; 1805–6, July 1870
FO 65 (reports from St Petersburg), 697–704, February 1866–February 1867; 802–6, 820, May 1870–March 1871
FO 181 (St Petersburg drafts), 440–5, March–October 1866
FO 519 The Cowley Papers:

France, semi-official and private correspondence

171–81, from Earl of Clarendon, 1855–69
182, from Lord Stanley, 1859, 1866–7
184, from Earl Granville, 1852–71
205–6, from British Diplomats, 1852–67

Entry Books of Out-Letters to Secretaries of State for Foreign Affairs and others

216–22, to Earl of Clarendon and others, 1855–7
230–1, to Earl Russell and others, 1862–5
232, to Earl Russell, Earl of Clarendon and others, 1865–6
233, to Earl of Clarendon, Lord Stanley and others, 1866–7
234, to Lord Stanley, 1867

PRO 30/22   The Russell Papers:

14, Correspondence and Papers, 1860–3
21–3, Correspondence Cabinet Viscount Palmerston, 1863–5
26, Correspondence Cabinet other Members, 1863–5
27, Memoranda Cabinet Opinions, 1859–65
30, Drafts, the Queen, Cabinet, Viscount Palmerston, 1859–65
31, Drafts, Cabinet, various members, 1859–65
84, Correspondence British Embassy in St Petersburg, etc., 1863–5

(C) HAUS- HOF- UND STAATSARCHIV, WIEN

PAR x 49–61, Russie, Rapports, Expéditions, Varia, 1863–71
PAR ix 84 and 86, France, Rapports, Expéditions, Varia, 1867
xxxx 275, Ministerratsprotokolle (minutes of meetings of Imperial Council), 1869–71

(D) WÜRTTEMBERGISCHES STAATSARCHIV, STUTTGART

cccxiv, Gorchakov's letters to Olga Nicolaevna, 1855–71

II MANUSCRIPTS

(A) CLARENDON MSS., BODLEIAN LIBRARY, OXFORD

These were first used whilst still in the possession of the Seventh Earl of Clarendon and later during the period of reclassification in Oxford. No references can therefore be given. These papers are particularly valuable for Clarendon's private and semi-official correspondence with Lord Lyons (Paris) 1867–70.

(B) BROADLANDS MSS., BROADLANDS

It was impossible to visit Broadlands, but many documents for the period 1848–65 were made available by the kindness of the present owner.

(C) HENDERSON MSS., UNIVERSITY LIBRARY, CAMBRIDGE

Transcripts dealing mainly with the period 1855–6 made in Vienna, Berlin, Dresden and Hanover by the late Gavin B. Henderson.

III PRINTED SOURCES

Peter von Meyendorff, *Ein russischer Diplomat an den Höfen von Berlin und Wien. Politischer und privater Briefwechsel 1826–1863*, ed. O. Hoetzsch (Leipzig, 1923).

Die Grosse Politik der europäischen Kabinette, ed. A. Mendelssohn-Bartholdy, I. Lepsius and F. Thimme. 40 vols. in 54 (Berlin, 1922–6).

Lettres et Papiers du Chancelier Comte de Nesselrode 1760–1856, ed. A. de Nesselrode (Paris, n.d.).

Die Politischen Berichte des Fürsten Bismarck aus Petersburg und Paris 1859–1862, ed. L. von Raschdau (Berlin, 1920).

Die Auswärtige Politik Preussens 1858–1871, ed. E. Brandenburg and others, 10 vols. (Oldenburg, 1932 *et seq.*).

Russia and Prussia in the Schleswig-Holstein Question (in Russian), ed. S. Lesnik, *Krasny Arkhiv 2 (93)*, (Moscow, 1939).

The Letters of Queen Victoria
  First Series 1837–1861, ed. A. C. Benson and Viscount Esher (London, 1908).
  Second Series 1861–1885, ed. G. Buckle (London, 1926).

The later Correspondence of Lord John Russell 1840–78, ed. G. P. Gooch (1925).

British and Foreign State Papers, vols. 53, 60 and 61 dealing with the years 1863, 1870 and 1871.

Hansard, *Parliamentary Debates*, Third Series
  Vols. 169–70 (Poland, 1863).
  Vols. 172–6 (Schleswig-Holstein, 1863–4).

The Political Correspondence of Mr Gladstone and Lord Granville, ed. A. Ramm (London, 1952), vol. 1, 1868–71.

Les Origines diplomatiques de la guerre de 1870–71. Recueil de documents. 29 vols. (Ministère des Affaires Etrangères, Paris, 1910 *et seq.*).

IV SECONDARY SOURCES

A. Scharff, *Die Europäischen Grossmächte und die Deutsche Revolution 1848–1851* (Leipzig, 1942).

L. B. Namier, *1848: The Revolution of the Intellectuals* (London, 1946).

Ch. Friese, *Russland und Preussen vom Krimkrieg bis zum Polnischen Aufstand* (Berlin, 1931).

G. B. Henderson, 'The Diplomatic Revolution of 1854' in *Crimean War Diplomacy* (Glasgow, 1947).

R. H. Lord, 'Bismarck and Russia in 1863' in *The American Historical Review*, XXIX (Oct. 1923–July 1924).

L. D. Steefel, *The Schleswig-Holstein Question* (Cambridge, Mass., 1932).

F. Charles-Roux, *Alexandre II, Gortchakoff et Napoléon III* (Paris, 1913).

R. H. Lord, *The Origins of the War of 1870* (Cambridge, Mass., 1924).

Other works are mentioned in the text. For a general bibliography of the subject, the reader is referred to the relevant portions of the bibliography in A. J. P. Taylor, *The Struggle for Mastery in Europe 1848–1918* (Oxford, 1954), pp. 569 ff.

INDEX